THE MODERN CAFÉ

THE MODERN CAFÉ IS AN IMPRESSIVE VOLUME IN BOTH BREADTH AND DEPTH THAT ELEVATES STANDARD CAFÉ FARE TO SOMETHING WORTHY OF THE TERM CUISINE. FRANCISCO MIGOYA GENEROUSLY SHARES HIS YEARS OF EXPERIENCE AND RESEARCH, OFFERING **A FRESH, CONTEMPORARY APPROACH TO CASUAL DINING.** HIS TECHNICAL SKILL AND EYE FOR DETAIL ARE INSPIRING, RESULTING IN RESPECTFUL YET INVENTIVE INTERPRETATIONS OF THE CLASSICS. MIGOYA HAS GIVEN ALL OF US PROFESSIONAL COOKS, PASTRY AND SAVORY ALIKE, **ANOTHER INVALUABLE RESOURCE.**

—MICHAEL LAISKONIS
EXECUTIVE PASTRY CHEF, LE BERNARDIN

WHAT A HIGH LEVEL OF PROFESSIONALISM IN **A BOOK FULL OF ORIGI-NALITY AND CREATIVITY!** FRANCISCO MIGOYA HAS CREATED A NEW WORK WITH TECHNOLOGY, SENSITIVITY, AND PASSION—AN INVALU-ABLE CONTRIBUTION TO THE WORLD OF GASTRONOMY. **ENJOY IT!**

—ORIOL BALAGUER
PASTRY CHEF AND OWNER, ORIOL BALAGUER BOUTIQUES

FRANCISCO MIGOYA'S THE *MODERN CAFE* IS A BEAUTIFUL BOOK THAT WILL BE USED AS **A PRACTICAL GUIDE AND INSPIRATION** FOR PROFES-SIONALS AND HOME COOKS ALIKE.

—GRANT ACHATZ
CHEF AND OWNER, ALINEA

THIS BOOK IS JUST AMAZING—THERE IS SO MUCH INFORMATION, DETAIL, AND INSPIRATION. YOU CAN REALLY SEE FRANCISCO'S PASSION FOR PASTRY. THIS IS **AN OUTSTANDING FOLLOW UP TO HIS FIRST BOOK,** *FROZEN DESSERTS.*

—PATRICK COSTON
PASTRY CHEF AND CHOCOLATIER

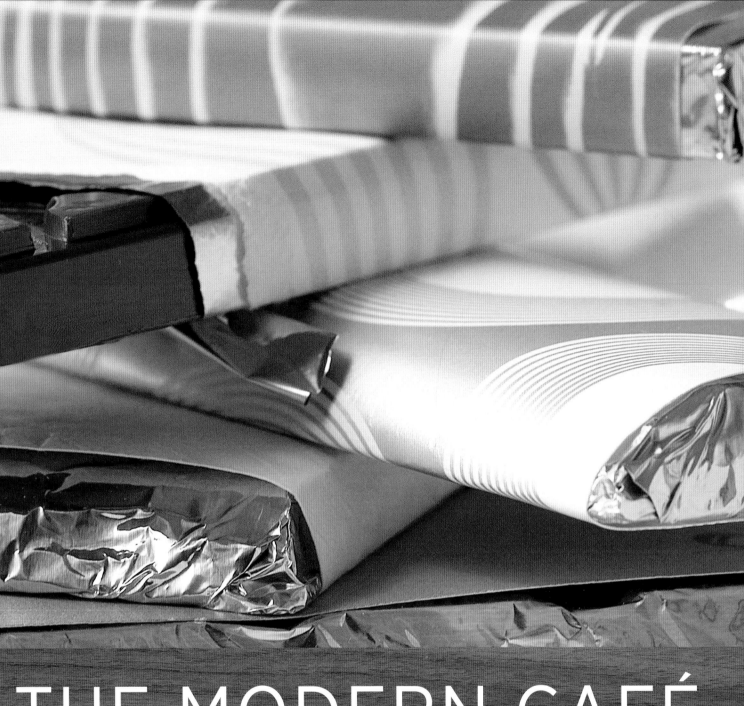

THE MODERN CAFÉ

FRANCISCO J. MIGOYA THE CULINARY INSTITUTE OF AMERICA

PHOTOGRAPHY BY BEN FINK

WILEY

JOHN WILEY & SONS, INC.

THE CULINARY INSTITUTE OF AMERICA®

THE CULINARY INSTITUTE OF AMERICA

PRESIDENT	Dr. Tim Ryan '77
VICE-PRESIDENT, DEAN OF CULINARY EDUCATION	Mark Erickson '77
SENIOR DIRECTOR, CONTINUING EDUCATION	Susan Cussen
DIRECTOR OF PUBLISHING	Nathalie Fischer
EDITORIAL PROJECT MANAGER	Margaret Wheeler '00
EDITORIAL ASSISTANTS	Shelly Malgee '08
	Erin Jeanne McDowell '08

This book is printed on acid-free paper. ∞

Photography copyright © 2010 by Ben Fink.

Published by John Wiley & Sons, Inc., Hoboken, New Jersey

Published simultaneously in Canada

Limit of Liability/Disclaimer of Warranty: While the publisher and author have used their best efforts in preparing this book, they make no representations or warranties with respect to the accuracy or completeness of the contents of this book and specifically disclaim any implied warranties of merchantability or fitness for a particular purpose. No warranty may be created or extended by sales representatives or written sales materials. The advice and strategies contained herein may not be suitable for your situation. You should consult with a professional where appropriate. Neither the publisher nor author shall be liable for any loss of profit or any other commercial damages, including but not limited to special, incidental, consequential, or other damages.

For general information on our other products and services or for technical support, please contact our Customer Care Department within the United States at (800) 762-2974, outside the United States at (317) 572-3993 or fax (317) 572-4002.

Wiley also publishes its books in a variety of electronic formats. Some content that appears in print may not be available in electronic books. For more information about Wiley products, visit our Web site at www.wiley.com.

Design by Vertigo Design NYC

LIBRARY OF CONGRESS CATALOGING-IN-PUBLICATION DATA:

Migoya, Francisco J.
  The modern café / Francisco Migoya ; photography by Ben Fink.
     p. cm.
  Includes bibliographical references and index.
  ISBN 978-0-470-37134-3 (cloth)
  1. Restaurants--United States. 2. Restaurant management--United States. I. Culinary Institute of America. II. Title.
  TX945.M535 2009
  647.9573--dc22

                    2009001798

Printed in China

10 9 8 7 6 5 4 3 2 1

ACKNOWLEDGMENTS

I would like to thank the following people, in no particular order:

Tom Vaccaro, Associate Dean of Baking and Pastry at The Culinary Institute of America, for being so supportive of this project and for his assistance in making it happen the way I wanted.

Yohan Lee, Café Coordinator for the Apple Pie Bakery-Café at The Culinary Institute of America, for procuring the beautiful props and special ingredients used in this book.

Mr. John Miles, President of Steelite International, for his generous donation of porcelain plates. The plates used for the photos on pages 317, 325, 326, 333, 336, 341, 351, 353, 357, 384, and 390 are part of their Montgatina collection. Thank you.

Maggie Wheeler, who once again has shown her eye for detail and patiently received all of my corrections and rewrites and last-minute adjustments. Thank you to Shelly Malgee, who was invaluable throughout the photo shoots.

Ben Fink, the best food photographer around, hands-down.

Kathryn Gaffney, Bryan Graham, Raewyn Horton, Sean Pera, Nelson Salsa, Matthew Siciliano, Erin Snyder, Adam Starowicz, and Christopher Teixeira. All of you were instrumental in the testing of recipes and production of the food photographed in this book. Without you this would not have been possible. Remember these names, because you will certainly hear about them in the future.

Dr. Tim Ryan and Mark Erickson, for supporting this project.

Nathalie Fischer, for her help and insight.

Pam Chirls from John Wiley & Sons, for her help in coordinating this book.

My parents, who gave me all the tools I ever needed and more.

My wife, Kris, and my daughter, Isabel; you are the reason for this.

INTRODUCTION

In my years in the industry I have seen, lived, and been part of much of the recent evolution of food in the United States. I am not referring to trends, which seem to come and go at an increasingly fast rate, but to the increased appreciation that the consumer has developed for good, accessible, moderately inexpensive food. I have also realized that even though consumers have very high expectations, they would like their food promptly expedited so they can get on with their lives. You don't always have the time (or the means) for a Michelin three-star experience. Enter *The Modern Café*.

What defines a café? A café can offer a variety of items, such as:

- BREAKFAST ITEMS (VIENNOISERIE)

- ARTISAN BREADS

- PASTRY ITEMS (CAKES OR ENTREMETS AND INDIVIDUAL DESSERTS)

- SAVORY ITEMS

- CONFECTIONS AND CHOCOLATES

- PACKAGED SHELF-STABLE FOODS

- ICE CREAM AND OTHER FROZEN DESSERTS

- BEVERAGES

Not all cafés will offer all of the above-mentioned items, but in order to be financially healthy, there should be at least a combination of two or three of them. This book contains all of them. All of the products included are special, meaning that they are not strictly traditional; they are also refined and require precise execution, care for technique, and quality of ingredients. The craft of the baker, pastry chef, and chef is evident in them, and they all have elements that make them stand out. Each and every finished product has an important reason for being included. I believe that this book will offer many ideas, techniques, and recipes, and that most importantly, it will be inspirational.

In order to operate a successful café, one must be a master of many trades and have a profound understanding of quality, refinement, and business sense. Customers have become more sophisticated, and in order to meet their needs, there are many more well-trained bakers, pastry chefs, and chefs than there were in the past decade. Culinary and pastry schools have become very popular, and though this mini career explosion is great, it also means that there is a lot of talent out there. It keeps getting harder and harder to be financially successful and keep up with the competition. One of the key aspects in the big picture of a café's financial success is the way in which the product is sold, from how it should be displayed to how it is taken away. This is also included in the book, not as a chapter in itself, but in sidebars throughout the different chapters.

While there is an emphasis on technique and execution, this book is not going to focus on basic educational information. It is geared toward professionals, not students. For example, scientific explanations of the functions of ingredients, definitions of basic equipment, and the history of each item will not be covered. In certain cases when it is necessary to talk about a specific ingredient or a piece of equipment like the immersion thermocirculator, there will be sidebars to provide explanation.

As diversified as a modern café can be, there really are three major categories: baked goods (breakfast pastries, artisan breads, and other various baked goods), pastries, and savory items. Breakfast pastries (viennoiserie) hold a very important place in the café and for me in my career. When I was hired to be the executive pastry chef for Thomas Keller's restaurants in Yountville, California (The French Laundry, Bouchon Bistro, and

Bouchon Bakery), I was initially very hesitant about the bakery aspect, since it was not part of my "comfort zone" at the time. I was actually more concerned about producing for the Bouchon Bakery than The French Laundry itself. There were many months spent developing recipes, especially for the perfect croissant, which is one of Mr. Keller's benchmarks for a quality bakery, along with éclairs and chocolate chip cookies. We accomplished that goal not only for croissants, but also with every item that came out of that bakery. I learned how to transform something ordinary into something extraordinary.

Though there is certainly a wide variety of breads made today, I will focus on two "mother" doughs in the book: lean dough and sourdough. For me, the fewer breads offered, the better. A good example is Poilâne in Paris. They are famous for making a single kind of bread. The breads and their variations in Chapter 1 will be featured as loaves to be sold as is, but they will also be used in the savory kitchen for sandwiches or to accompany a finished appetizer. This is not a book about bread; it is particularly its role in the café in which we are interested.

Cakes (entremets), which can also be modified into individual desserts, are one of the pastry chef's most technically involved procedures. In this book, I will show how to compose and build a large array of cakes and individual desserts that combine a variety of textures with straightforward flavors, and are finished in a clean, simple, elegant way. Beautiful, sophisticated, and flavorful cakes are the focus of Chapter 2. The same goes for tarts, which will be shown in large sizes that can be modified for individual portions as well. There will also be a few specialty cookies, such as French macarons.

The savory component of this book is as important as the baked goods and pastry aspect. The crucial difference is that many savory items require an à la minute pickup. The items in this book have been thoroughly thought out, with a focus on advanced preparation and a quick finish with a well-planned *mise en place*. This food is intimately connected to the other elements of the book in regard to its refined simplicity and use of quality ingredients. There is a way to achieve a happy medium between quick and excellent. Most of this food is inspired by my favorite restaurants, which are not precisely cafés but whose philosophy and approach to food is in tune with my interpretations of café food. Eating at those restaurants is an easy way to have excellent food without breaking the bank.

Diversifying a café's offerings is a smart way to increase sales. This is why I decided that there should be a chapter devoted to the retail shelf. The more needs you can fulfill, the better, even if your customer doesn't know before they walk into your café that they need a box of chocolates with that cup of coffee. They see it, they might buy it, or at least they'll know that when they need it, you have it available.

Finally, there are a few sidebars in the book that refer to packaging products for sale and to how to set up a display case, since knowing how to make a cake is only part of the equation. I have always thought that the right packaging can make a world of difference. When you buy an expensive pair of shoes, you walk into an immaculate store where all the shoes are neatly arranged and easy to see. You pay for them and they are placed in a nice box inside a nice bag. Now imagine if they had been shoved into a nondescript brown paper bag after you paid all that money. It is the same for a cake or a box of French macarons. Throughout each chapter, there will be sidebars that refer to one of the most crucial aspects of a café, which is its image and how the product is presented. A clean display case filled with beautiful desserts, symmetrically laid out with clear, attractive signs, speaks volumes to the customer.

My expectation for this book is for it to be a pioneer in the realm of modern café food. There are many books available that are very specific to the different categories I will include, but this is the only book where it all comes together seamlessly.

—FRANCISCO J. MIGOYA

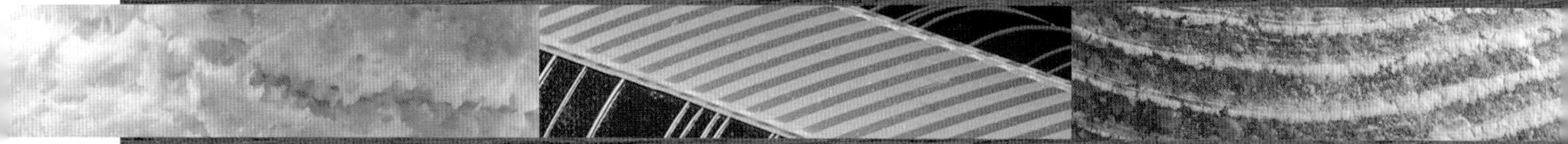

THE BAKERY

"SIMPLE" IS OFTEN THE HARDEST ACT TO PULL OFF, and nowhere in the café is that more evident than in the bakery. There are seven basic ingredients that are the backbone of most baked goods (in no particular order): flour, eggs, sugar, salt, a leavener (chemical, such as baking powder and baking soda, or biological, such as yeast), a fat (butter and oil), and a liquid (water, milk, and heavy cream). These seven key ingredients, in different proportions and combinations, can produce thousands of varieties of breads and viennoiserie. They are by no means the only ingredients, but they are the most utilized. While some items contain all seven ingredients and some may contain even more, we'd be hard pressed to find a recipe with less than three of them.

THIS CHAPTER focuses only on the methods for specific varieties of bread or viennoiserie. What makes them special? A combination of a consistent respect for technique and execution, an understanding of the product's origin, the use of high-quality ingredients, and a refined finished product that always has the right texture and the right flavor. There is always a way to make things better, and it only takes a few more steps to make them that way. But it has to be done consistently.

The bakery is typically a low-cost/high-profit area, where money is made on volume production. A large quantity of bread can be produced at a low cost. This is not necessarily the same in other areas of the shop, such as pastry, which has a low food cost and high labor cost, or savory items, which have a high food cost. Once the product is baked and, in some cases, garnished, it needn't be refrigerated, and it is sold as is. The basic ingredients are generally inexpensive, except perhaps for butter. And this is where trouble usually begins. The biggest mistake any establishment can make is to cut corners on quality ingredients. Margarine will never be all that butter is, as far as flavor, texture, quality of the finished product, and nutritional value.

It is by no means easy to produce high quality-baked goods. However, it is very easy to produce average to ordinary baked goods. Unfortunately, a lot of the basic techniques are often overlooked by bakers in order to trim down food costs and labor expenses; the clearest example is in laminated products, where technique is key and so many variables need to be controlled (see lamination, page 40). This practice could ultimately hurt the bottom line, though, because it is not business-smart, at least not in an obvious way. Why is your customer going to come to your establishment and not the one across the street? The answer is very simple: Your product is better. It can be better because it is made by following production techniques consistently and utilizing quality ingredients. Consumers are becoming more and more sophisticated and understand that the quality of what they eat is very important, and not just for health reasons. If they like the food, they'll come back. This is not a book on healthy eating—the recipes feature butter and fat. However, all good things can be enjoyed in small amounts.

While the emphasis here is primarily on technique and execution, there is another side to baked goods that is very hard to teach and is perhaps a reason why some bakeries and cafés aren't successful. Baked goods, especially those that contain yeast, almost have a life of their own, and it is the baker's job to coax and manipulate them in the right direction. For me, the number-one baked good, the king of the bakery if you will, is the croissant. It is the benchmark of the bakery and, as a result, of the baker as well. The information on croissants on page 38 will certainly get you started and point you in the right direction, but practice is imperative to actually make the perfect croissant. In the bakery you don't only use the recipe; you need to use all of your senses. You need to feel the dough; see it; hear it as it mixes; smell it when it is raw, when it is baking, and when it is done baking; and finally, taste it. When you do this hundreds of times, you will understand the croissant completely, and even then you will still continue to learn about it throughout your life as a baker.

There are very few things in life that I think are as beautiful as a box full of fresh baked goods. Early in the morning, you go to the café, order one of this and two of that and a jar of marmalade or jam, you get some coffee and quickly take it all home, where ideally there is some good butter sitting out. You sit at your kitchen or dining room table by yourself, or with your family, friends, or whoever happens to be home, and take a bite, and then it all clicks. You realize that the baker is a true craftsman because that bite of Danish you just took is perhaps the best you have had in your life, and there is nothing better in the world at that moment, except for the next bite.

THE SEVEN KEY INGREDIENTS

The following are the basic properties of the different ingredients used for yeast-raised breakfast pastries as well as all chemically leavened items and bread items in this book. It is important to understand how these ingredients interact with each other and how they are mixed, retarded, fermented, shaped, proofed, baked, and finished.

leaveners

YEAST

Yeast is what will make the dough grow and expand through proofing (fermentation). CO_2 and alcohol, which are responsible in part for flavor as well, are by-products of fermentation; they are trapped by the dough and are eventually expelled from the dough during the baking process. There are two different kinds of yeast.

commercial yeast: Commercial yeast is available in three different forms: fresh (or compressed), instant, and active dry. The latter is the kind found at the supermarket and is not recommended for commercial baking. The recipes in this book use instant yeast for all dough. Instant dry yeast can be incorporated directly into the dry ingredients of a recipe right before mixing, while fresh yeast and active dry yeast need to be dissolved in a warm liquid such as water or milk before they can be combined with the other ingredients. The most commercially available brand of yeast is SAF, which produces "red label" instant yeast and "gold label" instant yeast (see Resources, page 540). The red label is better for lean dough (baguette, ciabatta, Breton, Francese, country), and the gold label is best for dough with a high sugar percentage or acidity, such as brioche, croissant, and Danish. The strain of yeast used in gold-label yeast can withstand larger amounts of sugar and acidity than red-label yeast. Yeast eats sugar, which promotes fermentation; too much sugar leads to too much fermentation and overproofing.

If fresh (compressed) yeast is all that is available, simply multiply the amount of instant yeast in the recipe by three. The resulting number will be the amount of fresh yeast needed for the recipe. However, since fresh yeast contains a percentage of water, water needs to be subtracted from the recipe. To do this, calculate the amount of fresh yeast to add, and then subtract the amount of instant dry yeast originally needed. The resulting number will be the amount of liquid that will need to be taken out of the recipe.

For example:

A recipe calls for 100 g/3.5 oz instant dry yeast.

100 x 3 = 300 g/10.5 oz. This is the amount of fresh yeast needed for the recipe. To calculate how much liquid to subtract from the recipe:

300.03 – 100 = 200 g/7 oz. This is the amount of liquid that needs to be taken away from the recipe.

Active dry yeast is available in supermarkets for the home baker. It lacks the strength and quality that instant dry yeast has. Since the process required to produce this yeast is very aggressive, most of the yeast found in a package is dead. It is not recommended for use, even at home.

wild yeast: Wild yeast is obtained from ambient yeast, or yeast that is found in the environment. Certain foods like grapes, grape juice, raisins, whole grains and flours, yogurt, and honey contain a proportion of this wild yeast. In order to harness it, one of the ingredients mentioned above is combined with an equal amount (by weight) of water and is left to ferment for 4 to 6 days, after which it is strained. Some bakers add a small amount of sugar, about 5 percent of the total weight, to speed up the fermentation process. This resulting liquid is known as a "chef," and it can be used to make any variety of pre-ferment (see below). The chef can be used in combination with commercial yeast, but purists will argue that the very best way to make bread is by using a chef in the pre-ferment instead of commercial yeast.

PRE-FERMENTS (a.k.a. Starters or Levains)

These are used to improve the character of bread (flavor, crumb, texture, crust, and aroma), but more importantly they are used to "seed" another dough to begin the fermentation process. They are used occasionally for viennoiserie but are mostly used for breads. In this book pre-ferments are used in the sourdough and the lean dough breads.

There are four basic types of pre-ferments, which can be tweaked and modified to create hundreds of varieties. Pre-ferments do not have the gassing strength that straight commercial yeast has, but they make up for it by improving the finished item's flavor, since fermentation takes longer. The longer the fermentation, the more time the starches in the flour have to break down, and this has a direct result on the flavor, crumb, crust, and color. It is important to remark that flavor comes from the flour and the by-products of yeast fermentation (CO_2 and alcohol), not from the yeast itself, which is why some bakers will only use pre-ferments for their dough. The strength of a pre-ferment will depend on the environmental conditions in which it is kept as well as the ingredients used to make it. For viennoiserie like croissants, which are very finicky, straight instant yeast (gold label) is used instead of pre-ferments in order to maintain a consistent product.

pâte fermentée: Pâte fermentée is a dough in itself, made with yeast (fresh or instant), flour, eggs, butter, salt, sugar, and water. It is mixed until full gluten development is obtained (see Full Gluten Development, page 10), fermented, and then added to other ingredients (such as more flour, eggs, butter, and sugar), mixed again, and then fermented again to obtain a second dough.

Some bakers simply reserve some dough from one batch and add it to another new dough, then save a piece of that dough for the next dough, and so on.

Use pâte fermentée for lean dough. It contributes body and flavor and helps strengthen the dough.

biga: A biga is similar to pâte fermentée but contains no salt. As noted below, salt controls or slows down the yeast. Since there is no salt, a biga will move (proof) the dough a lot faster. Bigas are also made expressly to be a pre-ferment, unlike pâte fermentée, which can be a piece of ready-made dough. Both the biga and pâte fermentée are firm in consistency compared to the two following pre-ferments. Use firm pre-ferments for firm doughs and looser pre-ferments for looser doughs; keep in mind that pre-ferments can be combined to obtain the desired result.

Use the biga for lean dough. It contributes more flavor than other pre-ferments as well as acidity. It also helps strengthen the dough.

poolish: A poolish is a type of starter made by combining equal parts (by weight) of water and flour, and a small amount of yeast (.25 percent of the weight of the flour if it is fresh yeast and .08 percent if it is instant). Dough that will have a poolish added as a pre-ferment will typically have another amount of yeast added before it is mixed. Use poolish-style starters for lean dough (see recipes on page 109). A poolish contributes high gassing power for loose doughs such as ciabatta, which will result in a very open crumb. Sometimes it is used in combination with other pre-ferments for firmer doughs. The flavor is typically mild. A poolish helps to denature doughs and, as a result, tenderize them.

sponge (a.k.a. regular sponge): The ratio for a sponge is typically one part water to two parts flour, with a larger percentage of yeast added than for a poolish. This pre-ferment is a lot faster than poolish precisely because of the yeast, and it doesn't need as much time to ferment before it is mixed into a dough. There is also a small percentage of yeast that is added to the dough before mixing. This dough will also proof a lot faster than a dough made with poolish, which will have a negative impact on the final flavor.

Use a sponge for enriched doughs. It helps to jump-start the fermentation process and should be used for doughs that need to move quickly, or at least faster than lean-type doughs.

CHEMICAL LEAVENERS

The most important function of chemical leaveners is to increase the size or volume of a dough or batter. They do so when they break down and form carbon dioxide (a gas) during the mixing process but more so while baking, therefore expanding the batter or dough. This increase in volume (or leavening) also contributes to the tenderness of the baked product, since the expanding carbon dioxide will thin out the cell walls of the baked product. Finally, they affect the pH of a batter or dough and, depending on the leavener, will decrease the pH (baking powder) or increase the pH (baking soda). These adjustments in pH have a direct result on the crumb, crust, color, flavor, and general texture of the baked dough or batter.

baking soda: Baking soda is activated through interacting with an acidic liquid, such as buttermilk, yogurt, or crème fraîche; and heat. Baking soda will produce carbon dioxide on its own when it comes in contact with moisture, but it will require copious amounts of moisture to leaven a dough or a batter properly. When it is combined with an acidic liquid, baking soda breaks down more efficiently into carbon dioxide. Be careful, though; it reacts to its fullest capacity within a couple of minutes of being incorporated into a batter or dough, so speed is of the essence. Rarely is baking soda used on its own; it is usually combined with baking powder.

baking powder: Single-acting baking powder is a combination of baking soda, cream of tartar (an acid), and cornstarch. The ratio is 1:2:1. "Single-acting" refers to baking powder that contains one acid that dissolves in water and will immediately react with the baking soda. This gives the baker or pastry chef very little time to make the batter or dough and bake it without the baking powder adversely affecting the finished baked product. Single-acting baking powder is not sold anymore, but it is a kind of baking powder that one could make at home. Thankfully, there is double-acting baking powder, which contains two acids (sometimes more). One acid dissolves in the presence of moisture (and therefore reacts with the baking soda), and another acid reacts with heat during baking. There are some baking powders that contain a single acid but are treated so that some of it dissolves in moisture and the rest will dissolve in the presence of heat. This will result in a better finished product.

There are two other types of leavening agents: water and air. Water in the form of steam (see Water, page 6) is considered a physical leavener. Air leavens batters in the form of bubbles trapped in a foam, such as aerated egg whites (or yolks to a lesser extent) in a batter, soufflé, or génoise (sponge cake). Air is known as a mechanical leavener, since air is produced by mechanical means, such as a whip or an electric mixer.

eggs

While one could spend a good amount of time studying to understand all of the properties that eggs have, only those that are relevant to this book are discussed here, and even then only briefly. These are their main functions:

- **Aerator:** Eggs have the capacity to trap air through foaming, which will have a leavening effect on baked goods. This applies primarily to egg whites, but egg yolks can be foamed as well to a lesser extent.

- **Integral part of the structure of baked goods:** Structure occurs when the egg proteins coagulate in the batter or dough after coming in contact with heat. This occurs in custards and some dessert preparations as well.

- **Flavor:** Eggs carry a distinctive flavor depending on the preparation. A scrambled egg doesn't have the same flavor as the egg inside brioche, for example. If the brioche didn't contain eggs, besides its appearance being off, the flavor would be noticeably different.

- **Emulsifier (especially egg yolks):** Eggs have a direct effect on binding the ingredients in a batter or dough, which affects not only texture but flavor as well. For blended batters such as muffins (see page 89), it is especially important to have a proper emulsion.

- **Color:** Eggs add color not just as an egg wash for baked items but in the dough or batter itself, which browns while baking. This browning is called a Maillard reaction (or Maillard browning), which should not be confused with caramelization. Caramelization is exclusive to sugar, while Maillard is the caramelization of sugar in the presence of a protein.

- **Add nutritional value:** Eggs contain proteins and vitamins.

flour

The main purpose of flour is to provide the structure or body (along with eggs) in a dough or batter. Gluten (a protein) is mostly responsible for the structure of a dough or batter, but flour in itself does not contain gluten. It contains glutenin and gliadin (both proteins), which together will produce gluten when they come in contact with water and during the mixing process. The longer a dough mixes, the more gluten will develop in a given dough or batter. While gluten development is desired in certain doughs, like brioche, it is not needed in batters, like muffins. For example, a bread, which will usually require medium to full gluten development, needs the strength that results from gluten formation in order to form a firm structure throughout the dough. For items that are more delicate, like muffins, if they are overmixed, they will become tough.

Different varieties of flour will have different percentages of protein. Flour also contributes to flavor (see yeast on page 2), and in conjunction with sugar produces color through the Maillard browning mentioned above, and absorbs liquids, which helps bind all of the ingredients together in a dough or batter. Flour provides some nutritional value, especially whole wheat varieties, but to a much lesser extent when compared to dairy and eggs.

The following is a list of the types of flours that are used in this book, along with the average protein content for each.

- **High-gluten flour:** 13.5 to 14.5 percent protein

- **White whole wheat flour:** 13 to 14 percent protein (used for sourdough)

- **Bread flour:** 11 to 13.5 percent protein (used for viennoiserie, sourdough in combination with white whole wheat flour, and lean dough breads)

- **All-purpose flour:** 9 to 10.5 percent protein (used for batters and dough). All-purpose flour can be made by combining 70 percent bread flour with 30 percent cake flour (by weight, not by volume).

- **Cake flour:** 7 to 8 percent protein (used for various sponge cakes)

- **Pastry flour:** 8 to 9 percent protein (used for muffins)

The recipes in this book use malted flour. There are some flours, most of them organic, that are not malted. Always check the specs of the flour; this information should be available from the flour mill. If the flour is not malted, malt syrup can be added to the recipe; it is usually about 1 percent of the total weight of the flour. Malt syrup acts as a tenderizer, but mostly it provides maltose and glucose for moisture retention and yeast growth.

All recipes that contain yeast or a starter in this book (brioche, croissant dough, Danish dough, sourdough, and lean dough breads) are calculated according to what is called the "bakers' percentage." There is a column of percentages in some of the recipes in this chapter, and the total percentages add up to above 100 percent; for example, the brioche recipe on page 10 adds up to 232.25 percent. The basic principle is that the flour amount (usually bread flour) is always 100 percent. To determine the rest of the percentages, simply divide the weight of the other ingredients by the weight of the flour, and multiply that result by 100. In all other recipes, the percentage is determined by the total amount of the recipe (all ingredients). Bakers' percentage is an excellent tool for bakers, and it has many other possibilities than just determining the percentages in a recipe.

butter

If you overwhip heavy cream, two products will form: butter and buttermilk. The solid component is butter and the liquid is buttermilk. Butter is essentially a water-in-fat emulsion, and it is graded according to the fat percentage it contains. "Premium" butters will contain at least 82 percent fat. (The USDA allows rounding numbers up to the closest whole number, so butter with 81.6 percent fat will be considered premium, and so will one with 82.5 percent fat, even though there is almost a whole percentage number between them.) Butter will provide flakiness, flavor, moisture, and volume, and it acts as a tenderizer in baked goods. It "softens" a baked product by interfering with the structure formation achieved by the flour and eggs. Butter fat will coat the gluten strands, reducing gluten development since glutenin and gliadin will not be able to come in contact with the water. Remember that water is partially responsible for gluten development. So instead of having long gluten strands, the dough will have shorter strands, which means the product has been tenderized.

salt

The main function of salt is flavor enhancement, but when it is used in a dough that contains yeast of any variety, it will help to control and slow down fermentation. Other functions include increased color of crust and strengthening of gluten bonds, which makes the dough more uniform. If there is too much salt in a dough, it will slow down yeast growth and cause the dough to proof more slowly.

sugar

The most important purpose of sugar is to sweeten, but it also has other contributions to baked goods. In yeasted doughs, it promotes or speeds up fermentation, since sugar is the food yeast uses to ferment. It also acts as a tenderizer since, like butter, it interferes but doesn't prevent gluten strand formation by delaying the formation of structure. The more sugar is in a dough or batter, the more tender it will be. However, too much sugar will overtenderize the dough, making it a spongy, soft mess; additionally, if the dough contains yeast, it will also grow too quickly. Sugar will also contribute to color by browning easily in conjunction with the flour proteins (Maillard browning). In foamed sponge cakes, it will assist in stabilizing the egg foam by slowing the unfolding of the egg proteins, which will prevent the overwhipping of egg foams, especially egg white foams. It also stabilizes the foam because as the sugar comes in contact with the moisture found in eggs, it will dissolve, and this liquid sugar will help trap and support air bubbles.

liquids

WATER

Water serves to hydrate a dough (it is not used frequently in batters), which means it will moisten the glutenin and gliadin to promote the formation of gluten. It helps dissolve solids, such as sugar and salt, in doughs and batters, and it also contributes to the activation of chemical leaveners by dissolving them. It hydrates fresh yeast, thereby allowing fermentation to happen. Water will affect the consistency of a dough (too much will make the dough too loose). It produces steam when it comes in contact with heat, which contributes to crumb formation and the expansion of a dough. For this reason it is also known as a physical leavener. The clearest example of its role as a physical leavener is in pâte à choux, which expands so much because of its high water content that it becomes virtually a hollow shell when baked. Water helps with crust formation in breads (and some viennoiserie such as croissants and Danish), as it evaporates from the surface of the dough when the vent is opened in an oven, drying out the surface and forming a hard shell.

MILK

Milk contains a type of sugar called lactose. When lactose comes in contact with gluten, it will produce Maillard browning on the crust of the dough as it bakes, which will make the crust darker than when water is used in a dough or batter. This crust will also be softer than if water had been used, since milk proteins absorb water, which will slow down its evaporation from the dough's surface. All of the above properties of water are the same for milk, but milk is used primarily for enriched dough, such as brioche, croissant, and Danish. An enriched dough is a dough that contains one or more of the following ingredients: milk instead of water, butter (or other fats), and eggs. All of these ingredients contain a proportion of fat. They differ from lean dough (see page 109) in that lean dough will contain no fat at all, hence the name.

HEAVY CREAM

Heavy cream is obtained from milk and contains 35 to 40 percent fat. It is used mostly for quick breads, such as biscuits and scones, because it contains not only moisture but fat as well. This will result in a homogeneous dough that is not too wet. If an equal amount of milk or water is substituted for heavy cream, it would result in a "wet" dough. The dough can retain the moisture from the heavy cream without it feeling too wet because of its high fat content.

choosing the right butter

NOT ALL BUTTERS ARE MADE THE SAME WAY. The basic steps are as follows: Milk is poured into a machine known as a separator. The cream rises to the top and is skimmed off and then pasteurized. Some manufacturers let it sit overnight to stabilize the fat globules, which will control the crystallization of fat, which in turn will determine the consistency of the butter. What remains in the separator is skim milk. Once the heavy cream has been pasteurized and the fat globules have stabilized, it is transferred to a churn, where it spends anywhere from thirty minutes to an hour, depending on how quickly or slowly the moisture separates from the milk solids. In the churn, the solids are separated from the liquid, which is known as buttermilk. The churn agitates the cream to the point where the fat globules bind to each other, squeezing the moisture out. The resulting butter is then mixed to form the finished product.

Some butters are more elastic than others, meaning they can be stretched to a certain extent before they crack. This quality is called plasticity and is not to be confused with spreading ability, which is how easily it can be spread on, say, a piece of bread. The relative amounts of fat molecules with a high melting point found in a particular butter will determine how hard or soft the butter will be. Soft butter has a high content of crystallized low-temperature-melting fat molecules, while harder butter has a high content of high-temperature-melting fat molecules. The size of the fat crystals depends on how quickly the heavy cream was cooled down after pasteurization. The faster it is cooled down, the smaller the fat crystals will be, and therefore the butter will be softer. The slower it cools down, the larger the fat crystals will be, and therefore the butter will be firmer. The balance between the sizes of both types of fat crystals is what makes the difference between one type of butter and another. The proportion of both types of fat crystals can differ from maker to maker, and it is not necessarily a determining factor in the quality of the butter. It has to do with how quickly the cream is cooled down after pasteurization, before it is churned. Butter plasticity is a prized quality for the lamination process because the butter will be easier to roll out without it cracking. You can get away with the butter being on the colder side, which makes it easier to roll out than when it is soft. It doesn't mean that the butter can be too cold, though, because then it will crack or break no matter how good the plasticity of the butter. For a list of butters with good plasticity for lamination, see Resources, page 540.

BUTTERMILK

Buttermilk is used as an acidic liquid in certain recipes to activate chemical leaveners, and it is also used because its acidity acts as a tenderizer in items such as biscuits. The enzymes in the buttermilk break down flour proteins, making them tender. Buttermilk also contributes a certain flavor. Modern buttermilk production consists of adding lactic acid bacteria to milk; it was originally the liquid that was "squeezed" out of butter after it was churned. Both of these are considered buttermilk, but the latter has a much shorter shelf life.

When weighing any of the recipes in this book, it is fine to round the amounts up to the nearest whole number. All liquids are measured by weight, not volume. It is more efficient to have one type of measuring tool (a scale) than two (a scale and a measuring cup).

The baking (and in some occasions, cooking) times are relative and imprecise. They are only meant to give a general time frame. The most reliable measure to tell when anything is baked or cooked is experience, which can only be acquired through time. All ovens, even those made by the same manufacturer, will be slightly different.

yeast-raised breakfast pastries (viennoiserie)

It is important to know and understand the term *viennoiserie,* since it is truly the origin of all yeast-raised breakfast pastries. This term is used to describe all yeast-raised baked goods that are not bread. They may contain a higher proportion of sugar than bread (they are considered sweet), they are mostly but not exclusively laminated (see the definition of lamination on page 537), and they are typically but not exclusively eaten for breakfast.

As far as the origin of the word itself, it is closely linked to the origin of croissants (see sidebar, page 39), but there is neither solid evidence nor a specific date for when it originated. It is only known that viennoiserie did in fact originate in Vienna, Austria. But viennoiserie as we know it today was influenced by many different countries, such as France, Italy, Germany, Switzerland, Belgium, Denmark, Poland, and, of course, Austria, among other European countries.

There are two major categories of yeast-raised breakfast pastries: those that are leavened by yeast, and those that are leavened by yeast and steam produced by laminating a yeasted dough with butter.

yeast-raised pastries

This refers to breakfast pastries that are leavened exclusively by yeast and are enriched. They contain a proportion of fat given by one or a combination of the following ingredients: milk, eggs, and/or fat (butter). This book will focus on brioche.

BRIOCHE

Brioche is one of the most versatile doughs available. It can be seen as a workhorse dough because it can be used for sweet items as well as savory; it is relatively easy to make, shape, proof, and bake; and it holds well under refrigeration for about two days and frozen as a raw dough for about a week, if it is tightly wrapped.

The mixing method used for brioche is called the "straight" method, which consists of placing all of the ingredients in a bowl and mixing until full gluten development is achieved. Though the ingredients can technically be placed in the bowl in a random order, for best results the ingredients should be placed in the bowl in the following order:

- **Liquid:** It will be milk in most cases, ideally at 21°C/70°F. If fresh (compressed) yeast is being used, it should be dissolved in this liquid.

- **Eggs:** They should be at room temperature, or 21°C/70°F, so that they do not bring the temperature of the liquid and, as a result, the dough down to where it is too cold. It is *very important* not to add all of the eggs in the recipe at this point. Withhold 10 to 15 percent of the eggs, and then add those to the dough after the dough has been well mixed and achieved full gluten development. This way the gluten can properly develop before the eggs have a chance to interfere with the process. Since the fat found in yolks will have a similar effect to that of butter, it will coat the proteins in the flour, which will hinder or slow down gluten development.

- **Flour:** If instant dry yeast is being used, put half of the flour in first, then the yeast, then the rest of the flour.

- **Salt:** Make sure there are no clumps of salt. Keep it separate from the yeast if scaling ahead of time.

- **Sugar:** Make sure there are no clumps of sugar. Keep it separate from the yeast if scaling ahead of time.

- **Butter:** This should be added once the previous ingredients have started mixing and have formed a uniform mass. If butter is added too soon, it will interfere with the hydration of the other ingredients (salt, sugar, flour, instant yeast) and gluten development will take much longer (see "butter" in the ingredients section of this chapter, page 5). The recipe for brioche in this book contains close to 50 percent of the total weight in butter.

A hook is the proper attachment to use for the straight mixing method, since it will mix the ingredients without ripping the dough apart as a paddle would. Always make sure to use an adequately sized bowl for mixing. If the bowl is too small, the dough won't mix well and some of it might come out. If the bowl is too big, it will take too long for the dough to reach gluten development, since the revolution of a large hook takes much longer to complete a full circle than a smaller hook in a small bowl. Be careful that the dough does not exceed 27°C/80°F, since the butter might start melting away from the dough; this can have terrible consequences for the dough, since it can't be fixed at this point.

possible defects of yeast-raised products

defect	cause(s)	solution (the appropriate steps need to be taken beforehand)
Pale crust	Not egg-washed or not egg-washed sufficiently	Make sure to apply the correct amount of egg wash before baking. Once the item has been baked there is no way to fix it.
	Recipe was improperly scaled and has the incorrect amount of sugar or salt	Make sure that all of the ingredients are scaled correctly before making the product.
Thick crust	Overbaked	Have timers available and check the ovens frequently.
Cracked crust	Crust dried out from insufficient egg-washing or there wasn't enough humidity in the proof box	Egg-wash the product as needed during the proofing process (two to three times). Make sure there is enough moisture in the proof box.
Tight crumb	Underproofed*	Bake products when they have achieved adequate proofing. Typically the item should have doubled in size.
Surface looks ripped	Underproofed*	Bake products when they have achieved adequate proofing. Typically the item should have doubled in size.
Crumb is too open (large air pockets)	Overproofed*	When an item is overproofed, it will look deflated.
Surface is not smooth	Dough got too warm from sitting out too long or being excessively handled.	Do not let the dough sit uncovered for long periods of time.
	Warm hands can also damage a dough if they are in contact with the dough for extended periods of time.	Do not overhandle the dough.
Pastry looks deflated	Overproofed*. Excessive fermentation and CO_2 overinflated the pastry with large gas pockets, which deflated during the baking process.	When an item is overproofed, it will look deflated. Bake the item when it is properly proofed.
Pastry smells like alcohol	Overproofed*. Excessive fermentation produced too much alcohol.	Bake the item when it is properly proofed.
Pastry has a ring of egg wash underneath it	Excessive egg wash	Apply just enough egg wash to coat the item to be baked without it pooling down the sides.
Looks flat	Insufficient yeast (improperly weighed-out yeast)	Make sure that all of the ingredients are scaled correctly before making the product.
	Insufficient fermentation	Bake the item when it is properly proofed.
	Oven was at the wrong temperature	Always check the oven before loading it with product.

*Adequate proofing (fermentation) will vary from item to item. In most cases, the product will double in size, but it is not a set rule for all items. Knowing when a dough is proofed requires extensive experience gained through trial and error. Touching the dough to test for proof and having it double in size are two ways to tell if the dough is ready to bake or not.

BRIOCHE "MOTHER" RECIPE

yield: 5 kg/11 lb.3 oz dough

INGREDIENT	METRIC	U.S.	BAKERS' %
Bread flour	2.15 kg	4 lb 12 oz	100%
Salt	56 g	2 oz	2.62%
Sugar	321 g	11.3 oz	14.91%
Instant dry yeast (red label)	26 g	.9 oz	1.2%
Milk, at 21°C/70°F	499 g	1 lb 1.6 oz	23.16%
Eggs, at 21°C/70°F	862 g	1 lb 14.4 oz	40.06%
Butter, diced, pliable but not soft	1.08 kg	2 lb 6.2 oz	50.3%
Total	5 kg	11 lb .3 oz	232.25%

1. Combine the flour, salt, sugar, and yeast.

2. In a 20-qt mixing bowl, pour in the milk and 750 g/1 lb 11 oz of the eggs and stir to combine. Pour the dry ingredients on top. Mix on low speed until just incorporated.

3. Add one-third of the butter and switch the mixer to medium speed. Once that butter has been incorporated, add another third of the butter. Wait until it has been completely mixed in, then add the remaining butter.

Basic Method for Making Brioche Dough

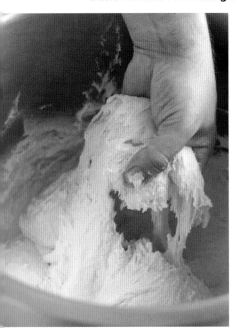 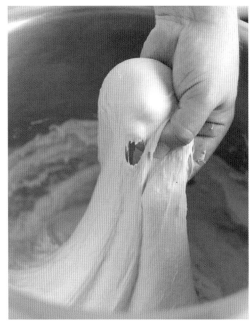 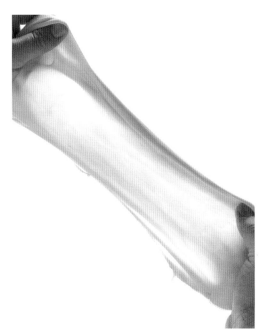

FROM LEFT TO RIGHT:
1. After incorporating the butter, the dough will show minimal gluten development.
2. Midway through the mixing process, the dough will have developed enough gluten to begin to exhibit elasticity when stretched.
3. Use the window test to determine when the dough has reached full gluten development.

4. Continue to mix on medium speed until full gluten development is achieved. To check for gluten development, perform a "window test." Stretch a small amount of dough with your hands. It should be elastic enough to be pulled until it is very thin and you can see through it without it ripping.

5. Add the remaining eggs and mix until just incorporated. At this point, the final dough temperature should not exceed 27°C/80°F.

6. Take the dough out of the bowl and place on a floured surface. Cover with plastic wrap. Allow it to bulk ferment for 45 minutes.

7. Transfer the dough to a sheet pan lined with silicone paper or greased parchment paper to prevent it from sticking. Wrap the sheet pan with plastic wrap and refrigerate. It is ready to be shaped when it is has firmed up and relaxed for at least an hour. At this point it can be reserved in the refrigerator for 12 hours before shaping, or it can be frozen for later use.

notes Never handle brioche above 27°C/81°F, since this temperature will cause the large amount of butter in the dough to soften and separate from the dough, thereby breaking the emulsion. This will result in a brioche with poor crumb structure and an uneven baking surface (cracked and lumpy rather than smooth). If the bakeshop is too hot, keep the dough as cold as possible (freezing it for short periods of time) and only shape a few pieces at a time. Work as far away from the oven or any other heat source as possible. The temperature 27°C/81°F is only good for proofing; since the dough will not be manipulated (touched) any further, the butter has a chance to slowly expand with the dough as it proofs, and there is no separation. The brioche should be proofed at 27°C/81°F, with a humidity of 65 to 70 percent.

CRAQUELIN

yield: 40 pieces

INGREDIENT	METRIC	U.S.
Sugar cubes	80	80
Lemon zest	6 lemons	6 lemons
Tahitian vanilla powder	10 g	.35 oz
Brioche Dough (page 10)	3.64 kg	8 lb .4 oz
Egg Wash for Brushing (page 13)	as needed	as needed
Sanding sugar	as needed	as needed

1. Cut the sugar cubes in half and combine them with the lemon zest and vanilla powder in a bowl. Toss until all of the ingredients are uniformly mixed. It is a good idea to prepare this ahead of time. A large amount of this mixture can be made and stored at room temperature in an airtight container for further use. This will also help the sugar cubes absorb the flavors of the lemon zest and vanilla powder.

2. Weigh out forty 63-g/2.25-oz pieces of brioche and refrigerate. Weigh out forty 28-g/1-oz pieces of brioche and refrigerate.

3. Shape the larger pieces of brioche into balls and refrigerate.

4. Roll the smaller pieces of brioche out into 7.5-cm/3-in discs.

5. Place 40 mini panettone cups on a sheet pan.

6. Remove the larger brioche balls from the refrigerator. Push 4 sugar cube halves into each ball, and reshape into a ball.

7. Brush the exposed surface of the brioche discs with egg wash. Place a large brioche ball at the center of each disc.

8. Carefully wrap the larger balls with the brioche discs, making sure that they are completely enclosed.

9. Place each craquelin inside a panettone cup, with the seam resting on the base of the cup. Brush the top of each craquelin with egg wash.

10. Place the sheet pan inside a large plastic bag and tie it shut. Proof at room temperature (21° to 22°C/70° to 72°F) until the craquelin rises to the top of the panettone molds. This can take up to 3 hours; alternatively, proof inside a proof box at 27°C/81°F with 70 percent humidity, until the craquelin reaches the top of the panettone molds, about 1½ hours.

11. Preheat a convection oven to 185°C/365°F.

12. Brush the top of the craquelin with egg wash one more time and sprinkle sanding sugar generously on top, enough to cover the exposed surface. Score the center of the craquelin using a pair of scissors. The score should be about the size of a dime in diameter, and 1.25 cm/.5 in deep.

13. Bake until the craquelin is golden brown on top, about 12 minutes.

Basic Method for Shaping Craquelin

FROM LEFT TO RIGHT:
1. Press the halved sugar cubes into the centers of the larger balls of brioche dough.
2. Gently wrap the brioche balls in discs of dough, ensuring that each ball is completely encased.
3. The abundance of sugar tenderizes the dough and fuels yeast activity, creating a hollow within the finished craquelin's delicate crumb.

note For this particular item, it is very important that it be completely finished the same day that the dough is made, or it will not hold its shape when it bakes. The large amount of sugar in the dough provides plenty of food for yeast development, but don't forget that sugar is also a tenderizer (it can weaken the gluten in the dough). The delicate outer shell of the craquelin needs to withstand the interior expansion of the dough without ripping while it bakes. The dough is strongest when it is recently made. The older it is, the weaker it will become.

variations Use brown sugar cubes instead of white sugar cubes. However, brown sugar cubes can be very expensive.

Any citrus zest will work; add 20g/.70 oz per 5 kg/11 lb .32 oz batch of brioche dough.

Sugar cubes can also be flavored with ground spices such as cinnamon, nutmeg, and cloves; simply toss them with the cubes to coat them.

Cubes can be drizzled with liquor, such as rum or Amaretto, but they need to be placed in an oven to dry them out; otherwise they will dissolve.

Substitute English toffee pieces for the sugar cubes.

EGG WASH FOR BRUSHING

yield: 1 kg/2 lb 3.2 oz

INGREDIENT	METRIC	U.S.	%
Whole eggs	658 g	1 lb 7.2 oz	65.79%
Egg yolks	263 g	9.28 oz	26.32%
Milk	66 g	2.32 oz	6.58%
Salt	13 g	.46 oz	1.32%

Combine all of the ingredients in a bowl using a whisk. Pass through a fine-mesh sieve and pour into an airtight container. Refrigerate. Discard after 3 days.

note This will need to be made in advance, before shaping pastries.

Pearl Sugar Brioche (page 15) on the left and Huckleberry Compote and Lemon Curd Brioche (page 16) in the center.

PEARL SUGAR BRIOCHE

yield: 40 pieces

INGREDIENT	METRIC	U.S.	%
Brioche Dough (page 10)	2.8 kg	6 lb 2.77 oz	90.9%
Egg Wash for Brushing (page 13)	as needed	as needed	
Pearl sugar, or as needed	284 g	10 oz	9.1%

1. Place 40 fluted paper cup molds (see picture at left) on a sheet pan. Spray lightly with vegetable spray.

2. Divide the brioche into forty 70-g/2.5-oz pieces. Shape each piece into a ball on a lightly floured surface.

3. Preheat a convection oven to 185°C/365°F.

4. Place each ball inside the prepared molds. Make sure they are centered in the mold so that when they bake, they bake upward and not lopsided. Wrap the entire sheet pan and freeze or refrigerate if not using right away, or brush with egg wash and proof at 27°C/81°F with 70 percent humidity for 2 hours or until nearly doubled in size. Brush the brioche with egg wash again. Make sure not to brush the brioche too heavily, since any egg wash that trickles down will puddle and bake. Brush on just enough to coat the surface.

5. Once the brioche has fully proofed, brush with egg wash once again. Sprinkle about 7 g/.25 oz of pearl sugar on top of each brioche. Use more if necessary to coat the entire surface.

6. Bake until golden brown, 10 to 12 minutes. Cool on a wire rack.

BRIOCHE À TÊTE

yield: 40 pieces

INGREDIENT	METRIC	U.S.
Brioche Dough (page 10)	2.8 kg	6 lb 2.75 oz
Egg Wash for Brushing (page 13)	as needed	as needed

1. Place 40 fluted tinned-steel brioche molds on a sheet pan. Spray lightly with vegetable spray.

2. Divide the brioche into forty 70-g/2.5-oz pieces. Shape each into a ball on a lightly floured surface and refrigerate covered until firm to the touch.

3. Roll each piece into a cylindrical shape with the palm of your hand on a lightly floured surface. The approximate dimension will be 7.5 cm long by 2.5 cm in diameter/3 by 1 in. Visually divide each piece into thirds and, using your hand as if it were a knife, roll the dough back and forth until it is almost divided into 2 pieces one-third from one end of the cylinder.

4. Lift the dough from the smaller piece and press down into the larger piece of dough in a circular motion; this will form the large rounded base and the smaller rounded top.

5. Place the shaped têtes inside the prepared molds. Make sure they are centered in the molds so that when they bake, they bake upward and not lopsided. Wrap and freeze or refrigerate if not using right away, or brush with egg wash and proof at 27°C/81°F with 70 percent humidity for 2 hours or until nearly doubled in size.

6. Meanwhile, preheat a convection oven to 185°C/365°F.

7. Once the têtes have proofed, brush with egg wash again and bake until golden brown, 10 to 12 minutes. Remove from the molds immediately after they bake, otherwise the steam from the brioche will be trapped and the base of the brioche will collapse.

8. Cool on a wire rack.

HUCKLEBERRY COMPOTE AND LEMON CURD BRIOCHE

yield: 40 pieces

INGREDIENT	METRIC	U.S.	%
LEMON CURD			
Lemon juice	218 g	7.68 oz	18.18%
Sugar	218 g	7.68 oz	18.18%
Eggs	218 g	7.68 oz	18.18%
Butter	545 g	1 lb 3.2 oz	45.45%
HUCKLEBERRY COMPOTE			
Huckleberries (see Note)	840 g	1 lb 13.6 oz	70%
Sugar	240 g	8.45 oz	20%
Water	120 g	4.22 oz	10%
Salt	pinch	pinch	
Brioche Dough (page 10)	2.4 kg	5 lb 4.66 oz	47.06%
Egg wash for Brushing (page 13)	as needed	as needed	1.97%
Pearl sugar	200 g	7.05 oz	3.92%

1. **FOR THE LEMON CURD:** Combine the lemon juice, sugar, and eggs in a bowl and cook over a double boiler, whisking constantly, until the mixture reaches 80°C/175°F.

2. Remove from the heat and transfer to a mixer bowl fitted with a whip attachment. Whip on high speed, and add the butter in small pieces. Whip until the curd has cooled down.

3. Reserve refrigerated in an airtight container. Place a piece of plastic wrap directly over the surface of the lemon curd to prevent a skin from forming.

4. **FOR THE HUCKLEBERRY COMPOTE:** Combine all of the ingredients in a pot and bring to a slow boil, stirring occasionally. Turn off the heat. Do not boil too quickly or stir aggressively, in order to keep the integrity of the huckleberries as much as possible (they burst easily).

5. Cool the huckleberry compote over an ice bath. Adjust the sweetness by adding more sugar if necessary. Reserve refrigerated in an airtight container.

6. **FOR THE ASSEMBLY:** Remove the brioche from the refrigerator and roll the dough to a thickness of 5 mm/.25 in using a sheeter, preferably, or a rolling pin. Let the dough relax for 30 minutes in the freezer. This will help it hold its shape when cut.

7. Meanwhile, grease forty 113-g/4-oz disposable aluminum soufflé tins or stainless-steel rings 7.5 cm diameter by 3.75 cm high/3 by 1.5 in with nonstick spray. Place them on a sheet pan, with parchment paper if using stainless-steel rings.

8. Cut out brioche circles using a 10-cm-/4-in-diameter ring cutter. If the dough is still cold by the time the last piece is cut out, line the inside of the soufflé tins or the rings with the dough, making sure that the dough is flush with the base of the tin or ring and that it comes up just above the rim. At this point the shaped brioche can be wrapped and refrigerated or frozen. If not, brush the exposed border of the dough with egg wash and proof at 27°C/81°F at 70 percent humidity for about 2 hours or until nearly doubled in size.

9. Meanwhile, preheat a convection oven to 185°C/365°F.

10. Brush the exposed border of the dough with egg wash again and sprinkle a small amount (about 5 g/.18 oz) of pearl sugar around the rim of the brioche.

11. Bake until the brioche is golden brown, 10 to 12 minutes.

12. Take the tins or ring molds off of the sheet pan and cool them on a wire rack.

13. Once they have cooled, push down the center of the dough with your index finger, wearing a glove, to make room for the lemon curd. Pipe 30 g/1.06 oz of lemon curd into the baked brioche, and then spoon 30 g/1.06 oz of huckleberry compote on top of the lemon curd.

14. Tie a ribbon around the finished brioche, and reserve in a cool, dry place for up to 12 hours. Discard any remaining brioche after service.

note Huckleberries usually come with a few stems and leaves. Make sure to pick through them before cooking. This task can be very laborious, but it is necessary.

FOIE GRAS, RAINIER CHERRY, AND SICILIAN PISTACHIO BRIOCHE

yield: 40 pieces

INGREDIENT	METRIC	U.S.	%
Foie gras (Grade A duck), cleaned	1.2 kg	2 lb 10.32 oz	23.53%
POACHED RAINIER CHERRIES			
Rainier cherries, stemmed and pitted	1.4 kg	3 lb 1.28 oz	44.4%
Sugar	750 g	1 lb 10.4 oz	23.79%
Water	1 kg	2 lb 3.2 oz	31.72%
Salt	3 g	.11 oz	.10%
Madagascar vanilla pods, split and seeds scraped	4	4	
TOASTED SICILIAN PISTACHIOS			
Sicilian pistachios	203 g	7.15 oz	100%
Brioche Dough (page 10)	2.4 kg	5 lb 4.66 oz	47.06%
Egg Wash for Brushing (page 13)	as needed	as needed	1.97%

1. Place the foie gras in a Thermomix cup. Press the 60°C/140°F button, turn the speed dial to speed 6, let it run for 2 minutes, and then turn the speed to 10 for 10 seconds. Transfer the foie gras to a bowl because the carryover heat in the cup might melt the foie gras.

2. Transfer the foie gras to a piping bag. Pipe it into 28-g/1-oz muffin fleximolds, smoothing out the tops with a small offset spatula. The shape of the muffin is ideal for the foie gras, since it will be placed inside the brioche.

3. Freeze the foie gras until hardened. Unmold and reserve frozen in an airtight container.

4. **FOR THE POACHED RAINIER CHERRIES:** Place all of the ingredients in a 6-qt sauce pot and bring to a boil over high heat. Turn the heat down to low and cook for 20 minutes, or until the cherries are tender. Skim the surface of the pot while the cherries are cooking.

5. Take the pot off the heat and transfer the contents to a hotel pan. Remove the vanilla pods. Let them cool at room temperature, then transfer to an airtight container and refrigerate.

6. **FOR THE TOASTED SICILIAN PISTACHIOS:** Preheat a convection oven to 162°C/320°F. Line a half sheet pan with parchment paper.

7. Chop the pistachios coarsely by hand and place on the sheet pan.

8. Toast until you can smell the pistachios (smelling them from the oven is a good gauge to determine if they are done). They will lose some weight due to evaporation while toasting.

9. Cool on a speed rack and transfer to an airtight container. The toasted nuts will keep for 5 to 7 days at room temperature.

10. **FOR THE ASSEMBLY:** Take the brioche out of the refrigerator and roll the dough to a thickness of 5 mm/.25 in using a sheeter or a rolling pin. Let the dough relax for 30 minutes in the freezer. This will help it hold its shape when it is cut out.

11. Place 40 mini panettone paper baking cups on a full-size sheet pan. Cut out brioche circles using a 12.5-cm-/5-in-diameter ring cutter. If the dough is still cold by the time the last piece is cut out, line the inside of the mini panettone cups, making sure that the dough is flush with the

base of the cup and that it comes up just above the rim. At this point the shaped brioche can be wrapped and refrigerated or frozen. Or brush the exposed border of the dough with egg wash and proof at 27°C/81°F at 70 percent humidity for about 2 hours or until nearly doubled in size.

12. Meanwhile, preheat a convection oven to 185°C/365°F.

13. Brush the exposed border of the dough with egg wash again.

14. Bake for 6 to 7 minutes until the top of the brioche is golden brown. Once the brioche has cooled off, place the foie gras inside it; you may need to make room for it with your fingers. Strain the liquid out of the cherries and reserve for another use. Spoon 28 g/1 oz of poached cherries onto the foie gras and top with 5 g/.18 oz of toasted Sicilian pistachios. Optionally, tie a ribbon around the finished brioche. Reserve in a cool, dry place for up to 12 hours. Discard any remaining brioche after service.

note Even though the cherries will start out at a larger amount than the final weight needed, they will lose volume due to evaporation, even with the addition of sugar. The final yield is the weight of the cherries once they are cooked and drained from their poaching liquid.

DOUGHNUTS

yield: 40 pieces

INGREDIENT	METRIC	U.S.
Brioche Dough (page 10)	3.2 kg	7 lb .64 oz

1. Roll out the cold brioche dough to a thickness of 2 cm/.75 in using a rolling pin or, preferably, a sheeter for consistency. Let the dough relax for 30 minutes in the freezer. If the dough is cut before this time, the gluten will pull back too quickly and will result in oval doughnuts.

2. Flour the work surface (preferably wood) lightly with bread flour. Line 4 sheet pans with parchment paper and spray the paper with nonstick oil spray.

3. Place the chilled dough on top of the floured surface and lightly dust flour over the exposed surface of the dough. Dip a 7.5-cm-/3-in-diameter doughnut cutter (or use larger or smaller cutters, as desired) in bread flour and cut into the dough, making sure the cutter goes straight down and is not lopsided. Do not twist the cutter, since this will affect the shape of the doughnut as well. If the doughnut did not come out clean, the cutter needs more flour.

4. Place the cut doughnuts on the prepared sheet pans. There should be 12 to 15 pieces per sheet pan.

5. Proof at 27°C/81°F with 70 percent humidity for 2 to 3 hours, or until almost doubled in size. You can tell they are proofed by gently pressing down with your finger. If the dough springs back, it is ready to fry.

6. While the doughnuts proof, heat a fryer to 182°C/355°F, or bring oil up to that temperature in a large rondeau.

7. When the doughnuts are ready to fry, line 2 sheet pans with a wire rack and have a spider ready to turn the doughnuts around in the fryer and to spoon them out. Gently lift the parchment paper under a doughnut and place the doughnut on the palm of your hand, then carefully drop it into the hot oil. This is another way to prevent the doughnut from becoming misshapen, since pulling on any part of it will make it lose its "O" shape.

8. Add 4 or 5 more doughnuts to the fryer. Once the doughnut gets a golden brown color on one side, flip it over and fry until golden on the other side, about 3 minutes per side. If you are also frying the doughnut centers, you must move them around in the oil constantly with a spoon, since they won't turn on one side or the other because they are round. Moving them constantly will give them an even color. The trick is to get the doughnut to be the same color on both sides, and for all the doughnuts to be the same color as well. Practice makes perfect.

9. Place the fried doughnuts on the wire racks to cool.

notes You can reserve the doughnut centers, fry them, and finish them as you would the actual doughnuts, but with less frying time since they are considerably smaller. These can be given out as samples or used to actually finish the doughnuts by placing them in the center of the finished doughnut, as with the Meyer Lemon Doughnuts on page 23.

It is desirable to have a white ring around the doughnut. This is a sign of proper proofing and frying. Some mass-produced doughnuts are uniformly browned throughout, and it is because they are fried in conveyor-belt type fryers that completely submerge the doughnut in hot oil for quicker frying.

Although there are variations on the dough used to make doughnuts, brioche is preferred because it produces a very delicate and light doughnut when it is fried. As commonplace as doughnuts are, it takes only a little more effort and a few extra steps to make them special. The preferred oil for frying doughnuts (or anything in this book, for that matter) is peanut oil, but there are two factors to consider with peanut oil. The first, and perhaps not as important as the second, is the cost factor. Peanut oil is expensive. The second factor is that there are many people with nut allergies. The second-best oil to use is straight canola oil. Never use shortening or lard.

FOR GLAZING DOUGHNUTS WITH POURING FONDANT

This procedure will apply to any item that uses pouring fondant to glaze, and this includes doughnuts, éclairs, and religieuses. Each variety will have specifics, such as a particular flavor or color or garnish, but all of the principles for working correctly with fondant are described in this section.

Place the fondant in a bowl and soften it using a hot water bath while stirring with a rubber spatula. Better yet, use a wooden spoon, but never a whisk. It can be hard to stir the fondant since it is very stiff when it is at room temperature. To help with this, add a small amount of simple syrup or water (about 100 g/3.53 oz for each 1 kg/2 lb 3.2 oz of fondant). Some chefs prefer to add water in order not to increase sweetness of the glaze, since fondant is already very sweet, but simple syrup and corn syrup can improve the shine of the glaze. This simple syrup should be made by boiling equal parts (by weight) of sugar and water. Make sure it is at room temperature when adding it to the fondant. One of the most important things to know about glazing an item with fondant is that it should warmed to between 35° and 40°C/95° and 105°F to obtain the shiniest glaze.

Fondant is made by boiling sugar and glucose syrup in order to concentrate it. It is then cooled down through agitation, which will result in very fine sugar crystals with delicate bonds that stay aligned a certain way. When fondant gets too hot, the bonds separate, and they give the glaze the impression of being bloomed (cracked and dull). It is for this reason that the water in the hot water bath should never boil, nor should the simple syrup or chocolate be added when they are hot, since this could bring the temperature of the fondant above 40°C/105°F. If making chocolate fondant glaze, when the fondant is fluid, add the melted but cool chocolate and stir until a uniform mixture is obtained.

The second most important aspect of glazing is getting the fondant to the right consistency. The final consistency should be semifluid. If it is too firm, it will not glaze the doughnut smoothly and evenly, and it will have ripples and spikes. If it is too loose, it will drip down the sides of the item. To fix these problems, if the glaze is too thick, add some simple syrup, and then measure the temperature again. Since the simple syrup is at room temperature, it will drop the temperature of the glaze. Warm the fondant over a water bath if necessary. If it is too loose, add more fondant (which will lighten the color of the glaze) or more chocolate (which will make it dull). Ideally, add a small amount of both, check the temperature, and reheat the glaze if necessary.

Remember that while you are glazing, the temperature of the glaze will drop. Check the temperature frequently and always have a hot water bath going to reheat the glaze when needed.

It is always nice to obtain an even coat of glaze on an item, a practically perfect straight line across it, but sometimes there will be a runaway drop going down the side of the doughnut. You can always use your finger to wipe it off, but make sure you are wearing gloves.

MEYER LEMON DOUGHNUTS

yield: 40 pieces

INGREDIENT	METRIC	U.S.
MEYER LEMON GLAZE		
Pouring fondant	1.33 kg	2 lb 14.88 oz
Meyer lemon juice	667 g	1 lb 7.52 oz
Brioche Doughnuts (page 21)	40	40
Brioche Doughnut Centers, fried (page 21)	40	40
Silver dragées	40	40

1. **FOR THE MEYER LEMON GLAZE:** Follow the instructions for glazing with fondant on page 22. Adjust the consistency of the glaze by adding more juice to loosen the glaze or more fondant to thicken it, if necessary. This glaze can be piped on instead of dipped for a "dripping" look (see photo).

2. **FOR THE ASSEMBLY:** Dip a doughnut horizontally into the glaze until it almost reaches its midsection, about one-third of the way. For the centers, dip them in the same glaze. The glaze will need to be reheated at this point.

3. Put a silver dragée on top of the freshly glazed centers before the glaze sets; otherwise it will not adhere. Place the finished centers in the hole in the center of the finished doughnuts.

4. Display for 16 hours maximum. Discard any left over after this period of time.

note There will be some leftover glaze, but it is necessary to make more than will actually coat the doughnuts. The doughnuts need to be dipped in a certain volume of glaze so that it can completely surround the doughnuts' surface.

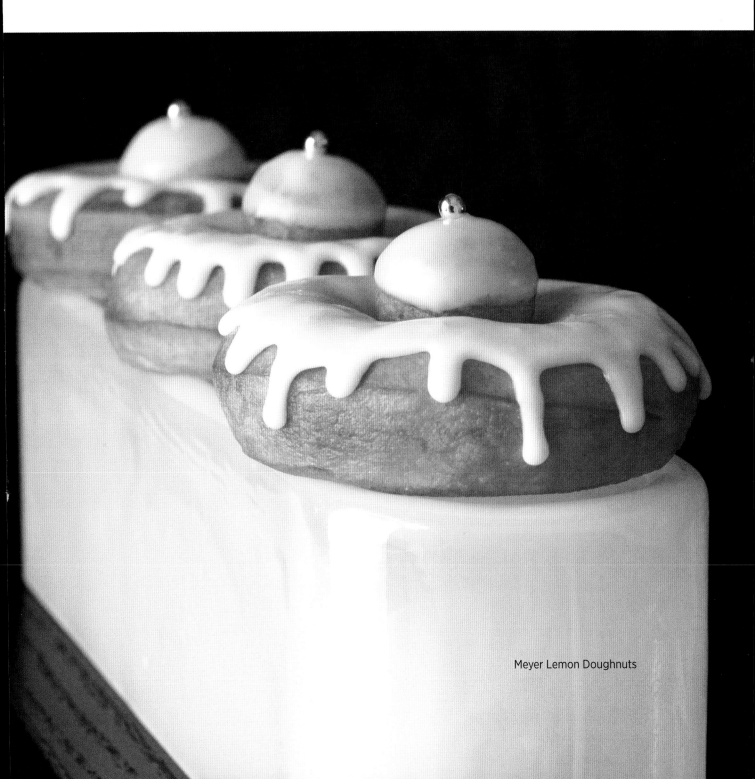

Meyer Lemon Doughnuts

CHOCOLATE-GLAZED AND COCONUT DOUGHNUTS

yield: **40 pieces**

INGREDIENT	METRIC	U.S.
CHOCOLATE GLAZE		
Pouring fondant	1.21 kg	2 lb 10.72 oz
Dark chocolate (64%), melted but cool	606 g	1 lb 5.28 oz
Simple syrup, water, or corn syrup	182 g	6.4 oz
Brioche Doughnuts (page 21)	40	40
Shredded coconut	500 g	1 lb 1.63 oz
Gold leaf	1 sheet	1 sheet

1. **FOR THE CHOCOLATE FONDANT GLAZE:** Follow the instructions for glazing with fondant on page 22, adding chocolate to the finished fondant.

2. **FOR THE ASSEMBLY:** Dip a doughnut horizontally into the glaze until it almost reaches its midsection, about one-third of the way.

3. Before the glaze sets, sprinkle one-half of the doughnut with shredded coconut and garnish the other half with a small piece of gold leaf. It is a good idea to have 2 people work on this so that one can glaze and another can garnish.

4. Display for 16 hours maximum. Discard any left over after this period of time.

STRAWBERRY SUGAR DOUGHNUTS WITH CRYSTALLIZED BERRIES

yield: 40 pieces

INGREDIENT	METRIC	U.S.
STRAWBERRY SUGAR		
Granulated sugar	900 g	1 lb 15.75 oz
Strawberry powder (see Note)	95 g	3.35 oz
Vanilla powder (see Note)	5 g	.18 oz
CRYSTALLIZED ROSE PETALS		
Rose petals	40	40
Pasteurized egg whites	91 g	3.2 oz
Superfine sugar	909 g	2 lb
CRYSTALLIZED BERRIES		
Freeze-dried raspberries	40	40
Freeze-dried strawberries	40	40
Freeze-dried blueberries	40	40
Egg whites	91 g	3.2 oz
Superfine sugar	909 g	2 lb
Brioche Doughnuts (page 21)	40	40
Brioche Doughnut Centers, fried (page 21)	40	40

1. **FOR THE STRAWBERRY SUGAR:** Combine all of the ingredients thoroughly in a bowl and then pass them through a drum sieve. Reserve in an airtight container at room temperature. The strawberry sugar will keep indefinitely if kept in a cool, dry place.

2. **FOR THE CRYSTALLIZED ROSE PETALS:** Brush each petal lightly with egg whites and then coat them with the superfine sugar. Brush the excess sugar off so that each petal has a uniform coating of sugar. If there is too much egg white, the sugar will clump up on the petal; if there is too little, the sugar will not adhere to the petal.

3. Place the petals on a sheet pan lined with parchment paper. Let them dry for at least 6 hours before using. Once they are dry, transfer to an airtight container and reserve in a cool, dry place. They will keep indefinitely if kept in these conditions.

4. **FOR THE CRYSTALLIZED BERRIES:** Insert the tip of a toothpick into each berry, being careful to not break it. Brush the egg whites onto the berry and then coat it in the superfine sugar. Stick the other end of the toothpick into a piece of Styrofoam (or similar item) to let the berries dry completely.

5. **FOR THE ASSEMBLY:** As soon as the doughnuts and the centers come out of the fryer, they need to be gently tossed in the strawberry sugar. If they are not coated immediately, the sugar will not adhere to the doughnut. Once the doughnuts have cooled, place one brioche center in the hole in the center of each doughnut. One crystallized rose petal should be wedged between the doughnut and the brioche center at an angle. Place one of each crystallized berry between the petal and the brioche centers.

note Strawberry powder and vanilla powder are available through specialty purveyors. See Resources on page 540. See the resource list on page 540 to obtain freeze-dried berries.

CHANTILLY CREAM BRIOCHE BERLINERS WITH ALMOND STREUSEL

yield: 40 pieces

INGREDIENT	METRIC	U.S.
CHANTILLY CREAM		
Heavy cream	1.8 kg	3 lb 15.36 oz
Superfine sugar	162 g	5.7 oz
Heavy cream stabilizer (liquid; see Note)	22 g	.76 oz
Vanilla paste (see Note)	18 g	.63 oz
AMARETTO ICING		
Confectioners' sugar	385 g	13.54 oz
Heavy cream	77 g	2.71 oz
Amaretto	39 g	1.35 oz
ALMOND STREUSEL		
Almond flour	249 g	8.78 oz
Pastry flour	249 g	8.78 oz
Sugar	249 g	8.78 oz
Butter	249 g	8.78 oz
Salt	3 g	.09 oz
FRIED BERLINERS		
Brioche Dough (page 10)	3.2 kg	7 lb .64 oz

1. **FOR THE CHANTILLY CREAM:** Combine all of the ingredients in a mixer bowl. Using the whip attachment, whip the mixture until it almost reaches stiff peaks. Completely stiff heavy cream does not pipe very smoothly.

2. Reserve refrigerated in an airtight container. The cream will keep for 3 to 4 days in the refrigerator, but it will need to be rewhipped it every day.

3. **FOR THE AMARETTO ICING:** Combine all of the ingredients in a bowl and whisk until an even, thick paste forms. Adjust the consistency by adding more confectioners' sugar if it is loose or more liquid if it's too thick.

4. Use the icing right away or transfer it to an airtight container and refrigerate for up to 3 weeks. The very high sugar content prevents it from spoiling.

5. **FOR THE ALMOND STREUSEL:** Combine all of the ingredients in a mixer bowl. Mix on low speed using a paddle attachment until a homogeneous mass is obtained.

6. Pass the streusel through a grid wire rack to obtain evenly sized pieces (this won't work if the streusel is refrigerated). Freeze the streusel until hardened. It can be baked right away or kept frozen for up to 6 months.

7. **TO BAKE THE STREUSEL:** Preheat a convection oven to 160°C/320°F.

8. Spread the streusel onto a parchment paper–lined sheet pan in a single layer. Bake the streusel until golden brown, about 7 minutes.

9. Place the parchment paper on a cooling rack to cool to room temperature. Reserve in an airtight container in a cool, dry place. The baked streusel will hold for up to 1 week.

10. **FOR THE BERLINERS:** Follow the procedure for doughnuts on page 21, but use a plain 8.75-cm/3.5-in ring cutter to cut out the brioche dough instead of a doughnut cutter.

11. Using a Bismarck piping tip (also known as a filling tip because it has a long, thin tube attached to a regular shaped piping tip), make a hole in side of the fried Berliner. Once the Bismarck tip is in, swirl it around to make room for the filling. Fit the Bismarck tip inside a piping tip using a coupler.

12. **FOR THE ASSEMBLY:** Fill the piping bag with just-whipped Chantilly cream.

13. Fill the Berliner until it can hold no more filling (about 50 g/1.76 oz).

14. Spread the Amaretto icing on top of the Berliner using a gloved finger or a rubber spatula, then immediately dip it in the almond streusel. The top of the Berliner should be generously coated with streusel. The icing is only a "glue" to keep the streusel on the Berliner.

notes Superfine sugar is used because it dissolves faster than larger-crystal sugars.

Ideally, only fill as many Berliners as you think you can sell in 2 hours, since it is not a good idea to refrigerate Berliners, and you can refill the case as the day progresses. As long as you have the mise en place, it is easily done. Always let your customers know to consume the Berliners right away or to refrigerate them if they are not planning to eat them in the very near future.

The stabilizer is used to maintain the volume of the whipped heavy cream throughout the day and through temperature changes, since heavy cream only stays whipped when it is at or below 4°C/39°F (without reaching freezing temperatures). Stabilizers are, in fact, natural products, and most of them are derived from sea algae and plants, not chemicals.

Heavy-cream stabilizers can be found in liquid or powdered form, and neither is better than the other. Check the label of the stabilizer to see how much is required for a specific amount of heavy cream (it might be different from the amount used above).

Vanilla paste is precisely that, a semiliquid paste made with pulverized vanilla beans. In cold preparations such as this one, it helps distribute the vanilla beans more evenly than those of an actual vanilla pod, whose beans are clumped up. Never use vanilla extract. Even the more expensive ones will never taste as good as vanilla paste, vanilla powder, or actual vanilla beans.

A Berliner is a disc of dough (in this case brioche) that is fried and then filled. Here we fill the Berliners with Chantilly cream, but they can be filled in many other ways, such as with pastry cream, raspberry jam, or chocolate ganache.

BRIOCHE LOAVES

INGREDIENT	METRIC	U.S.
Brioche Dough (page 10)	1.4 kg	3 lb 1.38 oz
Egg Wash for Brushing (page 13)	as needed	as needed

1. Grease 2 stainless-steel ring molds 10 cm tall by 15 cm in diameter/4 by 6 in (see Resources, page 540) lightly with nonstick oil spray, and line the inside of them with silicone paper cut to fit inside the ring mold. Place both ring molds on a half sheet pan lined with silicone paper or a nonstick rubber mat.

2. Make the brioche dough. Weigh out two 700-g/1 lb 8.64-oz pieces of brioche. Flour a work surface with bread flour. Roll out each piece to 2.5 cm/1 in thick, trying to keep it as round as possible.

3. Place the garnish at the center of the dough and fold in the ends to encase the desired garnish (see the table on page 30).

4. Roll the dough into a ball and place one inside each mold with the seam facing down, pressing down with your knuckles so that the dough covers the entire bottom surface of the mold. Try not to leave any garnish exposed or protruding through the surface because it might burn when it bakes. Brush the top with egg wash.

5. Proof at 27°C/81°F with 70 percent humidity for 2½ to 3 hours.

6. Meanwhile, preheat a convection oven to 160°C/320°F.

7. Once proofed, brush the top again with egg wash and add any toppings or glazes if required. Score the dough with a pair of scissors, cutting an "X" that is about 5 cm/2 in long straight down the middle of the top.

8. Bake for 16 minutes, and then turn the temperature down to 150°C/300°F. Bake for about 30 more minutes, or until the internal temperature of the dough reaches 95°C/203°F. The brioche loaves can be taken out of the oven if they are slightly under the desired temperature, since there will be carryover heat that will finish the baking process. Some loaves will require to be glazed at this point while they are still hot.

9. Take the ring molds off the baked brioche while they are still hot and let them cool at room temperature over a sheet pan lined with a cooling rack.

10. Finish the loaves with the appropriate garnish. Display in a cool, dry area. Discard after 16 hours.

Praline Brioche (page 31)

brioche loaf variations

The total amount in the brioche loaf recipe is for 2 loaves, each weighing 700 g/1 lb 8.64 oz before baking. They will lose 3 percent of their weight once they have baked and cooled. This weight does not include added garnish, which can add 15 percent to 20 percent to the total weight. All added garnishes should not weigh more than 20 percent of the total weight of the dough to prevent the risk of the dough collapsing from excess added weight. Recipes for garnishes follow.

	internal garnish	amount (for 2 loaves; divide in half for each loaf)	coating/glaze/other	amount (for 2 loaves; divide in half for each loaf)	special instructions
Dark Chocolate and Toffee Brioche	Dark chocolate pistoles (72%)	100 g/3.53 oz	Salted Caramel	400 g/14.11 oz	Brush the caramel on after the ring mold has been taken off and while the brioche is still warm. Brush it on all the sides and top of the brioche cube. Return to the oven for 5 minutes. Sprinkle 5 g/.18 oz of Maldon sea salt and 75 g/2.64 oz of toasted pecans on top of each brioche. Finish with the appropriate ribbon.
	English Toffee	100 g/3.53 oz	Toasted pecans (chopped)	150 g/5.3 oz	
			Maldon sea salt	10 g/.35 oz	
Banana, Brown Sugar, and Macadamia Nut Brioche	Rum-Scented Sugar Cubes	100 g/3.53 oz	Rum Icing	300 g/10.58 oz	Once the loaves have cooled, dip the tops of the brioche into the rum icing (it should just coat the top). Coat the icing with 200 g/7.05 oz chopped candied macadamia nuts for each loaf. Finish with the appropriate ribbon.
	Caramelized Bananas	100 g/3.53 oz	Candied Macadamia Nuts (chopped)	400 g/14.11oz	
Luxardo Cherry and Milk Glaze Brioche	Luxardo cherries (see Note)	200 g/7.05 oz	Condensed milk (warmed to 50°C/122°F)	600 g/1 lb 5.15 oz	Take the molds off the brioche while they are hot. Using a thin skewer, make small holes in the brioche throughout the top (about 25 each); place the still-warm brioche on a sheet pan lined with a wire rack and slowly pour the condensed milk over the top using a funnel or ladle. Repeat until all of the condensed milk has been absorbed. Put the brioche on a sheet pan lined with a nonstick rubber mat. Return the brioche to the oven for 7 minutes. Garnish with a sheet of silver leaf (1 per loaf) and finish with the appropriate ribbon.
			Silver leaf (edible)	2 sheets (1 per brioche)	

	internal garnish	amount (for 2 loaves; divide in half for each loaf)	coating/glaze/other	amount (for 2 loaves; divide in half for each loaf)	special instructions
Blueberry, Almond and Vanilla Brioche	Blueberries (dried)	125 g/4.41 oz	Pearl sugar	200 g/7.05 oz	Apply the pearl sugar after proofing and the second coat of egg wash has been applied. Finish with a ribbon tied across the front.
	Vanilla beans (Tahitian, split and scraped, beans only; reserve pods for other uses)	2 pods			
	Toasted chopped almonds	75 g/2.64 oz			
Chocolate Truffle Brioche	Milk Chocolate Truffles	180 g/6.35 oz About 18 pieces at 10 g/.35 oz each. Use 9 pieces per cube. Place the truffles in a 3x3 grid (per piece of dough) on the flattened dough, and then fold the corners in.	Chocolate Glaze	250 g/8.82 oz	Apply a coat of chocolate glaze instead of the second coat of egg wash (before baking), and then another coat 2 to 3 minutes before it is finished baking (use a pastry brush to apply the glaze). Once they have cooled, garnish with the chocolate croquant and the chocolate-covered puffed rice. Finish with the appropriate ribbon.
			Chocolate Croquant	4 pc	
			Chocolate-Covered Puffed Rice (see Resources, page 540)	100 g/3.53 oz	
Praline Brioche	Praline croquant (see Resources, page 540)	180 g/6.35 oz	Almond Topping Pipe onto brioche once it is proofed.	200/7.05 oz	Finish with a wide brown ribbon tied around the middle of the loaf.
			Praline croquant Sprinkle on top of the almond topping to cover the surface.	200/7.05 oz	

note Luxardo cherries are marasca cherries, used to make maraschino liqueur. This particular brand (made in Italy) is of exceptional quality.

garnish recipes

Many of these recipes are simpler if made in larger batches because it is easier to prepare them, take their temperature, etc. Such recipes note whether or not they will keep well if stored.

ENGLISH TOFFEE

yield: 100 g/3.53 oz

INGREDIENT	METRIC	U.S.	%
Butter, salted	34 g	1.19 oz	33.68%
Sugar	57 g	2.01 oz	57.03%
Water	9 g	.33 oz	9.28%

1. Line a half sheet pan with a nonstick rubber mat.

2. Combine all of the ingredients in a sauce pot and cook over medium-high heat until the mixture reaches 152°C/305°F. Immediately pour onto the prepared sheet pan. Let it cool, and then break into small pieces using the back of a chef's knife.

3. Place inside a zip-close bag or an airtight container and reserve in a cool, dry place. The toffee will keep indefinitely if stored this way.

RUM-SCENTED SUGAR CUBES

yield: 100 g/3.53 oz

INGREDIENT	METRIC	U.S.	%
Brown sugar cubes	95 g	3.34 oz	95%
Dark rum	5 g	.18 oz	5%

1. Place the sugar cubes on a sheet pan lined with a nonstick rubber mat in a single layer and touching each other. Sprinkle the rum on top of the sugar cubes. Dry on top of an oven, uncovered, or in a dehydrator overnight. If too much rum is used, the sugar cubes will melt and lose their shape.

2. Once they are dry again, transfer to an airtight container and reserve in a cool, dry place. The sugar cubes will keep indefinitely if stored this way.

RUM ICING

yield: 300 g/10.58 oz

INGREDIENT	METRIC	U.S.	%
Confectioners' sugar	231 g	8.12 oz	76.92%
Heavy cream	46 g	1.62 oz	15.38%
Dark rum	23 g	.81 oz	7.69%

Combine all of the ingredients in a bowl and whisk until an even, thick paste forms. Adjust the consistency by adding more confectioners' sugar if it is loose or more liquid if it is too thick.

SALTED CARAMEL

yield: 400 g/14.11oz

INGREDIENT	METRIC	U.S.	%
Sugar	162 g	5.7 oz	40.46%
Glucose syrup	81 g	2.85 oz	20.23%
Heavy cream	101 g	3.56 oz	25.28%
Butter	51 g	1.78 oz	12.64%
Salt	6 g	.20 oz	1.39%

1. In a 2-qt sauce pot, combine the sugar with enough water to obtain a "wet sand" texture (about one-quarter of the weight of the sugar), using your hands. Pour in the glucose. Clean the sides of the pot so that there are no sugar crystals on it by using a clean pastry brush dipped in water. Cook over high heat.

2. While the sugar cooks, bring the cream, butter, and salt to a simmer in a small sauce pot.

3. Once the sugar reaches a dark amber color (170°C/338°F), slowly whisk in the hot cream and butter mixture.

4. Pour the caramel into an adequately sized stainless-steel container and cool at room temperature. Once cool, transfer to an airtight container and reserve in a cool, dry place. The caramel will keep indefinitely if stored this way.

CARAMELIZED BANANAS

yield: 100 g/3.53 oz

INGREDIENT	METRIC	U.S.	%
Bananas	150 g	5.28 oz	50%
Sugar	100 g	3.53 oz	33.33%
Butter	50 g	1.76 oz	16.67%

1. Cut the bananas into 5-mm-/.25-in-thick discs.

2. In a small sauté pan, make a dry caramel with the sugar over high heat, stirring constantly with a spoon. Once the sugar turns a medium amber brown, stir in the butter.

3. When the sugar starts bubbling again, turn the heat down to low and add the bananas. When the side that faces the sugar has been caramelized, turn the discs over and cook until they are caramelized as well.

4. Spoon the bananas out of the caramel and place them onto a sheet pan lined with silicone paper. Place the sheet pan in the freezer, since the caramelized banana discs need to be frozen hard when they are mixed into the brioche to prevent them from breaking up too much.

note Even though the total weight of the ingredients is larger than the yield, we will only be using the drained mass—in other words, only the bananas, which will lose a large amount of moisture during the cooking process.

CANDIED MACADAMIA NUTS

yield: 400 g/14.11 oz

INGREDIENT	METRIC	U.S.	%
Whole macadamia nuts	209 g	7.35 oz	52.17%
Sugar	139 g	4.9 oz	34.78%
Water	52 g	1.84 oz	13.04%

1. Preheat a convection oven to 160°C/325°F.

2. Grease a marble surface with a small amount of nonstick oil spray.

3. Line a sheet pan with parchment paper and a wire rack. Grease the wire rack with nonstick oil spray.

4. Combine the sugar and water in a small sauce pot and cook over high heat. Meanwhile, toast the macadamia nuts in the oven. The trick is to coordinate the cooking of the sugar with the toasting of the nuts. The sugar should be started first since it takes longer to cook than the macadamia nuts do to toast, but with such small amounts it will take practically the same time. If per chance the nuts are toasted before the sugar is caramelized, leave them on top of the oven to keep them warm. The intention is that when they are stirred into the sugar they are not cold, because if they are, they will bring the temperature of the sugar down so drastically that it will crystallize.

5. Cook the sugar to 170°C/338°F. When making small amounts such as this, it is best to tell the temperature by the color of the sugar, since a thermometer probe is too big to submerge into the boiling sugar and will therefore not provide an accurate reading. You could also make more than you need for 1 batch. The color of the cooked sugar syrup should be amber brown.

6. Remove the syrup from the heat and stir in the macadamia nuts. Continue to stir until the macadamia nuts are completely coated in sugar.

7. Pour the macadamia nuts onto the greased wire rack. The parchment paper below the wire rack will catch the caramelized sugar and make cleanup easier.

8. Put on 3 gloves per hand. Spray each hand with nonstick oil spray. Separate the slivered macadamia nuts and place them on the greased marble surface to cool.

9. Once the macadamia nuts have cooled down, chop them coarsely with a chef's knife. Reserve them in an airtight container at room temperature in a cool, dry place. The nuts will keep for up to 2 weeks if stored in these conditions.

CHOCOLATE GLAZE

yield: 250 g/8.82 oz

INGREDIENT	METRIC	U.S.	%
Almond flour	47 g	1.65 oz	18.77%
Cocoa powder	7 g	.24 oz	2.68%
Sugar	134 g	4.72 oz	53.62%
Cornstarch	5 g	.19 oz	2.14%
Egg whites	57 g	2.01 oz	22.79%

1. Combine the flour, cocoa, sugar, and cornstarch in a Robot Coupe and grind for about 1 minute (to obtain a homogeneous mixture).

2. Slowly pour in the egg whites through the top of the Robot Coupe while it is running. Turn the Robot Coupe off as soon as all of the whites have been incorporated.

3. Reserve in an airtight container in the refrigerator. This glaze will keep for up to 1 week.

MILK CHOCOLATE TRUFFLES

yield: **18 truffles**

INGREDIENT	METRIC	U.S.	%
GANACHE (TRUFFLE FILLING)			
Milk chocolate	424 g	14.93 oz	56.54%
Sugar	27 g	.93 oz	3.53%
Pectin, universal (see Note)	11 g	.37 oz	1.41%
Heavy cream	265 g	9.33 oz	35.34%
Glucose syrup	24 g	.84 oz	3.18%
Truffle shells	18	18	
Tempered dark chocolate (64%)	100 g	3.53 oz	

1. **FOR THE GANACHE:** Place the chocolate in a medium-small stainless-steel bowl, anchored down with a damp towel to keep it in place.

2. Combine the sugar with the pectin in another small bowl; make sure they are uniformly combined, or else the pectin will clump up on contact with the cream.

3. Place the cream in a small sauce pot over medium heat. When the cream reaches room temperature, stir in the sugar-pectin mix. Whisk in the glucose syrup. Bring the mixture to a boil and pour it over the milk chocolate in a slow, steady stream, stirring constantly with a rubber spatula.

4. Let the mixture cool to room temperature in a shallow hotel pan.

5. **FOR THE ASSEMBLY:** Transfer the ganache to a piping bag and fill the truffle shells to the top. Let the ganache set at room temperature, at least 2 to 3 hours.

6. Coat the truffles in tempered dark chocolate. Reserve them in an airtight container at room temperature in a cool, dry place. They will keep for 1 week if stored this way.

note It is crucial to use universal pectin, also known as NH95 pectin (see Resources, page 540), since regular pectin gels in the presence of sugar, liquid, and an acid. Since there is no acid here to gel the pectin, universal pectin is required because it gels in presence of the liquid and calcium found in the heavy cream and milk chocolate. We add pectin to this ganache because it will stabilize it while it is baking and will prevent ingredient separation. Another notable quality of universal pectin is its "thermoreversible" gelling properties. Once it has gelled, it can be melted and softened again through heat, unlike regular pectin. Regular pectin has irreversible gelling; once it gels it cannot be melted again.

CHOCOLATE CROQUANT

yield: 2 large pieces or 4 small pieces (500 g/1 lb 1.6 oz)

INGREDIENT	METRIC	U.S.	%
Sugar	204 g	7.18 oz	40.82%
Glucose syrup	204 g	7.18 oz	40.82%
Cocoa paste	92 g	3.23 oz	18.37%

1. Line a sheet pan with a nonstick rubber mat and set aside.

2. In a 2-qt sauce pot, combine the sugar with enough water so that it feels like "wet sand" (about one-quarter of the weight of sugar), then pour the glucose syrup on top. Do not stir, mix, or agitate in any way after this point. Place a thermometer in the pot.

3. Cook the mixture until the sugars reach 163°C/325°F, then shock the pot in a cold water bath for 20 seconds to keep the sugar from cooking any further. Stir in the cocoa paste with a wooden spoon and pour onto the prepared sheet pan.

4. When the sugar is pliable, start pulling it. Pull until the sugar is paper thin and you can see through it. The end product will have very abstract shapes, but the pieces should be somewhat similar in look and size. The most important factor is that they be very thin so that they are easy to eat. If the sugar is too hot to handle, put on 2 or 3 pairs of latex gloves, and lightly spray the gloves with nonstick oil spray. If the sugar is too hot, you will not be able to stretch it properly. An ideal temperature is around 50°C/122°F; you can take the temperature with a surface (infrared) thermometer. If the sugar hardens and is not pliable any more, microwave it in 4-second intervals.

5. Keep the croquant in an airtight container at room temperature in a cool, dry place. With cooked sugar pieces, use silica gel packs (see Resources, page 540), which absorb moisture in the environment, keeping the sugar pieces dry. They will keep indefinitely if stored this way.

ALMOND TOPPING

yield: 200 g/7.05 oz

INGREDIENT	METRIC	U.S.	%
Sugar	93 g	3.28 oz	46.51%
Almond flour	53 g	1.87 oz	26.51%
Canola oil	7 g	.26 oz	3.72%
Semolina	4 g	.13 oz	1.86%
Egg whites	43 g	1.51 oz	21.4%

1. Combine all of the ingredients in a bowl. If the mixture is too thick, add some more egg whites.

2. Reserve in an airtight container in the refrigerator for up to 5 days.

note When this topping is baked it becomes very crisp, especially with the addition of the praline croquant, which gives the soft brioche a nice texture balance.

PULLMAN LOAF

yield: 2 loaves

INGREDIENT	METRIC	U.S.
Brioche Dough (page 10)	2 kg	4 lb 6.54 oz

1. Divide the dough into two equal 1 kg/2 lb 3.26 oz pieces. Roll out each piece to the length of the Pullman mold (see note below). Let it relax in the refrigerator for 20 to 30 minutes, covered in plastic wrap. Meanwhile, grease the inside of each loaf pan and the lids with a light coating of nonstick oil spray. Roll the dough out to the same length as before and place it inside the loaf pans, flattening them with your knuckles so they occupy the entire base of the pan. Place both pans on a sheet pan.

2. Proof at 27°C/81°F with 70 percent humidity. This can take between 2 and 3 hours.

3. Meanwhile, preheat a convection oven to 190°C/375°F.

4. When the brioche is ready, slide the lid on top of the pan.

5. Bake until the brioche reaches an internal temperature of 95°C/203°F. It can be baked to a few degrees cooler, since there will be some carryover heat that will finish baking the brioche.

6. As soon as the loaves come out of the oven, unmold the brioche onto a wire rack to cool them quickly. If they are left to cool in the pan, they will collapse onto themselves and will not have an even rectangular shape; they will resemble the letter "X" when cut horizontally.

7. Once they have cooled, wrap them tightly in plastic wrap and freeze. They should be frozen in order to obtain a clean, even, straight cut. Always cut with a good serrated knife.

notes A Pullman loaf (also known as pain de mie or sandwich loaf) refers to the mold in which the brioche is baked. This recipe uses a 1-kg pan (known as a 2-lb pan in the U.S.), but there are smaller molds available. This particular mold measures 10 by 40 by 10 cm/4 by 16 by 4 in. It resembles a long rectangle and it has a lid (often sold separately from the pan). The lid keeps the brioche flat on all sides (no crown on top) and creates a tight, compact crumb. This shape is why this loaf is ideal for cutting slices of bread with an even square (or rectangular) shape, with little to no waste. This bread can be used in applications such as the tea sandwiches, pain perdu (similar to French toast), croutons, and bread pudding.

This bread should be cut when it is frozen; this will almost guarantee a clean, straight, even cut with no crumbs falling out. I prefer to cut the crust off for certain sandwich applications and for pain perdu, since it tends to be somewhat dry.

yeast- and steam-raised breakfast pastries (laminated viennoiserie)

These pastries are not only leavened by yeast, but also by steam. This steam comes primarily from butter that is laminated into the dough but also, to a lesser extent, from other moisture like milk and another amount of butter that is mixed into the actual dough. The basic principle of lamination is that very thin layers of dough alternate with very thin layers of butter through a series of specific folds (some call them turns), and it is that butter that produces the steam that leavens the product. The dough basically has the butter "trapped" within itself, in many layers of equal thickness, but the amount of dough layers (81) is larger than the amount of butter layers (78). It is the evenness of these layers and the equal distribution of butter within the dough that will be one of the determining factors of a quality laminated pastry. An example of a steam-raised laminated dough that contains no yeast but is laminated is puff pastry.

These laminated pastries have very different qualities than yeast-raised pastries. Laminated pastries are flaky on the outside, which is a direct result of the butter layers, and light and soft on the inside. There are many signs to look out for in a quality laminated pastry, but the single most valued sign is called the "honeycomb." A laminated pastry honeycomb is a series of irregular cells or air pockets, which have a distinct pattern that is never the same from one item to the other, but when it is done right, they are all similar in principle.

The following is a list of the most valuable quality aspects of laminated, yeast-raised pastries:

- **Flakiness:** The crust of the pastry should easily crumble when gentle pressure is applied, and pieces should flake off, making a crunchy sound. If it doesn't make that sound, it means the pastry is soft, which is a clear sign that something was not done correctly or that the pastry is old. There will be a very fine coating of butter on your fingers when you break through the crust.

- **Lightness:** The pastry is lighter in weight than it looks; this is because it is not a solid piece of dough, but is full of air cells (the honeycomb).

- **Texture contrast:** The flaky crust combines with a light, delicate interior.

- **Yeasty flavor:** Through bulk fermentation and proofing, the dough develops a unique yeasted flavor.

In this book, classic French croissants and pain au chocolat are made with the same dough as Danish pastries. It is important to note that usually pain au chocolat is incorrectly called "chocolate croissant." *Croissant* refers to only one variety of laminated pastry, the croissant, even though other laminated pastries are made with croissant dough.

In this book, Danish distinguishes itself from croissant-dough items with the addition of a garnish, which can be a pipeable filling (jam, cream cheese, or curd), cooked fruit, nut pastes, batters, and so on. Personally, I like to have a 60/40 ratio of dough to garnish (sometimes 70/30); this allows garnish and dough to be eaten together in every bite from beginning to end. This book does not use any "wet" fillings (such as pie filling–style fillings or pastry cream), and most garnish is not added until after the Danish is baked. There is a very simple reason for

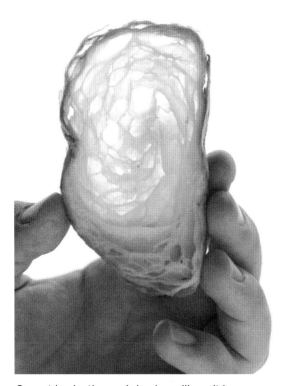

Correct lamination and shaping will result in a perfect honeycomb structure.

this. When the dough is proofed with the garnish, the garnish will weigh the dough down, compromising the proper leavening of the dough since it is too delicate to push most garnishes up. The Danish will usually end up flatter, with little flakiness around the area where the garnish is placed. We will be piping the garnish inside and/or on top of the baked pastry, thus maintaining its flakiness for a longer period of time. In this section are different ways to shape and garnish Danish that greatly increase its shelf life and flakiness. Furthermore, there is a section of Danish titled "Advanced Viennoiserie" on page 62, which is a step up from an already high-quality Danish.

When baked, laminated pastries should have a deep golden brown color, which translates into a flaky product, even once it cools down. When the baked product is pale and yellowish, the pastry will have a soft, bun-like consistency, and all the work that went into making all of those layers is rendered useless.

As seen in the diagram on page 41, there is a dough portion and a butter portion (also known as a butter block), which accounts for over 60 percent of the weight of the flour. This means that for nearly every part of butter there are two parts of dough.

the story behind croissants and lamination

UNFORTUNATELY, THERE IS NO SOLID EVIDENCE that tells us where the croissant as we know it today came from. The shape, however, can be traced to the seventeenth century. It is said that a baker in either Vienna or Budapest working the night shift heard noises coming from underground. The noises turned out to be a group of Turks trying to besiege the city. The baker stopped the attempted invasion by sounding the alarm. He asked for no reward, but he was offered the honor of creating a pastry that would commemorate the occasion. The Turkish flag has a crescent moon on it, so the baker created a pastry in that crescent shape.

According to *The Oxford Companion to Food,* croissants as the flaky, delicate pastry we know today are mentioned for the first time in 1906 in a publication titled *Nouvelle Encyclopedie Culinaire.* This means that the croissant could be just over a hundred years old. However, puff pastry has been around for centuries. The first published mention of puff pastry (or "butter paste") can be traced to 1596 in a book titled *The Good Housewife's Jewel,* by Thomas Dawson. It employed a method similar to the one known today as the "blitz" method for puff pastry. Instead of using a butter block, the dough is dotted with pieces of butter, then folded over to trap the butter, then rolled out again and folded again, for a total of five folds. It is curious that the principle of laminating butter and dough has been around for so long, but that using a yeasted dough took over three centuries to happen. One can actually trace the origins of puff pastry, specifically with the blitz method, to short-crust pastry (a rudimentary form of pie dough). Short-crust pastry is made in much the same way that the cut-in method dough is, in which butter is interspersed through the dough to create pockets of steam and thus produce a flaky pastry. The size of the butter will determine the flakiness of the dough (the smaller it is, the crumblier it will be; the larger it is, the flakier it will be).

TECHNIQUES

the lamination process

FORMATION OF THE BUTTER BLOCK

In order to obtain a rectangle of butter for laminating dough, there are three approaches:

1. Have a frame made that will hold the exact amount of butter needed. For the amount needed in the recipe on page 53, the frame should measure 37.5 by 25.5 by 1.25 cm/14.75 by 10 by .5 in on the interior; the width of the frame should be no more than 2 cm/.75 in thick so that it can fit inside a sheet pan if necessary. Place the frame on top of one side of a sheet of silicone paper. Place the butter inside the frame and spread it out evenly with an offset spatula. Close the other half of the silicone paper on top of the butter and, using a rolling pin, even it out. At this point you can pass the back of a paring knife around the inside of the frame, take the frame off, and make another butter block, or, if you are just doing one frame, close up the silicone paper borders as if you were folding an envelope closed. Refrigerate until ready for further use, or freeze if stocking up on butter blocks. Make sure to place them on a flat surface while they firm up, and don't stack blocks on top of each other if the one directly underneath has not firmed up yet.

   If the butter block is still at 21°C/70°F or slightly colder and the croissant dough is cold, at refrigeration temperature, the lamination can be started right away. Otherwise, chill the butter block completely, and then pull it out of the refrigerator a couple of hours before using it. If you forget to do so (which is a possibility you need to allow for), then take the following steps. Remove the butter block from the refrigerator and microwave it on high power for 10 seconds. Pound it lightly with a French rolling pin (or thick wooden dowel) in even strokes from one direction to the other (left to right, for example), flip the block over, and tap it again in the same way. Reshape the butter block with the rolling pin and with your hands, evening out the borders. If it is still too hard, repeat this process until it reaches the right temperature. If it gets too soft, refrigerate the block again to get it completely cold. The reason for this is that butter will get colder at different rates in different areas of the block, which will give it an uneven consistency. The middle of the block might still be soft while the exterior is already firm.

The success or failure of lamination partially depends on the dough and butter block being of the same consistency, so that when they are rolled out (or sheeted if using a sheeter) they both extend at the same rate, thus keeping the dough from ripping or the butter from cracking. Even layers will produce the much-coveted honeycomb. The only downside of this frame is that it can be costly. Plexiglas is an adequate material for this frame.

2. Another method for making a butter block if you have no frame is to place the softened butter on one half of a sheet of silicone or parchment paper and close the other half of the paper on top of the butter. Close or seal the open ends of the paper by folding it onto itself (the top half over the bottom half), creating a package. With a rolling pin, flatten the butter into a block, rolling it toward the border of the package, trying to keep an even thickness throughout the block. The disadvantage of this method is difficulty in keeping the thickness consistent, but with practice it can be done.

THE LOCK-IN

1. The next step in the lamination process is the lock-in. This refers to locking the butter inside the dough. The dough should be cold (refrigeration temperature) and the butter block should be pliable (21°C/70°F) but not soft.

2. Flip the dough onto a floured surface, preferably wood, and remove the silicone paper. The wrinkled side of the dough should face up.

3. Place the butter block on the right half of the dough. There should be about 2.5 cm/1 in of dough around the butter block. If the butter is at the right consistency, you can move it around the dough in case it is slightly askew.

   If it is too soft it will be impossible to move, but this is also part of a bigger problem. If the dough is firmer than the butter, it will not extend at the same rate as the butter when it is rolled out. Make sure that the dough that "frames" the butter block is no wider than 2.5 cm/1 in, since this is dough that will never be layered with butter (a.k.a. dead dough).

4. Roll the left side of the dough onto the butter block with your hands underneath it. The dough should completely cover the butter block. The reason to roll the dough onto the butter is that if the corners of the dough are pulled over the butter, the dough will become misshapen and the chances of getting air pockets in the dough

increase. If the dough is flush on the butter, there will be a minimal chance of air pockets getting trapped. Air pockets can show up in the final product, greatly deforming it.

5. Press down on the border of the dough with the heel of your hand without pressing on the butter. This will seal the border of the dough and keep the butter in place. The dough borders that were sealed need to be tucked under the "package." Make sure there is no flour under the dough, because if you try to tuck the dough flaps under the dough and it has flour, these flaps will not adhere to the package and will be loose.

6. Reshape the package to an even rectangle with your hands. It should be even on the sides and on the top as well (where it should not be thinner in one corner and thicker in another). Lightly dust the sheeter's surface.

7. Place the dough on the sheeter with the spine facing the rollers. Make sure that the dough isn't too thick; otherwise it will get caught on the protective guides and tear. Roll it down by hand if it is too thick. Make sure the rollers are on the largest setting as well. Lightly flour the surface of the dough. Start the sheeter and pass the dough through twice on the same number in both directions, then turn the dial down to the next number. Decrease the rollers by two or three numbers at a time; there is really no point in going in small increments. Keep going until the dough is as wide as a sheet pan. Rotate the dough 90 degrees to your left, and continue to sheet the dough down until it is 1.25 cm/.5 in thick.

8. Relax the dough by placing your palms completely underneath the dough and pulling it up from the sheeter in a delicate but assertive way. Make sure your palms or fingers do not damage the dough, but lift the dough up enough from the sheeter so that it literally will pull in. This will help the gluten relax and assure an evenly shaped pastry. Brush any excess flour off the dough with a bench brush.

9. Reshape the dough into a rectangle, using your hands. Do not tug on the corners to do so, since this will only make the corners very thin in relation to the rest of the dough (a.k.a. dog ears). Instead, pull the dough with both hands from the middle of the border out toward the corners; do this on each corner and the dough will maintain an even thickness.

10. Visually divide the dough into three equal parts vertically. Brush any excess flour off the dough. Fold the right third over the middle third. Brush any excess flour from the dough that has just been folded. Fold the left third of the dough on top of the previously folded dough, and brush off any excess flour. This is called a "three-fold."

11. Reshape the dough into an even rectangle and carefully transfer it to the sheet pan that it was on originally. Make sure that the silicone paper is lightly coated in flour; always use bread flour for dusting.

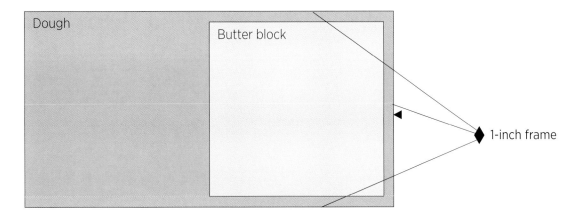

Place the butter block on the right half of the dough. There should be about 2.5 cm/1 in of dough around the butter block.

12. Reshape into a rectangle again while on the sheet pan, straightening out the borders with a bench knife by pushing into the dough with the bench knife at a 90-degree angle. Key point: It is crucial for a successful lamination that the dough be kept in an even rectangle shape throughout the entire process. This will ensure evenly thin layers of dough and butter.

13. Cover the dough with plastic wrap, tucking the plastic under the dough to keep it from drying out.

14. Relax and chill the dough (if necessary). There will be a total of four three-folds for both items, but between each of them, the dough needs to relax (the gluten needs to regroup and pull in). This is achieved through letting the dough sit on its own for at least 15 minutes. The dough will spend this time in the reach-in and/or at room temperature, depending on its consistency. The ideal consistency is the same as that of the thumb muscle on the palm of your hand when you bend or flex it. Do not let the dough stay cold for too long, since the butter will harden much more than the dough will,

and don't forget that for successful lamination, the dough and the butter need to extend at the same rate. If the butter is too hard, it will crack as the dough is stretched. Common sense might tell you to just leave the dough to sit out at room temperature for the butter to soften, but by the time the butter is pliable (soft) again, the dough will be even softer, and again, the consistency of both will be different, and they will not extend evenly. If the butter can be felt through the dough, it has gotten too hard and the lamination is compromised. There is no way to fix this but to throw the dough out and start again (which is slightly unreasonable) or to soldier on and expect that the final product will not be of adequate quality. Hard butter will damage the dough by breaking through it, but so will soft butter that will "squish" its way through the fine layers of dough. When this occurs, the butter will "flood" into the dough, since the layer of dough has ripped (or cracked) and now there are two layers of butter. This makes the interior honeycomb look gummy and wet, and it is, since all the butter

Basic Method for Laminating Dough

FROM LEFT TO RIGHT:

1. When locking in, carefully roll the dough over the butter block to avoid air bubbles and misshapen dough.
2. After executing a three-fold, it is critical to reshape the dough into an even rectangle.
3. Properly laminated dough is composed of thin, uniform layers of dough and butter that allow the pastry to evenly expand upward as it bakes.

was too much for the delicate layers of dough to handle and the excess was absorbed into it instead of baking off as steam, thus preventing the formation of a fine air-cell network.

The time between folds is at least 15 minutes, but it can be 30 or 45 minutes if the dough does not feel right and is too soft. This time can be spent completely in refrigeration or at room temperature, or in some combination thereof, whatever is needed to achieve that right consistency. Typically after it has been rolled down and sheeted, the dough is soft from the friction from the roller or rolling pin, so it will typically have to spend some time in the reach-in. Again, it all depends on the consistency of the dough; soft yet firm, not squishy soft and not hard.

15. The dough is ready for the second three-fold when it has relaxed for at least 15 minutes and is at the right consistency (see above). Lightly flour the surface of the sheeter and place the dough on top with the spine toward the rollers. Do not flip or turn the dough over; it should be as it was on the sheet pan.

16. Sheet the dough until it is as wide as a sheet pan, then rotate 90 degrees to your left. It is very important to always start the dough with the spine first toward the rollers, then to always rotate it toward the same direction. In this case it will be 90 degrees to the left. You could always do 90 degrees to the right if you wanted to, so long as you always do it that way; the reason is that the direction of the layers should be consistent so that when the pastry bakes, it will bake upward and not in a zigzag fashion or slanted or falling on its side. This is another key point to successful lamination. Sheet the dough down to 1.25 cm/.5 in thick and perform another three-fold exactly as before: right third on top of the middle third, and the left third folded on top of that. It is also important to do this consistently the same way.

17. Relax and chill as in step 14 (see the special precautions).

18. Perform another three-fold as in steps 7 through 10. I like to roll it down further when it is on the sheet pan so that it is on the thin side (about 2.5 cm/1 in). The thinner the dough is rolled, the more evenly dispersed the general temperature will be. If it is too thick, the exterior will get cold before the center of the dough does. Even sheeting or laminating depends greatly on the consistency of the butter and the dough, and they should both be at the same consistency. Perform another

three-fold after this dough relaxes and reaches the correct consistency, for a total of four three-folds; after the last three-fold, continue with the following instructions. This time, instead of refrigerating it, freeze it for at least an hour enclosed in plastic wrap. The butter needs be firm throughout but not hard to the point of cracking. Once the entire dough has firmed up but is not frozen solid, cut it into halves using a sharp chef's knife. Sheet each square down to the specific thickness, rotating it as needed so that it is about the size of a sheet pan. Remember, make sure the dough is firm but not rock hard; otherwise it will get damaged (cracked) as it is sheeted down. If it is very hard, simply place it in the refrigerator until it softens throughout before sheeting. Some cracking will inevitably happen around the border of the dough, but it is dough that will be used for other purposes (see page 50 for notes on dough trimmings). Conversely, if the dough is not firm enough yet, it will certainly get damaged while you are sheeting it down to the desired thickness.

During this last sheeting is when most doughs get damaged. Be careful, gentle, and aware of your dough. Use flour generously if necessary on both sides of the dough while sheeting the dough down. Croissant and pain au chocolat will be sheeted to 5 mm. Danish, depending on the style, will be shaped to either 5 mm, 7 mm, or 10 mm. Once it has been sheeted, relax it by lifting it up from the sheeter with the palms of your hands, delicately but assertively, then transfer it to a silicone-lined sheet pan. Brush off the excess flour on both sides of the dough—or it will dry out the dough and then it will crack—and cover it with plastic wrap completely. Let it harden again for 30 to 45 minutes or up to an hour, but do not let it get hard to the point where it will crack when you try to cut it. The ideal consistency to cut laminated dough is semi-frozen.

One of the unfortunate effects of the environment on laminated items is that in a matter of hours, most of the flakiness and crisp exterior can soften due to moisture in the environment as well as the moisture inside the item. A croissant that is fresh out of the oven won't be same four hours later, much less eight hours later. A croissant during spring will not be the same as a croissant in a hot and humid summer, where its lifespan is dramatically decreased.

I once took home a dozen croissants that I had made that day, for the weekend. Not that I was going to eat all twelve during the weekend, or even more than two. At most, half would be eaten by my family, and the rest I could freeze. I knew that the croissants would be like brioche buns the next day and perhaps worse the day after that, so it has always been a common practice for me to refresh any flaky laminated dough in a hot oven for a few minutes. Once they came out of the oven warm, crisp, and refreshed, it was like nothing had happened. They were almost perfect. In fact, they were perhaps slightly better, since they were not only flaky again, but they were also warm. Some Danish pastries couldn't be refreshed if they had a topping such as a ganache or other heat-sensitive item on their surface, but if it were inside the pastry would crisp up just as well.

This all made me wonder if this technique could transfer to a café environment with fresh croissants and pain au chocolat. A small, high-quality convection oven was purchased and installed close to the pastry display case, away from the customers' view. The oven was set to 230°C/445°F, and multiple timers were installed on a wall next to the oven, each one set for 45 seconds, so that each time a croissant was placed in the oven and the door was closed, the person who loaded the oven could easily start the timer. Every order for Danish, croissant, and pain au chocolat was recrisped in the oven, regardless of the time of day, but they would always be freshly made Danish pastries, croissants, and pain au chocolat (day-old croissants were not served; for these purposes, see the almond croissant recipe on page 54). This technique makes a great product even better—sort of like warm chocolate chip cookies.

SPECIFIC LAMINATED PASTRY SHAPES

croissant

The recipe on page 53 yields about 60 croissants (80 g/2.82 oz each). There will be some dough trimmings that cannot be used for croissant but that can be used for other items (see page 50). The final baked weight of these croissants is about 73 g/2.57 oz on average. They will lose 9 to 10 percent of their weight in the form of steam.

1. Place the semi-frozen croissant dough sheet on a lightly floured surface. Using a croissant cutter with triangles that measure 8 by 21 cm/3.15 by 8.27 in (see Resources, page 540), cut out the croissants by pushing down hard with the cutter as you roll it away from you. If you do not get a clean cut, the croissant won't proof and bake well because the layers of dough will bind to each other. The croissant triangles may not detach from each other. If this happens, separate the triangles by cutting them

with a knife; do not pull the triangles apart. Do not flour the croissant's surface heavily, since this will only dry out the dough's surface, and the rolled-up layers of dough need to adhere to each other when they proof and bake; use a very light layer of bread flour. If the croissants don't come off the cutter easily, pry them out with the tip of a paring knife or a small offset spatula tip. Do not force them out with your fingers. If you have little practice shaping croissants, place them on a sheet pan covered with plastic wrap to keep them from drying out. Refrigerate them because, don't forget, you are working with a delicate product that contains yeast, and the longer it sits out, the softer it will get, and the yeast will start proofing (fermenting) the dough.

2. For the amount of croissant dough on page 53, line 5 sheet pans with silicone paper.

3. Stack as many croissants as you feel comfortable shaping on the wooden worktable. Start with 5 or 6 triangles. Do not flour the table, since doing so will only make you chase the dough around the table and make it hard to shape the croissant.

4. Place the wide end of the croissant in one hand and very gently tug on the croissant from its center toward the tip, using your thumb on top and index finger at the bottom and sliding them toward the tip in a tugging motion to stretch out the triangle. It should stretch to 2.5 to 3.75 cm/1 to 1.5 in longer than its original shape and no more, since doing so will cause serious damage to the layers of dough.

5. When you are done stretching the triangle, place it on the table. The wide end of the triangle (or the top, if you will) will have a small incision made by the croissant cutter, which will create two distinct "flaps." Roll them out outward. These will be the tips of the croissant; do not pull too hard or it will rip the croissant dough; this will show in the honeycomb as a large air pocket. Gently roll the triangle up, pushing it away from you (some people are more comfortable rolling the triangle toward them instead of away). Try to make it as even as possible, so the segments are evenly sized. If they are correctly rolled up, there will be 5 distinct segments: 1 in the middle (which is somewhat triangular and part of the tip of the croissant) and 2 on each side of this triangle. The tip of the croissant should be tucked under, because as the croissant proofs and bakes, it will want to unroll, but if the tip is secured under the croissant, it won't. Place the croissants with the tips facing down, looking almost like an airplane, making sure that the tip is tucked under. See the Note on page 45.

Basic Method for Shaping Croisssants

FROM LEFT TO RIGHT:

1. To avoid damaging the dough's layers, use extreme care when stretching the croissant triangles before shaping.
2. Beginning with the wide end of the triangle, roll the dough to create five uniform segments.
3. Properly proofed croissants

6. Place the croissants on the sheet pan as you shape them (the less you touch them and handle them, the better), in a 4x3 grid (12 croissants per sheet pan maximum) in a diagonal slant. Evenly distributed croissants will bake evenly since there will be similar heat flow passing through them as they bake; randomly placed croissants will not bake evenly or well.

7. Once the croissants are shaped, they can be retarded in refrigeration for a few hours or proofed. Try not to freeze them for further use, since yeast will not react well to this. If proofing them, brush them with egg wash beforehand so that they won't develop a skin on top. Make sure to brush them with the right amount of egg wash; if there is too much, it will accumulate at the bottom of the croissant and it will look like scrambled eggs when it is baked. If retarding them in the refrigerator, wrap them loosely or place the sheet pan in a large plastic bag and tie it shut.

notes A croissant cutter is an invaluable investment. Cutting croissants by hand is inefficient, and most of the time it will yield poor results, since the dough needs to sit out at room temperature while it is measured and cut, the person doing the cutting hoping all the while that each triangle is the same as the next. With a cutter, the croissants are consistent and they are cut in a fraction of the time that it would take to cut them by hand.

Some bakers prefer to stretch the croissant longer and obtain 7 visible segments instead of 5. This could thin out the dough too much, risking rupture and damage of not only the exterior of the croissant but the interior as well, thus damaging the potential honeycomb. Seven segments will also take away from the dramatic look of the baked, thin laminated layers you worked so hard to achieve. Five is ideal.

See the Note on page 48 for advice on using day-old croissants.

pain au chocolat

The recipe on page 53 yields about 40 pieces. The raw weight is 102 g/3.6 oz each, plus 3 chocolate batons per pastry (5 g/.18 oz each) = 117 g/4.13 oz. For the chocolate batons, see Resources, page 540. The final weight of a baked pain au chocolat is about 109 g/3.84 oz. It loses

laminating dough with foie gras instead of butter

IT SEEMED LIKE A TRULY INSPIRED IDEA: Use duck foie gras instead of butter to laminate croissant dough. The plan was to come up with a flaky, croissant-like bun that would be used for a duck confit sandwich. What better than foie gras to laminate the dough? After doing some research, I found that Grade A foie gras has the same fat content as premium European butter, 82 percent. I have some experience with foie gras, and I know that it is somewhat pliable when it is semi-cold, such as butter can be if handled properly. Grade A foie gras is also easier to clean (it is not too veiny) and has fewer bruises than lower-grade lobes.

I ordered two 680-g/1.5-lb Grade A foie gras lobes, proceeded to clean them, and then passed them though a drum sieve to obtain a smooth paste, which I could easily shape into a rectangle. I weighed out the resulting block, then made enough croissant dough to obtain the right ratio of dough for the amount of fat I had.

Lamination went pretty much the same as it does with butter. I had no fat cracks or dough damage. I was concerned with maintaining the integrity of the dough, for no other reason than if the dough were to get damaged, I would ruin a rather expensive product that could not be fixed.

After the final sheeting I could see the foie gras through the dough, which was very exciting. After shaping the dough, I proofed it, and then I baked it. I could smell the foie gras as the dough baked. The whole shop smelled like foie gras, which I assumed meant that the croissant would be packed with foie gras flavor, and this was a great thing. Why had no one thought of this before?

After cooling the croissant, I tasted it. One bite, then two, three. Where did the foie gras go? The croissant had absolutely zero foie gras taste. The flavor had escaped along with the steam. It was still a flaky croissant, but a truly expensive one at that, with none of the foie gras goodness left behind.

between 8 and 10 percent of its original weight in the form of steam.

1. Line 4 sheet pans with silicone or parchment paper.

2. This will require 4 sheets of semi-frozen croissant dough. Each sheet will yield 9 to 10 pain au chocolat. Remove 1 sheet from the freezer and, if it is too hard, let it soften for a few minutes. If possible, use a thick Plexiglas guide to cut the croissants because it will be faster and more precise (measuring with a ruler takes too long). Make sure the guide is as long as a sheet pan and at least 1.3 cm/.5 in thick (ideally 2.5 cm/1 in thick) so that it will be sturdy enough and so that the side of the wheel cutter can lean on it to give a perfect 90-degree angle. In this case, the pain au chocolat will measure 8.75 by 12.5 cm/3.5 by 5 in.

3. Place the 12.5-cm/5-in guide on top of the dough and cut as many "columns" of dough as possible, then use the 8.75-cm/3.5-in guide to cut as many rows as possible. Use a wheel cutter (a.k.a. pizza cutter or rolling knife) that is sharp and not dull or damaged. Use as much of the dough as possible; there might be an extra piece or two gained by just cutting the dough in a different direction. One key point for all laminated dough cutting—use a sharp wheel cutter at an exact 90-degree angle so that the dough will be cut straight down. You can ensure that this will happen by leaning the wheel cutter on the Plexiglas frame. If the dough

Basic Method for Shaping Pain au Chocolat

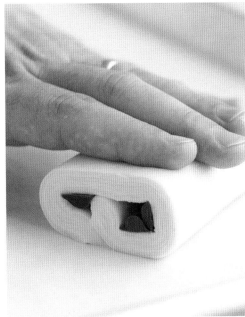

FROM LEFT TO RIGHT:

1. To begin, roll the bottom edge of the dough toward the middle of the dough rectangle, over the two batons.
2. Once shaped, the dough should be rolled securely, yet loosely enough that steam can still escape during baking.
3. Properly proofed pain au chocolat

is cut in a slant, it will bake as a slant and will only get bigger as it bakes. A large wheel cutter is preferred over smaller ones.

4. There should be 9 to 10 pieces of dough on the sheet of parchment paper. They don't need to be separated or moved around; in fact, it is best that they are kept together. The short sides of the rectangles should face you. Brush the top half of these rectangles with egg wash and visually divide the rectangles in 3 pieces horizontally.

5. Place 1 chocolate baton (see Note) where the top third of the rectangle begins, closest to you, not on the furthest end, then 2 pieces where the bottom third begins. Repeat with all of the rectangles.

6. To shape the pain au chocolat, roll the bottom end of the rectangle up toward the middle of the rectangle (the bottom end will be between the top and bottom chocolate batons), and then roll all the way up. Do not roll the pain au chocolat too tight. Otherwise the steam inside will have no way to escape and it will produce a very large and unsightly air pocket. Place the rolled-up dough on a silicone-lined sheet pan, with the seam on the

bottom and right in the middle. If the seam is not centered, the pain au chocolat will open up and unroll as it proofs and bakes.

7. Push the rolled-up dough down slightly from the top. Push gently with the tips of your fingers so as to not damage the dough. If you look at it from the side it should almost look like a pretzel. Repeat with the remaining dough rectangles and the other sheets of semi-frozen dough.

8. There should be 12 pieces per sheet pan, evenly placed in a 4x3 grid, all the pieces going in the same direction (diagonally) for an even bake. Wrap or bag the sheet pans and refrigerate to proof at a later time, or brush with egg wash and proof immediately. Make sure to brush with the right amount of egg wash; if there is too much, it will accumulate at the bottom of the pain au chocolat and it will look like scrambled eggs when it is baked.

note A good pain au chocolat requires good-quality chocolate. Try to use chocolate pieces that are specifically intended for this purpose. These are called chocolate *batons,* or, roughly translated, chocolate sticks, and they come in a variety of sizes, but they are all essentially the same shape: a long, thin rectangle. Most importantly, they are bake-proof, meaning they have a higher fat content and won't melt away and disappear as the pain au chocolat bakes. The ones used in the recipe on page 54 come in a 300-count box (300 batons per box), each measuring .8 by 7.8 cm/.31 by 3.08 in and containing a minimum of 44 percent chocolate liquor.

DAY-OLD CROISSANTS AND PAIN AU CHOCOLAT

The reality is that sometimes there will be leftover croissants and pain au chocolat. They can in fact be used the following day, but not as croissants or pain au chocolat. They can be revived by making almond croissants and almond pain au chocolat (see page 54).

danish

The true distinction between an actual croissant or pain au chocolat and a Danish is the fact that Danish pastries typically have the following additions (one of them or a combination):

- Filling (such as marmalade, curd, cream cheese)

- Topping or Garnish (such as nuts, pearl sugar, cooked fruit)

- Glaze (such as apricot jam, fondant)

While the simplicity of a croissant is valued, Danish opens a whole new set of opportunities for flavor and texture combinations. Don't forget that the finished product should have a ratio of 60 percent dough/ 40 percent added ingredients (fillings, toppings, glazes), so that every bite has a little of both. All Danish pastries will have an initial weight of about 120 g/4.25 oz but, as with croissants, they will lose between 8 and 10 percent of their weight once they are baked. They will also increase about 3 times in volume, while the croissant increases by about 100 percent. There is a slight increase in weight while they proof because of the egg wash that is applied. Brush the pastry with egg wash 3 times before it is baked: right after shaping, when it is halfway proofed, and right before it is baked. Egg wash contributes to the final color and shine of the baked Danish, and every time it is applied, it will be absorbed. If the Danish is not brushed with egg wash three times, the skin of the Danish can also become dry and it will crack as it proofs, even in a proofer with controlled humidity.

PROOFING INSTRUCTIONS FOR ALL LAMINATED PASTRIES (except Advanced Viennoiserie)

Ideally the pastries will be proofed in a proof box with temperature and humidity control. If so, set the temperature to 27°C/81°F and the humidity to 85 percent. It can fluctuate between 80 and 90 percent humidity maximum. The proofing time for croissants and pain au chocolat is between 2 and 3 hours depending on how cold the dough was when it went into the proof box. The proofing time for Danish is between 1 and 2 hours. This dough moves very fast since it has a high percentage of yeast; the proofing time depends on how cold the dough was when it went into the proof box. If the Danish is just shaped and it is going to be proofed and baked the same day, it will spend less time in the proofer; if retarding the Danish overnight, it will be colder once it gets in the proofer and will take longer to bake. Try to get the pastries up to room temperature before they are placed in the proofer, or the high heat will damage the exterior layers of dough. Proofer-retarders are ideal, since you can place the finished pastries in them and program the machine so that it stays cold for a certain amount of time, and then slowly starts warming up to the desired temperature and humidity. These can be costly, though.

1. Once the pastries are shaped, brush them with a coat of egg wash. Use a pastry brush with very soft bristles that won't damage the pastry. Place the pastries in the proof box.

2. After about an hour of proofing, brush the pastries with another coat of egg wash.

Most laminated breakfast pastries will take between 2 and 3 hours to proof. One of the hardest things for a baker to know is when the dough has reached its maximum fermentation point. After this point, the dough will plateau and then the yeast will die. This is called "overproofed," and a telltale sign is a very strong smell of alcohol coming from the pastries, which is one of the by-products of fermentation: alcohol and CO_2. The key to knowing when a dough is properly proofed is a developed sense of touch. When an item is properly proofed and you push on it gently, it will spring back. Having said this, there are degrees of proofing, meaning that the dough will spring back at many stages of proofing. In this case, go by the size of the pastry, which should ideally double in size. If it is underproofed or overproofed, it will not spring back. Additionally, the surface of the overproofed pastry will have a bubbly appearance, the pastry will have an alcoholic smell, and its size will be more than twice the size of the original. Why bother with the finger-pushing test? It is a way to gauge when the pastry is getting close. Once this occurs, it won't be long before the pastry is ready for the oven.

notes If you do not have a proof box, try using a Cres Cor cabinet or similar cabinet. Place one or two lit Sternos at the base of the cabinet. Above the Sternos, place a sheet pan; and on that, a hotel pan filled with hot water. Place the sheet pans with pastries in the cabinet. Keep a thermometer probe inside the cabinet so that you can monitor what is going on inside without having to open the cabinet door too frequently. It is also a good idea to have a humidity meter, or better yet a hygro-thermometer, which is a device that can measure both. If it is getting too hot in the cabinet, use only one Sterno, or place the cap on the Sterno halfway so that only half the flame is visible.

If you do not have a Cres Cor cabinet, there are plastic bags that are big enough to fit an entire speed rack. Alternatively, there is a heavier-duty version that is made out of canvas, shaped like a speed rack, and has a zipper that goes from top to bottom for easy access. Use the same setup of Sterno, water bath, and hygro-thermometer to create a proof box.

Ultimately, the proof box is the best method for proofing, but not everyone can afford or fit such a piece of equipment in their shops. If that is the case, you just have to pay closer attention and monitor your measuring instruments carefully.

BAKING INSTRUCTIONS

Always bake croissants with croissants, pain au chocolat with pain au chocolat, and Danish with Danish (the same varieties at the same time). The main reason for this is that each type of pastry bakes at its own pace, and it is detrimental to the pastry if the oven door is opened and closed to remove finished pastries before others are ready. Croissants and items made with that dough are very delicate, and this should not be taken for granted at any time during the process.

The only appropriate oven to use for laminated pastries is a convection oven, since it has better temperature control and will give a fast, direct heat from the fan that spins the heat around the pastries, causing the pastry to puff up quickly, known as "oven-spring."

croissants

1. Preheat the convection oven to 227°C/440°F.

2. Load the oven with a maximum of 4 sheet pans of croissants as quickly as possible to prevent the oven's temperature from dropping too much.

3. As soon as the oven door is closed, press the steam button. It should be programmed to deliver 1.25 L/1.32 qt of steam when the steam button is pushed; or, depending on the oven, press the steam button for 5 seconds.

4. Lower the temperature to 190°C/375°F.

5. Continue to bake. At the onset of color, after 3 to 5 minutes, open the vents and continue to bake for 5 more minutes or until they turn amber golden brown.

6. Once they are baked, slide the baked croissants onto a metro shelf to cool. Slide them off the sheet pan with the parchment paper they are on; don't try to pick them up individually. This prevents them from getting soggy at the base, since steam will be able to escape properly. If you do not have metro shelving, slide the baked pastries onto wire racks. Once they have cooled, they can be returned to a sheet pan.

pain au chocolat and all danish (except Advanced Viennoiserie on page 62)

1. Follow steps 1 through 3 for baking croissants.

2. Lower the temperature to 185°C/365°F.

3. Continue to bake. At the onset of color, after 3 to 5 minutes, open the vents and continue to bake for 5 to 7 more minutes or until they turn an amber golden brown.

4. For Danish: Once the Danish pastries come out of the oven, brush them with a hot mixture of 90 percent apricot jam and 10 percent water. Combine the apricot jam with the water in a sauce pot and bring to a simmer. Keep the glaze covered to prevent excess evaporation. It is very important that the hot liquid is brushed onto hot Danish, so that the moisture evaporates from the surface of the Danish and doesn't make it soggy. This layer of jam makes the Danish shiny and keeps it crisp for a longer period of time because it seals the outside of the pastry. Glaze the Danish pastries as they are cooling on a metro shelf or wire rack.

For pain au chocolat: Once the pain au chocolat are baked, slide the baked pastries onto a metro shelf to cool. Slide them off the sheet pan with the parchment paper they are on; don't try to pick them up individually.

5. Once the Danish pastries have cooled, you can split them in half and fill them with their respective fillings, reassemble them, and then glaze and apply any final garnishes.

Danish must be sold the day it is it baked. Any leftover pastries must be discarded. Unfortunately, when it comes to Danish, there is nothing similar to the almond cream for Croissant and Pain au Chocolat, since Danish already has the addition of a filling or glaze and it cannot be removed (without damaging the Danish). It is not worth trying to rescue them for next-day use.

UTILIZING CROISSANT DOUGH TRIMMINGS

When cutting out any laminated pastry from a sheet of dough, there will necessarily be some trimmings that cannot be used for their intended purpose. One way to not let this dough go to waste is to make a cinnamon-Danish loaf.

The method principles are as follows:

1. Place all of the dough trimmings on a sheeter. Make sure the dough is cold.

2. Start sheeting the trimmings at the highest number. The trimmings will start to fuse to one another as the dough gets thinner. The goal is to have a piece of dough that is about the same dimensions as a sheet pan and about 5 mm/ .25 in thick. This will depend on how much trimming you have. You will need about 2.7 kg/6 lb of dough to make one full sheet pan at the above dimensions. If there is very little, freeze what you have and add the next day's trimmings to it, and so on, until there is enough to make at least 4 or 5 loaves. It is a good idea to offer these types of loaves for the weekend. That way you can build up your trimmings during the week by adding to them every day so that you can make and finish them on Fridays.

3. Once there is a sheet of dough the size of a sheet pan, let it relax and chill again in refrigeration for 30 minutes.

4. In the meantime, grease 1.36-kg/3-lb loaf pans that are 11.5 by 21.5 by 7.5 cm/4.5 by 8.5 by 3 in using nonstick oil spray.

5. Line the inside of the pans with paper loaf-pan liners with the same dimensions as the pans.

6. Remove the sheet of chilled dough from the refrigerator. Spread a thin layer of Cinnamon Smear (page 55) on it and roll the dough up loosely. Trim the ends off and cut the roll in half. Place each roll in one pan, with the seam at the bottom of the pan. Brush with egg wash and proof (see proofing instructions for Danish on page 48).

7. Preheat a convection oven to 160°C/320°F.

8. Bake until the internal temperature of the loaf reaches 95°C/203°F. Brush a layer of hot apricot glaze on the loaf as soon as it comes out of the oven. Sprinkle about 50 g/1.76 oz per loaf of toasted pecans on top.

Other options: Coat the loaf in fondant glaze drizzle and pecans. Warm some pouring fondant with a little corn syrup to loosen it up, and then drizzle it on the loaf pan in straight or crisscrossed lines. Sprinkle pecans (or any other nut) on top before the glaze sets. You can flavor the glaze with cinnamon or any other spice.

Cut the roll of dough with the layer of cinnamon smear into 5-cm-/2-in-thick pieces instead of loaf portions and finish them as sticky buns with the fondant glaze as above.

possible defects of yeast- and steam-raised (laminated) products

defect	cause(s)	solution (the appropriate steps need to be taken beforehand)
Very greasy pastry	Underproofed*. When the pastry was baking, the dough had not developed enough structure during the proofing process to support the butter as it melted during the baking, so the butter melted out of the pastry instead of inside it to create steam pockets (honeycomb). There will also be a large amount of butter on the sheet pan.	Bake the product when properly proofed. The pastry should have doubled in size before baking.
	Dough may have been damaged to the point where the butter leaked out. It could have been damaged during shaping (it was too cold or too soft) and the outer layer of dough was ripped, causing the butter directly underneath it to melt out.	Handle the dough carefully.
Flat pastry	Possibly overproofed* Yeast could have been inactive or improperly scaled out.	Bake the product when properly proofed. The pastry should have doubled in size before baking. Make sure to scale out all of the ingredients properly.
	The oven temperature was too low. Speed is of the essence when you are loading a convection oven, since the longer the door is open the more the temperature will drop, and to obtain proper volume, the pastries need to get a quick oven-spring from a hot oven. Always use a convection oven on the highest fan speed to get the best oven-spring and highest volume for the pastries.	Check the oven temperature before baking. Load the oven quickly.
Gummy interior and/ or honeycomb	There was dough damage during the lamination process, in which the dough may have been ripped, and the butter flooded from one layer to another. The honeycomb will have a "wet" look instead of a dry one.	Handle the dough carefully.
Too small	Did not proof long enough*. Don't forget that proof time is between 2 and 3 hours. If you try to rush, it won't work.	Bake the product when properly proofed. The pastry should have doubled in size before baking.
	There was insufficient humidity in the proofer. Humidity should be between 80 and 90%. This will help moisten the exterior of the pastry, which will help it expand as it bakes.	Make sure the proofer is adequately set for the correct humidity. It is a good idea to have a humidity meter in the proof box to monitor humidity accuracy.
Too big	Overproofed*. You will also notice an alcoholic smell from the yeast overfermenting and producing excess CO_2 and alcohol.	Bake the product when properly proofed. The pastry should have doubled in size before baking.

(continued)

defect	cause(s)	solution (the appropriate steps need to be taken beforehand)
Honeycomb looks like the crumb of brioche, but is not gummy or wet looking.	The butter that was used to make the butter block was overpaddled and therefore trapped too much air, and that air stayed in the butter. Usually this butter is overpaddled when it is too cold; some bakers just let the machine do the softening, but this only incorporates air into the butter. Plan ahead and use soft, room-temperature butter to make the butter blocks.	Mix the butter until it is pliable and soft.
Layers are indistinct inside or outside the pastry.	Severe dough damage, where there are no distinguishable layers of dough.	Handle the dough with care.
The pastry lost its shape after baking (round pastries are oval, square pastries are rectangular).	The dough was not relaxed enough either during lamination (between folds) or after it was sheeted. Always make sure to relax the dough as much as possible. Try to get your hands completely underneath the dough and lift it up from left to right or right to left—it doesn't matter which, as long as you go from one end to the other to relax the entire sheet of dough, and then perform the fold. When performing the final sheeting (after the last three-fold, when the dough is cold throughout), relax the dough in the same way, and then place it on a sheet pan to get cold again.	Relax the dough throughout the entire laminating process.
Crust looks like bark from a tree.	The pastry was not brushed with egg wash enough and dried out when it proofed, or it was left exposed in the refrigerator or in a freezer for too long without being wrapped.	Egg wash the pastries two to three times during proofing to keep the outer skin from drying out.
	The proof box did not have the correct setting for humidity (it needs to be between 80 and 90%).	Make sure the proofer is adequately set for the correct humidity. It is a good idea to have a humidity meter in the proof box to monitor humidity accuracy.

*Adequate proofing (fermentation) will vary from item to item. In most cases, the product will double in size, but it is not a set rule for all items. Knowing when a dough is proofed requires extensive experience gained through trial and error. Touching the dough to test for proof and having it double in size are two ways to tell if the dough is ready to bake or not.

croissants

CROISSANT AND DANISH DOUGH

yield: 5 kg/11 lb .32 oz

INGREDIENT	METRIC	U.S.	%
DOUGH			
Bread flour	2.13 kg	4 lb 11.1 oz	100%
Salt	53 g	1.87 oz	2.5%
Sugar	256 g	9.03 oz	12%
Instant dry yeast (gold label)	43 g	1.52 oz	2%
Water, at 21°C/70°F	1.02 kg	2 lb 4 oz	48%
Butter, soft	426 g	15.03 oz	20%
Butter block	1.06 kg	2 lb 5.4 oz	50%

1. **FOR THE DOUGH:** Combine all of the ingredients except the softened butter in a 20-qt mixer bowl using the hook attachment. Mix on low speed until the mixture reaches a shaggy mass, about 1 minute.

2. Add the softened butter and mix for 3 to 4 minutes on low speed. Switch to medium speed and mix for 3 to 4 more minutes, or until the stage of medium gluten development.

3. Line a sheet pan with silicone paper and lightly flour it. Place the dough on the prepared sheet pan, cover with plastic wrap, and bulk ferment for 45 minutes. Punch the dough down and shape into an evenly sized rectangle with your hands.

4. Cover with plastic wrap again and freeze for 45 minutes. Turn the dough around after 20 minutes for even temperature distribution. You can start laminating this dough right after this step, or reserve it frozen, very well wrapped with plastic, and then thaw it in the refrigerator.

5. **TO MAKE THE BUTTER BLOCK:** Weigh the butter. It is always best to keep some butter at room temperature for this purpose, or to pull it out of the refrigerator a few hours before using. If room-temperature butter is not available, weigh out the butter and dice it, then microwave it in a bowl at 10-second intervals until it reaches 21°C/70°F. Alternatively, pound the butter with a French rolling pin until it is malleable. The butter block should be half the size of the dough, and at least an inch smaller lengthwise and widthwise.

6. Follow the instructions for the lamination process on page 44.

Croissant

ALMOND CROISSANTS OR PAIN AU CHOCOLAT

yield: about 40 pieces

INGREDIENT	METRIC	U.S.	%
ALMOND CREAM			
Butter, diced, at 21°C/70°F	479 g	16.9 oz	23.93%
Sugar	479 g	16.9 oz	23.93%
Eggs, at 21°C/70°F	479 g	16.9 oz	23.93%
Almond flour	479 g	16.9 oz	23.93%
Cake flour, sifted	85 g	3.01 oz	4.27%
Day-old Croissants (page 53)	40 pieces	40 pieces	
Almonds (slivered or sliced)	400 g	14.11 oz	16.67%

1. **FOR THE ALMOND CREAM:** Cream the butter and sugar in a mixer bowl using the paddle attachment until it is light and fluffy.

2. Add the eggs in 4 additions, scraping the bowl between each addition.

3. Add the almond flour and the cake flour and mix for a few more seconds, or until a homogeneous mass is obtained.

4. Transfer to an airtight container and refrigerate. The almond cream will keep for a week if stored this way.

5. **FOR THE ASSEMBLY AND FINISHING:** Preheat the convection oven to 150°C/300°F.

6. Pipe about 50 g/1.76 oz of almond cream on top of each croissant or pain au chocolat.

7. Sprinkle about 10 g/.35 oz of slivered or sliced almonds on top of each pastry.

8. Bake until the almond cream and the almonds are golden brown, about 10 minutes.

note Can also be made with Pain au Chocolat.

CINNAMON SMEAR

yield: 1.8 kg/3lb 15.52 oz (enough for 4 loaves at 450 g/15.87 oz each)

INGREDIENT	METRIC	U.S.	%
Butter, melted	646 g	1 lb 6.78 oz	35.88%
Brown sugar	618 g	1 lb 5.8 oz	34.32%
Light corn syrup	70 g	2.47 oz	3.9%
Pastry flour	90 g	3.17 oz	5.01%
Ground cinnamon	90 g	3.17 oz	5.01%
Vanilla paste	15 g	.53 oz	.84%
Eggs	271 g	9.55 oz	15.04%

1. Combine the butter, brown sugar, and corn syrup in an electric mixer bowl. Mix with the paddle attachment on low speed until smooth.

2. Add the flour and cinnamon and mix until smooth.

3. Add the vanilla paste, then the eggs one by one, scraping the sides to ensure an even mix.

4. Refrigerate or use right away. If refrigerating, you will need to paddle it for a few seconds before you spread it on the dough so that it is smooth and easy to spread.

5. The cinnamon spread will keep in an airtight container in the refrigerator for up to 1 week.

danish

KEY LIME CURD DANISH

yield: about 40 pieces

INGREDIENT	METRIC	U.S.	%
KEY LIME CURD			
Key lime juice	273 g	9.63 oz	18.18%
Sugar	273 g	9.63 oz	18.18%
Eggs	273 g	9.63 oz	18.18%
Butter	682 g	1 lb 8 oz	45.45%
KEY LIME GLAZE			
Key lime juice	750 g	1 lb 10.4 oz	78.95%
Confectioners' sugar	200 g	7.05 oz	21.05%
Danish Dough, semi-frozen (page 53)	5 kg	11 lb .32 oz	
Egg Wash for Brushing (page 13)	as needed	as needed	
Poppy seeds	80 g	2.82 oz	

1. **FOR THE KEY LIME CURD:** Follow the method for lemon curd on page 16.

2. **FOR THE KEY LIME GLAZE:** Combine all of the ingredients in a bowl and whisk until evenly combined. If the mixture is too thick, add more lime juice. The consistency should be as thick as pouring fondant. If using immediately, pour the glaze into a piping bag. Otherwise, transfer to an airtight container and cover the surface directly with plastic wrap. Reserve in the refrigerator; discard after 2 weeks.

3. **FOR THE ASSEMBLY:** Sheet the semi-frozen dough to 5 mm/.2 in on the sheeter. Return to the freezer for about 1 hour, or until semi-frozen. Use a wheel cutter and a ruler or a guide to cut out 9-cm/3.6-in squares. Dip the wheel cutter in flour before each cut.

4. Dip a half-circle cutter in bread flour and cut out half-circles on the diagonal in the square. Brush the borders of each square with egg wash.

5. Bring one corner of the square over to reach the other tip of the square, leaving the cutout semicircle down the middle of the square. Brush with egg wash.

6. **TO FINISH:** Follow the proofing instructions for laminated pastries on page 44.

7. When fully proofed, follow the baking instructions on page 49.

8. Once the pastries have cooled, place the Key lime curd inside a piping bag with a Bismarck tip (or a long, thin tip). Pipe the curd into the Danish in the center, where the semicircle meets the triangle.

9. Drizzle the Key lime glaze over the entire surface of the Danish in a thin, steady stream, creating very fine, straight lines. Sprinkle about 2 g/.07 oz of poppy seeds over the Danish before the glaze sets, trying to disperse them as much as possible.

STRAWBERRY D'ARTOIS DANISH

yield: about 40 pieces

INGREDIENT	METRIC	U.S.	%
STRAWBERRY JAM			
Strawberries, stemmed and hulled	750 g	1 lb 10.5 oz	50%
Sugar	750 g	1 lb 10.5 oz	50%
Tahitian vanilla pods	2	2	
CREAM CHEESE FILLING			
Cream cheese, at room temperature	708 g	1 lb 8.96 oz	70.82%
Superfine sugar	283 g	9.99 oz	28.33%
Tahitian vanilla powder	9 g	.30 oz	.85%
Danish Dough (page 53)	5 kg	11 lb .32 oz	
Egg Wash for Brushing (page 13)	as needed	as needed	
Dextrose powder	100 g	3.53 oz	

1. **FOR THE STRAWBERRY JAM:** Combine the strawberries and the sugar in a 4-qt sauce pot. Split and scrape the vanilla pods; add both the pods and seeds to the pot.

2. Start cooking over high heat. Once the mixture comes to a boil, turn the heat down to medium.

3. Continue to cook until the jam reaches 108°C/226°F. Remove the vanilla pods. Pour into a hotel pan to cool to room temperature. Once it has cooled, transfer to an airtight container and refrigerate. The jam will keep for up to 3 weeks if properly stored.

4. **FOR THE CREAM CHEESE FILLING:** Combine all of the ingredients in a mixer bowl fitted with the paddle attachment. Mix on low speed until the sugar has dissolved and the mix is homogeneous. Adjust the sweetness if necessary. Reserve refrigerated, but in order to be soft enough to pipe, it needs to soften for a few hours at room temperature. If kept refrigerated, the filling will keep for up to 1 month.

5. **FOR THE ASSEMBLY:** Sheet 3.75 kg/8 lb 4.28 oz of the semi-frozen laminated dough to 5 mm/.2 in and the remaining dough to 3 mm/.12 in. Place in the freezer for 45 minutes or until semi-frozen.

6. Remove the thinner piece of dough from the freezer. Dip a rolling lattice cutter in bread flour and roll it over the dough, pressing down firmly so that it cuts through the dough. Gently pull the dough so that the cuts open up. It will look like a honeycomb. Return to the freezer to harden.

7. Meanwhile, remove the thicker piece of dough from the freezer and cut into 9-cm/3.6-in squares using a wheel cutter and a ruler or a guide.

8. Score each square with a 5-cm/2-in round cutter in the middle of the square. Brush the borders of each square with egg wash. Place the squares in the refrigerator.

9. Cut the lattice into 9-cm/3.6-in squares. Place each lattice square on top of each thicker square, making sure that they are evenly lined up.

10. **TO FINISH:** Follow the proofing instructions for laminated pastries on page 44.

11. When fully proofed, follow the baking instructions on page 49.

12. Once they are baked and cooled, transfer the strawberry jam to a piping bag with a Bismarck piping tip or similar long, thin piping tip. Do the same with the cream cheese filling.

13. Insert the piping tip through the side of the Danish and fill with 30 g/1.05 oz strawberry jam. Once all of the Danish have been filled with strawberry jam, finish filling them with about 25 g/.88 oz each of the cream cheese filling. Insert the piping tip in the same spot used to insert the strawberry jam.

14. Place the dextrose powder in a small sifter. Sift over all of the Danish; try to coat each piece evenly.

note This cream cheese filling recipe is a no-bake filling, which can and will be applied once the Danish is baked, but it can also be used before it is baked if needed. Traditional cream cheese fillings are made with eggs, which easily curdle at high baking temperatures, resulting in a grainy and unpleasant mouthfeel.

CANDIED MEYER LEMON AND GRAPEFRUIT MARMALADE DANISH

yield: about 40 pieces

INGREDIENT	METRIC	U.S.	%
GRAPEFRUIT MARMALADE			
Grapefruit, sliced 5 mm/.2 in thick	1.25 kg	2 lb 12.16 oz	55.56%
Sugar	1 kg	2 lb 3.2 oz	44.44%
Danish Dough (page 53)	5 kg	11 lb .32 oz	
Candied Meyer Lemon Zest (page 215)	200 to 280 pieces	200 to 280 pieces	

1. **FOR THE GRAPEFRUIT MARMALADE:** Place the grapefruit discs in a 4-qt sauce pot and cover with hot water; bring to a boil. Drain. Repeat 5 more times, changing the water each time. This will remove the bitter taste from the rind. This should yield about 1 kg/2 lb 3.2 oz of grapefruit once is has been blanched, but weigh it out to make sure because it needs to be cooked with an equal amount of sugar.

2. Combine the blanched rind with an equal amount of sugar in the same pot in which the rind was blanched.

3. Cook over medium-low heat until the skin is translucent, about 2 hours. Alternatively, measure the sugar density with a refractometer. It should measure 69° Brix, at which point the marmalade will be at the ideal consistency.

4. Once it reaches the desired Brix or the rind is translucent, pour it into a hotel pan and let it cool to room temperature. Transfer to an airtight container. If it is kept refrigerated, the rind will keep for up to 3 months.

5. **FOR THE ASSEMBLY:** Sheet the semi-frozen dough to 5 mm/.2 in. Return it to the freezer for 45 minutes or until it is semi-frozen again.

6. Cut discs out of the dough using a 12.5-cm/5-in ring cutter, and then cut them in half, in order to obtain 2 half-circles.

7. **TO FINISH:** Follow the proofing instructions for laminated dough on page 44.

8. When fully proofed, follow the baking instructions on page 49.

9. Fill a piping bag with the grapefruit marmalade; no tip is needed.

10. Once the pastries have cooled, cut them in half vertically with a sharp serrated knife; try to cut in a very straight line. If done properly, once both pieces are put back together, the cut will not be noticeable. Pipe about 50 g/1.76 oz of marmalade onto the bottom half of each Danish, and then put the top, or lid, back on.

11. Garnish with 5 to 7 pieces of Candied Meyer Lemon Zest, randomly spread out.

CHOCOLATE GANACHE AND CHERRY COMPOTE DANISH

yield: about 40 pieces

INGREDIENT	METRIC	U.S.	%
GANACHE			
Dark chocolate coins (64%)	686 g	1 lb 8.16 oz	42.86 %
Heavy cream	762 g	1 lb 10.88 oz	47.62 %
Butter, diced, at 21°C/70°F	152 g	5.38 oz	9.52 %
Danish Dough, semi-frozen (page 53)	5 kg	11 lb .32 oz	
CHERRY GLAZE			
Cherry poaching liquid	500 g	1 lb 1.6 oz	22.22%
Confectioners' sugar	1.75 kg	3 lb 13.76 oz	77.78%
Poached Rainier Cherries (page 19)	1 kg	2 lb 3.2 oz	
Gold leaf	as needed	as needed	

1. **FOR THE GANACHE:** Place the chocolate in a small stainless-steel bowl.

2. Bring the heavy cream to a boil, pour half of it onto the chocolate, and wait 45 seconds (this helps get the melting process started). Stir the mixture with a rubber spatula until most of the chocolate is incorporated (it won't dissolve completely with only half the heavy cream). Bring the other half of the heavy cream up to a boil again and pour over the chocolate mixture, stirring with a rubber spatula until completely incorporated.

3. Stir in the butter and mix until it has dissolved.

4. Transfer to an airtight container and reserve at room temperature. The ganache can only be used once it has set at room temperature, about 6 hours after it has been made. It will keep for 4 days at room temperature. If refrigerated, it can keep up for to 2 weeks, but it will need to

be pulled out and warmed up to room temperature at least 4 hours before it is needed so that it will be soft enough to pipe and hold its shape.

5. **FOR THE ASSEMBLY:** Sheet the semi-frozen dough to 5 mm/.2 in on the sheeter. Return the dough to the freezer for about 45 minutes or until it is semi-frozen.

6. Cut rectangles 5 by 12.5 cm/2 by 5 in out of the dough using a wheel cutter and a ruler or guide.

7. **TO FINISH:** Follow the proofing instructions for laminated pastries on page 44.

8. When fully proofed, follow the baking instructions on page 49.

9. **FOR THE CHERRY GLAZE:** Mix both ingredients together in a bowl. Adjust the consistency with poaching liquid or with confectioners' sugar; it should be as thick as pouring fondant. Pour into a piping bag and reserve while filling the Danish with ganache and the poached cherries. It will keep for 3 weeks in an airtight container in the refrigerator.

10. Once the Danish have cooled, fill a piping bag fitted with a Bismarck tip or other long, thin tip with the chocolate ganache.

11. Cut the baked Danish rectangles in half horizontally using a sharp serrated knife. When done properly, both pieces should fit together seamlessly.

12. Pipe 40 g/1.41 oz of ganache onto each bottom piece of Danish. Place 25 g/.88 oz of poached cherries on top of the ganache. Put the lids on the Danish. Drizzle the cherry glaze on top of each Danish to create a very tight pattern of thin lines. Garnish with a small fleck of gold leaf.

note Ganache is an emulsion, and this is why we add the heavy cream in 2 additions. If it is added all at once, the ganache might have a grainy consistency once it sets. This is an indication of a broken emulsion.

BLACK CURRANT AND GIANDUJA CREAM DANISH

yield: about 40 pieces

INGREDIENT	METRIC	U.S.	%
BLACK CURRANT FILLING			
Almond paste	508 g	1 lb 1.92 oz	50.85%
Sugar	254 g	8.97 oz	25.42%
Black currant purée	169 g	5.98 oz	16.95%
Egg yolks	68 g	2.39 oz	6.78%
GIANDUJA CREAM			
Gianduja, coarsely chopped	1.6 kg	3 lb 8.48 oz	66.67%
Heavy cream	800 g	1 lb 12.16 oz	33.33%
Danish Dough, semi-frozen (page 53)	5 kg	11 lb .32 oz	
Dark chocolate (64%), melted	200 g	7.05 oz	
Praline croquant	400 g	14.11 oz	

1. **FOR THE BLACK CURRANT FILLING:** In a 5-qt mixer bowl fitted with the paddle attachment, mix the almond paste, sugar, and black currant purée on low speed until a homogeneous mass is obtained. Add the egg yolks and continue to mix until completely incorporated. If making larger amounts, add the eggs in 4 additions so that they can incorporate evenly and not break the mixture.

2. Once mixed, transfer to an airtight container and refrigerate. The filling will keep for 8 to 10 days.

3. **FOR THE GIANDUJA CREAM:** Place the gianduja in a small stainless-steel bowl.

4. Bring the cream to a boil and pour over the gianduja. Wait for 45 seconds, then stir with a rubber spatula until a homogeneous mass is obtained.

5. Transfer to an airtight container and refrigerate. Pull it out at least 4 hours and up to the night before it is needed so that it is soft enough to pipe and hold its shape. It will keep for 2 weeks refrigerated and for 4 days if left at room temperature.

6. **FOR THE ASSEMBLY:** Sheet the semi-frozen dough to 5 mm/.2 in and return to the freezer for about 45 minutes or until it is semi-frozen again.

7. Spread the black currant filling across the entire surface of the dough, leaving a 2.5-cm/1-in border around the filling; it should be a very thin layer.

8. Cut out rectangles 9 by 12.5 cm/3.6 by 5 in using a wheel cutter and a guide or ruler. Roll the Danish rectangles up loosely. Place them on a sheet pan with the seam centered directly at the base.

9. **TO FINISH:** Follow the proofing instructions for laminated pastries on page 44.

10. When fully proofed, follow the baking instructions on page 49.

11. Once the pastries have cooled, fill a piping bag fitted with a Bismarck tip or other long, thin piping tip with gianduja cream. Insert the tip into the side of the Danish and pipe about 60 g/2.11 oz into each piece.

12. Place the melted chocolate in a piping bag and cut a hole to make a very small tip. Drizzle the chocolate quickly across the top of the Danish to create a very tight pattern of thin lines.

13. Sprinkle praline croquant across the left half of the Danish.

14. Refrigerate for 5 minutes to set the chocolate, but no longer; otherwise the flaky layers of Danish will soften with condensation.

notes If desired, substitute any other fruit purée (apple, raspberry, strawberry, pear, etc.) for the black currant purée as long as it is of purée consistency (thick).

Gianduja is a type of chocolate (usually milk) that has a percentage of hazelnut paste added, giving it a distinct flavor. It is very high in fat, which is why it doesn't need to be emulsified like ganache does.

advanced viennoiserie

These Danish varieties embody a slightly higher degree of complexity as far as how they are finished. The lamination process is the same, but they are assembled and finished differently. There is a quick-bread element (frangipane and pound cake) incorporated into each recipe, which is piped into the Danish before it is baked. This contributes two things. It adds texture and can also add a secondary flavor, but most importantly, it helps support the central structure of the Danish. As it bakes, it pushes up at the same rate as the Danish dough and, once the Danish cools, it stays in place. It helps the Danish cool without a chance of it deflating or collapsing onto itself.

The finishing is also more involved. There is a fruit component that is always cooked beforehand, a glaze, and a decorative garnish, which is not just for visual appeal, but also adds texture and flavor. These are very special Danish pastries that combine the wonderful flaky texture of Danish with a combination of textures and flavors that make a good thing even better.

POACHED PEAR, FRANGIPANE, CASSIS PÂTE DE FRUIT, AND GUINNESS GLAZE DANISH

yield: about 40 pieces

INGREDIENT	METRIC	U.S.	%
POACHED PEARS			
Water	2 kg	4 lb 6.56 oz	44.44%
Guinness beer	1.5 kg	3 lb 4.96 oz	33.33%
Sugar	1 kg	2 lb 3.2 oz	22.22%
Vanilla pods, split and scraped	3	3	
Bosc pears, semi-ripe	14	14	
FRANGIPANE			
Almond paste	219 g	7.71 oz	21.85%
Butter, at 21°C/70°F	219 g	7.71 oz	21.85%
Sugar	219 g	7.71 oz	21.85%
Eggs, at 21°C/70°F	251 g	8.85 oz	25.08%
Cake flour, sifted	94 g	3.3 oz	9.36%
GUINNESS GLAZE			
Guinness beer	396.04 g	13.97 oz	24.75%
Confectioners' sugar	1.18 kg	2 lb 9.62 oz	74.26%
Lemon juice	15.84 g	.56 oz	.99%
Danish Dough (page 53), **semi-frozen**	5 kg	11 lb .32 oz	
Apricot Glaze (page 49), **warm**	as needed	as needed	
Black Currant Pâte de Fruit (page 480), **cut into 3-cm/1.2-in squares**	40	40	

1. **FOR THE POACHED PEARS:** In a medium sauce pot, combine the water, beer, sugar, and vanilla pods and seeds. Bring to a boil over high heat.

2. Meanwhile, peel the pears, cut them into quarters (or eighths if they are large), and remove the cores with a knife. Once the liquid reaches a boil, turn off the heat and place the pears in the liquid. Cover them with a cloth or heavy-duty paper towel and let them cool to room temperature.

FROM TOP TO BOTTOM: Fig Jam, Roasted Fig, Stone Pine Liqueur Glaze, and Toasted Almond Danish (page 69), Pineapple Jam, Coconut Ganache, and Dark Rum Glaze Danish (page 67), Apple Butter, Candied Apple, Applejack Glaze, and Caramel Danish (page 65), Poached Pear, Frangipane, Cassis Pâte de Fruit, and Guiness Glaze Danish (page 62)

This should be enough heat to cook the pears through. If not, return them to cook over low heat until they are tender. Cool them quickly over an ice bath or in a hotel pan in the refrigerator. Remove the vanilla pods.

3. Once they have cooled, transfer to an airtight container and refrigerate. The poached pears will keep for up to 1 week.

4. **FOR THE FRANGIPANE:** Combine the almond paste, butter, and sugar in the bowl of an electric mixer fitted with the paddle attachment. Mix on low speed until it forms a homogeneous mass.

5. Add the eggs 1 at a time. Scrape the sides of the bowl and the paddle and mix for a few more seconds.

6. Add the cake flour and pulse the mixer until incorporated.

7. If ready to use, pour into a piping bag and reserve at room temperature for ease of piping (it hardens when it is refrigerated); otherwise reserve refrigerated in an airtight container. The frangipane will keep for up to 2 weeks in the refrigerator.

8. **FOR THE GUINNESS GLAZE:** Whisk together the beer, sugar, and lemon juice in a bowl until thoroughly combined. Adjust the consistency until it is similar to warm pouring fondant. Adjust the thickness if necessary by adding more beer. Transfer to a piping bag if using soon. Otherwise, reserve in an airtight container at room temperature. It will keep for up to 1 month in the refrigerator.

9. **FOR THE ASSEMBLY:** Sheet the semi-frozen dough to 7 mm/.3 in thick. Return the dough to the freezer for about 45 minutes or until it is semi-frozen again.

10. Use an oval cutter measuring 5 by 15 cm/2 by 6 in with a corner radius of 2.5 cm/1 in (see Resources, page 540, for custom-made cutters) to cut out the sheet of dough.

11. Cut a slit lengthwise down the middle of the oval using a paring knife, starting 2.5 cm/1 in from the top and ending 2.5 cm/1 in from the bottom.

12. Pull one end of the dough down and twist it in through the slit, then pull it out. Repeat with the remaining pieces of dough. Place the shaped dough on a sheet pan lined with parchment paper.

13. Pipe about 25 g/.88 oz of frangipane down the opening of the oval. It should be just enough to fill the gap. Wrap the sheet pans loosely and let the Danish retard overnight in the refrigerator.

14. **TO FINISH:** Proof the Danish for 45 minutes to 1 hour at 27°C/80°F with 80 to 90 percent relative humidity.

15. Heat a convection oven to 226°C/440°F. Load the oven and press the steam button for 3 seconds. Once the steam button has been pressed, set the temperature to 185°C/365°F.

16. On the onset of color, open the vent. This helps develop a flaky crust and a deep golden brown color. Bake until the Danish achieve a deep brown golden color, 8 to 12 minutes depending on the oven. Remove the Danish from the oven and slide the parchment paper and Danish onto a sheet pan fitted with a cooling rack or onto a metro shelf. While they cool, brush the pastries with hot apricot glaze.

17. Once they have cooled, drizzle a random thick line of Guinness glaze across the middle of each Danish. Place 2 or 3 pieces of pear on top of the glaze. Place 3 pieces of cassis pâte de fruit in a random pattern over each Danish.

note Some ovens, such as the one used to bake Danish, dispense a preset amount of steam each time the steam button is pressed and can be programmed to release a specific amount. In this case, the oven should be set to dispense 1 L/1.06 qt of steam for a fully loaded oven of 5 sheet pans.

APPLE BUTTER, CANDIED APPLE, APPLEJACK GLAZE, AND CARAMEL DANISH

yield: about 40 pieces

INGREDIENT	METRIC	U.S.	%
CINNAMON POUND CAKE			
Butter	364 g	12.85 oz	24.29%
Sugar	383 g	13.5 oz	25.51%
Eggs	292 g	10.29 oz	19.44%
Salt	7 g	.23 oz	.43%
Pastry flour	364 g	12.85 oz	24.29%
Baking powder	4 g	.12 oz	.23%
Ground cinnamon	5 g	.18 oz	.34%
Crème fraîche	82 g	2.89 oz	5.47%
APPLE BUTTER			
Granny Smith apples	1.16 kg	2 lb 9.12 oz	66.62%
Butter	117 g	4.11 oz	6.66%
Sugar	350 g	12.34 oz	19.99%
Maple sugar	117 g	4.11 oz	6.66%
Salt	1 g	.04 oz	.07%
Cinnamon sticks	7	7	
Tahitian vanilla pods, split and scraped	3	3	
APPLEJACK GLAZE			
Applejack	200 g	7.05 oz	15.27%
Confectioners' sugar	900 g	1 lb 15.68 oz	68.7%
Heavy cream	200 g	7.05 oz	15.27%
Lemon juice	10 g	.35 oz	.76%
Danish Dough (page 53), **semi-frozen**	5 kg	11 lb .32 oz	
Apricot Glaze (page 49), **warm**	as needed	as needed	
Caramel (page 446)	1 kg	2 lb 3.27 oz	
Candied Apples (pages 81-82)	500 g	1 lb 1.64 oz	
Edible gold leaf	1 sheet	1 sheet	

1. **FOR THE POUND CAKE:** Follow the creaming method on page 76; add the cinnamon with the dry ingredients. Then add the crème fraîche. Once the batter is made, pour it into a piping bag if using soon. Otherwise, reserve in an airtight container in the refrigerator. Discard after 5 days.

2. **FOR THE APPLE BUTTER:** Coarsely chop the apples into about 8 pieces each and place all of the pieces, as well as the seeds, stems, and cores, in a 4-qt sauce pot. Dice the butter and add it to the apples. Place the remaining apple butter ingredients in the pot.

3. Bring the mixture to a boil over high heat, and then turn the heat down to medium low. If the apples begin to scorch, turn the heat down to low, stirring the pot every few minutes to ensure there is no scorching.

4. Cook until all the apples have cooked through and turned brown, about 3 hours. The mixture will look almost like a paste, and there will be no discernible pieces of apple. Remove the vanilla pods.

5. While the apple butter is still warm, pass it through a ricer or a drum sieve. The ricer is better because the mixture is hot, and a ricer will lessen the chance of burns. If using a drum sieve, use gloves and a bowl scraper to push the apples through. Let the apple butter cool to room temperature in a hotel pan covered with plastic wrap. Once cool, transfer to an airtight container and refrigerate. The apple butter will keep for up to 3 weeks in the refrigerator.

6. **FOR THE GLAZE:** Whisk all of the ingredients in a bowl until thoroughly combined. Adjust the texture if necessary; it should be thick like warm pouring fondant.

7. **FOR THE ASSEMBLY:** Sheet the semi-frozen dough to 7 mm/.3 in. Return the dough to the freezer for 45 minutes or until it is semi-frozen again.

8. Meanwhile, spray 40 tart rings with nonstick oil spray and place them on sheet pans (10 per sheet pan).

9. Cut the dough out using a 9-cm/3.6-in ring cutter. Cut a 4-cm-/1.6-in-long slit down the middle of each disc. Using your thumbs, push out on the discs through the slit, so it looks like an open mouth.

10. Place inside the prepared tart shells. Pipe about 30 g/1.06 oz of pound cake batter inside the opening of each Danish. Wrap the sheet pans loosely and let the pastries retard overnight in the refrigerator.

11. **TO FINISH:** Proof the Danish for 45 minutes to 1 hour at 27°C/80°F with 80 to 90 percent relative humidity.

12. Heat a convection oven to 226°C/440°F. Load the oven and press the steam button for 3 seconds. Once the steam button has been pressed, set the temperature to 185°C/365°F.

13. On the onset of color, open the vent. This helps develop a flaky crust and a deep golden brown color. Bake until the Danish achieve a deep brown golden color, 8 to 12 minutes depending on the oven. Remove the Danish from the oven and slide the parchment paper and Danish onto a sheet pan fitted with a cooling rack or onto a metro shelf. While the pastries cool, brush them with hot apricot glaze.

14. Once they have cooled, fill a piping bag fitted with a Bismarck piping tip or other thin, long tip with the caramel. Using the tip, make a hole on the top of the Danish and pipe about 25 g/.88 oz into each Danish. Fill another piping bag with the apple butter and pipe 25 g/.88 oz into the same hole used to pipe in the caramel.

15. Drizzle the applejack glaze on one side of each Danish.

16. Using a spoon, place 10 g/.35 oz of candied apples on top of each Danish.

17. Garnish with a fleck of gold leaf.

PINEAPPLE JAM, COCONUT GANACHE, AND DARK RUM GLAZE DANISH

yield: about 40 pieces

INGREDIENT	METRIC	U.S.	%
COCONUT POUND CAKE			
Butter	351 g	12.37 oz	23.37%
Sugar	368 g	12.98 oz	24.54%
Eggs	281 g	9.9 oz	18.7%
Salt	6 g	.22 oz	.41%
Pastry flour	351 g	12.37 oz	23.37%
Baking powder	3 g	.12 oz	.22%
Crème fraîche	79 g	2.78 oz	5.26%
Shredded coconut	62 g	2.18 oz	4.12%
PINEAPPLE JAM			
Pineapple, peeled, cored, and finely chopped	874 g	1 lb 14.88 oz	69.93%
Sugar	350 g	12.33 oz	27.97%
Lemon juice	26 g	.93 oz	2.1%
COCONUT-WHITE CHOCOLATE GANACHE			
White chocolate, chopped or in pistoles	600 g	1 lb 5.12 oz	60%
Heavy cream	200 g	7.05 oz	20%
Shredded coconut	200 g	7.05 oz	20%
RUM GLAZE			
Myers's dark rum	200 g	7.05 oz	15.27%
Confectioners' sugar	900 g	1 lb 15.75 oz	68.7%
Heavy cream	200 g	7.05 oz	15.27%
Lemon juice	10 g	.35 oz	.76%
CANDIED PINEAPPLE			
Pineapple, peeled	1	1	
Sugar	1 kg	2 lb 3.2 oz	
Candied macadamia nuts	400 g	14.11 oz	
Danish Dough (page 53), semi-frozen	5 kg	11 lb .32 oz	
Apricot Glaze (page 49), warm	as needed	as needed	
Shredded coconut	as needed	as needed	
Edible gold leaf	as needed	as needed	

1. **FOR THE COCONUT POUND CAKE:** Follow the creaming method on page 76 with the dry ingredients, and then add the crème fraîche. Add the shredded coconut after the crème fraîche; mix until just combined. If using immediately, pour into a piping bag. Otherwise, refrigerate in an airtight container.

2. **FOR THE PINEAPPLE JAM:** Combine all of the jam ingredients in a 4-qt sauce pot and cook over high heat until it comes to a boil.

3. Turn the heat down to medium and cook, stirring with a wooden spoon every few minutes to prevent it from scorching at the bottom. When the mixture reaches 72° Brix, take it off the heat and pour the jam into a hotel pan.

4. Let it cool to room temperature. After it has cooled, transfer the mixture to an airtight container and refrigerate. The jam will keep for up to 2 months in the refrigerator.

5. **FOR THE COCONUT-WHITE CHOCOLATE GANACHE:** Set up a hot water bath with simmering, not boiling, water.

6. Place the chocolate in a small stainless-steel bowl along with the cream; stir until the chocolate has melted and a homogeneous mass is obtained. Make sure the water does not boil, or it will overheat the chocolate and make it seize. White chocolate tends to thicken when it is overheated.

7. Take the bowl off the heat and stir in the coconut.

8. Transfer to an airtight container and refrigerate. The ganache will keep for up to 2 weeks in the refrigerator. It will need to be pulled out at least 3 hours before it is needed so that it is soft enough to pipe.

9. **FOR THE RUM GLAZE:** Whisk all of the glaze ingredients together in a bowl until thoroughly combined. The glaze should be the consistency of warm pouring fondant. Adjust consistency if needed. If it is too loose, add more sugar; if it is too thick, add more cream or rum. Transfer to a piping bag if using immediately. Otherwise, place the glaze in an airtight container in the refrigerator. The glaze will keep for 2 months in the refrigerator.

10. **FOR THE CANDIED PINEAPPLE:** Cut the pineapple into 1.25-cm/.5-in discs. Cut the pineapple slices using a 7.5-cm/3-in ring cutter to get evenly sized discs. Using a 2.5-cm/1-in ring cutter, remove the core from each disc. Put the sugar in a medium rondeau and make a dry caramel over high heat (see page 446 for the procedure for dry caramel). Once the sugar achieves an amber brown color, add the pineapple slices. Cook them for 4 minutes on each side or until they absorb the caramel color. Spoon the slices onto a silicone paper–lined sheet pan to cool. If not using right away, wrap the sheet pan and place in the refrigerator. Discard after 3 days.

11. **FOR THE CANDIED MACADAMIA NUTS:** Follow the procedure on page 34 for candied macadamia nuts.

12. **FOR THE ASSEMBLY:** Sheet the semi-frozen dough to 10 mm/.4 in thick on a sheeter. Return the dough to the freezer for 45 minutes or until it is semi-frozen again.

13. Cut rectangles 5 by 12.5 cm/2 by 5 in out of the dough using a wheel cutter and a ruler or guide. Cut a slit down the middle of each rectangle, starting 2.5 cm/1 in from the top and ending 2.5 cm/1 in from the bottom.

14. Open the rectangle from the slit outward, so that it looks like an open mouth. Place 12 Danish on each sheet pan. Pipe about 30 g/1.06 oz of coconut pound cake batter down the center of each Danish, inside the opening. Wrap each sheet pan loosely and retard overnight in the refrigerator.

15. **TO FINISH:** Proof the Danish for 1½ to 2 hours at 27°C/80°F with 80 to 90 percent relative humidity.

16. Heat a convection oven to 226°C/440°F. Load the oven and press the steam button for 3 seconds. Once the steam button has been pressed, set the temperature to 185°C/365°F.

17. On the onset of color, open the vent. This helps develop a flaky crust and a deep golden brown color. Bake until the Danish achieve a deep brown golden color, 8 to 12 minutes depending on the oven. Remove the Danish from the oven and slide the parchment paper and Danish onto a sheet pan fitted with a cooling rack or onto a metro shelf. While the pastries cool, brush them with hot apricot glaze.

18. Once they have cooled, put the pineapple jam in a piping bag fitted with a Bismarck tip or other long, thin piping tip. Insert the tip through the slit and pipe about 30 g/1.05 oz of jam inside each Danish. Repeat this procedure with the ganache, piping into the same slit as the jam.

19. Pipe the rum glaze widthwise across the middle of the Danish from one end to the other in a semi-wide strand, about 1 cm/.4 in wide. Sprinkle shredded coconut on top of the glaze before it sets; when it dries it will not adhere. Cut a pineapple disc into quarters and place one quarter on top of the Danish. Place a candied macadamia nut on top of the pineapple and a fleck of the gold leaf on top of the candied nut.

FIG JAM, ROASTED FIG, STONE PINE LIQUEUR GLAZE, AND TOASTED ALMOND DANISH

yield: **about 40 pieces**

INGREDIENT	METRIC	U.S.	%
VANILLA POUND CAKE			
Butter	290 g	10.23 oz	24.17%
Sugar	305 g	10.74 oz	25.38%
Eggs	232 g	8.19 oz	19.34%
Salt	5 g	.18 oz	.43%
Pastry flour	290 g	10.23 oz	24.17%
Baking powder	3 g	.1 oz	.23%
Crème fraîche	65 g	2.3 oz	5.44%
Vanilla paste	10 g	.36 oz	.85%
FIG JAM			
Black Mission figs, ends trimmed	1.2 kg	2 lb 10.4 oz	48.98%
Sugar	1.2 kg	2 lb 10.4 oz	48.98%
Lemon juice	50 g	1.76 oz	2.04%
ROASTED FIGS			
Zirbenz Stone Pine liqueur	750 g	1 lb 10.4 oz	48.39%
Sugar	800 g	1 lb 12.16 oz	51.61%
Cinnamon sticks	5	5	
Tahitian vanilla pods, split and scraped	2	2	
Black Mission figs, ends trimmed and cut in half lengthwise	20	20	
PINE LIQUEUR GLAZE			
Zirbenz Stone Pine liqueur	200 g	7.05 oz	16.53%
Confectioners' sugar	900 g	1 lb 15.75 oz	74.38%
Heavy cream	100 g	3.53 oz	8.26%
Lemon juice	10 g	.35 oz	.83%
Danish Dough (page 53), semi-frozen	5 kg	11 lb .32 oz	
Apricot Glaze (page 49), warm	as needed	as needed	
Toasted sliced almonds	200 g	7.05 oz	
Silver dragées	100 g	3.53 oz	

1. **FOR THE POUND CAKE:** Follow the creaming method on page 76. Add the vanilla paste with the crème fraîche. Transfer to a piping bag if using immediately. Otherwise, reserve the batter in an airtight container in the refrigerator. Discard after 5 days.

2. **FOR THE FIG JAM:** Combine all of the jam ingredients in a sauce pot and bring to a boil over high heat, stirring frequently. Turn the heat down to medium-low and cook until the mixture reaches 65° Brix. Test the jam with a refractometer.

3. Cool the jam in a hotel pan over an ice bath. Once it has cooled down, transfer it to a piping bag fitted with a Bismarck tip or other long, thin piping tip if using soon. Otherwise, transfer it to an airtight container and refrigerate. It will keep for up to 1 month in the refrigerator.

4. **FOR THE ROASTED FIGS:** Combine the Stone Pine liqueur, sugar, cinnamon sticks, and vanilla pods and beans in a sauce pot and bring to a boil over high heat. Turn the heat down to medium. Continue to cook until the liquid is reduced by half. Remove the pan from the heat and remove the cinnamon sticks and vanilla pods.

5. Preheat a convection oven to 160°C/320°F.

6. Pour the reduced liquid into a hotel pan. Place the halved figs into the hotel pan, cut side down. Roast until tender, about 7 minutes. Once they are cooked, transfer them onto a sheet pan lined with silicone paper or a nonstick rubber mat and cool in the refrigerator. Reserve the cooking liquid at room temperature in an airtight container. It will keep for up to 2 months, since it has such a high sugar concentration. The consistency should be that of a thick glaze.

7. **FOR THE PINE LIQUEUR GLAZE:** Whisk all of the glaze ingredients together in a bowl until thoroughly combined. Adjust the consistency if necessary. If it is too thick, add more heavy cream; if it is too thin, add more confectioners' sugar. It should have the consistency of warm pouring fondant. If using soon, transfer to a piping bag with no tip and reserve at room temperature. Otherwise, transfer to an airtight container and refrigerate. It will keep for up to 1 month in the refrigerator.

8. **TO ASSEMBLE:** Sheet the semi-frozen dough to 10 mm/.4 in thick on a sheeter. Return the dough to the freezer for 45 minutes or until it is semi-frozen again.

9. Cut rectangles 5 by 12.5 cm/2 by 5 in using a wheel cutter and a ruler or guide. Cut a slit down the middle of each rectangle, starting 2.5 cm/1 in from the top and ending 2.5 cm/1 in from the bottom.

10. Open up the rectangle from the slit outward, so that it looks like an open mouth. Take the top end and twist it inward, toward the center of the Danish. It should look like a heart. Place 10 pieces on each sheet pan. Pipe about 30 g/1.06 oz of vanilla pound cake batter down the center of each Danish, inside the opening. Wrap each sheet pan loosely and retard the Danish overnight in the refrigerator.

11. Proof the Danish for 1½ to 2 hours at 27°C/80°F with 80 to 90 percent relative humidity.

12. Heat a convection oven to 226°C/440°F. Load the oven and press the steam button for 3 seconds. Once the steam button has been pressed, set the temperature to 185°C/365°F.

13. On the onset of color, open the vent. This helps develop a flaky crust and a deep golden brown color. Bake until the Danish achieve a deep brown golden color, 8 to 12 minutes depending on the oven. Remove the Danish from the oven and slide the parchment paper and Danish onto a sheet pan fitted with a cooling rack or onto a metro shelf. While the pastries cool, brush them with hot apricot glaze.

14. Once they have cooled, pipe the fig jam into the Danish. Insert the tip through the slit and pipe about 30 g/1.05 oz of jam inside each Danish. Pipe a straight line of pine tree glaze widthwise across the center of the Danish from end to end. Place about 10 g/.35 oz of sliced almonds across the center of the Danish on top of the stone pine glaze before it sets; otherwise they will not adhere. Spoon about 15 g/.52 oz of the fig roasting liquid onto the front end of the Danish. It should be thick enough to cling to the Danish and not slide off. Sprinkle about 2 g/.07 oz of silver dragées onto the glaze. Place a single roasted fig half on top of the Danish.

laminated brioche

Laminated brioche brings together delicate, soft brioche with the flaky crispness of laminated pastries. The end result is not quite a brioche and not quite a laminated pastry. It is, in fact, a whole different pastry with many possibilities.

When we laminate croissant dough, we take a dough with little gluten development and develop that gluten through lamination (turns and folds). When laminating brioche, we start the process with dough that has full gluten development. This in itself makes

it much easier to handle than croissant dough, since brioche will be more elastic and pliable.

A laminated brioche is one of the most decadent and richest pastries out there. The dough itself contains about 50 percent butter (in relation to 100 percent bread flour), and more butter will be added in the form of a butter block, which is 33 percent of the total weight of the dough. This will result in an extremely flaky pastry with a very moist interior.

LAMINATED BRIOCHE

yield: 5 kg/11 lb .32oz

INGREDIENT	METRIC	U.S.	%
Brioche Dough (page 10)	3.76 kg	8 lb 4.64 oz	75.19%
Butter block	1.24 kg	2 lb 11.84 oz	24.81%

1. See the procedures for butter blocks on page 40 and croissant lamination on page 44. All the principles are the same.

2. Follow the procedures for proofing on page 48 and baking on page 49.

note The most important thing to keep in mind is that brioche is a fully developed dough with gluten at its maximum development. It is much stronger and therefore more forgiving than croissant dough, but it is also harder to manage; since the gluten is already so strong, the dough tends to pull back much more after being rolled out. To correct this, simply relax the dough as much as possible while sheeting it and between folds.

FLEUR DE SEL, ROASTED GARLIC, SAGE, AND PECORINO TARTUFO BRIOCHE

yield: about 40 pieces

INGREDIENT	METRIC	U.S.
ROASTED GARLIC		
Garlic heads	4	4
Olive oil	200 g	7.05 oz
FRIED SAGE LEAVES		
Canola oil	500 g	1 lb 1.6 oz
Sage leaves	40	40
Laminated Brioche (page 71), semi-frozen	5 kg	11 lb .32 oz
Pecorino Tartufo, grated with a rasp	926 g	2 lb .64 oz
Fleur de sel	74 g	2.61 oz

1. **FOR THE ROASTED GARLIC:** Cut off the top of each garlic head to expose all of the cloves. Place the heads in a half hotel pan and drizzle them with the olive oil. Roast in a 200°C/392°F deck oven for about 30 minutes or until the garlic cloves have turned golden brown.

2. Let the heads cool to room temperature in the roasting pan. Once cooled, peel the skin off the cloves; it should come off easily. Reserve at room temperature. Refrigerate if not using soon. Discard after 2 days.

3. **FOR THE FRIED SAGE:** Heat the canola oil to 180°C/356°F in a 4-qt sauce pot. Fry 5 leaves at a time until crispy, about 1 minute. Discard after 24 hours.

4. Place 40 mini panettone molds on 2 sheet pans (see Resources, page 540). Space them evenly.

5. Sheet the semi-frozen dough to 5 mm/.2 in. Cut widthwise into 3 evenly sized sheets and return to the freezer for about 45 minutes or until the dough is semi-frozen. Cut it into 40-cm-/16-in-wide sheets (they should already be the length of a sheet of parchment paper from the original sheeting), using a Plexiglas guide and a wheel cutter.

6. Sprinkle the cheese over the entire surface of all 3 sheets of laminated brioche dough in an even layer.

7. Roll the sheets up away from you. Trim an end off of each roll, and cut each one into 5-cm-/2-in-thick pieces. Place each piece inside a mini panettone mold.

8. Follow the proofing instructions for Danish on page 48.

9. Preheat the convection oven to 175°C/350°F.

10. Before baking, sprinkle a pinch (about 2 g/.07 oz) of fleur de sel on top of each proofed laminated brioche and insert 1 roasted garlic clove into each piece, at the center of the spiral.

11. Bake until the internal temperature of the brioche is 95°C/203°F, 10 to 13 minutes. Once cooled, tear the paper off and insert a fried sage leaf next to the garlic clove.

notes Pecorino Tartufo is an Italian sheep's milk hard cheese from the Umbria region that has black truffle trimmings added to it, which infuse their flavor to create a unique cheese.

The ratio of dough to garnish is not the usual 60 percent to 40 percent in this recipe (it is 80 percent to 20 percent), because if there were any more cheese it would weigh the brioche down too much.

SLOW-POACHED QUINCE AND CURRANT BRIOCHE

yield: about 40 pieces

INGREDIENT	METRIC	U.S.
SLOW-POACHED QUINCE AND CURRANTS		
Quince, large, peeled	40	40
Dried currants	300 g	10.58 oz
Water	2 kg	4 lb 6.4 oz
Elderflower liqueur (St-Germain)	1 kg	2 lb 3.2 oz
Sugar	2 kg	4 lb 6.4 oz
Cinnamon sticks	10	10
Orange zest	3 oranges	3 oranges
Vanilla pods	2	2
Cloves	5	5
Laminated Brioche (page 71), semi-frozen	5 kg	11 lb .32 oz

1. **FOR THE SLOW-POACHED QUINCE AND CURRANTS:** In a medium sauce pot, combine all of the ingredients. Cover with a clean kitchen towel and place over medium-low heat.

2. Cook until the quince are tender and a skewer slides through them with little resistance.

3. Remove from the heat and allow to cool to room temperature. Remove the cinnamon sticks, vanilla pods, and cloves.

4. Cut the quince into quarters and remove the cores. Cut into an even medium dice and return to the liquid.

5. Transfer to an airtight container and reserve in the refrigerator. The quince can keep for up to 1 week in the refrigerator.

6. **FOR THE ASSEMBLY:** Remove the required 1.8 kg/3 lb 15.36 oz of diced quince and poached currants from their poaching liquid. Pat them dry between sheets of paper towels.

7. Sheet the semi-frozen dough to 5 mm/.2 in thick on a sheeter. Divide the dough widthwise into 3 evenly sized sheet, using a wheel cutter. If you have a sheet of dough this long, you will cut it into 3 same-sized pieces. Return the dough to the freezer for 45 minutes or until it is semi-frozen again.

8. Distribute equal parts of the quince-currant mixture in a single layer on each sheet of dough.

9. Roll each laminated brioche sheet up to form an even roll. Don't roll it too tight; otherwise the brioche will "telescope" when it bakes; it will shoot out from the center of the mold and look like a telescope. Trim one of the ends off of each roll, and cut each one into 2.5-cm/1-in-thick pieces. Place each piece inside a paper baking mold that measures 9 cm/3.6 in diameter and 2.5 cm/1 in deep (see Resources, page 540).

10. **TO FINISH:** Follow the proofing instructions for Danish on page 48.

11. Preheat the convection oven to 175°C/350°F.

12. Bake until the brioche takes on a dark amber brown color, 10 to 12 minutes.

note The weight of the currants will increase because they will hydrate once they are cooked. The yield is the resulting drained mass; it does not include the cooking liquid, since it is not an actual part of the brioche. Save this liquid for future use. The flavor will continue to improve as it is stored.

MANCHEGO CHEESE AND SERRANO BRIOCHE

yield: 45 to 50 pieces

INGREDIENT	METRIC	U.S.	%
Laminated Brioche (page 71), semi-frozen	5 kg	11 lb .32 oz	
Serrano ham, thinly sliced	1.6 kg	3 lb 8.48 oz	80%
Sage leaves, small	45 to 50	45 to 50	
Manchego, grated finely on a rasp	400 g	14.11 oz	20%
Egg Wash for Brushing (page 13)	as needed	as needed	

1. Line 5 sheet pans with silicone paper.

2. Cut the laminated brioche dough as for pain au chocolat into rectangles 8.75 by 12.5 cm/ 3.5 by 5 in using a Plexiglas guide and a wheel cutter.

3. The rectangles should be placed with the short sides facing you, right next to each other. Do not separate them after cutting them or brushing the egg wash on them. Brush the top half of the rectangles with the egg wash.

4. Place a few slices of Serrano ham widthwise on top of each rectangle (about 80 g/2.8 oz per rectangle of dough).

5. Roll up the dough away from you, but not too tightly, and place on a silicone paper–lined sheet pan. Make sure the seam is directly at the middle-bottom of the brioche. Press down gently with your fingertips. Repeat until all the pieces have been shaped, then brush with egg wash and proof, or wrap and refrigerate or freeze.

6. **TO FINISH:** See the instructions for proofing laminated pastries on page 44. When the brioche is done proofing and the last layer of egg wash has been applied, place a small leaf of sage on top of the proofed dough, and then sprinkle about 20 g/.7 oz of the grated cheese on top.

7. Bake as for Danish, following the baking instructions on page 49.

note This will exceed the recommended ratio of 60 percent dough to 40 percent garnish by 10 percent, but if you are already splurging on the butter, why not splurge on the Serrano too?

chemically leavened breakfast pastries (quick breads)

Chemically leavened breakfast pastries are also known as "quick breads" because they can be made quickly and you don't have to wait for the yeast to proof the dough. The type of leavening agent is the way in which they differ from what we have covered so far in that they are raised chemically by baking powder and/or baking soda, and not biologically by yeast. Structurally, chemically leavened products are completely different from yeast-risen products, not only because of the leavener used, but also because chemically leavened products are typically not mixed long enough to develop any gluten, while yeast leavened doughs are mixed long enough. This will have a dramatic difference on the end product, not only in the crumb but also in the crust and the texture of the finished product.

CREAMED BUTTER BATTERS (Pound Cakes)

The method used to make pound cakes is known as the creaming method. It begins with softening the butter by paddling it with the sugar. This first step helps the sugar to dissolve, the eggs to incorporate more readily, and the dry ingredients to be distributed evenly. The butter must be soft so that it mixes easily with tempered eggs; it would be very complicated to combine hard butter with eggs. The process is quick: Once the butter and sugar have been creamed to the correct consistency (fluffy) and the eggs have been added, the dry ingredients are mixed only until just incorporated and a homogeneous mass has been formed. It is at this point that overmixing can develop unwanted gluten and produce a tough final product.

The method principles are as follows:

1. Scale out the ingredients. Make sure to use a fine-grain sugar such as superfine or bakers' sugar. It will dissolve more readily in the butter than larger crystal sugars. Combine the flour with the leaveners and salt, and if there is a powdered flavor such as ground spices, combine it with these ingredients. Sift them twice, preferably, and right before they are needed. If they are sifted an hour or a day before using, they might clump up again. The purpose of sifting is threefold: It gets rid of any solid clumps that may make their way into the batter; it aerates the dry ingredients, making them lighter and therefore easier to incorporate into the batter; and finally, it causes the ingredients to combine into a homogeneous mass.

2. Prepare the baking pans by greasing them with a nonstick oil spray. Paper pan liners can be used as well, but a well-seasoned pan won't need them.

3. Cut the butter into medium dice and bring it up to 21°C/70° by leaving it at room temperature for a couple of hours, depending on the temperature of the bakeshop. Try to keep it close to the desired temperature. If it is too hot in the bakeshop, keep the butter refrigerated until 30 minutes before it is needed and then pull it out to warm up. If it is too cold in the shop, keep the butter close (but not too close) to a heat source, such as a stovetop or oven. The butter needs to be pliable, not melted or too soft.

4. Warm the eggs up to the same temperature as the butter. Crack the eggs into a bowl over a slightly warm water bath 30 minutes before using. Always take their temperature just before using to get the most accurate read. Whisk the eggs slightly to create a uniform mass, which will make it easier for the butter to combine with the eggs.

5. Place the butter and sugar in the bowl of an electric mixer and mix on medium speed using the paddle attachment. If the butter is at the right temperature, it will become soft, white in color, and fluffy within a few minutes of mixing. This is where many bakers make the mistake of overmixing their butter. Two events are occurring while the butter and sugar are mixing: The sugar is dissolving into the butter and the butter is trapping air, which will result in better leavening and an even crumb. If too much air is trapped, there will not be enough structure from the flour and egg proteins in the batter to hold that much air, and the pound cake will collapse. Keep in mind that mixing a pound cake is different in a 5-qt, 12-qt, 20-qt, or 40-qt mixer. Don't go by how long it takes to cream the butter (the larger the bowl, the longer it will take); go by how it looks, which should be fluffy, light, and white.

6. Add the eggs in 4 additions. After every addition, stop the machine, drop the bowl, and scrape the bowl and paddle with a rubber spatula. If the mixture looks separated by the time the last of the eggs has been added, it means the emulsion is broken. The reason for this is that one of the

ingredients (the eggs or the butter) was at the wrong temperature. Some bakers say that it's not a big deal because when the flour is added, the emulsion comes back together. This is not true. At a glance it might look fine, like nothing happened, but when the pound cake is baked, it will have a greasy-oily feel, which is precisely because of all the fat that separated from the eggs.

7. Once all the eggs have been added and there is a smooth emulsion, add the flour mixture in 2 additions. After the first addition, pulse the machine so that the flour doesn't go everywhere. Immediately after the first addition is incorporated, stop the machine, drop the bowl, and scrape the bowl and paddle with a rubber spatula. Add the remaining flour mixture and mix until just incorporated. Stop the machine, drop the bowl, and scrape the bowl and paddle with a rubber spatula again. Mix for 2 or 3 more seconds. Be careful not to overmix.

8. It is at this point that solid garnishes are added (see Notes). There are many options available for garnishes. The key is to add them right at the end and then to mix the batter just long enough so that the garnish is evenly dispersed, which should take no more than a few seconds. Do not add more than 250 g/8.8 oz of solid garnish per 800-g/1-lb 12-oz loaf. Otherwise, the garnish will weigh down the batter, it will not form a crown, and it will have a very tight and dense crumb.

9. Once the batter has been made, scale out the desired weight and pour into the prepared baking or loaf pans. It is important that they be the same weight so that they bake at the same time.

10. Preheat a convection oven to 175°C/350°F.

11. Place the pans in the oven. After 20 minutes, when the crust starts to form on top of the pound cake, cut a straight line through the crust with a razor blade. This will help the pound cake form a nice, even crown, with a straight slit right down the middle. A properly made pound cake will form a good crown as it bakes either way, but the razor cut makes it look slightly better.

12. After 10 minutes, drop the temperature to 160°C/325°F. Bake for 20 more minutes, then

drop the temperature to 150°C/300°F, and bake for about 20 more minutes or until the cake springs back at the center of the crown when gentle fingertip pressure is applied. The intent of all of these different temperatures is to at first achieve a tall crown and maintain it, then to assure that the pound cake gets completely baked through without drying out or burning the crust. It is acceptable to insert a thin skewer through the pound cake to check whether it is baked all the way (it will come out dry if it is), but this will leave a hole in the final product. Check for doneness with your fingertips; if it springs back at the center of the crown, it is done.

notes If adding nuts, toast them before adding them to the batter, since they will be trapped by the batter for the most part (unless they are on the surface) and won't get toasted while baking.

If adding any other garnish, such as dried fruit, candied fruit, or candied citrus zest, toss it in bread flour before adding it to the batter. This will help keep the pieces uniformly dispersed throughout the batter; otherwise they tend to sink to the bottom of the pan. Using fresh fruit such as berries will release a large amount of moisture when they are baked into the pound cake. This will give the finished product a wet feel, and it keeps the batter from baking properly since there is so much moisture present. Some berries explode into the batter, creating large gaps of air, and other berries such as raspberries turn some batters green when they come into contact with baking powder.

If adding a very lightweight garnish such as lemon zest, add it with the butter and sugar when they are first being creamed.

If using cocoa powder, combine it with the flour and the leavener, and then sift them together so that they can be added to the batter together.

The pound cake in this book calls for crème fraîche, which also needs to be brought up to 21°C/70°F, then added at the very end and quickly mixed in. It is intended to give flavor and to tenderize the product, as well as to help hydrate and react with the baking powder to leaven the batter (an acidic liquid; see ingredients, page 4.)

savory breakfast pastries

KNOW THIS: Savory breakfast pastries will be some of your top-selling items. The reason it is so important to know this is that sometimes as bakers or pastry chefs we lose sight of the savory world and its possibilities in the bakeshop. Not every one of your customers has a sweet tooth, and not all of them will always want something sweet for breakfast. A lot of people would much rather have a plate of scrambled eggs than a doughnut for breakfast. The problem is that not everyone has the time to sit down and wait for those eggs to be made. But you can order a savory scone and a glass of orange juice and be on your way.

In every bakeshop I have worked in, at least 10 to 15 percent of the product mix sold has been savory, and they consistently rank among the top-ten sellers.

A few ideas for savory breakfast pastries:

Savory scones: For the recipe on page 100, reduce the sugar by half and use the same percentage of garnish as for a sweet scone. Some possible examples are Cheddar and bacon, chorizo and manchego, and caramelized shallots and Parmesan.

Brioche: The recipe on page 10 stays the same. Some possible examples are Brie and spinach turnovers (brush the tops with egg wash and sprinkle sesame seeds on top), olive and goat cheese mini pizzas (cut out rounds of brioche and top with sliced, pitted black olives and crumbled goat cheese), and mushroom and Stilton tarts (line a mini pie tin with brioche and sautéed mushrooms, and top with cheese).

Laminated brioche: See the items on pages 72 and 75.

It is a good idea to invest in a commercial toaster with a conveyor belt–like system, since many people enjoy their pastries toasted, and not only savory items but sweet ones as well. One of the best things to eat, at least in my opinion, is a warm croissant with butter and jam, or a hot biscuit with some butter and marmalade.

Always keep in mind that whatever you put into the savory pastries must be shelf stable.

possible defects of chemically leavened pastries

defect	cause(s)	solution (the appropriate steps need to be taken beforehand)
No crown	Oven temperature was too low.	Make sure the oven is at the right temperature when loading it.
	Batter was overmixed.	Do not overmix the batter; it should be mixed until it comes together and forms a homogeneous mass.
	Butter was overcreamed (too much air was incorporated). It will form a large crown when it is baking, but when it cools off, the crown collapses; there wasn't enough structure in the batter to support so much air.	Do not overcream the butter. It should only be mixed until it is light and fluffy in the case of the creaming method.
	Insufficient leavener.	Weigh out the ingredients accurately.
Grainy-looking surface	This occurs with granulated sugar. Use sugars with smaller crystals such as bakers' sugar or superfine sugar, which dissolve easily and quickly into the batter.	Use a smaller size of sugar crystal.
Tunnels throughout the crumb	The batter was overmixed, which in turn caused excess gluten development. When the leavener was activated through heat, the gas that it produced had to push its way through the batter to come out, thus creating the tunnels. Overmixed batters tend to not be as light as properly mixed batters.	Mix the batter until ingredients are just incorporated and become a homogeneous mass.
Greasy- or wet-looking crumb	The emulsion was not properly made. One of the ingredients was not at the right temperature, which makes it impossible to create a proper emulsion.	Add the ingredients in the right order and at the correct temperature.
Thick crust	Pastry was overbaked.	Bake until just done. Test the product when you think it is almost ready.
Dip in the center of the crown	Pastry was underbaked; might be raw down the middle.	Bake until just done. Test the product when you think it is almost ready.
Muffin overflowed (looks like magma rippling around the muffin)	Usually the culprit is a chunk of butter or a sugar bomb (a sugar cluster) that was not completely incorporated into the batter.	Make sure all of the ingredients are homogeneously mixed.
	It may also be that there was too much batter inside the baking cup.	Pour the same amount of batter into each pan or baking cup. Weighing them out helps with consistency.
Flour pockets throughout the crumb	Dry ingredients were not sifted. Dry ingredients were not mixed in all the way.	Make sure all of the ingredients are homogeneously mixed.

BASIC POUND CAKE RECIPE

yield: 3 kg/6 lb 9.76 oz

INGREDIENT	METRIC	U.S.	%
Pastry flour	733 g	1 lb 9.76 oz	24.38%
Baking powder	7 g	.24 oz	.23%
Salt	13 g	.46 oz	.43%
Butter	733 g	1 lb 9.76 oz	24.38%
Eggs	587 g	1 lb 4.64 oz	19.51%
Superfine or bakers' sugar	770 g	1 lb 11.04 oz	25.6%
Crème fraîche, at 21°C/70°F	165 g	5.8 oz	5.48%

1. Combine the flour with the baking powder and salt. Sift them twice, preferably right before they are needed.

2. Prepare the baking pans by greasing them with a nonstick oil spray. Paper pan liners can be used as well, but a well-seasoned pan won't need them.

3. Cut the butter into medium dice and bring it up to 21°C/70°F by leaving it at room temperature for a couple of hours, depending on the temperature of the bakeshop. The butter needs to be pliable, not melted or too soft.

4. Warm the eggs to the same temperature as the butter. Crack the eggs into a bowl over a slightly warm water bath 30 minutes before using. Whisk the eggs slightly to create a uniform mass.

5. Place the butter and sugar in the bowl of an electric mixer and mix on medium speed using the paddle attachment. If the butter is at the right temperature, it will become soft, white in color, and fluffy within a few minutes of mixing.

6. Add the eggs in 4 additions. After every addition, stop the machine, drop the bowl, and scrape the bowl and paddle with a rubber spatula.

7. Once all the eggs have been added and there is a smooth emulsion, add the flour in 2 additions. After the first addition, pulse the machine so that the flour doesn't go everywhere. Immediately after the first addition is incorporated, stop the machine, drop the bowl, and scrape the bowl and paddle with a rubber spatula. Add the remaining flour and mix until just incorporated. Stop the machine, drop the bowl, and scrape the bowl and paddle with a rubber spatula again. Mix for 2 or 3 more seconds. Be careful to not overmix.

8. Add the crème fraîche and gently but quickly mix it in.

9. Lightly grease 3 half tube molds (also known as terrine molds) that are 7.5 by 22.5 by 7.5 cm/3 by 9 by 3 in (see Resources, page 540). Brush the molds with softened butter, and then coat them with a light layer of bread flour. Tap the excess off. Each mold should be filled with 1 kg/2 lb 3.2 oz of batter.

10. Preheat a convection oven to 175°C/350°F.

11. Place the filled molds in the oven. After 20 minutes, when the crust starts to form on top of the pound cake, cut a straight line through the crust with a razor blade.

12. After 10 more minutes, drop the temperature to 160°C/325°F. Bake for 20 more minutes, then drop the temperature to 150°C/300°F, and bake for about 20 more minutes or until it springs back at the center of the crown when gentle fingertip pressure is applied.

13. Cool to room temperature, and then trim the crown off using a serrated knife. This will be the base and therefore needs to be flat.

CINNAMON POUND CAKE WITH CANDIED APPLES, CINNAMON GLAZE, AND OATMEAL STREUSEL

yield: 3 cakes

INGREDIENT	METRIC	U.S.
CANDIED APPLES		
Sugar	908 g	2 lb
Water	272 g	9.59 oz
Lemon juice	20 g	.72 oz
Granny Smith apples, peeled and cut into medium dice	400 g	14.11 oz
OATMEAL STREUSEL		
Butter, at 21°C/70°F	160 g	5.64 oz
Sugar	160 g	5.64 oz
Pastry flour	160 g	5.64 oz
Old-fashioned oats	112 g	3.95 oz
Salt	2 g	.08 oz
Ground cinnamon	3 g	.11 oz
Vanilla powder	3 g	.11 oz
CINNAMON POUND CAKE BATTER		
Basic Pound Cake Batter (page 80)	3 kg	6 lb 9.76 oz
Ground cinnamon	5 g	.18 oz
Candied Apples	500 g	1 lb 1.6 oz
APPLEJACK SOAKING LIQUID		
Applejack	108 g	3.81 oz
Simple syrup	432 g	15.24 oz
APPLEJACK GLAZE		
Confectioners' sugar	960 g	2 lb 1.92 oz
Buttermilk	192 g	6.77 oz
Applejack	48 g	1.69 oz
GARNISH		
Vanilla pods	3	3
Cinnamon sticks	3	3
Star anise	3	3
Ground cinnamon	15 g	.52 oz

1. FOR THE CANDIED APPLES: Combine the sugar, water, and lemon juice in a 4-qt sauce pot. Stir until the sugar has been completely dissolved.

2. Clean the sides of the pot by brushing them with a wet pastry brush. Cook over high heat. When the sugar starts turning a pale yellow color, add the diced apples, and turn the heat down to medium-low. Cook very slowly until the pectin in the fruit has been activated, and the fruit is translucent and has taken on the caramelized sugar color. The sugar will continue to cook even after the apples have been added, and it will turn a dark brown color; cook until the temperature reaches about 160°C/320°F.

3. Remove the apples from the liquid by scooping them out with a slotted spoon, and then place them in a hotel pan to cool. Once cooled, transfer to an airtight container and refrigerate. The apples will keep for 3 weeks in the refrigerator.

4. **FOR THE OATMEAL STREUSEL:** Preheat a convection oven to 160°C/325°F. Combine the butter and the sugar in an electric mixer bowl. Mix using a paddle attachment on low speed. Continue to mix until a homogeneous mass is obtained.

5. Add the pastry flour and pulse the mixer until all of the flour has been incorporated. Add the oats, salt, cinnamon, and vanilla powder, and pulse until just combined.

6. Rub the streusel through a wire rack to obtain evenly sized morsels of streusel.

7. Bake until golden brown, about 7 minutes. Cool to room temperature.

8. Transfer to an airtight container and reserve for up to 5 days.

9. **FOR THE POUND CAKE:** Combine the cinnamon with the flour, salt, and baking powder for the batter and sift them together twice. Proceed with the batter as directed on page 80.

10. Before adding the candied apples to the batter, toss them in bread flour (just enough to be able to toss them in it). Any excess will be discarded. They are rather sticky, so try to separate them when tossing them in the bread flour so that they do not clump up. Shake off the excess flour by placing the apples on a drum sieve and shaking. Remember, the apples should go in after the dry ingredients have been incorporated, but before the crème fraîche.

11. Divide the batter between three 1-kg/2 lb- 3.2-oz cake molds. The total yield of the recipe will have gone up to 3.4 kg/7 lb 8.09 oz with the addition of the candied apples and the cinnamon. Pour 1.13 kg/2 lb 8.03 oz of batter into each loaf pan. Follow the baking instructions on page 80.

12. **FOR THE APPLEJACK SOAKING LIQUID:** Combine both ingredients in a bowl. Reserve the mixture in an airtight container at room temperature. The soaking liquid will keep indefinitely in these conditions. The sugar might crystallize over time, but the chances of that are slim. If and when that happens, bring the mixture up to a boil over high heat until the crystals dissolve again.

13. Divide the soaking liquid into 3 equal parts (180 g/6.35 oz).

14. Place all the pound cakes on a wire rack. Poke 12 small holes in the crown of each pound cake using a thin skewer.

15. Pour one-third of the divided soaking liquid portion over 1 pound cake, let it absorb, pour another one-third of the liquid over the cake, let it absorb, and then pour the last one-third over the cake. Repeat with the other pound cakes. Leave the loaves on the rack for glazing.

16. **FOR THE APPLEJACK GLAZE:** Combine all of the ingredients in a medium bowl using a whisk. Mix until smooth. You may store the glaze in the refrigerator for up to 1 month, or at room temperature for 5 days. Pour 400 g/14.1 oz over each loaf.

17. Apply one-third of the streusel to the sides of each just-glazed pound cake. If the glaze dries, then the streusel will not stick to it.

18. **TO FINISH THE CAKE:** Once the pound cake is glazed and the sides are coated with the oatmeal streusel, place 1 vanilla pod, 1 cinnamon stick, and 1 piece of star anise on each pound cake. Arrange them so they have height and balance. Sprinkle a pinch of powdered cinnamon across the surface.

19. Finally, if desired, wrap a ribbon around the base of the pound cake. Since this pound cake is soaked and is coated in glaze, it will stay moist and will not dry out quickly. It has a lifespan on the retail shelf of up to 3 days.

notes Although the recipe for candied apples calls for only 400 g/14.11 oz of diced apples, they will increase in weight from cooking, because they absorb a percentage of the sugar in which they are being cooked. This is a form of cooking apples, but also of preserving them, since the water they contain is replaced by sugar. The cooking process, along with the lemon juice, activates the natural pectin in the apples, which give them a gummy, candy-like texture with a very strong and concentrated candied apple taste.

If the apples were cooked too much, they might hold their shape, but the sugar will have turned too hard. Don't throw them out; you can add a little water, which will soften the sugar and the apples. If the apples are mushy, it means they were old and were in storage for too long. At this point, discard them or add them to the apples for Apple Butter (page 65).

Use ripe apples. The best kind of apples to use for candying are those that have a high pectin content and low moisture content, such as Granny Smith, Ginger Gold, and Honeycrisp apples.

LEMON AND POPPY SEED POUND CAKE

yield: 3 cakes

INGREDIENT	METRIC	U.S.
LEMON POPPY SEED POUND CAKE BATTER		
Lemon zest	8 lemons	8 lemons
Basic Pound Cake Batter (page 80)	3 kg	6 lb 9.76 oz
Poppy seeds	18 g	.63 oz
LEMON SOAKING LIQUID		
Lemon juice	144 g	5.08 oz
Simple syrup	576 g	1 lb 4.32 oz
LEMON GLAZE		
Confectioners' sugar	1.28 kg	2 lb 13.2 oz
Buttermilk	256 g	9.03 oz
Lemon juice	64 g	2.26 oz
LEMON CHIPS		
Lemons	2	2
Simple syrup	500 g	1 lb 1.6 oz

1. **FOR THE POUND CAKE:** Zest the lemons using a rasp into the mixer bowl that you will use to paddle the sugar and the butter for the pound cake. This will keep all of the oils from the lemon in the bowl. Cream the butter and sugar as per the creaming method in step 5 of the Basic Pound Cake on page 80. Proceed with the recipe on page 80. Add the poppy seeds once all of the dry ingredients have been incorporated but before the crème fraîche is added.

2. Lightly grease 3 half tube molds (also known as terrine molds) that measure 7.5 by 22.5 by 7.5 cm/3 by 9 by 3 in (see Resources, page 540). Brush the molds with softened butter, and then coat them with a light layer of bread flour. Tap the excess off. Each mold should be filled with 1 kg/2 lb 3.2 oz batter.

3. Preheat a convection oven to 175°C/350°F.

4. Place the filled molds in the oven. After 20 minutes, when the crust starts to form on top of the pound cake, cut a straight line through the crust with a razor blade.

5. After 10 minutes, drop the temperature to 160°C/325°F. Bake for 20 more minutes, then drop the temperature to 150°C/300°F, and bake for about 20 more minutes or until the cake springs back at the center of the crown when gentle fingertip pressure is applied. Cool to room temperature, and trim the crown off using a serrated knife. This will be the base and therefore needs to be flat. Flip the pound cake over so that the top is now the bottom.

6. **FOR THE LEMON SOAKING LIQUID:** Combine the lemon juice and simple syrup in a bowl. Transfer to an airtight container and refrigerate. The soaking liquid will keep for up to 5 days. If using right away, divide the liquid into 3 equal parts.

7. Put the 3 loaves on a a wire rack set over a sheet pan lined with parchment paper. Let them reach room temperature, because they cut well when they are cold, but they do not absorb liquids as efficiently.

8. Make 12 even perforations over the surface of each loaf using a thin skewer.

9. Pour one-third of the divided soaking liquid portion over each cake, let it absorb, then pour another one-third of the liquid over the cake, let it absorb, and then apply the last one-third to the cake. Leave the cakes on the rack for glazing.

10. **FOR THE LEMON GLAZE:** Combine all of the ingredients in a bowl. Mix until smooth using a whisk. Reserve refrigerated in an airtight container, or use immediately. The glaze will keep for up to 2 weeks in the refrigerator.

11. Pour the glaze over each pound cake. Try to obtain an even coat on all sides of the loaf by pouring the glaze down the middle and letting it pour down the sides.

12. Before the glaze sets, sprinkle 3 g/.11 oz of poppy seeds down the middle of the loaf in a thin, straight line.

13. **FOR THE LEMON CHIPS:** Freeze the lemons until hard. Fill a medium pot two-thirds full with water and bring to a boil. Slice the lemons very thinly on an electric slicer. Blanch in hot water until the water comes back to a boil. Remove from the pot with a spider and repeat. Place the slices in a hotel pan.

14. Bring the simple syrup to a boil, and pour it over lemon slices so that they are generously coated. Let them absorb the syrup for at least 45 minutes.

15. Place the lemon slices in a dehydrator at 57°C/135°F until dry, about 4 hours. Make sure there are no lemon seeds in the slices. To keep the slices flat, place them on a sheet of silicone paper that is cut to fit inside the dehydrator (see Note).

16. Store the lemon chips in an airtight container at room temperature. The chips will keep for at least 1 week in a cool, dry environment.

17. To garnish the pound cake, place 3 lemon chips in a standing position on top of the cake in a straight line, next to the poppy seeds. If desired, tie a ribbon around the pound cake next to the poppy seeds. Discard after 2 days; the lemon chips can get soggy.

note If you do not have a dehydrator, dry the lemon chips in a very low oven (82°C/180°F) for 3 hours or until dry.

CHOCOLATE POUND CAKE

yield: **3 cakes**

INGREDIENT	METRIC	U.S.	%
CHOCOLATE POUND CAKE			
Butter, soft	471 g	1 lb .64 oz	15.7%
Sugar	544 g	1 lb 3.2 oz	18.12%
Light brown sugar	170 g	6 oz	5.67%
Eggs, at 21°C/70°F	398 g	14.05 oz	13.28%
Chocolate liquor, melted but cool (21°C/70°F)	73 g	2.56 oz	2.42%
Pastry flour	685 g	1 lb 8.16 oz	22.82%
Baking powder	4 g	.13 oz	.12%
Baking soda	10 g	.35 oz	.33%
Salt	6 g	.21 oz	.2%
Cocoa powder	81 g	2.85 oz	2.7%
Vanilla paste	9 g	.33 oz	.31%
Buttermilk	550 g	1 lb 3.36 oz	18.33%
Shiny Dark Chocolate Glaze (page 148), **warm**	1.2 kg	2 lb 10.33 oz	
Dark chocolate (64%), melted	300g	10.58 oz	
Chocolate décor chips (see Resources, page 540)	1.2 kg	2 lb 10.4 oz	
Dark Chocolate Plaques (page 529; 2.5 by 21.5 cm/1 by 8.5 in)	3	3	
Gold leaf	1 sheet	1 sheet	

1. **FOR THE POUND CAKE:** Make the recipe according to the creaming method on page 76. The melted chocolate liquor is added after the eggs have been completely incorporated. Combine the vanilla paste with the buttermilk and add at the end of the mixing process (as you would with the crème fraîche).

2. Lightly grease 3 half tube molds (also known as terrine molds) that measure 7.5 by 22.5 by 7.5cm/3 by 9 by 3 in (see Resources, page 540). Brush the molds with softened butter, and then coat them with a light layer of bread flour. Tap the excess off. Each mold should be filled with 1 kg/2 lb 3.2 oz of batter.

3. Preheat a convection oven to 175°C/350°F.

4. Place the filled molds in the oven. After 20 minutes, when the crust starts to form on top of the pound cake, cut a straight line through the crust with a razor blade.

5. After 10 minutes, drop the temperature to 160°C/325°F. Bake for 20 more minutes, then drop the temperature to 150°C/300°F, and bake for about 20 more minutes or until it springs back at the center of the crown when gentle fingertip pressure is applied.

6. Cool to room temperature, and trim the crown off using a serrated knife. This will be the base and therefore needs to be flat.

7. **FOR THE ASSEMBLY/FINISHING:** Flip the pound cake over so that the top is now the bottom.

8. Pour 400 g/14.1 oz of ganache over each cake and let it set in the refrigerator. Pour the melted chocolate into a piping bag. Drizzle the melted chocolate over the entire surface of the pound cakes in thin lines.

9. Surround the pound cake with chocolate décor chips, pressing them gently into the ganache so that they stick.

10. Place a chocolate plaque and then a fleck of gold leaf on top of the pound cake.

notes This recipe is slightly different from the regular pound cake recipe. The chocolate cake is moist, flavorful, and delicate at the same time.

Ganache is an emulsion, and this is why we add the heavy cream in 2 additions; if you add it all at once the ganache might have a grainy consistency once it sets (an indication of a broken emulsion).

MADELEINES

INGREDIENT	METRIC	U.S.	%
Butter	281 g	9.9 oz	23.38%
Brown sugar	31 g	1.1 oz	2.6%
Sugar	265 g	9.35 oz	22.08%
Eggs	312 g	10.99 oz	25.97%
Vanilla paste	16 g	.55 oz	1.3%
Lemon zest	5 g	.16 oz	.39%
Salt	3 g	.11 oz	.26%
All-purpose flour	281 g	9.9 oz	23.38%
Baking powder	8 g	.27 oz	.65%
Orange blossom water	50 g	1.76 oz	
Confectioners' sugar	as needed	as needed	

1. Preheat the oven to 160°C/320°F. Lightly grease five 12-piece madeleine pans with nonstick oil spray.

2. Make the madeleine batter according to the creaming method on page 76.

3. Pour the batter into a piping bag. Pipe the batter into the madeleine pans, filling each impression three-quarters of the way full.

4. Bake until the madeleines are golden brown, 5 to 7 minutes.

5. Put a sheet of parchment paper on a work surface.

6. Turn the pans over onto the parchment paper and tap the molds gently onto the table so that the madeleines pop out easily.

7. Brush each madeleine bottom with a small amount of orange blossom water.

8. Turn the madeleines over so that the textured surface is facing up. Dust the madeleines with confectioners' sugar.

note The best way to enjoy a madeleine properly is to have it warm and fresh out of the oven. That will not always be possible if you insist on selling madeleines. You can always refresh them in a hot oven for a couple of minutes before serving them.

BLENDED BATTERS

The blending method by definition is a mixing method in which two or more ingredients are combined just until they are evenly mixed. But there is more to it than that. Typically, the liquid ingredients and dry ingredients are mixed separately and then combined. Liquid ingredients generally mean eggs plus dairy (milk and/or heavy cream and/or buttermilk) and/or melted butter or another liquid fat such as canola oil. What you are trying to accomplish at this point in the recipe is an emulsion. In order to do this, all of the ingredients should be at the same temperature, ideally 21°C/70°F, so that the fat globules will bind with each other more readily than when they are at different temperatures (cold fat globules are firm, while warm fat molecules are softer). For the liquid ingredients, place the warmed eggs in a mixer bowl and slowly pour in the melted but cool butter in a slow, steady stream until they form a homogeneous mass or emulsion. If warm butter is poured into cold eggs, the butter will seize and it will not combine uniformly with the eggs. This will also result in a greasy-looking baked pastry, since the emulsion was never formed in the beginning. The fat will not bind with the other ingredients and will be "loose" in the batter when it bakes, instead of baking into the other ingredients. If the recipe calls for heavy cream, it should be added in the same way, in a constant slow stream. Some recipes will call for eggs, butter, and heavy cream, and they should be added in that order. Always keep a close eye on their temperature and add them in a slow, steady stream. Some recipes will require that the eggs be combined with sugar at the beginning of the recipe before emulsifying anything into them. This is typically when the recipe calls for large amounts of sugar, and this will help dissolve the sugar better than if it were added with the other dry ingredients later in the recipe.

The method principles are as follows:

1. Combine all of the liquid ingredients on medium speed using a paddle attachment (some recipes that require more thorough mixing will use a whip instead). For the amounts in this book, the ingredients can be mixed by hand (use a whisk and a bowl large enough to fit all the ingredients).

2. Sift all of the dry ingredients together. Remember that there are three main reasons for sifting: to break up any clumps, to aerate the dry ingredients (which makes them lighter and easier to incorporate), and to obtain a homogeneous mix (they are evenly distributed within their mass).

3. Add the dry ingredients to the liquid ingredients and mix on low speed.

4. Mix until just incorporated, scraping the bowl as necessary. Don't overmix. Overmixing will cause the gluten in the flour to develop too far, making the batter tough. A sure sign of overmixing is a series of small air tunnels throughout the crumb. This is because the carbon dioxide produced by the leavener needs to push its way out through a tough batter, and the more gluten development, the tougher the batter.

5. Add the garnish at the end (dried fruit, toasted nuts, chocolate chips).

PUMPKIN MUFFINS WITH CRANBERRY GLAZE

yield: 5.6 kg/12 lb 5.6 oz (at 140 g/4.93 oz each)

INGREDIENT	METRIC	U.S.	%
PUMPKIN MUFFINS			
Eggs	528 g	1 lb 2.56 oz	9.43%
Canola oil	499 g	1 lb 1.6 oz	8.91%
Pumpkin purée	1.32 kg	2 lb 14.56 oz	23.6%
Baking soda	28 g	1 oz	.5%
Bread flour	698 g	1 lb 8.64 oz	12.47%
Pastry flour	698 g	1 lb 8.64 oz	12.47%
Ground cinnamon	19 g	.66 oz	.33%
Ground nutmeg	6 g	.22 oz	.11%
Ground cloves	3 g	.11 oz	.06%
Ground allspice	3 g	.11 oz	0.06%
Sugar	1.79 kg	3 lb 15.36 oz	32.07%
CRANBERRY GLAZE			
Confectioners' sugar	870 g	1 lb 14.72 oz	86.96%
Cranberry juice	130 g	4.6 oz	13.04%
Ground cinnamon	40 g	1.41 oz	

1. **FOR THE PUMPKIN MUFFINS:** Divide 40 mini panettone cups (see Resources, page 540) between 2 sheet pans.

2. Bring the eggs, oil, and pumpkin purée to 21°C/70°F.

3. Sift together the baking soda, flours, cinnamon, nutmeg, cloves, and allspice.

4. Combine the eggs with the sugar in a bowl large enough to fit all of the ingredients. Emulsify the eggs and the oil by slowly whisking in the oil. Stir in the pumpkin purée.

5. Whisk in the dry ingredients.

6. Portion 140 g/4.93 oz of the batter into each of the mini panettone cups, or fill the cups to within .5 cm/.25 in of the top. Freeze the muffins if not baking them right away.

7. Preheat a convection oven to 160°C/320°F.

8. Bake for 15 to 20 minutes, turning the pan halfway through the process to ensure an even bake. Check for doneness with a skewer or by pressing the center of the muffin's crown with a finger; if it springs back, it is done. Cool to room temperature on a speed rack.

9. **FOR THE CRANBERRY GLAZE:** In a stainless-steel bowl, combine the confectioners' sugar with three-quarters of the cranberry juice. The glaze should be thick, not thin such as the one used for the pound cakes (see page 83). If the glaze is too thick, add more cranberry juice. If the glaze is too thin, add more confectioners' sugar.

10. **FOR THE ASSEMBLY:** Dip the crown of the pumpkin muffins into the glaze. Let the excess drip off as much as possible before turning the muffin back over so that the glaze won't trickle down the sides.

11. Sprinkle a pinch of cinnamon on top of the glaze (about 1 g/.04 oz per muffin). Discard after 1 day.

BLUEBERRY MUFFINS WITH OATMEAL STREUSEL

yield: 40 muffins

INGREDIENT	METRIC	U.S. (LBS)	%
Cake flour	1.42 kg	3 lb 2.24 oz	25.4%
Sugar	593 g	1 lb 4.96 oz	10.58%
Baking powder	43 g	1.55 oz	.76%
Salt	6 g	.22 oz	.11%
Butter, melted	474 g	1 lb .8 oz	8.47%
Eggs	418 g	14.75 oz	7.47%
Heavy cream	1.99 kg	4 lb 6.24 oz	35.56%
Vanilla paste	21 g	.74 oz	.37%
Dried blueberries (not fresh or frozen)	632 g	1 lb 6.24 oz	11.29%
Oatmeal Streusel (page 81)	1 kg	2 lb 3.2 oz	

1. Divide 40 mini panettone cups between 2 sheet pans.

2. Sift together the flour, sugar, baking powder, and salt.

3. Emulsify the butter and eggs as per the blending method on page 89 in a bowl large enough to fit all the ingredients in the recipe. Whisk in the cream and the vanilla paste.

4. Whisk in the sifted dry ingredients. Whisk until a homogeneous mass is obtained. Stir in the blueberries.

5. Portion 140 g/4.93 oz of the batter into each of the panettone cups, or fill them to within .5 cm/.25 in of the top. If you aren't baking the muffins right away, freeze them.

6. Sprinkle 25 g/.88 oz of the oatmeal streusel on top of each muffin.

7. Preheat a convection oven to 160°C/320°F.

8. Bake for 15 to 20 minutes, turning the tray around halfway through the process to ensure an even bake. Test for doneness with a skewer, or press the crown of a muffin with your finger; if it springs back, it is done. Discard after 1 day.

BANANA MUFFINS WITH TURBINADO SUGAR

yield: 40 pieces

INGREDIENT	METRIC	U.S.	%
Cake flour	675 g	1 lb 7.84 oz	10.55%
Bread flour	675 g	1 lb 7.84 oz	10.55%
Baking powder	32 g	1.12 oz	.49%
Baking soda	16 g	.56 oz	.25%
Bananas	1.35 kg	2 lb 15.68 oz	21.11%
Brown sugar	675 g	1 lb 7.84 oz	10.55%
Sugar	675 g	1 lb 7.84 oz	10.55%
Eggs	596 g	1 lb 4.96 oz	9.31%
Canola oil	338 g	11.91 oz	5.28%
Buttermilk	675 g	1 lb 7.84 oz	10.55%
Salt	16 g	.56 oz	.25%
Walnuts, chopped and toasted	675 g	1 lb 7.84 oz	10.55%
Turbinado sugar	1 kg	2 lb 3.2 oz	

1. Divide 40 mini panettone cups (see Resources, page 540) between 2 sheet pans.

2. Sift both flours together with the baking powder and baking soda.

3. Purée the bananas with both sugars, and make sure there are no banana chunks left.

4. Emulsify the eggs with the oil following the blending method on page 89.

5. Whisk the buttermilk into the eggs, then whisk in the puréed bananas.

6. Whisk in the sifted dry ingredients and the salt. Mix until a homogeneous mass is obtained.

7. Stir in the walnuts.

8. Portion 160 g/5.64 oz of the batter into each prepared ring. If not baking the muffins right away, freeze them.

9. Sprinkle 25 g/.88 oz of turbinado sugar on top of each muffin.

10. Preheat a convection oven to 160°C/320°F.

11. Bake for 15 to 20 minutes, turning the tray around halfway through the process to ensure an even bake. Test for doneness with a skewer, or press the crown of a muffin with your finger; if it springs back, it is done. Discard after 1 day.

CORN MUFFINS

yield: 40 muffins

INGREDIENT	METRIC	U.S.	%
Bread flour	876 g	1 lb 14.88 oz	12.89%
Pastry flour	876 g	1 lb 14.88 oz	12.89%
Cornmeal	730 g	1 lb 9.76 oz	10.74%
Salt	3 g	.11 oz	.04%
Baking powder	5 g	.16 oz	.07%
Eggs	609 g	1 lb 5.44 oz	8.95%
Canola oil	876 g	1 lb 14.88 oz	12.89%
Sugar	1.36 kg	3 lb .16 oz	20.05%
Milk	1.46 kg	3 lb 3.52 oz	21.48%

1. Divide 40 mini panettone cups between 2 sheet pans.

2. Sift the flours, cornmeal, salt, and baking powder together.

3. Temper the eggs with the oil following the blending method on page 89. Whisk in the sugar and milk.

4. Whisk in the dry ingredients. Mix until a homogeneous mass is achieved.

5. Portion 170 g/5.99 oz of batter into each of the prepared panettone cups. If not baking them right away, freeze them.

6. Preheat a convection oven to 160°C/320°F.

7. Bake for 15 to 20 minutes, turning the pan halfway through the process to ensure an even bake. Test for doneness with a skewer, or press the crown of a muffin with your fingers; if it springs back, it is done. Discard the muffins after 1 day.

RASPBERRY MUFFINS WITH RASPBERRY GLAZE

yield: 40 pieces

INGREDIENT	METRIC	U.S.	%
Butter	716 g	1 lb 9.28 oz	11.19%
Eggs	631 g	1 lb 6.24 oz	9.87%
Raspberry purée	1.36 kg	3 lb .16 oz	21.32%
Elderflower liqueur (St-Germain)	325 g	11.45 oz	5.08%
Sour cream	260 g	9.16 oz	4.06%
Sugar	1.59 kg	3 lb 8 oz	24.82%
All-purpose flour	1.44 kg	3 lb 2.72 oz	22.52%
Baking powder	62 g	2.2 oz	.97%
Vanilla powder	10 g	.35 oz	.16%
RASPBERRY GLAZE			
Pouring fondant	1.54 kg	3 lb 6.24 oz	76.92%
Raspberry purée	462 g	1 lb .32 oz	23.08%
Crystallized violets	40	40	
Gold leaf	2 sheets	2 sheets	

1. Divide 40 stainless-steel rings 7 cm in diameter by 7.5 cm high/2.75 by 3 in between 2 sheet pans lined with parchment paper. Lightly spray the interior of each ring with nonstick oil spray. Cut out 40 pieces of parchment paper that measure 7.5 by 25 cm/3 by 10 in. Line the inside of each ring with a piece of parchment paper.

2. Make sure the butter, eggs, raspberry purée, elderflower liqueur, and sour cream are at 21°C/70°F.

3. Sift the sugar, flour, baking powder, and vanilla powder together.

4. Emulsify the butter and eggs according to the blending method on page 89 in a bowl large enough to fit all the ingredients in the recipe.

5. Whisk in the raspberry purée along with the elderflower liqueur and sour cream.

6. Stir in the dry ingredients. Mix until just combined and a homogeneous mass is achieved.

7. Portion 160 g/5.64 oz of the batter into each of the prepared rings. If not baking the muffins right away, freeze them.

8. Preheat a convection oven to 160°C/320°F.

9. Bake for 15 to 20 minutes, turning the pan halfway through the process to ensure an even bake. Test for doneness with a skewer, or press the crown of a muffin with your fingers; if it springs back, it is done.

10. **FOR THE RASPBERRY GLAZE:** Combine the pouring fondant with the raspberry purée in a bowl. Bring the mixture up to 37°C/99°F over a hot water bath. If it is too thick, add a little more purée. If it is too thin, add more pouring fondant.

11. Dip the crown of each muffin all the way into the glaze. Let the excess glaze drip off, and then turn the muffin back over and let it set.

12. Place the crystallized violets and gold leaf on the glaze before it sets. Let it set for 30 minutes before displaying the muffins.

notes You only need about 30 g/1.05 oz of glaze per muffin, but you will need more than just the exact amount of glaze, since you need to dip the crown of the muffin completely into the glaze so that it can get properly coated.

An alternative glaze can be used for this product (see below).

variation For Bosc Pear Muffins, substitute pear purée for the raspberry purée in the batter, elderflower syrup for the raspberry purée in the glaze, and Crystallized Rose Petals (page 25) for the crystallized violet and gold leaf garnish.

SUPER-SHINY THICK GLAZE

yield: 2 kg/4 lb 6.4 oz

INGREDIENT	METRIC	U.S.	%
Pouring fondant	1.62 kg	3 lb 9.28 oz	81.08%
Simple syrup, 50° Brix	216 g	7.63 oz	10.81%
White or milk chocolate, melted to 40°C/104°F	162 g	5.72 oz	8.11%
Red food coloring (alcohol or water based)	as needed	as needed	

1. Combine the fondant and simple syrup in a bowl and warm up over a simmering water bath to 35°C/95°F, stirring frequently. Do not exceed 40°C/104°F; otherwise the fondant will bloom and once it sets, it will be dull. Stir in the chocolate once the other ingredients have reached 35°C/95°F.

2. Add the food coloring just before glazing. Adjust color as needed.

3. Dip the raspberry muffins in up to the crown only. Let all excess glaze drip off before turning them back over, or turn them over and let the excess drip off the sides to give it a drip-down look.

4. Place the garnish (the crystallized violets and gold leaf) on the glaze before it sets. Let it set for 30 minutes before displaying the muffins. Discard the muffins after a day. This glaze can keep indefinitely as long as it is kept covered in an airtight container at room temperature.

note This glaze can be used for many pastries, like doughnuts, muffins, scones, and cookies.

RUBBED BUTTER OR CUT-IN BUTTER QUICK BREADS

This method consists of cutting or rubbing butter or another solid fat into flour. The butter is not mixed in all the way, but is left in pea-size pieces that, when baked, result in a delicate and flaky pastry.

The method principles are as follows:

1. Place all of the dry ingredients in a bowl (typically a type of flour, salt, and a leavener). If making large amounts, mix the dough in an electric mixer using a paddle attachment; otherwise use your hands. If making very large amounts, consider freezing the flour and other dry ingredients to keep them very cold while mixing. Large batches need to mix longer, and longer mixing results in more friction, which produces heat that will melt or soften the butter, having an adverse effect on the final flakiness of the scones.

2. The fat needs to be diced into about 2.5-cm/1-in cubes, and they need to be kept cold until the last minute. Examples of fat used in these items are butter, lard, and shortening. Use butter.

3. To cut the butter in by hand, toss the cold diced fat in the dry ingredients, so that each cube gets coated. Rub the cubes with the palms of your hands with some of the flour, flattening the cubes as you press them into the flour. This is also known as "shingling." The cubes will become flat and part of them will be mixed into the dry ingredients. Repeat with all of the fat in the bowl. To cut the butter in with an electric mixer, mix the dry ingredients with the cold diced fat using a paddle attachment on low speed. Mix until the fat cubes are about the size of a pecan. The flakiness of the dough depends on the size of the butter: The smaller the butter, the more it was mixed into the dough, and the less flaky it will be.

4. If the recipe calls for a garnish such as nuts or dried fruit, add it once all of the fat has been cut in. Be careful to not overmix, since the fat will continue to cut into the flour every time it is mixed and produce a crumbly pastry instead of a flaky one. You might want to add the garnish by hand and give it a quick mix. Items such as biscuits will never have any garnish added.

5. Add the liquid. For biscuits, it is usually buttermilk, which in part is what gives them their characteristic flavor, but also acts as a tenderizer (the acid in the buttermilk tenderizes the gluten strands in the dough). For scones, the liquid is typically heavy cream combined with eggs (sometimes milk is used). Be careful when adding the liquid, since overmixing occurs very easily. If you are mixing by hand, turn the dough onto itself a few times (about eight) until you obtain what is called a "shaggy mass." This is not a uniform dough but only a cohesive dough. A smooth, uniform dough is the most obvious sign of overmixing.

6. Turn the dough onto a floured surface. Using a rolling pin, roll out the dough to the desired thickness. Try to be consistent throughout the entire dough so that you obtain even pieces that bake evenly.

7. Cut the dough out to the desired shape using a floured cutter or knife, depending on the desired shape. If you are not baking it right away, place the dough on a sheet pan lined with parchment paper, wrap, and freeze until needed.

FINANCIERS

yield: 40 pieces

INGREDIENT	METRIC	U.S.	%
Butter	300 g	10.58 oz	17.76%
Egg whites	341 g	12.03 oz	28.42%
Sugar	355 g	12.53 oz	29.6%
Almond flour	142 g	5.01 oz	11.84%
Cake flour	142 g	5.01 oz	11.84%
Baking powder	6 g	.23 oz	.53%
Financier Garnishes (below)			

1. Melt the butter over high heat in a small sauté pan. Continue to cook the butter until the solids caramelize and turn brown. The recipe requires 213 g/7.52 oz of brown butter.

2. Warm the egg whites to 21°C/70°F.

3. Sift together the dry ingredients. Add brown butter and mix until evenly combined. Scrape down the sides of the bowl. Add the egg whites to the mixture. In this case, it is necessary to add the egg whites to the dry ingredients instead of the other way around in order to prevent the dry ingredients from clumping.

4. If not baking right away, refrigerate the batter.

5. Grease financier molds (see Resources, page 540; or use fleximolds) with a light coat of nonstick oil spray. These fleximolds come in small sheets of 12 pieces and up to 72 pieces. Use the smaller sheets if baking small batches at a time, or the larger one if baking them all at once.

6. Preheat a convection oven to 160°C/320°F.

7. Pour the financier batter into a piping bag.

8. Pipe the batter into the molds, filling them three-quarters of the way full.

9. Place the desired garnish at the center of the mold.

10. Bake until the financiers turn a deep golden brown around the border, about 8 to 12 minutes.

financier garnishes

item	garnish
Almond Financier (use almond flour)	40 raspberries (1 raspberry per financier)
Pistachio Financier (use pistachio flour)	40 Luxardo cherries (1 cherry per financier) or other type of cherry in syrup
Macadamia Nut Financier (use macadamia nut flour)	40 macadamia nuts (untoasted)
Hazelnut Financier (use hazelnut flour)	40 pieces hazelnuts, (untoasted)

BASIC SCONES

yield: 40 scones

INGREDIENT	METRIC	U.S.	%
Pastry flour	1.34 kg	2 lb 15.36 oz	37.32%
Salt	24 g	.84 oz	.66%
Baking powder	48 g	1.69 oz	1.33%
Sugar	144 g	5.08 oz	4%
Butter	576 g	1 lb 4.32 oz	16%
Garnish (see page 101)	576 g	1 lb 4.32 oz	16%
Eggs (whole)	102 g	3.58 oz	2.82%
Egg yolks	68 g	2.39 oz	1.88%
Heavy cream	720 g	1 lb 9.44 oz	19.99%
Egg Wash for Brushing (page 13)	as needed	as needed	

1. Make the scones following the cut-in method on page 97.

2. Roll the dough to 2.5 cm/1 in thick. Use a 7.5-cm/3-in diameter ring cutter dipped in bread flour to cut out the scones. Do not twist the cutter, just cut straight down. Twisting the cutter will seal the scone and keep it from puffing up properly when it bakes.

3. Use an offset spatula to gently pick up the scones and place them on a sheet pan lined with parchment paper. Each sheet pan should have 15 scones in a 3x5 grid. If not baking them right away, wrap and freeze them.

4. Once the scones have been cut out, brush them with egg wash.

5. Preheat a convection oven to 160°C/320°F.

6. Bake until they turn a light golden brown on the top and bottom rim, 15 to 20 minutes. If the top surface is brown, the scones have been overbaked.

7. Transfer the scones to a cooling rack to cool.

note Classic English scones have only currants added as the garnish. See page 101 for suggestions for other scone garnishes.

Never use fresh fruit to make scones; they will add unwanted moisture to the scone, making it a wet, soggy scone.

When using cheese in savory scones, use cheeses that aren't too creamy, since they will melt away from the scone as opposed to into the scone. Hard cheeses are best. Always grate them with the largest opening on the grater. Never cube them, since it is time-consuming and the cheese, even if it is a hard cheese, will melt out of the scone.

scone variations

Use about 576 g/1 lb 4.32 oz for the amount in the recipe above, or about 16 percent of the total weight. The garnish is added once the butter is cut in but before adding the eggs and heavy cream.

garnish	amount
Chocolate and Espresso	Dark chocolate chips (64%): 550 g/1 lb 3.36 oz Soluble coffee crystals: 25 g/.88 oz
Almond and Cherry	Slivered almonds, toasted: 400 g/14.11 oz Dried cherries, coarsely chopped: 175 g/6.17 oz
Pecan and Orange	Pecans, chopped and toasted: 550 g/1 lb 3.36 oz Orange zest: 25 g/.88 oz
Blueberry and Vanilla	Dried blueberries: 560 g/1 lb 3.68 oz Vanilla powder: 15 g/.52 oz
Macadamia Nut and White Chocolate Chips	Macadamia nuts, coarsely chopped and toasted: 350 g/12.35 oz White chocolate chips (ovenproof): 220 g/7.76 oz

savory scones

For savory scones, reduce the amount of sugar to half of the original amount. Add the garnish as for a sweet scone and in the same proportions (16 percent of the total weight).

Some flavor combinations for savory scones are:

garnish	amount
Caramelized Onions and Gruyère	Caramelized onions: 400 g/14.11 oz Gruyère, grated: 175 g/6.17 oz
Serrano Ham and Manchego	Serrano ham, thinly sliced and cut into julienne: 400 g/14.11 oz Manchego, grated: 175 g/6.17 oz
Bacon and Idiazabal	Bacon, parcooked: 400 g/14.11 oz Idiazabal cheese, grated: 175 g/6.17 oz
Prosciutto and Parmesan	Prosciutto, thinly sliced and cut into julienne: 400 g/14.11 oz Parmesan, grated: 175 g/6.17 oz
Black Olive, Basil, and Drunken Goat Cheese	Black olives, coarsely chopped: 280g/9.88 oz Basil, coarsely chopped: 15 g/.52 oz Drunken goat cheese, grated: 280 g/9.88 oz
Ham, Cheddar, and Green Onion	Ham, diced: 280 g/9.88 oz Vermont Cheddar, grated: 280 g/9.88 oz Green onions, coarsely chopped: 15 g/.53 oz

BISCUITS

yield: 40 pieces

INGREDIENT	METRIC	U.S.	%
White Lily Flour (see Resources, page 540)	1.95 kg	4 lb 4.8 oz	54.22%
Baking powder	95 g	3.36 oz	2.65%
Salt	64 g	2.24 oz	1.77%
Butter, chilled and cut into medium dice	400 g	14.12 oz	11.12%
Buttermilk	1.09 kg	2 lb 6.4 oz	30.24%
Butter, melted	100 g	3.53 oz	

1. Sift the flour, baking powder, and salt together.

2. Cut in the butter following the cut-in method on page 97.

3. Stir in the buttermilk (do not use a whisk) and mix until the dough forms a cohesive mass (a shaggy mass). Transfer the dough to a floured surface and pack it down with your hands, just until it comes together. Roll the dough to 2.5 cm/1 in thick with a rolling pin.

4. Dock the dough with a fork in a uniform, symmetrical pattern.

5. Dip a 7.5-cm/3-in ring cutter in bread flour and cut circles out of the dough. Do not twist the cutter as you cut down, since twisting the cutter will seal the rim of the dough and prevent the biscuits from puffing up properly when they bake.

6. Carefully transfer the biscuits to a sheet pan lined with parchment paper. If not baking them right away, wrap and freeze them.

7. Preheat a deck oven to 237°C/460°F.

8. Bake the biscuits until the top and bottom rim of the biscuits turn golden brown, 10 to 12 minutes, rotating the sheet pan halfway through the process to ensure an even bake.

9. When the biscuits come out of the oven, brush them with the melted butter.

breads

This is by no means a book about breads. The breads that are covered in this section are merely two basic varieties from which we will make different shapes and add different garnishes. Their main purpose is to serve as sandwich bread (see page 360) and, for some varieties, to be sold as loaves. In order to keep this section simple, only the basic principles of making these two varieties of bread are covered.

Making good bread is a matter of being well organized, making sure to follow instructions, and being very precise when weighing out recipes. Good bread is also the result of how the dough is handled and proper fermentation. As with laminated dough, every single step is important, and you cannot skip one or cut a corner here or there if you want to make good bread.

Following are the twelve steps of bread making:

1. **Mise en place:** Have all the ingredients, tools, and equipment ready to go. This means that the pre-ferments have had the time they need to ferment, the ingredients are weighed out, the liquids are at the right temperature, and you have a thermometer, a floured or greased surface or bin, depending on the bread, and a plastic bag or plastic wrap (to cover the dough) ready.

2. **Mixing (or kneading):** The purpose of mixing is to develop gluten, distribute ingredients evenly, and start the fermentation process. Mixing time depends on the type and the amount of dough. While mixing by hand has its place, using an electric mixer to mix the dough will expedite the process and ensure uniform mixing. Dough can be mixed to three stages of gluten development:

   Short mixing method (minimal gluten development/soft dough): When the dough is mixed to this stage, it needs to go through a long first fermentation to strengthen the dough. The gluten bonds are strengthened during this fermentation. It can take up to 3 hours, and the dough will need to be folded onto itself two or three times to degas it and to get the dough to have an even temperature distribution (see next step). This is very good for the actual dough, since it will develop its flavors better (long and slow fermentation is always better for flavor development than short and fast fermentation), and it extends the shelf life of the finished bread. The only disadvantage is that it takes a lot of time, especially if there are many breads in the shop that go through the same process.

   Intense mixing method: This mixing method achieves full gluten development. This speeds up the fermentation process and, as a result, the baking. However, it is not ideal for bread flavor and texture.

   Improved mixing method: This is a combination of the first two methods. It does not achieve full gluten development, but the dough will be have enough gluten development to be extensible and medium-soft (medium gluten development). The dough will strengthen during a semi-long first fermentation of about 1½ hours (see step 3). The improved mixing method is a happy compromise between a long and slow fermentation and full gluten development. This method is recommended for most doughs.

3. **First (or primary) fermentation:** Here is where fermentation begins, and it is a crucial step toward dough and flavor development. After the dough is mixed, it is left to ferment, covered, at room temperature on a floured surface. The fermentation time depends on the type of bread.

4. **Degassing or punching down the dough:** This is a literal term. The dough is punched down, and this process has four purposes: to relax the dough, to expel excess carbon dioxide (CO_2 and alcohol are produced during the fermentation process), to even out the dough temperature (the exterior dough will be cooler than the dough at the center of the mass), and finally, to redistribute the ingredients in the dough, which kicks off a second round of yeast feeding.

5. **Dividing the dough:** The dough is cut out, preferably with a bench knife to avoid tearing the dough apart, and scaled to the desired weight. If dividing large amounts of dough, keep the scaled pieces covered and on a floured surface.

6. **Rounding the dough:** This will preliminarily shape the dough into the desired form (miche, boule, bâtard, baguette, etc.).

7. **Benching the dough:** The dough and specifically the gluten is left to relax a little longer. The amount of time depends on the type of dough.

8. **Shaping:** The dough is reshaped to its final shape.

9. **Second (secondary) fermentation:** This is yet another step toward flavor development through fermentation and is also known as proofing. The proofing time depends on the desired final size. For the most part, the dough will be about 85 percent

of the desired finished size when it is ready to be baked. Proofing can take place in a variety of environments (see proof box in lamination proofing instructions, page 48). Not all doughs go through this step; it depends on the mixing method and the duration of the first fermentation.

10. **Scoring and baking:** Before bread is baked, it needs to be scored. Scoring helps the dough expand without ripping by giving it a vent to let the steam from the dough escape. The ability to score a dough properly (just deep enough and at the right angle) is something that comes with practice. The angle and depth of the score depends on the baker, and it will determine the final look of the dough. The preferred oven for baking bread is a hearth oven, where there is direct bottom heat, which will give the dough a good initial rise (known as oven-spring) and help form a crisp crust. These ovens are equipped with a steam button, which is crucial for color development and crust formation, as well as a vent, which is also responsible for color and crust formation. The amount of steam used depends on the baker and the oven. The bread can be loaded into the oven by a peel that is dusted with flour or semolina, or by a loader. If using a loader, make sure that the bread is evenly spaced to ensure even heat flow. How do you know when the bread is baked? One way to tell is if you tap the bottom of the loaf with your hand and it produces a hollow sound. This works for larger loaves like boules, but how do you tell if a baguette is done? The clearest way to tell is by the color of the crust and the darkening of the ears (the exposed part of the dough where it was scored). Another way to tell that is somewhat foolproof but may damage the bread is to insert a probe thermometer into a loaf. If it reads 93°C/200°F to 96°C/205°F, it is done.

11. **Cooling:** You won't be able to tell if the crumb is good if you cut bread while it is still hot, since steam is still escaping and the crumb is still forming. Some say that you should wait for the bread to cool in order to appreciate its flavors to the fullest.

12. **Storing:** While as a rule of thumb you should sell bread the day you make it, some sourdoughs actually improve after a couple of days. Bread should be displayed as is, but should be packed in paper bags to ensure that the crust will stay crisp longer. Plastic bags make the crust soggy quickly because the bread cannot breathe. Day-old bread is good for croutons, bread crumbs, and in some cases bread pudding.

note The breads we cover in this book are derived from lean dough and sourdough. It is important to mention that we will also be using brioche for sandwiches (see Pullman Loaf, page 37).

DETERMINING THE DESIRED DOUGH TEMPERATURE (DDT) TO OBTAIN THE REQUIRED WATER TEMPERATURE FOR A DOUGH

When mixing bread dough, don't just weigh or measure the water and add it to the remaining ingredients. It is important to first take the temperature of the water and adjust it so that it is at the correct temperature before adding it to the remaining ingredients. The water temperature will have an effect on mixing (colder water extends mixing time), proofing (warmer water accelerates fermentation), and baking (as a result of the effect of water on mixing time and proofing time). In order to obtain the ideal water temperature, the Desired Dough Temperature needs to be established. The ideal DDT for most dough is between 23°C/74°F and 25°C/77°F. In order to calculate the DDT, consider three factors:

- Room temperature

- Flour temperature: This is usually the same as room temperature.

- Friction temperature: As the dough is mixed, the friction created by the movement of the dough hook (or spiral mixer hook and bowl), increases the temperature of the dough. Typically, the dough will increase 3.6°C/2°F for every minute of mixing.

Formula:
To obtain the water temperature, first multiply the DDT by the number of factors that will affect the DDT: 3 (room temperature, flour temperature, and friction temperature). Next, subtract the room temperature, flour temperature, and friction temperature. The result will be the required water temperature.

Example:
DDT: 23°C/73°F
Multiply the DDT by the amount of factors that will contribute to the DDT:
23 x 3 = 69
Subtract room temperature: −20°C
Subtract flour temperature: −20°C
Subtract friction factor: −14.4°C
Water temperature: 14.6°C/58.3°F

possible defects of breads

defect	cause(s)	solutions (the appropriate steps need to be taken beforehand)
Loaf looks like a mushroom cap or is not tapered around the base	Dough was overproofed* (particularly for a boule, miche, or bâtard).	Proof until the dough springs back when gentle fingertip pressure is applied; the dough should be roughly twice its original size.
Tight crumb	Dough was underproofed*.	See note above.
	Dough was mixed too long.	Mix to the required gluten development.
	There is too much salt in the dough.	Scale the ingredients out carefully.
Dough looks ripped	Underproofed*.	Proof until the dough springs back when gentle fingertip pressure is applied; the dough should be roughly twice its original size.
	Improperly scored (score was not deep enough or in the wrong area of the bread).	Scoring also takes much practice. Scoring too deep can deflate the dough, but not scoring deep enough can make the dough look like it is ripped since the trapped steam will expand the score in order to escape.
Bread has little or no color on the surface	Bread was not vented while it baked.	Always vent the oven during the last few minutes of baking.
	Salt may have been scaled incorrectly.	Scale the ingredients out carefully.
Surface is cracked	Steam was not applied at the beginning of the baking process.	Make it a habit to apply steam just after the bread is loaded into the oven.
Score is barely noticeable	Score was not deep enough.	Score the dough to the correct depth; only practice can determine how deep you need to score each dough.
Bread is flat	Underproofed/overproofed*.	Proof until the dough springs back when gentle fingertip pressure is applied; the dough should be roughly twice its original size
	Oven was not hot enough (no oven-spring).	Always check the oven temperature before loading it.
Bread smells like alcohol	Overproofed*; crumb will also be very large; also, see first defect in this table.	Proof until the dough springs back when gentle fingertip pressure is applied; the dough should be roughly twice its original size.
Crumb feels wet or gummy	Dough was undermixed.	Mix to the required gluten development.
	Dough has the wrong amount of water added.	Always scale out ingredients carefully.
	Water temperature was incorrect when mixing the dough.	Take the temperature of the water before adding it to the other ingredients in the mixer.

defect	cause(s)	solutions (the appropriate steps need to be taken beforehand)
Dough is tough	Too much salt was added.	Always scale the ingredients out carefully.
	Dough was overmixed (gluten developed too much).	Mix to the required gluten development.
Crust is too thick	Overbaked.	Have timers available by the oven; always check the oven during baking.

*Adequate proofing (fermentation) will vary from item to item. In most cases, the product will double in size, but it is not a set rule for all items. Knowing when a dough is proofed requires extensive experience gained through trial and error. Touching the dough to test for proof and having it double in size are two ways to tell if the dough is ready to bake or not.

displaying and packaging bread and breakfast pastries

PRETEND THAT YOU WALK INTO A VERY EXPENSIVE STORE that carries very expensive shoes, and the shoes are strewn around the floor instead of neatly placed on the shelves, there is dust on the shelves, and the salesperson is loudly chewing gum. You spot a really nice pair of shoes amid the mess, and they are very expensive. You really like them, but the price tag seems out of place for the establishment. You pay for them anyway, since you can see that the quality of the shoe is outstanding, even though they were sitting in a pile of dirt. The salesperson takes your money and gives you the shoes in a crumpled-up brown paper bag with a grease stain. Something feels very wrong. It is still the same great pair of shoes and you are going to get rid of the bag once you get home regardless of what it looks like. It's not that you need the bag. But the experience seems off-kilter. All of this is to illustrate a point: Displaying and packaging are 50 percent of the sale, especially for new customers. Neatly lined-up breads, pastries, and desserts make a world of difference. The process doesn't end when your product comes out of the oven. It is wise to invest in quality, solid packaging. I am not going to preach about using eco-friendly materials or not—that is up to you—but the image of your packaging is the image of your establishment that the customers take wherever they go. If you are selling a $2 croissant, for example, don't just stuff it in a generic brown paper bag. Have bags made with your logo or your colors, and the customer won't think twice about paying $2 for a croissant. People will fall in love with what they see first, and then with how it tastes. If it is visually appealing, symmetrical, and clean, it makes people happy. Of course taste and texture are the ultimate determining factors, but how do you get someone to taste what you make in the first place? What do you need to do to get them to give you their money and keep giving it to you every day of the week? Well, a good start is an impeccable display case and appealing packaging. Of course, knowing how to make all of those things that will go into those shelves and packages is of equal importance. Don't forget, also, that even though your packaging needs to be visually appealing, the ultimate function of packaging is that it needs to get the product safely from point A to point B.

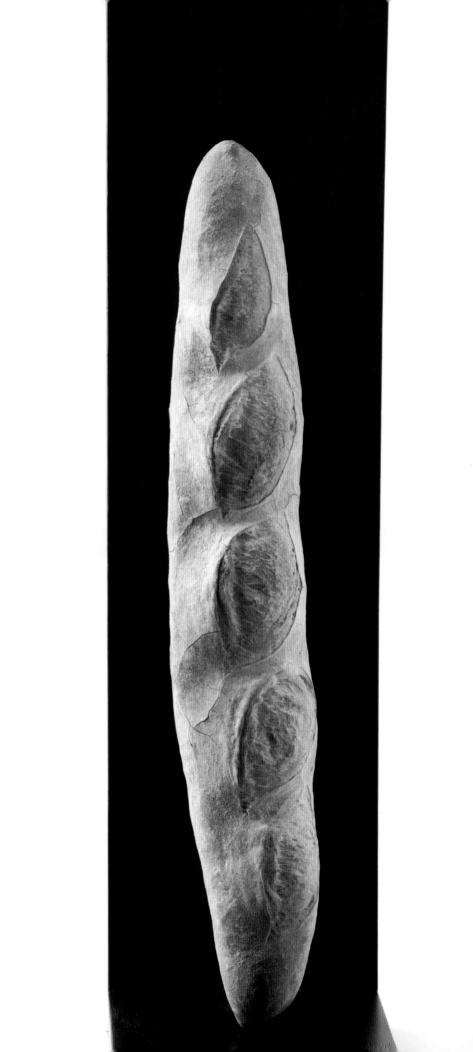

LEAN DOUGH

yield: 3.7 kg/8 lb 2.4 oz dough

INGREDIENT	METRIC	U.S.	%
POOLISH			
Bread flour	743 g	1 lb 10.24 oz	100%
Instant yeast (red label)	3 g	.12 oz	.45%
Water	743 g	1 lb 10.24 oz	100%
FINAL DOUGH			
Bread flour	1.43 kg	3 lb 2.24 oz	100%
Poolish	1.48 kg	3 lb 4.48 oz	104.3%
Water, at 21°C/70°F	739 g	1 lb 10.08 oz	51.83%
Instant yeast (red label)	3 g	.12 oz	.23%
Salt	43 g	1.52 oz	3.03%

1. **FOR THE POOLISH:** The DDT for the poolish is 21°C/70°F. Mix the flour with the yeast, and then add to the water. This can be mixed by hand in a bowl. The poolish should be left to ferment at room temperature for at least 4 hours but ideally up to 12 to 18 before it is needed.

2. **FOR THE FINAL DOUGH:** The DDT for the dough is 25°C/77°F. Use the improved mixing method on page 104. Combine the flour, poolish, water, and yeast in a mixer. Mix for 3 minutes on low speed. Allow it to rest, covered, for 15 minutes. Add the salt and mix for 4 to 5 minutes on low speed. If making larger amounts of dough, for example, twice as much, the dough will require more mixing time during the second mixing, just enough until full gluten development is reached.

3. Transfer the dough to a floured wooden table and let it bulk ferment for 1 hour covered with a plastic bag.

4. Punch the dough down, and fold it onto itself. Keep it covered.

5. Bulk ferment for 45 more minutes.

6. Divide the dough into 370-g/13.05-oz pieces for baguettes, or 370-g/13.05-oz pieces for épi.

7. To preshape the baguettes and épis, push the dough down with the heel of your hand and brush the excess flour off the dough. Roll the dough in toward you (vertically), pushing the dough down with your fingertips as you roll it up to tighten the roll and to help degas it. Make sure that there isn't too much flour on the dough; brush it off if you can see it. Roll it out to a 40-cm/16-in oblong with slightly tapered ends.

The intermediate fermentation for all of the shapes should be 15 minutes. Keep them covered with plastic.

8. **FOR THE FINAL SHAPING OF THE BAGUETTE AND ÉPI:** Roll the dough out to 57.5 cm/23 in long. Try to get an even roll with tapered ends. Place a linen couche on a wooden board and coat the couche with some bread flour. Start placing the baguettes on the linen with the seams facing the linen, making sure that you pull the linen in to "cradle" each baguette; this will keep them separate from each other and will also keep them straight.

9. Proof épis and baguettes for 1½ hour to 2 hours at room temperature, or in a proof box for 1 hour to 1 hour and 15 minutes at 30°C/86°F with 80 percent humidity.

10. **FOR BAKING THE BAGUETTE:** Preheat a hearth oven to 250°C/482°F. Flip each baguette onto a wooden paddle by pulling on the side of the linen, then flip the baguette onto a loader. The seam of the baguette should be on the bottom again. Make five to six 45-degree-

angle scores of even lengths (about 7.5 cm/3 in long) down the length of the dough with a lame. Load all 10 baguettes into the oven at the same time (5 baguettes at a time on the loader; 5 on the left side of the deck, 5 on the right side). Make sure they are evenly spaced. Load the baguettes into the oven and press the steam button for 5 to 10 seconds, depending on the oven. Bake for about 20 minutes, and then open the vent and bake for 5 more minutes. Take the bread out of the oven with a peel and slide onto a metro shelf to cool.

FOR BAKING THE ÉPI: Preheat a hearth oven to 250°C/482°F. Flip each piece of dough onto a wooden paddle, and then flip the dough onto the loader. Once all the "baguettes" are on the loader, cut the baguette using scissors into 6 evenly spaced pieces at a 45-degree angle; be careful to not cut all the way through the dough. All cuts should be evenly spaced and the same size. Turn one tip gently to one side, and then pull the next tip in the opposite direction, and so on. Do this as you are cutting the dough. Load the épis into the oven (5 épis at a time on the loader; 5 on the left side of the deck, 5 on the right side) and press the steam button for 5 seconds. Bake for about 20 minutes, and then open the vent and bake for 5 more minutes. Take the bread out of the oven with a peel and slide onto a metro shelf to cool.

notes The practice of resting the dough before adding the salt and mixing to full gluten development is known as "autolysis." It was discovered by Professor Raymond Calvel in France, who realized that this rest period improves the links between starch, gluten, and water and improves the extensibility (stretchiness) of the dough. As a result, when the mixing is resumed, the dough forms a mass and becomes smooth more quickly, reducing mixing time by about 15 percent. This produces bread with more volume, better crumb, and better structure. Mixing the dough for too long can also cause it to oxidize, turning it a pale white.

Basic Method for Shaping and Cutting Épi

FROM LEFT TO RIGHT:

1. Use the palms of your hands to roll the baguette dough into an oblong shape with slightly tapered ends.
2. Instead of scoring the baguette, you can instead use a pair of sharp scissors to snip the dough into the classic épi shape.
3. A well-baked épi or baguette will have a hard, brown crust that produces a hollow sound when the bottom of the loaf is tapped.

Épis

CIABATTA

yield: 12.5 kg/27 lb 8.96 oz (ten 1.25-kg

INGREDIENT	METRIC	U.S.	%
POOLISH			
Bread flour	1.74 kg	3 lb 13.28 oz	100%
Water	1.74 kg	3 lb 13.28 oz	100%
Instant yeast (red label)	14 g	.48 oz	.79%
FINAL DOUGH			
Bread flour	5.18 kg	11 lb 6.56 oz	100%
Water, at 26°C/80°F	3.62 kg	7 lb 15.52 oz	69.84%
Poolish	3.49 kg	7 lb 10.88 oz	67.3%
Instant yeast (red label)	34 g	1.21 oz	.66%
Salt	162 g	5.7 oz	3.12%

1. **FOR THE POOLISH:** The DDT for the poolish is 21°C/70°F. Mix the flour and the yeast, and then mix it into the water. Make the poolish 18 hours before it is needed and leave it covered at room temperature.

2. The DDT for the final dough is 23°C/74°F. Bulk ferment the dough for 40 minutes. For the final dough: In a large bowl, combine the flour, water, poolish, and yeast and mix with your hands for 3 minutes.

3. Let the dough sit in the bowl for 15 minutes, covered with a plastic bag.

4. Add the salt and mix again by hand for 5 more minutes. Cover the bowl with a lid or a plastic bag.

5. Fold the dough onto itself and bulk ferment for 10 more minutes.

6. Transfer the dough to a heavily floured surface. If the dough is being used for loaves, roll it out to 2.5 cm/1 in thick; if it is for individual pieces, roll it out to 1.25 cm/.5 in thick.

7. Using a bench knife, cut the dough. For loaves, cut the dough into pieces 12.5 by 30 cm/ 5 by 12 in (each about 1.25 kg/2 lb 12.08 oz). For individual pieces, cut the dough into pieces 7.5 by 12.5 cm/3 by 5 in (each about 125 g/4.41 oz).

8. Transfer the dough pieces to a wooden board lined with a linen couche that is coated in an abundant amount of bread flour. This will keep the dough from sticking to the linen. Reshape each piece into a rectangle. The dough is very wet, which makes it practically impossible to form a perfectly even rectangle. However, this is fine because ciabattas should have a somewhat rustic look.

9. Dust the top of the ciabatta with a generous amount of bread flour. Proof in a proof box set to 30°C/86°F with 80 percent humidity for 45 minutes to 1 hour.

10. Preheat a hearth oven to 250°C/480°F.

11. Dust the loader with semolina. Flour the top of the ciabattas generously with semolina, flip them onto a wooden paddle dusted with semolina, and then slide them (not flip them) onto the loader. The surface that was at the bottom in contact with the linen will have the characteristic flour pattern of a ciabatta and the top will not. Make sure the loader is coated with plenty of semolina so that the ciabattas don't stick. Make sure that the ciabattas are evenly spaced. If you made loaves and individual pieces, do not bake them in the same deck. They will take slightly different times to bake and it will affect even heat flow.

12. Load the oven and press the steam button for 5 to 10 seconds, depending on the oven.

13. Bake the loaves for 20 minutes, and then open the vent and bake for 5 more minutes. Bake the individual pieces for 15 minutes, and then open the vent and bake for 5 minutes.

14. Using a peel, take the bread out of the oven and slide it onto a metro shelf to cool.

variation: For Dill Ciabatta Buns, add 120 g/4.23 oz chopped dill with salt in step 4.

COUNTRY BREAD

yield: 10 bâtards

INGREDIENT	METRIC	U.S.	%
PRE-FERMENT			
Bread flour	1.87 kg	4 lb 1.6 oz	100%
Water	1.21 kg	2 lb 10.56 oz	65.03%
Instant yeast (red label)	23 g	.79 oz	1.21%
Salt	37 g	1.29 oz	1.97%
FINAL DOUGH			
Bread flour	3.71 kg	8 lb 3.04 oz	89.9%
Medium rye flour	412 g	14.55 oz	11.1%
Water	2.61 kg	5 lb 12.32 oz	70.48%
Instant yeast (red label)	50 g	1.76 oz	1.35%
Salt	81 g	2.87 oz	2.19%
Pre-ferment	3.12 kg	6 lb 14.24 oz	84.1%

1. **FOR THE PRE-FERMENT:** The DDT for the pre-ferment is 21°C/70°F. Mix all the ingredients in an electric mixer on low speed using a dough hook until a homogeneous mass is obtained.

2. Allow it to ferment for 1 hour at room temperature, and then refrigerate overnight. The following day, let the pre-ferment reach room temperature (1 to 2 hours) before mixing the dough.

3. **FOR THE FINAL DOUGH:** The DDT for the final dough is 23°C/74°F. Mix all of the ingredients in an electric mixer on low speed using a dough hook until full gluten development is achieved.

4. Bulk ferment the dough for 1 hour on a floured surface, covered with plastic.

5. Divide the dough into 10 pieces that are 1 kg/2 lb 3.2 oz each.

6. Preshape pieces of dough into tight balls. Let the dough relax for 30 minutes.

7. Flour 2 couches and place them on wooden planks. You will place 5 bâtards on each couche setup.

8. Flatten the dough balls with the heel of your hand and roll them up toward you, pressing down the border or rim of the roll onto the bottom part of the dough as you roll it in to form a tight oval. Roll the oval out to form a bâtard that is 50 cm/20 in long. Place each piece on the floured couches with the seam facing down and cradle them with the couche.

9. Proof for 1 hour and 15 minutes at 27°C/80°F and 60 to 70 percent humidity.

10. Preheat a hearth oven to 260°C/500°F.

11. Dust the loader with semolina. Turn the bâtards onto a wooden paddle and place them on the loader. Score three 7.5-cm-/3-in-long cuts down the middle at a 45-degree angle.

12. Load the oven and press the steam button for 3 seconds.

13. Bake for 30 to 35 minutes or until the crust is a dark golden brown. Open the vent for the last 4 minutes of baking.

note Country bread is a type of bread that can be shaped into many different forms. The dough is often used to make what are known as French regional breads, as with baguette dough, but I prefer to use much simpler shapes. For the country bread in this section we will be shaping the bread into bâtards that are 1 kg/2 lb 3.2 oz each.

BRETON BREAD

yield: 12 kg/26 lb 7.36 oz dough (or four 3 kg/6 lb 9.76 oz miches)

INGREDIENT	METRIC	U.S.	%
PÂTE FERMENTÉE			
Bread flour	891 g	1 lb 15.43 oz	100%
Instant yeast (red label)	7 g	.5 oz	.8%
Salt	17 g	.6 oz	2%
Water	624 g	1 lb 6 oz	70%
FINAL DOUGH			
Bread flour	5.42 kg	11 lb 15.2 oz	76.19%
Light buckwheat flour	1.03 kg	2 lb 4.48 oz	19.05%
Medium rye flour	258 g	9.11 oz	4.76%
Instant yeast (red label)	21 g	.73 oz	.38%
Pâte fermentée	1.54 kg	3 lb 6.32 oz	28.57%
Water	3.61 kg	7 lb 15.52 oz	66.67%
Gray salt, ground to powder in a spice or coffee grinder	103 g	3.64 oz	1.9%

1. **FOR THE PÂTE FERMENTÉE:** The DDT for the pâte fermentée is 21°C/70°F. Mix all of the ingredients on low speed until medium gluten development is reached. Let it relax for up to 5 hours before it is needed or until it has doubled in volume. Alternatively, let it sit at room temperature for 1 hour, and then refrigerate it for up to 48 hours. Pull it out of the refrigerator 2 hours before it is needed so that it can reach room temperature.

2. **FOR THE FINAL DOUGH:** The DDT for the final dough is 23°C/74°F. Mix on medium speed until the dough achieves medium gluten development (also known as improved mix). The dough can stretch, but it will not have the strength of dough with full gluten development. It will rip before it forms a window.

3. Bulk ferment the dough for 1 hour, covered with plastic. Fold the dough onto itself and bulk ferment for 45 more minutes.

4. Dust 4 miche baskets with bread flour.

5. Divide the dough into pieces that are 3 kg/6 lb 9.76 oz each.

6. Bench rest for 15 minutes, and then shape into large boules. Put the shaped pieces into the dusted baskets, seams facing up.

7. Proof at 27°C/81°F with 60 to 70 percent humidity for 1 hour to 1 hour and 15 minutes.

8. Preheat a hearth oven to 250°C/482°F.

9. Dust the loader with semolina. Turn the baskets carefully onto the loader. Space the bread out evenly (staggered in a 2x2 grid) and score it with a crisscross across the top.

10. Load the bread into the oven and press the steam button for 2 seconds. After 5 minutes, lower the temperature to 200°C/390°F. Once the loaves have turned golden brown, open the vent and bake until the miches reach an internal temperature of 96°C/205°F. Since it is such a large piece of bread, be sure to always take the internal temperature. Baking times can fluctuate wildly depending on the oven.

note This recipe contains gray sea salt from Brittany, France. It produces a bread with a slightly greenish-gray hue, with a mineral taste from the salt. This is a terrific bread to bake in large pieces, such as a miche.

weekend breads and pastries

A GREAT SALES OPPORTUNITY IS PRODUCING WEEKEND PRODUCTS. Weekend products can be extremely profitable, since typically it can be whatever you make during the week but bigger, because these items are meant to be shared. During the week, individual or small pastries or breads will be the most requested items. But from Thursday to Sunday, many people partake in social gatherings with friends and family. This means that they will need something big enough to serve a larger group of people.

Ideally, you would know in advance exactly what your customers will need for any given day, but that won't be the case most of the time. In fact, your customers may not know exactly what they want most of the time until they see it.

First and foremost, if you have established a loyal customer following, they will know what kind of products you have. They will show up and see what you have to offer for the weekend, like a large miche, a chocolate pound cake or two, a dozen breakfast pastries for the next morning, a cake for dessert, a box of chocolates, or a pound of coffee. This is your favorite customer. Your job is to make sure you always have that particular kind of product available at the right time of the week.

Most of your customers know what they need beforehand when it comes to simple items like a cup of coffee and a muffin. But never underestimate the power of impulse buying. Ideally your establishment is a busy one where there is a line of people waiting to pay. Set up a table next to that line with a variety of weekend items, all packaged and ready to go, and you will surely sell out by the end of the day.

FRANCESE

yield: 10 loaves

INGREDIENT	METRIC	U.S.	%
SPONGE			
Bread flour	449 g	15.85 oz	100%
Water	449 g	15.85 oz	100%
Instant yeast (red label)	.88 g	.03 oz	.2%
FINAL DOUGH			
Bread flour	1.49 kg	3 lb 4.64 oz	79.54%
Whole wheat flour	306 g	10.78 oz	20.46%
Water	1.25 kg	2 lb 12.48 oz	84.34%
Instant yeast (red label)	6 g	.22 oz	.42%
Salt	36 g	1.28 oz	2.43%
Sponge	900 g	1 lb 15.02 oz	60.26%

1. **FOR THE SPONGE:** The DDT for the sponge is 21°C/70°F. Mix the ingredients until well incorporated by hand. Cover with a damp cloth and allow to pre-ferment at room temperature for 1 hour. Refrigerate overnight.

2. Pull the pre-ferment out of the refrigerator to reach room temperature 2 hours before mixing the dough.

3. **FOR THE FINAL DOUGH:** The DDT for the dough is 23°C/74°F. Mix for minimum gluten development (also known as short mix) , about 5 minutes by hand in a bowl or a plastic tub, as you would with ciabatta, stirring to incorporate the ingredients. Place the dough on a wooden table that is generously floured.

4. Bulk ferment the dough for 3 hours, covered with a damp cloth that is not directly in contact with the dough's surface; put it over the bowl or tub used to mix the dough. Fold the dough 3 times during the bulk ferment (once each hour). Keep the dough covered with plastic. Meanwhile, flour 2 couches generously and place each one on a wooden board.

5. Divide the dough into 400-g/14.11-oz pieces. This dough does not need to be preshaped or bench rested. Shape into a long strip and place it on the prepared linen; cradle each piece with the couche. A rough measurement for the strip is about 7.5 by 45 by 2.5 cm/3 by 18 by 1 in.

6. Proof at 27°C/80°F for 45 minutes at 60 to 70 percent humidity.

7. Preheat a hearth oven to 240°C/464°F.

8. Dust the loader with semolina. Carefully put the bread on the loader using a wooden paddle. This bread does not need to be scored. Load the oven and press the steam button for 2 seconds.

9. Bake for 35 to 38 minutes, opening the vent for the last 4 minutes. This bread comes out very dark.

notes To make this Francese with caramelized onions, add 400 g/14.11 oz of caramelized onions to the dough by hand once it has finished mixing.

Francese is a rustic Italian bread that is not scored like ciabatta. It means "French bread" in Italian. It goes through a very long first fermentation in order to develop the best flavor. This is why the dough is mixed with minimum gluten development, so that it can develop its flavor and strengthen during that first fermentation.

sourdough

The varieties of sourdough covered on pages 121 through 122 are plain sourdough boule, bacon and caramelized onion bâtard, chorizo boule, and wild mushroom miche.

Sourdough can be shaped in many ways, but for our needs, the boule (ball), bâtard (oval oblong), and miche (large ball) are the most useful for slicing and selling whole. It is important, as with any bread, to make sure that you are performing proper shaping in order to obtain an evenly shaped, properly baked sourdough. Shaping should make the bread as tight as possible to avoid any unwanted air pockets inside the bread; this will also help degas the bread.

You will need to have a white sour starter, and you will need to feed it on a daily basis. The sourdough recipe contains only wild yeast.

WHITE SOUR STARTER

A white sour starter takes 5 days to make, but once you have it you can keep it alive by feeding it every day, and this way it can be used for daily bread production. Many bakeries have had their white sour starter for years, some for decades, and some for even more than that. This starter uses wild yeast, which is why it takes so many days to make.

DAY 1

INGREDIENT	METRIC	U.S.	%
Bread flour	200 g	7.05 oz	100%
Water, at 30°C/86°F	200 g	7.05 oz	100%

Mix the flour and water together. Let sit overnight at room temperature, covered.

DAY 2

Stir the mixture from day 1.

DAY 3

INGREDIENT	METRIC	U.S.	%
Day 1 mix	200 g	7.05 oz	100%
Water, at 30°C/86°F	200 g	7.05 oz	100%
Bread flour	200 g	7.05 oz	100%

Weigh out the necessary amount of day 1 mix and discard the leftovers. Stir in the water. Mix in the flour. Reserve overnight at room temperature, covered.

DAY 4

INGREDIENT	METRIC	U.S.	%
Day 3 mix	400 g	14.11 oz	100%
Water, at 30°C/86°F	200 g	7.05 oz	100%
Bread flour	200 g	7.05 oz	100%

Weigh out the necessary amount of day 3 mix and discard any leftovers. Stir in the water. Mix in the flour. Reserve at room temperature, covered.

INGREDIENT	METRIC	U.S.	%
Day 4 mix	200 g	7.05 oz	33.33%
Water, at 30°C/86°F	400 g	14.11 oz	66.66%
Bread flour	600 g	1 lb 5.12 oz	100%

Weigh out the necessary amount of day 4 mix and discard any leftovers. Stir in the water. Mix in the flour. Reserve at room temperature, covered.

FOR THE DAILY FEEDING

INGREDIENT	METRIC	U.S.	%
Water, at about 9°C/48°F	1.45 kg	3 lb 3.2 oz	100%
White sour starter (see page 118)	251 g	8.87 oz	17.33%
Bread flour	1.45 kg	3 lb 3.2 oz	100%

1. **TO FEED THE SOUR:** Place the cold water (from the tap) in a mixing bowl and dissolve the sour starter in it.

2. Add the flour and mix until a homogeneous mass is obtained.

3. Leave at room temperature (21°C/70°F).

4. Make sure to feed this white sour starter 18 hours before mixing the dough and on a daily basis.

Basic Method for Shaping and Scoring a Boule

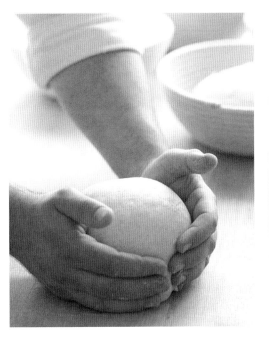  

FROM LEFT TO RIGHT:
1. To create a boule, use your hands to shape the sourdough into a round ball.
2. Before baking, score each boule as desired.
3. A properly baked loaf of sourdough.

Sourdough Boules

SOURDOUGH

yield: 13.5 kg/29 lb 12.16 oz dough

INGREDIENT	METRIC	U.S.	%
Bread flour	5.39 kg	11 lb 13.76 oz	76.62%
Whole wheat flour	630 g	1 lb 6.24 oz	11.69%
Medium rye flour	630 g	1 lb 6.24 oz	11.69%
White sour starter	3.15 kg	6 lb 14.88 oz	58.45%
Water, at 21°C/70°F	3.46 kg	7 lb 10.08 oz	64.28%
Salt	227 g	7.99 oz	4.2%

1. **FOR THE SOURDOUGH:** Make sure to feed the white sour starter 18 hours before mixing the dough.

2. Add the flours, starter, and water to the mixer bowl. Mix on low speed for 3 minutes, and then let rest for 15 minutes, covered with plastic. Add the salt and mix for 5 more minutes on low speed. The dough should achieve full gluten development; check the gluten development by performing a window test (see page 10).

3. Transfer the dough to a floured wooden worktable and bulk ferment for 1 hour. Punch the dough down and fold it onto itself. Bulk ferment for 1 more hour.

4. Fold the dough onto itself one more time and let it bench rest for 15 minutes.

5. Divide the dough. For miche, scale out pieces that are 2.7 kg/5 lb 15.2 oz each.

For boules, scale out pieces that are 900 g/1 lb 15.68 oz each.

For bâtards, scale out pieces that are 675 g/1 lb 7.68 oz each.

6. **FOR SHAPING THE MICHE:** Round the dough into a ball, pulling toward you to tighten it. Transfer to heavily floured miche baskets; the smooth top goes in the basket first.

FOR THE BOULE: The shaping is the same as for the miche.

FOR THE BÂTARD: Shape into an oblong oval, then roll it up vertically toward you the length of the basket. Place the dough into a heavily floured basket, with the smooth side facing the basket. Bulk ferment at room temperature for 2 hours, covered with plastic.

7. Retard overnight in the refrigerator.

8. Pull the dough out of the refrigerator 1 to 2 hours before baking and check the proof. The dough should spring back when you apply gentle pressure to it with your fingertips.

9. **FOR BAKING THE MICHE:** Preheat a hearth oven to 255°C/490°F. Flip the baskets onto the loader and gently let the dough come out. Make sure that all the loaves are evenly spread out; score the dough as desired. Load the oven and press the steam button for 5 to 10 seconds, depending on the oven. Lower the temperature to 200°C/390°F. Bake for 25 minutes, and then open the vent and bake for 10 to 15 more minutes or until the bread reaches an internal temperature of 93°C/200°F. Take the bread out of the oven with a peel, and then slide it onto a metro shelf to cool.

FOR BAKING THE BOULES AND BÂTARDS: Preheat a hearth oven to 255°C/490°F. Flip the baskets onto the loader gently, making sure that all the loaves are evenly spread out; score the dough as desired. Load the oven and press the steam button for 5 to 10 seconds. Bake for 20 minutes, and then open the vent and bake 10 to 15 more minutes or until the bread reaches an internal temperature of 93°C/200°F. Take the bread out of the oven with a peel, and then slide it onto a metro shelf to cool.

note This recipe makes 5 miches at 2.7 kg/5 lb 15.2 oz, 15 boules at 900 g/1 lb 15.68 oz, or 20 bâtards at 675 g/1 lb 7.68 oz.

garnished sourdough

The garnish for a flavored sourdough is added during the last minute of mixing. The amounts of garnish are for 13.5 kg/29 lb 12.16 oz of dough, and the breads can be shaped into any of the previously described shapes (miche, boule, and bâtard).

garnish	amount	procedure
Chorizo	1.15 kg/2 lb 8.48 oz	Cut the chorizo into small dice, then render it in a hot sauté pan and cook it until crisp. Transfer to paper towels and pat dry to remove excess fat. Let cool before adding it to the bread.
Bacon and caramelized onions	Bacon: 900 g/1 lb 15.68 oz Caramelized onions: 900 g/1 lb 15.68 oz	Place the bacon on a sheet pan lined with a wire rack. Bake at 160°C/325°F for 10 to 15 minutes or until crisp. Once the bacon has cooled, break it into small pieces. Thinly slice the onion. Cook it in a sauté pan with very hot oil until the onions turn brown (caramelize).
Wild mushrooms	Black trumpet mushrooms: 400 g/14.1 oz Wood ear mushrooms: 400 g/14.1 oz Porcini mushrooms: 400 g/14.1 oz	Chop the mushrooms coarsely. Cook in a sauté pan with very hot olive oil until tender. Season with salt and pepper as they cook. Pat dry with paper towels and allow to cool before adding to the dough.

Sourdough Miche

THE PASTRY SHOP

THIS CHAPTER WILL FOCUS ON CAKES (molded varieties and layered varieties), individual desserts, tarts, and some specialty cookies. The pastry shop is a different world than that of the bakery discussed in Chapter 1, but some items will utilize the mixing methods covered in Chapter 1, such as sponge cakes made with the blending method. In pastry there is more control over the final product than with baked goods, especially those that contain yeast, which practically makes them living things, susceptible to the many variables that can affect the finished product. Not to say that pastry does not contain a degree of complexity, but if there is an understanding of how to use and control the ingredients and the techniques involved, positive results can easily be achieved on a consistent basis.

ANOTHER FACTOR that makes pastry production different from bakery production is the financial aspect. In general terms, baked goods have a low food cost and low labor cost, which make them high-profit-margin items. Pastry items, in general terms, have a low to medium food cost but a high labor cost. This makes the profit margin medium to high. The reason for the high labor cost is that pastry requires much more manual labor to produce a specific item than do most breads. For example, making twenty baguettes from beginning to end, without counting fermentation time, can take a total of two hours of actual hands-on dough manipulation. The cost is marginal. But to make twenty individual desserts with two to three components can take perhaps twice as long as that. This influences how much to charge for a small dessert. Generally speaking, the food cost for baked goods could be between 15 and 20 percent, while desserts are closer to 20 to 28 percent.

It is important to remark on an obstacle that is not only present in a café environment, but also can be found in most food preparation establishments: the balance between quality and value. It is important to consider the amount that can be charged for an item when determining the ingredients that will be used. Although it is not always possible to use the highest-quality ingredients due to the amount that the clientele is willing to pay, it is important to use the best ingredients possible.

One of the most important factors to consider is that these items are made ahead of time. Most of them will be displayed or kept under refrigeration and completely exposed for a period of time so they will typically have an ideal shelf life of one day from the moment they are finished and ready to be sold. That said, the pastry display case does not need to be completely full at ~6 A.M.; between ~10 and 10:30 A.M. would suffice, since most people rarely eat desserts that early. Furthermore, an early schedule would need to be established for the pastry cooks in order to have the pastry case full by the time you open. While this looks great, if you are open until late afternoon or early evening, those desserts will already be six hours old by the time anyone orders one, and by the time you close, much older. As long as your bread and breakfast pastry displays are ready by the time you open, it is understandable that the pastry display case is not full yet.

After a maximum of thirty-six hours, any dessert that has been assembled and garnished and is displayed in exposed refrigeration should be discarded. If there is a dessert that in fact makes it to thirty-six hours without selling, you might need to think about reducing the par stock or changing the dessert to one that sells more. There may not be anything intrinsically wrong with the dessert, but most refrigeration units have a fan circulating cold air throughout the interior of the display case or refrigerator. This circulating air tends to dry out whatever comes in contact with it. This is why sheet pans with mise en place are covered with plastic wrap or some of this mise en place is reserved in airtight containers, where it can remain cold but not exposed to air circulation. Air circulation can also make an item take on a variety of unpleasant flavors, such as the very distinct "refrigerator" taste.

Since these items are made ahead of time to be sold during the day, they are completely finished and ready to be eaten or packaged to go. This is the essential and most important difference between these types of pastries (individual desserts and cakes) and restaurant desserts, which typically require a few more touches before they go out to the dining room. A pastry chef should never forget that the product needs to hold for a certain period of time in the display case and that each of the pastry's components must hold up in the refrigerator's conditions during that time. For example, never use components that are susceptible to deterioration in the presence of moisture, such as sugar decorations or baked items such as tuiles. Both of these items will become soggy and highly unpalatable after a few hours. Form and function are both essential to success, since a beautiful cake that has inedible garnishes can be a tremendous disappointment to a customer, no matter how many bells and whistles it has.

Having said that, the biggest challenge is to produce items that will have a variety of textures (soft, smooth, firm, crunchy) that won't succumb to their environment. In addition to utilizing textural differences, understanding flavor combinations is imperative. A good rule of thumb is never to use more than three or four flavors in a single dessert, since the tongue cannot distinguish more than that and it will then only be able to taste sweet or sour, whichever is the dominant taste. Both of these factors were taken into consideration when formulating the pastries in this chapter.

One question that is frequently asked is, "How do you come up with the right flavor combinations?" First of all, there really isn't such a thing as the "right" flavor combination, because it all comes down to what you like. What flavors do you like? If you are not sure whether a particular flavor goes with another, taste them and see. Most of this comes with experience and with tasting as many different foods (not just pastry) as possible. This is how your palate becomes educated and trained, if you will, to your likes and dislikes. It's as simple as that: You make what you like, and hopefully there are many hundreds of people who share your taste. A word to the wise: Unusual flavors do not sell. Some chefs can get away with it, but not everyone can or should. Customers might try a few eccentricities once in a while, but "shock value" pastries have a very short life span. People don't necessarily want their palates challenged all the time. Again, it's good to experiment and test new ingredients out, but do yourself a favor and taste it for yourself first with your staff and then with a few loyal customers. These loyal customers are usually the most honest of the bunch, since they have nothing to gain or lose by giving you their opinion. But they might just save you from shooting yourself in the foot.

THE KEY INGREDIENTS

The ingredients used in the pastry shop can easily outnumber those found in the bakery. This section cannot cover every single ingredient used because of the sheer number of possibilities. Instead, here is a brief overview of the most widely used ingredients that focuses on their properties with regard to pastry production. These items, in no particular order, are:

eggs

Besides the baking properties mentioned on pages 4 to 5, which apply to some items in this chapter such as the baked cake or sponge components of some entremets, the most important egg functions specific to pastry production are:

AERATOR

Both the yolk and the white, and the yolk and white together, have the capacity to trap air in the form of very small bubbles. The egg whites have the most capacity to trap air, thanks to a protein called globulin. Egg yolks contain a percentage of fat, which prevents them from being capable of trapping as much air as egg whites do. While egg whites can increase in volume up to eight times, egg yolks can only increase in volume up to four times. Aeration produces light and delicate products, and these products range from baked items, such as sponge cakes, to mousses, which contain aerated egg yolks and sometimes aerated or whipped egg whites. Always keep in mind that if using a raw egg product, it should be cooked or at least pasteurized.

THICKENER

Eggs and particularly egg yolks are used for making custards. Egg proteins begin to coagulate at 60°C/145°F; when these egg proteins begin to cook, they will thicken the liquid they are in, typically a dairy product such as milk and/or heavy cream when making custard. There are three types of custards:

- **Stirred custards**, such as crème anglaise. This is a custard made on the stovetop by boiling a combination of milk and heavy cream with sugar and then tempering in egg yolks that have been whisked together with another part of sugar. This mixture is cooked, stirring continuously, on the stovetop until it reaches 80°C/180°F and is then cooled immediately over an ice bath. Crème anglaise will have the consistency of a semifluid liquid and can be used as a sauce or as the base for a cream (see page 137). Stirred custards can also be cooked over a hot water bath, which take longer to cook but are easier to control. Cooking custards over a direct flame can easily result in an overcooked custard. An example of a stirred custard cooked over a hot water bath is a curd (see page 17), which is an acidic fruit juice thickened by eggs.

- **Boiled custards** are similar in principle to stirred custards, but they are cooked until they come to a boil. Since they not only contain eggs to thicken the custard, but also a starch, such as cornstarch or flour, the liquid must be boiled to cook these starches, or they will not hydrate, coagulate, and thicken the custard, and the finished product will have a grainy consistency as a result of the raw starch. The best example of a boiled custard is pastry cream (see page 519).

- **In baked custards**, the egg proteins are cooked, or rather baked, in a water bath in an oven, which provides indirect rather than direct heat. A dairy product such as milk and/or heavy cream is combined with sugar and egg yolks and then transferred to a baking vessel such as a porcelain ramekin or mason jar (see Maple Pot de Crème on page 247). This ramekin is then placed in a hot water bath, typically in a hotel pan or any pan that will hold the entire ramekin. Finally, the custard is baked in a low oven. Baking custards through indirect heat will result in a very smooth finished product if properly baked; when overbaked, they are like rubber. Other examples of baked custards include crème brûlée, pumpkin pie, and bread pudding.

sugar

Sugar has physical effects on baked goods (see Chapter 1, page 6), but its main function in pastry is to sweeten. Desserts aren't desserts without sugar. The addition of sugar will also have physical effects on pastry items. For example, it helps to stabilize a foam in an egg white meringue if and when it is added at the correct time during the whipping process, it can thicken liquids, and it can be cooked to produce confections in a variety of textures. Depending on the type of sugar, it can contribute to the texture of the finished item and it can depress the freezing point in frozen desserts such as ice cream. The preferred type of sugar for pastries is not granulated sugar but a finer-crystal sugar, such as baker's sugar, or superfine sugar, which has an even smaller crystal. The reason is that the smaller the crystal, the better and the quicker it will dissolve. The larger the crystal, the longer it will take to dissolve, which translates to longer mixing times that can have a negative effect on the final product.

heavy cream

Heavy cream contains a considerable amount of fat. The most common percentage available in the United States is 40 percent fat by weight, but in Europe, lower-fat heavy cream is the standard and it contains closer to 36 percent fat by weight. In many preparations such as mousses, parfaits, creams, and crème Chantilly, it is one of the ingredients that is "aerated," meaning air is incorporated into it through whipping. This aeration is directly responsible for the light texture and smooth mouthfeel in the finished product. Heavy cream can be combined with another aerated item such as eggs (yolks, whites, or both), depending on the type of dessert. Examples of items that use heavy cream as a foam are ice creams, some gelatos, and most still-frozen desserts.

Whipped cream is a foam composed of water and air and is stabilized by the fat molecules found in heavy cream. As the cream is whipped, the fat globules trap the air bubbles and strengthen the foam. Heavy cream needs to be very cold (ideally 4°C/39°F) to whip properly, otherwise the structure will not hold. When the cream is warmer, the fat globules get soft and are not capable of trapping air.

Heavy cream is not just used as a foam. It can be the main ingredient in a panna cotta (which literally translated from Italian means "cooked cream"), where one need only add a flavor, sugar, and silver gelatin (see page 228). Heavy cream is also a main component in certain custards, such as crème anglaise (English cream), pot de crème (cream pot), and crème brûlée (burnt cream). And last but not least, it is also used in confections such as caramels.

chocolate

Chocolate is one of the essential ingredients in the pastry shop, and some would argue that it is the pastry chef's best friend. However, it can easily be overused. To properly handle chocolate and to execute high-quality pastries using it can be challenging.

There are two basic types of chocolate: dark (which ranges from "bitter chocolate" to "semisweet") and milk. White chocolate is not chocolate, since chocolate requires cocoa liquor (or cocoa solids) in order to be considered chocolate, and white chocolate does not have any cocoa liquor. Dark and milk chocolate are categorized by percentages, and those percentages represent the amount of cocoa beans used, which is inversely proportionate to the amount of sugar in the chocolate. For instance, a 64 percent chocolate contains about 36 percent sugar. The higher the percentage of cocoa beans, the more intense the taste of the chocolate, but also the more bitter it will be. Cocoa powder, an essential ingredient in baking and pastry, comes from cocoa beans as well. In pastry, chocolate is incredibly versatile. In this book it will be used to make cakes, mousses, creams, décor, glazes, and velour (spray).

A very important feature of chocolate is that it can be used to garnish desserts that will be held in refrigerated display cases without losing its consistency. Remember that this type of environment can be harsh on certain garnishes, negatively affecting their texture. Chocolate, if properly tempered, will retain its snap. But be careful to not overdo it; you don't want to have chocolate on too many of your desserts.

fruit

Fruit by definition is the ovary of a flowering plant that contains a seed or seeds. If it does not contain a seed it cannot technically be called a fruit. For the pastry chef, fruit is available fresh, preserved (canned or jarred in syrup, water, or liquor), candied (there are many varieties of candied fruit available), dried (partially dehydrated, dehydrated, or freeze-dried, whole or powdered), juiced, or puréed. Ideally, fresh ripe fruit would be used on a consistent basis, but there are some very high-quality fruit purées available (see Resources, page 540). Keep in mind that purées have a percentage of sugar added to them and that they can be of a thin liquid consistency, such as passion fruit purée, or thick from pulpy fruit, such as raspberry purée. The consistency needs to be taken into consideration when making fruit creams and mousses, since thinner liquids will require more body (from foams such as egg yolks, egg whites, and heavy cream, and gelling agents such as gelatin) to remain firm than thicker liquids.

Try to use only seasonal fruit. A pastry chef who uses strawberries in winter does not give a very good impression to educated customers. Not only that, but strawberries that are available during the winter taste awful, which should be the main deterrent to ever using fruit that is out of season.

While no items in the pastry section of this book utilize vegetables, they are widely used in the savory section and to a much lesser degree in the bakery section in the form of onions, garlic, and mushrooms. When using vegetables in nontraditional preparations such as desserts, keep in mind that many customers will not be used to seeing them mixed in with their favorite cake. It's good to experiment and test the waters, but be aware that you might not sell a large amount of those items.

flavors

Flavors are ingredients that can contribute texture as well the obvious flavor. Flavors are not the same thing as flavorings, since flavorings contribute only flavor and not texture, much like infused flavors. Flavorings are usually extracts or compounds, such as vanilla extract, almond extract, or coffee extract. Flavors can be categorized in the following way:

- Liquid flavors: These contribute flavor and moisture. Examples are fruit juices and purées and liquors.

- Paste flavors: These contribute flavor and body. Examples include nut pastes, chocolate, and vanilla paste.

- Infused flavors: Infused flavors contribute just flavor. Examples of flavors that are infused are herbs, spices, teas, vanilla beans, and coffee beans.

flour

For information on the characteristics of flour as well as information on other varieties, see the notes on page 5. The most common flours used in pastry are:

PASTRY FLOUR

The most delicate of all commercially available flours with the lowest percentage of protein (glutenin and gliadin), pastry flour is used to make a variety of sponges and cakes.

CAKE FLOUR

Cake flour is slightly stronger than pastry flour, with a slightly higher percentage of protein. It is ideal for sponges, since it doesn't toughen batters as much when they are mixed. The more the batter is mixed, the tougher a batter or dough will become; the higher the protein content, the faster this strengthening or toughening will occur.

ALL-PURPOSE FLOUR

All-purpose flour is a combination of bread flour and pastry flour and a decent replacement for cake or pastry flour. It is a generally acceptable workhorse flour, but if possible, use cake flour or pastry flour when called for in order to obtain the best results. Some recipes in this book call for all-purpose flour, since it has the right amount of strength needed for the particular recipe.

gelatin

Gelatin is extracted from animals and mainly from pigskin. It is used because of its gelling and stabilizing properties. It can make a foam permanent, such as in the Peanut Butter Mousse with Milk Chocolate Chantilly, Peanut Brittle, and Chocolate Cake on page 168. A liquid or semiliquid can be gelled into a firmer, more solid state depending on the amount of gelatin used, making it easier to handle and use. Gelatin melts between 26° and 32°C/80° and 90°F and is easily incorporated into recipes. It needs first to be hydrated or bloomed in very cold water, and then strained, the excess water squeezed off and finally melted and incorporated into another ingredient or ingredients. The preferred type of gelatin used in this book is sheet gelatin, not powdered.

All gelatin will be measured by weight, not by the sheet. Since it will contribute to the total weight of the finished product, and because the actual sheets may vary in weight from one manufacturer to another, it needs to be included in the recipe as a weight measure. It is crucial for recipes to have each ingredient represented not only by its weight but also by its percentage of the total weight of the recipe in order to calculate different yields depending on the needs of the user. There are three types of gelatin: gold, silver, and bronze. This book uses a specific type of gelatin sheet, silver, and they each weigh approximately 3.5 g/.12 oz. Before making the recipes in this book, weigh a sheet of gelatin from the brand that you are going to use. If it is significantly lower or higher in weight than 3 to 3.5 g/.10 to .12 oz, you will have to make adjustments to the recipe. The gelling power or quality of gelatin is measured in "blooms," named for Oscar Bloom, inventor of the device that measures gelatin quality; the higher the bloom number, the higher the strength or quality. The gold variety has the strongest gelling power (200 to 225 bloom), silver the next strongest (160 to 180 bloom), and bronze the least strong (120 to 150 bloom). Silver sheets weigh 3 g to 3.5 g/.10 to .12 oz each, and the number of sheets required for a recipe can be determined by dividing the weight called for in the recipe by 3.5. Ordinarily, gelatin sheets are made with the intention of counting them, not weighing them, so that if a given recipe requires five sheets of gelatin it will be the same gelling strength no matter what type of gelatin sheets you use. This, as much as it is convenient, is imperfect and impractical because weighing the sheets is faster than counting forty-two sheets of gelatin, and it is more precise to weigh them out because the weight per sheet can vary from maker to maker, and the sheets can be broken up if needed. An extra sheet of gelatin, or part of it, can make a small difference in the final result of a product, but when you are making large amounts of a product with gelatin, the difference in texture will be much more pronounced.

Silver gelatin sheets are the most commonly used and the most widely available, but if you cannot

chocolate décor

CHOCOLATE DÉCOR IS SIMPLY A CHOCOLATE DECORATION for a dessert or cake. It is typically a piece that embellishes the cake that can contribute to texture and obviously flavor, but its main purpose is to be a decorative piece.

Having said that, there are a few aspects to consider when making chocolate décor. First and foremost, it should make sense as a flavor component with the rest of the dessert. Do not use chocolate just for the sake of using chocolate. For example, if the cake has no chocolate in any of its components, then it makes no sense to use chocolate décor.

Second, any and all chocolate décor must be as thin as paper. Anyone can make thick décor, but it is the experienced pastry chef who can execute and produce chocolate décor with finesse. Pastry ingredient catalogs for professionals offer a variety of shapes and colors of chocolate décor, and they are usually very thick. There are two reasons for this: One, they are most likely made by a machine, and two, they are made to withstand transportation. Their thickness will help in maintaining their integrity. You can immediately tell someone's skill level by something as simple as the décor. This is why it is so important to practice as much as you can to get the thickness right. However, there is also such a thing as décor that is too thin; so thin that you can see through the chocolate is going a little too far.

Always keep your tools clean, especially the offset spatula used to spread the chocolate. I have often seen the same mistake happen over and over again. Someone will spread chocolate onto a sheet of acetate and then put the offset spatula down. The chocolate left on the spatula will set, and when the person spreads more chocolate onto another sheet of acetate using the chocolate-covered offset spatula, the result is a bumpy, smeared coat. Always scrape the chocolate off your tools as soon as you are done with them. Chocolate ideally should be stored in a Cres Cor environment, with no plastic wrap, but with a door to keep it protected.

Customized Silk Screens for Chocolate Décor

As with outsourced chocolate décor, transfer sheets look like a machine made them and, as with fleximolds (see page 134), they take away from the technique and creative resources pastry chefs have at their disposal. With that in mind, you can make your own transfer sheets. The process is not very complicated and the result is completely unique, since the design is of your own making. These are the steps:

find them, use bronze or gold. However, make the necessary adjustments based on the weight of each type of sheet. All of the recipes in this book that call for gelatin intend for silver to be used. Try not to use powdered gelatin, but if it must be used, 10 sheets of silver gelatin or 14 sheets of bronze gelatin have the same gelling strength as 28.34 g/1 oz of powdered gelatin.

CAKES (Entremets)

Cakes will be divided into two categories: molded and layered. They are categorized by the way they are assembled. These types of pastries are formulated in larger sizes that are meant to be shared. All of the cakes can be made into individual portions provided there is an adequate mold available. It is useful to have both sizes available in the display case, which also makes mise en place more efficient.

1. Choose the design you like from a digital source, such as an image found online or a photograph taken with a digital camera. It can also be as simple as text. The more defined the design is, the better. If it has too many shadows, shades, and thin lines, chances are they won't show up on the chocolate. Transfer this image to a word-processing application document.

2. Send this image to a custom silk screen maker (see Resources, page 540). They typically make full-, half-, and quarter-letter-size screens (based on a sheet of paper 8.5 by 11 in). Anything larger may become prohibitively expensive. This image is transferred to a silk screen via a Thermofax, which literally burns the image onto the silk screen. This silk screen is then attached to a screen. The process is quite quick.

3. Once the silk screen is ready, grease a marble surface, spreading the oil out evenly using a paper towel. Line up as many acetate sheets as you think you will need to make.

4. Melt some chocolate liquor or some very low-viscosity chocolate. The thickness of the chocolate is crucial to the success of the transfer sheet. It is not necessary to temper it; since it is such a thin layer that will be needed, it will set quickly.

5. Put the silk screen over the acetate and then pour some chocolate over the top end of the screen. It will take some practice to get the right amount (in other words, just enough to cover the entire image once it is scraped), but start with 100 g/3.53 oz. Using a chocolate scraper, pull the chocolate toward you, pressing down as hard as you can. The harder you press, the cleaner the image will come out. The reason you need to have a thick chocolate is so that it doesn't leak out of the design on the silk screen and it only gets the chocolate on the design.

6. Once you have scraped the chocolate all the way down the screen, lift the screen up and continue with the other sheet of acetate. Work quickly so that the chocolate on the screen doesn't set and clog the image on the screen.

7. Once you are done with all the acetates, clean the screen off by using a paper towel soaked in hot water. Do not apply hot water directly to the screen, since it will warp the frame and the screen itself.

8. Once the transfer sheets are done, you can apply a tempered chocolate of a different color over it, spreading it thinly and evenly with an offset spatula. Let it set and, using a ruler and a paring knife or a cutter in any shape, cut it out to the desired shape.

note There are no names given to any cakes in this book that do not already have a pre-existing and commonly known name, such as the Black Forest Cake v2.0 on page 143, which shares the flavors of the original Black Forest Cake but is more modern. One cannot assume that the name properly describes the contents of the cake and that your customers can be asked to memorize these names. All of the items in this book are named after what they are composed of, for the sake of clarity and simplicity.

molded cakes

The basic characteristic of molded cakes is that they are assembled in a mold. This mold can be made of a variety of materials like stainless steel, heavy-grade aluminum, semirigid acrylic plastic, or silicone. Stainless steel is widely used because it transfers temperature very well, which is convenient when assembling the cake. A stainless-steel mold will set the contents faster while it freezes and, when unmolding the ring with a torch, or a hot water bath if it is a dome-shaped mold, is also very strong and more resistant to heavy use than aluminum, which tends to bend and lose its shape easily. One way to avoid using a torch to unmold a cake is to line the interior of the mold with a piece of acetate cut out to the same height and slightly longer than the mold. In this case, just push the cake out of the mold and take the acetate off. This method does not work very well with straight corners; acetate needs to be folded by hand in order to get it into the corners of the mold. Aluminum is an economical mold option (see Resources for custom-made aluminum molds on page 540), and it also transfers temperature well. Semirigid acrylic plastic molds are not recommended since they easily lose their shape even when they are being washed with hot water, they do not transfer temperature well, they are very hard to unmold, and they are very hard to clean well since acrylic is porous. They also tend to crack and break after a few uses, and some acrylic might get into the finished product.

Silicone molds, commercially known as fleximolds, are very convenient because they hold their shape well regardless of the temperature (you can bake in them as well) and also because of their flexibility. They make unmolding very easy; just pop the cake out. They are also relatively inexpensive considering how much use you can get out of them. The downside is that they are not very good at transferring heat or cold, since the material they are made with is a poor temperature conductor. Items take longer to set and bake in them. Baked items don't get a very good color from them since the silicone insulates the baked item to a certain degree, preventing a proper Maillard reaction.

Another downside is that they absorb strong flavors, which is a problem when they get washed with strong detergents since they can take on a soapy flavor; hot water is usually enough to clean fleximolds.

Molded cakes are typically composed of:

- **A cake or sponge:** This is typically the base or support of the cake.

- **At least one insert:** An insert is a component that is placed inside the body of the cake. It cannot be seen from the outside and is typically a different flavor than that of the body of the cake. These inserts are an opportunity for the pastry chef to introduce a texture and a flavor that is different from that of the body.

- **The body:** This is the main component of the cake, which will contain all other components and is the dominant flavor. It is usually what the cake is named after. For example, if the body is a chocolate mousse, the cake will be described as a chocolate mousse cake first, and then the other components will be listed.

- **A coating:** The coating's main purpose is to protect the cake from the external elements such as circulating air, but it is also an opportunity to add another texture or to enhance the flavor of the other components of the cake. Types of coatings include glazes, velour (or chocolate spray), and actual chocolate in a variety of forms. There may be other types of coating, but these are the most common.

- **Garnish:** This is an extra component that should allude to the flavors used in the cake. For example, a coconut cake might have coconut chips, coquitos (baby coconuts), or shredded coconut on top. If there is a passion fruit insert in the cake, use a passion fruit gelée or passion fruit seeds to garnish the top. For the most part, cake garnishes should be edible; otherwise, advise your customers to take the garnish off before they cut into it. Nonedible garnishes refer to ingredients that can be used to prepare foods but are not eaten as is, such as whole spices; they do not refer to nonfood items (such as wood, for example). Do not use cooked sugar decorations, since they will get tacky in the refrigerator. Sugar has a property know as hygroscopicity, which means that it pulls or absorbs moisture from its surroundings: salt does the same. If the cake can be garnished right before it is presented to a customer in the dining room, as in a restaurant, sugar decorations can work as an à la minute garnish because the sugar will not be affected. Some pastry chefs will garnish the cake so that each slice gets a garnish. It is up to you how you want to garnish your cake.

Basic Method for Assembling Molded Cakes

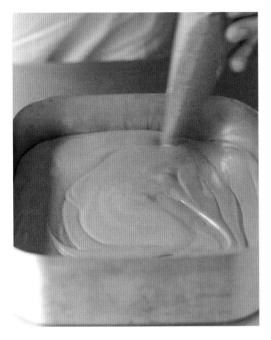  

FROM LEFT TO RIGHT:

1. To begin assembly, pipe a layer of the mousse, which will compose the body of the cake, into the stainless-steel mold.
2. Place the insert into the center of the mold, applying gentle pressure to make sure the layer is level.
3. Because molded cakes are assembled upside down, the cake's base is the final layer to be placed into the mold.

the craft of the pastry chef and why fleximolds should be used in moderation

I WAS LOOKING AT A PASTRY EQUIPMENT CATALOG NOT TOO LONG AGO. It had a large selection of fleximolds. These molds are made out of heat- and freezer-resistant rubber and are also nonstick. You can bake in them as well as freeze mousses and ice creams in them, which makes them incredibly practical and convenient. Anything frozen or baked in them will pop right out. I was looking at a new line of these molds and they were truly beautiful molds, in a variety of forms and shapes. One of my colleagues was looking at the molds over my shoulder and pointed out that you didn't really need to have much technique or knowledge to use those molds, since they did most of the work for you, including determining the aesthetic component to an extent. Why spend so much time and money becoming technically proficient, when a rubber mat will do most of the work for you?

I agree with him to an extent. If everything can be assembled or baked in fleximolds, then you aren't truly practicing your craft. But there is a gray area because of the level of convenience. For example, with small dome fleximolds versus stainless-steel domes, especially the really small ones (2.5 cm/1 in diameter), if you try unmolding the stainless-steel domes with a torch or a hot water bath, it takes a very long time to finish the job. With a fleximold, you can unmold dozens in a few minutes. The problem comes when these molds have all the finishing touches that a pastry chef should know how to do quickly and efficiently. In this case, the key is moderation. Also keep in mind that these molds absorb flavors easily. Therefore, when they are washed it must be done properly; otherwise future molded items will absorb that soapy flavor. Also, if an item is baked in these molds, it will never obtain the browning that is achieved with a metal mold, since they do not transfer heat as quickly and efficiently. On the other hand, the molds do not have to be greased. It's a tradeoff, but you have to decide when it is best to use a fleximold and when it is best to use metal.

Molded cakes are typically assembled upside down, meaning that the base of the cake, generally a sponge cake, will be the last item to go into the mold, on the top. The cake is then frozen, flipped over onto a cake board, and then unmolded, glazed, and garnished. More specific assembly and finishing techniques are covered from pages 132 to 133; also see the photos on page 133.

MILK CHOCOLATE MASCARPONE CREAM, CRÈME BRÛLÉE CREAM, AND HAZELNUT CRUNCH CAKE WITH VELOUR AND MILK CHOCOLATE MOLECULES

yield: 6 cakes

components

3.00 kg/6 lb 9.76 oz Milk Chocolate Mascarpone Cream

600 g/1 lb 5.12 oz Crème Brûlée Cream Demi-Spheres

6 Hazelnut Crunch Cake discs

6 Bubble Milk Chocolate Discs

Six 2.5-cm/1-in Milk Chocolate Molecules

Six 2-cm/.75-in Milk Chocolate Molecules

Six 1.25-cm/.5-in Milk Chocolate Molecules

200 g/7.05 oz milk chocolate, melted

200 g/7.05 oz Milk Chocolate Velour Spray

6 Milk Chocolate Curved Triangles

1. **TO ASSEMBLE THE CAKES:** Pull the mascarpone cream out of the refrigerator 4 hours before using so that it can reach room temperature.

2. Place six 7.5-cm-/3-in-diameter stainless-steel rings on a sheet pan. Place 6 stainless-steel demi-sphere molds that are 13.75 cm/5.5 in diameter and 10 cm/4 in high on the stainless-steel rings.

3. Unmold the crème brûlée demi-spheres; reserve frozen and covered to prevent frosting on their surface.

4. Set aside the cake discs and bubble milk chocolate discs within reach.

5. Pour the mascarpone cream into the stainless-steel dome molds, filling them only two-thirds of the way.

6. Place the frozen crème brûlée inserts into the cream, domed side first, pushing them in gently so that the dome is completely immersed in the mascarpone cream.

7. Pour in enough milk chocolate mascarpone cream to just cover the insert. Place a bubble milk chocolate disc on top of the cream in each mold. Pour in enough cream to come up within 6 mm/¼ in from the top of the dome mold.

8. Place a hazelnut crunch cake disc on top of the cream in each mold, with the bottom part of the cake facing up. Push down gently until the base of the cake is flush with the top of the dome mold. Using an offset spatula, even out any excess milk chocolate mascarpone cream.

9. Place a sheet of acetate on top of the cakes, and then put a sheet pan on top with a cutting board or other flat piece of equipment that will weigh the sheet pan down on top of the pan. Freeze the cakes until hardened.

10. **TO FINISH THE CAKES:** Set up a spray area. Use a spray paint gun or a compressor to spray the chocolate velour. Spraying chocolate can make a big mess. To reduce this mess, cover the table and the wall where you will be spraying with plastic bags, taping them into place so they will stay put.

11. Line a sheet pan with parchment paper and place a wire rack on top of it.

12. Unmold the bubble milk chocolate spheres (molecules) and reserve refrigerated.

13. Fill a piping bag one-third of the way with melted milk chocolate; reserve in a warm area to keep it from setting.

14. **TO UNMOLD THE CAKES:** Fill a bowl that is twice as large as the assembled cake domes with very hot water.

15. Assemble 6 cake boards that are slightly smaller than the base diameter of the cake. Ideally, trim 2.5 cm/1 in off a 15-cm/6-in cake board using a pair of scissors. Set them aside.

16. Unmold 1 dome at a time. Place a dome in the hot water, submerging it up to the top rim; be careful not to flood the exposed base of the cake with water. Let it warm up for about 10 seconds. Remove the dome from the water. Turn the stainless-steel dome with one hand while keeping the cake in place with the other hand, going in a circular motion. The mold should slide right off. If it doesn't, put it back in the water to soften the cream more. Once the mold has come off, place the cake on the sheet pan fitted with the wire rack. Unmold all of the cakes following this procedure. The hot water bowl may need to be changed a few times during the process.

17. Once all the cakes have been unmolded, freeze them again for about 1 hour, until hardened completely.

18. Drizzle some of the warm melted milk chocolate on top of the domes; they do not need to be identical from cake to cake. Try to keep the drizzle on one side of the cake.

19. Remove the bubble milk chocolate spheres from the freezer. Using some of the same melted milk chocolate from the piping bag, adhere the spheres to the cakes. Each cake gets one of each size of the spheres. Return the cakes to the freezer for 10 minutes.

20. Place the chocolate spray in the spray gun or compressor gun.

21. Take the cakes out of the freezer and spray the chocolate evenly on the cakes, turning the sheet pan 90 degrees every few seconds.

22. Once the cakes have an even coat of spray, transfer them to the cake base or board they will be displayed on. The cake board they have had until now was merely to support them and keep them in place. Use a large, wide, firm offset spatula to carefully lift the cakes and gently slide them from the original board to their clean, new one.

23. Place the chocolate curved triangles on top of each cake. They will need to be glued into place with a small dot of melted chocolate. Once the cakes are finished, they should no longer be kept frozen, since they can develop frosting, which will turn to condensation when they thaw.

24. Sell or serve within 36 hours. The cake should ideally be tempered for 30 to 45 minutes before consuming. Advise your customers of this.

MILK CHOCOLATE MASCARPONE CREAM

yield: 3.00 kg/6 lb 9.76 oz

INGREDIENT	METRIC	U.S.	%
MILK CHOCOLATE CRÈME ANGLAISE			
Milk	197 g	6.95 oz	26.28%
Heavy cream	197 g	6.95 oz	26.28%
Sugar	99 g	3.48 oz	13.14%
Egg yolks	116 g	4.1 oz	15.49%
Milk chocolate coins	141 g	4.98 oz	18.81%
MILK CHOCOLATE MASCARPONE CREAM			
Milk Chocolate Crème Anglaise	734 g	1 lb 9.92 oz	24.47%
Gelatin sheets, bloomed (4.33 sheets)	15 g	.52 oz	.49%
Mascarpone	2.25 kg	4 lb 15.36 oz	75.04%

1. **FOR THE MILK CHOCOLATE CRÈME ANGLAISE:** Prepare an ice bath.

2. Combine the milk, heavy cream, and half of the sugar in a small sauce pot.

3. Combine the egg yolks with the other half of the sugar in a bowl.

4. Bring the contents of the sauce pot up to a boil and slowly pour two-thirds of the hot liquid into the egg yolk–sugar mix in the bowl, whisking constantly.

5. Pour the contents of the bowl back into the pot and cook over medium heat until the liquid reaches 82°C/180°F. Immediately after, strain the crème anglaise through a fine-mesh sieve into a small bowl and stir in the milk chocolate until it is melted. Place the bowl over the prepared ice bath and cool the contents down as quickly as possible.

6. Transfer to an airtight container and refrigerate if not using immediately. The cream will hold for up to 4 days in the refrigerator.

7. **TO FINISH THE CREAM:** Place the milk chocolate anglaise and the bloomed gelatin in a bowl over a simmering water bath. Stir with a whisk until the gelatin has melted and a homogeneous mass has been obtained. Don't let it get too hot; it should be just warm enough to melt the gelatin completely (about 45°C/110°F). Stir in the tempered mascarpone with a whisk. (To temper the mascarpone, pull it out and let it sit at room temperature for 3 hours before using.) Adding the mascarpone must be done immediately before use.

note This cream must be made right before the cake is to be assembled, since it is necessary for it to be fluid.

CRÈME BRÛLÉE CREAM DEMI-SPHERES

yield: 600 g/1 lb 5.12oz

INGREDIENT	METRIC	U.S.	%
Milk	266 g	9.39 oz	29.57%
Heavy cream	512 g	1 lb 2.05 oz	7.39%
Salt	.34 g	.01 oz	.04%
Vanilla pod, split and scraped	1	1	
Sugar	50 g	1.76 oz	5.54%
Egg yolks	53 g	1.88 oz	5.91%
Cornstarch	10 g	.35 oz	1.11%
Sugar, to caramelize	100 g	3.53 oz	
Gelatin sheets, bloomed in cold water (2.33 sheets)	8 g	.28 oz	.88%

1. Combine the milk, 66 g/2.35 oz heavy cream, salt, vanilla pod, and half of the sugar in a small sauce pot.

2. In a small bowl, combine the egg yolks and the cornstarch, stirring well with a whisk until a smooth paste is obtained. Whisk in the rest of the sugar.

3. Bring the ingredients in the sauce pot to a boil. Pour about two-thirds of the milk mixture into the egg yolk mixture slowly while whisking, then pour the contents of the bowl back into the pot. Cook over medium heat while stirring constantly until the custard thickens and the first bubble appears. This signals that the starch is cooked through.

4. Remove the pan from the heat and stir off the heat for 30 more seconds. Pour the contents into a half hotel pan and remove the vanilla pod. Cover the custard with plastic wrap and let it cool in the refrigerator.

5. Sprinkle the remaining sugar to caramelize over the entire surface of the cooled custard. Using a blowtorch, caramelize the sugar.

6. Let the custard sit uncovered in the refrigerator until the caramelized sugar dissolves. It will absorb some moisture from the custard and turn into liquid.

7. **TO FINISH THE CREAM:** Set six 7-cm-/2.75-in-diameter demi-sphere molds in a half sheet pan.

8. Whip the remaining heavy cream to medium-stiff peaks and reserve in the refrigerator.

9. Transfer the crème brûlée custard to a bowl.

10. Place 200 g/7.05 oz of the crème brûlée custard in a small sauce pot with the bloomed gelatin. Melt over medium heat, stirring constantly with a whisk.

11. Pour the contents of the pot into the bowl with the crème brûlée custard and whisk vigorously.

12. Quickly fold the whipped heavy cream into the custard in 2 separate additions.

13. Transfer the finished cream to a piping bag.

14. Pipe the cream into the demi-sphere molds, and smooth out the top with a small offset spatula. Freeze the finished cream.

15. Once frozen, the demi-spheres can be unmolded and returned to the freezer, or they can be reserved in the molds wrapped tightly in plastic for future use. They will hold for up to 2 months frozen.

note This recipe makes enough for 6 demi-sphere molds at 100 g/3.53 oz each.

HAZELNUT CRUNCH CAKE

yield: 1 half sheet pan (6 cake discs)

INGREDIENT	METRIC	U.S.	%
Cake flour	179 g	6.32 oz	17.93%
Almond flour	83 g	2.91 oz	8.26%
Baking powder	14 g	.48 oz	1.37%
Eggs	206 g	7.28 oz	20.65%
Brown sugar	179 g	6.31 oz	17.9%
Milk	138 g	4.86 oz	13.76%
Hazelnut oil	165 g	5.83 oz	16.52%
Hazelnuts, toasted and coarsely chopped	24 g	.85 oz	2.41%
Hazelnut croquant	12 g	.42 oz	1.2%
Milk chocolate, melted	100 g	3.53 oz	

1. Line a half sheet pan with a nonstick rubber mat. Lightly spray the borders with nonstick oil spray.

2. Preheat a convection oven to 160°C/320°F.

3. Sift the cake flour, almond flour, and baking powder together.

4. Whip the eggs with the brown sugar on high speed in an electric mixer until they have quadrupled in size and have reached the ribbon stage. The yolks will turn a pale yellow color from the incorporation of air, and they will thicken in consistency.

5. Turn the mixer down to medium speed and slowly add in the milk.

6. Pour in the sifted dry ingredients and mix just until a homogeneous mass is obtained; scrape the bottom and sides of the bowl to ensure that there are no lumps. On low speed, slowly pour in the oil.

7. Pour the batter onto the prepared sheet. Spread the batter in an even layer using an offset spatula. Sprinkle the hazelnuts and the hazelnut croquant on top of the cake.

8. Bake until the cake turns a deep golden brown, 12 to 15 minutes.

9. Cool to room temperature, and then freeze. Once frozen, flip the cake onto another sheet pan lined with parchment paper. Peel the silpat off. Spread the melted chocolate quickly in a thin layer using an offset spatula, coating the entire base.

10. Once the layer of chocolate has set, cut out discs using a 12.5-cm/5-in ring cutter. If not assembling the cakes the same day the sponge is made, wrap each piece individually, label, date, and freeze. If frozen, they can keep for up to 2 months, or they can be refrigerated for up to 1 week. Keep these cakes frozen in a single layer; do not stack them.

MILK CHOCOLATE MOLECULES AND BUBBLE MILK CHOCOLATE DISCS

yield: 500 g/1 lb 1.6 oz (see Note)

INGREDIENT	METRIC	U.S.	%
Milk chocolate, melted but cool	417 g	14.7 oz	83.33%
Hazelnut oil	83 g	2.94 oz	16.67%

1. Assemble silicone sphere molds with the following diameters: 2.5 cm/1 in (6 molds), 2 cm/.75 in (6 molds), 1.25 cm/.5 in (6 molds). See Resources on page 540; these sphere molds will have a varying number of cavities. The larger ones typically have 5 cavities, and smaller ones can have up to 15. You would be hard-pressed to find single-cavity silicone sphere molds. These sphere molds are seamless, resulting in a near-perfect sphere shape. Gather 6 stainless steel or PVC rings with a 10-cm/4-in diameter and a height of at least .5 cm/.2 in. Line the inside of each ring with a strip of acetate to cover the interior of the ring completely. Have a ½-liter heavy cream whipper and three whipped cream charges on hand (see Resources, page 540).

2. Place the silicone molds on a half sheet pan. Place the stainless-steel rings on a sheet pan lined with a nonstick rubber mat.

3. Combine the melted but cool chocolate with the hazelnut oil.

4. Pour the mixture into the whipper canister and screw the top on; screw in the tip with the smallest spout. Load one charge and shake the whipper vigorously for 10 seconds. Load a second charge and whip vigorously again.

5. Gently pour the chocolate into the silicone molds, filling them to the top. Fill the stainless-steel rings as well, up to .5 cm/.2 in high.

6. Freeze the spheres and refrigerate the rings. If not using them soon, wrap them tightly with plastic once they have set. In these conditions they can keep for up to 2 months.

note This recipe is sufficient for 18 spheres (3 per cake, 3 different sizes, from large to small) and 6 inserts measuring 10 cm/4 in diameter and .5 cm/.2 in thick; one insert per cake.

MILK CHOCOLATE VELOUR SPRAY

yield: 200 g/7.05 oz

INGREDIENT	METRIC	U.S.	%
Milk chocolate coins	100 g	3.53 oz	50%
Cocoa butter (powder)	100 g	3.53 oz	50%

1. Combine both ingredients in a bowl and melt over a hot water bath.

2. Pass through a fine-mesh sieve and reserve in an airtight container in an area that is warm enough to keep the chocolate and the butter melted, ideally around 38°C/100°F. If kept in an airtight container, it can keep for up to 1 year.

note This velour or spray can be reserved at room temperature, but it will need to be remelted before using. The frosted or velour look is the result of spraying a warm or hot chocolate spray over a cold or preferably frozen cake.

variations For dark chocolate velour spray, substitute an equal amount of dark chocolate for the milk chocolate.

For white chocolate velour spray, substitute an equal amount of white chocolate for the milk chocolate.

MILK CHOCOLATE CURVED TRIANGLES

yield: **about 10 triangles**

INGREDIENT	METRIC	U.S.
Tempered milk chocolate	200 g	7.05 oz

1. Spread a thin layer of tempered chocolate over an acetate sheet using a small offset spatula. It will need to be spread at least 25 cm long by 15 cm wide/10 in long by 6 in wide.

2. When the chocolate is semi-set, cut out triangles that measure 20 cm long by 1.25 cm wide/8 in long by .5 in wide at the base. Use a ruler and the back of a paring knife to cut a straight line through the chocolate.

3. Before the chocolate sets, place it over a PVC tube or tube made from another material that is 12.5 cm/5 in diameter and at least 12.5 cm/5 in wide, with the chocolate side on the tube. Let the chocolate set on the tube so it will take on its curved shape.

4. Reserve in a cool, dry area. In these conditions they can keep for a year. Chocolate should be stored ideally in a Cres Cor environment without plastic wrap, but with a door to keep it protected.

note The recipe only requires 6 triangles, 1 for each cake; use the remaining triangles for future cakes.

BLACK FOREST CAKE V2.0

yield: 6 cakes

components

4 kg/8 lb 13.12 oz Devil's Food Cake

500 g/1 lb 1.6 oz Vanilla Chantilly rectangles

600 g/1 lb 5.12 oz Shaved Dark Chocolate Curls

1.2 kg/2 lb 10.4 oz Luxardo Cherries

4 kg/8 lb 13.12 oz Dark Chocolate Mousse

3 kg/6 lb 9.76 oz Shiny Dark Chocolate Glaze

100 g/3.53 oz white chocolate, chopped

12 "Tree" Imprint Chocolate Plaques

6 sheets gold leaf

1. Place 6 stainless-steel oblong oval molds 25 cm by 7.5 cm x 7.5 cm/10 in by 3 in by 3 in on a flat sheet pan lined with a sheet of acetate. Place this entire setup in a freezer.

2. Unwrap the devil's food cake cutouts and reserve frozen.

3. Unmold the vanilla Chantilly rectangles from the frames if they are not already unmolded. Use a torch to apply heat to the frame so that it slides out easily but not so much that it melts the Chantilly. Return the Chantilly rectangles to the freezer and keep them well covered so that they do not get frost on them. Have the shaved chocolate curls and cherries on hand.

4. Remove the frozen stainless-steel oblong molds from the freezer. Pipe chocolate mousse around the interior border of the mold first and then in an even layer over the base. This first layer should be about 2.5 cm/1 in thick.

5. Remove the vanilla Chantilly inserts from the freezer and place them over the mousse in the molds. Make sure they are centered, and push them down gently until enough mousse comes up the sides of the Chantilly insert to completely envelop its sides but not the top.

6. Pipe enough mousse on top of the Chantilly inserts to just cover them.

7. Gently place the shaved chocolate curls (except for the 18 reserved) on top of the mousse. To prevent air pockets from forming, make sure they do not come in contact with the mold.

8. Place a single layer of Luxardo cherries over the shaved chocolate, also making sure that they do not come in contact with the mold. Pipe more mousse around and on top of the cherries, making sure that this last layer is not too thick. There should be enough mousse so that when the devil's food cake is placed on top of it, the mousse comes up as evenly as possible with the top border of the mold.

9. Place the devil's food cake on top of the last layer of mousse, with the chocolate side facing up. Push in gently; this helps prevent air pockets because it will push down on the mousse and push any air pockets out. The cake and the mousse must be flush with the top of the mold. It's always better to have to pour some mousse out of the mold because there is too much than not to have enough. Also, it won't matter if the cake and some mousse come up slightly above the mold, because next you place a sheet of acetate on top of the cakes, and then a sheet pan on top of the acetate, and then a weight on top of that.

10. Freeze until hardened. Once frozen, take the weight and the top sheet pan off. Leave the acetate on for extra freezer protection, then wrap the entire sheet pan well with plastic and label it. The better it is wrapped, the longer it will keep in the freezer. The wrapping will keep frost from forming on the cake.

11. **TO FINISH THE CAKE:** Melt the shiny chocolate glaze over a hot water bath. Don't stir too much; this will prevent small bubbles from forming. It will be ready for glazing when it reaches between 38°C and 43°C/100°F and 110°F.

12. Meanwhile, line a sheet pan with parchment paper and place a wire rack on top of it. Have a torch and a cake stand ready.

13. Cut out 6 pieces of cake cardboard that measure 13.75 by 5 cm/8.25 by 2 in.

14. Melt the white chocolate and put it in a cornet; keep it warm to prevent it from setting.

15. Remove the cakes from the freezer. Place one cake on a previously cut cake cardboard and then place this setup on a cake stand.

16. Using a torch, gently warm only the mold just enough so that it can easily be pulled up without damaging the smoothness and integrity of the cake. Be sure to spin the cake stand and keep the torch steady. This step takes some practice to gauge how much heat to apply, since too much will melt the cake, but too little will prevent the mold from coming out cleanly and leave marks on the cake. Place the unmolded cake on the prepared sheet pan with the wire rack.

17. Repeat this step with the remaining cakes. Return them to the freezer for 30 minutes.

18. By this time the glaze should have reached the ideal temperature. Pour the glaze into a funnel and place the funnel on its stand.

19. Remove the cakes from the freezer. Pour the glaze over the cakes in an even coat. Make sure that the entire surface (top and sides) is covered. If the glaze is at the right temperature, the mousse will not be seen through it and it won't have trickle marks down the base; it will have a smooth, clean, even look. Do not return the cakes to the freezer to set the glaze. The gelatin in the glaze will set on the cakes without any trouble, since the cakes should be frozen. If the cakes are returned to the freezer, they will get frost on them and take on a dull look. If there are some trickle drops down the base of the cake, simply dip a paring knife in warm water, dry it, and cut through the trickle marks to even the glaze out.

20. Once the glaze is set, cut a small tip off the cornet with white chocolate. Draw a single thin, straight, vertical line across all of the cakes. It is important that the glaze is set so that the line of white chocolate does not sink into the glaze.

21. Place 3 of the reserved chocolate curls on top of each cake, close to the front end. Stack the curls to give them height. Lean a "tree" plaque against the stacked curls, so that it is standing at a 90-degree angle.

22. Place a sheet of edible gold leaf on the front end of the cake.

23. Before the cakes thaw completely, transfer them to the cake boards on which they will be displayed. Carefully lift each cake with a large, flat, wide, sturdy, stainless-steel offset spatula and gently slide it onto the desired cake board.

24. Let the cakes thaw in the refrigerator before serving. Display them for a maximum of 36 hours. The cakes should ideally be tempered for 30 to 45 minutes before eating for the best texture. Advise your customers of this.

DEVIL'S FOOD CAKE

yield: 4 kg/8 lb 13.12 oz

INGREDIENT	METRIC	U.S.	%
Sugar	1.12 kg	2 lb 7.52 oz	28.03%
Pastry flour	323 g	11.4 oz	8.08%
Bread flour	323 g	11.4 oz	8.08%
Cocoa powder	303 g	10.69 oz	7.58%
Baking soda	10 g	.36 oz	.25%
Baking powder	5 g	.18 oz	.13%
Salt	3 g	.11 oz	.08%
Eggs	356 g	12.57 oz	8.91%
Egg yolks	143 g	5.03 oz	3.56%
Butter, melted but cool	152 g	5.34 oz	3.79%
Buttermilk	654 g	1 lb 7.04 oz	16.35%
Coffee, freshly brewed	607 g	1 lb 5.44 oz	15.17%
Dark chocolate (64%) coins, melted	500 g	1 lb 1.6 oz	

1. Line a sheet pan with a nonstick rubber mat; spray the borders with nonstick oil spray.

2. Preheat a convection oven to 160°C/320°F.

3. Sift all of the dry ingredients onto a sheet of parchment paper.

4. Bring all of the liquids, including the melted butter, up to 21°C/70°F. Place the eggs and the egg yolks in a bowl large enough to hold all of the ingredients in the recipe, and then slowly whisk in the melted butter. Slowly whisk in the buttermilk and, finally, the coffee.

5. Whisk the dry ingredients into the emulsified liquid, whisking constantly until a homogeneous mass is obtained.

6. Pour the batter onto the prepared sheet pan and spread it out evenly using an offset spatula.

7. Bake for 10 minutes, rotate the sheet pan, and bake for 7 to 9 more minutes or until the cake springs back when gentle pressure is applied with the fingertips. Check for doneness with a toothpick at the center of the sheet pan if you are not sure. Alternatively, press the middle of the cake with your finger; if it springs back, it is done.

8. Let the cake cool to room temperature, and then freeze it. It cuts a lot more cleanly once it is frozen. Flip the cake over and peel the nonstick rubber mat off. Pour the dark chocolate all over the cake once the cake is frozen. Try to obtain a thin coat of chocolate all over the cake by spreading it with an offset spatula. This thin layer of chocolate will keep the cake from sticking to the board it will be presented and sold on. Place the cake back in the freezer.

9. Once it is frozen hard, cut out 6 cakes that measure 21 by 5 cm/8.25 by 2 in.

10. Wrap the cutout cakes individually with plastic, label, and reserve frozen. They will keep for up to 2 months frozen. Do not stack them.

VANILLA CHANTILLY

yield: 500 g/1 lb 1.6 oz

INGREDIENT	METRIC	U.S.	%
UHT heavy cream	452 g	15.96 oz	90.5%
Tahitian vanilla powder	1 g	.05 oz	.27%
Superfine sugar	41 g	1.44 oz	8.14%
Heavy cream stabilizer	5 g	.19 oz	1.09%

1. Place 6 stainless-steel or aluminum frames 13.75 by 5 by 1.25 cm/8.25 by 2 by .5 in on a half sheet pan lined with a sheet of acetate.

2. Whip all of the ingredients together to stiff peaks. Pipe the whipped Chantilly into the prepared frames, making sure to get into all the corners. Even out the top with a small offset spatula. Cover with acetate, place a flat half sheet pan on top of the acetate, and then freeze until hardened.

3. Once the Chantilly is frozen, wrap the entire sheet pan with plastic, label it, and reserve frozen. Alternatively, unmold the rectangles by warming the frame with a torch with just enough heat so that the frames slide off without melting the Chantilly. Harden them again in the freezer, wrap them tightly in plastic, label the sheet pan, and freeze it. The Chantilly rectangles will keep for up to 2 months frozen.

SHAVED CHOCOLATE CURLS

yield: 600 g/1 lb 5.12 oz

INGREDIENT	METRIC	U.S.
Dark chocolate (60%) block	5 kg	11 lb .32 oz

1. Place the full block of dark chocolate on a sheet of parchment paper.

2. Using a chef's knife, in a curved front-to-back motion and pressing down firmly with the knife, scrape the knife against the block, pulling the knife toward you to obtain as many curls as you need. Reserve in a single layer; if they are stacked they will get damaged. Avoid handling them with your hands, since they are so thin that your hands can melt them.

3. Set 18 of the largest curls aside; they will be used to garnish the top of the cake. Reserve all of the curls refrigerated until needed.

note The recipe requires about 100 g/3.53 oz of chocolate curls per cake. It is better not to move the curls around too much. For example, moving them to a container to weigh them will damage them. Shave a test batch, weigh it to see what it looks like, then make similar amounts for the actual cakes so that they don't have to be weighed out. For the best results, this step should be done right before assembling the cake to maintain the integrity of the curls.

LUXARDO CHERRIES

INGREDIENT	METRIC	U.S.
Luxardo cherries, drained	1.2 kg	2 lb 10.4 oz

After straining the cherries out of the syrup, pat the cherries dry. Reserve the cherries, covered, at room temperature until needed.

notes Luxardo is a name brand, not a variety of cherry. These cherries come in a jar; they are of the highest quality as far as preserved cherries go (see Resources, page 540). If you cannot find them, there are other suitable replacements. However, do not substitute with maraschino cherries.

The required weight refers to the drained mass of cherries, not the cherries with the liquid.

DARK CHOCOLATE MOUSSE

yield: 4 kg/8 lb 13.12 oz

INGREDIENT	METRIC	U.S.	%
Eggs	810 g	1 lb 12.48 oz	20.24%
Sugar	333 g	11.76 oz	8.33%
Dark chocolate (64%) coins	1.07 kg	2 lb 5.76 oz	26.79%
Heavy cream	1.78 kg	3 lb 15.04 oz	44.64%

1. Combine the eggs with the sugar in a bowl and bring the mixture up to 60°C/140°F over a hot water bath while stirring constantly.

2. Remove the mixture from the heat and pour it into the bowl of an electric mixer. Whip on high speed until it cools to 35°C/95°F and creates ribbons, about 10 minutes. Meanwhile, melt the chocolate over a hot water bath or in a microwave. Let it cool to 35°C/95°F.

3. Once both the egg mixture and the chocolate are at the right temperature, strain the egg mixture through a sieve over the chocolate and mix with a whisk until a homogeneous mass is obtained.

4. Whip the heavy cream to medium peaks.

5. Fold half of the whipped cream into the chocolate mixture. Fold in the remaining whipped cream. Fill a piping bag with the mousse and follow the instructions for finishing the cake.

SHINY DARK CHOCOLATE GLAZE

yield: 3 kg/6 lb 9.76 oz

INGREDIENT	METRIC	U.S.	%
Sugar	1.24 kg	2 lb 11.84 oz	41.49%
Water	657 g	1 lb 7.2 oz	21.9%
Cocoa powder	380 g	13.42 oz	12.68%
Crème fraîche	380 g	13.42 oz	12.68%
Dark chocolate (55%) coins	277 g	9.75 oz	9.22%
Gelatin sheets, bloomed in cold water (17.5 sheets)	61 g	2.15 oz	2.03%

1. Bring the sugar, water, cocoa powder, and crème fraîche to a boil while stirring constantly.

2. Once the mixture comes to a boil, stir in the chocolate and mix until dissolved.

3. Squeeze the excess water off the bloomed gelatin, add it to the pot, and stir until dissolved.

4. Pass the mixture through a fine-mesh sieve.

5. Cool over an ice bath until completely cool.

6. Once cooled, transfer to an airtight container and refrigerate. The glaze will keep for up to 10 days in the refrigerator.

note Each cake will need about 500 g/1 lb 1.6 oz of glaze, including the runoff. It is always necessary to make more glaze than needed, because the entire cake needs to be covered with glaze. As the glaze is poured over the cake, some will pour off, resulting in an even coat. The total amount that will stay on each cake is about 300 g/10.58 oz.

"TREE" IMPRINT CHOCOLATE PLAQUES

yield: about 12 plaques

INGREDIENT	METRIC	U.S.	%
Dark chocolate (72%), low viscosity, melted	50 g	1.76 oz	20%
White chocolate, tempered	200 g	7.05 oz	80%

1. Place a silk screen (see Note) over an acetate sheet that measures 21.5 by 28.75 cm/8.5 by 11 in, or about the same as a regular sheet of paper. It will be the same size as the silk screen. Tape the border of the silk screen down to the work surface to keep it from moving.

2. Pour the dark chocolate over the top part of the screen. Using a bench knife, spread the chocolate toward the bottom, pushing down firmly, keeping the frame steady with your other hand.

3. Lift the silk screen carefully. The chocolate will set very quickly because it is very thin; this is why there is no need to temper it.

4. Once the "tree" images have set, pour the tempered white chocolate over them, and spread it very thin using an offset spatula.

5. When the white chocolate is semi-set, using the back of a paring knife and a ruler, cut the tree plaques out. Each plaque should have the complete image of one tree, and all plaques should be the same size.

6. Flip the acetate over onto a flat sheet pan lined with a sheet of parchment paper and place a weight on top of it, such as stack of nonstick rubber mats, to keep the décor flat. Let it set at room temperature. The plaques will keep for up to a year in a cool, dry place.

note This plaque requires a custom-made silk screen. Silk screens are typically used to transfer precise images onto clothing or paper, but they work very well with chocolate as long as it is of high viscosity (thick rather than thin; thin or low-viscosity chocolate will not leave a proper imprint). For custom-made silk screens, see Resources, page 540. The image of the tree can be obtained on the Internet, and it can be any tree, but the size should be about 3.75 cm tall by 2.5 cm wide/1.5 in tall by 1 in wide. Paste the images into a regular Word document in such a way that they are evenly spaced out and that twelve (3x4) images can fit on a sheet of paper. This will be the image that the manufacturer will use to make the silk screen. This method is very useful for any other custom-made transfer sheets (see sidebar, page 130).

ESPRESSO CREAM, CRISP CHOCOLATE MERINGUE, AND FLOURLESS CHOCOLATE CAKE

yield: **6 cakes**

components

6 Flourless Chocolate Cake discs

4.5 kg/9 lb 14.72 oz Espresso Cream

6 Crisp Chocolate Meringue discs

600 g/1 lb 5.12 oz Dark Chocolate Velour (page 140–141)

300 g/10.58 oz White Chocolate Velour (page 140–141)

200 g/7.05 oz dark chocolate, chopped

120 g/4.23 oz white, milk, and dark chocolate-covered puffed rice (see Resources, page 540)

1. Assemble 6 silicone molds (or any other cake mold) on a sheet pan. Unwrap the flourless chocolate cake discs, but keep them frozen until the last minute.

2. Place a thick, square silicone insert 5 by 1.25 cm/ 2 in by .5 in inside each silicone mold, directly in contact with the base of the cake mold. This will be taken off once the cake is ready to be sprayed, giving the cake an inverted square where the chocolate-covered puffed rice will be placed.

3. Pipe the espresso cream into the mold, filling it one-third of the way and making sure to get into all the nooks to prevent any air pockets from forming. It helps to have the tip of the piping bag completely submerged in the cream, which will decrease the formation of air pockets coming out of the bag.

4. Place a disc of chocolate meringue on top of the cream, making sure it is centered. Pipe more cream in, around, and on top of the meringue, until the mold is filled to about 3 mm/ .12 in from the top.

5. Place a disc of flourless chocolate cake on top of the cream and press down gently. It is fine if there is some cream coming up the sides of the cake, overflowing the mold.

6. Place a sheet of acetate on top of the cakes, then a flat sheet pan on top. Place a weight such as a heavy cutting board on top of the top sheet pan, and freeze until hardened.

7. **TO FINISH THE CAKE:** Freeze the cakes in a blast freezer set at −38°C/−36°F. This type of mold might crack the cake while it is being removed, so the cakes need to be frozen hard to unmold.

8. Set up an area for spraying the chocolate. Warm both the dark and white chocolate velours to 37°C/100°F.

9. Line a sheet pan with parchment paper and place a wire rack on top of it.

10. Melt the dark chocolate and keep it in a piping bag in a warm place to prevent the chocolate from setting.

11. Once the cakes have completely hardened, peel the silicone molds off carefully and place the cakes on the wire rack. Remove the silicone squares carefully from the tops of the cakes, trying not to damage the surfaces of the cakes. Use the tip of a paring knife or a scribe (a pin-like instrument with a handle). Since the cakes are still frozen, they don't need to be refrozen to spray them.

12. Spray a coat of dark chocolate spray all over the cakes, rotating the sheet pan 90 degrees at even intervals to give the cake an even coat.

13. Switch to white chocolate spray, and spray only on one half of each of the cakes.

14. Transfer the cakes to the cake board or base on which they will be displayed or presented. Use a wide, sturdy, stainless-steel offset spatula to carefully lift the cakes from the wire rack and slide them onto the cake board or base.

15. Pipe about 25 g/.88 oz of the melted chocolate into the inverted square (the imprint that the silicone square left once it was removed), and then pour in about 20 g/.7 oz of white, milk, and dark chocolate–covered puffed rice on top of the chocolate. Do this with one cake at a time since the frozen cake will set the melted chocolate very quickly.

16. Thaw the cakes in the refrigerator before presenting or placing them in the display case. The cake should ideally be tempered for 30 to 45 minutes before it is eaten. Advise your customers of this.

the blast freezer

AS I WAS WRITING THIS BOOK, I kept saying to myself, "Everyone should have a blast freezer." As I wrote the recipes that required that items be frozen, and frozen hard, I was only hoping that all of the people reading this book would at least have a solid, dependable freezer, a good degree of patience, and good timing skills so as to have their product nice and frozen before proceeding to the next step.

There are three negative sides to owning a blast freezer. They are big, so they take up a lot of space, and in many restaurants every square foot is prime real estate. Even the smallest blast freezers take up a lot of room because, in order to be able to freeze at the temperatures they freeze (on average they can drop to –38°C/–36°F in fifteen minutes), they need to have massive compressors. Another downside is the level of noise they produce as they blast-freeze. You find yourself shouting to a person standing two feet from you. The third negative aspect is the actual cost of a quality blast freezer. It is certainly in the five digits.

However, I will take those negative points any day for the convenience these freezers can provide. It takes a relatively short amount of time to assemble cakes and petits plaisirs when their components can harden quickly and then be ready for the next component to be poured in. The blast freezer is really a tool of efficiency and speed. It is still worth every penny to invest in one.

FLOURLESS CHOCOLATE CAKE

yield: 1 sheet pan (about eight 15-cm/6-in cake discs; the recipe requires six)

INGREDIENT	METRIC	U.S.	%
Egg yolks	200 g	7.05 oz	15.09%
Sugar	150 g	5.29 oz	11.32%
Dark chocolate (64%) coins	450 g	15.87 oz	33.96%
Butter	225 g	7.94 oz	16.98%
Egg whites	300 g	10.58 oz	22.64%
Dark chocolate (55%), melted	500 g	1 lb 1.6 oz	

1. Grease a sheet pan with a coat of nonstick oil spray. Line the sheet pan with a sheet of silicone paper, smoothing the paper with your hands or a bench knife so that there are no air pockets or wrinkles in the paper.

2. Preheat a convection oven to 160°C/320°F.

3. Whip the egg yolks with 120 g/4.23 oz sugar until thickened and pale yellow in color (the ribbon stage) with a mixer on high speed. Meanwhile, melt the chocolate with the butter over a hot water bath.

4. Once the chocolate and butter are melted, combine them with the ribboned egg yolks, using a whisk to obtain a homogeneous mass.

5. Whip the egg whites with the remaining sugar on high speed until the meringue achieves a medium-stiff peak. Fold the whipped whites into the chocolate-egg mixture in 2 additions.

6. Pour the batter into the prepared sheet pan and even it out using an offset spatula.

7. Bake until firm, 7 to 9 minutes. The cake will bubble while it bakes because there is no flour to keep the structure of the cake from doing so. Do not test the doneness with a toothpick; when it is done, there will be no wet spots on the surface.

8. Once the cake is baked, cool it to room temperature, and then freeze it.

9. Once frozen, pass the back of a paring knife around the border of the cake and remove the cake from the sheet pan. Flip it over onto a cutting board, peel the silicone paper off, and quickly spread the melted chocolate evenly in a thin coat all over the cake using an offset spatula. The chocolate will set on contact with the frozen cake.

10. Cut the cake into 15-cm/6-in discs using a ring cutter. Reserve the cakes, individually wrapped, in a freezer. Keep them flat; do not stack them because they will lose their shape easily. The cakes will keep for up to 2 months frozen.

ESPRESSO CREAM

yield: 4.5 kg/9 lb 14.72 oz

INGREDIENT	METRIC	U.S.	%
ESPRESSO ANGLAISE			
Heavy cream	1.41 kg	3 lb 1.8 oz	28.51%
Milk	912 g	2 lb .16 oz	28.51%
Espresso coffee beans	128 g	4.52 oz	4.01%
Sugar	684 g	1 lb 8.16 oz	21.38%
Egg yolks	563 g	1 lb 3.84 oz	17.6%
ESPRESSO CREAM			
Heavy cream	1.75 kg	3 lb 13.92 oz	38.99%
Heavy cream stabilizer (liquid)	35 g	1.24 oz	.78%
Gelatin sheets, bloomed in cold water (22.5 sheets)	79 g	2.78 oz	1.75%
Espresso Anglaise	2.63 kg	5 lb 12.8 oz	58.48%

1. **TO MAKE THE ESPRESSO ANGLAISE:** Bring the heavy cream and the milk to a simmer. Grind the coffee beans finely in a coffee grinder just before using to obtain the best flavor possible. Ideally, use a dark French roast type of coffee bean, which has a more pronounced flavor. Add the freshly ground coffee beans to the simmered heavy cream and milk off the heat. Stir, cover with plastic wrap, and steep for 10 minutes. Strain the coffee cream through a fine-mesh sieve and cool over an ice bath.

2. Once the heavy cream has reached 4°C/39°F, weigh out 912 g/2 lb .17 oz of the steeped cream. The extra heavy cream was used because when steeping or infusing any ingredient, the solids will absorb some of the liquid, subtracting from the amount needed in the recipe. It's always good to add a little more than what is needed. If there is some steeped liquid left over, save it for future use.

3. Prepare an ice bath.

4. Place the steeped cream mixture, and half of the sugar in a sauce pot. Bring to a boil over high heat.

5. Meanwhile, combine the remaining sugar with the egg yolks in a bowl. Once the cream mixture has boiled, temper the egg yolk–sugar mixture into it (see page 138).

6. Bring the liquid up to a nappé consistency (82°C/180F°) while stirring continuously. Remove the pot from the heat and stir for 2 more minutes. Strain the finished anglaise through a fine-mesh sieve and cool it over the prepared ice bath.

7. Once the anglaise has cooled down, make the espresso cream or transfer it to an airtight container. It can be refrigerated for 4 days. Alternatively, seal the anglaise using Cryovac and freeze it. It will keep for up to 2 months in the freezer.

8. **TO MAKE THE ESPRESSO CREAM:** While the anglaise is cooling off, whip the heavy cream with the liquid stabilizer to medium peaks. Reserve refrigerated until needed.

9. Squeeze the excess water off the bloomed gelatin sheets. Place one-quarter of the anglaise in a bowl with the gelatin. Place the bowl over a hot water bath and stir until the gelatin has dissolved. Once the gelatin has melted, remove the bowl from the heat. Add the remaining anglaise to the bowl and whisk to incorporate. If it feels too warm, let the anglaise cool for a few minutes until it reaches 30°C/86°F.

10. Fold in the whipped heavy cream in 2 additions. Fill a piping bag with the cream and follow instructions for assembling cake.

note You will need less espresso anglaise (2.63 kg/5 lb 12.8 oz) to make the espresso cream than the recipe yields (3.7 kg/8.16 lb), but there will be some evaporation during the cooking and cooling-down process.

CRISP CHOCOLATE MERINGUE

yield: 6 meringue discs (900 g/1 lb 15.68 oz; 150 g/5.3 oz per disc)

INGREDIENT	METRIC	U.S.	%
Confectioners' sugar	150 g	5.29 oz	16.67%
Cocoa powder	150 g	5.29 oz	16.67%
Egg whites (at 21°C/70°F)	300 g	10.58 oz	33.33%
Superfine or bakers' sugar	300 g	10.58 oz	33.33%
Dark chocolate couverture, melted	500 g	1 lb 1.6 oz	

1. Using a 15-cm/6-in cake ring and a marker, draw 6 evenly spaced circles on a sheet of parchment paper. Put the sheet of parchment paper on a sheet pan, and then place a nonstick rubber mat on top of the stencil.

2. Preheat a convection oven to 85°C/185°F. Open the vent.

3. Sift the confectioners' sugar and the cocoa powder separately. Whip the egg whites and superfine sugar together on high speed in an electric mixer. Once the whites have reached the stiff-peak stage, turn the mixer down to low speed and slowly pour in the sifted confectioners' sugar. Continue to whip until the meringue thickens, 5 to 7 minutes. The egg whites will not overwhip at this point; since there is such a large amount of sugar in the whites, the meringue is completely stabilized.

4. Take the whipped egg whites off the mixer and fold in the cocoa powder by hand. Transfer the meringue to a piping bag fitted with a #4 plain piping tip.

5. Pipe the meringue in a spiral shape onto the prepared stencils.

6. Bake the meringues until they are crisp and completely dried out, about 2 hours.

7. Let the meringues cool to room temperature. Once they have cooled, gently take them off the nonstick rubber mat and coat each one in the melted couverture. Dip each meringue individually and then return the coated meringues to the nonstick rubber mat so that the couverture can set.

8. Once set, wrap the entire sheet pan with plastic and reserve at room temperature in a cool, dry place. The meringues will keep for 3 months.

note When making the meringue, it is important to add the superfine sugar to the egg whites at the beginning so that it can dissolve completely in the egg whites. General meringue mixing principles dictate to add the sugar once the egg whites have almost reached full volume. This holds some truth to it, but the egg whites with the sugar added at the beginning will eventually achieve the same volume as that of the whites with the sugar added later, plus they will be more stable, since sugar acts as a stabilizer. Also, the sugar will not be dissolved completely.

TAHITIAN VANILLA CREAM, LEMON CURD, HUCKLEBERRY COMPOTE, AND CRÈME FRAÎCHE CAKE WITH CRÈME FRAÎCHE DOMES AND PURPLE VELVET

yield: 6 cakes

components

9 kg/19 lb 13.44 oz Tahitian Vanilla Cream

6 Huckleberry Compote squares

6 Lemon Curd squares

6 Crème Fraîche Cake squares

24 Crème Fraîche Domes

600 g/1 lb 5.12 oz Purple Velvet

30g/1.06 oz Pistachio Powder

6 letter "H" Huckleberry Gelées

30 g/1.06 oz crystallized mimosa flowers (see Resources, page 540)

1. Assemble 6 curved-square stainless-steel or aluminum molds (see Resources, page 540), 17.5 cm square by 6.25 cm deep/7 by 2.5 in, on a large sheet pan lined with acetate. Place this setup in the freezer.

2. Pipe the vanilla cream into the frozen square frames until it comes 2.5 cm/1 in up the sides of the molds.

3. Place the frozen huckleberry compote squares on top of the piped vanilla cream and gently press them in.

4. Pipe more vanilla cream around and on top of the huckleberries until it comes two-thirds of the way up the mold. Place the lemon curd squares on top of the second layer of vanilla cream, making sure they are centered in the molds. Press them down gently until the vanilla cream comes halfway up the lemon curd squares.

5. Pipe more vanilla cream only around the curd, not on top. Place a square of crème fraîche cake directly on the curd. Push down until the cake is flush with the top of the mold.

6. Once all of the molds are filled, place an acetate sheet on top of the cakes, then a flat sheet pan, and then a heavy cutting board on top of that to level out the cakes. Freeze until hardened.

7. Once they have hardened, wrap each cake individually in plastic, label it, and freeze it. The cakes will keep for up to 2 months in the freezer.

8. **TO FINISH THE CAKES:** Unmold the cakes by applying direct heat to the frames with a torch. Place the cake on a cake board that is smaller than its base, then place it on a cake stand and spin it while applying heat to the frame. Apply enough heat so that the mold slides off easily.

9. Place the cakes on a sheet pan lined with parchment paper with a wire rack set on top of it. Place 4 crème fraîche domes on top of each cake, each within 2.5 cm/1 in from the corner. Return the cakes to the freezer to harden.

10. Set up a spray area (see page 135). Warm the purple velvet spray to 38°C/100°F in a microwave or over a hot water bath.

11. Fill the spray paint gun or a compressor tank with the purple velvet.

12. Spray the cakes only when they are completely frozen. Spray an even coat of purple velvet over the entire surface of the cakes; rotate the cakes 90 degrees every time one side has been completely coated in purple spray.

13. Transfer the cakes to the cake board or base on which they will be displayed or presented.

14. Place a rectangular stencil or cutter 5 by 7.5 cm/2 by 3 in on top of the cake. Sprinkle about 5 g/.2 oz of pistachio powder into it. Place a frozen huckleberry "H" on top of the cake. Sprinkle about 5 g/.2 oz of candied mimosas randomly around the surface of the cake.

15. Wrap the base of the cake with the ribbon of your choice.

16. Thaw them in the refrigerator before they are displayed. The cakes should ideally be tempered for 30 to 45 minutes before they are eaten. Advise your customers of this.

LEMON CURD

yield: 3 kg/6 lb 9.76

INGREDIENT	METRIC	U.S.	%
Lemon juice	456 g	1 lb .16 oz	15.21%
Sugar	913 g	2 lb .16 oz	30.42%
Eggs	456 g	1 lb .16 oz	15.21%
Gelatin sheets, bloomed (9.7 sheets)	34 g	1.19 oz	1.13%
Butter	1.14 kg	2 lb 8.32 oz	38.03%

1. To make the curd, see the procedure on page 16. Add the gelatin to the mixture before adding the butter. Stir until it has dissolved, and then add the butter.

2. Once the curd has cooled, place 6 frames measuring 12.5 cm square by 2.5 cm deep/5 by 1 in on a half sheet pan lined with acetate. Pipe the curd into the frames and even out the top with an offset spatula. Freeze until hardened.

3. Once the squares have hardened, unmold them if using right away. Otherwise, wrap the sheet pan with plastic, label it, and freeze it. The curd will keep for up to 2 months in the freezer.

4. **TO UNMOLD:** Place a curd square on a cake stand and apply direct heat to the frame while spinning the cake stand and keeping the torch in place. Take the frame off the curd and return the curd to the freezer. Once all of the curd squares have been unmolded, cover them in plastic and reserve them frozen until needed.

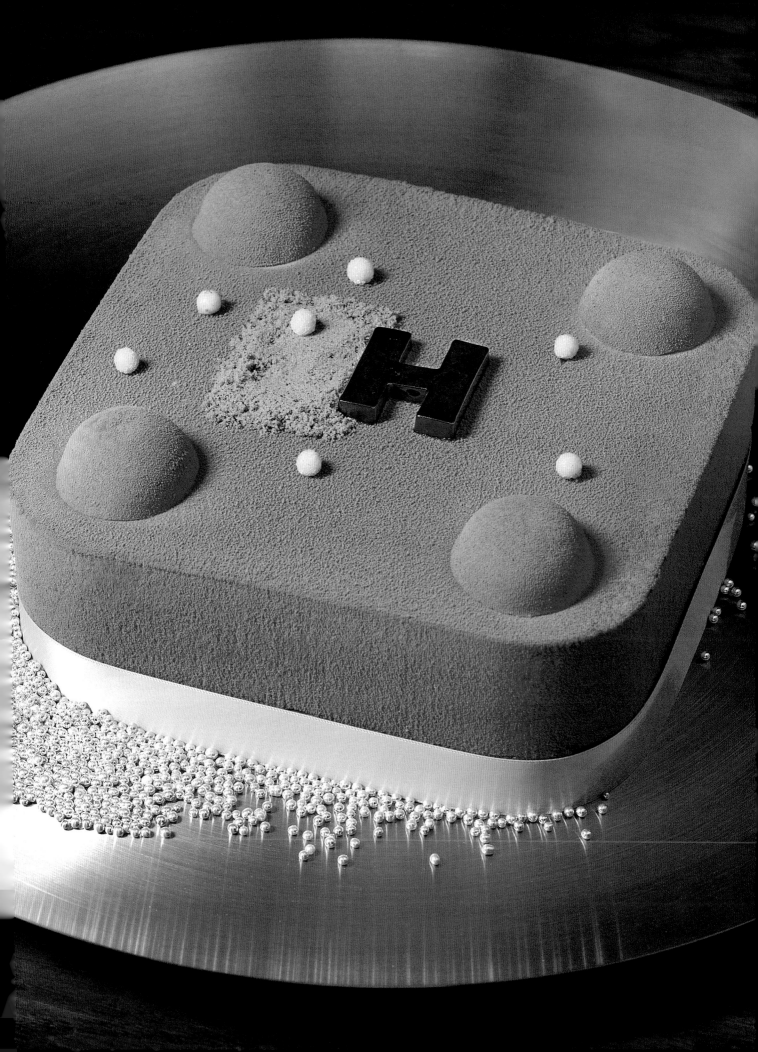

TAHITIAN VANILLA CREAM

yield: 9 kg/19 lb 13.44 oz

INGREDIENT	METRIC	U.S.	%
VANILLA ANGLAISE			
Milk	2.17 kg	4 lb 12.8 oz	29.03%
Heavy cream	2.17 kg	4 lb 12.8 oz	29.03%
Sugar	1.8 kg	3 lb 15.52 oz	24.01%
Tahitian vanilla pods, split and scraped	7	7	
Egg yolks	1.34 kg	2 lb 15.36 oz	17.93%
TAHITIAN VANILLA CREAM			
Heavy cream	3.52 kg	7 lb 12.48 oz	39.22%
Heavy cream stabilizer (liquid)	71 g	2.49 oz	.78%
Gelatin sheets, bloomed (30.3 sheets)	106 g	3.73 oz	1.18%
Vanilla Anglaise	5.29 kg	11 lb 10.72 oz	58.82%

1. **FOR THE VANILLA ANGLAISE:** Prepare an ice bath.

2. Place the milk, cream, and half of the sugar in a sauce pot with the vanilla pods and seeds and bring to a boil.

3. Meanwhile, combine the remaining sugar with the egg yolks in a bowl. Once the milk mixture has boiled, temper in the egg yolk–sugar mixture (see page 138).

4. Bring the liquid to 82°C/180°F, or nappé consistency, while stirring constantly. Remove the pot from the heat and stir for 2 more minutes. Strain the finished anglaise through a fine-mesh sieve and cool it over the prepared ice bath.

5. Once it has cooled, make the cream, or transfer the anglaise to an airtight container. It can be refrigerated for 4 days. Alternatively, it can be sealed by Cryovac and frozen. It will keep for up to 2 months in the freezer.

6. **FOR THE TAHITIAN VANILLA CREAM:** Whip the cream and the stabilizer to medium peaks; reserve refrigerated.

7. Squeeze the excess water off the bloomed gelatin sheets. Place one-quarter of the anglaise in a bowl with the gelatin sheets. Place the bowl over a hot water bath and stir until the gelatin has dissolved.

8. Once the gelatin has melted, remove the bowl from the heat. Add the remaining anglaise to the bowl and whisk to incorporate. If it feels too warm, let the anglaise cool for a few minutes, until it reaches 30°C/86°F.

9. Fold in the whipped heavy cream to the anglaise in 2 additions. Fill a piping bag with the cream. Immediately follow the instructions for finishing the cake.

note The vanilla cream will need less crème anglaise than the recipe makes, but there will be some evaporation during the cooking and cooling process.

HUCKLEBERRY COMPOTE

INGREDIENT	METRIC	U.S.	%
Huckleberries	1.3 kg	2 lb 13.92 oz	50%
Sugar	1 kg	2 lb 3.2 oz	38.46%
Water	300 g	10.58 oz	11.54%

1. Combine all of the ingredients in a sauce pot and bring to a boil. Lower the heat to a simmer and cook for 5 more minutes. The once-plump huckleberries will now resemble raisins. Remove the pot from the heat and transfer the contents to a hotel pan to cool.

2. Once the mixture has cooled, strain out the liquid and reserve it in a container in the refrigerator. This liquid will be used to make the huckleberry gelée letters.

3. Pat the huckleberries dry with paper towels.

4. Place a sheet of acetate on a sheet pan and 6 frames measuring 12.5 cm square by 2.5 cm/5 by 1 in deep on the acetate.

5. Put a single layer of huckleberries into each frame and freeze them. Once they are frozen, take the frames off, and place another sheet of acetate on top of them. Wrap the sheet pan with plastic, label it, and reserve it frozen. The compote will keep for up to 2 months frozen.

note The recipe total is larger than the yield because the yield accounts for the drained mass, and there also will be some water evaporation.

CRÈME FRAÎCHE DOMES

INGREDIENT	METRIC	U.S.	%
Crème fraîche	611 g	1 lb 5.6 oz	40.74%
Heavy cream	611 g	1 lb 5.6 oz	40.74%
Sugar	278 g	9.8 oz	18.52%

1. Place all of the ingredients in the bowl of an electric mixer fitted with the whip attachment and whip on high speed until stiff.

2. Place the whipped crème fraîche into a piping bag.

3. Put a demi-sphere fleximold sheet with 3.13-cm-/1.25-in-diameter domes on a sheet pan. Pipe the whipped crème fraîche into the domes and smooth out the tops with an offset spatula. Freeze until hardened.

4. Once they have hardened, wrap the sheet pan with plastic, label it, and freeze it for up to 2 months. Otherwise, if assembling the cakes, unmold the domes, cover them with plastic, and reserve them frozen until needed.

note This recipe yields enough to make about 54 domes, and each cake uses 4 domes.

CRÈME FRAÎCHE CAKE

yield: 1.5 kg/3 lb 4.96 oz (1 half sheet pan)

INGREDIENT	METRIC	U.S.	%
All-purpose flour	264 g	9.31 oz	17.6%
Baking powder	22 g	.78 oz	1.47%
Salt	4 g	.13 oz	.25%
Tahitian vanilla powder	2 g	.06 oz	.12%
Butter, at 21°C/70°F	278 g	9.8 oz	18.53%
Superfine or bakers' sugar	250 g	8.82 oz	16.67%
Eggs, at 21°C/70°F	184 g	6.48 oz	12.26%
Crème fraîche, at 21°C/70°F	497 g	1 lb .96 oz	33.11%

1. Spray the inside border of a half sheet pan with nonstick oil spray, then place a half sheet nonstick rubber mat on the sheet pan.

2. Preheat a convection oven to 160C°/320°F.

3. Sift the flour, baking powder, salt, and vanilla powder together.

4. Cream the butter with the sugar in an electric mixer fitted with the paddle attachment on high speed until it is light and fluffy, 4 to 5 minutes.

5. Add the eggs in 4 additions; stop, drop the bowl, and scrape down the bowl and paddle between each addition.

6. Add the dry ingredients and pulse the mixer until a homogeneous mass is obtained. Be careful to not overmix the batter.

7. Add the crème fraîche and pulse the mixer until a homogeneous mass is obtained.

8. Pour the batter onto the prepared sheet pan and spread it out in an even layer using an offset spatula.

9. Bake until golden brown, 13 to 15 minutes.

10. Cool to room temperature, and then refrigerate. Once the cake is cold, flip it over onto a cutting board and cut out 12.5-cm/5-in squares. Reserve covered in plastic wrap in a freezer in a single layer. Do not stack them or they will stick to each other. The cakes will keep for up to 2 months in the freezer and 1 week in the refrigerator.

PURPLE VELVET

yield: 600 g/1 lb 5.12 oz

INGREDIENT	METRIC	U.S.
Cocoa butter (Mycryo)	600 g	1 lb 5.12 oz
Violet food coloring (liquid, fat based)	as needed	as needed

1. Melt the cocoa butter over a hot water bath. Stir in enough drops of purple food coloring to obtain a deep purple color. It will keep for up to 6 months at room temperature.

2. The purple velvet spray can be made ahead of time and melted to 38°C/100°F as needed.

PISTACHIO POWDER

yield: 30 g/1.06 oz

INGREDIENT	METRIC	U.S.	%
Pistachio flour	41.67	1.47 oz	83.33%
Bread flour	8.33	.29 oz	16.67%

1. Combine both ingredients in a Robot Coupe. Blend until a homogeneous mix is obtained. Pass it through a fine-mesh sieve. The recipe is larger than what is needed because there will be some residue in the sieve that cannot be used.

2. The powder will keep for 2 weeks at room temperature or for up to 6 months in the freezer.

note The flour is used to keep the pistachio powder dry.

"H" HUCKLEBERRY GELÉES

yield: about 12 letters

INGREDIENT	METRIC	U.S.	%
Huckleberry compote cooking liquid	200 g	7.05 oz	91.95%
Gelatin sheets, bloomed (5 sheets)	18 g	.62 oz	8.05%

1. Combine both ingredients over a bowl over a hot water bath. Stir until the gelatin is dissolved.

2. Portion into the letter "H" silicone molds and freeze. Once they are frozen, push them out of the molds. Reserve them frozen until needed. If they are well wrapped, they can be kept frozen for up to 2 months.

note The cake recipe uses only 6 of the gelées, but making a smaller recipe is very unproductive and might not yield very good results.

COCONUT AND VANILLA CREAM WITH PASSION FRUIT CURD AND ANGEL FOOD CAKE

yield: 6 cakes

components

6 kg/13 lb 3.68 oz Light Coconut Cream

6 Passion Fruit Curd rectangles

6 Angel Food Cake rectangles

400 g/14.11 oz White Velvet Spray

6 Passion Fruit Gelée oblong ovals

6 small basil leaves

3 baby coconuts (coquitos), cut in half

1. Assemble six stainless-steel or aluminum rectangular cake molds measuring 6.25 by 20 by 10 cm/2.5 by 8 by 4 in. Place these on a flat sheet pan lined with acetate. Tape the molds to the acetate around the base to prevent the coconut cream from seeping. Place this setup in the freezer. Place six silicone rectangles measuring 2.5 by 7.5 by .63 cm/1 by 3 by ¼ in inside the molds, against the top right corner, with the long side of the silicone mold against the long side of the cake mold and the width of the silicone mold against the width of the cake mold. It will be in the front, right side corner of the mold. Place this setup in the freezer.

2. Pipe the coconut cream into the frozen prepared molds, filling them two-thirds of the way full. Make sure to pipe the cream with the tip of the piping bag submerged in the cream to prevent air pocket formation. Make sure to get into every corner, including the silicone rectangles.

3. Place the frozen passion curd inserts on top of the coconut cream, making sure they are centered. Press down until the coconut cream comes up the sides of the passion fruit curd.

4. Put the angel food cake on top of the curd and push it down until it is flush with the border of the cake mold. Ideally the coconut cream is also flush with the border of the mold, but this is very hard to achieve. If the cream is under the rim of the mold, pipe some more coconut cream around the angel food cake. If it overflows (which is better than putting too little in), clean the sides of the cake mold before returning the assembled cakes to the freezer.

5. Once all the molds have been filled, place a sheet of acetate on top of them, then a flat sheet pan on top of the acetate, and then a heavy cutting board on top of that to weigh the cakes down and even out the base. Freeze to harden. Once they have hardened, wrap them individually with plastic, label them, and freeze them. The cakes will keep for up to 2 months in the freezer.

6. Set up a spray station (see page 135). Fill the spray paint gun or a compressor canister with the white velvet spray; if using a compressor, turn it on. Warm the velvet spray to 38°C/100°F.

7. Line a sheet pan with parchment paper and freeze it. Place 6 cake boards or bases on a sheet pan. They should be slightly smaller than the dimensions of the base of the cake.

8. Cut the acetate around the base of the cakes, making sure to cut right against the mold using a sharp paring knife so that there is no excess. This rectangle of acetate will stay on the cake until it is time to place it on a cake board or base. This makes the process easier since the cake won't stick to any surface it is on, and it is easier to move the cake without damaging it.

9. Making sure it is hardened enough from being frozen, take the silicone rectangle off the top of the cake by gently prying it off with the tip of a paring knife or a scribe. It is crucial that the cake be very hard in order to prevent any damage while removing the silicone rectangle.

10. Place a cake on the cake stand and apply direct heat to the mold with a torch while spinning the cake stand. Apply enough heat so that the mold slides off easily.

11. Transfer the cake to the prepared sheet pan in the freezer. Return the cake to the freezer to reharden. Repeat this process with the remaining cakes.

12. Once all the cakes have hardened, spray them with the white velvet spray, rotating the sheet pan 90 degrees every few seconds to obtain an even coat.

13. Once they are sprayed, lift each one of the cakes from the cake cardboard base using a wide, sturdy, stainless-steel offset spatula, sliding it halfway only so that you can peel the acetate off. With a gloved hand, hold the cake by the base and peel off the rest of the acetate. Quickly and gently slide the cake onto the prepared cake display board with the help of the offset spatula, but be careful not to damage the exterior of the cake.

14. When all the cakes are on their boards, place a passion fruit gelée oval on the long side of the top of the cake, opposite from where the silicone rectangle imprint is, and then put a basil leaf on top of the gelée; place a baby coconut half inside the silicone rectangle imprint. They can be glued down with a small amount of white chocolate or neutral mirror glaze.

15. Let the cakes thaw in the refrigerator before displaying them. Display for up to 36 hours only. The cake should ideally be tempered for 30 to 45 minutes before eating. Advise your customers of this.

LIGHT COCONUT CREAM

yield: 6 kg/13 lb 3.68 oz

INGREDIENT	METRIC	U.S.	%
Coconut purée	3.18 kg	7 lb .48 oz	53.16%
Superfine or bakers' sugar	319 g	11.25 oz	5.32%
Egg whites	159 g	5.62 oz	2.65%
Heavy cream	1.75 kg	3 lb 13.92 oz	29.24%
Sugar	478 g	1 lb .8 oz	7.97%
Heavy cream stabilizer (liquid)	26 g	.9 oz	.43%
Gelatin sheets, bloomed (21 sheets)	73 g	2.59 oz	1.22%

1. Pour the cold coconut purée into a large bowl and warm it up to 15°C/60°F over a warm water bath. Reserve at room temperature until needed.

2. Combine the sugar with one-quarter of its weight in water in a small sauce pot. Bring the sugar up to 121°C/250°F over high heat. Meanwhile, whip the egg whites to stiff peak.

3. Once the sugar has reached the correct temperature and the egg whites have reached stiff peaks, pour the sugar into the egg whites as they whip on medium-high speed. Continue to whip until the meringue cools to room temperature.

4. Combine the cream, sugar, and stabilizer in the bowl of an electric mixer and whip on high speed until the mixture reaches medium peaks. Reserve in the refrigerator until needed.

5. Place 10 percent of the tempered coconut purée in a small bowl along with the bloomed gelatin. Place the mixture over a hot water bath and stir until the gelatin dissolves.

6. Pour this mixture into the larger amount of coconut purée. Fold in the Italian meringue in 2 additions.

7. Fold in the whipped heavy cream in 2 additions. Follow the instructions for assembling the cake.

PASSION FRUIT CURD

yield: 1.8 kg/3 lb 15.52 oz

INGREDIENT	METRIC	U.S.	%
Passion fruit purée (see Note)	238 g	8.39 oz	13.21%
Lemon juice	24 g	.84 oz	1.32%
Sugar	301 g	10.63 oz	16.74%
Salt	.4 g	.01 oz	.02%
Egg yolks	317 g	11.19 oz	17.62%
Butter, diced	912 g	2 lb .16 oz	50.65%
Gelatin sheets, bloomed (2.3 sheets)	8 g	.28 oz	.44%

1. Place 6 stainless-steel, aluminum, or Plexiglas frames 3.75 by 17.5 by 3.75 cm/1.5 by 7 by 1.5 in on a half sheet pan lined with acetate and freeze them.

2. In a small sauce pot, combine the passion fruit purée with the lemon juice and bring to a boil.

3. Meanwhile, place the sugar, salt, and egg yolks in a bowl and whisk to combine.

4. Prepare a hot water bath.

5. Pour the boiling passion fruit mixture into the yolk mixture while whisking vigorously. Place on top of the prepared hot water bath and stir occasionally until the curd thickens.

6. Once it has thickened (it will reach about 90°C/195°F), take the curd off the hot water bath and stir in the butter in small increments. Make sure it is all melted, and then stir in the bloomed gelatin until completely dissolved.

7. Strain the curd through a fine-mesh sieve into a hotel pan and cover it with plastic wrap. Let it cool to room temperature, stirring every 5 minutes. A curd is an emulsion; if it is refrigerated while it is cooling down or if it is cooled over an ice bath, the emulsion will break and the curd will be grainy.

8. After the curd has cooled, pipe it into the prepared frames. Even out the top with an offset spatula and place in the freezer to harden.

9. Once hardened, wrap the sheet pan tightly with plastic, label it, and freeze it. The curd will keep for up to 2 months. Otherwise, if assembling the cakes, unmold the curd. Place a frame on a cake stand and apply direct heat only to the frame with a torch while spinning the cake stand. Apply enough heat so that the mold slides off easily. Too much heat will melt the curd; too little will not release the mold well.

10. Once all of the curd has been unmolded, return it to the freezer to harden, then cover with plastic wrap and keep frozen until ready to assemble the cake.

note If the passion fruit purée is concentrated, use half passion fruit purée and half orange juice.

ANGEL FOOD CAKE

yield: 2 kg/4 lb 6.4 oz (1 half sheet pan)

INGREDIENT	METRIC	U.S.	%
Pastry flour	315 g	11.1 oz	15.74%
Sugar	419 g	14.78 oz	20.95%
Egg whites	840 g	1 lb 13.6 oz	41.99%
Superfine or bakers' sugar	419 g	14.78 oz	20.95%
Cream of tartar	2 g	.07 oz	.09%
Salt	6 g	.2 oz	.28%
Sugar, for sprinkling on cake	100 g	3.53 oz	

1. Line a sheet pan with a nonstick rubber mat. Do not spray the border of the sheet pan, since angel food cake needs something to adhere to as it bakes; otherwise it will pancake while it cools down.

2. Preheat a convection oven to 160°C/320°F.

3. Sift the flour and sugar together.

4. Whip the egg whites on high speed with the superfine sugar, cream of tartar, and the salt.

5. Fold in the sifted dry ingredients by hand.

6. Pour the batter into the prepared pan and spread it out in an even layer using an offset spatula.

7. Bake until the surface turns golden brown, 20 to 25 minutes.

8. Once the cake is baked, sprinkle its surface with sugar. Place a sheet of silicone paper on top of it, and then a sheet pan, and flip this setup over. Let the angel food cake cool to room temperature.

9. Once the cake has cooled, freeze it. This cake cuts much more easily once it is frozen.

10. Cut the cake into 6 rectangles 5 by 18.75 by 2.5 cm/2 by 7 by 1 in. Wrap them tightly with plastic, label them, and freeze them until needed. The cakes will keep for up to 2 months in the freezer.

note Adding the sugar at the beginning of the meringue process will weigh down the whites and slow down the whipping process, but it will eventually reach its full volume. The reason the sugar is added at that point is so that it can dissolve completely into the egg whites. The later the sugar is added, the less it will dissolve, and the angel food cake might end up with a grainy consistency.

WHITE VELVET SPRAY

yield: 400 g/14.11 oz

INGREDIENT	METRIC	U.S.	%
Cocoa butter, chopped	398 g	14.04 oz	99.5%
White food coloring (oil based)	2 g	.07 oz	.5%

1. Melt the cocoa butter in a bowl over a hot water bath.

2. Stir in the food coloring until evenly mixed.

3. Reserve at 38°C/100°F on top of an oven that is warm enough to keep the cocoa butter from setting.

4. It will keep for up to 1 month if melted or up to 6 months at room temperature.

PASSION FRUIT GELÉE

yield: 400 g/14.11 oz

INGREDIENT	METRIC	U.S.	%
Passion fruit purée (concentrated)	125 g	4.4 oz	31.2%
Orange juice	125 g	4.4 oz	31.2%
Sugar	137 g	4.84 oz	34.31%
Gelatin sheets, bloomed (3.7 sheets)	13 g	.46 oz	3.29%
Passion fruit seeds	60	60	

1. You will need a flexible rubber ice tray that is a set of ten oblong ovals 1.25 by 10 cm/.5 by 4 in (see Resources, page 540).

2. Bring the purée, orange juice, and sugar up to a boil, and boil for 10 seconds. Adjust the sugar if necessary.

3. Add the gelatin sheets and stir until dissolved.

4. Fill the flexible ice trays halfway with the gelée. Let it set in the refrigerator.

5. Once it is set, evenly space 10 passion fruit seeds on top of each set gelée. Pour in enough gelée to cover the seeds, and allow it to set in the refrigerator.

6. Once it is set, dip the ice tray in a warm water bath just enough to loosen the gelée from the mold without getting the exposed part of the gelée wet.

7. Slide the gelée out of the mold onto a sheet pan lined with acetate. Pat dry any melted liquid and reserve, covered in plastic wrap, in the refrigerator. The gelée will keep for 36 hours covered and refrigerated. If the gelée is stored in the ice trays it will keep for 4 more days, but once it is melted and unmolded it will start to dry out.

PEANUT BUTTER MOUSSE WITH MILK CHOCOLATE CHANTILLY, PEANUT BRITTLE, AND CHOCOLATE CAKE

yield: 6 cakes

components

3.5 kg/7 lb 11.52 oz Peanut Butter Mousse

600 g/1 lb 5.16 oz Peanut Brittle pieces

6 Milk Chocolate Chantilly rectangles

6 Chocolate Cake rectangles

600 g/1 lb 5.16 oz Milk Chocolate Velvet Spray (page 140)

120 g/4.23 oz Super-Shiny Glaze (page 96) **1 sheet gold leaf**

1. Place the silicone molds on a sheet pan.

2. Pipe enough peanut butter mousse to fill the silicone molds halfway (see Note). Place about 100 g/3.53 oz of the peanut brittle into each mold. Pipe in enough mousse to cover the brittle.

3. Place the milk chocolate Chantilly inserts on top of the mousse and push down gently until the mousse covers the sides of the Chantilly.

4. Place the chocolate cake rectangles on top of the Chantilly and push down gently until the cake is lined up with the top of the mold. Ideally, the peanut butter mousse will come up exactly to the top of the mold. If it doesn't, pipe some mousse around the cake until it does. If there is too much mousse, even it out with an offset spatula.

5. Place a sheet of acetate over the cakes, and then a sheet pan on top of the cakes, and then a heavy cutting board on top of that. Freeze it to harden.

6. Once they have hardened, wrap all of the cakes individually with plastic, label them, and freeze them. The cakes will keep for up to 2 months in the freezer.

7. **TO FINISH THE CAKES:** Place the cakes in a blast freezer until hardened. Cakes that are assembled in uneven silicone molds such as this one need to be rock hard in order to come cleanly out of the molds. If a blast freezer is not available, try to get the cakes as cold as possible in a freezer to avoid damaging them.

8. Set up a spray station (see page 135).

9. Drizzle some corn syrup on a sheet pan, and then glue a sheet of parchment paper on the sheet pan. Freeze it.

10. Place 6 cake boards or bases on a sheet pan big enough to fit the cakes.

11. Once the cakes have hardened in the blast freezer, unmold them and place them on the frozen sheet pan with the glued parchment paper. Keep them frozen.

12. Warm the chocolate spray to 38°C/100°F. Fill the spray paint gun tank or the compressor's canister with the chocolate spray. Spray the cakes in an even coat, rotating the sheet pan 90 degrees every few seconds. Immediately after spraying the cakes, transfer them to the prepared cake boards.

13. Drizzle 20 g/.71 oz of shiny glaze across the top of the cake; place a piece of gold leaf on top of the glaze.

14. Let the cakes thaw in the refrigerator before displaying them or serving them. The cakes should ideally be tempered for 30 to 45 minutes before eating. Advise your customers of this.

The silicone molds need to be made at least 48 hours in advance. Use food-grade silicone (see sidebar and Resources on pages 191 and 540). This particular mold is cast out of Plexiglas, using 12 pieces that measure 5 by 12.5 by .6 cm/2 by 5 by ¼ in. Glue the pieces together with epoxy glue in sets of 2. Then glue them all together, offsetting each pair by 2.5 cm/1 in to create a zigzag pattern.

Line a very flat surface, like a sheet of Plexiglas, with acetate. Once the glue is dry, spread some petroleum jelly over the bottom surface of the mold to keep it in place on the acetate. If it moves, the silicone will flood under the Plexiglas shape. Place the Plexiglas shape on the acetate. Place a stainless-steel square frame around each Plexiglas shape that is large enough to fit the Plexiglas plus about 1.25 cm/.5 in to spare around its border. It is crucial to line the frame with a sheet of acetate for easy removal of the frame.

Mix the silicone and pour it in the frame until it covers the Plexiglas shape. Let it cure for 24 hours. Remove the frame, and then push the Plexiglas out and let the silicone cure for 24 more hours. Make sure the mold is washed well before using it.

PEANUT BUTTER MOUSSE

yield: 3.5 g/7 lb 11.52 oz

INGREDIENT	METRIC	U.S.	%
Eggs	1.06 kg	2 lb 5.44 oz	30.32%
Confectioners' sugar	714 g	1 lb 9.12 oz	20.4%
Peanut butter	955 g	2 lb 1.76 oz	27.28%
Heavy cream	714 g	1 lb 9.12 oz	20.4%
Gelatin sheets, bloomed (16 sheets)	56 g	1.96 oz	1.59%

1. Combine the eggs with the confectioners' sugar in a bowl and place it over a hot water bath. Stir them together with a whisk until they reach 60°C/140°F. Continue to whisk for 10 more seconds, and then remove the bowl from the hot water bath. Transfer the mixture to the bowl of an electric mixer and whip on high speed until it reaches the ribbon stage.

2. Meanwhile, place the peanut butter, 142 g/5 oz cream, and the gelatin sheets in a bowl over a hot water bath. Whisk them until the gelatin dissolves and the peanut butter softens.

3. Pour the peanut butter mixture into the ribboned yolks and whip until the mixture reaches 30°C/86°F.

4. Whip the remaining heavy cream to medium-stiff peaks.

5. Fold the whipped heavy cream into the peanut butter base in 2 additions.

6. Transfer the mousse to a piping bag and follow the instructions for assembling the cake.

PEANUT BRITTLE

yield: 750 g/1 lb 10.4 oz

INGREDIENT	METRIC	U.S.	%
Roasted salted peanuts	207 g	7.3 oz	27.59%
Sugar	169 g	5.97 oz	22.55%
Corn syrup	183 g	6.47 oz	24.45%
Baking soda	12 g	.43 oz	1.62%
Milk chocolate couverture coins	178 g	6.29 oz	23.79%

1. Line a half sheet pan with a nonstick rubber mat.

2. Combine the peanuts with the sugar and corn syrup in a small sauce pot. Cook over high heat while stirring with a wooden spoon until the mixture reaches 170°C/338°F.

3. Remove the pan from the heat and then vigorously stir in the baking soda. Immediately pour it onto the prepared sheet pan and even it out with the spoon. Let it cool to room temperature.

4. While the peanut brittle cools, melt the chocolate couverture.

5. Once the brittle has cooled, crush it with a wooden dowel until there are pieces that are about 1.25 cm/.5 in. Place them in the bowl with the couverture, and stir with a wooden spoon until they are completely coated with the couverture. Pour them back onto the nonstick rubber mat and try to separate the pieces as much as possible.

6. Once the couverture has set, wrap the sheet pan tightly with plastic, label it, and store it at room temperature. The brittle will keep for about 1 month before the peanuts become stale.

MILK CHOCOLATE CHANTILLY

yield: 1 kg/2 lb 3.2 oz

INGREDIENT	METRIC	U.S.	%
Heavy cream	750 g	1 lb 10.56 oz	75%
Milk chocolate coins	250 g	8.77 oz	25%

1. Bring the cream to a boil and pour it over the chocolate in a bowl. Combine the cream and the chocolate using a handheld blender. Blend until uniform, then refrigerate.

2. Line a sheet pan with a nonstick rubber mat. Place a stainless-steel, aluminum, or Plexiglas frame measuring 20 by 37.5 by 2 cm/8 by 15 by .75 in on top of the rubber mat, and place this setup in the freezer.

3. Once the milk chocolate mixture has reached 4°C/39°F, whip it in an electric mixer on medium-high speed until stiff peaks are achieved.

4. Pipe the Chantilly into the prepared frozen mold. Even out the top with an offset spatula. Reserve the leftover Chantilly in the refrigerator; it will be used to garnish the cake. Freeze the Chantilly until hardened. Place another sheet pan lined with a sheet of acetate in the freezer.

5. Once the Chantilly has hardened, remove it from the frame. Use the tip of a paring knife to cut around the inside border of the frame, but be careful not to cut the nonstick rubber mat. Flip the Chantilly onto the frozen sheet pan with the acetate.

6. Cut out 6 rectangles 10 by 12.5 cm/4 by 5 in using a warm knife and a ruler. At this point, reharden the Chantilly in the freezer. Wrap it, label it, and return it to the freezer. The frozen Chantilly will keep for up to 2 months in the freezer.

CHOCOLATE CAKE

yield: 1 kg/2 lb 3.2 oz (1 half sheet pan)

INGREDIENT	METRIC	U.S.	%
Butter, at 21°C/70°F	157 g	5.54 oz	15.7%
Sugar	181 g	6.39 oz	18.12%
Light brown sugar	57 g	2 oz	5.67%
Eggs, at 21°C/70°F	133 g	4.68 oz	13.28%
Chocolate liquor, melted but cool	24 g	.85 oz	2.42%
Pastry flour	228 g	8.05 oz	22.82%
Baking powder	1 g	.04 oz	.12%
Baking soda	3 g	.12 oz	.33%
Salt	2 g	.07 oz	.2%
Cocoa powder	27 g	.95 oz	2.7%
Vanilla paste	3 g	.11 oz	.31%
Buttermilk	183 g	6.46 oz	18.33%
Milk chocolate, melted	100 g	3.53 oz	

1. Grease the inside border of a half sheet pan with nonstick oil spray, and then line it with a nonstick rubber mat.

2. Preheat a convection oven to 160°C/320°F.

3. Make the cake according to the creaming method on page 88. Add the chocolate liquor after the eggs have been completely incorporated. Combine the vanilla paste with the buttermilk and add in alternating intervals with the dry ingredients once the chocolate liquor has been added.

4. Bake the cake until it has a crown down the center, about 12 minutes. It is fully baked when you press the crown with your finger tips it spring back. Alternately check the doneness with a toothpick or knife.

5. Cool the baked cake to room temperature. Once it has cooled, flip it over and spread the melted milk chocolate over it in a very thin, even layer with an offset spatula. Freeze the cake.

6. Once it has hardened, cut out 6 rectangles 10 by 12.5 by .5 cm/4 by 5 by .25 in. Use a 6 mm-/.25-in-thick guide to cut the cake to the proper thickness.

7. Place the cake rectangles on a half sheet pan lined with parchment paper, wrap it tightly with plastic, label it, and freeze it. The cakes will keep for up to 2 months in the freezer.

PEAR CREAM, VANILLA AND HONEY–SCENTED POACHED BOSC PEAR, CARAMEL CHANTILLY, AND PEAR CAKE WITH CARAMEL GLAZE

yield: 6 cakes

components

3.8 kg/6 lb 9.76 oz Pear Cream

4 Vanilla and Honey–Scented Poached Bosc Pears

6 Caramel Chantilly squares

6 Pear Cake squares

1.5 kg/3 lb 4.96 Caramel Glaze

1.2 kg/2 lb 10.24 oz caramelized puffed rice (see Resources, page 540)

454 g/1 lb honeycomb

30 g/1.07 oz acacia honey

3 Tahitian vanilla pods

12 g/.42 oz vanilla powder

1. Assemble six 10-cm/4-in stainless-steel or aluminum cube cake molds on a flat sheet pan lined with acetate. Tape the cubes down to the acetate around the base to keep any liquid from seeping. Place the molds in the freezer.

2. Take the frozen molds out of the freezer. Pipe the pear cream into the molds so that it comes 2.5 cm/1 in up the sides of the molds.

3. Place the equivalent of half a diced pear on top of the cream for each cake. Keep them centered; they should not touch the cake mold. Pipe in enough pear cream to fill the mold two-thirds of the way.

4. Place the frozen caramel Chantilly inserts into the molds and push them in until the pear cream comes up the sides of the insert. Pipe enough pear cream to cover the Chantilly inserts.

5. Place the pear cake on top of the pear cream with the chocolate-coated side facing out. Push it down until it is level with the top of the mold. The pear cream should come up exactly to the top of the mold. If a small amount overflows, even it out with an offset spatula. If there is not enough, pipe enough cream around the cake so that it is flush with the mold. Place a sheet of acetate on top of the cakes, and then a flat sheet pan on top of the acetate, and then a heavy cutting board on top of that. Freeze until hardened.

6. Once hardened, wrap each cake individually with plastic, label it, and freeze it. The cakes will keep for up to 2 months in the freezer.

7. Place six 8.75-cm/3.5-in square cake boards or bases on a sheet pan. Line a sheet pan with parchment paper, and freeze it. Line another sheet pan with parchment paper, and place a wire rack on top of it.

8. Melt the caramel glaze in a bowl over a hot water bath, and then cool it to 22°C/72°F.

9. Cut the honeycomb to obtain 6 rectangles that measure 4 by 5 by 2 cm/1.6 by 2 by .8 in. Keep them on a sheet of parchment paper.

10. Unmold the cakes by applying direct heat from a torch to the molds. Place the molds on a cake stand and spin it while holding the torch flame in one place. Apply enough heat so that the mold slides off easily. Place the unmolded cake on the cake cardboard, and then put it on the frozen sheet pan.

11. Once all of the cakes have been unmolded and have rehardened in the freezer, place them on the sheet pan with the wire rack. Pour the warm glaze over the cakes in an even coat using a funnel gun. The glaze will set a few minutes after it is applied, since the gelatin in the glaze will react to the frozen cake.

12. Once the glaze has set, transfer the cake without the cardboard to the cake boards on which they will be displayed or presented.

13. Coat all 4 sides of each cake with the caramelized puffed rice.

14. Place the honeycomb on the cake. Brush each reserved slice of pear with acacia honey, and then lean it on the honeycomb. Cut the vanilla pods in half. Lean 1 half on the honeycomb. Sprinkle 2 g/.07 oz of vanilla powder next to the poached pear in a thin, straight line across the entire surface.

15. Let the cake thaw in the refrigerator before displaying or presenting it. The cakes should ideally be tempered for 30 to 45 minutes before eating. Advise your customers of this.

PEAR CREAM

yield: 3.8 kg/6 lb 9.76 oz

INGREDIENT	METRIC	U.S.	%
Bosc pear purée	2.02 kg	4 lb 7.2 oz	53.16%
Heavy cream	1.11 kg	2 lb 7.2 oz	29.24%
Sugar	303 g	10.69 oz	7.97%
Heavy cream stabilizer	16 g	.57 oz	.43%
Gelatin sheets, bloomed	46 g	1.64 oz	1.22%
Italian Meringue (page 245)	303 g	10.69 oz	7.97%

1. Warm the pear purée to 15°C/60°F over a warm water bath. Reserve at room temperature.

2. Combine the cream, sugar, and stabilizer in an electric mixer bowl on medium-high speed and whip until it reaches medium peak. Reserve refrigerated.

3. Place 10 percent of the tempered pear purée and the bloomed gelatin in a small bowl. Place both over a hot water bath and stir until the gelatin dissolves. Pour this mixture into the larger amount of pear purée.

4. Fold in the Italian meringue in 2 additions. Fold in the whipped heavy cream in 2 additions. Place in a piping bag, and follow the instructions for assembling the cake.

note Make the Italian Meringue just after warming the pear purée.

VANILLA AND HONEY–SCENTED POACHED BOSC PEARS

yield: **3 poached pears**

INGREDIENT	METRIC	U.S.	%
Bosc pears, ripe	4	4	
Simple syrup, at 50° Brix	1 kg	2 lb 3.2 oz	74.07%
Acacia flower honey	350 g	12.35 oz	25.93%
Vanilla pods, split and scraped	4	4	

1. Peel the pears and keep them covered with a damp cloth.

2. Bring the simple syrup, honey, and the vanilla pods and seeds to a boil in a small sauce pot.

3. Once the liquid boils, take the pot off the heat and place the pears inside the liquid. Cover them with a clean towel and let them cool in the liquid. This will allow them to cook through without overcooking them. Remove the vanilla pods.

4. Keep them in the liquid in the refrigerator in an airtight container, covered with the same towel. They will keep for up to 1 week.

5. When using the pears to assemble the cake, remove them from the liquid, pat them dry, and cut them into 1.75-cm/.5-in cubes. Discard the cores. Reserve a 1.75-cm-/.5-in-wide wedge to garnish each cake.

CARAMEL CHANTILLY

yield: **850 g/1 lb 13.92 oz (there might be some left over)**

INGREDIENT	METRIC	U.S.	%
Heavy cream	641 g	1 lb 6.56 oz	75.41%
Caramel (page 446)	192 g	6.78 oz	22.62%
Gelatin sheets, bloomed (2.6 sheets)	9 g	.32 oz	1.06%
Heavy cream stabilizer	8 g	.27 oz	.9%

1. Assemble a rectangular frame 17.5 by 26.5 by 2.5 cm/7 by 10.5 by 1 in on a sheet pan lined with acetate. Use steel caramel bars or a Plexiglas frame. Place this setup in the freezer.

2. Combine the cream, caramel, and bloomed gelatin in a bowl. Place the mixture over a hot water bath and stir until they are evenly mixed and the gelatin has dissolved. Cool to 4°C/39°F in an ice bath. Once the mixture has reached this temperature, place it in the bowl of an electric mixer with the stabilizer and whip to stiff peaks on medium-high speed.

3. Pour the whipped caramel Chantilly into the prepared frozen frame and even out the top with an offset spatula. Freeze it to harden.

4. Once it has frozen, remove the frame using the tip of a paring knife. Cut out 6 squares that measure 8.75 cm square by .5 cm thick/3 by 3 by 1 in using a long slicing knife dipped in hot water to warm the blade. There should be a 3x2 grid. Freeze the Chantilly again.

5. Once it has rehardened, try to separate the frozen squares carefully so as to not break them; there should be 6 distinct and even squares.

6. Wrap the sheet pan tightly with plastic, label it, and freeze it. The Chantilly will keep for up to 2 months in the freezer.

PEAR CAKE

yield: 2 kg/4 lb 6.4oz

INGREDIENT	METRIC	U.S.	%
Butter	224 g	7.89 oz	11.19%
Eggs	197 g	6.96 oz	9.87%
Bosc pear purée	508 g	1 lb 1.92 oz	25.39%
Elderflower liqueur (St-Germain)	102 g	3.58 oz	5.08%
Sugar	496 g	1 lb 1.44 oz	24.82%
All-purpose flour	450 g	15.89 oz	22.52%
Baking powder	20 g	.69 oz	.97%
Vanilla powder	3 g	.11 oz	.16%
White chocolate, melted	100 g	3.53 oz	

1. Grease the border of a half sheet pan with nonstick oil spray, and then line it with a nonstick rubber mat.

2. Preheat a convection oven to 160°C/320°F.

3. Prepare the recipe as per the blending method on page 88.

4. Pour the batter into the prepared pan and spread it out evenly with an offset spatula.

5. Bake until golden brown, about 17 minutes.

6. Let the cake cool to room temperature.

7. Once it has cooled, flip it onto a cutting board and spread the melted white chocolate in a thin, even layer over the exposed base. Refrigerate it to set the chocolate. Cut out 8.75-cm/3.5-in squares, and then cut the squares to 2.5- cm/1- in thick using a guide.

8. Transfer all the squares to a half sheet pan lined with parchment paper, wrap it tightly in plastic, label it, and freeze it. The squares will keep for up to 2 months in the freezer.

note This will make a half sheet pan and will yield 12 squares that are 8.75- cm/3.5- in and 2.5 cm/1 in thick, although the recipe only requires 6 squares. Save the rest for assembling more cakes.

CARAMEL GLAZE

yield: 1.5 kg/3 lb 4.96 oz

INGREDIENT	METRIC	U.S.	%
Salt	14 g	.49 oz	.93%
Water	62 g	2.19 oz	4.13%
Cornstarch	43 g	1.52 oz	2.87%
Sugar	740 g	1 lb 10.08 oz	49.33%
Heavy cream	620 g	1 lb 5.92 oz	41.33%
Gelatin sheets, bloomed in cold water (6 sheets)	21 g	.74 oz	1.4%

1. Combine the salt, water, and cornstarch in a bowl to make a slurry. Mix until the cornstarch and salt dissolve.

2. Combine the sugar with one-quarter of its weight in water (or enough to obtain a "wet sand" consistency) in a small pot. Cook the sugar to 170°C/338°F, or until it becomes a medium amber–colored caramel. Meanwhile, bring the cream to a simmer.

3. Once the sugar reaches the desired temperature, slowly stir in the cream with a whisk. Stir in the slurry, and bring to a boil to cook off the cornstarch and thicken the caramel.

4. Remove the pan from the heat. Squeeze the excess water from the bloomed gelatin sheets and stir the gelatin into the hot pan until it dissolves.

5. Pass the glaze through a fine-mesh sieve and cool over an ice bath.

6. Reserve in an airtight container in the refrigerator. The glaze will keep for up to 1 week.

MONT BLANC: CHESTNUT FINANCIER, SABLÉE, CRISP MERINGUE, CRÈME FRAÎCHE CHANTILLY, MILK CHOCOLATE MOUSSE, AND SWEET CHESTNUT JAM

yield: **6 cakes**

components

6 Crème Fraîche Chantilly cylinders

6 Chestnut Financier discs

3.3 kg/7 lb 4.43 oz Milk Chocolate Mousse

900 g/1 lb 15.68 oz Sablée pieces

450 g/15.84 oz Crisp Meringue "kisses"

600 g/1 lb 5.12 oz chestnut jam (see Resources, page 540)

6 Milk Chocolate Plaques

1.85 kg/4 lb 1.08 oz milk chocolate, at 43°C/110°F

600 g/1 lb 5.12 oz Milk Chocolate Velour Spray (page 140)

1. Line 12 stainless-steel or heavy-gauge aluminum cake rings 10 cm tall by 10 cm diameter/4 by 4 in with a sheet of acetate of the same height. Place the cake molds on a flat half sheet pan lined with acetate. Tape the base of the molds to the acetate with electrical tape or transparent tape. Place this setup in the freezer.

2. Unwrap the Chantilly cylinders, but keep them in the freezer. Do the same with the financier cake bases.

3. Pipe the milk chocolate mousse into the prepared cake molds until it is 2.5 cm/1 in up the side of the molds. The mousse might be somewhat loose to hold the Chantilly insert without it sinking. Refrigerate the molds for a few minutes to set the mousse slightly before putting in the insert.

4. Place the Chantilly inserts in the cake molds directly on top of the mousse, making sure to keep them centered. Push in slightly, just enough to keep the insert in place (about 5 mm/.25 in).

5. Pipe more mousse around and on top of the insert, or just enough to cover it. Sprinkle 150 g/5.29 oz of sablée morsels on top of the mousse, keeping them away from the cake mold. Push the sablée in gently, then place 5 meringue "kisses" in a circle on top of the sablés, away from the mold.

6. Pipe a small amount of mousse on top of the meringue. Place a financier disc on top of the mousse, chocolate side up, and push it in gently until the base of the financier is flush with the top of the mold. The mousse should come up to the top of the mold as well. If there is some excess it will just spill down the sides; if there is not enough, pipe some more mousse around the cake until it is at the same level as the top of the mold.

7. Place a sheet of acetate on top of the cake, and then a flat sheet pan on top of that, and then a heavy cutting board on top of that, and freeze the cakes until hardened. Once they have hardened, wrap each one individually with plastic, label it, and freeze it The cakes will keep for up to 2 months in the freezer.

8. Place 6 rectangles of marble, 15 by 45 by 2.5 cm/6 by 16 by 1 in each, in a freezer.

9. Place the chestnut jam in a piping bag.

10. Place 6 cake boards or bases on a sheet pan. They should be slightly larger than the base diameter of the cakes.

11. Have the milk chocolate plaques on hand, plus a small cornet filled with 45 g/1.58 oz melted milk chocolate (to stick the plaques to the cake).

12. Set up a spray station (see page 135). Have a spray paint gun or compressor ready. Warm the milk chocolate velour spray to 38°C/100°F. Place a wire rack on a sheet tray lined with parchment paper. Place a sheet pan lined with parchment paper in a freezer.

13. Remove the cakes from the freezer and push them out of the molds. Place them onto the sheet pan in the freezer, spacing them out evenly.

14. Remove 1 chilled slab of marble from the freezer. Pour a thin, even layer of about 300 g/10.58 oz melted milk chocolate over it. Spread it quickly with an offset spatula. Make sure the spatula is longer than the marble is wide to ensure a quick, efficient spread.

15. Cut a straight line about 2.4 cm/1 in from both wide ends of the marble slab. A 40-cm/14-in piece of chocolate is the ideal length to wrap the cake, but it may need to be longer to compensate for uneven ends, which occur frequently.

16. Lift the chocolate with your hands, using gloves so as to not melt the chocolate. This might require an offset spatula to remove the chocolate from the marble. Quickly surround or enrobe one of the cakes in the freezer with the strip of chocolate. Gently press the top of the chocolate in toward the middle of cake with the index fingers and thumbs from both hands. It should look like a four-leaf clover. Repeat the same process with the other cakes, using a fresh slab of frozen marble each time.

17. Once all the cakes have been covered with the milk chocolate robe, spray them with the milk chocolate velour spray. Once they have been sprayed, transfer each cake to a cake board or base, carefully using an offset spatula to move them.

18. Pipe 100 g/3.53 oz of chestnut jam into the top of the cake. It will not be seen from the outside. There is enough room inside the top of the chocolate and the actual top of the cake to fit this amount of chestnut jam.

19. Stick the chocolate plaques onto the cakes using the cornet of melted chocolate.

20. Let the cakes thaw in the refrigerator before displaying or serving them. The cakes should ideally be tempered for 30 to 45 minutes before eating. Advise your customers of this.

CRÈME FRAÎCHE CHANTILLY

yield: 575 g/1 lb 4.32 oz

INGREDIENT	METRIC	U.S.	%
Crème fraîche	234 g	8.26 oz	40.74%
Heavy cream	234 g	8.26 oz	40.74%
Sugar	106 g	3.76 oz	18.52%

1. Line 6 PVC or stainless-steel tubes 5 cm tall by 5 cm diameter/2 by 2 in with a strip of acetate of the same height. Place these tubes on a half sheet pan lined with acetate or a nonstick rubber mat.

2. Whip all of the ingredients together to stiff peaks, and pipe into the prepared tubes, making sure they are completely filled and there are no air pockets at the base. Even out the top with an offset spatula. Freeze the tubes.

3. Once frozen, wrap the entire sheet pan with plastic, label it, and freeze it. The Chantilly will keep for up to 2 months in the freezer. Alternatively, push the inserts out of their tubes and freeze them unwrapped. This method of storage is more convenient when assembling.

CHESTNUT FINANCIER

yield: 1.5 kg/3 lb 4.96 oz (1 half sheet pan)

INGREDIENT	METRIC	U.S.	%
Sugar	408 g	14.39 oz	27.19%
Almond flour	163 g	5.75 oz	10.88%
Cake flour	163 g	5.75 oz	10.88%
Baking powder	7 g	.26 oz	.49%
Brown Butter (page 98), **melted but cool**	245 g	8.63 oz	16.31%
Egg whites	392 g	13.81 oz	26.1%
Candied chestnuts, coarsely chopped (see Resources, page 540)	122 g	4.32 oz	8.16%
Milk chocolate, melted	100 g	3.53 oz	

1. Grease the border of a half sheet pan with nonstick oil spray, and then line it with a nonstick rubber mat.

2. Preheat a convection oven to 160°C/320°F.

3. Place the sugar, almond flour, cake flour, and baking powder in the bowl of an electric mixer fitted with the paddle attachment. Paddle for a few seconds until all the ingredients are evenly mixed, then pour in the brown butter, and then the egg whites.

4. Once a homogeneous mass is achieved, pour the batter into the prepared sheet pan and spread it in an even layer with an offset spatula. Sprinkle the candied chestnuts evenly across the surface of the financier.

5. Bake the financier until it is golden brown, about 6 minutes.

6. Cool the cake to room temperature.

7. Once it cools, flip the cake over onto a sheet of parchment paper and spread the melted milk chocolate all over the cake in a thin, even layer using an offset spatula.

8. Place the financier in a freezer. Once it has hardened, cut out six 8.7-cm/3.5-in discs using a ring cutter. Place the cakes on a sheet pan lined with parchment paper, wrap it with plastic, label it, and place it in the freezer. The cakes will keep for up to 2 months in the freezer.

MILK CHOCOLATE MOUSSE

yield: 3.3 kg/7 lb 4.43 oz

INGREDIENT	METRIC	U.S.	%
Milk	592 g	1 lb 4.88 oz	17.93%
Milk chocolate	1.11 kg	2 lb 7.15 oz	33.78%
Gelatin sheets, bloomed (4.3 sheets)	15 g	.53 oz	.47%
Heavy cream	1.57 kg	3 lb 7.38 oz	47.82%

1. Bring the milk to a boil and pour it over the milk chocolate in a bowl. Stir until the chocolate dissolves. Let the mixture cool to 30°C/82°F.

2. Squeeze the excess water off the gelatin sheets. Combine about 200 g/7.05 oz of the cream with the gelatin in a small sauce pot. Melt the gelatin over low heat, and then stir it into the milk and chocolate mixture.

3. Whip the remaining cream to medium peaks, and fold it into the milk chocolate mixture in 2 additions.

4. Pour some of the mousse into a piping bag. Follow the instructions for finishing the cake.

SABLÉE

yield: 750 g/1 lb 10.4 oz

INGREDIENT	METRIC	U.S.	%
All-purpose flour	103 g	3.64 oz	13.76%
Cake flour	249 g	8.79 oz	33.21%
Butter, at 21°C/70°F	171 g	6.03 oz	22.78%
Salt	3 g	.09 oz	.36%
Confectioners' sugar	128 g	4.52 oz	17.08%
Almond flour	25 g	.88 oz	3.32%
Eggs, at 21°C/70°F	71 g	2.51 oz	9.49%

1. Sift the all-purpose flour and cake flour together.

2. Combine the butter, salt, confectioners' sugar, and almond flour in the bowl of an electric mixer fitted with the paddle attachment. Paddle them until a homogeneous mass is achieved.

3. Add the eggs in 2 additions. For larger amounts, add them in more additions. Always stop the mixer, drop the bowl, and scrape it between additions.

4. Stop the mixer and add the sifted flours. Pulse the mixer a few times, then mix until a homogeneous mass is obtained. Be careful to not overmix the dough.

5. Remove the dough from the mixer and shape it into a 1.25-cm-/.5-in-thick flat square. Wrap it in plastic and refrigerate it for at least 1 hour so that the butter firms up.

6. Preheat a convection oven to 160°C/320°F.

7. Roll the dough out to .3 cm/.12 in with a rolling pin or a sheeter. The shape doesn't matter because it will be broken up once it bakes and cools. Place the dough on a sheet pan lined with parchment paper and dock it with a fork. Freeze it until it hardens again.

8. Bake until golden brown, about 7 minutes. Let cool to room temperature.

9. Once it has cooled, break it up by hand into about 1.75-cm/.5-in pieces. Reserve in an airtight container at room temperature. It will stay crisp for up to 3 days.

CRISP MERINGUE

yield: 450 g/15.84 oz

INGREDIENT	METRIC	U.S.	%
Egg whites	150 g	5.29 oz	33.33%
Superfine or bakers' sugar	150 g	5.29 oz	33.33%
Confectioners' sugar, sifted	150 g	5.29 oz	33.33%
Cocoa butter, in a spray can (see Resources, page 540)	as needed	as needed	

1. Whip the egg whites with the superfine sugar to stiff peaks on an electric mixer on high speed. Stop the mixer, and then put it on low speed. Pour in the confectioners' sugar and whip until the meringue is a bright shiny white and holds stiff peaks.

2. Pipe the meringue into 2.5-cm-/1-in-wide "kisses" on a sheet of silicone paper. Place them in a dehydrator set at 63°C/145°F or in an oven at the same temperature. Dehydrate or bake until dry on the inside, about 3 hours. Allow the meringue to cool.

3. Once they have cooled, spray the meringues on top and on bottom with a light mist of cocoa butter spray. This will extend its crispness in a moist environment, such as the interior of a cake.

4. Let the cocoa butter set, and keep the meringues in an airtight container in a cool, dry place. The meringues will keep for up to 1 year if stored in these conditions.

note This recipe will yield much more than needed, but making a smaller amount is more difficult since whipping egg whites can get complicated if there is very little to whip.

MILK CHOCOLATE PLAQUES

yield: 6 plaques

INGREDIENT	METRIC	U.S.
Milk chocolate, tempered	100 g	3.53 oz

1. Grease a marble surface with a mist of nonstick oil spray. Spread the spray out evenly with a paper towel.

2. Place a piece of acetate 7.5 by 18.75 cm/3 by 7 in on the marble and smooth it out with a paper towel so that it is flat against the marble with no air pockets or wrinkles. Spread the tempered chocolate into a thin, even layer using a small offset spatula.

3. When the chocolate is semi-set, lift up the acetate from the base and place it on another part of the marble to get rid of the excess chocolate frame.

4. Using a ruler and the back of a paring knife, cut out rectangles 2.5 by 5 cm/1 by 2 in.

5. Flip the whole acetate over onto a flat surface and place a nonstick rubber mat on it as a weight so that the chocolate plaques don't bow when they set.

6. Once the plaques are set, store them in an airtight container in a cool, dry place. The plaques will keep for up to 1 year.

PUMPKIN SPICE CREAM, PUMPKIN CREMEUR, PUMPKIN BREAD, AND MOLASSES AND CRÈME FRAÎCHE QUENELLES WITH PUMPKIN SEED VELVET

yield: 6 cakes

components

1 kg/2 lb 3.2 oz Pumpkin Bread rectangles

2.5 kg/4 lb 8.16 oz Pumpkin Cremeur cylinders

5.25 kg/11 lb 9.12 oz Pumpkin Spice Cream

1.25 kg/2 lb 12 oz Pumpkin Seed Velvet

2 kg/4 lb 6.56 oz Molasses and Crème Fraîche Quenelles

200 g/7.05 oz molasses

1. Place 6 rectangular molds with rounded corners measuring 7.5 by 30 by 7.5 cm/3 by 12 by 3 in on a flat sheet pan lined with acetate. Tape the base of the molds to the acetate on the sheet pan. Place this setup in the freezer.

2. Unwrap the pumpkin bread and reserve frozen. Unwrap the pumpkin cremeur inserts and peel the acetate wrap off.

3. Pipe the cream into the frozen cake molds and fill them halfway. Place the pumpkin cremeur tube directly on top of the cream, making sure it is centered. Push the insert in gently until the cream comes halfway up the tube.

4. Pipe more cream on top and around the insert until the mold is filled to within 2.5 cm/1 in from the top. Place the pumpkin bread on top of the cream, chocolate side up, and push down until the cake is flush with the top of the cake mold. Repeat with all of the cakes.

5. Place an acetate sheet on top of the assembled cakes, place a sheet pan on top of the acetate, and then place a heavy cutting board on top. Place in the freezer to harden.

6. Once the cakes have hardened, wrap them individually with plastic, label them, and freeze them. The cakes will keep for up to 2 months in the freezer.

7. Line a sheet pan with parchment paper and place 6 cake cardboards measuring 6.25 by 28.75 cm/2.5 by 11.5 in on it. Place the set up in the freezer.

8. Set up a spray station (see page 135). Make sure the pumpkin seed velvet spray is warmed to 38°C/100°F.

9. Unmold the cakes by applying direct heat to the cake mold with a torch. Place the cake on a cake stand and spin it as you hold the flame in one place. Apply enough heat so that the mold slides off easily.

10. Once the cake has been unmolded, place it on one of the cake cardboards on the frozen sheet pan and return the sheet pan to the freezer. Repeat the same procedure with all the cakes. Freeze them until they have hardened.

11. Re-whip the molasses crème fraîche to make sure it is stiff. Dip a soupspoon into a hot water bath and make 3 large quenelles, placing them directly on the cake once they are scooped. Scoop 3 quenelles with a smaller spoon and place them on the cake. Scoop 3 quenelles with an even smaller spoon and place them on the cake. Place them in an asymmetrical but even pattern, trying to have an even distribution of quenelle sizes across the top of the cake. Return the cakes to the freezer to harden the quenelles.

12. Fill the spray paint gun or the compressor's canister with the melted pumpkin seed velvet spray. Spray an even coat of velvet spray all over the cakes, rotating the sheet pan 90 degrees every few seconds to ensure an even layer of spray.

13. Drizzle the molasses with a soupspoon horizontally across the top of the cake in thin lines.

14. Transfer the cakes to the prepared cake boards or bases carefully, using a wide, sturdy offset spatula.

15. Let the cake thaw in the refrigerator before displaying or serving it. The cakes should ideally be tempered for 30 to 45 minutes before eating. Advise your customers of this.

PUMPKIN SPICE CREAM

yield: 5.25 g/11 lb 9.12 oz

INGREDIENT	METRIC	U.S.	%
PUMPKIN SPICE MIX			
Ground cinnamon	29 g	1.05 oz	52.45%
Ground ginger	12 g	.44 oz	21.68%
Grated nutmeg	10 g	.35 oz	17.48%
Ground cloves	5 g	.17 oz	8.39%
PUMPKIN SPICE ANGLAISE			
Milk	1.28 kg	2 lb 13.44 oz	28.67%
Heavy cream	1.28 kg	2 lb 13.44 oz	28.67%
Sugar	1.06 kg	2 lb 5.6 oz	23.7%
Pumpkin Spice Mix	57 g	2.01 oz	1.26%
Egg yolks	796 g	1 lb 12.16 oz	17.7%
PUMPKIN SPICE CREAM			
Heavy cream	2.05 kg	4 lb 8.64 oz	39.22%
Heavy cream stabilizer (liquid)	41 g	1.45 oz	.78%
Gelatin sheets, bloomed (17.7 sheets)	62 g	2.18 oz	1.18%
Pumpkin Spice Anglaise	3.08 kg	6 lb 12.96 oz	58.82%

1. **FOR THE PUMPKIN SPICE MIX:** Combine all of the ingredients in a coffee grinder. Pulse for a few seconds, until all of the spices are evenly mixed. Reserve the mixture in an airtight container at room temperature. The spice mix will keep for up to 6 months.

2. **FOR THE PUMPKIN SPICE ANGLAISE:** Prepare an ice bath.

3. Place the milk, cream, and half of the sugar in a sauce pot with the spice mix and bring to a boil.

4. Meanwhile, combine the remaining sugar with the egg yolks in a bowl. Once the liquid has been brought to a boil, temper the egg yolk–sugar mixture with it. Pour the mixture back into the sauce pot.

5. Bring the liquid up to 82°C/180°F (nappé consistency) while stirring continuously. Take the pot off the heat and stir for 2 more minutes. Strain the finished anglaise through a fine-mesh sieve, and cool it over the prepared ice bath.

6. Once it has cooled, make the cream or transfer the anglaise to an airtight container and refrigerate it for 4 days. Alternatively, Cryovac and freeze the mixture. The anglaise will keep for up to 2 months in the freezer.

7. **FOR THE PUMPKIN SPICE CREAM:** Whip the cream with the stabilizer until the mixture achieves medium peaks.

8. Squeeze the excess water from the gelatin sheets. Combine one-quarter of the anglaise in a bowl with the bloomed gelatin sheets, and place the bowl over a hot water bath. Stir until the gelatin has dissolved.

9. Once the gelatin has melted, remove the bowl from the heat. Add the remaining anglaise to the bowl and whisk to incorporate. If it feels too warm, let the anglaise cool for a few minutes, until it reaches 30°C/86°F.

10. Fold the whipped heavy cream into the anglaise in 2 additions. Fill a piping bag with the cream and follow the assembly instructions for the cakes.

note The anglaise recipe makes more than what is needed, but there will be some evaporation during the cooking and cooling process.

PUMPKIN BREAD

yield: 1 kg/2 lb 3.2 oz

INGREDIENT	METRIC	U.S.	%
Butter	112 g	3.95 oz	11.19%
Eggs	99 g	3.48 oz	9.87%
Bourbon	51 g	1.79 oz	5.08%
Pumpkin purée	254 g	8.95 oz	25.39%
Sugar	248 g	8.75 oz	24.82%
All-purpose flour	225 g	7.94 oz	22.52%
Baking powder	10 g	.34 oz	.97%
Ground cinnamon	2 g	.06 oz	.16%
Milk chocolate, melted	100 g	3.53 oz	

1. Grease the border of a sheet pan with nonstick oil spray, and then line it with a nonstick rubber mat.

2. Preheat a convection oven to 160°C/320°F.

3. Make sure all of the liquids (butter, eggs, bourbon, and pumpkin purée) are warmed to 21°C/70°F.

4. Sift all of the dry ingredients together.

5. Pour the butter into the eggs slowly while whisking constantly to emulsify them together, in a bowl that is large enough to fit all of the ingredients in the recipe.

6. Whisk in the bourbon and the pumpkin purée.

7. Stir in the dry ingredients. Mix until just combined and a homogeneous mass is obtained.

8. Pour into the prepared pan and spread it in an even layer with an offset spatula.

9. Bake until golden brown, about 17 minutes.

10. Let the bread cool to room temperature.

11. Once it has cooled, flip it onto a cutting board, peel off the nonstick rubber mat, and spread the melted milk chocolate in a thin, even layer all over the exposed base. Refrigerate it to set the chocolate. Cut out 8 pieces 6.25 by 18.75 by 6 mm/2.5 by 7.5 by .25 in. The recipe makes 8 pieces, but the assembled entremets only require 6 pieces. Save the remaining pieces for future cakes. Put the bread on a sheet pan.

12. Wrap the pan with plastic, label it, and freeze it. The bread will keep for up to 2 months in the freezer.

PUMPKIN CREMEUR

yield: 2.5 kg/4 lb 8.16 oz

INGREDIENT	METRIC	U.S.	%
Sugar	264 g	9.32 oz	17.62%
Egg yolks	298 g	10.53 oz	19.9%
Heavy cream	458 g	16.16 oz	30.55%
Milk	247 g	8.7 oz	16.45%
Pumpkin purée	211 g	7.46 oz	14.1%
Gelatin sheets, bloomed (6 sheets)	21 g	.73 oz	1.38%

1. Line 6 PVC tubes 18.75 cm long by 3.75 cm diameter/7.5 by 1.5 in with acetate. Stand the tubes on a flat half sheet pan lined with acetate. Tape the base of the tubes with electrical tape or transparent tape to the acetate on the sheet pan. Place this setup in the freezer.

2. Whip the sugar and the yolks together on high speed in an electric mixer until they reach the ribbon stage.

3. Bring the cream, milk, and pumpkin purée to a boil. Temper the yolk and sugar mixture into the milk mixture. Cook over medium heat while stirring constantly until it reaches 82°C/180°F (the nappé stage), and then pour the liquid into the bowl of an electric mixer. Put the bloomed gelatin in the bowl and whip on low speed until the mixture cools.

4. Pour the cremeur into the prepared tubes until they are filled to the top and even them out with an offset spatula. Place in the freezer until hardened.

5. Once hardened, remove the frozen cremeur from the tubes. The tubes may need to be warmed under running warm water; this will help the cremeur slide out. Keep the acetate on the cremeur and place them all on a sheet pan. Wrap the sheet pan with plastic, label it, and freeze it. The cremeur will keep up for 2 months in the freezer.

note This will produce 6 inserts at 350 g/12.35 g each; there will be some extra.

PUMPKIN SEED VELVET

yield: 1.25 kg/2 lb 12 oz

INGREDIENT	METRIC	U.S.	%
Cocoa butter powder (Mycryo)	878 g	1 lb 15.04 oz	70.27%
Pumpkin seed oil	372 g	13.11 oz	29.73%

1. Combine the cocoa butter with the pumpkin seed oil in a bowl and heat over a hot water bath until the cocoa butter has melted.

2. Reserve in a warm place (at least 40°C/104°F) to keep the cocoa butter fluid. It will keep for 2 weeks if kept warm or 2 months if it is allowed to set and is reserved at room temperature.

MOLASSES AND CRÈME FRAÎCHE QUENELLES

yield: 2 kg/4 lb 6.56 oz

INGREDIENT	METRIC	U.S.	%
Crème fraîche	889 g	1 lb 15.36 oz	44.44%
Heavy cream	889 g	1 lb 15.36 oz	44.44%
Molasses powder	222 g	7.84 oz	11.11%

1. Combine all of the ingredients in the bowl of an electric mixer and whip until stiff peaks form. Reserve in the refrigerator.

2. The mixture will need to be re-whipped just before scooping the quenelles onto the cake.

layered cakes

The main differences between molded cakes and layered cakes are as follows. Layered cakes are typically exposed, meaning that the layers or components can be seen. They are not or should not be built individually. They are built in a series of stacked frames and are then cut out to a particular shape and size, typically a rectangle, square, or triangle. Layered cakes are built right side up as opposed to upside down like molded cakes. They generally have a shorter shelf life, since their layers are exposed; the cake component dries out and other components, such as mousse or glaze, develop a skin.

All layered cakes are built in a frame; each layer will have its own frame and the components will be stacked one on top of the other using the frames. For example, the base cake is cut 1.25 cm/.5 in thick, and a frame with the same thickness is placed around it. Another frame, of any thickness, is placed on top of that and filled with mousse, for example. This is evened out, and then another frame is stacked on top of that component, and so on. These cakes can be built with great precision, which is what makes them very visually appealing.

Plexiglas frames are easily made and are much more economical than stainless-steel frames. Plexiglas frames can be custom made to your specifications, as can stainless steel, but the latter are prohibitively expensive. If building a cake in a full-size sheet pan, use frames that fit inside the sheet pan and have a 2.5 cm/1 in width. The same applies to a half sheet pan. It is important that the frame fits inside the pan.

It is highly likely that well-used sheet pans might not be 100 percent flat. It is the nature of a sheet pan to warp. Building a cake on this type of surface is not recommended unless there is no other alternative. Some practical alternatives are cutting boards or marble; Plexiglas can also be used as a base for assembling layered cakes. Whatever you choose to do, make sure that the base fits inside the reach-in and can be placed on a rolling rack shelf. It should be the same size as a full or half sheet pan. An important tip when using Plexiglas is to never run it through very hot water or an industrial dishwasher; always wash it with slightly warm water and soap to prevent it from warping.

When a liquid is poured into a frame, it will need to be smoothed out and even on top. For this, use a sturdy, flat, stainless-steel or plexiglass bar. It needs to be wider than the frame so that it can lean on the frame to even out the poured liquid.

The actual components of layered cakes are similar to those of molded cakes, but a layered cake will not have a body or component that surrounds it. The component that would typically be considered the body in a molded cake would simply be another layer in a layered cake.

FRAME AND BASE DIMENSIONS

Some cakes will be assembled in a half sheet pan and others in a full sheet pan in order to obtain a yield of 6 cakes.

For a cake assembled on a half sheet pan:

Frame dimensions (interior): 22.5 by 35 cm/9 by 14 in

Frame dimensions (exterior): 27.5 by 40 cm/11 by 16 in (frame is 2.5 cm/1 in wide all around)

At least 3 frames with the above dimensions are needed, and they should be .6 cm/.25 in thick, 1.25 cm/.5 in thick, 1.9 cm/.75 in thick, and 2.54 cm/1 in thick. Plexiglas base dimension: 30 by 41.25 by .5 cm/11.75 by 16.5 by .25 in.

For a cake assembled on a full-size sheet pan:

Frame dimensions (interior): 33.75 by 53.75 cm/13.5 by 21.5 in

Frame dimensions (exterior): 38.75 by 58.75 cm/15.5 by 23.5 in (frame is 2.5 cm/1 in wide all around)

At least 3 frames with the above dimensions are needed and they should be .6 cm/.25 in thick, 1.25 cm/.5 in thick, 1.9 cm/.75 in thick, and 2.54 cm/1 in thick. Plexiglas base dimension: 38.75 by 58.75 by .5 cm/15.5 by 23.5 by .25 in.

possible defects of molded and layered cakes

defect	cause	solution
Specks of undissolved gelatin in a cream or mousse	The gelatin was not melted properly or entirely.	Make sure the gelatin is completely melted before adding it into another liquid. Make sure the liquid is not too cold; otherwise the gelatin might set on contact.
The insert(s) sunk to the bottom of the cake or is slanted.	The body of the cake (either a mousse, cream, chiboust, or other foamed item) was overmixed or warm and was therefore too loose (fluid). It did not have enough surface tension to support the weight of the insert.	The body should be semi-cold and its foamed component whipped properly and folded in properly to keep it from deflating.
The cake exterior is wet or has condensation on it.	Excessive frost accumulated on its surface while freezing because it was not wrapped properly. The frost then melted on the cake or the cake wasn't thawed properly.	Always keep the cakes or their components properly covered with plastic wrap. Cakes should be thawed in the refrigerator, not at room temperature.
The body is bowing (it doesn't keep its shape).	The gelling agent (usually gelatin) was not measured out properly. There is insufficient gelatin or the cake is in an environment that is too warm for it.	Double-check the mise en place before proceeding with a recipe. Always keep the finished cakes in a refrigerated environment for storage.
When the cake is cut open, the body does not have a uniform look (it is swirled).	The components of the body were not folded in properly.	Fold the components of the body completely, just until they form a homogeneous mass. Be careful to not overmix.
A chocolate mousse has chocolate "chips" in it.	The chocolate was not melted all the way or the chocolate was very cold when the cold whipped cream was folded into it, setting it almost immediately.	Always melt the chocolate to at least 37°C/100°F; cool it to 30°C/82°F when folding other ingredients, such as whipped cream, into it.
The body is grainy.	The cream or the meringue was overwhipped.	Be careful to whip heavy cream only to medium peaks and to whip egg whites only to stiff peaks.

Basic Method for Assembling Layered Cakes

 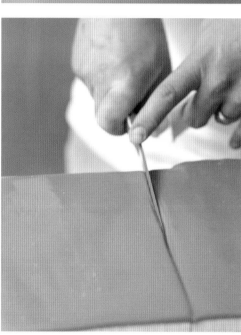 

TOP ROW, FROM LEFT TO RIGHT:

1. Since layered cakes are built right side up, cut the base layer to size and place it into the frame first.
2. After piping a filling into the frame, level it off using a flat-edged stainless-steel or Plexiglas bar.
3. When assembling several layers of filling, use multiple Plexiglas frames to achieve the proper thickness for each layer.

BOTTOM ROW, FROM LEFT TO RIGHT:

4. With the cake still in the frame, pour on a layer of glaze and quickly even out the surface with an offset spatula.
5. Remove the assembled cake from the frame and use a warm slicing knife to cut out individual cakes to size.
6. To finish, garnish the cakes as desired.

making your own molds with silicone

THERE IS A TYPE OF FOOD-GRADE SILICONE that goes by the trade name CopyFlex that can be used to make molds. There are many different kinds of silicone that are used to make molds, but CopyFlex is very fluid, which means it can get into all the nooks and crannies and not have air pockets. There are many methods to make your own molds, and there are entire books dedicated to this, but this method is the one used to make the cakes on page 150 and page 168.

Start with a cast or original shape. Plexiglas is the straightest and cleanest material that is easily cut to exact specifications and is economical, to an extent. Since Plexiglas is generally available in .6-cm-/.25-in-thick sheets, the cut pieces may need to be glued together to form the cast. The best glue to use is epoxy, which will bind two pieces of Plexiglas together practically permanently.

Once the cast is made, spray some nonstick oil spray on a very flat surface, such as marble. Smooth the oil out with a paper towel, and then put a sheet of acetate on top of the greased surface, smoothing it out as well with a clean paper towel. Rub some petroleum jelly on the base of the cast only. Put the cast down on the acetate with the petroleum jelly side in contact with the acetate. This will keep the mold in place.

Put a frame around the cast that is big enough to fit the cast inside comfortably and high enough that it is taller than the cast. The frame can be made out of Plexiglas or stainless steel or aluminum. If the frame is too big, there will be a lot of wasted silicone, which is very expensive. Tape the border of the frame to the acetate with electrical tape. CopyFlex comes in two separate containers with different liquids that have to be mixed to obtain the silicone mixture. One of the liquids is the catalyst that makes the silicone set. Mix the two liquids, in equal proportions by weight, using a disposable wooden dowel such as those used to mix paint. Stir until they are evenly mixed, and then pour the liquid on top of the cast. Fill the frame until it covers the cast. It takes about six hours to set the silicone, but leave it overnight just to make sure.

The silicone mold will come right off the cast once it has set. Use these molds for cold products only, since they are too thick to bake anything in them properly. If you have assembled a cake in this mold, freeze it as hard as possible (ideally in a blast freezer) so that it comes out as cleanly as possible.

BUTTERNUT SQUASH BUTTER AND CARAMEL MOUSSE CAKE WITH GINGERBREAD GÉNOISE AND GINGER SPICE GLAZE

yield: **6 cakes**

components

Assembled Butternut Squash Butter and Caramel Mousse Cakes

600 g/1 lb 5.12 oz caramelized puffed rice (see Resources, page 540)

1. Prepare a hot water bath.

2. Assemble a ruler longer than the length of the frame, a paring knife, a slicing knife, 2 heavy-duty paper towels, and a sheet pan with 6 cake boards or bases (17.5 by 20 cm/7 by 8 in) where the cakes will be displayed.

3. **TO FINISH THE CAKE:** Cut around the inside of the frames using a paring knife. Carefully take off the frames.

4. Slide the cake onto a cutting board by pulling it from the parchment paper.

5. Dip the slicing knife in the hot water bath and dry it with the paper towel. Cut a straight line along one of the short ends of the cake. Repeat this procedure, but this time cut on one of the long ends. On the straight wide end, measure 15-cm/6-in pieces (there will be 2), and on the straight long end, measure 17.5-cm/7-in pieces (there will be 3).

6. Mark each piece with the tip of the paring knife. Measure the same distances on the opposite side of the length and the width. Score the cake with the long ruler where the measurements are marked. There will be a 3x2 grid, with some excess.

7. Cut the cakes using the slicing knife; dip it in the hot water and dry it each time in order to get a clean cut. When cutting, bring the knife down and then pull it toward you; do not lift the knife up again. Turn the cake around 180 degrees to cut the other side. This also helps to get a clean cut. After cutting 1 cake, transfer it to the prepared cake board or base, gently lifting it from the cutting board with 2 medium offset spatulas. Repeat for all of the remaining cakes.

8. Have a square grid stencil (4x5) made of rigid plastic, where each square measures 2.5 cm/1 in and is separated 1.25 cm/.5 in from the next square in any direction. Once all of the cakes are on the cake boards or bases, place the plastic stencil over the glaze, being careful not to touch it since it will damage the glaze but getting as close to it as possible. Sprinkle the caramelized puffed rice over the stencil, making sure all of the squares are completely filled.

9. Display the cakes for a maximum of 24 hours.

10. The cake should ideally be tempered for 30 to 45 minutes before eating. Advise your customers of this.

note: Assemble the components in the following order.

GINGERBREAD GÉNOISE

yield: 2 kg/4 lb 6.4 oz (1.75-cm-/.5-in-thick full sheet pan cake)

INGREDIENT	METRIC	U.S.	%
Salt	6 g	.21 oz	.3%
Bread flour	246 g	8.68 oz	12.31%
Pastry flour	246 g	8.68 oz	12.31%
Ground ginger	12 g	.41 oz	.58%
Ground cinnamon	6 g	.2 oz	.29%
Ground cloves	3 g	.12 oz	.17%
Grated nutmeg	2 g	.08 oz	.11%
Eggs	880 g	1 lb 15.04 oz	43.98%
Dark brown sugar	493 g	1 lb 1.44 oz	24.63%
Crystallized ginger, finely chopped	24 g	.83 oz	1.17%
Butter, melted but cool	83 g	2.93 oz	4.15%

1. This cake will be assembled in a full sheet pan, and each cake will measure 15 by 17.5 cm/ 6 by 7 in. Grease the border of a sheet pan with nonstick oil spray and line it with a nonstick rubber mat.

2. Preheat a convection oven to 160°C/320°F.

3. Sift the salt, flours, and spices together.

4. Whip the eggs with the brown sugar on high speed until they reach the ribbon stage.

5. Fold in the dry ingredients by hand and then the ginger. Mix in the butter.

6. Pour the génoise into the prepared frame and spread in an even layer with an offset spatula.

7. Bake until golden brown, about 15 minutes.

8. Cool to room temperature.

9. Once it has cooled, flip the cake onto a cutting board lined with silicone paper, peel off the rubber mat, and then flip it back onto a clean sheet pan also lined with silicone paper.

10. Take the top sheet of silicone paper off and reserve for another use. Place a 1.25-cm-/ .5-in-thick frame on top of the cake. Trim the borders so that the cake is inside the frame and the frame is not on top of the cake.

11. Use a long serrated knife to cut the cake to the same thickness as the frame. The knife should be longer than the frame is wide so that the blade can use the frame as a guide to lean on while cutting it. If the cake is not staying flat as you cut it, press down with your hand close to the blade as you cut it.

12. Place this cake with the frame on a Plexiglas base lined with acetate. Keep it covered with plastic wrap until needed.

BUTTERNUT SQUASH BUTTER

yield: 1.5 kg/1 lb 10.4 oz

INGREDIENT	METRIC	U.S.	%
Butternut squash, peeled, seeded, and diced	1.68 kg	3 lb 11.36 oz	56.05%
Butter	411 g	14.5 oz	13.71%
Sugar	907 g	2 lb	30.23%
Vanilla pods, split and scraped	4	4	
Cinnamon sticks	8	8	

1. Bring all the ingredients to a boil in a 4-qt sauce pot. Reduce the heat to medium-low.

2. Cook until the squash is tender and broken down, about 2 hours. Stir often and reduce the heat if necessary to prevent scorching.

3. Cool the butter to room temperature in a hotel pan. Remove the vanilla pods.

4. Place a .6-cm-/.25-in-thick frame on the frame that holds the pumpkin cake. Pour the pumpkin butter in and spread it in an even layer. Freeze these items together uncovered.

note The ingredients call for twice the amount that this recipe yields because there will be lot of evaporation that occurs during the cooking process.

CARAMEL MOUSSE

yield: 2 kg/4 lb 6.4 oz

INGREDIENT	METRIC	U.S.	%
Sugar	370 g	13.05 oz	18.5%
Butter	123 g	4.35 oz	6.17%
Heavy cream warmed to 21°C/71°F	288 g	10.15 oz	14.39%
Eggs	247 g	8.7 oz	12.33%
Gelatin sheets, bloomed (9.8 sheets)	17 g	.61 oz	.86%
Heavy cream	945 g	2 lb 1.28 oz	47.27%
Heavy cream stabilizer (liquid)	10 g	.35 oz	.49%

1. **FOR THE CARAMEL:** In a small sauce pot, cook the sugar over high heat, stirring constantly until it turns to a medium amber (170°C/338°F). Stir in the butter until thoroughly incorporated, and then stir in the warm heavy cream. Remove the caramel from the heat.

2. Place the eggs over a hot water bath and warm them to 60°C/140°F while stirring constantly. Transfer them to an electric mixer bowl and whip until they have cooled down to room temperature. While the eggs are whipping and before they have cooled, stream the caramel in. Add the gelatin and whip until the gelatin dissolves and the mixture has cooled down to 21°C/70°F.

3. Whip the remaining heavy cream and the stabilizer in an electric mixer to medium peaks. Fold the whipped cream into the caramel in two additions.

4. Place a 1.25-cm/.5-in frame on top of the butternut squash butter frame. Pour the mousse in and spread in an even layer using an offset spatula or Plexiglas and the frame as a guide.

5. Freeze this setup; make the gingerbread glaze. Do not cover until it has hardened in the freezer. Otherwise the plastic wrap will make it uneven.

GINGER SPICE GLAZE

yield: 1.5 kg/3 lb 4.96 oz

INGREDIENT	METRIC	U.S.	%
Fresh ginger, peeled	2.5-cm/1-in piece	2.5-cm/1-in piece	
Heavy cream	720 g	1 lb 9.4 oz	41.33%
Cinnamon sticks, toasted	4	4	
Cloves, toasted	8	8	
Nutmeg, crushed and toasted	1	1	
Sugar	620 g	1 lb 5.92 oz	41.33%
Molasses	120 g	4.23 oz	8%
Salt	14 g	.49 oz	.93%
Water	62 g	2.19 oz	4.13%
Cornstarch	43 g	1.52 oz	2.87%
Gelatin sheets, bloomed (6 sheets)	21 g	.74 oz	1.4%

1. Grate the ginger into the cream in a small sauce pot.

2. Add the cinnamon sticks, cloves, and nutmeg. Bring the liquid to a boil, and then remove it from the heat. Cover it with plastic wrap and let it steep for 30 minutes.

3. Once steeped, strain the cream through a fine-mesh sieve and measure out 620 g/1 lb 5.92 oz of steeped cream.

4. Add the sugar and the molasses to the measured cream and bring it to a boil again.

5. Meanwhile, combine the salt, water, and cornstarch in a bowl. Whisk to obtain a slurry. Pour this mix into the boiling cream and, stirring constantly, bring it back to a boil. This is necessary to cook off the starch and thicken the liquid.

6. Squeeze the excess liquid from the gelatin sheets. Remove the pot from the heat and stir in the gelatin until it has dissolved. Strain the liquid through a fine-mesh sieve and cool it over an ice bath.

7. When it reaches 19°C/66°F, pour it over the caramel mousse with the frame still on. Spread it evenly with an offset spatula and tap the sheet pan down to even out the glaze.

8. Let the glaze set on the cake in the refrigerator. Reserve until needed.

MACADAMIA NUT CRÈME BRÛLÉE, CARAMELIZED PUFF PASTRY, BANANA CREMEUR, AND DARK CHOCOLATE TILES

yield: 6 cakes

components

6 Caramelized Puff Pastry squares

18 Dark Chocolate Tiles

6 Macadamia Nut Crème Brûlée squares

6 Banana Cremeur squares

200 g/7.05 oz Candied Macadamia Nuts

1. Assemble 6 square cake boards or bases on a sheet pan that measures 17.5 cm/7 in long. Place a drop of corn syrup on the cake boards or bases. This is to hold the puff pastry in place.

2. Place the puff pastry squares on top of the cake boards or bases.

3. Place a chocolate tile on top of the puff pastry, then top with the frozen crème brûlée squares. Place another chocolate tile on top, and then place a square of banana cremeur on top of the tile. Make sure that each layer is lined up evenly and straight.

4. Place a final chocolate tile on top of the banana cremeur. Finally, put a drop of corn syrup or glucose in the top right corner of the top tile and put a candied macadamia nut on it.

5. Thaw the cakes in the refrigerator before displaying or serving. Ideally, this cake is not tempered before serving, since the crème brûlée and the cremeur would get too soft. Advise your customers of this.

note These cakes will not be assembled in a frame; they will be layered individually.

CARAMELIZED PUFF PASTRY

yield: 2 kg/4 lb 6.4 oz

INGREDIENT	METRIC	U.S.	%
Cake flour	200 g	7.05 oz	10%
Bread flour	820 g	1 lb 12.96 oz	41%
Salt	30 g	1.06 oz	1.5%
Cold water, at 10°C/50°F	510 g	1 lb 1.92 oz	25.5%
Butter, at 21°C/70°F	440 g	15.52 oz	22%
Corn syrup	300 g	10.58 oz	

1. Combine the flours and salt in the bowl of an electric mixer. Start mixing on low speed with the paddle attachment.

2. Pour in the cold water and mix until a smooth, homogeneous dough is achieved. Be careful not to overmix the dough in order to keep gluten development at a minimum.

3. Transfer the dough to a sheet pan lined with silicone paper and lightly dusted with flour. Cover it with plastic and let the dough relax for 30 minutes.

4. Roll the dough out on the sheet pan to a rectangle 20 by 30 cm/8 by 12 in. Cover it in plastic wrap and refrigerate it. While the dough chills, make the butter block.

5. Shape the soft but pliable butter into a rectangle 12.5 by 17.5 cm/5 by 7 in on a sheet of parchment paper. If the butter is too soft, refrigerate it.

6. To make the puff pastry, see the procedure for lamination on page 40.

7. Once the dough is made and cold enough to roll out, roll it to a thickness of .5 cm/.25 in, preferably on a sheeter to ensure an even thickness.

8. Relax the dough for 30 minutes, and then transfer it to a sheet pan lined with parchment paper. Cover the dough with plastic wrap and freeze it. The ideal working consistency is semi-frozen. This generally occurs within 30 to 45 minutes of putting the dough in the freezer.

9. Preheat a hearth oven to 220°C/430°F.

10. Remove the dough from the freezer and dock it with a docker or a fork. Place a sheet of silicone on top of it and then 5 sheet pans on top of that.

11. Bake the dough until it turns amber brown. This can take anywhere from 30 minutes to 1 hour. When the pastry starts to turn golden brown, slide another sheet pan underneath it to keep the base from burning before the top of the pastry is fully baked.

12. Take the sheet pans and the top sheet of silicone off the pastry.

13. Brush half of the corn syrup on the surface and bake it for 5 minutes, or until it caramelizes. Flip the pastry over carefully onto another sheet pan lined with silicone paper, brush the remaining corn syrup on top, and bake it for 5 more minutes, or until caramelized.

14. Let the baked puff pastry cool to room temperature. Once it has cooled, put it in the freezer.

15. Once it has frozen, remove it from the freezer and put it on a cutting board. Cut out a total of six 15-cm/6-in squares using a sharp serrated knife.

16. Keep the baked puff pastry squares on a sheet pan covered with plastic in a cool, dry place. The squares will keep for up to 2 days.

MACADAMIA NUT CRÈME BRÛLÉE

yield: 6 squares measuring 12.7 cm/5 in square by 1.25 cm/.5 in thick

INGREDIENT	METRIC	U.S.	%
Heavy cream	2.1 kg	4 lb 10.08 oz	49.96%
Macadamia nut paste (see Resources, page 540)	900 g	1 lb 15.75 oz	21.41%
Egg yolks	600 g	1 lb 5.16 oz	14.28%
Sugar	600 g	1 lb 5.16 oz	14.28%
Salt	3 g	.11 oz	.07%

1. Preheat a convection oven to 135°C/275°F.

2. Lightly grease 3 half hotels pans with nonstick oil spray and then line them with plastic wrap.

3. Combine all of the ingredients in a bain marie and mix them together using a beurre mixer. Pass the liquid through a fine-mesh sieve.

4. Divide the liquid into 3 equal parts of 1.4 kg/3 lb 1.28 oz and pour into the 3 prepared hotel pans.

5. Put 3 full-size hotel pans in the oven and fill them halfway with hot water. Place the half hotel pans with the brûlée inside each full-size hotel pan.

6. Bake for 40 to 45 minutes or until the custard is set. It will have a gelatinous jiggle when the pan is gently tapped; if it is not done, it will slosh around the pan.

7. Once baked, take the brûlée out of the oven and out of the full-size hotel pans. Cool them down quickly in a freezer.

8. Once they are set and frozen, remove them from the pan and cut them into 12.5-cm/5-in squares with a warm slicing knife.

9. Put them on a sheet pan lined with acetate and cover them with plastic wrap. Reserve frozen.

BANANA CREMEUR

yield: 1.75 kg/3 lb 13.76 oz

INGREDIENT	METRIC	U.S.	%
Heavy cream	569 g	1 lb 4.16 oz	32.53%
Milk	307 g	10.81 oz	17.52%
Banana purée	263 g	9.27 oz	15.01%
Vanilla pods, split and scraped	2	2	
Egg yolks	371 g	13.08 oz	21.19%
Sugar	219 g	7.72 oz	12.51%
Gelatin sheets, bloomed (6.3 sheets)	22 g	.76 oz	1.24%

1. Place a 1.25-cm-/.5-in-thick frame on top of a full-size Plexiglas base lined with an acetate sheet. Tape the frame to the base on the outside border to prevent the cremeur from leaking out.

2. Combine the cream, milk, banana purée, and vanilla pods and seeds in a saucepan and bring to a boil.

3. In the meantime, whip the egg yolks with the sugar in the bowl of an electric mixer until they reach the ribbon stage.

4. Temper them into the liquid and cook until the mixture reaches 82°C/180°F (nappé consistency). Remove the vanilla pods from the mixture.

5. Squeeze the excess water from the gelatin sheets. Remove the pot from the heat and stir in the bloomed gelatin until dissolved.

6. Transfer the liquid to the bowl of an electric mixer and whip on low speed until the liquid cools down.

7. Pour into the prepared frame and freeze it. Once the creamer has frozen, remove the frame with the help of a paring knife. Cut along the inside border of the frame.

8. Dip a knife in hot water, and then dry it with a paper towel. Using the warm knife and a ruler, cut out 12.5-cm/5-in squares. Keep them frozen and covered in plastic until ready to assemble the cake.

DARK CHOCOLATE TILES

yield: 18 tiles

INGREDIENT	METRIC	U.S.
Dark chocolate (72%), tempered	500 g	1 lb 1.6 oz

1. Grease a marble surface lightly with nonstick oil spray. Spread the oil out evenly with a paper towel.

2. Place 9 sheets of crocodile-textured acetate sheets or other textured acetate sheets on the marble.

3. Spread the tempered chocolate on top in a thin, even layer. When the chocolate is semi-set, transfer the acetate sheets to another section of the marble so that the excess chocolate frame will remain on the sheet pan or marble.

4. Using a ruler and the back of a paring knife, cut out two 15-cm/6-in square tiles from each acetate sheet. Flip each tile onto a sheet pan lined with parchment paper, and alternate each sheet of acetate with a sheet of parchment paper.

5. Reserve in a cool, dry place in an airtight container for up to one year.

CANDIED MACADAMIA NUTS

yield: 200 g/7.05 oz

INGREDIENT	METRIC	U.S.	%
Macadamia nuts	183 g	6.43 oz	52.17%
Sugar	122 g	4.29 oz	34.78%
Water	46 g	1.61 oz	13.04%

See the procedure for candied almonds on page 23.

PRALINE MASCARPONE CREAM CAKE WITH FRANGIPANE, PRALINE CRUST, AND CARAMEL GLAZE

yield: **6 cakes**

components

6 assembled Praline Mascarpone Cream Cakes

6 sheets gold leaf

12 chocolate décor curved triangles

1. Assemble a long slicing knife, a ruler, a paring knife, 2 heavy-duty paper towels, 2 large offset spatulas, a hot water bath large enough to fit the entire blade of the knife, and a cutting board large enough to fit the whole cake. Place 6 cake boards or bases on a sheet pan that measures 10 by 32.5 cm/4 by 13 in.

2. Remove the frame from the cake by passing a paring knife along the inside border of the cake. Gently slide the cake onto a large cutting board by pulling on the silicone paper under the cake.

3. Trim a vertical border on one of the long ends (about 1 cm/.4 in wide) and a horizontal border on one of the short ends (about 1 cm/.4 in wide). To do this, dip a long, thin slicing knife into hot water and dry with a paper towel. Cut straight down and then pull the knife back toward you.

4. Once the two borders have been trimmed, measure the pieces to be cut. Begin measuring on the trimmed borders. Each cake will measure 7.5 cm by 30 cm/3 by 12 in. To cut the cakes, use the same knife. Dip it in very hot water, dry it with a paper towel, and then make a cut. Repeat this procedure every time in order to get a clean cut. Make sure the knife is at a perfect 90-degree angle to get a straight cut down. Bring the knife down, and then pull it toward you to get the cleanest cut.

5. Transfer the cakes to a cake board or base by lifting it from the cutting board using 2 large offset spatulas.

6. Place a full sheet of gold leaf on the left end of the cake, then place 1 curved chocolate triangle on its side, and another on top of it, curving toward the cake like an upside-down "U."

7. Discard after 24 hours. The cake should ideally be tempered for 30 to 45 minutes before eating. Advise your customers of this.

note Assemble the components in the following order.

PRALINE

yield: 1.5 kg/3 lb 4.96 oz

INGREDIENT	METRIC	U.S.	%
Sugar	661 g	1 lb 7.36 oz	44.05%
Water	165 g	5.83 oz	11.01%
Lemon juice	13 g	.47 oz	.88%
Almonds	330 g	11.65 oz	22.03%
Hazelnuts	330 g	11.65 oz	22.03%

1. In a 4-quart sauce pot, combine the sugar and water. Add the lemon juice. Cook over high heat until it reaches 182°C/360°F.

2. Meanwhile, toast the nuts in a 160°C/325°F oven until they turn golden brown.

3. When the sugar has reached the proper temperature, stir in the nuts while they are still hot. Otherwise the sugar will crystallize.

4. Turn off the heat and continue to stir until you hear a popping sound.

5. Pour the praline onto a sheet pan lined with parchment paper.

6. Once the praline has cooled, break it up into 2.5-cm/1-in pieces. Grind the praline in a Robot Coupe until it acquires a sandy texture, but do not grind it to a paste.

7. Reserve in an airtight container. The praline will keep for up to 1 month in a cool, dry place.

PRALINE CRUST

yield: 1 kg/2 lb 3.2 oz

INGREDIENT	METRIC	U.S.	%
Praline (recipe above)	371 g	13.08 oz	37.06%
Almond paste	370 g	13.06 oz	37.03%
Milk chocolate (40%), at 40°C/104°F	185 g	6.53 oz	18.51%
Butter, at 40°C/104°F	74 g	2.61 oz	7.4%

1. Combine the praline and almond paste in the bowl of an electric mixer fitted with a paddle attachment. Mix until uniformly combined. Pour in the chocolate and mix until thoroughly combined, and then add the butter. It is crucial that the chocolate and butter not be too hot; otherwise the ingredients, especially the fat, will separate.

2. Shape into a flat square, wrap, and refrigerate.

3. Once cold and firm, roll out to a rectangular shape 40 by 47.5 by .3 cm/16 by 19 by .11 in on a sheet of silicone paper. Try to roll it out to the size of the sheet of silicone paper. This will help to move the crust without damaging it and in eventually assembling the cake. Slide the rolled-out praline crust onto a flat sheet pan.

4. Place a .6-cm-/.25-in-thick Plexiglas frame over the crust. Trim the crust so that it fits inside the frame and the frame is not lying on the crust. Refrigerate until needed, covered in plastic wrap.

FRANGIPANE

yield: 1.5 kg/3 lb 4.96 oz

INGREDIENT	METRIC	U.S.	%
Almond paste (50% nuts)	415 g	14.65 oz	27.68%
Sugar	415 g	14.65 oz	27.68%
Butter, at room temperature	415 g	14.65 oz	27.68%
Eggs, at room temperature	140 g	4.94 oz	9.34%
Cake flour	114 g	4.03 oz	7.61%
Simple syrup	200 g	7.05oz	
Natural almond extract, or as needed	3 g	.11 g	

1. Line a sheet pan with a nonstick rubber mat.

2. Preheat a convection oven to 160°C/320°F.

3. Combine the almond paste and sugar in the bowl of an electric mixer fitted with the paddle attachment. Mix until sandy, 10 to 15 minutes. Add the butter, and cream for 5 minutes on medium speed until a homogeneous mass is obtained.

4. Slowly incorporate the eggs in 2 additions. Scrape the sides of the bowl after each addition.

5. Add the flour and mix until just incorporated.

6. Pour the batter onto the prepared sheet pan. Using a 40.64 by 48.26 by .6 cm/16 by 19 by .25 in Plexiglas frame, spread the batter evenly with an offset spatula. Remove the Plexiglas frame.

7. Bake until slightly golden brown around the border. Cool to room temperature.

8. Place a .6-cm-/.25-in-thick frame over the frame that holds the praline crust.

9. Once cooled, trim the borders of the frangipane so it will fit inside the frame on top of the praline crust.

10. Slide the cake on top of the praline crust. Combine the simple syrup and almond extract. Soak the frangipane with the simple syrup using a pastry brush.

11. Place a 1.25-cm-/.5-in-thick frame on top of the praline and frangipane frames for the praline mascarpone cream. Set aside, covered with plastic wrap.

PRALINE MASCARPONE CREAM

yield: 2.5 kg/5 lb 8.16 oz

INGREDIENT	METRIC	U.S.	%
Mascarpone	1.71 kg	3 lb 12.32 oz	68.73%
Praline paste (50% nuts)	382 g	13.47 oz	15.27%
Superfine or bakers' sugar	382 g	13.47 oz	15.27%
Gelatin sheets, bloomed (5.1 sheets)	18 g	.64 oz	.73%

1. Soften the mascarpone in a bowl over a hot water bath. Combine the soft mascarpone with the praline paste and the sugar. Mix over a warm, not hot, water bath with a whisk until the sugar is dissolved and all of the ingredients are evenly incorporated.

2. Place one-quarter of the mixture in a small pot with the bloomed gelatin. Melt over low heat, and then mix into the remaining mascarpone-praline cream.

3. Pour into the frame with the soaked frangipane and praline crust. Spread the cream in an even layer using an offset spatula and the frame as a guide. Remove any excess from the top so that it is even with the top of the frame. Let it set completely in the freezer before glazing.

note Use a high-quality mascarpone; low-end mascarpone breaks or separates easily when hot.

CARAMEL GLAZE

yield: 1 kg/2 lb 3.2 oz

INGREDIENT	METRIC	U.S.	%
Salt	9 g	.33 oz	.93%
Water	41 g	1.46 oz	4.13%
Cornstarch	29 g	1.01 oz	2.87%
Sugar	493 g	1 lb 1.44 oz	49.33%
Heavy cream	413 g	14.58 oz	41.33%
Gelatin sheets, bloomed (4 sheets)	14 g	.49 oz	1.4%

1. Combine the salt, water, and cornstarch in a bowl. Mix until the cornstarch and salt dissolve.

2. In a small pot, combine the sugar with one-quarter of its weight in water, or enough to obtain a "wet sand" consistency. Cook to 170°/338F° or to a medium amber–colored caramel.

3. Meanwhile, bring the cream to a simmer. Once the sugar reaches the desired temperature, slowly stir in the cream with a whisk. Stir in the cornstarch slurry and return the mixture to a boil to cook off the cornstarch and thicken the caramel.

4. Remove from the heat and stir in the gelatin until it dissolves.

5. Pass the glaze through a fine-mesh sieve and cool over an ice bath. Store in an airtight container in the refrigerator. Discard after 8 days.

6. To glaze the cake, bring the glaze to 22°C/72°F, which is the ideal glazing temperature. Pour it over the entire surface of the frozen cake and spread evenly with an offset spatula. Glaze the cake with the frame still in place. Tap the sheet pan down gently to even out the glaze. If there are bubbles on the surface, briefly heat them with the flame of a torch and they will pop.

7. Refrigerate the cake to let the glaze set.

CHOCOLATE DÉCOR

yield: **about 20 curved dark chocolate triangles**

INGREDIENT	METRIC	U.S.
Tempered dark chocolate (60%)	**200 g**	**7.05 oz**

1. Cut a full-size acetate sheet into 7.5-cm-/3-in-wide strips. A full-size sheet of acetate is about the same size as a sheet pan and will yield about 6 strips.

2. Place the strips on a flat surface such as the back of a sheet pan or a marble surface, leaving about 2.5 cm/1 in between each strip.

3. Spread the tempered chocolate in an even and very thin layer over all of the acetate strips using an offset spatula.

4. When the chocolate begins to set, transfer the strips to another flat surface, such as another sheet pan or another section of the marble surface. This is so that you will have an even, clean rectangle to work with and all of the excess chocolate frame will remain on the sheet pan or marble.

5. Using a ruler and the back of a paring knife, cut 3.8-cm-/1.5-in-wide triangles. Before the chocolate sets, transfer the strip to a curved surface, such as a PVC tube. Ideally, the PVC tube will have a 5-cm/2-in diameter in order to obtain a pronounced curve. Make sure to tape the tube down so that it won't roll. Once the chocolate is set, remove the acetate from the finished triangles.

6. Reserve the finished triangles in an airtight container in a cool, dry place. They will keep in these conditions for up to 1 year.

SWEET VANILLA-MASCARPONE CREAM WITH RASPBERRY CAKE AND FRESH RASPBERRIES

yield: **6 cakes**

components

12 Raspberry Cake rectangles

200 g/7.05 oz dark chocolate, melted

2.00 kg/4 lb 6.4 oz Sweet Vanilla-Mascarpone Cream

50 g/1.76 oz corn syrup

12 Chocolate Tiles

6 fresh raspberries

6 Raspberry Macarons (page 276)

1. This cake will be assembled in a full-size sheet pan. Place 1 sheet of raspberry cake over a full-size Plexiglas base; do not remove it from the nonstick rubber mat. Spread the melted chocolate over the entire surface in a thin, even layer using an offset spatula.

2. Place a sheet of silicone paper on top of the chocolate once it has set and flip it over so that the chocolate side is facing the Plexiglas. Remove the nonstick rubber mat from the cake. Place a .6-cm-/.25-in-thick frame on top of the cake.

3. Pour in half of the vanilla-mascarpone cream and spread in an even layer using an offset spatula.

4. Place the second sheet of raspberry cake (still in the frame, nonstick rubber mat removed) on top of the mascarpone.

5. Place another .6-cm-/.25-in-thick frame on top of the second sheet of raspberry cake and fill it with the remaining vanilla-mascarpone cream. Spread the cream in an even layer with an offset spatula and freeze it.

6. Place 6 cake boards or bases on a sheet pan, measuring 10 by 32.5 cm/4 by 13 in. Assemble a slicing knife, a hot water bath in a bain marie deep enough to fit the entire blade of the knife, a heavy-duty paper towel, a ruler, a paring knife, 2 large offset spatulas, and a cutting board.

7. Draw a thin line of corn syrup on the cake boards or bases to keep the cakes in place.

8. Remove the cake from the freezer. Only cut it once the vanilla-mascarpone cream has hardened.

9. Using a paring knife, cut around the inside border of the frame and remove the frame.

10. Slide the cake onto a cutting board by pulling it by the silicone paper on the base. Trim a horizontal border on one of the short ends, about 1 cm/.4 in wide, and a vertical border of the same width on one of the long ends. To do this, dip a long, thin slicing knife into hot water and dry with a paper towel. Cut straight down and then pull the knife back toward you.

11. Once the borders have been trimmed, measure the pieces to be cut. Begin the measurements on the trimmed borders. Each cake will measure 7.5 by 30 cm/3 by 12 in. To cut the cake, use the same knife. Dip it in very hot water, dry it with a paper towel, and then cut. Repeat this procedure every time in order to get a clean cut. Make sure the knife is at a perfect 90-degree angle to get a straight cut. Bring the knife down, and then pull toward you to get the cleanest cut.

12. Transfer each cake to a cake board or base by lifting it from the cutting board using 2 large offset spatulas.

13. Place a chocolate tile, shiny side up, on top of each cake, evenly lined up.

14. Place 1 raspberry on top of the chocolate tile.

15. Put a raspberry macaron next to the raspberry.

16. Let the cake defrost in the refrigerator before displaying it or presenting it. The cake is ideally tempered for 30 to 45 minutes eating. Advise your customers of this.

note: Assemble the components in the following order.

RASPBERRY CAKE

yield: 4 kg/8 lb 13.12 oz

INGREDIENT	METRIC	U.S.	%
Butter	448 g	15.79 oz	11.19%
Eggs	395 g	13.93 oz	9.87%
Raspberry purée	1.01 kg	2 lb 3.84 oz	25.39%
Chambord	203 g	7.16 oz	5.08%
Sugar	993 g	2 lb 3.04 oz	24.82%
All-purpose flour	901 g	1 lb 15.84 oz	22.52%
Baking powder	39 g	1.38 oz	.97%
Vanilla powder	7 g	.23 oz	.16%

1. Grease the border of 2 full sheet pans with nonstick oil spray and then line them with a nonstick rubber mat.

2. Preheat a convection oven to 160°C/320°F.

3. To make the raspberry cake, see the procedure for the pear cake on page 175.

4. Divide the raspberry cake batter into 2 equal amounts and pour them each into a prepared sheet pan. Spread the batter in an even layer using an offset spatula.

5. Bake until the cake springs back in the middle when you apply gentle pressure with your fingertips.

6. Cool the cakes to room temperature.

7. Place a .6-cm-/.25-in-thick frame on top of each raspberry cake. Trim the cake so that it fits inside the frame, and remove the trimmings.

8. Put a sheet of silicone paper on top of each cake and use a rolling pin to even out the cake.

9. Place a flat, heavy cutting board that is as big as the frame on top of each cake and freeze both of them. If the cake is tightly wrapped, it can keep for up to 2 months in the freezer.

SWEET VANILLA-MASCARPONE CREAM

yield: 2 kg/4 lb 6.4 oz

INGREDIENT	METRIC	U.S.	%
Gelatin sheets, bloomed (4.3 sheets)	15 g	.53 oz	.75%
Mascarpone	1.64 kg	3 lb 9.92 oz	82.06%
Tahitian vanilla paste	54 g	1.91 oz	2.71%
Superfine or bakers' sugar	290 g	10.21 oz	14.48%

1. Squeeze the excess water off the gelatin sheets. Combine all of the ingredients in a bowl, and place the bowl over a hot water bath.

2. Stir with a whisk until the gelatin is dissolved. Take the bowl off the hot water bath. Follow the instructions for making the cakes.

CHOCOLATE TILES

yield: 6 tiles

INGREDIENT	METRIC	U.S.
Dark chocolate (64%), tempered	300 g	10.58 oz

1. Grease a marble surface lightly with nonstick oil spray and smooth it out with a paper towel. Place a sheet of acetate on it and smooth it out as well with a clean paper towel to avoid air pockets and wrinkles.

2. Pour the chocolate over the acetate and spread it out in a thin, even layer using an offset spatula.

3. When the chocolate is semi-set, transfer the acetate to another area of the marble so that the excess chocolate frame will remain on the sheet pan or marble.

4. Using a ruler and the back of a paring knife, cut out rectangles 7.5 by 30 cm/3 by 12 in.

5. Flip the rectangles onto a sheet pan lined with parchment paper and let them set at room temperature.

6. Reserve in a cool, dry place in an airtight container for up to one year.

CHOCOLATE MOUSSE, CHOCOLATE GANACHE, AND CHOCOLATE CAKE WITH CHOCOLATE TILES

yield: 6 cakes

components

6 Chocolate Cake rectangles

24 Chocolate Tiles

12 Chocolate Mousse rectangles

6 Chocolate Ganache rectangles

1. Place 6 cake boards or bases on a sheet pan that measures 10 by 20 cm/4 by 8 in, and have some corn syrup in a squeeze bottle on hand. Place a small drop of corn syrup on the cake boards to keep the cakes in place.

2. Place a chocolate cake layer on the cake board. Layer the following components in order, making sure to keep the edges lined up: chocolate tile, chocolate mousse, chocolate tile, chocolate ganache, chocolate tile, chocolate mousse, and then a chocolate tile. Repeat with the remaining cakes.

3. Allow the cakes to thaw in the refrigerator before displaying or presenting. This cake is ideally tempered for 30 to 45 minutes before eating. Advise your customers of this.

CHOCOLATE CAKE

yield: 2 kg/4 lb 6.4 oz

INGREDIENT	METRIC	U.S.	%
Egg yolks	302 g	10.65 oz	15.09%
Sugar	226 g	7.97 oz	11.32%
Dark chocolate (64%) coins	680 g	1 lb 8 oz	33.96%
Butter	340 g	12 oz	16.98%
Egg whites	453 g	15.97 oz	22.64%
Dark chocolate (64%), melted	200 g	7.05 oz	

1. Grease the border of a full sheet pan with nonstick oil spray, and then place a nonstick rubber mat on it.

2. Preheat a convection oven to 160°C/320°F.

3. Whip the egg yolks with 181 g/6.39 oz sugar to the ribbon stage. Meanwhile, melt the chocolate with the butter over a hot water bath.

4. Once the chocolate mixture is melted, add it to the egg yolks and stir until they are evenly mixed.

5. Whip the egg whites with the remaining 45 g/1.6 oz sugar until stiff peaks form. Fold the meringue into the chocolate–egg yolk mixture in 2 additions.

6. Pour the batter into the prepared sheet pan and spread it out in an even layer with an offset spatula.

7. Bake until the cake springs back when gently pressed with your fingers in the middle of the cake, 12 to 15 minutes.

8. Once the cake is baked, let it cool to room temperature. Once it has cooled, flip it over onto a sheet of parchment paper and spread the melted chocolate over the entire surface in a thin, even layer.

9. Let the chocolate set in the refrigerator. Remove the cake from the refrigerator and flip it back over onto a sheet of silicone paper on a sheet pan, so that the chocolate is on the bottom.

10. Place a full-size .6-cm-/.25-in-thick frame on top of the cake. Using a paring knife, trim the cake so that the cake is inside the frame, not under it. Remove the trimmings.

11. Place a sheet of silicone paper on top of the cake and, using a rolling pin and the frame as a guide, gently even out the surface of the cake. Place the cake with the frame and the silicone paper in the freezer.

12. Once it has hardened, cut out pieces 7.5 by 17.5 cm/3 by 7 in, using a ruler and a wheel cutter. Reserve the chocolate cake rectangles in the refrigerator until ready to assemble the cakes.

CHOCOLATE TILES

yield: 24 tiles

INGREDIENT	METRIC	U.S.
Dark chocolate (72%), tempered	700 g	1 lb 8.64 oz

1. Grease a marble surface lightly with nonstick oil spray. Spread it out evenly with a paper towel.

2. Place 6 sheets of textured acetate sheets (or other) on the marble. Each sheet should measure 25 by 40 cm/10 by 16 in (see Resources, page 540).

3. Spread the tempered chocolate on top of the acetate in a thin, even layer. When the chocolate is semi-set, transfer the acetate sheets to another section of the marble so that the excess chocolate frame will remain on the sheet pan or marble.

4. Using a ruler and the back of a paring knife, cut out four tiles 10 by 20 cm/4 by 8 in from each acetate sheet.

5. Flip each tile onto a sheet pan lined with parchment paper, and alternate each sheet of acetate with a sheet of parchment paper.

6. Place a weight on top of the acetate, such as a flat cutting board, to keep the tiles from bowing when they set.

7. Reserve in a cool, dry place in an airtight container for up to one year.

CHOCOLATE MOUSSE

yield: 1.5 kg/3 lb 4.96 oz

INGREDIENT	METRIC	U.S.	%
Eggs	304 g	10.71 oz	20.24%
Sugar	125 g	4.41 oz	8.33%
Dark chocolate (64%)	402 g	14.17 oz	26.79%
Heavy cream	670 g	1 lb 7.68 oz	44.64%

1. Grease a full-size Plexiglas base with a small amount of nonstick oil spray, and then line it with a sheet of acetate. Place a .6-cm-/.25-in-thick frame on top of the acetate.

2. To make the mousse, see the procedure for dark chocolate mousse on page 147.

3. Pour the mousse into the frame and spread it in an even layer using an offset spatula.

4. Cover the mousse with acetate and freeze.

5. Once it is frozen, remove the frame by cutting the mousse around the inside of the frame with the tip of a paring knife.

6. Cut the mousse into rectangles 7.5 by 17.5 cm/3 by 7 in using a warm slicing knife and a ruler. There should be very little waste.

7. Reserve the mousse rectangles in the freezer covered with plastic wrap until ready to assemble the cake. Discard after 2 months.

CHOCOLATE GANACHE

yield: 1.05 kg/2 lb 4.96 oz

INGREDIENT	METRIC	U.S.	%
Heavy cream	500 g	1 lb 1.6 oz	47.62%
Dark chocolate (64%)	450 g	15.87 oz	42.86%
Butter, soft	100 g	3.53 oz	9.52%

1. Grease a full-size Plexiglas base with a light coat of nonstick oil spray, and spread it out evenly with a paper towel. Line the Plexiglas with a sheet of acetate. Smooth out the surface with another paper towel to prevent air pocket formation and wrinkles.

2. Bring the cream to a boil, and then stir it into the chocolate in 2 additions.

3. Stir in the softened butter until it is dissolved completely.

4. Wait for the ganache to cool; 30°C/86°F is ideal. If the ganache is poured into the frame while it is still very hot, it will wrinkle the acetate.

5. Pour the ganache into the frame and spread in an even layer using an offset spatula. The frame should be the size of a full-size sheet pan frame and .6 cm/.25 in thick.

6. Let the ganache set at room temperature for 2 hours, then freeze it until it has hardened.

7. Once it has hardened, remove the frame from the ganache, using the tip of a paring knife to cut around the inside border of the frame.

8. Using a warm slicing knife and a ruler, cut out rectangles 7.5 by 17.5 cm/3 by 7 in. Keep them frozen and wrapped in plastic until ready to assemble the cakes. Discard after 2 months.

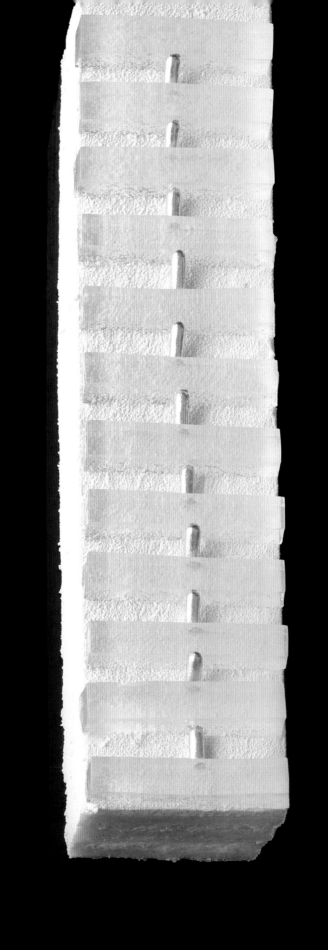

LEMON CURD, TAHITIAN VANILLA CREAM, AND CRÈME FRAÎCHE CAKE

yield: **6 cakes**

components

1.5 kg/3 lb 4.96 oz Lemon Velvet

3 assembled Crème Fraîche cakes

1.5 kg/3 lb 4.96 oz Lemon Jelly

66 oval silver dragées

1. Place 6 cake boards or bases on a sheet pan. The boards should be 10 by 32.5 cm/4 by 13 in.

2. Set up a spray area (see page 135). Warm the lemon velvet to 38°C/100°F.

3. Cut 6 pieces of acetate to cover the front of the cakes, about 7.5 by 5.62 cm/3 by 2.25 in.

4. Remove the cakes from the freezer and place a sheet of the cut acetate on the front end of each one. Rub the acetate gently so that it adheres to the cakes.

5. Spray the cakes evenly with the lemon velvet on every side and on top, rotating the sheet pan 90 degrees every few seconds.

6. Transfer the cakes to the cake boards or bases and remove the acetate. The intention of this acetate is to keep the front end from getting sprayed, and thus show the even layers that make up the cake.

7. Cut the lemon jelly to the following dimensions: 1.25 by 5.62 cm/.5 by 2.25 in. Each time the jelly is cut, place the cut piece directly on top of the cake. In this case, it is not efficient to cut all of the pieces first and then place them on the cakes. There will be 12 pieces per cake, each separated by 1.25 cm/.5 in. Lean a silver dragée on each slice of lemon jelly.

8. Let the cakes thaw in the refrigerator before serving or presenting. The cake should be tempered for 30 to 45 minutes before eating. Advise your customers of this.

note Assemble the components in the following order.

This cake will be assembled in a full-size frame.

CRÈME FRAÎCHE CAKE

yield: 6 kg/13 lb 3.68 oz

INGREDIENT	METRIC	U.S.	%
Butter, at 21°C/70°F	1.11 kg	2 lb 7.2 oz	18.53%
Sugar	1 kg	2 lb 3.36 oz	16.67%
Tahitian vanilla powder	7 g	.26 oz	.12%
Eggs, at 21°C/70°F	735 g	1 lb 9.92 oz	12.26%
All-purpose flour	1.05 kg	2 lb 5.28 oz	17.6%
Baking powder	88 g	3.11 oz	1.47%
Salt	15 g	.52 oz	.25%
Crème fraîche	1.98 kg	4 lbs 6.08 oz	33.11%
Lemon Syrup (page 215)	600 g	1 lb 5.16 oz	
Lemon Curd (page 156)	4 kg	8 lb 13.12 oz	
Tahitian Vanilla Cream (page 158)	3 kg	6 lb 9.76 oz	

1. Grease the borders of 3 full-size sheet pans with nonstick oil spray, and then line them with nonstick rubber mats.

2. Preheat a convection oven to 160°C/320°F.

3. To make the cake, see the procedure for crème fraîche cake on page 160. Divide the batter into 3 equal amounts, and spread each in an even layer in a prepared sheet pan using an offset spatula.

4. Bake until golden brown, 12 to 15 minutes. Cool the cakes to room temperature.

5. Place a .6-cm-/.25-in-thick frame on top of each cake and cut around the inside of the frame so that the cakes are inside their respective frames and not under them. Be careful to not cut in to the nonstick rubber mat.

6. Place a sheet of silicone paper on top of each cake and, using a rolling pin, even them out. Soak each cake with 200 g/7.05 oz of lemon syrup using a pastry brush.

7. Place another .6-cm-/.25-in-thick frame on top of the cake; this frame will be for the lemon curd.

8. Pour the curd into the prepared frames on top of the crème fraîche cake. Spread the curd in an even layer using an offset spatula. Freeze the cakes.

9. Place a .6-cm-/.25-in-thick frame on top of the crème fraîche cake–lemon curd setups.

10. Divide the vanilla cream into 3 equal parts by weight, and pour each part into the frames. Spread in an even layer using an offset spatula. Place the setups in the freezer until they have hardened.

11. Remove the frames from each setup by using a paring knife to cut along the inside of each frame. The 3 set cakes will be stacked on top of each other to form the final cake. It doesn't matter which cake will be the base, but all of cakes must be flipped over onto a sheet of silicone paper. One of the cakes needs to have a sheet of silicone paper placed on top of it while flipped over, and then it needs to be flipped back onto a cutting board large enough to hold it. Remove all of the rubber mats.

12. Remove the top layer of silicone paper from the cake on the cutting board and lightly torch the surface. This will soften the surface just enough to adhere the next cake to it. Flip another cake onto the cake on the cutting board, remove the silicone paper, and torch it as well. Flip the last cake onto the previous 2 assembled cakes. Cover the assembled cake with plastic wrap and freeze it to re-harden once again.

13. Use a 35-cm/14-in double-handled cheese knife to cut 7.5-cm-/3-in-wide rows of cake. Trim the wide ends off so that each column measures 30 cm/12 in long. There may be more than 6 cakes to finish. Flip all the cakes on their sides by 90 degrees, so that the layers of the cake can be seen on top.

14. Glue a piece of parchment paper down to a sheet pan with corn syrup all around the border. Place all of the cakes on the prepared sheet pan with at least 5 cm/2 in between each cake. Another sheet pan may be needed to accommodate all of the cakes.

15. Freeze the cakes uncovered to harden. Once hardened, wrap them with plastic wrap, label them, and reserve them in the freezer. Discard after 2 months.

note You will need less anglaise than this recipe states in its yield to make the cream, but there will be some evaporation during the cooking and cooling down process.

LEMON SYRUP

yield: 600 g/1 lb 5.12 oz

INGREDIENT	METRIC	U.S.	%
Sugar	250 g	8.82 oz	41.67%
Water	250 g	8.82 oz	41.67%
Lemon juice	100 g	3.53 oz	16.67%

1. Bring the sugar and water to a boil in a sauce pot.

2. Let it cool completely, and then stir in the lemon juice. Reserve refrigerated. The syrup will keep for up to 10 days in the refrigerator.

note For Candied Meyer Lemon Zest: Peel 10 Meyer lemons. If the pith on the lemons is too thick, cut it off and discard. Stack 5 pieces of the lemon peel with the pith facing up and cut into a thin chiffonade. Blanch the zest 3 times in water, changing the water each time. Place the blanched zest in a pot with the lemon syrup. Cook over medium-low heat until the zest is translucent. Strain the zest out of the syrup and let it cool on a plastic-wrap lined sheet pan, refrigerated. Act quickly and make sure to refrigerate the zest, otherwise the sugar might crystallize. Once cool, reserve in an airtight container in the refrigerator.

LEMON JELLY

yield: 1.5 kg/3 lb 4.96 oz

INGREDIENT	METRIC	U.S.	%
Water	1 kg	2 lb 3.2 oz	66.67%
Sugar	286 g	10.08 oz	19.05%
Lemon juice	143 g	5.04 oz	9.52%
Vegetable gelling agent (see Note)	71 g	2.52 oz	4.76%

1. Lightly grease a flat wooden board with nonstick oil spray. Spread it out evenly with a paper towel. Place a sheet of acetate over the greased board and smooth it out with a clean paper towel.

2. Build a frame with caramel bars with the following measurements: 17.5 by 40 by 1.25 cm/ 7 by 16 by .5 in. Tape the bars down to the acetate with electrical tape to prevent the liquid from seeping out of the frame.

3. Combine the water and the sugar in a sauce pot. Whisk over medium-high heat until the sugar has dissolved. Add the lemon juice, and then stream in the vegetable gelling agent while whisking constantly.

4. Bring the liquid to above 65°C/149°F minimum to fully hydrate and activate the gelling agent. It begins to set at 60°C/140°F.

5. Let the liquid cool down if it went too far above hydrating temperature, but do not let it cool so much that it will set before pouring it into the frame. Pour the liquid into the frame and let it set for about 10 minutes, and then place it in the refrigerator.

6. Once the jelly has set, cover it with plastic wrap. It will keep for up to 3 days in the refrigerator. Freezing is not recommended because it will turn the jelly dull and wrinkled.

note The vegetable gelling agent is a mixture of carrageenan gum and locust bean gum. See Resources on page 540.

LEMON VELVET

yield: 1.5 kg/3 lb 4.96 oz

INGREDIENT	METRIC	U.S.	%
Cocoa butter powder (Mycryo)	1.45 kg	3 lb 1.84 oz	96.67%
Lemon oil	50 g	1.76 oz	3.33%

1. Melt the cocoa butter over a hot water bath. Once it has melted, stir in the lemon oil.

2. Reserve in a warm place to keep the velvet fluid (melted).

3. The velvet will keep for 1 week if kept warm, or for up to 1 month if it is left to set and stored at room temperature.

petits plaisirs and other individual desserts

Petits plaisirs literally translates to "small pleasures" from the French. These are a series of desserts that all share the same essential principle: They are small. These desserts step away from the classic pâtisserie format of individual desserts, which are really just small versions of cakes. I wanted to produce desserts that could be put inside a display case and just as well be served in a restaurant environment. Of course, there are limitations. These petits plaisirs still have to subscribe to all of the display-case principles mentioned at the beginning of this chapter. No components can get soggy or suffer from the display-case environment, and of course there are no frozen components. But these types of desserts have achieved a happy medium. And considering how much these desserts are exposed (as is anything that is kept in a display case without being covered), I thought it might be a good idea to put desserts in a jar, or a beautiful clear plastic box. These desserts are ready to go (*prêt à partir,* if you will) and need nothing else but the box or bag in which they are to be taken away. Furthermore, a dessert in a jar allowed me to do something not very common in a display case, and that was to have desserts that would actually have a sauce. Desserts could have a variety of components, like a plated dessert in a restaurant, and could be presented in a jar because they wouldn't suffer the impact of the conditions of the display case.

While cakes typically have a coating to protect them from the circulating air in the display case, most of the desserts that are not in a box or a jar will be affected. In these cases it is important to always have the top component be a moist one that can withstand many hours in the case, like a jelly, fruit compote, or honeycomb. It is a good idea to use chocolate as a protective coat as well, but not all your desserts will be made with chocolate, and using chocolate haphazardly is not a good idea.

Another important consideration for the presentation of these desserts is the environmental impact it will have. It is better to use more organic materials, such as glass, or, if using plastic, it should either be recyclable or an item that could be used by the customer for another purpose. The secondary effect of using these types of organic packaging is that they are visually arresting. They are environmentally friendly, they preserve desserts longer, and they make them look beautiful. The downside is that the packaging can be expensive, but this can always be included in the price of the dessert, especially if the customer can take the packaging home.

Small desserts are also more approachable. Customers will be inclined to purchase a variety of small desserts when perhaps they would buy only one if it were a slightly larger individual portion. The petits plaisirs were inspired by restaurants that sell small portions of tapas-style food. It is great to taste as much as possible and have a large variety of flavors and textures to sample, as opposed to one big item, which limits the experience. For some customers there is also less guilt involved in ordering something that is eaten in three or four bites rather than in six or seven (or more).

packaging cakes and individual pastries (petits plaisirs)

THE JOB IS NOT OVER once the products are packaged and ready to be taken away. Technically it is over once the last piece is eaten. One of the links in the chain between the café and the consumer is the transportation of the product to wherever the customer is taking it. Customers will assume and expect that if they purchase a cake, go directly home, and keep it in the refrigerator, it will be fine for at least two days. If they open the box and the cake or desserts have fallen over or gotten damaged, it is usually too late for them to run out and get another cake, since this box will probably be opened just before dinner or even just at the moment dessert is served.

Whenever a new dessert is implemented, think about this part of the puzzle: How will it be packaged so that it makes it safely to someone's home? If it cannot be packaged at all (either because it is too tall or it contains a liquid, for example), be honest with your customers and make a different suggestion. The box a cake is packaged in should be about .5 cm/.2 in bigger than the cake board, and it should be front loading, not top loading. It will be nearly impossible to take the cake out without damaging it if it is in a top-loading box. For petits plaisirs and other individual desserts, box each dessert individually in same-size boxes, and then put those boxes in a larger box to keep them in place. It is good to have an all-purpose box for small desserts, medium desserts, and cakes, and some of varying sizes. Try to stick to a general dessert dimension so that there is always a box available. Of course, if you just have to have a particular item on your menu and no box you have in stock will do, then plan ahead and purchase the correct size boxes for when the dessert or cake comes out on the menu. In some cases, use tissue to wrap certain desserts to cushion them in the box; just make sure that the tissue does not damage the dessert. This technique is used mostly for desserts that are assembled and displayed or served in a glass vessel. It is a good idea to anchor down the dessert if it is assembled on a cake board, a small board, or a flat base of any sort. Use a sticker with the establishment's logo on it. This will keep it from moving around the box.

Always use sturdy boxes and packaging and never flimsy, cheap boxes that will fall apart or disassemble easily. Imagine the potential tragedy if all the desserts end up on the floor and create a very unhappy customer. I also strongly suggest using either recyclable or biodegradable materials.

possible defects of individual desserts

defect	cause	solution
A skin has formed on the outer layer.	The dessert has begun to dry out due to long exposure in the refrigerator to circulating air.	Discard desserts within 24 to 36 hours of being made. Always taste them on a daily basis.
Condensation has formed on the dessert.	The display case is not functioning properly (it is not venting properly).	Have the display case fixed.
The desserts have a refrigerator taste.	The display case is not clean.	Deep clean the display case once a week and do a regular cleaning on a daily basis.
Desserts seem loose (fluid).	The display case is running warm. Ingredients were not weighed out properly.	Adjust the thermostat; if that doesn't work, the display needs to be fixed by a technician.

COCONUT TAPIOCA WITH PASSION FRUIT CURD AND PASSION FRUIT GELÉE

yield: 20 portions

components

400 g/14.11 oz Passion Fruit Gelée

900 g/1 lb 15.68 oz Passion Fruit Curd (page 165)

600 g/1 lb 5.12 oz Coconut Tapioca

100 g/3.53 oz Basil Seeds

20 strands very fine basil chiffonade

1. Assemble twenty 75-mL/2.5-fl-oz oval glasses.

2. Place the passion fruit gelée in a freezer to harden so that it will be easier to unmold.

3. Meanwhile, fill the glasses one-third of the way full with the passion fruit curd.

4. Fill the glass halfway up with the coconut tapioca (about 30 g/1.06 oz per glass).

5. Push the passion fruit gelée out of the fleximolds and put one on top of the coconut tapioca

6. Spoon 5 g/.17 oz basil seeds over the top.

7. Place a strand of basil chiffonade directly over the passion fruit gelée.

note This dessert must be discarded the day after it is made if there is any left in the display case, since the tapioca will continue to absorb water even after it has fully cooked. It will go from being chewy to crumbly, like wet cooked rice.

PASSION FRUIT GELÉE

yield: 400 g/14.11 oz

INGREDIENT	METRIC	U.S.	%
Passion fruit juice	319 g	11.26 oz	79.82%
Sugar	64 g	2.25 oz	15.96%
Gelatin sheets, bloomed in cold water (4.8 sheets)	17 g	.59 oz	4.21%

1. Place 2 fleximolds with 12 rectangular cavities 2.5 by 3.75 by .62 cm/1 by 1.5 by .25 in each on a half sheet pan.

2. Bring the passion fruit juice and sugar to a boil. Let it boil for 5 seconds, and remove the pot from the heat. Squeeze the excess water from the bloomed gelatin. Stir in the gelatin until it has dissolved.

3. Portion the gelée into the fleximolds using a funnel gun, filling the cavities up to the top. Only fill 20 cavities for 20 portions (1 gelée rectangle per portion). Refrigerate the gelée until it sets.

4. Cover the fleximolds with plastic wrap. The gelée will keep for up to 3 days in the refrigerator if covered in plastic.

note If the passion fruit juice is a concentrated purée, use half passion fruit purée and half orange juice.

COCONUT TAPIOCA

INGREDIENT	METRIC	U.S.	%
Tapioca (small pearls)	120 g	4.23 oz	19.97%
Unsweetened coconut milk	360 g	12.68 oz	59.92%
Sugar	120 g	4.23 oz	19.97%
Salt	.8 g	.03 oz	.13%

1. Place the tapioca in a small pot and cover it with cold water. Bring the mixture to a boil, and strain out the resulting liquid. Return the tapioca to the pot, cover with fresh cold water, return to a boil, and strain the resulting liquid again. Repeat this procedure 4 times or until the tapioca is translucent.

2. Rinse the tapioca in cold water to rinse the mucilaginous coating off the pearls and to stop the cooking process.

3. Put the tapioca in a bowl with the coconut milk, sugar, and salt. Mix until the sugar has dissolved. Adjust sweetness if necessary by adding more sugar.

notes This recipe will yield more than the total weight of the recipe, since tapioca absorbs close to 3 times its weight in water while it is cooking.

The tapioca must be made just before assembling these desserts to prevent it from clumping.

BASIL SEEDS

INGREDIENT	METRIC	U.S.	%
Basil seeds (see Resources, page 540)	50 g	1.76 oz	50%
Hot water, at 80°C/176°F	50 g	1.76 oz	50%

Combine both ingredients in a small cup and let them sit for at least 1 hour uncovered at room temperature before using. Basil seeds will absorb the water and form a gelatinous shell around them. This gives the seeds 2 textures: crunchy and chewy. Discard after 24 hours.

CHOCOLATE POT DE CRÈME IN AN EGGSHELL

yield: 20 portions

components

50 g/1.76 oz melted dark chocolate

20 Eggshells

900 g/1 lb 15.68 oz Chocolate Pot de Crème Base

20 printed rooster images on sugar paper (see Note)

100 g/3.53 oz dark chocolate décor chips (see Resources, page 540)

1. Assemble 20 curved triangle plastic plates and 1 can of cold spray (see Resources, page 540). Place the 20 curved triangle plastic plates on a work surface.

2. Place the melted dark chocolate in a cornet. Pipe a small dot of dark chocolate from the cornet in the center of each plate.

3. Place an eggshell on the dark chocolate dot and spray it with the cold spray so that it sets quickly. This has to be done 1 egg at a time.

4. Place the chocolate pot de crème in a piping bag and pipe about 45 g/1.6 oz into each eggshell. The pot de crème should come within .3 cm/.1 in of the top of the egg.

5. Place a white chocolate décor rectangle into each of the filled eggshells diagonally.

6. Put about 5 g/.18 oz chocolate décor chips into each eggshell. Try to cover the entire surface of the pot de crème.

7. Discard after 36 hours.

note For the rooster images: These images are printed on edible sugar paper with edible ink. You can purchase all the necessary items (the printer, the paper, and the ink; see Resources, page 540) and do it yourself, or you can order the images online (see Resources, page 540).

EGGSHELLS

yield: 20 eggshells

INGREDIENT	METRIC	U.S.	%
Eggs	20	20	100%

1. Bring the eggs to room temperature either by leaving them out for a few hours or by placing them in a warm oven for a few minutes. This will help to cleanly remove the top.

2. Using an egg topper, top the narrow tip end of the eggshell. Be very careful to apply the right amount of pressure, since the eggs can easily break. It might take a few tries before getting it right, so plan on making a few extra eggshells just in case. Reserve the eggs to make the pot de crème base or for other uses.

3. Place the empty eggshells in a large sauce pot filled with hot water and bring them to a boil. Boil them for 15 seconds. Remove the eggshells from the water and rinse them off.

4. Peel off the inside membrane. Let the eggshells dry at room temperature.

CHOCOLATE POT DE CRÈME BASE

yield: 900 g/1 lb 15.68 oz

INGREDIENT	METRIC	U.S.	%
Heavy cream	438 g	15.45 oz	48.67%
Milk	120 g	4.22 oz	13.29%
Sugar	80 g	2.8 oz	8.83%
Egg yolks	79 g	2.78 oz	8.75%
Dark chocolate (64%)	184 g	6.49 oz	20.45%

1. Prepare an ice bath.

2. Combine the cream, milk, sugar, and egg yolks in a small sauce pot over medium heat. Bring the mixture slowly to 82°C/180°F while whisking constantly.

3. Remove the pot from the heat and add the chocolate. Mix using a handheld immersion blender.

4. Pass the liquid through a fine-mesh sieve and cool it over the prepared ice bath.

5. Once it has cooled, transfer it to an airtight container and reserve in the refrigerator. The pot de crème base will keep for up to 5 days in the refrigerator.

note Pot de crème is typically baked in the oven as crème brûlée is, but for this recipe, it is cooked in a pot on the stove.

VANILLA PANNA COTTA WITH YUZU CURD, RUBY SIPPERS GELÉE, AND A SHOT OF YUZU

yield: **20 portions**

components

900 g/1 lb 15.75 oz Vanilla Panna Cotta

600 g/1 lb 5.12 oz Yuzu Curd

300 g/10.58 oz Ruby Sippers Gelée

200 g/7.06 oz white chocolate–coated puffed rice
(see Resources, page 540)

1 sheet gold leaf

300 g/10.58 oz Yuzu Shot

1. Soften the panna cotta in a bowl over a warm, not hot, water bath until it is a pourable consistency. It should be about 21°C/70F. It is important not to let it get it too hot or else the vanilla beans will not be evenly dispersed throughout the panna cotta. They will settle at the bottom of the liquid.

2. Soften the curd using the same procedure and to the same temperature.

3. Melt the ruby sippers gelée using the same procedure, but it will need to come to 30°C/82°F to be of an adequate pouring temperature.

4. Pour all of the melted ruby sippers gelée inside twenty 2-cm/.8-in diameter silicone sphere molds and freeze to harden.

5. Place 20 glasses (120 ml/4 fl oz) on a half sheet pan. Pour about 20 g/.7 oz of curd into each glass, and let it set in the refrigerator for about 45 minutes or until firm.

6. Pour about 45 g/1.6 oz of the panna cotta into each glass. Freeze the glasses until the panna cotta has set, but is not hardened. Once it sets, put 10 g/.35 oz of the chocolate-coated puffed rice over the entire surface of the panna cotta.

7. Push the frozen ruby sippers spheres out of the silicone molds and place them on top of the puffed rice.

8. Garnish the top of each sphere with a small piece of gold leaf.

9. Place the yuzu shot pipette in the perforation on the glass.

10. Display or serve. Discard after 36 hours.

note The order in which the components are made doesn't matter, but the order in which the dessert is assembled does matter.

VANILLA PANNA COTTA

yield: 900 g/1 lb 15.68 oz

INGREDIENT	METRIC	U.S.	%
Heavy cream	814 g	1 lb 12.8 oz	90.48%
Sugar	77 g	2.72 oz	8.57%
Tahitian vanilla pods, split and scraped	2	2	
Gelatin sheets, bloomed (2.6 sheets)	9 g	.3 oz	.95%

1. Prepare an ice bath.

2. Place the cream, sugar, and vanilla pods and seeds in a small sauce pot. Bring the liquid to a boil, and remove the pot from the heat. Let the vanilla pods steep for 10 minutes off the heat.

3. Squeeze the excess liquid from the gelatin sheets. Add the gelatin to the cream mixture and stir until it has dissolved.

4. Strain the liquid through a fine-mesh sieve and place over the prepared ice bath to cool. Stir it as it cools, so that the vanilla seeds will be evenly distributed throughout the panna cotta. Otherwise they will settle at the bottom of the liquid.

5. Once the panna cotta has cooled down, transfer it to an airtight container and refrigerate it. The panna cotta will keep for up to 5 days in the refrigerator.

YUZU CURD

yield: 600 g/1 lb 5.12 oz

INGREDIENT	METRIC	U.S.	%
Yuzu juice	55 g	1.92 oz	9.09%
Lemon juice	55 g	1.92 oz	9.09%
Sugar	109 g	3.85 oz	18.18%
Eggs	109 g	3.85 oz	18.18%
Butter	273 g	9.62 oz	45.45%

To make the curd, see the procedure for passion fruit curd on page 165.

RUBY SIPPERS GELÉE

yield: 300 g/10.58 oz

INGREDIENT	METRIC	U.S.	%
Water	211 g	7.43 oz	70.24%
Ruby sippers tisane (see Resources, page 540)	50 g	1.76 oz	
Sugar	77 g	2.7 oz	25.54%
Gelatin sheets, bloomed (3.7 sheets)	13 g	.45 oz	4.21%

1. Bring 261 g/9.2 oz water to a boil. Add the tisane and let it steep for 5 minutes. Strain the resulting liquid out, and measure out 211 g/7.43 oz of the infusion. Add the sugar while the infusion is still hot and stir until it dissolves completely.

2. Squeeze the excess water from the gelatin sheets. Add the gelatin sheets to the hot liquid and stir until they dissolve. Adjust sweetness if necessary by adding more sugar.

3. Let the infusion cool to room temperature. Transfer to an airtight container and refrigerate. The gelée will keep for up to 2 weeks in the refrigerator.

YUZU SHOT

yield: 300 g/10.58 oz

INGREDIENT	METRIC	U.S.	%
Yuzu juice	60 g	2.12 oz	20%
Simple syrup, at 50° Brix	240 g	8.47 oz	80%

1. Combine the yuzu juice with the simple syrup. Adjust sweetness if necessary.

2. Assemble 20 pipettes (see Resources, page 540). Squeeze the large end of the pipette and suction about 15 g/.52 oz yuzu shot per pipette. Reserve in the refrigerator. This item will keep for up to 10 days in the refrigerator.

LEMONGRASS PANNA COTTA WITH BUBBLE TAPIOCA AND FIJI TEA

yield: **20 portions**

components

1.2 kg/2 lb 10.24 oz Lemongrass Panna Cotta

600 g/1 lb 5.12 oz Bubble Tapioca

600 g/1 lb 5.12 oz Fiji Tea

1. Assemble 20 rectangular glasses (see Resources, page 540) on a sheet pan.

2. Warm the panna cotta over a warm, not hot, water bath until it is a pourable consistency. Fill the glasses halfway with panna cotta (about 60 g/1.6 oz per glass).

3. Let the panna cotta set in the refrigerator.

4. Strain the tapioca pearls from the corn syrup and pat them dry with a clean, heavy-duty paper towel. Place 30 g/1.05 oz of bubble tapioca into each glass.

5. Pour 30 g/1.05 oz of the Fiji tea into each glass.

6. Place a bubble tapioca straw into each glass (see Resources, page 540).

7. Display or serve. Discard after 24 hours. Ordinarily a dessert has a shelf life of up to 36 hours, but tapioca tends to break down and become crumbly as opposed to staying chewy which is the desired texture once it is just cooked.

note The ideal way to eat this dessert is to stir the panna cotta with the tapioca and Fiji tea using the straw, and then drink the contents through the straw. Advise your customers to do so.

LEMONGRASS PANNA COTTA

yield: 1.2 kg/2 lb 10.24 oz

INGREDIENT	METRIC	U.S.	%
LEMONGRASS-INFUSED CREAM			
Lemongrass	900 g	1 lb 15.68 oz	45%
Heavy cream	1.1 kg	2 lb 6.88 oz	55%
LEMONGRASS PANNA COTTA			
Lemongrass-Infused Cream	1.08 kg	2 lb 6.09 oz	90.2%
Sugar	103 g	3.62 oz	8.55%
Gelatin sheets, bloomed (4.3 sheets)	15 g	.53 oz	1.25%

1. Crush the lemongrass with a wooden dowel on a marble surface. Combine it with the cream in a sauce pot.

2. Bring the cream to a simmer, stir the liquid, and then remove the pan from the heat. Let it steep for 20 minutes off the heat with the pot covered with plastic wrap.

3. Strain the liquid and measure the amount of cream needed for the panna cotta. Add the sugar and the bloomed gelatin. The cream should still be hot enough to dissolve both ingredients.

4. Cool over an ice bath, and then transfer to an airtight container and refrigerate. Discard after 5 days.

BUBBLE TAPIOCA

yield: 600 g/1 lb 5.12 oz

INGREDIENT	METRIC	U.S.	%
Water	2.1 kg	4 lb 10.08 oz	77.78%
Bubble tapioca	300 g	10.58 oz	11.11%
Light corn syrup	300 g	10.58 oz	11.11%

1. Bring the water to a boil in a sauce pot, and then pour in the tapioca, stirring gently so that the pearls do not scorch or stick to the bottom of the pot.

2. Wait until the tapioca pearls float to the top, and then cover the pot with a lid. Cook for 25 to 30 more minutes over low heat.

3. Remove the pot from the heat and let it sit for 25 to 30 minutes with the lid still on it.

4. Strain the pearls and rinse them in cold water to stop the cooking process.

5. Toss them in a bowl with the corn syrup. They must be used within 24 hours of being made; otherwise they will go from being pleasantly chewy to unpleasantly crumbly.

note The total weight of the recipe is much larger than the yield, because the water used to cook the bubble tapioca will be discarded. Consider that the bubble tapioca will absorb twice its weight in water as well. This bubble tapioca should be the parcooked variety (see Resources, page 540).

FIJI TEA

yield: 600 g/1 lb 5.12 oz

INGREDIENT	METRIC	U.S.	%
Water	500 g	1 lb 1.6 oz	83.33%
Fiji tea (see Resources, page 540)	100 g	3.53 oz	
Sugar	100 g	3.53 oz	16.67%

1. Bring the water to a boil, and take it off the heat. Pour in the Fiji tea and stir for a few seconds. Let the tea steep for 5 minutes.

2. Strain the liquid out and add the sugar. Stir until it has dissolved. Adjust sweetness if necessary.

3. Cool and reserve at room temperature until needed. Discard after 24 hours.

note This tea should be used the same day it is brewed.

ACACIA HONEY CREAM WITH RAW MOLASSES JELLY AND HONEYCOMB

yield: 20 portions

components

1.2 kg/2 lb 10.4 oz Acacia Honey Cream

600 g/1 lb 5.12 oz Raw Molasses Jelly

20 honeycomb squares (3.75 cm/1.5 in)

1. Bring the acacia honey cream and molasses jelly to room temperature. Make sure that both are of a pourable consistency. If they are too cold and the gelatin in them begins to set, simply warm them up slightly over a warm, not hot, water bath or in a microwave for a few seconds.

2. Place 20 slanted glasses on a half sheet pan (see Resources, page 540).

3. Pour a .6-cm/.25-in layer of acacia cream into each glass and let it set in the refrigerator.

4. Pour .2 cm/.08 in of raw molasses jelly on top of the acacia cream once it is set. Let it set in the refrigerator. Repeat this process until there are 5 layers of acacia honey cream alternating with 5 layers of raw molasses jelly. The last layer should be molasses jelly.

5. Place a square of honeycomb directly on top of the jelly. Display or serve. Discard after 36 hours.

ACACIA HONEY CREAM

yield: 1.2 kg/2 lb 10.4 oz

INGREDIENT	METRIC	U.S.	%
Heavy cream	953 g	2 lb 1.16 oz	86.36%
Acacia honey	181 g	6.37 oz	8.18%
Honey powder (see Resources, page 540)	50 g	1.77 oz	4.55%
Gelatin sheets, bloomed (4.6 sheets)	16 g	.57 oz	.91%
Yellow food coloring (water based)	as needed	as needed	

1. Bring the cream, honey, and honey powder to a simmer in a sauce pot. Be sure to pour in the honey powder while stirring to prevent clumping.

2. Squeeze the excess water from the gelatin sheets. Remove the pot from the heat and stir in the gelatin sheets until they have dissolved. Stir in the yellow food coloring until a bright yellow is obtained.

3. Cool the mixture to 21°C/70°F over a cold water bath. Do not use an ice bath, since the temperature will make the cream set too fast.

note For the honey powder, use Crumiel (see Resources, page 540).

RAW MOLASSES JELLY

yield: 600 g/1 lb 5.12 oz

INGREDIENT	METRIC	U.S.	%
Water	456 g	1 lb .16 oz	75.99%
Molasses	114 g	4.02 oz	19%
Gelatin sheets, bloomed	30 g	1.06 oz	5.02%
Black food coloring	as needed	as needed	

1. Combine the water with the molasses in a sauce pot and bring it to a simmer. Remove the pot from the heat. Squeeze the excess water from the gelatin sheets and stir in the gelatin until dissolved.

2. Add a few drops of food coloring, until the liquid turns a deep black. Cool the jelly to 21°C/70°F over a cold water bath. Do not use an ice bath, because the temperature will make the jelly set too fast.

RED VELVET CAKE

yield: 45 portions

components

3 Red Velvet Sponge Cakes

5 kg/11 lb .32 oz Coconut-Pecan Filling

1. Place a sheet of silicone paper on a flat full-size sheet pan or cutting board. Assemble 11 Plexiglas frames with exterior dimensions of 27.5 by 40 by 1.25 cm/11 by 16 by .5 in and interior dimensions of 22.5 by 35 cm/9 by 14 in. The frame is 2.5 cm/1 in wide all around.

2. Remove the nonstick rubber mats from the cakes before cutting. Cut all of the red velvet cakes in half widthwise, and then cut around their borders so that they will fit inside the Plexiglas frames.

3. Place the first frame on the prepared sheet pan or cutting board. Place the first layer of cake inside it. If the cake is thicker than the frame, use a long serrated knife to trim off the top, using the frame as a guide to cut the cake to an even thickness. Lean the blade of the knife on the frame and slowly cut the cake in short sawing motions.

4. Put another frame on top of the evened-out cake, and fill it with one-quarter of the coconut-pecan filling. Spread the filling in an even layer using an offset spatula, and place another frame on top of it. Place a layer of cake inside the frame. Repeat this procedure until there is a total of 5 layers of cake alternating with 4 layers of coconut-pecan filling. Once the cake is assembled, cover it with plastic wrap and freeze it.

5. Remove the cake from the freezer, and remove all of the frames one by one by cutting around the inside border of the frame with a paring knife. Transfer the cake to a cutting board if it is not already on one.

6. Cut rectangles out of the cake that are 3.75/1.5 in squares. The easiest way to cut it, since it is such a thick cake, is to make a grid on the top of the cake with the above measurements using a ruler and a paring knife. Use a 30-cm/12-in double-handled cheese knife, making sure to cut straight down so that the rectangles will stand straight up.

7. Display or present. Discard after 72 hours.

note Due to the fact that the most efficient way to assemble this cake is by using frames the size of half sheet pans, this recipe will yield a much larger amount than the more common 20-portion recipes. However, this cake freezes very well, so it can be portioned and the remainder can be frozen.

RED VELVET SPONGE CAKE

yield: 6 kg/13 lb 3.68 oz

INGREDIENT	METRIC	U.S.	%
Butter, at 21°C/70°F	975 g	2 lb 2.4 oz	16.24%
Superfine or bakers' sugar	1.72 kg	3 lb 12.96 oz	28.83%
Eggs, at 21°C/70°F	430 g	15.16 oz	7.16%
Red food coloring	122 g	4.3 oz	2.03%
Cocoa powder	129 g	4.55 oz	2.15%
All-purpose flour	1.41 kg	3 lb 2.08 oz	23.63%
Salt	13 g	.45 oz	.21%
Vanilla powder	21 g	.76 oz	.36%
Buttermilk	1.05 kg	2 lb 5.44 oz	17.66%
Baking soda	39 g	1.36 oz	.64%
White vinegar	64 g	2.27 oz	1.07%

1. Grease 3 full-size sheet pans with nonstick oil spray around the border, and then line each sheet pan with a nonstick rubber mat.

2. To make the cakes, see the procedure for red velvet cupcakes on page 269.

3. Divide the batter into 3 equal parts, pour each one into a prepared sheet pan, and spread it in an even layer using an offset spatula.

4. Bake until the cakes spring back when gentle pressure is applied, about 15 to 17 minutes per cake. Let the cakes cool to room temperature.

COCONUT-PECAN FILLING

yield: 5 kg/11 lb .32 oz

INGREDIENT	METRIC	U.S.	%
Milk	1.31 kg	2 lb 14.24 oz	26.22%
Bread flour	51 g	1.79 oz	1.01%
Cake flour	41 g	1.43 oz	.81%
Butter, soft	1.31 kg	2 lb 14.24 oz	26.22%
Superfine or bakers' sugar	1.16 kg	2 lb 9.28 oz	23.40%
Tahitian vanilla paste	15 g	.54 oz	.3%
Shredded sweet coconut	413 g	14.57 oz	8.26%
Pecans, chopped and toasted	688 g	1 lb 8.32 oz	13.76%

1. Combine the milk with the flours and bring to a boil in a sauce pot, whisking constantly. Boil until it thickens to a paste, and let it cool to room temperature.

2. Meanwhile, cream the butter and the sugar in a mixer using a paddle attachment until light and fluffy, 4 to 5 minutes. Add the vanilla paste.

3. Add the cooled flour paste and paddle until smooth.

4. Fold in the coconut and pecans.

ANGEL FOOD CAKE WITH VANILLA CRÈME ANGLAISE, WILD BLUEBERRY COMPOTE, AND VANILLA CHANTILLY

yield: 20 portions

components

400 g/14.11 oz Vanilla Anglaise (page 158)

1 Angel Food Cake

400 g/14.11 oz Wild Blueberry Compote

300 g/10.58 oz Vanilla Chantilly (page 146)

1. Assemble 20 mason jars measuring 150 mL/5 fl oz and arrange them on a half sheet pan.

2. Pour about 60 g/2.1 oz of crème anglaise into each jar.

3. Cut 20 squares of angel food cake that are 2.5 cm/1 in thick. Place 1 piece of angel food cake in each jar.

4. Drain the wild blueberry compote from its cooking liquid with a slotted spoon and pat dry on a clean piece of heavy-duty paper towel. Each jar will need 20 g/.7 oz of compote. Spoon it next to the angel food cake. Spoon or pipe 15 g/.52 oz of vanilla Chantilly on top of the compote and angel food cake.

5. Close the lids on the mason jars. Display or serve. Discard after 48 hours.

note The order in which the components are made is not important.

ANGEL FOOD CAKE

yield: 550 g/1 lb 3.34 oz

INGREDIENT	METRIC	U.S.	%
Pastry flour	87 g	3.05 oz	15.74%
Sugar	230 g	8.11 oz	41.9%
Egg whites	231 g	8.15 oz	41.99%
Cream of tartar	.51 g	.02 oz	.09%
Salt	2 g	.05 oz	.28%

1. Preheat a convection oven to 160°C/320°F.

2. Place a 20-cm/8-in angel food cake pan on a half sheet pan.

3. Sift the pastry flour with 115 g/4.06 oz sugar.

4. Whip the egg whites with the remaining sugar, cream of tartar, and salt on high speed until stiff peaks form.

5. Fold in the sifted dry ingredients.

6. Pour into the ungreased angel food cake pan.

7. Bake until golden brown and the crown of the angel food cake springs back when gentle pressure is applied to the surface.

8. Flip the angel food cake over onto the sheet pan it was baked on. These pans have a tube-like opening down the center that is higher than the outside of the pan, so when it is flipped over, the cake will not touch the surface of the sheet pan. This will cool the cake faster and prevent sticking, and it is also what gives the cake its characteristic shape. The tube is also there to ensure an even bake. These pans are typically made of aluminum, and they are not greased because the cake needs something to "adhere to" while it bakes; otherwise it would collapse onto itself if the cake mold had a slippery surface.

9. Once the cake has cooled, pass a paring knife between the cake and all sides of the pan. Tap the cake out gently.

10. The cake can be wrapped with plastic, labeled, and refrigerated or frozen. The cake will keep in the refrigerator for up to 4 days or in the freezer for up to 2 months.

WILD BLUEBERRY COMPOTE

yield: 400 g/14.11 oz drained mass (see Note)

INGREDIENT	METRIC	U.S.	%
Wild blueberries	300 g	10.58 oz	42.86%
Sugar	300 g	10.58 oz	42.86%
Water	100 g	3.53 oz	14.29%
Tahitian vanilla pod, split and scraped	4	4	0.00%

1. Combine all of the ingredients in a pot and bring to a boil over high heat.

2. Turn off the heat and let the pot stand for about an hour. Remove the vanilla pod. Cool the compote over an ice bath, and then transfer to an airtight container and refrigerate. Discard after 8 days.

note The recipe itself is larger than 400 g/14.11 oz, but once the blueberries are drained, they will yield about this amount.

PEANUT BUTTER AND MILK CHOCOLATE "SNOW CONE"

yield: 20 portions

components

900 g/1 lb 15.68 oz Peanut Butter Powder

900 g/1 lb 15.68 oz Milk Chocolate Powder

1. Assemble 20 bamboo cornets (see Resources, page 540) on a Plexiglas (or other material) stand.

2. Spoon 45 g/1.6 oz of peanut butter powder in one half of the cornet, and then spoon 45 g/1.6 oz of milk chocolate powder in the other half of the cornet, so that both components are distinguishable.

3. Display or serve. Discard after 48 hours.

PEANUT BUTTER POWDER

yield: 900 g/1 lb 15.68 oz

INGREDIENT	METRIC	U.S.	%
Peanut butter	600 g	1 lb 5.12 oz	66.67%
Tapioca maltodextrin (see Note)	300 g	10.58 oz	33.33%

1. Place the peanut butter and tapioca maltodextrin in a Robot Coupe and grind together until a homogeneous mass is obtained; it should look like a ball of clay. If it is too wet and it does not hold its shape, add more tapioca maltodextrin.

2. Pass the resulting mixture through a drum sieve.

3. Let it dry for a few hours at room temperature, and then transfer it to an airtight container. Reserve in a cool, dry place. The powder will keep for 1 week before it starts to dry out.

MILK CHOCOLATE POWDER

INGREDIENT	METRIC	U.S.	%
Milk chocolate coins	500 g	1 lb .16 oz	55.56%
Canola oil	100 g	3.53 oz	11.11%
Tapioca maltodextrin	300 g	10.58 oz	33.33%

1. Melt the milk chocolate with the canola oil over a hot water bath. Transfer to a Robot Coupe and grind together with the tapioca maltodextrin until a homogeneous mass is obtained. If it is too wet, add more tapioca maltodextrin.

2. Pass the resulting mixture through a drum sieve.

3. Let it dry out at room temperature for a few hours, and then transfer it to an airtight container. Reserve in a cool, dry place. It will keep for 1 week before it starts to dry out.

notes Tapioca maltodextrin is a modified tapioca starch that thickens and stabilizes fatty compounds. It is flavorless. One of its properties is that when mixed with any ingredient, for example peanut butter and milk chocolate, and then dried briefly, it will reconstitute in your mouth. It has to be mixed with an ingredient that contains some fat in order to produce the "snow" (or some might say, "dirt") look. However, it also works with nonfat liquids. For example, it can gel in cold water.

LEMON CURD WITH SHORTBREAD AND ITALIAN MERINGUE

yield: 20 portions

components

1.2 kg/2 lb 10.4 oz Lemon Curd (page 156)

600 g/1 lb 5.12 oz Shortbread

270 g/9.52 oz Italian Meringue

1. Assemble 20 votive glasses measuring 90 mL/ 30 fl oz on a sheet pan.

2. Smooth the lemon curd in a bowl using a whisk. Fill the glasses halfway full with lemon curd.

3. Place 30 g/1.05 oz of shortbread on top of the curd. Make sure the shortbread is not visible; it should be inside the boundaries of the curd.

4. Fill to the top with lemon curd and smooth the top with an offset spatula. Reserve in the refrigerator.

5. Pipe enough meringue onto each glass to cover the entire surface. Try to give the meringue as much height as possible.

6. Using a torch, brown the meringue lightly.

7. Display or serve. Discard after 36 hours.

SHORTBREAD

yield: 600 g/1 lb 5.12 oz

INGREDIENT	METRIC	U.S.	%
All-purpose flour	245 g	8.65 oz	40.89%
Rice flour	35 g	1.24 oz	5.84%
Salt	4 g	.15 oz	.7%
Butter, soft	210 g	7.42 oz	35.05%
Superfine or bakers' sugar	105 g	3.71 oz	17.52%
Superfine or bakers' sugar, for sprinkling the dough	75 g	2.64 oz	

1. Sift the flours and the salt together.

2. Cream the butter and the sugar together in the bowl of an electric mixer fitted with the paddle attachment until a homogeneous mass is obtained. Be careful to not over-cream the mixture.

3. Add the sifted dry ingredients to the mixer and mix on low speed until incorporated.

4. Roll the dough into a 1.25-cm-/.5-in-thick rectangle on a sheet pan lined with parchment paper. Cover with plastic wrap and refrigerate for 1 hour or until hardened.

5. Preheat a convection oven to 160°C/320°F.

6. Dock the firm shortbread with a fork, making sure to go all the way through the dough. Sprinkle the sugar on top of the dough.

7. Bake until golden brown, 7 to 9 minutes.

8. Cool to room temperature.

9. Once the shortbread has cooled, cut it into 1.25-cm/.5-in pieces with a knife. Reserve at room temperature in an airtight container. The shortbread will keep for up to 1 week at room temperature.

ITALIAN MERINGUE

yield: 270 g/9.52 oz

INGREDIENT	METRIC	U.S.	%
Sugar	180 g	6.35 oz	66.67%
Egg whites	90 g	3.17 oz	33.33%

1. Combine the sugar with one-quarter of its weight in water in a small sauce pot. Mix well until all of the sugar has been hydrated.

2. Cook over high heat until it reaches 121°C/250°F. Meanwhile, whip the egg whites until stiff peaks form. If the sugar reaches the desired temperature before the egg whites are fully whipped, shock the pot in a cold water bath to stop the cooking process.

3. Pour the hot sugar into the whipping egg whites. Continue to whip until the meringue cools completely.

4. Once it cools, transfer the meringue to a piping bag fitted with a large coupler or a large plain piping tip. Follow the instructions for finishing on page 244.

MAPLE POT DE CRÈME

yield: **20 portions**

components

1.5 kg/3 lb 4.96 oz Maple Pot de Crème

100 g/3.53 oz Grade A maple syrup

1. Pour 5 g/.18 oz of maple syrup on top of the baked maple pot de crème.

2. Close the lids of the mason jars.

3. Display or serve. Discard after 36 hours.

MAPLE POT DE CRÈME

yield: 1.5 kg/3 lb 4.96 oz

INGREDIENT	METRIC	U.S.	%
Heavy cream	969 g	2 lb 2.24 oz	64.58%
Maple sugar	326 g	11.51 oz	21.75%
Salt	1 g	.04 oz	.07%
Egg yolks	204 g	7.19 oz	13.6%

1. Place 20 mason jars with a 90-mL/3-fl-oz capacity in a 10-cm-/4-in-deep full-size hotel pan.

2. Preheat a convection oven to 135°C/275°F.

3. Bring the cream, 293 g/10.34 oz sugar, and the salt to a boil.

4. Whisk the egg yolks with the remaining sugar in a bowl. Temper the hot cream into the yolks.

5. Strain through a fine-mesh sieve, and then place about 75 g/2.65 oz into each mason jar, using a funnel gun. Try to bake the pot de crème immediately. This will cut the baking time in half because the base is already hot.

6. Place the hotel pan in the oven, and then pour enough hot water into it to come up to the same level as the pot de crème in the jars.

7. Bake for 15 to 20 minutes or until the pot de crème is set. It will still have a slight jiggle when it is properly baked. If it sloshes around in the jar, it needs to bake longer; if it doesn't jiggle at all, it is overbaked.

8. Once the pot de crème is baked, take the jars out of the hot water bath and refrigerate them immediately to stop the cooking process.

9. They will keep in peak freshness for 36 hours in the refrigerator. They can also be frozen; discard after 2 months.

tarts

The use of tarts opens up a whole world of possibilities. The actual tart shell provides all the texture needed; it holds the fillings in place, plus it provides crunch. Think of it as a vessel, and what you put in this vessel is limited only by your creativity and, of course, your common sense. Tarts can be shaped in many forms; the ones in this chapter are shaped in traditional round tart rings as well as in rectangles, ovals, and squares. They can also be shaped for individual tarts or larger tarts. In any case, always consider the following:

- A tart is eaten with a fork, and because of this, the shell should be firm enough to hold the contents of the tart in place, but also yield to the fork with gentle pressure. You should not need to use a knife to eat a tart.

- Make sure that the tart fillings aren't fluid. When the tart is cut, nothing should pour out of it.

Otherwise it becomes a challenge to eat the tart. This is even more the case when it comes to large tarts, because they will be cut into individual portions and the potential for a mess is greatly increased.

The sablée dough recipe for tarts (page 250) can withstand refrigeration for up to 48 hours. The biggest concern is to prevent the shell from getting soggy. It is an acceptable practice to brush the inside of the tart shell with melted chocolate to insulate it. However, what if chocolate doesn't make sense with the fillings? Keep that in mind as well.

Refer to the photographs below for instructions on shaping tarts.

Basic Method for Lining a Tart Ring

 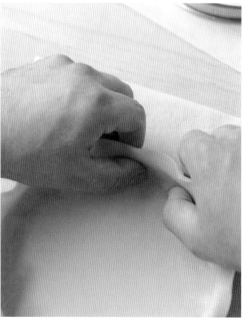 

FROM LEFT TO RIGHT:
1. Carefully place a disc of dough into the round tart mold.
2. Use your thumbs to press the dough into the mold, eliminating any gaps, cracks, or air pockets.
3. Holding the blade flush against the mold, run a sharp paring knife around the top edge of the ring to remove any excess dough.

possible defects of tarts

defect	cause	solution
The shell is hard to cut through.	The dough was sheeted too thick, and therefore the tart was thick.	Always sheet the dough to 2.5 to 3 mm/ .1 to .12 in maximum.
	The dough has been sheeted more than twice.	Sheet the dough only twice (the second sheeting will be the trimmings from the first sheeting).
	The dough was overmixed.	Mix the dough until it just comes together.
The shell is seeping liquid.	The tart shell was not shaped properly, and there is a crack or cracks where liquid is seeping out.	Ensure that you have an even shell; inspect each tart after it is shaped.
The shell is cracking.	The filling is too heavy for the shell and is pushing on it, or the shell is too thin.	Never overfill a tart shell.
		Sheet the dough out to the correct thickness.
The shell is soggy in a filled tart.	The tart is old, and the moisture from the filling is softening the tart shell.	Discard tarts after 24 to 36 hours. Always taste tarts before displaying them.
The shell looks uneven or the rim is jagged.	The shell should be even, and the rim was probably cut when the dough was still soft.	Practice. Know how to handle the dough.

BASIC SABLÉE DOUGH

yield: 3 kg/6 lb 9.76 oz

INGREDIENT	METRIC	U.S.	%
All-purpose flour	413 g	14.57 oz	13.76%
Cake flour	996 g	2 lb 3.13 oz	33.21%
Butter	683 g	1 lb 8.1 oz	22.78%
Salt	11 g	.38 oz	.36%
Confectioners' sugar	512 g	1 lb 2.1 oz	17.08%
Almond flour	100 g	3.53 oz	3.32%
Eggs, at room temperature	285 g	10.05 oz	9.49%

1. Sift the all-purpose and cake flours together.

2. Combine the butter, salt, confectioners' sugar, and almond flour in the bowl of an electric mixer fitted with a paddle attachment. Mix them together until a homogeneous mass is achieved.

3. Add the eggs in 4 additions. Stop the mixer and add the sifted dry ingredients. Pulse the mixer a few times, and then mix until a homogeneous mass is achieved. Be careful to not overmix.

4. Remove the dough from the mixer bowl and shape it into a flat square. Wrap it in plastic and refrigerate it for at least 1 hour so that the butter firms up.

5. Roll the dough out to 3 mm/.11 in with a rolling pin or a sheeter, but preferably a sheeter to ensure an even thickness. Let the dough firm up again in the refrigerator.

6. Cut the dough to the desired shape and size. Line the tart molds with the dough on a piece of parchment paper; make sure that the dough is flush with the mold and the sheet pan with no gaps, cracks, or air pockets. Make sure that the thickness is even throughout. This will take some time and practice, but it is crucial, not only for visual appeal but also because a thick piece of baked dough is hard to cut through with a fork. Always keep that in mind. Tarts are eaten with a fork alone, not a fork and a knife; they should cut easily and with little effort.

7. Do not trim the excess off the top of the tart mold yet.

8. Freeze the tart shells for a few minutes, until the dough hardens.

9. Preheat a convection oven to 160°C/320°F.

10. Trim off the excess from the top of the tart mold with a sharp paring knife. Make sure that the blade is flush (perpendicular) with the top of the mold and not at an angle.

11. Dock the center of the raw tart shell with a fork. If it is still frozen, bake it. If not, return it to the freezer until it is frozen.

12. Bake until golden brown, about 7 minutes.

13. Cool to room temperature, and reserve on a sheet pan, tightly wrapped with plastic. The tart shells will keep for up to 5 days once they are baked. However, refresh them in a hot oven for 5 minutes as needed to ensure that they will be crisp for at least 48 hours once they are filled and garnished.

notes Keep this dough sheeted out in a freezer. It will keep for 3 to 4 months, but try not make so much that it sits in the freezer that long. Having the dough sheeted will make it easy to cut and shape the tarts as needed. Once the dough is sheeted, always keep 2 sheets of parchment paper or silicone between the sheets of dough, because the dough sheets tend to stick to each other.

This recipe yields more than needed to make the tarts that follow, but it's always a good idea to make more since it holds so well baked and frozen.

Save any trimmings from shaping the tart shells and re-sheet or reroll them one more time. This will reduce waste. Note that this will have an effect on gluten development, and the second-roll tarts will be slightly firmer and will pull in from the tart mold a little more than first-roll tarts.

CARAMELIZED PEARS AND BROWN BUTTER PASTRY CREAM TART WITH CRÈME FRAÎCHE QUENELLES

yield: 6 tarts

components

1.2 kg/2 lb 10.24 oz Basic Sablée Dough (page 250)

900 g/1 lb 15.68 oz Brown Butter Pastry Cream

6 Caramelized Pears

540 g/1 lb 3.04 oz Crème Fraîche Quenelles

1. Cut 6 pieces of dough that measure 12.5 by 35 cm/5 by 14 in. Line 6 tart molds that measure 2.5 by 25 by 2.5 cm/1 by 10 by 1 in.

2. Bake according to the instructions on page 250.

3. Draw a line of corn syrup on 6 cake boards or bases as long as the tart shell. Place the tart shells on the cake boards.

4. Pipe 150 g/5.3 oz of brown butter pastry cream into each tart shell.

5. Cut the pears into quarters and core them. Cut each quarter in half lengthwise.

6. Place each wedge in a standing position in the tart shell, making sure they are evenly spaced.

7. Prepare the crème fraîche by whipping it to stiff peaks in a mixer or by hand just before using. Using a medium (20-g/.71-oz capacity) spoon, make small quenelles and put them between each piece of pear so that the pears and crème fraîche are alternating on the tart. There should be a total of 8 slices of pear and 7 quenelles per tart.

8. Display or serve. Discard after 36 hours.

note This amount of tart dough is more than what is needed, since it will be used to sheet the dough and fill the tarts, and excess will be trimmed.

BROWN BUTTER PASTRY CREAM

yield: 900 g/1 lb 15.68 oz (150 g/5.3 oz per tart)

INGREDIENT	METRIC	U.S.	%
Milk	505 g	1 lb 1.76 oz	56.09%
Sugar	125 g	4.42 oz	13.92%
Salt	3 g	.1 oz	.31%
Tahitian vanilla pod, split and scraped	1	1	
Eggs	167 g	5.89 oz	18.55%
Cornstarch	50 g	1.77 oz	5.57%
Brown Butter, melted but cool (page 98)	50 g	1.77 oz	5.57%

1. Combine the milk with half of the sugar, the salt, and the vanilla pod and seeds in a sauce pot. Bring the mixture to a boil.

2. Meanwhile, whisk the eggs together with the cornstarch until it achieves a smooth paste. Stir in the other half of the sugar.

3. Once the milk mixture comes to a boil, temper in the egg yolk slurry.

4. Return the mixture to the pan over medium-low heat. Stir constantly and vigorously until the pastry cream thickens and comes to a boil.

5. Remove the pan the heat and stir for 30 seconds. Stir in the brown butter and pour the pastry cream into a hotel pan. Remove the vanilla pod.

6. Cover the pastry cream with plastic wrap directly on its surface. Refrigerate until completely cooled (see Note).

7. Once cold, transfer it to an airtight container and refrigerate it with plastic directly covering its surface. The pastry cream will keep for up to 4 days in the refrigerator.

note If making larger batches, cool the pastry cream in an ice bath.

CARAMELIZED PEARS

yield: 6 caramelized pears (1 per tart)

INGREDIENT	METRIC	U.S.	%
Bosc pears, ripe	6	6	
Sugar	600 g	1 lb 5.12 oz	23.08%
Water, hot	2 kg	4 lb 6.56 oz	76.92%

1. Peel the pears and cut them in half. Keep them covered with a damp paper towel.

2. Make a dry caramel with the sugar in a saucepan over high heat; cook it to a dark amber brown (178°C/353°F).

3. Add the hot water to the caramel slowly. Bring it to a boil, and make sure all of the sugar has dissolved in the water.

4. Turn off the heat, put the pears in the syrup, and cover them with a heavy-duty paper towel or clean cloth towel.

5. Let them sit in the hot liquid while they cool at room temperature; reserve the pears refrigerated in the caramel liquid in an airtight container. They will keep for up to 1 week in the refrigerator.

CRÈME FRAÎCHE QUENELLES

yield: 540 g/1 lb 3.04 oz

INGREDIENT	METRIC	U.S.	%
Crème fraîche	234 g	8.26 oz	40.74%
Heavy cream	234 g	8.26 oz	40.74%
Sugar	106 g	3.76 oz	18.52%

Whip all the ingredients together to obtain stiff peaks. Follow the instructions for finishing on page 251.

RASPBERRY COMPOTE, VANILLA MASCARPONE, AND SWEET RHUBARB TART WITH RASPBERRY COULIS AND TRUE WHITE VELVET

yield: 6 tarts

components

1 kg/2 lb 3.2 oz Basic Sablée Dough (page 250)

600 g/1 lb 5.12 oz Sweet Rhubarb

600 g/1 lb 5.12 oz Raspberry Compote

1.2 kg/2 lb 10.4 oz Vanilla Mascarpone

1 kg/2 lb 3.2 oz True White Velvet

200 g/7.05 oz Raspberry Coulis

6 raspberries

6 pieces Rhubarb Skin

1 sheet silver leaf

1. Cut the dough into 6 pieces 20 by 25 cm/8 by 10 in. Line 6 oval tart shell molds 5 by 12.5 by 2.5 cm/ 2 by 5 by 1 in.

2. Finish and bake as per the instructions on page 250.

3. Place 100 g/3.53 oz of diced sweet rhubarb across the base of each baked tart shell. Place 100 g/3.53 oz of raspberry compote on top of the rhubarb.

4. Pour enough finished vanilla mascarpone into the tart shell to cover the raspberries. It should come up to the top of the tart shell. Smooth the surface with an offset spatula if necessary.

5. Put all the tarts on a sheet pan lined with parchment paper (glue the paper down with corn syrup). Reserve the tarts in the refrigerator.

6. Thirty minutes before spraying the tarts, place the tarts in the freezer.

7. Meanwhile, set up a spray area (see page 135). Warm the white velvet to 35°C/95°F. Fill a spray paint canister with the white velvet or set up a compressor with its canister.

8. Remove the tarts from the freezer and spray them with an even coat of white velvet, rotating the sheet pan 90 degrees every few seconds.

9. Transfer the tarts on to cake boards that measure 7.5 by 15 cm/3 by 6 in.

10. Thaw in the refrigerator. Pour about 30 g/1.05 oz of raspberry coulis across the top of the tart. Place a raspberry over the coulis. Lean a strip of rhubarb skin against the raspberry. Place a small piece of silver leaf on the raspberry.

11. Display or serve. Discard after 48 hours.

note This amount of tart dough is more than what is needed, since it will be used to sheet the dough and fill the tarts, and excess will be trimmed.

SWEET RHUBARB

yield: 600 g/1 lb 5.12 oz

INGREDIENT	METRIC	U.S.	%
Rhubarb stalks, leaves removed	8	8	
Sugar	1 kg	2 lb 3.2 oz	100%

1. Preheat a convection oven to 160°C/320°F.

2. Rinse the rhubarb stalks under hot water. Peel the skin off with a peeler and reserve. Put the peeled rhubarb in a hotel pan and cover with the sugar.

3. Roast the stalks until tender, 12 to 15 minutes. They should be cooked through, but not mushy.

4. Cool the rhubarb stalks quickly in a blast freezer or a regular freezer to stop the cooking process.

5. Once they have cooled, cut them into 6-mm/.25-in cubes. Reserve the rhubarb in its cooking liquid in an airtight container in the refrigerator. The sweet rhubarb will keep for up to 4 days.

RASPBERRY COMPOTE AND RASPBERRY COULIS

yield: 800 g/1 lb 5.12 oz

INGREDIENT	METRIC	U.S.	%
Raspberries	400 g	14.11 oz	50%
Sugar	400 g	14.11 oz	50%
Tahitian vanilla pod, split and scraped	1	1	

1. Combine all of the ingredients in a small sauce pot. Bring them to a boil, and remove the pot from the heat. Remove the vanilla pod.

2. Cool the mixture over an ice bath.

3. Blend 200 g/7.05 oz of the compote until smooth, and then pass it through a fine-mesh sieve. Reserve the compote and the coulis separately in airtight containers. The compote and coulis will keep for up to 3 days in the refrigerator.

VANILLA MASCARPONE

yield: 1.2 kg/2 lb 10.4 oz

INGREDIENT	METRIC	U.S.	%
Mascarpone	992 g	2 lb 3.04 oz	82.68%
Tahitian vanilla paste	33 g	1.16 oz	2.73%
Superfine or bakers' sugar	175 g	6.17 oz	14.59%

1. Combine all of the ingredients in a bowl and place over a hot water bath.

2. Stir until the mixture becomes fluid and pourable, about 35°C/95°F. Follow the instructions for finishing the tart on page 255.

TRUE WHITE VELVET

yield: 1 kg/2lb 3.2 oz

INGREDIENT	METRIC	U.S.
Cocoa butter powder (Mycryo)	1 kg	2 lb 3.2 oz
White food coloring (fat based), or as needed	4 to 5 drops	4 to 5 drops

1. Melt the cocoa butter over a hot water bath, and stir in the food coloring. The velvet should be a bright white color.

2. Keep the cocoa butter in a warm place (such as the top of an oven) to keep it melted. It will keep for up to 1 month warm and melted and for up to 6 months at room temperature.

RHUBARB SKIN

yield: 6 to 10 pieces

INGREDIENT	METRIC	U.S.	%
Reserved peeled rhubarb skin	75 g	2.65 oz	42.86%
Grenadine	100 g	3.53 oz	57.14%

1. Heat the rhubarb skin and grenadine in a small pot over medium heat until the mixture comes to a simmer.

2. Let cool to room temperature, about 2 hours.

3. Remove the skins from the grenadine and pat them dry.

4. Place them in a dehydrator overnight to dry.

5. Once they are dry, reserve them in an airtight container in a cool, dry place. Discard after 1 month.

APPLE "MILLE FEUILLE" AND VANILLA BAVARIAN TART

yield: 6 tarts

components

1.3 kg/2 lb 13.76 oz Basic Sablée Dough (page 250)

6 Vanilla Cream squares

1 Apple "Mille Feuille"

300 g/10.58 oz neutral mirror glaze

6 mini apples (see Resources, page 540)

6 sheets gold leaf

6 cinnamon sticks

6 Tahitian vanilla beans

6 star anise

1. Cut the dough into six 22.5-cm/9-in squares. Line 6 tart shells 12.5 cm square by 2.5 cm deep/5 by 1 in with it.

2. Follow the finishing and baking instructions for tart shells on page 250. Allow the tart shells to cool.

3. Place the frozen vanilla cream squares inside the baked tart shells. Keep them refrigerated.

4. Remove the frozen apple "mille feuille" from the freezer. Using a ruler and a warm slicing knife, cut out six 12.5-cm/5-in squares. Place the frozen squares on top of the vanilla cream in the tart shells.

5. Mix the neutral glaze with 75 g/2.64 oz cold water. Brush the top of the "mille feuille" with neutral mirror glaze. Cover each mini apple with a sheet of gold leaf and place 1 on each tart. Dip the spices in the neutral mirror glaze, and then arrange them around the mini apple.

6. Let the tarts thaw in the refrigerator. Display or serve. Discard after 48 hours.

note This amount of tart dough is more than what is needed, since it will be used to sheet the dough and fill the tarts, and the excess will be trimmed.

VANILLA CREAM SQUARES

yield: 1.5 kg/3 lb 4.96 oz

INGREDIENT	METRIC	U.S.
Tahitian Vanilla Cream (page 158)	1.5 kg	3 lb 4.96 oz

1. Make a thick frame 20 by 30 by 1.75 cm/8 by 12 by .5 in with caramel bars over a sheet pan lined with a nonstick rubber mat. Freeze it. Pour the finished vanilla cream into the prepared frame; even out the top with an offset spatula. Freeze it. Freeze a cutting board as well.

2. Once it has hardened, flip the frozen vanilla cream onto the frozen cutting board lined with a sheet of silicone paper. Using a slicing knife and a ruler, cut out 12.5-cm/5-in squares.

APPLE "MILLE FEUILLE"

yield: 6 squares

INGREDIENT	METRIC	U.S.	%
Sugar	1 kg	2 lbs 3.2 oz	98.04%
Ground cinnamon	20 g	.71 oz	1.96%
Granny Smith apples	40	40	

1. Combine the sugar and cinnamon.

2. Peel the apples and slice them through the laminator (see Resources, page 540). This piece of equipment will slice an entire apple in 1 thin, long sheet.

3. Grease a hotel pan with nonstick oil spray and line it with a sheet of silicone paper.

4. Once all of the apples are prepared, arrange them in the prepared hotel pan. Place the apple slices or strips in 1 row horizontally the length of the hotel pan, and then add another row, slightly overlapping with the previous row, and so on until the entire width of the hotel pan is covered.

5. Once the entire width is covered, sprinkle about 50 g/1.76 oz of the cinnamon-sugar mix evenly over the apples.

6. Arrange another layer of apples in the hotel pan, and sprinkle more sugar on them. Repeat this process until all the apples are used up.

7. Put a sheet of plastic wrap on the apples and then another hotel pan on top of the plastic wrap. Lift both hotel pans and squeeze them together at an angle. Liquid should pour out of the pan. Save this liquid; it is full of apple and cinnamon flavor and makes very good sorbet or granité. This buildup of liquid will continue to occur for a few hours. Every hour or so, squeeze the excess liquid out.

8. Let the apples sit overnight in the refrigerator with a weighted hotel pan on top. Use weights such as balance-beam weights or a heavy cutting board.

9. The next day, squeeze all of the accumulated excess liquid out. Wrap the entire hotel pan in aluminum foil vertically and horizontally to trap the steam as it bakes.

10. Bake in a 135°C/275°F convection oven for about 8 hours, or until the apples are dark amber brown.

11. Take the foil off the hotel pan and let it cool to room temperature. Once it has cooled, flip it onto a large cutting board lined with silicone paper. Pull the "mille feuille" out of the pan by the silicone paper; it should come out easily and in 1 piece.

12. Wrap the entire cutting board in plastic wrap and freeze it. The "mille feuille" will keep for up to 2 months in the freezer.

DARK CHOCOLATE GANACHE AND SALTED CARAMEL TART WITH CRÈME FRAÎCHE

yield: 6 tarts

components

1.1 kg/2 lb 6.72 oz Basic Sablée Dough (page 250)

600 g/1 lb 5.12 oz Salted Caramel

900 g/1 lb 15.68 oz Chocolate Ganache (page 211)

300 g/10.58 oz melted chocolate (64%)

6 Large Chocolate Plaques

500 g/1 lb .16 oz Whipped Crème Fraîche Quenelles

600 g/1 lb 5.12 oz Dark Chocolate Spray

300 g/10.58 oz White Chocolate Velour Spray
(page 140–141)

1. Cut the dough into 6 rectangles 15 by 20 cm/6 by 8 in. Line 6 tart shell molds 10 by 15 by 2.5 cm/4 by 6 by 1 in with the sablée rectangles.

2. Bake as per the instructions on page 250. Cool the tarts to room temperature.

3. Pour about 100 g/3.53 oz salted caramel into each tart shell and spread it in an even layer.

4. Pour enough ganache into each tart shell so that it comes up to the top border. Let the ganache set at room temperature.

5. Place the melted chocolate in a piping bag.

6. Place the large chocolate plaques on top of the ganache on the tarts.

7. Drizzle some of the melted chocolate in a random pattern over the top of the tarts. Put the tarts in the refrigerator to set the chocolate. Keep the remaining chocolate in the piping bag warm, over a hot oven, for example.

8. Dip a soupspoon into hot water and scoop a quenelle of whipped crème fraîche, placing it on top of each tart vertically at the top end. Freeze the tarts for 20 minutes.

9. Set up a spray area (see page 135). Warm the dark chocolate spray to 38°C/100°F; do the same with the white chocolate spray. Fill the spray paint gun or compressor spray gun canister with the dark chocolate spray.

10. Spray the semi-frozen tarts with an even coat of spray, rotating the sheet pan 90 degrees every few seconds to ensure that the tarts get an even coat. Fill another canister for the spray gun with the white chocolate spray. Spray only the left side of the tarts (do not rotate them).

11. Transfer the tarts to a cake cardboard. Put a few drops of corn syrup on the cake boards to keep the tarts from sliding off.

12. Let the tarts thaw in the refrigerator.

13. Display or serve. Discard after 48 hours.

note This amount of tart dough is more than what needed, since it will be used to sheet the dough and fill the tarts, and the excess will be trimmed.

SALTED CARAMEL

yield: 600 g/1 lb 5.12 oz

INGREDIENT	METRIC	U.S.	%
Sugar	243 g	8.54 oz	40.46%
Glucose syrup	121 g	4.27 oz	20.23%
Heavy cream	152 g	5.34 oz	25.28%
Salted butter	76 g	2.67 oz	12.64%
Salt	8 g	.29 oz	1.39%

1. In a 2-qt sauce pot, combine the sugar with one-quarter of its weight in water, or enough to obtain a "wet sand" texture, using your hands.

2. Pour the glucose into the pot. Clean the sides of the pot so that there are no sugar crystals on it by using a clean pastry brush dipped in water. Cook over high heat until the mixture reaches 170°C/338°F, or a dark amber color.

3. While the sugar cooks, bring the cream, butter, and salt to a simmer in a small sauce pot.

4. Once the sugar reaches the desired temperature, slowly whisk in the hot cream-butter mixture.

5. Pour the caramel into an adequately sized stainless-steel container and cool to room temperature.

CRÈME FRAÎCHE QUENELLES

yield: 500 g/1 lb .16 oz

INGREDIENT	METRIC	U.S.	%
Crème fraîche	204 g	7.19 oz	40.74%
Heavy cream	204 g	7.19 oz	40.74%
Sugar	92 g	3.27 oz	18.52%

Whip all of the ingredients together until they are stiff. Be careful to not overwhip.

LARGE CHOCOLATE PLAQUES

yield: 6 large plaques

INGREDIENT	METRIC	U.S.
Dark chocolate (64%), tempered	1 kg	2 lb 3.2 oz

1. Lightly grease a marble surface with nonstick oil spray and spread it evenly with a paper towel. Put an acetate sheet over the greased area and smooth it out with a clean paper towel. Spread the tempered chocolate onto the acetate in a thin, even layer using an offset spatula.

2. Pour the chocolate onto the acetate and spread it out thinly and evenly with an offset spatula. Let them set at room temperature.

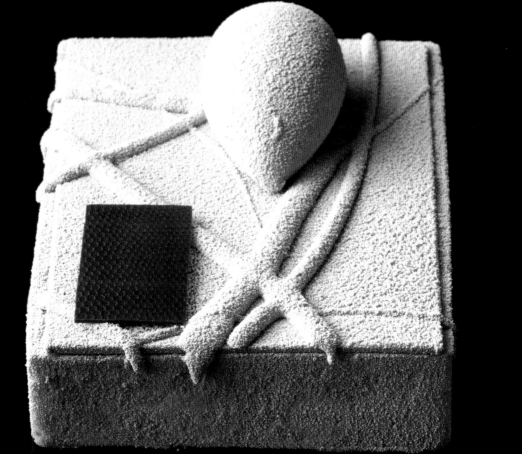

3. Once the chocolate is semi-set, take the acetate sheet off the marble and place it on a different section of the marble to avoid the chocolate frame setting around the acetate.

4. Using a ruler and the back of a paring knife, cut out plaques 15 by 20 cm/6 by 8 in.

5. Flip the acetate onto a sheet pan lined with parchment paper, and then place a nonstick rubber mat on top of the acetate to weigh it down to keep the chocolate plaques from bowing once they set. Reserve until needed.

DARK CHOCOLATE SPRAY

yield: 600 g/1 lb 5.12 oz

INGREDIENT	METRIC	U.S.	%
Dark chocolate (64%) coins	300 g	10.58 oz	50%
Cocoa butter powder (Mycryo)	300 g	10.58 oz	50%

Combine both ingredients in a bowl and melt them over a hot water bath. Keep the spray in a warm area to keep it fluid and melted.

cupcakes

Cupcakes are becoming increasingly popular. It's not that they ever went away; they just seem to be popping up everywhere, with some shops devoted entirely to their production. The reasons are quite simple: People like them, they are easy to make, they don't generally need to be refrigerated, and they don't take up too much space. It is important to keep the cupcakes simple, but there are ways to make them even more special (see recipes on pages 265 to 269).

The basic components are:

- **The cake portion:** This component can be anything; even a muffin batter might do. My personal preference is something that is more cake-like than sponge-like; in other words, it is crumbly. I like to soak the cake in a flavored syrup to ensure moistness.

- **The topping:** This second component should be shelf stable unless the cupcakes are being refrigerated. There are many types of toppings, but their main purpose besides flavor is to add moisture. Some examples of toppings are classic frosting, ganache, and meringue.

- **The garnish:** The third and final component is a garnish for the topping. It is not very common, but it will serve as not only a visual component but also a way to add texture, since the cake and the topping are usually soft in nature.

CHOCOLATE CUPCAKE WITH CHOCOLATE CREAM TOPPING

yield: 20 cupcakes

components

20 Chocolate Cupcakes

500 g/1 lb 1.64 oz Vanilla Soaking Syrup

2.95 kg/6 lb 8 oz Chocolate Cream Topping

60 g/2.11 oz multicolored dragées

1. Poke 5 holes in the top of each cupcake using a skewer.

2. Using a pastry brush, soak each cupcake with about 25 g/.88 oz of vanilla syrup.

3. Pour the chocolate cream into a piping bag fitted with a #864 fluted piping tip. Pipe a spiral around the cupcake.

4. Garnish with multicolored dragées. Wrap the cupcake with the cupcake wrappers (see Resources, page 540).

5. Discard after 48 hours. Advise your customers to consume them within a week or to refrigerate them, in which case they will keep for about 10 days. However, the buttercream will harden in the refrigerator.

CHOCOLATE CUPCAKES

yield: 20 cupcakes

INGREDIENT	METRIC	U.S.	%
Butter, at 21°C/70°F	341 g	12.04 oz	24.39%
Sugar	358 g	12.64 oz	25.6%
Eggs, at 21°C/70°F	273 g	9.64 oz	19.51%
Salt	6 g	.21 oz	.43%
Pastry flour	271 g	9.56 oz	19.36%
Cocoa powder	70 g	2.46 oz	4.99%
Baking powder	3 g	.11 oz	.23%
Crème fraîche, at 21°C/70°F	77 g	2.71 oz	5.49%

1. Make the batter as per the creaming method on page 88. The cocoa powder is sifted with the pastry flour, salt, and baking powder.

2. Preheat a convection oven to 160°C/320°F.

3. Spray 20 muffin cups with a light coat of nonstick oil spray and line them with cupcake paper cups.

4. Pour 65 g/2.3 oz of batter into each cup.

5. Bake until the center of the cupcake springs back when you apply gentle pressure with your fingertips. Alternatively, use a skewer or toothpick to check for doneness.

6. Cool them to room temperature.

VANILLA SOAKING SYRUP

yield: about 500 g/1 lb 1.64 oz

INGREDIENT	METRIC	U.S.
Simple syrup	500 g	1 lb .16 oz
Vanilla pods, split and scraped	2	2

1. Bring the simple syrup to a boil with the vanilla pods and seeds. Let the mixture cool to room temperature. Remove the vanilla pods.

2. Reserve in an airtight container in the refrigerator. The syrup will keep indefinitely.

CHOCOLATE CREAM TOPPING

yield: 2.95 kg/6 lb 8 oz

INGREDIENT	METRIC	U.S.	%
BUTTERCREAM			
Sugar	907 g	2 lb	30.77%
Water	227 g	8 oz	7.69%
Egg whites	454 g	1 lb	15.38%
Butter, soft	1.36 kg	3 lb	46.15%
CHOCOLATE CREAM			
Buttercream	873 g	1 lb 14.72 oz	72.73%
Pretacao cocoa paste	327 g	11.54 oz	27.27%

1. **FOR THE BUTTERCREAM:** Combine the sugar and the water in a pot and place it over high heat. Cook the mixture to 118°C/244°F. As the sugar gets close to the desired temperature, begin whipping the egg whites.

2. Once the sugar reaches the proper temperature, the egg whites should have formed stiff peaks. Pour the sugar down the side of the mixer bowl while mixing on medium speed.

3. Whip on high speed until the meringue cools to room temperature. Add the soft butter in small chunks and whip until all is combined.

4. Reserve covered in an airtight container at room temperature. The buttercream will keep for up to 1 month. It can keep for up to 6 months in the refrigerator, but it is always good to have soft buttercream ready to use.

5. **FOR THE CHOCOLATE CREAM:** Combine both ingredients in a bowl and stir with a rubber spatula to obtain a homogeneous mix.

6. Reserve in an airtight container at room temperature. Discard after 2 weeks.

LEMON MERINGUE CUPCAKE

yield: 20 cupcakes

components

20 Lemon Cupcakes

300 g/10.58 oz Lemon Syrup

400 g/14.11 oz Lemon Curd (page 156)

1.2 kg/2 lb 10.24 oz Italian Meringue (page 245)

100 g/3.53 oz silver dragées

1. Using an apple corer, remove the center of each cupcake without scooping to the bottom of the cupcake.

2. Brush 15 g/.52 oz of lemon syrup onto each cupcake using a pastry brush.

3. Pipe 20 g/.7 oz of lemon curd into the hollowed-out center of each cupcake.

4. Pipe Italian meringue over the crown of the cupcake with a #4 plain piping tip. Using a torch, carefully brown the meringue as evenly as possible.

5. Attach 2 g/.07 oz dragées to the meringue using tweezers.

6. Discard after 24 hours. Advise your customers to consume them the day of purchase, or to refrigerate them, in which case they will keep for up to 3 days.

LEMON CUPCAKES

yield: 20 cupcakes

INGREDIENT	METRIC	U.S.	%
Butter, at 21°C/70°F	340 g	11.99 oz	24.27%
Sugar	357 g	12.59 oz	25.49%
Lemon zest	6 g	.21 oz	.43%
Eggs, at 21°C/70°F	272 g	9.59 oz	19.42%
Salt	6 g	.21 oz	.43%
Pastry flour	340 g	11.99 oz	24.27%
Baking powder	3 g	.11 oz	.23%
Crème fraîche, at 21°C/70°F	76 g	2.7 oz	5.46%

1. Preheat a convection oven to 160°C/320°F.

2. Lightly spray 20 muffin cups with nonstick oil spray and line them with cupcake paper cups.

3. To make the cupcake batter, proceed as per the creaming method for pound cakes (see page 88). Add the lemon zest after the butter and sugar have been creamed.

4. Portion 65 g/2.3 oz of batter into each cup.

5. Bake until the center of the cupcake springs back when you apply gentle pressure with your fingertips. Alternatively, use a skewer or toothpick to check for doneness.

6. Cool the cupcakes to room temperature.

LEMON SYRUP

yield: 300 g/10.58 oz

INGREDIENT	METRIC	U.S.	%
Simple syrup, at 50° Brix	250 g	8.82 oz	83.33%
Lemon juice	50 g	1.76 oz	16.67%

Combine both ingredients and reserve in an airtight container. It will keep for 10 days in the refrigerator.

RED VELVET CAKE CUPCAKE WITH CREAM CHEESE AND COCONUT TOPPING

yield: 20 cupcakes

components

20 Red Velvet Cupcakes

300 g/10.58 oz Rum Soaking Syrup

1.65 kg/3 lb 10.24 oz Cream Cheese Topping

300 g/10.58 oz shredded sweet coconut, finely chopped by hand

1. Poke 5 holes in the crown of each cupcake.

2. Brush 15 g/.52 oz of rum syrup onto each cupcake.

3. Pipe a spiral of cream cheese topping around the crown of each cupcake using a plain #4 piping tip.

4. Coat the entire surface of cream cheese with the coconut.

5. Discard after 24 hours. Advise your customers to consume them the day of purchase, or to refrigerate them, in which case they will keep for up to 3 days.

RED VELVET CUPCAKES

yield: 20 cupcakes

INGREDIENT	METRIC	U.S.	%
Butter, at 21°C/70°F	340 g	12 oz	24.3%
Sugar	357 g	12.6 oz	25.52%
Eggs, at 21°C/70°F	272 g	9.6 oz	19.45%
Red food coloring	5 g	.17 oz	.34%
Salt	6 g	.21 oz	.43%
Pastry flour	270 g	9.53 oz	19.29%
Cocoa powder	70 g	2.46 oz	4.97%
Baking powder	3 g	.11 oz	.23%
Crème fraîche, at 21°C/70°F	77 g	2.7 oz	5.47%

1. To make the cupcakes, proceed as per the creaming method on page 88. The red food coloring is added in with the eggs, and the cocoa powder is sifted with the pastry flour, salt, and baking powder.

2. Preheat a convection oven to 160°C/320°F.

3. Put 20 paper brioche baking cups on a sheet pan.

4. Portion 50 g/1.76 oz of batter into each cup.

5. Bake until the center of the cupcake springs back when you apply gentle pressure with your fingertips. Alternatively, use a skewer or toothpick to check for doneness.

6. Cool them to room temperature.

note This recipe is different from the red velvet cake sheets on page 236. This recipe produces a good crown, while the other recipe is best for sheet cake.

RUM SOAKING SYRUP

yield: 300 g/10.58 oz

INGREDIENT	METRIC	U.S.	%
Simple syrup, at 50° Brix	250 g	8.82 oz	83.33%
Dark rum	50 g	1.76 oz	16.67%

Combine both ingredients. Reserve the syrup in an airtight container in the refrigerator. It will keep indefinitely in these conditions.

note If desired, cook off some of the alcohol from the rum on the stovetop before combining it with the simple syrup.

CREAM CHEESE TOPPING

yield: 1.65 kg/3 lb 10.24 oz

INGREDIENT	METRIC	U.S.	%
Cream cheese, at room temperature	1 kg	2 lb 4.2 oz	60.5%
Superfine or bakers' sugar	350 g	12.35 oz	21.17%
Tahitian vanilla powder	3 g	.11 oz	.18%

1. Combine all of the ingredients in the bowl of an electric mixer fitted with the paddle attachment. Mix together until smooth on medium speed. Adjust sweetness if necessary.

2. Transfer to a piping bag fitted with a plain #4 piping tip if using right away. Otherwise, place the topping in an airtight container in the refrigerator. It can keep for up to 2 weeks in the refrigerator. Soften it with a paddle every time it is used.

specialty cookies

There are many types of cookies. Hundreds, maybe even thousands, of them, and within each variety there might even be variations. Yet among all of these cookies, there are four types that exemplify the quality aspects that a cookie should have, and they are all very different in nature. These four types of cookies vary from simple execution, such as a shortbread cookie, to a more complicated and technically precise execution, such as the French macaron. Even the humble chocolate chip cookie has its place here (see page 288) in this selection.

This isn't to say that other cookies aren't good. There are many good varieties not included here, such as the Florentine, coconut macaroon (which is different than the French macaron), and even some Girl Scout cookies. But these don't make the cut because, in my opinion, they do not have what makes the selected cookies so special. As you read the recipes and see the photographs, you will see why.

FRENCH MACARONS

There is not much information available for the origin of this cookie. The actual shell is attributed to one of the chefs of Caterina de Medici, but this is more folklore than verifiable fact. What is known is that, around the beginning of the twentieth century, Frenchman Pierre Desfontaines was behind the idea of sandwiching chocolate ganache between two macarons. This implies that the actual cookie, even though it was not sandwiched, already existed. Mr. Desfontaines was a distant cousin of Louis Ernest Ladurée, the founder of Ladurée, which is credited with establishing the popularity of the macaron. This cookie became even more popular when Pierre Hermé, then a very young man, was hired to be the head pastry chef for Ladurée. His innovative flavors (some would say "bold," to put it mildly) had people forming a line out to the street to taste his newest

Basic Method for Piping and Assembling Macarons

FROM LEFT TO RIGHT:

1. After mixing, the macaron batter should be smooth, lump-free, and just loose enough for the surface to level itself out when it is piped.
2. When you first pipe a macaron, it will have a small peak at the center, but it should smooth itself out after just a few seconds.
3. It is best to refrigerate sandwiched macarons for 24 to 36 hours to give the filling time to meld with the cookies and soften their interiors.

creations. As popular as this cookie is in France, it never has become very popular here. In fact, the coconut macaroon is many times more popular.

One of the most fascinating characteristics of this cookie is how it can form such a firm, hard shell on the outside and still be moist and tender on the inside. They hold well under refrigeration; in fact, it is recommended to refrigerate them. They can even be frozen, which is something that is not done with other baked cookies because their quality will suffer. Some cookies hold up frozen, but none like the macaron. They can also be made quickly, since all that is required is to make the batter, pipe it, let it form a shell, and bake it. The filling is limited only by the chef's creativity. There are truffle macarons, foie gras macarons, and beet macarons; the sweet version is included in this chapter, but these varieties prove its versatility.

When coloring macarons, the amount of food coloring will vary from batch to batch. It is important to use water- or alcohol-based food coloring and to add it to the batter once the egg whites have been fully whipped to stiff peaks. If the food coloring is added before the whites have reached their full volume, they will not whip any higher. The coloring stabilizes the foam to the point that it cannot take in any more air. If fat-based food coloring is used, the egg whites will collapse. It is also important to use a very fine-grain sugar such as superfine or bakers' sugar when whipping the egg whites. It will dissolve faster than larger-crystal sugars, and it will melt quickly when the macaron is baked. For an even better result, grind the sugar in a coffee grinder. It will turn to powder, which will dissolve and melt very quickly. The faster the sugar dissolves and melts, the shinier the macaron will be. Do not grind the sugar too far ahead of time, since it will clump up from the moisture in the atmosphere. This leads us to the second sugar used in the recipe on page 275. Traditionally, confectioners' sugar is used, which is a very fine-crystal granulated sugar that contains on average 3 percent cornstarch by weight. However, cornstarch dulls the finished macaron, and some confectioners' sugars have more cornstarch than others. The fondant sugar used in the recipe on page 275 has the same-size sugar crystal as confectioners' sugar and no cornstarch. See Resources, page 540, for places to purchase fondant sugar.

For the almond flour in the recipe, spread it out on a sheet pan lined with parchment paper and leave it out the day before using it. This will dry it out and keep it from clumping. Also, always use finely ground blanched almond flour. The finer it is, the smoother the surface of the macaron will be.

SHORTBREAD COOKIES

Shortbread cookies are an exercise in simplicity. The method is important, as with anything, but what sets this cookie apart is that it is a perfect balance between firmness and fragility, since it holds its shape once it is baked, but it disintegrates once it is in your mouth. It is nearly half butter, which accounts for its flakiness but most importantly its flavor. Don't skimp on using a high-quality butter. Do not use this cookie for any other purpose than to eat it alone, as is. Spices or flavors do not need to be added either.

HAND-DECORATED SUGAR COOKIES

These cookies are included in the special group because they not only taste good, but they also can be truly unique, hand-crafted pieces once they are decorated with royal icing. This chapter includes three types of hand-decorated cookies. Two of them are the classic variety, completely filled and decorated by hand. The other variety is initially covered in royal icing but then is finished with either printed wafer paper (see Resources, page 540) or with sugar paper that has a printed image. This demonstrates the versatility of this cookie.

possible defects of specialty cookies

defect	cause	solution
They spread too much.	The dough was overcreamed.	Only cream the butter and the sugar long enough to make it light and fluffy, and use the butter at 21°C/70°F.
	There was too much baking soda.	Baking soda increases spreading, so make sure to measure it correctly.
	The dough was not chilled.	Make sure the dough was cold before baking and that the cookies were not put on a warm sheet pan before baking.
Cookies have excessive browning but don't taste overbaked.	An excess amount of baking soda was used.	Measure the baking soda properly.
Sugar granules are apparent on the cookies' surface. (If this is intentional, such as when sugar is sprinkled on shortbread cookies, it is not a problem.)	The butter was not creamed long enough with the sugar.	Cream the butter and the sugar long enough to make it light and fluffy.
	The sugar used had large crystals.	Use superfine sugar or bakers' sugar, which dissolves quickly and efficiently since it is such a small crystal.
Macarons are not round.	Batter was overmixed.	Mix batter to the right consistency (not too loose, not too firm).
Macarons cracked on the surface.	They did not form a shell.	Let the macarons sit for at least 20 minutes after they are piped before baking.
The color of the royal icing is dull.	The royal icing took too long to set.	Put a blow dryer or a fan directly over them once they are filled.
The colors look like they are bleeding.	The cookies were put away and wrapped before the icing could fully set.	Let the cookies sit overnight on a sheet pan before wrapping them so the icing can set.

BASIC MACARON

INGREDIENT	METRIC	U.S.	%
Fondant sugar	473 g	1 lb .64 oz	47.27%
Blanched almond flour	263 g	9.26 oz	26.26%
Salt	1 g	.04 oz	.11%
Egg whites, at 21°C/70°F	210 g	7.41 oz	21.01%
Superfine sugar, ground in a coffee grinder	53 g	1.85 oz	5.25%
Cream of tartar	1 g	.04 oz	.11%
Food coloring (water or alcohol based)	as needed	as needed	

1. Combine the fondant sugar, almond flour, and salt in a Robot Coupe until they are evenly mixed, and sift into a bowl using a drum sieve.

2. Make a French meringue with the egg whites, ground superfine sugar, and cream of tartar. When the whites are fully whipped, add a few drops of food coloring. Whip for about 15 seconds after adding the coloring.

3. Fold the meringue into the dry ingredients all at once, making sure that the batter has no lumps and is smooth but not runny. If undermixed, the surface of the macarons will not be smooth and will be lumpy. If overmixed, the macarons will run too much after piping and will not hold a round shape. The more you fold the batter, the looser it will get. Keep in mind that the foamed egg whites are not being folded in to make an airy sponge cake or soufflé; the whipped egg whites in this recipe are for binding the ingredients and providing moisture.

4. Line a very flat perforated sheet pan with silicone paper or a nonstick rubber mat. A perforated sheet pan will help speed up the baking process. Using a #4 straight tip, pipe a circle with a diameter of about 2.5 cm/1 in. The batter should run slightly but just enough so that the surface is smooth. When the macaron is first piped, it will have a small tip down the middle, but after a few seconds it will smooth itself out. If the peak stays, gently tap the sheet pan on a work surface with a cloth towel underneath it. If the peak does not budge or if the batter has a rippled look, it means that the batter is too stiff and is undermixed. Return the batter to a bowl and smooth it out some more. However, if the batter is too fluid and is overmixed, it can't really be fixed.

5. Pipe all the macarons, and let them dry for 20 minutes at room temperature so that they develop a shell. This shell is responsible for the macarons' signature look. It dries out somewhat on the surface, and this is what keeps the interior batter in check, expanding upward and forming a baked ring around the base of the macaron. In other words, the batter is pushed up and out slightly; the exterior becomes crisp, and the interior will stay moist and chewy.

6. Meanwhile, preheat a convection oven to 150°C/300°F.

7. Bake for 12 minutes. The macarons will have domed and lifted slightly from the sheet pan; they should have no color around the border (this means they are overbaked) and they shouldn't have a wet spot down the middle (this means they are underbaked). Make sure to let the macarons cool completely on the sheet pan before removing and filling. It is important to try to get the least amount of color on them as possible.

note If smaller or larger macarons are desired, make sure to adjust the baking times accordingly.

Chocolate Macarons

Add brown food coloring to the whipped egg whites.

Use 500 g/1 lb 1.64 oz Dark Chocolate Ganache (page 211) to fill the macarons.

Raspberry Macarons

Add red food coloring to the fully whipped egg whites.

Use 3 sheets of silver leaf to garnish the macarons. Once the macaron batter has been piped, put a small piece of silver leaf onto half of the macarons (these will be the top piece). Make sure to apply the silver leaf before the macaron surface dries; otherwise it won't stick.

Use 500 g/1 lb 1.64 oz Raspberry Jam (page 278) to fill the macarons.

Peach Macarons

Add peach-colored food coloring to the fully whipped egg whites.

Use 500 g/1 lb 1.64 oz Peach Butter (page 278) to fill the macarons.

Caramel Macarons

Add light beige food coloring to the fully whipped egg whites.

Use 500 g/1 lb 1.64 oz Caramel (page 446) to fill the macarons.

Mocha Macarons

Add light brown food coloring to the fully whipped egg whites.

Use 500 g/1 lb 1.64 oz Mocha Ganache (page 279) to fill the macarons.

Apple Macarons

Add a light green food coloring to the whipped egg whites.

Use 500 g/1 lb 1/64 oz Apple Butter (page 165) to fill the macarons.

Pear Macarons

Add yellow food coloring to the fully whipped egg whites.

Use 500 g/1 lb 1.64 oz Pear Butter to fill the macarons. For the Pear Butter, use the Apple Butter recipe on page 165 and substitute pears.

Use the Red Brush Stroke to garnish the macarons (page 280).

Banana Macarons

Add bright yellow food coloring to the whipped egg whites.

To garnish the banana macarons, sprinkle 100 g/3.53 oz of poppy seeds over the macarons just after they have been piped so that the poppy seeds stick to them.

Use 500 g/1 lb 1.64 oz Banana Butter (page 281) to fill the macarons.

Cassis Macarons

Add deep purple food coloring to the whipped egg whites.

Once the macaron batter has been piped, put a single oval silver dragée on half of the macarons. Make sure to do this before the macaron forms a shell so that the dragée adheres to the macaron.

Use 500 g/1 lb 1.64 oz Cassis Cream (page 280) to fill the macarons.

Peanut Butter and Jelly Macarons

Leave one-half batch of macarons plain, and then add a few drops of purple food coloring to the whipped egg whites for the other half of the batch.

Use 250 g/8.82 oz peanut butter and 250 g/8.82 oz Concord grape jelly to fill the macarons.

Flip the plain macarons over. Pipe a ring of peanut butter close to the outside border. Pipe the jelly inside the peanut butter ring. Assemble the sandwiches with the purple macarons.

Pumpkin Macarons

Add orange food coloring to the whipped egg whites.

To garnish the macarons, place a pumpkin seed on top of half of the macarons just after they have been piped so that they will bind to the macarons.

Use 500 g/1 lb 1.64 oz Pumpkin Butter (recipe follows) to fill the macarons.

Licorice Macarons

Add black food coloring to the whipped egg whites.

Use 500 g/1 lb 1.64 oz Licorice Cream to fill the macarons. To make the Licorice Cream, combine 498 g/1 lb 1.57 oz Buttercream (page 266) with 2 g/.07 oz licorice extract.

notes To sandwich macarons, flip half of the macarons over and pipe about 7 g/.24 oz of filling onto each flipped half, then sandwich them together. Ideally, once they are sandwiched, macarons are refrigerated for 24 to 36 hours before they are eaten. This gives the filling time to meld with the cookie base of the cookies and soften its interior. The shell will still remain crisp, though, even if the macarons have been frozen. If the cookies are in the refrigerator and not in a display case, always wrap them in plastic. They easily absorb flavors and aromas from the environment.

All the fillings yield 500 g/1 lb 1.64 oz, which is more than what is needed to assemble 112 to 125 macarons, but making smaller amounts properly is not efficient. The remaining filling can always be saved for a future batch of macarons.

RASPBERRY JAM

yield: 500 g/1 lb 1.64 oz

INGREDIENT	METRIC	U.S.	%
Raspberries	250 g	8.82 oz	50%
Sugar	250 g	8.82 oz	50%
Tahitian vanilla pod, split and scraped	1	1	

1. Combine all the ingredients in a small sauce pot. Bring to a boil, and then reduce the heat to a simmer. Cook until the liquid reaches 65° Brix.

2. Cool the jam over an ice bath. Remove the vanilla pod.

3. Once the jam has cooled, pipe it onto the macarons and sandwich them together. Refrigerate any leftover jam in an airtight container. It will keep for up to 1 month.

PEACH BUTTER

yield: 500 g/1 lb 1.64 oz

INGREDIENT	METRIC	U.S.	%
Peaches, peeled, pitted, and chopped	1.27 kg	2 lb 12. 96 oz	63.8%
Water	80 g	2.81 oz	3.99%
Lemon juice	6 g	.23 oz	.32%
Sugar	638 g	1 lb 6.56 oz	31.9%

1. Combine the peaches, water, and lemon juice in a pot. Bring the mixture to a boil over medium-high heat. Cook, stirring often, for about 20 minutes or until the peaches are soft. The cooking time depends on the ripeness of the peaches; the riper they are, the quicker they will cook.

2. Pass the peaches through a food mill, and then combine them with the sugar in a pot. Bring the mixture to a boil over medium-high heat, stirring occasionally.

3. Cook until the mixture thickens and holds its shape on a spoon, about 45 minutes.

4. Cool the mixture in a hotel pan over an ice bath.

5. Once it has cooled, pipe it onto the macarons and sandwich them. Place any remaining peach butter in an airtight container in the refrigerator. This will keep for up to 3 weeks in the refrigerator.

MOCHA GANACHE

yield: 500 g/1 lb 1.64 oz

INGREDIENT	METRIC	U.S.	%
Heavy cream	103 g	3.62 oz	20.55%
Glucose	171 g	6.04 oz	34.25%
Milk chocolate	103 g	3.62 oz	20.55%
Cocoa paste	86 g	3.02 oz	17.12%
Brandy	34 g	1.21 oz	6.85%
Coffee extract	3 g	.12 oz	.68%

1. Bring the cream and glucose to a boil in a sauce pot. Put the chocolate and cocoa paste in a bowl, and pour the cream mixture over it.

2. Add the brandy and coffee extract, and stir until a homogeneous mass is obtained.

3. Cool the ganache to room temperature.

4. Once it has cooled, pipe the ganache onto the macarons and sandwich them. Use the Espresso Brush Stroke (recipe follows) to garnish the macarons.

ESPRESSO BRUSH STROKE

yield: 15 g/.53 oz

INGREDIENT	METRIC	U.S.	%
Coffee extract	10 g	.35 oz	66.67%
Rum or vodka	5 g	.18 oz	33.33%

1. Mix both ingredients together in a bowl.

2. Once the macarons have been sandwiched, brush a small amount over each one on one side.

note The rum or vodka will help the liquid evaporate quickly and thus prevent the shell of the macaron from getting soggy.

RED BRUSH STROKE

yield: 10 g/.35 oz

INGREDIENT	METRIC	U.S.
Red food coloring (water or alcohol based)	2 drops	2 drops
Rum or vodka	10 g	.35 oz

Combine both ingredients in a bowl, and brush onto the macarons in a circular motion.

CASSIS CREAM FILLING

yield: 500 g/1 lb 1.64 oz

INGREDIENT	METRIC	U.S.	%
Buttercream (page 266)	1 kg	2 lb 3.27 oz	77%
Cassis purée	300 g	10.58 oz	23%

Combine the buttercream with the cassis purée in a bowl, and mix until fully incorporated.

BANANA BUTTER

yield: 500 g/1 lb 1.64 oz

INGREDIENT	METRIC	U.S.	%
Bananas, ripe	1.76 kg	3 lb 14.4 oz	88.4%
Butter	199 g	7.02 oz	9.94%
Ground cinnamon	20 g	.7 oz	.99%
Tahitian vanilla powder	13 g	.47 oz	.66%

1. Combine all of the ingredients in a 4-qt sauce pot. Cook over low heat until the contents reduce by half, about 4 hours.

2. Cool the mixture in a hotel pan over an ice bath.

3. Once the banana butter has cooled, pipe it onto the macarons and sandwich them.

PUMPKIN BUTTER

yield: 500 g/1 lb 1.64 oz

INGREDIENT	METRIC	U.S.	%
Sugar pumpkin, peeled, seeded, and diced	1.62 kg	3 lb 9.44 oz	65.18%
Butter	272 g	9.58 oz	10.86%
Sugar	599 g	1 lb 5.12 oz	23.95%
Tahitian vanilla pods, split and scraped	3	3	
Cinnamon sticks	7	7	

1. Combine all the ingredients in a 4-qt sauce pot and bring to a boil. Once the mixture has come to a boil, reduce the heat to medium-low.

2. Cook until the pumpkin is tender and broken down, about 2 hours. Stir often and reduce the heat if necessary to prevent scorching.

3. Cool the butter in a hotel pan over an ice bath and remove the vanilla pods. After it cools, pipe it into the macarons and sandwich them.

SHORTBREAD COOKIES

yield: **24 cookies**

INGREDIENT	METRIC	U.S.	%
All-purpose flour	1.05 kg	2 lb 4.96 oz	40.89%
Rice flour	150 g	5.29 oz	5.84%
Salt	18 g	.63 oz	.7%
Butter, soft	900 g	1 lb 15.75 oz	35.05%
Sugar	450 g	15.87 oz	17.52%
Superfine or bakers' sugar	as needed	as needed	

1. Place a 1.25-cm-/.5-in-thick Plexiglas frame on top of a sheet pan lined with silicone paper.

2. Sift the flours and the salt together.

3. Cream the butter and sugar together in an electric mixer fitted with the paddle attachment until just incorporated. Make sure not to cream the mixture for too long.

4. Add the sifted dry ingredients to the butter-sugar mixture. Mix on low speed until just incorporated.

5. Roll the dough out to fit into the frame on the prepared sheet pan. Chill until the dough has hardened.

6. Preheat a convection oven to 160°C/320°F.

7. Cut the cookies into 5-cm/2-in circles using a round cutter. Dock the dough with a fork in an "X" pattern, making sure the fork goes all the way through the dough.

8. Place the cookies on a sheet pan lined with parchment paper and sprinkle enough superfine or bakers' sugar on them to coat the surface. If the cookies are soft, chill them. These cookies need to be very cold, almost frozen, to bake properly.

9. Bake until they are golden brown around the border.

10. Cool to room temperature. If these cookies are baked properly, they will keep for up to 5 to 6 days in an airtight container at room temperature.

note These cookies originated in Scotland in the sixteenth century, and they were originally shaped into a round disc and then cut into triangles, as you would with a pizza.

HAND-DECORATED SUGAR COOKIES

yield: about 40 pieces, depending on the size

INGREDIENT	METRIC	U.S.	%
Tahitian vanilla powder	3 g	.11 oz	.17%
All-purpose flour	780 g	1 lb 11.52 oz	44.3%
Baking powder	18 g	.63 oz	1.02%
Salt	6 g	.21 oz	.34%
Butter	454 g	1 lb	25.76%
Superfine or bakers' sugar	400 g	14.11 oz	22.72%
Eggs, at 21°C/70°F	100 g	3.53 oz	5.68%

1. Sift the vanilla powder, flour, baking powder, and salt together.

2. Cream the butter with the sugar in an electric mixer fitted with the paddle attachment until light and fluffy, 4 to 5 minutes. Add the eggs 1 at a time, blending each in completely before adding another.

3. Stop the mixer, add the dry ingredients, and then pulse the machine until the ingredients just come together to form a uniform mass.

4. Shape the dough into a flat square and wrap it in plastic. Refrigerate for 2 hours.

5. Roll the dough to 1.25 cm/.5 in thick using a rolling pin or sheeter, but preferably a sheeter to ensure an even thickness.

6. Let the dough relax in the freezer until firm, at least 30 minutes.

7. Preheat a convection oven to 160°F/320°F.

8. Cut the dough into the desired shapes. Dock them down the center. How they are docked depends on the size of the cookies, but try to keep them 2.5 cm/1 in apart. Always bake this cookie when it is cold or even frozen to ensure it will keep its shape.

9. Bake just until the border, not the whole cookie, turns golden brown.

10. Cool to room temperature. If these cookies are kept in a cool, dry place, tightly wrapped in plastic or in an airtight container, they will keep for up to 6 days.

ROYAL ICING

yield: 2.16 kg/4 lb 12.48 oz

INGREDIENT	METRIC	U.S.	%
Confectioners' sugar	1.8 kg	3 lb 15.36 oz	83.03%
Cream of tartar	8 g	.28 oz	16.61%
Egg whites, pasteurized	360 g	12.7 oz	.37%

1. Sift the confectioners' sugar and cream of tartar together. Place the mixture in the bowl of an electric mixer fitted with the whip attachment.

2. Start mixing, and slowly pour in the egg whites. Mix until the sugar has dissolved and a homogeneous mix is achieved, about 2 minutes.

3. Pour the contents into an airtight container. Place a damp, heavy-duty paper towel directly over the royal icing. This will keep it from drying out or forming a skin on its surface. Put the lid on the container.

4. Make the royal icing the day before it is needed so that the sugar has time to completely dissolve. Royal icing requires the addition of an acid (in this case cream of tartar, but it can also be lemon juice or vinegar) because it helps the sugar crystallize quickly once it is piped and exposed to the air.

5. The royal icing will keep for up to 2 months in the refrigerator.

note Depending on the size of the cookie, this amount will be enough for about 100 cookies.

1. Draw an outline with the royal icing around the border of the cookie using a very small piping tip so that the outline is very thin. This border will keep the royal icing from flooding out.

2. At this point, if desired, color the royal icing. The border portion can also be colored, if desired. Always use water- or alcohol-based food coloring, never a fat-based coloring. Add as much or as little food coloring as necessary until the desired color intensity is achieved.

3. Transfer the royal icing to a piping bag. If using a piping tip, make sure the tip is covered between uses, since the icing will set when exposed to air and clog the tip.

4. Pipe the desired pattern; this is called "flooding." The entire surface doesn't always have to be piped; some icing can be piped onto the cookie and then dragged to the border with a scribe or toothpick. The consistency of the royal icing may need to be adjusted. If it is too thick, add a little water. If it is too thin, add more confectioners' sugar, but make sure the sugar is dissolved completely before using the icing.

Basic Method for Filling Hand-Decorated Cookies

DECORATING WITH ROYAL ICING, FROM LEFT TO RIGHT:

1. Use a small, round tip to pipe a very thin border of royal icing to keep the flooding in place.
2. When flooding with multiple colors, work on only a few cookies at a time so that the royal icing dries evenly.
3. You can gently drag a scribe or toothpick through the piping to create a marbleized effect.

5. Save any leftover royal icing covered with a damp paper towel. If swirling icings of different colors together, do only 2 or 3 cookies at a time so that the colors can swirl into each other without having a cracked, uneven look from the icing setting too quickly.

6. It is very important that the royal icing set quickly, though, in order to obtain a good shine; the slower it sets, the duller it will be. To achieve this, have 1 or 2 blow dryers pointing directly onto the cookies to speed up the drying process.

7. Once the cookies are decorated, let them dry completely for at least 8 hours without wrapping them or putting them in an airtight container. Once they have dried out completely, the cookies will keep for up to 4 days. After that point, the icing gets too hard and becomes unpalatable.

variations

Cow Cookies

1. Outline the cows with black royal icing.

2. Outline the spots with black royal icing.

3. Flood the black spots with black royal icing.

4. Flood the remainder of the cows with white or brown royal icing.

Swirled Icing Cookies (see photos on pages 284 and 286.)

1. Cut the dough so that the cookies are 5 by 10 cm/2 by 4 in.

2. Outline the cookies with brown royal icing.

3. Flood the cookies with brown royal icing.

4. Pipe pink polka dots inside the brown royal icing.

5. Pipe a line of turquoise royal icing and swirl it using a scribe or toothpick.

6. Put a silver oval dragée on top of each cookie before the icing sets.

Cookies with Wafer Paper

1. Cut the dough so that the cookies are 2.5 by 12.5 cm/1 by 5 in.

2. Cut the printed wafer paper into pieces 2.5 by 12.5 cm/1 by 5 in (see Resources, page 540).

3. Outline the cookies with white royal icing.

4. Flood the cookies with white royal icing.

5. Place the wafer paper on top of the wet royal icing. Flip the cookies over onto a flat surface and let them dry face down so that the paper doesn't wrinkle.

6. Once the royal icing and the wafer paper are dry, turn them back over.

Cookies with Printed Sugar Paper

1. Cut the dough so that the cookies are 6-cm/2.25-in squares.

2. Print the images onto the sugar paper, and cut them to the same size as the cookie. See Resources on page 540 for printers, edible ink cartridges, sugar paper, and custom-printed sugar paper.

3. Outline the cookies with orange royal icing.

4. Flood the cookies with orange royal icing.

5. Place the printed image directly over the royal icing as soon as it is flooded.

6. Let them dry at room temperature. This paper doesn't wrinkle, so it can be left to set facing up, rather than facing down like the wafer paper cookies.

THE ULTIMATE CHOCOLATE CHUNK COOKIE

yield: about 50 cookies

INGREDIENT	METRIC	U.S.	%
Butter, at 21°C/70°F	848 g	1 lb 13.92 oz	16.96%
Superfine or bakers' sugar	607 g	1 lb 5.44 oz	12.14%
Brown sugar	574 g	1 lb 4.32 oz	11.49%
Eggs, at 21°C/70°F	361 g	12.73 oz	7.22%
Baking soda	18 g	.64 oz	.36%
Salt	24 g	.86 oz	.49%
Tahitian vanilla paste	18 g	.64 oz	.36%
All-purpose flour	1.27 kg	2 lb 12.96 oz	25.49%
Semisweet chocolate chunks	1.27 kg	2 lb 12.96 oz	25.49%

1. Cream the butter and the sugars in an electric mixer fitted with the paddle attachment on medium speed until light and fluffy, about 4 minutes. Do not overcream; scrape the bowl and the paddle with a rubber spatula.

2. Stir the eggs so that they are homogeneous. Add the eggs in 3 or 4 additions. Stop the mixer, drop the bowl, and scrape the bowl and paddle after each addition.

3. Add the baking soda, salt, and vanilla paste, and mix until combined.

4. Add the flour and mix on low speed until just incorporated. Scrape the bowl and the paddle and mix for a few more seconds, until homogeneous.

5. Add the chocolate chunks and mix until just incorporated.

6. Scoop the cookie dough with a #16 scoop onto a sheet pan lined with parchment paper. Chill the scooped cookie dough or freeze it. The dough needs to be cold but not frozen hard before the cookies are baked.

7. Preheat a convection oven to 175°C/347°F.

8. Place 8 chilled scoops on a sheet pan lined with parchment paper, making sure they are evenly spaced. If the dough is frozen, thaw it on the sheet pan at room temperature. Press the cookies down slightly until they are about 2.5 cm/1 in thick.

9. Bake until the rim is golden brown and the center is still pale but baked through, 10 to 15 minutes. Rotate the sheet pan 180 degrees halfway through the baking process.

10. Cool the cookies to room temperature.

11. Bake the cookies throughout the day and discard any cookies that are left over at the end of the day.

notes There is no better chocolate chunk cookie than this one, at least in my opinion. If it is properly mixed and baked, it will be soft and chewy down the middle and crispy on the outside border. If it is kept in a warm spot, the chocolate will not set. Deliciousness ensues.

Raw cookies should be kept frozen on a sheet pan and tightly wrapped with plastic.

the display case

I HAVE OFTEN THOUGHT THAT IN A CAFÉ SETTING, you could practically do without a menu, since the menu is completely on display and people will order what they see. The first impact on a person is always a visual one, and this is why a lot of thought needs to be put into how the display case is presented.

First and foremost are the functional aspects. The case should always be functional and capable of a quick temperature recuperation time, since the door will be opened and closed many times during operation hours. There are many different kinds of display cases. There are front loading, rear loading, and top loading. The top-loading cases are exposed and easy to both fill and take desserts out of to sell or package. Always make sure that the actual case is clean. It is a good habit to take the desserts out of the case once the café is closed and perform a deep cleaning of the inside and outside of the case. Nothing turns people off more than a smudged, crumb-filled case. It is truly a reflection of the café.

Second, when you put your desserts in the case, try to always put them in the same place on a daily basis. It is important for your returning customers to know where to look for their favorite dessert. Try to keep the chocolate desserts in the furthest bottom corner in the case. Since chocolate desserts will usually be your best seller, you don't really need to show them off as prominently as you do other desserts. If someone wants chocolate they'll get chocolate, no matter where you place it, and that's fine, but you want to have a good sales mix and take some pressure and weight off of the chocolate items. This is a direct correlation to what occurs on printed menus. If you are in a restaurant environment, you would list the chocolate dessert(s) closer to the middle-bottom of the menu and not as the first option, since that will prompt many customers to not read any further.

Another important consideration is to try to have as many different shapes and colors as possible, and to mix them up. For example, don't have two square brown desserts next to each other, even if they are different flavors. Try to keep the colors in balance.

As far as placing the desserts in the case, always make sure that the signs are clear. They should say exactly what is in the dessert, its price, and, in the case of cakes, how many people it serves. Make sure that the desserts are symmetrical, straight, and perfectly lined up. The customers will notice this because it reflects care, precision, cleanliness, and finesse.

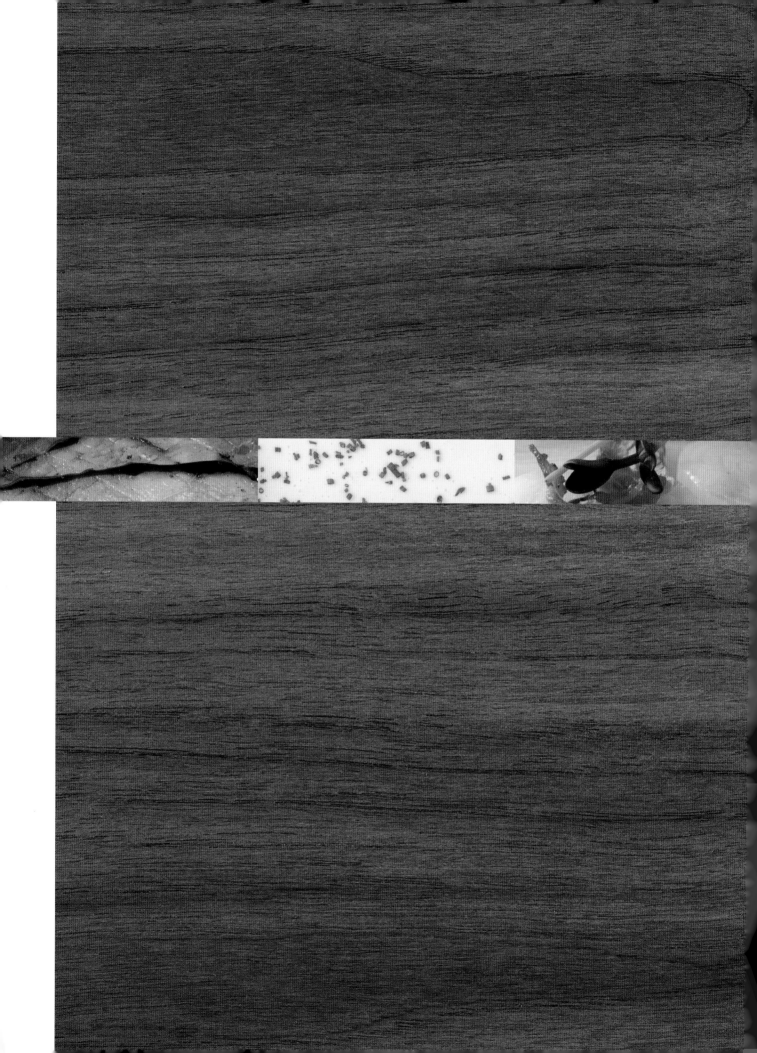

THE SAVORY KITCHEN

THE SAVORY KITCHEN is almost a completely different world from the bakeshop and the pastry kitchen. However, they do (or should) share a few essential principles. First and foremost, the quality of the ingredients plays an equally important role. Don't forget that high quality doesn't always equal high cost. It is entirely possible to find good products at a reasonable cost and keep the food cost in check. Second, the execution is just as crucial. It will determine the outcome of the products.

WHAT REALLY SETS the savory kitchen apart, other than the obvious fact that it turns out savory food, is that this area is an opportunity for à la minute preparations, whereas the bakeshop and the pastry shop feature ready-to-serve items. In fact, if the food isn't served à la minute, the quality will probably suffer. For example, if sandwiches are premade and held in the refrigerator, and they are not pressed or heated in some way (not in a microwave) before serving, the quality of the sandwich will be affected by its environment because the bread is in contact with moist ingredients, such as cured meat or a spread like mayonnaise. Ideally, any sandwich should be assembled to order.

There is a line here that needs to be understood. Café food should not be confused with cafeteria or diner food, which has its place. The food served in a café falls somewhere between a restaurant and a bistro, with an emphasis on speed and convenience. It is high-quality food delivered in an expeditious way that can be eaten in place or taken to go. Quality need not be sacrificed for the sake of speed. Mise en place is of the essence, as it is in any kitchen, but in this case think of efficiency and quality as the same thing. Do not confuse a café with a restaurant.

The items in this chapter are by no means the only variety of food a café should serve. They are simply foods that most properly suit a café environment. They are also foods that can be made in large quantities, within reason, and very few items are finished in a way that is too time-consuming. Consider the amount of customers that will be rotating through the dining room; it is not in your best interest to have pickups that are longer than ten or twelve minutes per item.

Mise en place is not exclusively having the ingredients and prep in place. It is also important to consider the equipment that will be used on the line. Newer technologies allow food to cook faster without sacrificing quality. The only downside is the initial investment. Combi ovens (combination cooking ovens), Alto-Shaams (cook and hold), CVap ovens (see sidebar, page 328), and immersion thermocirculators (see sidebar, page 383) all allow for a variety of items to be prepared ahead of time, cooked properly, and held for extended periods of time, again within reason. Purists will argue that there is nothing like cooking 100 percent to order. However, there are certain foods that, once cooked, can be held in adequate conditions for a few hours. You wouldn't sauté and hold a piece of foie gras, since it would melt completely if held at any temperature that would keep it warm; even if it could hold, the crisp exterior would get soggy. However,

you could hold duck confit in the fat in which it was cooked in an Alto-Shaam set to 60°C/140°F, and then finish it in a salamander, or better yet, an impinger oven. You wouldn't grill twenty porterhouse steaks and keep them in an Alto-Shaam, since they might keep their moistness but they wouldn't keep a crisp exterior. However, grilled flank steaks could be cooked to medium and held at 60°C/140°F, then sliced to order for a sandwich (see page 374). Don't pre-grill anything that would be served on its own. Other examples of items that can hold well in an Alto-Shaam are braised short ribs, pot roast, pulled pork, coddled eggs, and mashed potatoes. All they need in order to be picked up is to give them a quick burst of heat in a sauté pan, oven, salamander, or impinger oven to get them truly hot. It's all about getting the food out quickly and, most importantly, properly executed.

The recipes reflect an enthusiasm for seasoning with salt and pepper. Make the adjustments needed to season as desired. You can always adjust seasoning as you go, except with beans, which are seasoned once they are finished cooking. Salt is your friend.

MISE EN PLACE—KEY POINTS FOR MAXIMIZING EFFICIENCY

Soups: For hot soups, reserve them in a soup holder (similar to a bain marie); cold soups should be reserved refrigerated. Garnishes are to be added à la minute. Bowls and base plates should be kept warm if using for hot soups and cool if they are for cold soups.

Salads: Always dress them at the last minute. If there is a warm or hot component, get it up to temperature, and then dress the salad. Always use cool plates even when salads have a warm component.

Appetizers and side dishes: Keep the amount of components to a minimum; if they are cooked to order, make sure it's quick (such as frying).

Chilled sandwiches: Always assemble at the last minute; if they require cheese, make sure it is presliced and portioned so as to not have to separate the slices every time an order comes in. Try to keep all of the sandwich mise en place in one place.

Warm sandwiches: As with appetizers, the warm component should be warmed up to temperature quickly; assemble at the last minute as well.

organic food: is it always best?

THE SHORT ANSWER IS NO, NOT ALWAYS. You should not use organic food just for the sake of using organic food, because it is not always a higher-quality product. If it is a superior ingredient and it happens to be organic, all the better, but if it is organic and of poor quality, don't use it. Also, if a particular ingredient is not organic, it doesn't necessarily mean it will negatively impact the environment.

Organic food needs space, care, and special tending, which translates to a larger cost to those who produce/harvest it. This will impact the cost of the item being created in the kitchen and the price it is sold for in the café. This additional cost is something to consider when choosing to use organic foods and how to use them. Do the vegetables you use to make chicken stock need to be organic? Maybe not. It is these types of questions that you need to ask yourself. The most important aspects to consider are the ingredient's quality, flavor, and texture. There are other ways to be environmentally friendly as well, such as using recycled products and then recycling them, conserving energy, and not wasting water.

Hot sandwiches: On some occasions, you can preassemble the sandwiches and have them ready to be pressed or heated. This is if the filling is not too moist and won't moisten the bread significantly, such as with a grilled cheese sandwich. When pressing sandwiches with cheese, make sure the cheese is the top filling just before the top piece of bread, so that when it melts, it melts down into the other ingredients. Make sure the sandwich isn't too thick, so that it will get hot quickly, but nor should it be so thin that there's barely any filling. Use a good-quality press that will get the sandwich hot quickly (bread and filling all the way to the center) without burning it.

Entrées: Get as far ahead as you can in order to have a quick pickup, but never compromise the final product; advance mise en place is crucial.

As a general rule, always clean as you go.

soups

Soup is an item that can serve many purposes and be very versatile. It is relatively uncomplicated to make, easy to transport from kitchen to table or kitchen to home, easy to keep hot or cold, and easy to garnish. Thankfully, no matter where you live, there are many ingredients that can be used to make soups that do not depend on seasonality. Examples include potatoes, spinach, cauliflower, carrots, and leeks, which also happen to be relatively inexpensive. Soup can be a part of a meal or can be a meal in itself with nothing more than a good piece of bread.

It is a good idea to offer at least two to four types of soup per day. Among those choices, half should be creamed and half should be stock based (liquid plus solid garnish). If the season permits, it is a good idea to offer chilled soups. And on the flip side, what is better than a hot bowl of soup when it's cold outside? The ideal serving temperature for a hot soup is between a minimum of 80°C/176°F and a maximum of 87°C/189°F. Chilled soups should be served at 4°C/39°F and no lower than 2°C/36°F, since lower temperatures are too close to the freezing point (0°C/32°F).

If the soup includes a garnish, keep in mind that it should be on the small side or easy enough to break up with a spoon, such as a matzo ball, which is a large component but is easy to break with a spoon, or the gougères on page 301. Consider that any garnish that is temperature sensitive that goes into the soup should ideally be added right before the pickup. For example, if the soup contains pieces of cooked chicken, the chicken can be cooked in the soup to build flavor, but it should be taken out once it is fully cooked, and cooled down or kept at a more reasonable 60°C/140°F until needed for garnish.

the thermomix blender

THE THERMOMIX BLENDER is more powerful than most of the commercially available blenders in the United States, and it has two more wonderful features. It contains a heating element, and you can scale your ingredients directly into the cup while it is attached to the body of the mixer. The LCD display is mostly used as a timer, but when the balance beam button is pressed, it turns into a scale. As you mix, you can apply heat, from 37°C/99°F to 100°C/212°F. This opens up a whole world of possibilities. It is excellent for emulsions, sauces, pastry cream, and even ganache. For example, you can make a crème anglaise in it without having to temper the egg yolks. Simply increase the temperature of the mixer to 82°C/180°F and mix until the yolks have coagulated. It also makes sabayon a cinch.

When I first acquired this machine, the first item we tested out was a foie gras mousse. Typically this is a very delicate process because the foie gras can easily break or melt and a lot of money can be lost in a matter of seconds. After deveining and then soaking the foie overnight in milk to draw any excess blood and impurities out, I put pieces of foie gras in the Thermomix cup along with salt, pepper, and applejack apple brandy. I turned the mixer on to speed six for one minute, and then applied heat (60°C/140°F) for one more minute to cook the foie and make it food-safe. Finally I mixed the mousse for ten more seconds on the highest setting (ten). The heat, by the way, is instant. You do not need to wait for it to warm up. As the mixer applied heat, some of the foie started to melt, but not into a puddle. It was an even melting thanks to the speed of the blade, which kept the fat emulsified. The mousse at this point was perfectly smooth and it was of the consistency of soft butter, maybe a little looser. I lined a PVC tube 6.25 cm/2.5 in diameter by 30 cm/12 in long with acetate and placed it on a flat sheet pan lined with parchment paper. Once the mousse was done, I piped it into the prepared tube, covered it with plastic wrap and a cloth towel, and let it set in refrigeration. The result was a perfectly smooth foie gras with great flavor. Even better, it took three minutes to make. And all things considered, it is not a very expensive machine.

The only downside is that it has limited capacity (about 2 kg/4 lb 6.4 oz), so many products need to be made in small batches. Also, there aren't many qualified technicians who repair this machine in this country, so if it breaks down you have to send it off for a few weeks.

CHILLED CUCUMBER AND RADISH SOUP WITH WASABI CRÈME FRAÎCHE AND TOBIKO

yield: 20 portions

INGREDIENT	METRIC	U.S.
CUCUMBER SOUP		
English cucumbers, peeled and coarsely chopped (about 20)	8 kg	17 lb 10.08 oz
Green onions, ends trimmed and coarsely chopped (about 6)	540 g	1 lb 3.04 oz
Lime juice	50 g	1.76 oz
Salt	15 g	.53 oz
Red radishes	4	4
Crème fraîche	250 g	8.82 oz
Heavy cream	250 g	8.82 oz
Wasabi powder	3 g	.11 oz
Red tobiko	200 g	7.05 oz

1. **FOR THE CUCUMBER SOUP:** Combine the cucumbers, green onions, lime juice, and salt in a bain marie large enough to fit all of the ingredients. Using a beurre mixer, purée all of the ingredients until smooth.

2. Purée the mixture further in a commercial blender until smooth. Do not strain. Adjust the seasoning. Discard the soup after 24 hours.

3. Slice the radishes very thinly and reserve in chilled water.

4. **FOR THE WASABI CRÈME FRAÎCHE:** Combine the crème fraîche with the heavy cream and the wasabi and whip until stiff peaks form in an electric mixer or by hand. Reserve in the refrigerator. This item will keep for 2 days in the refrigerator, but it will need to be re-whipped a few times during the day so that it stays firm enough to form into quenelles.

5. **TO PICK UP:** Pour 350g/12.35 oz of cucumber soup into a soup bowl.

6. Using a warm spoon, scoop a 30-g/1.06-oz quenelle of crème fraîche and place it down the left side of the bowl. Put 3 to 5 slices of radish in the soup around the quenelle. Spoon 20 g/.70 oz of tobiko on top of the crème fraîche. Serve immediately.

GAZPACHO WITH CRAB, MIREPOIX SPROUTS, AND AVOCADO

yield: 20 portions

INGREDIENT	METRIC	U.S.
GAZPACHO		
Garlic cloves (about 4)	20 g	.7 oz
Beefsteak tomatoes, medium, very ripe (about 20)	5.1 kg	11 lb 3.84 oz
English cucumbers, peeled (about 2)	400 g	14.11 oz
Onion, peeled, ends trimmed (about 1)	320 g	11.29 oz
Red pepper, seeded and stemmed (about 3)	630 g	1 lb 6.08 oz
Paprika or pimentón dulce	30 g	1.06 oz
Freshly cracked black pepper, or as needed	4 g	.14 oz
Salt, or as needed	25 g	.88 oz
Sherry vinegar	75 g	2.64 oz
Brioche croutons (see method below)	200 g	7.05 oz
English cucumbers, peeled, seeded, and finely diced	200 g	7.05 oz
Red peppers, peeled, seeded, and finely diced	200 g	7.05 oz
Hass avocadoes, cut into 1.25-cm-/.5 in-wide wedges (to order)	1.17 kg	2 lb 9.44 oz
Spanish extra-virgin olive oil	100 g	3.53 oz
King crab legs, fully cooked	4	4
Mirepoix sprouts	100 g	3.53 oz
Extra-virgin olive oil for garnish	20 g	.7 oz

1. **FOR THE GAZPACHO:** Bring a small pot of water to a boil. Blanch the garlic cloves until tender, about 30 seconds.

2. Place the tomatoes, cucumbers, garlic, onion, red pepper, paprika, black pepper, salt, and sherry vinegar in a bain marie large enough to fit all of the ingredients. Using a beurre mixer, purée all of the ingredients until smooth.

3. Once the mixture is puréed, blend it further in a commercial blender until smooth. Do not strain this liquid.

4. **FOR THE BRIOCHE CROUTONS:** Use day-old brioche. Remove the crust and freeze it. Cut the brioche into small dice.

5. Toast the brioche cubes in a 160°C/320°F oven until light amber brown. Cool to room temperature and reserve in an airtight container at room temperature.

6. **TO PICK UP:** Place 10 g/.35 oz each of diced cucumbers and diced red peppers, and one slice of an avocado, inside a soup bowl.

7. Pour 350 g/12.35 oz of gazpacho into the bowl. Drizzle with 5 g/.17 oz of Spanish olive oil across the surface of the soup.

8. Place a 10-g/.35-oz mound of croutons at the center of the bowl. Place a crab leg on top of the croutons and a 5-g/.17-oz mound of mirepoix sprouts on top of the crab. Drizzle a few drops of extra-virgin olive oil over the soup (about 1 g/.03 oz per order). Serve immediately.

FROM TOP TO BOTTOM:
Avocado Soup with Smoked American Sturgeon and American Sturgeon Caviar (page 299), Watercress Soup with Greek Yogurt and Red Amaranth (page 298), Potato and Cauliflower Vichyssoise with Warm Truffle Béchamel–Filled Gougères and Chives (page 300), Chilled Cucumber and Radish soup with Wasabi Crème Fraîche and Tobiko (page 295), Gazpacho with Crab, Mirepoix Sprouts, and Avocado (opposite)

WATERCRESS SOUP WITH GREEK YOGURT AND RED AMARANTH

yield: 20 portions

INGREDIENT	METRIC	U.S.
WATERCRESS SOUP		
Watercress leaves with no stems	750 g	1 lb 10.4 oz
Butter, soft	130 g	4.58 oz
Leeks, ends trimmed and finely chopped	1.5 kg	3 lb 4.8 oz
Russet potatoes, peeled and cut into medium dice	1.7 kg	3 lb 12 oz
Chicken stock	4 kg	8 lb 13.12 oz
Heavy cream	400 g	14.11 oz
Salt	10 g	.35 oz
Greek yogurt	1 kg	2 lb 13.12 oz
Red amaranth sprouts	60 to 70	60 to 70

1. **FOR THE SOUP:** Bring a pot of heavily salted water to a boil.

2. Blanch the watercress until wilted, about 30 seconds. Shock the watercress in an ice bath to stop the cooking process. Squeeze off the excess water and keep the watercress refrigerated in an airtight container until needed.

3. Melt the butter in a sauce pot over medium-high heat and add the leeks. Sweat the leeks until translucent. Add the diced potatoes and stir to combine.

4. Add the chicken stock and bring the liquid to a boil. Reduce the heat to a simmer. Cook until the potatoes are tender, about 20 minutes.

5. Add the cream and bring to a boil again.

6. Remove the pot from the heat and purée the contents of the pot until smooth using a beurre mixer. Cool the soup over an ice bath.

7. Once the soup has cooled, add the cooked watercress and purée in a commercial blender at the highest speed until it is completely smooth, about 90 seconds. Pass the soup through a fine-mesh sieve, season with salt, and reserve in the refrigerator. Discard after 36 hours.

8. **TO PICK UP:** Dip a soupspoon in warm water, tap it dry on a clean paper towel, and scoop a 50-g/1.76-oz dollop of Greek yogurt into a soup bowl.

9. Pour 350 g/12.35 oz of soup into the bowl.

10. Garnish with a few stems of red amaranth on top of the yogurt. Serve immediately.

AVOCADO SOUP WITH SMOKED AMERICAN STURGEON AND AMERICAN STURGEON CAVIAR

yield: 20 portions

INGREDIENT	METRIC	U.S.
AVOCADO SOUP		
Hass avocados, ripe (about 20)	4.7 kg	10 lb 5.76 oz
Milk	3 kg	6 lb 9.76 oz
Heavy cream	200 g	7.05 oz
Lemon juice	100 g	3.53 oz
Salt	75 g	2.65 oz
Jalapeños, seeded, stemmed, and coarsely chopped (about 2)	70 g	2.47 oz
Ascorbic acid (vitamin C crystals)	10 g	.35 oz
Smoked American sturgeon, firm outer layer and skin (if any) removed	900 g	1 lb 15.68 oz
American sturgeon caviar	200 g	7.05 oz

1. **FOR THE SOUP:** Combine the avocados, milk, cream, lemon juice, salt, jalapeños, and ascorbic acid in a bain marie large enough to hold all of the ingredients. Use a beurre mixer to purée the ingredients until smooth.

2. Purée the ingredients further in a commercial blender. Adjust the consistency; if it is too loose, add more avocados, and if it is too thick, add more cream. Adjust seasoning and strain through a fine-mesh sieve.

3. Reserve in the refrigerator with a piece of plastic wrap directly on the surface of the soup to slow down oxidation. Discard the soup after 24 hours.

4. **TO PICK UP:** Pour 350 g/12.35 oz of avocado soup into a bowl.

5. Cut the sturgeon into .5-cm-/.2-in-thick slices. Place 45 g/1.6 oz of sliced sturgeon on top of the soup (4 to 5 slices per order).

6. Spoon 10 g/0.35 oz of caviar on top of the sturgeon. Serve immediately.

note Ascorbic acid, as unappetizing as it sounds, stops nearly all oxidation, and it is really only powdered vitamin C, a very concentrated and powerful acid.

POTATO AND CAULIFLOWER VICHYSSOISE WITH WARM TRUFFLE BÉCHAMEL–FILLED GOUGÈRES AND CHIVES

yield: **20 portions**

INGREDIENT	METRIC	U.S.
VICHYSSOISE		
Butter	150 g	5.3 oz
Onions, coarsely chopped (about 2)	640 g	1 lb 6.46 oz
Garlic cloves, coarsely chopped (about 8)	40 g	1.41 oz
Russet potatoes, peeled and cut into medium dice	1.4 kg	3 lb 1.44 oz
Cauliflower, coarsely chopped	1 kg	2 lb 3.2 oz
Chicken stock	3 kg	6 lb 9.76 oz
Heavy cream	1.1 kg	2 lb 6.88 oz
Salt	100 g	3.53 oz
Freshly ground white pepper	5 g	.17 oz
Gougères (page 301)	20	20
Truffle Béchamel (page 302)	600 g	1.32 oz
Chives, finely chopped	100 g	3.53 oz

1. **FOR THE SOUP:** Melt the butter in a sauce pot over medium-high heat. Sweat the onions and the garlic until tender.

2. Add the potatoes, cauliflower, and stock and bring to a boil. Reduce the heat to a simmer and cook until the potatoes and cauliflower are tender.

3. Add the cream and season with salt and white pepper. Bring to a boil quickly and remove from the heat.

4. Purée with a beurre mixer until a uniform mixture is obtained. Purée further in a commercial blender until smooth if the beurre mixer did not achieve the proper consistency.

5. Strain the soup through a fine-mesh sieve. Cool the soup over an ice bath.

6. **TO PICK UP:** Pour 350 g/12.35 oz of chilled vichyssoise into a soup bowl. Fill a gougère with about 15 g/.52 oz truffle béchamel and place it on top of the soup.

7. Sprinkle 5 g/.17 oz of diced chives over the soup and gougère. Serve immediately.

note The whole head of cauliflower will yield about 75 percent usable product.

GOUGÈRES (Gruyère Choux Puffs)

yield: about 80 pieces

INGREDIENT	METRIC	U.S.	%
GOUGÈRE BASE			
Water	338 g	11.91 oz	28.13%
Salt	3 g	.10 oz	.23%
Sugar	3 g	.11 oz	.26%
Butter, cut into medium dice	155 g	5.48 oz	12.94%
High-gluten bread flour	182 g	6.43 oz	15.19%
Gruyère, grated	135 g	4.76 oz	11.25%
Eggs	270 g	9.53 oz	22.51%
Egg Wash for Brushing (page 13)	as needed	as needed	
Freshly ground black pepper	.90 g	.03 oz	.08%
Freshly grated nutmeg	.45 g	.02 oz	.04%
Gruyère, grated	68 g	2.38 oz	5.63%

1. **FOR THE GOUGÈRE BASE:** Combine the water, salt, sugar, and butter in a sauce pot. Bring them to a full boil for 1 minute. Remove the pot from the heat and add the bread flour all at once while stirring constantly.

2. Return the pot to the heat and cook for about 1 more minute; stir constantly and vigorously with a wooden spoon. There should be a film that develops on the bottom of the pot; this is the sign that the starch in the flour has begun to gelatinize. At the first sign of this happening, flip the choux over as if it were a pancake and continue to stir vigorously with the wooden spoon.

3. Transfer this paste to an electric mixer and mix with the paddle attachment on medium-high speed for 30 seconds. This will cool down the paste somewhat, which may prevent the eggs from cooking on contact with the scalding hot paste and let some steam escape. Add the Gruyère before adding the eggs to the mixer.

4. Start adding the eggs to the mixer. Add them in 4 additions and, after each addition, wait for them to become completely incorporated before adding more. Stop the mixer, drop the bowl, and scrape the paddle and the bowl with a rubber spatula between each addition; this will ensure a homogeneous paste with no lumps.

5. Preheat a static oven to 220°C/428°F.

6. Using a #6 plain tip, pipe them to a 2.5-cm/1-in diameter over a nonstick rubber mat.

7. Brush the gougères with the egg wash once they have been piped. Grind the black pepper and grate the nutmeg directly over the gougères. Sprinkle the Gruyère on top of all the gougères.

8. Place the gougères in the deck oven. When they develop a medium amber-brown color, after about 5 minutes, open the vent and bake until the entire surface of the choux is golden brown, even on the seams on the sides, 15 to 20 more minutes.

9. To check if they are hollow, split one of the gougères from the middle of the sheet pan in half. There is no easier way to check the doneness. If they are not hollow, turn the oven down to 160°C/320°F and open the oven door. Slide the sheet pans toward the door of the oven so that they are still inside but so that all the excess steam will be able to escape, thus forming a hollow shell.

10. Cool the gougères to room temperature.

11. Reserve uncovered at room temperature during service; they will soften if wrapped. Discard after service.

note It is more efficient to make this yield; it becomes complicated to make a smaller amount, and the extra gougères can be frozen and refreshed in a hot oven as needed.

TRUFFLE BÉCHAMEL

yield: 900 g/1 lb 15.68 oz

INGREDIENT	METRIC	U.S.	%
Onion, finely diced	13 g	.44 oz	1.26%
Butter	68 g	2.4 oz	6.75%
Flour	98 g	3.45 oz	9.79%
Milk	786 g	1 lb 11.68 oz	78.54%
Black truffle trimmings, finely diced	21 g	.74 oz	2.09%
Black truffle salt	16 g	.55 oz	1.57%

1. Sweat the onion in 11 g/.38 oz butter over medium-high heat until translucent. Set aside.

2. Make a pale roux with the remaining butter and the flour in a sauce pot over high heat.

3. Pour the milk into the roux and stir vigorously until smooth. Add the sweated onions and the truffle trimmings. Simmer for 30 minutes or until the liquid has thickened.

4. Season with the black truffle salt. Adjust seasoning if necessary. Strain through 2 sheets of cheesecloth.

5. Transfer to a piping bag fitted with a #2 piping tip. Tie the large end of the piping bag with a rubber band. Keep hot (such as in an Alto-Shaam).

6. Discard any béchamel left over after service.

note The recipe weight is 1 kg/2 lb 3.2 oz, but there will be some weight loss due to evaporation.

For hot soups, always keep the bowls used to serve the soup in a hot area, such as next to an oven or grill. They need to stay hot so that the soup stays hot for a longer period of time. Make sure the bowls stay clean and are shielded from any splatter.

BREAD AND GARLIC SOUP WITH CANNELLINI BEANS, SWISS CHARD, AND POACHED EGG

yield: 20 portions

INGREDIENT	METRIC	U.S.
BEANS		
Cannellini beans	750 g	1 lb 10.5 oz
Chicken stock	3 kg	6 lb 9.8 oz
Carrots, coarsely chopped	150 g	5.29 oz
Onion, coarsely chopped	150 g	5.29 oz
Celery, coarsely chopped	150 g	5.29 oz
Garlic cloves	20 g	.71 oz
Slab bacon	250 g	8.82 oz
Salt	50 g	1.76 oz
POACHED EGGS		
Water	2 kg	4 lb 6.4 oz
White vinegar	250 g	8.82 oz
Eggs	20	20
SOUP		
Garlic	32 heads, skin on	32 heads, skin on
Chicken stock	4 kg	8 lb 12.96 oz
Swiss chard, stems removed, coarsely chopped, and rinsed in cold water	1 bunch	1 bunch
Salt	8 g	.28 oz
Freshly ground black pepper	3 g	.10 oz
Day-old sourdough bread, cut into 2.5-cm/1-in cubes	800 g	1 lb 12.16 oz

1. **FOR THE BEANS:** Soak the beans overnight in cold water.

2. Drain the beans and place them in a pot with the chicken stock, carrots, onion, celery, garlic, and slab bacon.

3. Bring to a boil, and then reduce the heat to a simmer.

4. Cook until the beans are tender, about 1 hour. Remove the pot from the heat and season the beans with the salt.

5. Cool the beans in a hotel pan over an ice bath to stop the cooking process. Reserve until needed.

6. **FOR THE POACHED EGGS:** Prepare an ice bath.

7. Bring the water and vinegar to a simmer that is just under a boil (about 98°C/208°F) in a pot or immersion thermocirculator (see sidebar, page 383).

8. Crack the eggs into 2-oz ramekins. Pour each egg into the water in 20-second intervals. Use a slotted spoon to "spin" the eggs in the water so that they don't spread out and so that they stay oval.

9. Once the egg whites are cooked, take them out of the simmering water with the slotted spoon and put them in the ice bath to stop the cooking process. The egg yolk should still be runny, but the egg whites should be fully cooked. Discard after 12 hours.

10. Before service, set up a pot with water or an immersion thermocirculator to 93°C/200°F. This will serve to reheat the poached eggs quickly.

11. **FOR THE SOUP:** Place the garlic in the chicken stock and bring to a boil, then reduce to a simmer. Cook until the garlic is tender, about 40 minutes. Strain the garlic out of the stock and return the stock to a simmer.

12. Pass the garlic through a food mill or sieve. Mix the garlic back into the stock and season with salt and pepper. Add the Swiss chard and cook until wilted, about 10 minutes, stirring frequently. Stir in the cooked cannellini beans. Hold hot in a soup warmer at 82°C/180°F. Discard the soup after 24 hours.

13. **TO PICK UP:** Place 40 g/1.4 oz of the diced sourdough bread in a soup bowl. Stir the hot soup and ladle 300 g/10.58 oz into the bowl on top of the bread (try to get an even mix of broth, beans, and Swiss chard). Let the bread soak up the soup.

14. Meanwhile, drop a poached egg into the pot with hot water or the thermocirculator and let it warm up for 1 minute.

15. Take the egg out of the water with the slotted spoon. Tap it gently on a paper towel, and then put the egg into the soup bowl. Serve immediately.

BLISS POTATO, BRAISED FENNEL, AND TASSO HAM SOUP

yield: 20 portions

INGREDIENT	METRIC	U.S.
BRAISED FENNEL		
Fennel bulbs, stems cut off and reserved, bulbs halved and cored (about 4)	620 g	1 lb 5.76 oz
Chicken stock	2 kg	4 lb 6.4 oz
Salt	50 g	1.76 oz
POTATOES		
Water	4 kg	8 lb 13.12 oz
Salt	200 g	7.05 oz
Bliss potatoes	2 kg	4 lb 6.4 oz
Tasso ham, finely diced	1.2 kg	2 lb 10.4 oz
Chicken consommé	4 kg	8 lb 13.12 oz
Salt	50 g	1.76 oz
Fennel fronds (reserved from the stems)	20	20

1. **FOR THE BRAISED FENNEL:** Preheat a convection oven to 149°C/300°F.

2. Place the prepared fennel bulbs in a hotel pan, flat side down. Make sure the core is entirely removed.

3. Pour half of the chicken stock into the hotel pan. It should come halfway up the fennel. Reserve the other half of the chicken stock hot in case more needs to be added to the fennel while it is braising. Sprinkle the salt over the fennel.

4. Place the hotel pan in the oven. Braise until the fennel bulbs are tender, about 45 minutes.

5. Remove the fennel from the oven and cool it off in an ice bath.

6. Cut the fennel into medium dice. Reserve the fennel in an airtight container in the refrigerator. Discard after 12 hours.

7. **FOR THE POTATOES:** Place the water and salt in a pot. Quarter the potatoes and place them in the water as they are cut.

8. Bring the liquid up to a boil, and then reduce the heat to a simmer. Simmer the potatoes until tender, about 20 minutes.

9. Using a slotted spoon, remove the potatoes from the hot liquid and place them in a hotel pan. Spread them out and cool them immediately in the refrigerator. Reserve in an airtight container in the refrigerator. Discard after 12 hours.

10. Preheat a convection oven to 160°C/320°F

11. Place the ham on a sheet pan lined with parchment paper. Cook it in the oven until crisp, about 12 minutes.

12. Pat it dry with a heavy-duty paper towel. Reserve covered at room temperature until needed. Discard after 12 hours.

13. Bring the chicken consommé to a boil, season with salt, and reserve hot in a soup warmer at 82°C/180°F; keep well covered.

14. **TO PICK UP:** Place 350 g/12.35 oz of the chicken consommé, 100 g/3.53 oz of the potatoes, and 50 g/1.76 oz of the braised fennel in a small sauté pan.

15. Bring the liquid to a boil over a high flame, and then pour it into a soup bowl.

16. Put a 60-g/2.11-oz mound of ham at the center of the bowl. Put a fennel frond on top of the ham. Serve immediately.

BRAISED PORK SHOULDER WITH HOMINY AND ANCHO CHILE SOUP

yield: 20 portions

INGREDIENT	METRIC	U.S.
Dried hominy	1 kg	2 lb 3.2 oz
PORK SHOULDER		
Pork shoulder	3 kg	6 lb 9.76 oz
Chicken stock	5 kg	11 lb .32 oz
Salt	100 g	3.53 oz
ANCHO CHILE SOUP		
Ancho chiles, toasted	120 g	4.23 oz
Onions, cut into medium dice	1.6 kg	3 lb 8.32 oz
Garlic, coarsely chopped	40 g	1.41 oz
Cilantro, coarsely chopped (about 1 bunch)	50 g	1.76 oz
Bay leaves	3	3
Tomato paste	200 g	7.05 oz
Chicken stock	5 kg	11 lb .32 oz
Salt	50 g	1.76 oz
Cilantro sprigs	20	20

1. Rinse the hominy under cold water until it runs clear. Soak in cold water for at least 12 hours in the refrigerator.

2. Strain the hominy, place it in a pot, and cover it with cold water. Bring to a boil and then reduce the heat to a simmer.

3. Cook, covered, until the hominy pops, about 1 hour. Season with salt and cool in a hotel pan over an ice bath or in a blast freezer for a few minutes. Reserve in the refrigerator.

4. **FOR THE PORK SHOULDER:** Combine the pork shoulder with the chicken stock and salt in a pot. The shoulder should be completely submerged in the stock.

5. Bring to a boil, and then reduce the heat to a simmer. Cook until the pork is fork-tender, 3 to 4 hours. Remove the pork from the chicken stock, and skim the fat off the stock.

6. Shred the pork with a fork into bite-size morsels and reserve in the chicken stock until needed in an Alto-Shaam oven or in a pot over low heat. Discard any left over after service.

7. **FOR THE SOUP:** Combine the ancho chiles with the onions, garlic, cilantro, bay leaves, tomato paste, chicken stock, and salt in a pot.

8. Bring to a boil, and then reduce the heat to a simmer until the onions and garlic are tender, about 20 minutes.

9. Strain the liquid and place it in a soup warmer set to 82°C/180°F. Keep it well covered. Return the hominy to a boil, strain it, and put it in the soup.

10. **TO PICK UP:** Stir the soup with a ladle and pour 350 g/12.35 oz into a soup bowl.

11. Spoon about 100 g/3.53 oz of shredded pork shoulder on top of the soup.

12. Put a cilantro sprig on top of the pork. Serve immediately.

CREAM OF ARTICHOKE SOUP WITH TRUFFLED CRÈME FRAÎCHE

yield: 20 portions

INGREDIENT	METRIC	U.S.
ARTICHOKE SOUP		
Artichokes, large	40	40
Butter	150 g	5.29 oz
Onion, cut into medium dice	200 g	7.05 oz
Garlic, coarsely chopped	15 g	.52 oz
Chicken stock	4.4 kg	9 lb 11.2 oz
Heavy cream	1.1 kg	2 lb 6.88 oz
Salt	75 g	2.64 oz
TRUFFLED CRÈME FRAÎCHE		
Crème fraîche	300 g	10.58 oz
Heavy cream	200 g	7.05 oz
Black truffle salt	3 g	.11 oz
Black truffle trimmings, finely chopped	20 g	.71 oz
Black truffle, thinly sliced	100 g	3.53 oz

1. **FOR THE SOUP:** Place the artichokes in a large pot with enough cold salted water to cover them. Bring them to a boil and then simmer until tender, 12 to 15 minutes.

2. Once they are cooked, remove the leaves, the stem, and the fibrous cap over the heart of the artichoke.

3. In a sauce pot, melt the butter over medium-high heat and sweat the onion and garlic until tender; stir in the artichokes and cook for 5 more minutes or until the onion is translucent.

4. Add the stock and the cream and bring to a boil. Purée with a beurre mixer until smooth, and then purée further with a commercial blender. Season with salt.

5. Pass the soup through a fine-mesh sieve. Cool over an ice bath or keep it hot, covered, in a soup warmer at 82°C/180°F. It will keep for 2 days in the refrigerator.

6. **FOR THE TRUFFLED CRÈME FRAÎCHE:** Combine all of the ingredients in a mixer bowl and whip until stiff peaks form. Reserve in the refrigerator during service. Adjust seasoning if needed. It may need to be re-whipped a few times during service. Discard after 48 hours.

7. **TO PICK UP:** Pour 350 g/12.35 oz of hot artichoke soup into a soup bowl.

8. Spoon a 45-g/1.58-oz quenelle of truffled crème fraîche down the center of the bowl. Place 3 or 4 slices of truffle next to the quenelle of crème fraîche. Serve immediately.

CREAM OF GREEN ASPARAGUS WITH MORELS AND FROMAGE BLANC

yield: 20 portions

INGREDIENT	METRIC	U.S.
ASPARAGUS SOUP		
Green asparagus, tough bottom ends trimmed	4 kg	8 lb 12.96 oz
Vegetable stock	2 kg	4 lb 6.4 oz
Salt	50 g	1.76 oz
MORELS		
Extra-virgin olive oil	150 g	5.29 oz
Morels, fresh	1.2 kg	2 lb 10.4 oz
Salt	15 g	.52 oz
Freshly ground black pepper	5 g	.17 oz
Fromage blanc	1.2 kg	2 lb 10.4 oz
Hawaiian black sea salt	20 g	.7 oz
Extra-virgin olive oil	20 g	.7 oz

1. **FOR THE SOUP:** Blanch the asparagus in boiling salted water until tender. Shock the asparagus in an ice bath.

2. Purée the asparagus in a blender with the vegetable stock and the salt. Blend thoroughly until very smooth.

3. Adjust the consistency if necessary with more vegetable stock and the seasoning with more salt if needed. The soup should be the consistency of cream; it should not be so thick that it can't be poured.

4. Cool over an ice bath. Reserve in an airtight container in the refrigerator. Discard after 48 hours. Do not reserve hot in a soup warmer.

5. **FOR THE MORELS:** In a large sauté pan, bring the olive oil to a shimmer (just before the smoking point).

6. Add the morels immediately and sauté until tender. Season the mushrooms with the salt and pepper.

7. Transfer to a hotel pan and reserve them hot in an Alto-Shaam. Discard after 12 hours.

8. **TO PICK UP:** Spoon 60 g/2.11 oz of fromage blanc into a soup bowl, on the side of the bowl. Pour 350 g/12.35 oz of soup into a sauté pan and bring to a quick boil. Pour the soup into the bowl.

9. Spoon 60 g/2.11 oz of morels (about 5 pieces) in a mound down the center of the bowl; try to keep them afloat, or at least pile them so that most of them come out above the surface of the soup. Sprinkle a pinch of Hawaiian black sea salt on top of the fromage blanc (about 1 g/.03 oz) and drizzle a few drops of extra-virgin olive oil over the soup (about 1 g/.03 oz). Serve immediately.

note Make sure the morels are properly washed and the stems are trimmed. Morels are notorious for harboring worms. If using dry morels, divide the amount by 3.5 (343 g/12.1 oz) and hydrate in hot water for 1½ hours.

WILD MUSHROOM AND THYME RAGOÛT WITH PORCINI CRÈME FRAÎCHE

yield: 20 portions

INGREDIENT	METRIC	U.S.	%
WILD MUSHROOMS			
Porcini mushrooms	600 g	1 lb 5.12 oz	6.91%
Cremini mushrooms	600 g	1 lb 5.12 oz	6.91%
Wood ear mushrooms	600 g	1 lb 5.12 oz	6.91%
Lobster mushrooms	600 g	1 lb 5.12 oz	6.91%
Black trumpet mushrooms	600 g	1 lb 5.12 oz	6.91%
Butter	150 g	5.29 oz	1.73%
Thyme sprigs	5 pc	5 pc	
Garlic, coarsely chopped	50 g	1.76 oz	.58%
Salt	9 g	.32 oz	
Chicken consommé	5 kg	11 lb .32 oz	57.6%
Salt	75 g	2.65 oz	.86%
PORCINI CRÈME FRAÎCHE			
Crème fraîche	200 g	7.05 oz	2.3%
Heavy cream	200 g	7.05 oz	2.3%
Porcini powder (see Resources, page 540)	4 g	.14 oz	.05%
Salt	2 g	.07 oz	.02%

1. **FOR THE MUSHROOMS:** Thoroughly rinse all the mushrooms in cold water, and pat them dry with heavy-duty paper towels. If the mushrooms are larger than bite-size, cut them down to the appropriate size. If they have tough stems, cut them off.

2. In a large sauté pan, melt the butter over medium-high until it starts to bubble. Add the thyme and garlic and stir for a few seconds.

3. Add the mushrooms and cook until they have browned. Season with salt. Taste and adjust seasoning as necessary.

4. Once cooked, cool them in a hotel pan and reserve in the refrigerator. Discard after 36 hours.

5. Combine the consommé with the salt and bring to a quick boil. Adjust seasoning. Transfer to a soup warmer and hold at 82°C/180°F.

6. **FOR THE PORCINI CRÈME FRAÎCHE:** Combine the crème fraîche with the heavy cream, porcini powder, and salt. Whip until stiff peaks form, and reserve in the refrigerator. This will need to be re-whipped throughout service, since it tends to loosen after about 30 minutes.

7. **TO PICK UP:** Reheat 80 g/2.8 oz of the cooked mushroom mixture on a sizzle platter in a hot salamander, or an oven or impinger set to 260°C/500°F, until crisp, about 5 minutes.

8. Place the mushrooms in a soup bowl in a pyramid shape.

9. Pour 300 g/10.58 oz of hot chicken consommé around the mushrooms.

10. Spoon a medium-size quenelle of porcini crème fraîche on top of the mushrooms. Serve immediately.

notes If using dried mushrooms, divide the amount in the recipe by 3. Soak the mushrooms in hot water until hydrated, about 1 hour. They will absorb 3 times their weight in water. Dry mushrooms do not need to be washed. Be careful when using this type of mushroom because while it is more economical, it will definitely have a different result. Some dry mushrooms can be rough, woody, and tough to eat even after soaking. Substitute other varieties of dried mushroom that hydrate well, such as shiitake and portobello; dried chanterelles and wood ear mushrooms can be tough even after soaking. Fresh mushrooms are always better to use.

Some chefs don't believe in washing mushrooms, since they tend to absorb water and become bloated. However, mushrooms are already close to 90 percent water, so a quick rinse won't hurt them. Rinsing them gets the dirt out more effectively than any other way of cleaning. The caveat is that they need to be cooked as soon as possible after rinsing and trimming, since they tend to discolor.

packaging hot and cold items to go

DON'T FORGET THAT ONE OF THE REASONS for going to a café is that it provides convenience. Not all your customers are going to sit down and enjoy an hour-long lunch; many of them will want their food packaged quickly so they can move on with their lives. This sounds much simpler than it is. These are the important aspects of packaging to consider:

- **Size:** Does the food fit snugly, or will it slide around in the container? Or is the container too small and will it smother or crush the contents?

- **Food-safe containers:** The food will usually be in direct contact with the packaging, which if it is cardboard or paper based needs to a have a coating that will make it somewhat resistant to moisture. If the package starts to show grease spots or wet spots, not only is it unsightly (especially if your café's name is on it), but it also means that the package might be weakened and could break. There's always the option of using plastic containers. Try to use recyclable/biodegradable products.

- **Keeping the food hot or cold:** You have to consider that the food will be consumed at a later time. Within reason, the food should arrive to the customer hot or cold, according to what her or she is looking for.

- **Containing the food:** If a hot soup is in a cup and the lid tends to loosen with the steam that comes from the soup, your customers will have a mess on their hands.

- **Storing the packaging:** Ideally the container used will be able to be stacked one inside the other, or they will be able to be stored flat and assembled as needed.

- **Cost of each package:** Whatever it is, it needs to be included in the price.

- **Packaging that fits in the to-go bag:** A customer will likely purchase more than one item, which will require putting them in a bag. They also need to fit snugly inside said bag.

The quality and look of the packaging directly reflects your establishment, but also keep in mind its functionality. If you have a beautiful bag but it breaks easily, you will have a very angry customer on your hands.

Not all food is meant to be to go. Make sure to make this clear on your menu. I would discourage you from having any entrées to go, because no matter how good the packaging, the contents will be a mess by the time they reach their destination.

Packaging can be a large investment, especially quality packaging, but the more volume you purchase, the lower the cost per piece will be.

salads

Salads don't need to be enormous to be satisfying. A salad can be a meal in itself without going into portion-size excess. Nor do salads need to have a leafy component. They do, however, need to have a dressing. Great salads incorporate a variety of textures along with warm and cold components. Although this is not always possible, a variety of textures and flavors can easily be achieved.

Mise en place for salads is relatively quick and easy, but one of the most important factors to consider is that salads are an extremely quick pickup. To pick up a salad properly, make sure to dress it right before it is plated. The general ratio for dressing salads is to use about 30 g/1.06 oz of dressing per portion; more than that and the components won't be able to hold it. Always keep in mind that once a salad is dressed, its lifespan is greatly reduced, especially if the dressing is vinegar based, such as a vinaigrette. The acid wilts all it comes in contact with, especially lettuce. Dressing a salad isn't something you can get ahead on.

If the salad has a warm component, such as the tarte flambé with poached egg or the crisp pork belly, always get that component hot, and dress the salad while that component is heating.

Traditional lettuce salads are not included in this section. Although these types of salad are delicious every now and then, there's only so much you can do with them, and it is limited by the particular format.

HEIRLOOM TOMATOES WITH BASIL, EXTRA-VIRGIN OLIVE OIL, AND MALDON SEA SALT

yield: 20 portions

INGREDIENT	METRIC	U.S.
Basil (about 1 leaf per portion)	20 g	.71 oz
Assorted heirloom tomatoes, ripe	7 kg	15 lb 6.88 oz
Extra-virgin olive oil, good quality	300 g	10.58 oz
Garlic, finely minced (about 1 garlic clove per portion)	100 g	3.53 oz
Maldon sea salt	40 g	1.41 oz

1. Roll up a leaf of basil and cut it into a very fine chiffonade.

2. Use about 350 g/12.35 oz of assorted heirloom tomatoes per portion. Heirloom tomatoes come in a large variety of sizes and shapes, so this ingredient cannot be measured by the piece; it has to be by weight. Cut the tomatoes into quarters or slices. Large tomatoes are typically sliced, while smaller ones are quartered. Place them on the desired plate or bowl. Arrange them so that they have some height.

3. Drizzle about 15 g/.53 oz of the olive oil over the tomatoes.

4. Sprinkle 5 g/.17 oz of the garlic over the tomatoes as evenly as possible. Do the same with the basil chiffonade and about 2 g/.07 oz of Maldon sea salt. Serve immediately.

GRILLED OCTOPUS WITH GIANT LIMA BEANS, CELERY SPROUTS, RED ONION, PARSLEY, AND LIME VINAIGRETTE

yield: 20 portions

INGREDIENT	METRIC	U.S.
LIMA BEANS		
Giant lima beans	2 kg	4 lb 6.56 oz
Chicken stock	4 kg	8 lb 13.12 oz
Onions, coarsely chopped (about 2)	640 g	1 lb 6.56 oz
Garlic head, cut in half widthwise (about 1 head)	100 g	3.53 oz
Slab bacon, cut in quarters	400 g	14.11 oz
Carrot (about 1)	150 g	5.29 oz
Salt	150 g	5.29 oz
OCTOPUS		
Baby octopus	2.5 kg	5 lb 8.16 oz
Water	2 kg	4 lb 6.4 oz
Salt	150 g	5.29 oz
Sugar	40 g	1.41 oz
LIME VINAIGRETTE		
Lime juice	200 g	7.05 oz
Garlic (about 2 cloves)	10 g	.35 oz
Canola oil	260 g	9.17 oz
Extra-virgin olive oil	140 g	4.94 oz
Salt	7 g	.25 oz
Freshly cracked black pepper	2 g	.07 oz
Dijon mustard	10 g	.35 oz
Celery leaves, coarsely chopped	120 g	4.32 oz
Red onion, thinly julienned (about 1)	320 g	11.29 oz
Parsley leaves, coarsely chopped	100 g	3.53 oz

1. **FOR THE BEANS:** Soak the lima beans (see Resources, page 540) in cold water overnight.

2. Strain the beans and combine with the chicken stock, onion, garlic, slab bacon, and carrot in a pot.

3. Bring to a boil, and then reduce the heat to a simmer. Keep the pot covered and cook until the beans are tender, about 2 hours.

4. Once the beans are cooked, transfer them to a hotel pan, add the salt, and stir to dissolve. Adjust seasoning if needed. Place the hotel pan over an ice bath and refrigerate to cool down quickly. Once the beans have cooled, strain them from the cooking liquid and reserve them in an airtight container in the refrigerator. Discard after 12 hours.

5. **FOR THE OCTOPUS:** Rinse the octopus in cold water.

6. Combine the water, salt, and sugar to create a brine, and stir to dissolve. Place the baby octopus in the brine for exactly 1 hour.

7. Remove the octopus from the brine and place them in a pot filled with simmering water. Gently simmer the octopus until tender, 55 minutes to 1 hour.

8. Remove the octopus from the simmering water and place them in a hotel pan in the refrigerator to stop the cooking process. Once they have cooled, keep them covered with a damp, clean kitchen towel or heavy-duty paper towel and reserve in the refrigerator. Discard after 12 hours.

9. **FOR THE VINAIGRETTE:** Place the lime juice and the garlic in a blender cup. Turn the blender on low speed, and then slowly increase the speed to high. Combine the canola and olive oil, and slowly pour it into the blender to create an emulsion. Add the salt, black pepper, and mustard. Adjust seasoning. Transfer to a squeeze bottle and reserve refrigerated. Discard after 3 days.

10. **TO PICK UP:** Grill 3 to 5 brined baby octopus, depending on the size, until slightly charred, 1 to 2 minutes per side.

11. In a small bowl, combine 180 g/6.35 oz of beans, 6 g/0.21 oz of celery leaves, 16 g/.56 oz of red onions, 5 g/.17 oz of parsley leaves, and 20 g/.7 oz of vinaigrette. Gently toss to combine. Put on the desired plate in a mound.

12. Place the grilled octopus on the dressed beans, making sure to get some height. Serve immediately.

TARTE FLAMBÉ SALAD: PUFF PASTRY BAKED WITH CRÈME FRAÎCHE, WILTED ONIONS, AND BACON WITH POACHED EGG, FRISÉE, AND SHALLOT VINAIGRETTE

yield: 20 portions

INGREDIENT	METRIC	U.S.
PUFF PASTRY TART FLAMBÉ		
Butter, soft	120 g	4.23 oz
Onions, julienned (about 2)	640 g	1 lb 6.56 oz
Puff Pastry (page 197)	20	20
Egg Wash for Brushing (page 13)	as needed	as needed
Crème fraîche	300 g	10.58 oz
Bacon, cooked until semi-crisp	300 g	10.58 oz
Eggs	20	20
SHALLOT VINAIGRETTE		
Shallots	100 g	3.53 oz
White vinegar	200 g	7.05 oz
Canola oil	240 g	8.47 oz
Extra-virgin olive oil	160 g	5.64 oz
Dijon mustard	10 g	.35 oz
Salt, or as needed	7 g	.25 oz
Freshly ground black pepper, or as needed	1 g	.04 oz
Frisée, cored, washed, spun dry in a salad spinner	4.00 kg	8 lb 13.12 oz
Gray sea salt	40 g	1.41 oz

1. **FOR THE PUFF PASTRY TARTE FLAMBÉ:** Preheat a convection oven to 160°C/320°F.

2. Melt the butter in a sauté pan over medium-high heat and sweat the onions until translucent. Cool to room temperature.

3. Cut the puff pastry sheet into 20 discs using a 7.5-cm/3-in ring cutter. Dock the puff pastry with a 6.25-cm/2.5-in ring cutter by cutting halfway into the puff pastry without going all the way through. Then dock the dough with a fork down the center ring, poking the dough 3 times, evenly spaced out. Always handle the puff pastry when it is semi-frozen, never when it is soft, since this will damage its delicate layering.

4. Brush the surface of the puff pastry with the egg wash, making sure it does not trickle down the sides, since this will anchor the dough down and keep it from puffing up when it bakes. Place 15 g/.53 oz of crème fraîche with a spoon in the middle of the puff pastry. Place 30 g/1.05 oz of the cooked onions on top of the crème fraîche, and finally 15 g/.53 oz of the bacon on top of the onions. Try to keep the ingredients inside the smaller ring of puff pastry. The intention is that the outer ring will bake upward as a vol-au-vent would, forming a shell or tart-like pastry around the filling.

5. Place the assembled tart flambés on a sheet pan lined with parchment paper as they are assembled. If they are still firm and chilled, bake them; otherwise freeze them until they are firm and chilled.

6. Bake them until they are golden brown, about 8 minutes.

7. Reserve at room temperature, uncovered, during service. Discard after 12 hours.

8. Poach the eggs according to the procedure on page 304.

9. **FOR THE SHALLOT VINAIGRETTE:** Place the shallots and white vinegar in a blender cup. Turn it on low speed and then turn it slowly up to high.

10. Combine the oils and pour them in slowly as the blender is running to create an emulsion. Add the mustard and season with salt and pepper. Adjust seasoning if needed.

11. **TO PICK UP:** Keep a pot with simmering water ready during service.

12. Place the puff pastry tart in a convection oven set to 160°C/320°F or an impinger oven set to 260°C/500°F for 3 to 4 minutes or until golden brown. Drop an egg gently into the simmering water.

13. Meanwhile, place 200 g/7.05 oz of frisée lettuce in a bowl and toss with 30 g/1.05 oz of shallot vinaigrette.

14. Place the dressed frisée on a plate. Place the warm puff pastry tart directly at the center of the plate.

15. Remove the egg from the simmering water with a slotted spoon. Tap it dry over a clean paper towel, then place it over the puff pastry tart. Sprinkle 2 g/.07 oz of gray sea salt over the egg. Serve immediately.

note For the puff pastry, omit the corn syrup and complete steps 1 through 8 of the Caramelized Puff Pastry recipe on page 197.

the vegetarian dilemma

LIKE MANY CHEFS I KNOW, I used to roll my eyes every time I received a special request from a vegetarian. I would huff and puff my way through it and serve it with a good dose of contempt. "Why don't they just have some fruit?" was my standard response. A few years ago I was working at a restaurant in New York City, and we had a request for a completely vegetarian meal that wasn't a mixed greens salad and grilled vegetables. While most of the cooks on the line, me as pastry chef included, grunted and frowned upon this request, the chef asked us to see these types of requests as opportunities to create items out of our regular comfort zone.

You could debate the fine points of vegetarianism for many hours and never come to an agreement. While I could never imagine my life without meat, I understand where my food comes from. Vegetarians choose to not eat meat, and from a practical perspective, they represent a percentage of your customer base. This is why it is always important to have a few vegetarian offerings that are truly intended for vegetarians; in other words, don't just slap some vegetables together and call it a meal. There is a way to make excellent vegetarian food that can in fact be appealing to all, even to us all-pork-product-loving people.

CRISP BERKSHIRE PORK BELLY WITH WILTED VEGETABLES AND BALSAMIC VINEGAR

yield: **20 portions**

INGREDIENT	METRIC	U.S.
Berkshire pork belly	6 kg	13 lb 3.68 oz
Garlic	300 g	10.58 oz
Shallots	200 g	7.05 oz
Salt	20 g	.71 oz
Thyme sprigs	60	60
Freshly ground black pepper	3 g	.1 oz
Brown sugar	200 g	7.05 oz
Chicken stock	3 kg	6 lb 9.76 oz
Extra-virgin olive oil	1.4 kg	3 lb 1.44 oz
Cherry tomatoes (about 5 per portion)	2 kg	4 lb 6.4 oz
Cucumbers (about 3), julienned on a mandolin	1.2 kg	2 lb 10.4 oz
Red onions, thinly sliced (about 2)	640 g	1 lb 6.56 oz
Balsamic vinegar	400 g	14.11 oz
Cyprus sea salt or other flake salt	60 g	2.12 oz
Freshly ground black pepper	4 g	.14 oz

1. **FOR THE PORK BELLY:** Trim the skin from the belly. Remove all but a .5-cm/.2-in layer of fat from the belly. Score the fat in a diamond grid, cutting all the way through just to the flesh but without cutting into the flesh. The diamonds should measure 1 cm/.4 in.

2. Smash the garlic coarsely and chop the shallots coarsely. In a roasting pan that will fit the belly completely, sprinkle the area where the belly will be placed with half of the salt. Spread one-third of the thyme, shallots, and garlic over the fat side of the belly.

3. Place the belly in the pan, fat side up. Sprinkle the other half of the salt, the black pepper, and the brown sugar evenly over the entire surface, and rub it into the scoring in the fat. Cover the belly with the rest of the garlic, shallots, and thyme, making sure to press them into the fat.

4. Preheat a static or deck oven to 150°C/302°F.

5. Pour the chicken stock into the roasting pan. It should come three-quarters of the way up the belly; all of the stock may not be needed. Wrap the pan in aluminum foil to keep the steam in.

6. Braise the pork belly for 3 to 4 hours, or until the meat is meltingly tender and most of the fat has rendered away. Check the pan at the 2-hour mark to make sure there is enough stock in the pan. If not, pour in more stock.

7. Cool the belly in the pan. Do not discard the liquid the belly was cooked in; keep it all together. Place a pan filled with ice underneath the roasting pan and place this setup in a reach-in or walk-in refrigerator.

8. Put plastic wrap directly on top of the belly. Place another pan on top of the belly with a weight on top (three #10 cans will work well). This will weigh the belly down and form it into an even piece. Allow it to chill overnight.

catering

PART OF THE FINANCIAL SUCCESS OF A CAFÉ is to look for as many effective ways to sell your food as possible. The dining room is only so big. As with breads, breakfast pastries, and desserts, which you can sell wholesale as another source of income, you can also provide catering services with not only savory offerings, but desserts as well. This generally works best if the location to be catered is close by.

You have to be very selective about what you offer and how you present it. One could write an entire book about catering, and there are many, but a café should focus on the "drop off and go" style of catering, not the fine china and wait-staff style of catering. Offices and small businesses are a good bet, but in order to get them to keep ordering from you, make sure that you can vary your offerings on a regular basis. Try having a ten- or fourteen- day (or twelve-day; whatever you decide) rotation menu with specific items that are popular, like a sandwich of the day or a salad of the day or a soup of the day.

Always consider that the food will need to be transported, which requires a different kind of packaging than for single to-go items. This falls more in the realm of large, moisture-resistant boxes with the food placed on disposable (and ideally recyclable) platters. The image of your café is very important and should be a part of everything you do, and therefore the box you pack your catering in and how you get it there is just as important as the food.

As with packaging individual items, you also have to consider that not every single item on the menu is suitable for catering. For example, consider not including anything that must be served hot, except for soup. Foods that are ideal for catering are soups, salads, sandwiches, and desserts. Anything else requires additional packaging, equipment, and attention.

9. Once it is chilled, cut the belly into 200-g/7.05-oz portions that measure about 4.5 by 11.25 cm/1.75 by 4.5 in. Trim enough fat from the top so that there is only about 3 mm/.11 in left. The portions can be reserved in the refrigerator at this point for up to 48 hours in an airtight container.

10. Thirty minutes before service, reheat the pork belly in a 160°C/320°F convection oven. Reserve the pork belly in an Alto-Shaam oven set to 60°C/140°F, covered with plastic.

11. **TO PICK UP:** Place a portion of pork belly on a sizzle platter. Place the sizzle platter in a hot salamander or 260°C/500°F oven or impinger oven until the pork belly gets hot and the fat crisps, about 5 minutes.

12. Meanwhile, pour 70 g/2.47 oz of extra-virgin olive oil into a sauté pan. Put the pan over high heat.

13. Combine 5 cherry tomatoes, 60 g/2.1 oz cucumbers, and 30 g/1.05 oz red onions in a bowl. Just before the oil starts smoking, add the vegetables.

14. Sauté for 20 seconds, remove the pan from the heat, and stir in 20 g/.7 oz of balsamic vinegar. Season with sea salt and black pepper.

15. Place the wilted vegetables in a bowl, and then put the crisp pork belly on top of them. Serve immediately.

FENNEL, CAULIFLOWER, GREEN BEANS, AND RADISHES WITH MEYER LEMON VINAIGRETTE

yield: 20 portions

INGREDIENT	METRIC	U.S.
Lemon juice	80 g	2.82 oz
Fennel bulbs (about 5)	4 kg	8 lb 12.96 oz
French butter radishes (about 30)	200 g	7.05 oz
Cauliflower, cut into small florets	2 kg	4 lb 6.4 oz
Green beans	2 kg	4 lb 6.4 oz
LEMON VINAIGRETTE		
Meyer lemon juice	300 g	10.58 oz
Canola oil	200 g	7.05 oz
Extra-virgin olive oil	100 g	3.53 oz
Salt	7 g	.25 oz
Freshly cracked black pepper	2 g	.07 oz

1. Fill a 10-cm-/4-in-deep hotel pan halfway with cold water and mix in the lemon juice.

2. Trim the tops and bottoms of the fennel bulbs. Peel off the outer layer. Trim any part of the fennel that is discolored or brown. Reserve 40 g/1.41 oz of fennel fronds in a damp paper towel during service. The fronds should be small, with 3 to 5 strands each.

3. Slice the fennel bulbs on an electric slicer to about 3 mm/.11 in thick, placing the fennel directly into the lemon juice bath as soon as it is sliced. Reserve the fennel in the lemon juice bath during service. Consolidate into a smaller hotel pan as needed for service.

4. Slice the radishes as thinly as possible on a mandoline. Reserve refrigerated and covered with a damp, heavy-duty paper towel.

5. Reserve the cauliflower in an airtight container in the refrigerator. The florets must be small because they will be served raw and are easier to eat that way.

6. Trim the ends of the green beans and cut them into 2.5-cm-/1-in-long pieces.

7. Bring a pot of abundantly salted water to a rolling boil. Have an ice bath ready.

8. Place the green beans in the boiling water and cook them until just tender. Shock them in an ice bath to stop the cooking process. Strain and reserve in an airtight container in refrigeration. Discard after service.

9. **FOR THE VINAIGRETTE:** Place the Meyer lemon juice in a blender cup and turn it on low speed. Slowly turn it up to high speed.

10. Combine both oils and slowly pour them into the blender. Add the salt and pepper, and adjust seasoning if needed. Reserve in the refrigerator. Discard after 4 days.

11. **TO PICK UP:** Pat 200 g/7.05 oz of fennel dry on a clean towel. Place it in a bowl with 10 g/ .35 oz of radish, 100 g/3.53 oz of cauliflower, and 100 g/3.53 oz of green beans. Toss with 30 g/1.05 oz of lemon vinaigrette. Put the salad on a plate and sprinkle 2 g/.07 oz of fennel fronds over the salad. Serve immediately.

note The vinaigrette in this recipe is not emulsified, so it will need to be stirred each time before using.

WHITE ASPARAGUS WITH SPANISH VINAIGRETTE

yield: 20 portions

INGREDIENT	METRIC	U.S.
White asparagus, ends trimmed	4 kg	8 lb 13.12 oz
SPANISH VINAIGRETTE		
Red pepper, cut into brunoise	200 g	7.05 oz
Cucumber, seeded but not peeled, cut into brunoise	200 g	7.05 oz
Egg whites, hard boiled and finely chopped	120 g	4.23 oz
Capers, finely chopped	100 g	3.53 oz
Garlic, finely chopped	10 g	.35 oz
Sherry vinegar	100 g	3.53 oz
Canola oil	200 g	7.05 oz
Extra-virgin olive oil	100 g	3.53 oz
Salt	3 g	.11 oz
Freshly cracked black pepper	1 g	.04 oz

1. **FOR THE ASPARAGUS:** Bring a large pot of salted water to a rolling boil The pot should be large enough to fit all the asparagus comfortably with abundant water.

2. Add the asparagus and cook just until tender, 3 to 4 minutes. Shock the asparagus in an ice bath to stop the cooking process.

3. Once they have cooled, store them in a hotel pan, lined and covered with a damp heavy-duty paper towel or a clean, damp kitchen towel. Discard after service.

4. **FOR THE SPANISH VINAIGRETTE:** Combine the red pepper, cucumber, egg whites, capers, and garlic in a bowl. Toss until evenly mixed. Reserve in an airtight container in the refrigerator. Discard after service.

5. Put the sherry vinegar in a blender cup and turn it on low. Slowly increase to high speed; combine the oils and slowly pour them into the vinegar. Season with salt and pepper; adjust seasoning if needed.

6. Reserve, covered, at room temperature. The vinaigrette will keep for at least 3 weeks. There is nothing in it that is perishable, but the oil can go rancid in a few weeks.

7. **TO PICK UP:** Place 30 g/1.06 oz of the cucumber mixture in a bowl with 20 g/.7 oz of the vinaigrette and stir until evenly mixed.

8. Place 5 asparagus spears on a plate. Spoon the vinaigrette directly over the asparagus. Serve immediately.

notes This vinaigrette is not emulsified.

Each asparagus spear weighs about 40 g/1.41 oz.

POACHED LEEKS WITH PANCETTA AND WHOLE-GRAIN MUSTARD VINAIGRETTE

yield: **20 portions**

INGREDIENT	METRIC	U.S.
POACHED LEEKS		
Chicken stock	4 kg	8 lb 13.12 oz
Salt	150 g	5.29 oz
Leeks, green ends and root ends trimmed, tough outer layers removed	80	80
Pancetta	2 kg	4 lb 6.4 oz
MUSTARD VINAIGRETTE		
Whole-grain mustard	50 g	1.76 oz
White vinegar	100 g	3.53 oz
Canola oil	200 g	7.05 oz
Extra-virgin olive oil	100 g	3.53 oz
Salt	8 g	.28 oz
Micro onion greens	40 g	1.41 oz
Kaiware shoots	40 g	1.41 oz

1. **FOR THE POACHED LEEKS:** Set an immersion thermocirculator to 70°C/158°F in a water bath. Combine the chicken stock with the salt and the leeks in a Cryovac bag. Place 8 leeks into a bag with 400 g/14.11 oz of chicken stock and 15 g/.52 oz of salt, for a total of 10 bags.

2. Cook them for 2 hours in the hot water bath, and then shock them in an ice bath to stop the cooking process. Reserve in the refrigerator until needed. Discard after 48 hours.

3. Preheat a convection oven to 160°C/320°F.

4. Freeze the pancetta. Slice it very thinly on an electric slicer. As they come off the slicer, place the slices directly on a sheet pan lined with a nonstick rubber mat.

5. Bake in the oven until crisp. Cool them to room temperature. The final yield of the pancetta will be about two-thirds of the original amount.

6. Reserve the pancetta slices flat in a single layer on a sheet pan lined with parchment paper. Do not refrigerate them. Discard after service.

7. **FOR THE WHOLE-GRAIN MUSTARD VINAIGRETTE:** Combine all of the ingredients in a bowl using a whisk. Adjust seasoning if necessary. Reserve at room temperature for at least 3 weeks. This vinaigrette has no components that are perishable, but the oil might go rancid after a few weeks.

8. **TO PICK UP:** Cut 2 to 3 poached leeks into 2.5-cm-/1-in-thick discs and place on a plate in a 4x3 grid.

9. Stir the mustard vinaigrette with a spoon and drizzle 20 g/.7 oz on top of the leeks.

10. Crumble 3 to 4 slices of crisp pancetta and evenly disperse them on top of the leeks.

11. Place 2 g/.07 oz of micro onions and 2 g/.07 oz of kaiware shoots on top of the leeks and pancetta, evenly spread out. Serve immediately.

HEARTS OF PALM WITH TRUFFLE VINAIGRETTE AND TRUFFLES

yield: 20 portions

INGREDIENT	METRIC	U.S.
Hearts of palm (inside the palm)	8 kg	17 lb 10.08 oz
TRUFFLE VINAIGRETTE		
Champagne vinegar	75 g	2.65 oz
Black truffle juice	100 g	3.53 oz
Canola oil	200 g	7.05 oz
Extra-virgin olive oil	100 g	3.53 oz
Truffle salt	9 g	.31 oz
Freshly ground black pepper	2 g	.07 oz
Whole black truffle	200 g	7.05 oz
Red amaranth sprouts	20 g	.71 oz
Popcorn shoots	20	20
Maldon sea salt	60 g	2.12 oz

1. Bring a pot of abundantly salted water just to a simmer. Cook the hearts of palm for 30 to 45 minutes, or until tender.

2. Shock the hearts of palm in an ice bath. Once they have cooled, push the cooked hearts out of the husks. The yield should be 4 kg/8 lb 12.96 oz. Do not cut them yet. Reserve the cooked hearts in an airtight container in the refrigerator. Discard after 2 days.

3. **FOR THE TRUFFLE VINAIGRETTE:** Pour the champagne vinegar and truffle juice in a blender cup and start it on low speed. Slowly turn the speed up to high.

4. Combine both oils and slowly pour them into the blender to create an emulsion. Season the vinaigrette with the truffle salt and black pepper. Reserve at room temperature until needed. It will keep for at least 3 weeks. It contains no perishable ingredients, but the oil can turn rancid.

5. Slice the truffles 2 mm/.08 in thick on a mandoline, and then cut them into julienne strips. Keep them covered with a slightly moistened heavy-duty paper towel during service. Do not discard leftovers after service; instead, use them to make more truffle vinaigrette.

6. **TO PICK UP:** Cut 250 to 300 g/8.82 to 10.58 oz cooked hearts of palm into cylinders and discs. If there are a variety of shapes, it makes for an appealing visual presentation. Place them on a plate and spoon 30 g/1.05 oz of truffle vinaigrette over them. Try to give the plate some height and movement if possible.

7. Sprinkle about 2 g/.07 oz of julienned truffles around the hearts of palm. Sprinkle 1 g/.03 oz of red amaranth sprouts on top of the truffles and hearts of palm. Place one popcorn shoot over a heart of palm. Sprinkle a pinch of Maldon sea salt (about 3 g/.1 oz) over all the components. Serve immediately.

notes Hearts of palm come inside the husk in which they grow. The only way to get them out is to cook them; their size varies wildly from pencil thin to about 10 cm/4 in diameter.

Do not use canned truffles since they are brined and have a sour taste. You might be tempted to use truffle oil. Don't. It does not contain truffles.

ovens in the savory kitchen

A TYPICAL OVEN USED IN A SAVORY KITCHEN IS A STATIC OVEN, which is much like a conventional oven but often larger and with a higher temperature capacity. There is nothing intrinsically wrong with a static oven, but there is newer technology that allows the chef and the cooks to produce large quantities of food with consistent results. The trick is to know how to adequately use them. Following are a few types of ovens.

The Impinger Oven

The first time I saw this oven was in a sandwich shop, and it was used to heat up open-faced sandwiches. While I don't think it is the best oven for a sandwich, it is very good for many other products. The way it works is by blowing hot air from the top and the bottom, while a conveyor belt moves the food along at a constant speed, which you can adjust. What this ensures is that if you set a certain temperature and a certain time, the product that you are trying to cook or crisp or bake will always come out the same. Plus, you can reduce human error, because whatever time you set on the oven is the time that the food will take to go from one end of the oven to the other. Once the food comes out, it is ready to go. I have found that this oven is terrific when it comes to crisping the skin of duck confit and pork belly (see recipes, pages 391 and 320), baking pizzas, and toasting bread, among other uses.

The Alto-Shaam Cook and Hold Oven

The Alto-Shaam cooks the food and then it holds it at a pre-set temperature. It works with radiant heat instead of circulating hot air, which is how convection ovens work. Circulating hot air can dry out whatever is in the oven, therefore convection ovens are better left to baked goods, not roasting meats. This oven can be used just as a holder as well, since it can hold food that has been cooked elsewhere, such as on a grill (see the flank steak on page 374) or in another oven (see the pork belly on page 320), and keep it from drying out. They also do not require a venting or hood system since they are self-contained. Setting this oven to 60°C/140°F will keep bacteria at bay, but it won't cook food further.

CVap Oven

The CVap oven is similar to the Alto-Shaam, but it cooks through steam. When you place an item such as a fish in the CVap oven, the cavity instantly fills with steam, which raises the temperature quickly and cooks the product evenly with no loss of moisture. This is great for items that would be steamed or even poached with great precision.

Combi Oven

The combi oven is a type of convection oven that can combine three modes of cooking in one oven at one time. It can poach, steam, roast, broil, bake, and reheat cooked food to the desired temperature. It can cook through hot air and steam or a combination of both, hence the name. It is a great piece of equipment, and the only downside is that it requires a large amount of space. However, so do most commercial ovens.

All of these ovens can also be used in combination, like in the pork belly recipe on page 320, which you cook in a deck or static oven, hold in an Alto-Shaam, and finish in an impinger oven.

small plates

As with small desserts (see petits plaisirs, page 217), this style of food, which is not really a style but merely an adjustment in portion size, is very popular since it allows a person to have a small, quick bite and be on his or her way. Small plates can also be served as a variety of small bites to be shared with other people in order to experience more flavors and textures. As a matter of practicality, small plates should be simple to prepare and execute. This is really the entire mantra for café food, but it is even truer for small plates. They need to not be too fussy or precious, just well done, with clear, simple flavors. It is also important to consider that there is an opportunity here to combine temperatures (cold and hot) and textures (crunchy and smooth).

Do not confuse small plates with tapas; while tapas are in fact small plates, the term refers specifically to Spanish bar food. Not all small plates should be called tapas.

With this type of food, since portion size is smaller, pickup times can be very fast, precisely because of their size; the smaller the surface area, the faster it will get hot.

appetizers

Appetizers are generally meant to be eaten before an entrée (or main course, if you will). However, this is not written in stone. I have had entire meals based on appetizers alone. They represent the essence of what small plates are, since their original reason for being is to entice the diner. In a classic sense, appetizers have always been intended to be a quick pickup. When you go to a restaurant (or a café, in this case), it is because you are hungry, and the faster you get some food the better. While you are eating your appetizer(s), the entrées are being finished in the kitchen, since they usually will take longer. It is more for practical reasons that appetizers came to be than for what we actually intend for them in this book, but in both cases they fulfill their purpose.

WARM GOAT CHEESE TART WITH ARUGULA, EXTRA-VIRGIN OLIVE OIL, AND FLEUR DE SEL

yield: 20 portions

INGREDIENT	METRIC	U.S.
GOAT CHEESE TARTS		
Goat cheese, triple cream	400 g	14.1 oz
Drunken goat cheese	400 g	14.1 oz
Caramelized Onions (page 331)	400 g	14.1 oz
Tart Shells (page 330)	20	20
Custard (page 331)	600 g	1 lb 5.16 oz
Arugula	900 g	1 lb 15.75 oz
Extra-virgin olive oil	200 g	7.05 oz
Fleur de sel	10 g	.35 oz

1. **FOR THE GOAT CHEESE TARTS:** Preheat a convection oven to 160°C/320°F.

2. Break the triple-cream goat cheese apart by hand into 2.5-cm/1-in morsels. Reserve refrigerated, covered with plastic wrap.

3. Remove the purple rind from the drunken goat cheese and grate. Reserve refrigerated in an airtight container.

4. Place 20 g/.7 oz of caramelized onions at the base of the tart shells. Place 20 g/.7 oz of triple-cream goat cheese on top of the onion.

5. Whisk the custard until foamy, and pour 30 g/1.05 oz on top of the cheese; this will make the custard lighter and more delicate than if it were added without foaming.

6. Sprinkle about 20 g/.7 oz of the grated goat cheese on top of each tart.

7. Bake until golden brown on top, about 8 to 12 minutes. Check the base of the tart shell and make sure it is baked as well (tip the tart over a little to check underneath). Cool to room temperature. Remove the rings carefully.

8. **TO PICK UP:** Place a goat cheese tart on a sizzle platter and put in a hot salamander or a 260°C/500°F oven or impinger oven for about 5 minutes, or until hot.

9. Meanwhile combine 45 g/1.6 oz of arugula, 10 g/.35 oz of extra-virgin olive oil, and .5 g/.02 oz of fleur de sel in a small bowl and toss to evenly coat the arugula. Put the dressed arugula on a plate.

10. Once the tart is hot, put it on the plate next to the arugula. Serve immediately.

TART SHELLS (PÂTE BRISÉE)

yield: **20 to 25 tarts**

INGREDIENT	METRIC	U.S.
Pastry flour	1.5 kg	3 lb 4.96 oz
Salt	36 g	1.28 oz
Frozen duck fat, cut into medium dice	750 g	1 lb 10.4 oz
Water, chilled	360 g	12.64 oz

1. Sift the flour and salt together.

2. Cut the duck fat into the flour in the bowl of an electric mixer fitted with the paddle attachment on low speed until it resembles coarse cornmeal.

3. On low speed, slowly add the chilled water; the dough may not need all the water. Mix just until the dough combines to form a homogeneous mass. Don't overmix.

4. Shape the dough into a 2.5-cm-/1-in-thick square patty and refrigerate for 1 hour before rolling out or sheeting.

5. Roll or sheet the dough down to 3 mm/.11 in, preferably using a sheeter to obtain an even thickness. Transfer the dough to a sheet pan lined with parchment paper and let it chill and relax in the refrigerator for at least 1 hour before shaping.

6. Place 20 stainless-steel rings, 5 cm/2 in high by 6.25 cm/2.5 in diameter, on a sheet pan lined with a nonstick rubber mat. Spray the inside of the rings with a light coat of nonstick oil spray.

7. Once the dough has chilled, cut out twenty 12.5-cm/4-in discs. Warm the dough lightly with your hands, and line the prepared tart rings with the dough. Make sure that the dough is flush with the ring and the base. Do not trim the tops yet.

8. Freeze the lined rings. Once the dough is firm, trim the tops off with a paring knife.

9. Reserve refrigerated, covered with plastic wrap.

note There will be some leftover dough; use it to make more tarts.

CARAMELIZED ONIONS

yield: 600 g/1 lb 5.16 oz

INGREDIENT	METRIC	U.S.
Canola oil	120 g	4.23 oz
Onions, thinly sliced	1.2 kg	2 lb 7.8 oz

1. Pour the canola oil in a large sauté pan over high heat. Once the oil is smoking, add the onions. Turn the heat down to medium-low.

2. Stir every few minutes to caramelize the onions evenly and to prevent them from burning.

3. Once the onions have caramelized, transfer them to a hotel pan to cool. Once cool, transfer to an airtight container and reserve in the refrigerator. Discard after 2 days.

CUSTARD FILLING

yield: 707.5 g/1 lb 8.96 oz

INGREDIENT	METRIC	U.S.
Milk	400 g	14.11 oz
Crème fraîche	100 g	3.53 oz
Salt	8 g	.26 oz
Eggs	200 g	7.05 oz

Combine all of the ingredients in a bowl, pass through a fine-mesh sieve, and reserve in the refrigerator in an airtight container. Discard after 4 days.

GRILLED SARDINES WITH PICKLED RED ONIONS, OLIVE OIL CRACKERS, AND CHERVIL

yield: 20 portions

INGREDIENT	METRIC	U.S.
OLIVE OIL CRACKERS		
Semolina flour	265 g	9.35 oz
Whole wheat flour	180 g	6.35 oz
Salt	6 g	.21 oz
Water, at 21°C/70°F	250 g	8.82 oz
Extra-virgin olive oil	70 g	2.47 oz
PICKLED ONIONS		
Water	300 g	10.58 oz
Red wine vinegar	600 g	1 lb 5.12 oz
Salt	20 g	.7 oz
Sugar	30 g	1.06 oz
Black peppercorns	5	5
Thyme sprigs	4	4
Red onions, sliced (about 1½)	600 g	1 lb 5.12 oz
SARDINES		
Sardines, gutted	60	60
Olive oil	1.5 kg	3 lb 4.96 oz
Salt	60 g	2.11 oz
Freshly ground black pepper	5 g	.17 oz
Fleur de sel	60 g	2.12 oz
Chervil sprigs	100	100
Lemon quarters	20	20

1. **FOR THE OLIVE OIL CRACKERS:** Place the flours and the salt in a the bowl of an electric mixer fitted with the hook attachment.

2. Turn the mixer on low speed and add the water. Once it has been incorporated, add the olive oil. Mix for about 5 minutes on medium speed. The dough will be slightly wet, but it should form a ball. If it is too dry, add some water until the dough is smooth. Take the dough off the mixer and let it relax in the bowl, covered with plastic, for about 30 minutes.

3. Preheat a convection oven to 160°C/320°F.

4. Using a pasta machine, sheet the dough as thinly as possible and as wide as the pasta machine. Place it on a sheet pan lined with parchment paper. Repeat as needed with all of the dough.

5. Bake the crackers until golden brown. Once they have cooled, break them up into 5-cm-/2-in-wide pieces. Reserve in an airtight container at room temperature in a cool, dry place. Discard after 1 week.

6. **FOR THE PICKLED ONIONS:** Bring the water, red wine vinegar, salt, sugar, peppercorns, and thyme sprigs to a boil.

7. Add the onions and reduce the heat to a simmer. Cook until the onions are wilted, about 5 minutes. Cool over an ice bath. Reserve in the refrigerator. Discard after 5 days.

8. **TO PICK UP:** Turn a grill on to high heat.

9. Brush 3 sardines with olive oil (about 75 g/2.64 oz per portion). Heavily season them on both sides with salt and pepper. Grill for 2 to 3 minutes on each side or until charred.

10. Put the sardines on a plate. Place 8 to 11 rings of pickled onion on top of them. Sprinkle 3 g/.1oz of fleur de sel over the sardines.

11. Place 5 to 7 chervil springs, evenly spaced, over the sardines. Put a lemon quarter on a side dish or ramekin. Put 3 crackers on a side dish. Serve immediately.

COD FRITTERS WITH SAFFRON MAYONNAISE

yield: 20 portions

INGREDIENT	METRIC	U.S.
COD FRITTERS		
Salt	150 g	5.29 oz
Chardonnay	400 g	14.11 oz
Water	4 kg	8 lb 12.96 oz
Cod, cut into 2.5-cm-/1-in-thick strips	2.7 kg	5 lb 15.2 oz
Eggs (about 12)	600 g	1 lb 5.12 oz
Green onions, finely chopped	50 g	1.76 oz
Parsley, finely chopped	75 g	2.65 oz
Bread crumbs	420 g	14.82 oz
SAFFRON MAYONNAISE		
Saffron strands	8	8
Corn oil	870 g	1 lb 14.56 oz
Egg yolks (about 4)	80 g	2.82 oz
Salt	20 g	.71 oz
Mustard	30 g	1.06 oz
Lemon juice	60 g	2.12 oz
Beer Batter (page 335)	1 kg	2 lb 3.2 oz

1. **FOR THE COD FRITTERS:** Combine the salt, white wine, and the water in a pot and bring it up to 62°C/145°F.

2. Once the liquid reaches that temperature, place the cod in the liquid and cook until done, 7 to 9 minutes. Remove the fish from the poaching liquid and let it cool in the refrigerator.

3. Combine cod with the eggs, green onions, parsley, and bread crumbs in a robot coup and grind until a homogeneous mass is obtained.

4. Transfer to a piping bag fitted with a #8 plain tip and pipe onto a sheet pan lined with a silicone rubber mat. Pipe into 7.5-cm-/3-in-long sticks, and then freeze.

5. **FOR THE SAFFRON MAYONNAISE:** Combine the saffron with the oil in a sauce pot and warm up to 80°C/176°F. Let it cool; cover and infuse overnight.

6. Place the egg yolks, salt, and mustard in a Robot Coupe and turn it on. Slowly pour the infused oil in to create an emulsion. Pour in the lemon juice.

7. Reserve refrigerated, with plastic wrap directly covering the surface. Discard after 4 days.

8. **TO PICK UP:** Heat a fryer to 180°C/360°F.

9. Dip 5 cod fritter sticks in the beer batter. Gently put them in the fryer and fry until golden brown, about 2 to 4 minutes.

10. Place 30 g/1.05 oz of saffron mayonnaise in a ramekin.

11. Put the finished cod fritters on a clean, heavy-duty paper towel to absorb the excess oil.

12. Put the cod fritters on a plate with the saffron mayonnaise and serve immediately.

BEER BATTER

yield: 1 qt/960 mL

INGREDIENT	METRIC	U.S.
Egg whites	60 g	2.12 oz
All-purpose flour	200 g	7.05 oz
Dark beer (such as Guinness)	340 g	11.99 oz
Extra-virgin olive oil	20 g	.71 oz
Salt	16 g	.56 oz

1. Whip the egg whites to stiff peaks just before they are needed.

2. Combine the flour with the beer in a bowl using a whisk. Fold in the whipped egg whites all at once, and then stir in the olive oil and salt. Reserve in the refrigerator.

note This batter might need to be made two or three times during service to keep it airy and light. Keep the mise en place for it at the ready.

CODDLED EGGS WITH MAPLE BACON AND TOASTED BRIOCHE

yield: 20 portions

INGREDIENT	METRIC	U.S.
Eggs (in their shells)	40	40
Slab bacon, cut into pieces 1 by 2.5 cm/.5 by 1 in	1 kg	2 lb 3.2 oz
Maple syrup	200 g	7.05 oz
Brioche Pullman loaf (page 37), cut into 2.5-cm-/1-in-thick slices	20	20
Clarified butter	200 g	7.05 oz

1. Set an immersion thermocirculator to 70°C/160°F.

2. Place half the eggs in the thermocirculator for 8 minutes, and then shock them in an ice bath. Repeat with the remaining eggs. Reserve in an Alto-Shaam set to 60°C/140°F during service. Discard the eggs after 12 hours.

3. Set the convection oven to 160°C/320°F.

4. Place the bacon on a sheet pan lined with silicone paper.

5. Bake until the bacon is crisp, about 15 minutes.

6. Remove the bacon from the oven and place it in a bowl. Toss it with the maple syrup and return to the oven on a sheet pan for 5 minutes so that the maple syrup bakes into the bacon. Reserve in a hotel pan at room temperature during service. Discard after service.

7. **TO PICK UP:** Keep a pot of water simmering over medium heat during service.

8. Place 2 coddled eggs in the pot until they are warm, about 2 minutes.

9. Meanwhile, brush both sides of the brioche with clarified butter. Toast it on both sides on the grill just enough to brown it and give it grill marks. Cut the bread in half diagonally to obtain 2 triangles.

10. Remove the eggs from the water and crack them into a French glass crock.

11. Place 50 g/1.76 oz of maple bacon on top of the eggs. Close the jar. Line a plate with a linen napkin.

12. Place the jar on the plate. Lay one of the grilled brioche triangles on the plate and place the other upright for height. Serve immediately.

ROASTED BONE MARROW WITH CELERY LEAVES, PARSLEY, AND PICKLED SPRING ONION SALAD WITH TOASTED CHALLAH AND MALDON SEA SALT

yield: 20 portions

INGREDIENT	METRIC	U.S.
Veal marrowbone, cut into 7.5-cm/3-in pieces	60	60
Challah bread, cut into 2.5-cm-/1-in-thick slices	60 slices	60 slices
Celery leaves	200 g	7.05 oz
Parsley leaves, coarsely chopped	100 g	3.53 oz
Pickled Spring Onions, thinly sliced (page 338)	200 g	7.05 oz
Extra-virgin olive oil	100 g	3.53 oz
Salt	7 g	.25 oz
Freshly ground black pepper	2 g	.07 oz
Maldon sea salt	200 g	7.05 oz

1. Preheat a static oven to 230°C/446°F.

2. Place the bone marrow pieces in a roasting pan. Roast the bones for about 20 minutes or until golden brown. Transfer them to a hotel pan and place them in an Alto-Shaam set to 60°C/140°F during service. Discard after 12 hours.

3. **TO PICK UP:** Place 3 pieces of bone marrow on a sizzle platter and put them in a 260°C/500°F oven or impinger oven for 3 minutes or until hot throughout.

4. Toast 3 challah slices in a hot salamander for up to 1 minute per side or just until the surface of the bread is brown.

5. Meanwhile, combine 10 g/.35 oz celery leaves, 5 g/.17 oz parsley, 10 g/.35 oz pickled onions, 5 g/.17 oz of extra-virgin olive oil, a pinch of salt, and pepper from 2 twists of a grinder in a bowl.

6. Toss until evenly mixed and the greens are coated with the oil and seasoning. Put them on a plate. Put 10 g/0.35 oz of Maldon sea salt in a ramekin on the plate.

7. Place the hot bone marrow on the same plate as the salad and sea salt and the toasted challah. Serve immediately.

PICKLED SPRING ONIONS

yield: 1 kg/2 lb 3.2 oz

INGREDIENT	METRIC	U.S.
White wine vinegar	250 g	8.82 oz
Water	250 g	8.82 oz
Sugar	200 g	7.05 oz
Mustard seeds	7 g	.25 oz
Black peppercorns	7 g	.25 oz
Celery seed	7 g	.25 oz
Coriander seed	7 g	.25 oz
Bay leaves	2	2
Salt	20 g	.71 oz
Spring onions, root ends trimmed, green ends cut off and reserved	1 kg	2 lb 3.2 oz

1. Bring a large pot with 4.00 kg/8 lb 12.96 of water and 100 g/3.53 oz of salt to a boil.

2. Meanwhile, combine the vinegar, water, sugar, spices, and salt in a separate sauce pot. Bring to a boil and turn down to very low heat.

3. Cook the spring onions in the boiling water until just tender, 3 to 5 minutes. Shock the onions in an ice bath to stop the cooking process.

4. Put the spring onions in a bain marie along with the trimmed green ends. Pour in the hot pickling liquid. Cool to room temperature uncovered, and then transfer to an airtight container. Pickle the onions for 4 days in the refrigerator before using.

5. These pickled onions will keep for over a year in the refrigerator.

notes This plate is eaten the following way: Using a butter knife, cut around the marrow inside the bone. It will slide out easily. Put it on a piece of toasted challah, sprinkle a pinch of Maldon sea salt over the marrow, and put some of the greens on top of it.

I would be remiss in not naming those who inspired this dish: Blue Ribbon Brasserie in SoHo, New York City, where the bone marrow is served with an oxtail marmalade; and Fergus Henderson from St. John in London, who serves his with a parsley salad. These interpretations are beyond improvement.

variation For pickled ramps, substitute ramps for the spring onions. Cut off the leafy part of the ramps and reserve for other uses.

HOUSE-CURED DUCK HAM WITH SAUCE GRIBICHE AND SOURDOUGH

yield: **20 portions**

INGREDIENT	METRIC	U.S.
DUCK HAM		
Duck breasts	8	8
Juniper berries	10 g	.35 oz
Star anise	10 g	.35 oz
Coriander seed	10 g	.35 oz
Bay leaves	4	4
Thyme sprigs	4	4
Garlic	30 g	1.06 oz
Salt	2 kg	4 lb 6.4 oz
Sugar	500 g	1 lb .16 oz
SAUCE GRIBICHE		
Hard-boiled eggs (about 6)	300 g	10.58 oz
Dijon mustard	15 g	.53 oz
Lemon juice	30 g	1.06 oz
Champagne vinegar	20 g	.71 oz
Kosher salt	5 g	.18 oz
Canola oil	370 g	13.05 oz
Gherkins, finely diced	100 g	3.53 oz
Small capers, finely chopped	80 g	2.82 oz
Parsley, finely chopped	5 g	.18 oz
Chervil, finely chopped	5 g	.18 oz
Tarragon, finely chopped	5 g	.18 oz
Freshly ground black pepper	2 g	.07 oz
Gherkins	100	100
Pickled Pearl Onions	100	100
Sourdough Boule (page 121), **sliced into 1.25-cm-/.5-in-thick slices, cut widthwise, then cut in half for a total of 4 half-slices per order**	80	80

1. **FOR THE DUCK HAM:** Freeze the duck breasts until semifirm. Using a very sharp knife, remove some of the top layer of fat, leaving about 6 mm/.25 in of fat on it. Cut a 1.25-cm-/.5-in crisscross grid over the fat.

2. Toast the juniper berries, star anise, and coriander seed in a 160°C/320°F oven until aromatic.

3. Cool the toasted spices, and then crush them. Crush the bay leaves and add them to the spice mix. Coarsely chop the thyme and garlic and add to the spice mix. Toss to evenly mix with the salt and sugar.

4. Put 8 pieces of plastic wrap on a worktable; each piece should be big enough to wrap a breast.

5. Spread 160 g/5.64 oz of the salt cure onto each piece of plastic wrap. Place the breasts on top of the cure, fat side down. Cover the breasts with the remaining mixture (160 g/5.64 oz on each breast), wrap them tightly, and let them cure for 4 days in the refrigerator.

6. Unwrap the breasts and rinse the cure off with water. Pat the breasts dry and wrap each one with 3 layers of cheesecloth. Tie the cheesecloth with twine, and hang the breasts in the refrigerator with the twine.

7. Let them cure for 3 weeks before using. They will hold for up to 3 more weeks in the refrigerator.

8. **FOR THE SAUCE GRIBICHE:** Separate the egg yolks from the whites. Finely chop the egg whites. Pass the cooked yolks through a drum sieve into a bowl. Add the mustard, lemon juice, champagne vinegar, and salt, and whisk to form a homogeneous mass. Put the bowl over a cloth towel or other surface that will keep the bowl steady.

9. Pour the oil into the bowl in a slow, steady stream while whisking vigorously to create an emulsion.

10. Stir in the chopped egg whites, diced gherkins, capers, herbs, and pepper. Adjust seasoning with salt and lemon juice, if necessary. Reserve in the refrigerator in an airtight container, with plastic wrap placed directly on the surface of the sauce. Put 45 g/1.6 oz of the sauce into jars with a lids; reserve refrigerated. Discard after 4 days.

11. **TO PICK UP:** Slice the cured duck breast as thinly as possible (about 120 g/4.23 oz per order) and lay it on a plate. Put 5 to 7 gherkins and 3 to 5 pickled onions next to the duck (the smaller they are, the more you will need). Put a jar of gribiche on the plate, along with the sliced sourdough. Serve immediately.

note The sauce gribiche recipe is based on Auguste Escoffier's original recipe, published in *The Complete Guide to the Art of Modern Cookery* in 1907. Some ingredients have been modified and adjusted.

GRIBICHE

PORK RILLETTES WITH SOURDOUGH AND GHERKINS

yield: **20 portions**

INGREDIENT	METRIC	U.S.
Gelatin sheets, bloomed	10 g	.35 oz
Sage leaves	60	60
PORK RILLETTES		
Pork butt, boned, cut into 5-cm/2-in pieces	4 kg	8 lb 13.12 oz
Onion, finely diced	400 g	14.11 oz
Carrot, finely diced	300 g	10.58 oz
Celery, coarsely chopped	250 g	8.82 oz
Garlic cloves, coarsely chopped	50 g	1.76 oz
Salt	100 g	3.53 oz
Chicken stock	2.5 kg	5 lb 8.16 oz
Black peppercorns	16	16
Bay leaves	6	6
Thyme sprigs	10	10
Pork butt cooking liquid (from above)	2 kg	4 lb 6.56 oz
Rendered pork or duck fat, melted (preferably pork)	500 g	1 lb 0.16 oz
Parsley, coarsely chopped	30 g	1.06 oz
Salt	9 g	.32 oz
Freshly ground black pepper	2 g	.07 oz
Rendered pork fat (to seal the rillettes)	300 g	10.58 oz
Gherkins	60	60
Sourdough Boules (page 121)	5	5

1. Wash twenty 340-g/12-oz French glass crocks thoroughly (see Resources, page 540). Wash the rubber seals separately. Once they are washed, air-dry the crocks and the rubber seals, and then put them together.

2. Melt the bloomed gelatin in a microwave or over a hot water bath. Brush the sage leaves with the melted gelatin and "glue" 3 of them inside each jar, evenly spaced and pointing up. Set the crocks aside while making the rillettes.

3. **FOR THE RILLETTES:** Preheat a convection oven to 160°C/320°F.

4. Put the pork butt in a pot and cover it with water. Bring it to a quick boil over high heat and drain off the liquid. This helps to remove some of the impurities from the pork.

5. Combine the pork butt, onion, carrot, celery, garlic, salt, chicken stock, peppercorns, bay leaves, and thyme in a large rondeau. Bring to a quick boil on the stove.

6. Cover the rondeau with a lid or aluminum foil and place it in the oven.

7. Braise the pork until it is tender and falling apart, about 2 hours. If it is not completely tender, continue to braise until it is.

8. Once the pork is cooked, remove the pork, garlic cloves, and carrots from the braising liquid. Place the pork and the garlic cloves in a 20-qt mixer bowl fitted with the paddle attachment. Place the carrots in a hotel pan in the refrigerator to stop the cooking process. Strain the braising liquid through a fine-mesh sieve and reserve at room temperature.

9. Mix the pork and garlic on low speed to break down the pork. Check the seasoning for salt and pepper.

10. Pour 284 g/10 oz braising liquid and 170 g/6 of pork fat slowly into the mixer while it is running. Alternate both ingredients in those amounts. The entire amount of braising liquid or pork fat may not be needed. The rillettes should be a moist and rich mixture. It should be able to hold the liquid. If it starts to look like it is puddling, there is too much liquid. To fix this, place the mixture over a perforated hotel pan or sheet pan, and in turn place that over a hotel pan or sheet pan with no perforations, and let the excess liquid strain out, stirring the rillettes frequently until they look drier.

11. Cut the cooked carrots into small dice. Put them in the mixer bowl on top of the pork, along with the chopped parsley. Grind 2 g/.07 oz of black pepper into the bowl. Mix for long enough to evenly incorporate all the ingredients.

12. Fill the glass crocks to within 2 cm/.75 in from the top with the rillettes mixture. Press down with your fingers so that it is compact. Clean the rim of the jar after filling, if necessary. Using a funnel, pour 15 g/.52 oz of melted pork fat into each crock, covering the entire surface (use the second amount of rendered pork fat). Close the lid on the crock.

13. Reserve in the refrigerator until needed. During service, keep the number of crocks that you think you will sell at room temperature. The fat hardens when it is cold and makes it very hard and unpleasant to eat. Rillettes will keep for up to 6 months in the refrigerator.

14. **TO PICK UP:** Place the tempered rillettes crock on a plate or wooden board lined with butcher paper, along with 3 gherkins in a ramekin and one-quarter of a boule of sourdough, cut in half. Always cut the bread to order to keep it from drying out. Serve immediately.

note Rillettes were originally made to preserve pork meat. The fat surrounding the pork acts as a barrier against bacteria growth. Nowadays we do it the same way, but for other reasons, namely flavor and texture. Some people, including me, eat the top layer of fat on the rillettes, which is packed with flavor and as smooth as butter.

FOIE GRAS "TORCHON" WITH MCINTOSH APPLE COMPOTE AND WARM TOASTED BRIOCHE

yield: **20 portions**

INGREDIENT	METRIC	U.S.
FOIE GRAS TORCHON		
Applejack brandy	50 g	1.78 oz
Calvados	25 g	.89 oz
Sweet sherry	25 g	.89 oz
Foie gras, Grade A, deveined and soaked in milk overnight (this helps pull any blood or impurities out of it)	1.86 kg	4 lb 1.6 oz
Salt	30 g	1.07 oz
Freshly ground black pepper	10 g	.36 oz
Ascorbic acid (or vitamin C crystals)	5.03	.18 oz
Brioche Tubes (page 346), **cut into 2.5-cm-/1-in-thick slices**	40	40
Clarified butter	100 g	3.53 oz
Freshly cracked black pepper	5 g	.17 oz
Maldon sea salt	20 g	.7 oz
McIntosh Apple Compote (page 346)	20 jars	20 jars

1. **FOR THE FOIE GRAS TORCHON:** Combine the applejack, Calvados, and sherry in a small sauté pan. Cook off the brandy over high heat until most of the alcohol evaporates, about 1 minute. It is a good idea to start with 25 percent more than is needed to make up for evaporation.

2. Line 2 PVC tubes 30 cm/12 in long by 6.25 cm/2.5 in diameter with acetate. Place them in a standing position on a flat sheet pan lined with parchment paper.

3. Place the brandy mixture, foie gras, salt, pepper, and ascorbic acid in a Thermomix cup.

4. Press the 60°C/140°F button, turn the speed dial to 6, let it run for 2 minutes, and then turn the speed to 10 for 10 seconds. Transfer the foie gras to a bowl because the carryover heat in the cup might melt the foie gras. Transfer the foie gras to a piping bag and pipe it into the prepared PVC tubes, filling them to just under 2.5 cm/1 in from the top of the tubes. The ascorbic acid is there to prevent the foie gras from oxidizing. It does not contribute flavor.

5. Form some plastic wrap into a ball that is big enough to fit inside the tubes. This will prevent the foie gras from oxidizing. Place the plastic wrap in tops of the tubes, cover both tubes with a towel, and refrigerate for at least 6 hours or until firm. Discard after 72 hours.

6. **TO PICK UP:** Brush both sides of 2 brioche slices with clarified butter and toast on both sides in a hot oven, a salamander, or an impinger oven until golden brown.

7. Meanwhile, cut the foie gras torchon. Dip a long, thin slicing knife in very hot water. Push the torchon 2.5 cm/1 in out of the tube. Using the end of the tube as a guide, cut the foie gras straight down, with the acetate still on, leaning the knife against the tube.

8. Remove the acetate from the foie gras and place it on a plate. Sprinkle cracked black pepper and Maldon sea salt over the foie gras. Put a jar of McIntosh apple compote on the plate.

9. Put both pieces of toasted brioche on a pocket-folded serviette. Serve immediately.

BRIOCHE TUBES

yield: 4 tubes

INGREDIENT	METRIC	U.S.
Brioche Dough (page 10)	2.04 kg	4 lb 7.84 oz

1. Spray a light coat of nonstick oil spray on both halves of each rib mold.

2. Weigh out four 510-g/1 lb 3.2-oz pieces of brioche. Flatten each piece and roll it up to the width of the pan. Place 1 roll in each rib pan. Close the pan and latch it.

3. Proof at 27°C/81°F for 3 hours at 80 percent humidity or until doubled in size.

4. Preheat a convection oven to 160°C/320°F.

5. Bake the brioche until it reaches an internal temperature of 96°C/205°F. Open the latch to lift the top of the rib pan in order to take a temperature reading with a probe thermometer.

6. Once it has baked, open the pan and let the brioche cool in the pan with the lid open; otherwise it might lose its shape.

7. Once it has cooled, wrap it and freeze it or use it for service. If kept at room temperature, it will keep for 48 hours.

note A rib pan is composed of 2 ribbed parts, a top part and a bottom part. Each part is a half cylinder, and when both halves are put together they form a ribbed cylinder or tube. They latch closed. See Resources, page 540, for places to find this pan.

MCINTOSH APPLE COMPOTE

yield: 20 jars

INGREDIENT	METRIC	U.S.
McIntosh apples, peeled, cored, and finely diced	961 g	2 lb 1.92 oz
Sugar	33 g	1.16 oz
Lemon juice	5 g	.19 oz
Salt	.55 g	.02 oz
McIntosh Apple Jelly (page 492)	1 kg	2 lb 3.27 oz

1. Sanitize the jars by placing them in boiling water for 10 minutes and then air-drying them.

2. Combine the apples, sugar, lemon juice, and salt in a sauté pan. Cook over medium-high heat until the apples are tender, about 7 to 10 minutes, depending on the water content of the apples. Cool to room temperature.

3. Portion 30 g/1.01 oz of apple compote into each jar.

4. Fill the jars to the top with jelly. Reserve in the refrigerator. The compote will keep for 2 months in the refrigerator.

SIDE DISHES

These items fall into a category all their own, since they are not exactly appetizers but they still qualify as small plate items. What distinguishes them is that they are meant to be eaten along with something else, most commonly with sandwiches and some entrées. Not that it's written in stone that they must be eaten with something else or they cannot be eaten at all. This type of food can also be considered "bar food" or even "bar snacks" since they are not part of a meal per se; they are meant to be nibbled on along with something else.

If appetizers are defined by their simplicity of execution and ease of preparation, side dishes take those principles even further with fewer ingredients and even faster preparations and pickups.

The following are not all the varieties of side dishes available; they simply represent my favorite ones. A simple green salad could be a side dish, but you aren't reading this book to learn about little salads. You will see an abundance of fried food because it just so happens that I love fried food. Who doesn't?

FRIED CHICKPEAS

yield: 20 portions

INGREDIENT	METRIC	U.S.
Chickpeas	2 kg	4 lb 6.4 oz
Chicken stock	4.5 kg	9 lb 14.72 oz
Salt	30 g	1.06 oz
Old Bay seasoning	30 g	1.06 oz
Limes, quartered	10	10

1. Soak the chickpeas overnight in cold water. Make sure it covers the chickpeas by about 5 cm/2 in. They will double in weight by the next day.

2. Strain the chickpeas. Put them in a pot with the chicken stock and bring them to a quick boil. Reduce the heat to medium-low and simmer until the chickpeas are tender, 1 to 2 hours.

3. Once the chickpeas are cooked, transfer them to a hotel pan and cool over an ice bath in refrigeration to stop the cooking process. Reserve in the refrigerator.

4. Once they are cooled, strain them from their cooking liquid and reserve in an airtight container in the refrigerator. Discard after 72 hours.

5. **TO PICK UP:** Heat a fryer to 190°C/375°F.

6. Place 200 g/7.05 oz chickpeas in a fryer basket and fry them until crisp, about 2 minutes.

7. Place the fried chickpeas in a bowl lined with a paper towel and season with 3 g/.11 oz salt and 3 g/.11 oz Old Bay seasoning.

8. Put the seasoned chickpeas in a bowl and serve with 2 lime quarters on the side.

the right frying oil

CHOOSING THE RIGHT FRYING OIL DEPENDS ON MANY FACTORS, but one of the most important considerations is the oil's smoke point. The smoke point is the highest temperature that the oil can reach before it starts to smoke. It will in fact begin to decompose well before that point. The higher the smoke point, the better the fry. Frying is a method of direct-heat cooking, since the hot oil will come in contact with whatever product is being fried. The temperature of the oil is well above the temperature of boiling water, and therefore it can cook a lot faster. This form of cooking will dry the surface of the food, crisp it, and brown it, while cooking it internally as well, practically sealing the moisture in.

Some commonly used oils with high smoke points are:

- Canola oil (204°C/400°F)

- Low acidity extra-virgin olive oil (high quality) (207°C/405°F)

- Sesame oil (210°C/410°F)

- Cottonseed oil (216°C/420°F)

- Peanut oil (227°C/440°F)

- Sunflower oil (227°C/440°F)

- Soybean oil (257°C/495°F)

- Safflower oil (266°C/520°F)

Any of these oils will work in a fryer, since you will rarely have to fry anything above 190°C/375°F. There are two questions to consider. Which one is the best for the food, and how much does it cost? If food cost is not an issue, the best choice is peanut oil, since it produces the crispiest fried food that stays that way longer. But, when taking food cost into consideration, use canola oil or sunflower oil for frying, since it will not only produce a crisp fried product but is also much more economical than peanut oil. Stay away from extra-virgin olive oil and sesame oil, since they impart their flavor to the foods as they are frying, unless that is the desired effect.

PICKLED VEGETABLES

INGREDIENT	METRIC	U.S.
Kirby cucumbers, ends trimmed and cut into 5-mm-/.25-in-thick discs	1 kg	2 lb 3.2 oz
Kosher salt	60 g	2.12 oz
Canola oil	60 g	2.12 oz
Garlic cloves, scored	25 g	.88 oz
Carrots, cut on a bias 1.25 cm/.5 in thick	450 g	15.87 oz
Red bell peppers, cut into batons	300 g	10.58 oz
Pearl onions	500 g	1 lb .16 oz
Cauliflower, broken into small florets	350 g	12.35 oz
Cider vinegar	1 kg	2 lb 3.2 oz
Brown sugar	350 g	12.35 oz
Fennel seed, toasted	15 g	.53 oz
Coriander seed, toasted	10 g	.35 oz
Bay leaves	2	2
Yellow mustard seed, toasted	15 g	.53 oz
Allspice, toasted	7 g	.25 oz
Cloves, toasted	5 g	.18 oz

1. Combine the sliced cucumbers with the salt and toss to coat in a bowl. Add 100 g/3.53 oz of crushed ice. Let them sit in the refrigerator for 2 hours.

2. Drain the excess moisture and rinse the cucumbers in cold water.

3. Put the oil in a large sauté pan over high heat. Once it begins to shimmer, add the garlic, carrots, red peppers, pearl onions, and cauliflower and turn the heat down to medium-low. Sweat the vegetables, stirring occasionally, for 10 to 15 minutes. Avoid caramelizing the vegetables.

4. Remove the pan from the heat and stir in the cucumbers.

5. Put the vinegar, sugar, and all the spices in a pot. Bring to a boil over high heat, stirring to dissolve the sugar, for about 5 minutes. Pour the boiling liquid over the sweated vegetables. Let them cool to room temperature.

6. Transfer to an airtight container and refrigerate. The pickled vegetables will hold for up to 1 month in the refrigerator.

7. **TO PICK UP:** Spoon 200 g/7.05 oz into a ramekin, using a slotted spoon to strain the liquid out. Serve cold.

note This item is a great side dish for any kind of sandwich or charcuterie. It may seem like a large amount of pickles, but they are very good and hold for a long time.

PAN-FRIED BABY ARTICHOKES WITH LEMON AÏOLI

yield: **20 portions**

INGREDIENT	METRIC	U.S.
Baby artichokes	100	100
LEMON AÏOLI		
Garlic cloves, peeled	10 g	.35 oz
Salt	4 g	.14 oz
Pasteurized egg yolks	170 g	6 oz
Red wine vinegar	7 g	.25 oz
Lemon juice	10 g	.35 oz
Lemon zest	3 g	.11 oz
Canola oil	720 g	1 lb 9.44 oz
Extra-virgin olive oil	240 g	8.47 oz
Extra-virgin olive oil	4 kg	8 lb 13.12 oz
Wondra flour	500 g	1 lb 1.6 oz
Salt	60 g	2.12 oz

1. Fill a large pot with cold water and 400 g/14.11 oz of salt. The pot should be large enough to hold all of the artichokes.

2. Trim the stems of the artichokes to within 2.5 cm/1 in of the base and about 1.75 cm/.5 in from the top. Put them in the water as soon as they are cut.

3. Prepare an ice bath large enough to hold all the artichokes; it can be more than one ice bath if need be.

4. Bring the water to a boil, and then reduce the heat to a simmer. Cook until the artichokes are tender, 12 to 20 minutes. Test the artichokes by inserting a paring knife through the base of the artichoke and into the stem; it should go in easily.

5. Remove the artichokes from the water with a spider and place them in the ice bath(s).

6. Once they have cooled, transfer them to a perforated hotel pan set over a regular hotel pan. This should allow the excess water to drip out from between the leaves. Reserve until needed. Peel off the outer leaves, which are tough and practically inedible, with your hands. Cut the artichokes in half lengthwise; reserve in an airtight container in refrigeration during service. Discard after 36 hours.

7. **FOR THE AÏOLI:** Chop the garlic very finely on a cutting board with a pinch of the salt. Make a paste with your knife, using the side of the blade against the cutting board. Alternatively, use a garlic press.

8. Place a bowl on a damp cloth towel to anchor it. Place the egg yolks, garlic, vinegar, lemon juice, lemon zest, and remaining salt in it. Whisk until evenly mixed.

9. Combine both oils, and slowly pour them into the bowl while whisking vigorously to create an emulsion.

10. Reserve in an airtight container with plastic wrap directly on the surface of the aïoli. Discard after 3 days.

11. **TO PICK UP:** Heat a fryer with the extra-virgin olive oil to 180°C/355°F. Have the Wondra flour available in a bowl.

12. When the oil is hot, place 10 cooked artichoke halves in the bowl with the Wondra flour, and toss them to coat completely in the flour. Shake the excess off each piece in a small sieve. Fry until they have browned evenly and the leaves are crisp, 2 to 3 minutes.

13. Transfer the artichokes to a bowl lined with a paper towel. Season with salt, about 3 g/.11 oz, or as needed. Put them on the desired plate.

14. Place 50 g/1.76 oz of aïoli in a ramekin or other serving container. Serve immediately.

MASHED POTATOES

yield: 20 portions

INGREDIENT	METRIC	U.S.
Yukon gold potatoes	2 kg	4 lb 6.4 oz
Butter, soft	1.5 kg	3 lb 4.96 oz
Crème fraîche, at room temperature	500 g	1 lb .16 oz
Salt	45 g	1.59 oz
Freshly ground black pepper	3 g	.11 oz

1. Preheat a static or deck oven to 230°C/450°F.

2. Line a half sheet pan with 2.5 cm/1 in of kosher salt. Place the potatoes on the salt.

3. Bake them until they are tender and a fork or a skewer can go though them easily.

4. Remove them from the oven and peel them immediately.

5. Pass the potatoes through a ricer. Put the potatoes and the remaining ingredients in the bowl of an electric mixer fitted with the paddle attachment. Mix them for a few seconds or just until they come together into a uniform mass.

6. Transfer them to a bain marie while hot and cover the potatoes. Make sure the surface is directly covered with plastic wrap. Keep the bain marie in a hot water bath during service.

7. To pick up: Spoon 200 g/7.05 oz of mashed potatoes into a ramekin. Serve immediately.

note This item is particularly good as a side dish for entrées.

FRIED PARSLEY WITH LEMON JUICE

yield: 20 portions

INGREDIENT	METRIC	U.S.
Parsley leaves	4 kg	8 lb 13.12 oz
Salt	80 g	2.82 oz
Lemons, cut into quarters	10	10

1. Heat a fryer to 190°C/370°F.

2. Place 200 g/7.05 oz of parsley leaves in a fryer basket. Fry the parsley for 3 or 4 seconds or until it no longer bubbles.

3. Remove the parsley from the fryer and transfer it to a bowl lined with a paper towel. Toss with 4 g/.14 oz of salt, or as needed.

4. Place the fried parsley in a bowl (75 g/2.64 oz per portion) and serve with 2 lemon quarters on the side.

notes There will be a large amount of evaporation during the frying process, which will result in a yield of about half of the original amount of parsley.

As an interesting note, this was one of Salvador Dali's favorite dishes.

Fried Parsley with Lemon Juice

DEVILED EGGS

INGREDIENT	METRIC	U.S.
Eggs	40	40
Capers	45 g	1.59 oz
Green onions, green part only, thinly sliced	45 g	1.59 oz
Aïoli (page 350); see Note	480 g	1 lb .93 oz
Paprika	28 g	.99 oz
Salt	8 g	.28 oz

1. Place the eggs in a single layer in a large rondeau. Fill the pan with cold water until it covers the eggs by 2.5 cm/1 in. Place the rondeau over medium-high heat and bring the water to a boil. Put a lid on the rondeau as it reaches a boil.

2. Remove the pan from the heat. Set a timer to 12 minutes for medium eggs, 15 minutes for large eggs, and 18 for extra-large eggs. Once the timer goes off, place the rondeau in a sink and run cold water over it until the eggs are cool. Drain the eggs. Reserve in the refrigerator for up to 1 week.

3. Heat a fryer to 190°C/370°F. Fry the capers until crisp in a fine-mesh sieve, about 45 seconds. (Regular fryer baskets have large openings through which the capers will fall.)

4. Put the capers in a bowl lined with a paper towel to absorb any excess oil. Reserve uncovered at room temperature during service. Discard after service. Repeat the frying and draining process with the green onions.

5. Peel the eggshells off of the eggs and cut the eggs in half. Scoop the yolks out and put them in the bowl of an electric mixer fitted with the paddle attachment.

6. Add the aïoli, paprika, and salt and mix until smooth. Adjust seasoning. Don't forget that the recipe also includes capers to garnish the eggs and that they are very salty, even after frying. Transfer to a piping bag fitted with a #864 fluted tip.

7. Place the egg white halves on a sheet pan lined with a heavy-duty paper towel. Pipe the egg yolk mixture into each cavity. Pipe up to 3.75 cm/1.5 in high above the egg white.

8. Cover loosely with plastic wrap to prevent a skin from forming on the piped egg yolk; try to keep the plastic from damaging the piped yolk.

9. **TO PICK UP:** Place 4 deviled egg halves on a plate. Sprinkle about 2 g/.07 oz fried capers and about 2 g/.07 oz green onions over the egg yolk. Serve immediately.

note Do not add the lemon to the aïoli on page 350.

GREEN BEAN SALAD

yield: 20 portions

INGREDIENT	METRIC	U.S.
DRESSING		
Sugar	15 g	.53 oz
Red wine vinegar	105 g	3.7 oz
English mustard	21 g	.74 oz
Garlic, finely chopped	36 g	1.27 oz
Extra-virgin olive oil	600 g	1 lb 5.12 oz
Kosher salt	12 g	.42 oz
Freshly ground black pepper	3 g	.11 oz
Green beans, blanched in salted boiling water and stems trimmed	1.8 kg	3 lb 15.52 oz
Cauliflower, small florets	1.5 kg	3 lb 4.96 oz
Red radishes, ends trimmed and thinly sliced on a mandoline	450 g	15.84 oz
Cucumbers, ends trimmed, cut into 3 equal parts, then sliced in half lengthwise, then each half cut into 3 long wedges	900 g	1 lb 15.68 oz
Red onions, thinly sliced	300 g	10.58 oz
Capers, coarsely chopped	150 g	5.29 oz

1. **FOR THE DRESSING:** Mix all of the ingredients in a blender on high speed. Taste and adjust seasoning with salt and black pepper. This dressing is not emulsified.

2. Place all of the vegetables and the capers in a bowl and toss with the dressing. Adjust seasoning again with salt and pepper if necessary.

3. Portion or serve. This salad tastes better 3 to 4 hours after it is assembled, because the vinaigrette tends to permeate the vegetables with a little sitting time. Discard after 12 hours.

POTATO AND SPANISH CHORIZO CROQUETTES WITH PECORINO TARTUFO AND DIJON MUSTARD

yield: 20 portions

INGREDIENT	METRIC	U.S.
Yukon gold potatoes	3 kg	6 lb 9.76 oz
Egg yolks	600 g	1 lb 5.12 oz
Chorizo, diced into small cubes	350 g	12.35 oz
Pecorino Tartufo cheese	400 g	14.11 oz
Kosher salt	20 g	.71 oz
Eggs, stirred to a uniform mass	200 g	7.05 oz
Cake flour	500 g	1 lb 1.64 oz
Panko, finely ground in a Robot Coupe	2 kg	4 lb 6.55 oz
Dijon mustard	600 g	1 lb 5.12 oz

1. Bake the potatoes as per steps 1 through 3 of the mashed potato recipe on page 352.

2. Peel the potatoes while they are hot and pass them through a ricer.

3. Place the peeled potatoes, egg yolks, chorizo, Pecorino Tartufo, and salt in the bowl of an electric mixer fitted with the paddle attachment. Mix just enough to combine all the ingredients into a homogeneous mass; be careful not to overmix.

4. Transfer the potatoes to a piping bag fitted with a #8 piping tip. Pipe them into 3.75-cm-/1.5-in-diameter spheres on a sheet pan lined with a nonstick rubber mat, making the spheres as even as possible. Place the sheet pan in the refrigerator to cool the potatoes. Once they are cold, round the spheres by hand, trying to get them as spherical as possible. Freeze the spheres. They can be reserved frozen for up to 3 months.

5. Once they are frozen, bread them. Dip the spheres into the eggs, then the cake flour, and finally the panko. Repeat so that the croquettes are coated twice. Reserve frozen during service.

6. **TO PICK UP:** Spoon about 20 g/.7 oz mustard into each ramekin or directly onto a plate. The Dijon mustard can be preportioned into ramekins before service.

7. Heat a fryer to 150°C/302°F.

8. Place 5 frozen croquettes in a fryer basket and fry them until golden brown.

9. Remove them from the fryer and place them on a heavy-duty paper towel to soak up the excess fryer oil.

10. Put the croquettes on a plate and serve immediately with a side of Dijon mustard.

TRUFFLED FRENCH FRIES

yield: 20 portions

INGREDIENT	METRIC	U.S.
Large russet potatoes (about 1 potato per portion)	20 to 25	20 to 25
Truffle salt	60 g	2.12 oz

1. Peel the potatoes, putting them in cold water as they are peeled.

2. Cut the potatoes lengthwise into 0.5-cm-/.25-in-wide sticks. It is important to always cut them to a consistent size, since different thicknesses will fry at different rates. Using a French fry cutter reduces the cutting time to a fraction of the time it takes to cut the potatoes by hand, plus it ensures consistency. Put the potatoes in cold water in a deep hotel pan as they are cut.

3. Change the water 5 times or until it comes out clear. Drain the water out each time, pouring the contents of the hotel pan into a large-mesh sieve or a colander. This will rinse all excess starch away.

4. Once the water runs clear, fill the hotel pan three-quarters of the way up with water and add enough ice to cover the entire surface of the hotel pan. Let the potatoes sit in this water for at least 30 minutes or up to 1 day in the refrigerator.

5. Heat a fryer to 160°C/325°F.

6. Remove the potatoes from the ice water and pat them very dry with a heavy-duty paper towel.

7. Pre-fry the potatoes a few batches at a time for 6 to 8 minutes. They shouldn't take on any color, they should just wilt. Always wait for the oil to return to the correct temperature before adding another batch. This pre-frying process step is essential to crisp French fries.

8. When the pre-fried potatoes come out of the fryer, place them on a sheet pan lined with a heavy-duty paper towel to absorb any excess fryer oil. Allow the fries to cool. Put them on a sheet pan lined with silicone paper or a nonstick rubber mat in a single layer, separate from each other.

9. Freeze the pre-fried potatoes, preferably in a blast freezer since this will ensure a quick and very hard freezing, and then consolidate them into a smaller container. Reserve frozen during service. They will keep for up to 6 months frozen, but they need to be well wrapped, otherwise they will have ice accumulation on the surface. This will melt into the fryer, and this can cause accidents such as the oil bubbling over the fryer and onto the floor or onto someone.

10. **TO PICK UP:** Heat a fryer to 190°C/375°F.

11. Fry 350 g/12.35 oz of frozen pre-fried potatoes until they are a deep golden brown and crisp.

12. Put them in a bowl lined with a paper towel and toss them with 3 g/.1 oz of truffle salt. Serve immediately.

note Try serving these fries with about 20 g/.7 oz aïoli, (see recipe on page 380; do not use lemon zest) and about 20 g/.7 oz malt vinegar. Try to always offer ketchup too.

If offering French fries on your menu, you have to really think about whether you want to make them from scratch or purchase them frozen and pre-fried. It takes time and space to make proper French fries. There are a few varieties of frozen French fries that are of good quality, but they are never as good as French fries from scratch.

TRUFFLED POTATO SALAD

yield: 20 portions

INGREDIENT	METRIC	U.S.
Fingerling potatoes	2.5 kg	5 lb 8.16 oz
Truffle Aïoli (see Note)	1.25 kg	2 lb 12.16 oz
Pecorino Tartufo cheese, finely grated with a rasp	350 g	12.35 oz
Parsley, coarsely chopped	30 g	1.06 oz
Red onion, thinly sliced	200 g	7.05 oz
Bacon lardons (see method on page 388)	750 g	1 lb 10.46 oz
Truffle salt	20 g	.7 oz
Hard-boiled eggs, coarsely chopped	500 g	1 lb 1.6 oz

1. Scrub the fingerling potatoes well and place them in a perforated full-size hotel pan.

2. Steam them in a steamer or combi oven until tender. The cooking times will vary depending on the cooking method. Test the potatoes by inserting a fork in them; if it slides in easily, they are done.

3. Cool the potatoes down to room temperature, and then slice them horizontally into 1-cm-/ .4-in-thick discs.

4. Combine the potatoes with all of the remaining ingredients in a bowl. Adjust seasoning with more truffle salt if necessary. Discard after 24 hours.

note For the truffle aïoli, see recipe for lemon aïoli on page 350. Do not add lemon, and replace the salt with truffle salt.

DILL POTATO CHIPS

yield: 20 portions

INGREDIENT	METRIC	U.S.
Yukon potatoes, large	6 kg	13 lb 3.68 oz
Kosher salt	35 g	1.23 oz
Dill, coarsely chopped	120 g	4.23 oz

1. Using a mandoline, slice the unpeeled potatoes as thinly as possible (about 1 mm/.04 in). Place them in a cold water bath and let them sit in it in the refrigerator overnight.

2. Drain the water and pat the slices dry.

3. Heat a fryer to 150°C/302°F.

4. Fry the potatoes in small batches of about 500 g/1 lb 1.6 oz. Move the chips around the fryer so that they take on an even color, which should be a medium-dark amber brown. The type of fryer will determine the time it takes to achieve this color. Remove the chips from the fryer and wait for the oil to come back up to temperature before frying more chips.

5. Season the chips as they come out of the fryer so that the salt adheres to them. Once the chips have cooled, toss them in the chopped dill. Discard after 12 hours.

sandwiches

In any way, shape, or form, sandwiches are one of the most popular things to eat. A sandwich can contain everything featured in a regular meal: starch (bread), vegetables (tomato, lettuce), protein (meats), and dairy (cheese). It is important to understand how to make a great sandwich and what makes a sandwich special. As with everything, a great sandwich starts with great ingredients. The following are the key points to consider.

bread type

There are two broad categories here: soft bread and crusty bread. There is a large variety of bread available within those two categories, but they are grouped this way because the texture will determine the type of sandwich you will end up with. When choosing a bread, you must make the decision according to what will go between the slices and how it is going to be eaten. The latter is a huge consideration: If you bite into it, will all of the filling come out? Is the bread going to hold the filling in place, or will it come out the sides when I bite into it? Is it so crusty that it will cut my palate? Will the bread toast well, or should it be left as is? Will the bread get too wet too quickly with the filling?

For the sandwiches included in this chapter, all of the breads can be made with the bread recipes in Chapter 1. Adjust the shape and size of each according to your preferences. For example, brioche buns are used for the braised pork shoulder sandwich on page 369, and they are made with the same recipe as in Chapter 1, but they will need to be portioned and shaped into 150-g/5-oz round buns.

sandwich temperature

There are three basic categories for sandwich temperatures: chilled, warm, and hot.

Chilled sandwiches are, as their name hints at, cold, and no heat is applied to any component, at least during sandwich assembly. One of the components could be precooked, such as a hard-boiled egg or a grilled vegetable, but it will be cold once the sandwich is assembled and served. Even though the components are cold, it doesn't mean that it's a good practice to preassemble chilled sandwiches and keep them refrigerated. Ideally they are assembled to order so that all the components are of top quality. The bread in premade sandwiches tends to get soggy or dense quickly, and there is always that refrigerator taste that is off-putting. Typically, these are the quickest sandwiches to assemble.

In warm sandwiches, one of the filling components will be hot while the remaining components are cold. For example, the warm component could be grilled flank steak or a fried egg. This type of sandwich is especially delicious precisely because it combines two temperatures, which also opens up textural variations. These can be the most complicated sandwiches to assemble, since one item needs to be cooked while the other ingredients are gathered and assembled.

Hot sandwiches are hot inside and out, and the result is typically a crisp exterior and a soft interior. There are a few ways to accomplish this. The first and perhaps most popular is by using a sandwich press (a.k.a. panini press), which flattens and compresses the sandwich. There is a fat component that is brushed on the exterior of the sandwich, such as clarified butter, olive oil, duck fat, or aïoli, which contributes an excellent garlic flavor in addition to producing a crisp exterior. Overly porous breads (those with an open crumb) are ideal since they allow for a proper heat transfer from the press to the center of the sandwich, which is good especially if there is cheese involved. A few examples of good breads for pressed sandwiches are:

- Brioche: Be careful, though, because brioche is a soft, tender bread that will toast much faster than firmer breads.

- Baguette: Ideally, it is cut in half and flipped over so that the crumb is facing the press. It also works the other way around, but it may take longer and the already firm crust can get even firmer due to toasting.

- Sourdough

- Francese

- Country bread

- Breton bread

- Ciabatta: As with baguette, it is ideally cut in half and flipped over to maximize heat transfer.

- Focaccia: Focaccia is firm yet soft at the same time. It can be pressed on either side with positive results.

- White bread

If the sandwich is to be pressed with cheese, the cheese should be placed directly below the top slice of bread so that it can melt down over the other ingredients. Another method for making hot sandwiches is to use a salamander, but the best tool is an impinger oven, which can strictly control time and temperature (see ovens sidebar, page 328). These sandwiches are typically heated open-faced and may be served open-faced or put back together once they are hot. Finally, a regular static oven or even a convection oven can be used, but these ovens aren't fast enough and don't evenly heat sandwiches through. The bread usually starts to burn before the middle of the sandwich gets hot. The preferred method for making hot sandwiches in this book is in a sandwich press.

type of filling

The types of filling placed on a sandwich are, for all intents and purposes, unlimited, but an important factor to consider is that it should be easy to bite through the filling. For example, if a sandwich is filled with thick slices of prosciutto, your teeth may not be able to cut through the meat and, as you pull away, the entire filling comes out. Another consideration is the amount of moisture in the filling. If it is too wet, it might moisten the bread enough to make the sandwich fall apart. Some typical fillings are:

- Cured meats: deli meats

- Charcuterie: duck confit, sausage (which also falls into the cured meats category), pâtés, or terrines

- Cooked meats: beef, chicken, turkey, pork, fish, seafood, etc.

- Cheese

- Vegetables: raw, cooked, or pickled

- Tofu: fresh, smoked, fried, or marinated

These are certainly the not the only types of fillings, but they are some of the most common. The possibilities are endless as long as you follow the important key points above.

SPREADS

Without a spread, most sandwiches would be bone-dry. A spread is necessary in order to add moisture and flavor to a sandwich. The most common spread is mayonnaise, followed by mustard. However, as with fillings, there are countless varieties of spreads. Whichever spread is used, use it in moderation since it is not a main ingredient in itself; it is just to add moisture and some flavor to the fillings and bread. Spreads are not always necessary. It isn't written in stone that each and every sandwich you make must have a spread. For example, if you use a very creamy cheese such as the triple-cream goat cheese used in the goat cheese tarts on page 329, or a smooth cheese such as a Boursin, you don't need a spread. If you believe the fillings have enough moisture, then a spread is not necessary.

There are two sandwiches that I know of and have eaten that are diametrically opposed to every key point above but are terribly popular in their country of origin. The first one is a Mexican creation that is very popular among street vendors. It is the tamal sandwich. A hot tamal (sweet or savory) is stuffed between two pieces of bread similar to a hoagie bun known as a *telera*. It is usually accompanied by a cornstarch-thickened drink (known as *atole;* more starch). The point of this sandwich is to fill you up for a few pesos, but it has almost no nutritional value whatsoever. The other sandwich is a British creation known as a *chip butty,* and it is French fries stuffed between two slices of plain, soft white bread and sometimes ketchup. Its purpose is the same as the tamal sandwich: to keep you full for little money.

SMOKED SALMON OPEN-FACED SANDWICH WITH PICKLED RAMPS, VIDALIA ONION MAYONNAISE, ARUGULA, AND DILL CIABATTA

yield: 20 sandwiches

INGREDIENT	METRIC	U.S.
VIDALIA ONION MAYONNAISE		
Mayonnaise	600 g	1 lb 5.12 oz
Vidalia onion, finely chopped	250 g	8.82 oz
Salt	3 g	.1 oz
Dill Ciabatta Buns (page 113)	20	20
Arugula	1 kg	2 lb 3.2 oz
Extra-virgin olive oil	140 g	4.94 oz
Fleur de sel	40 g	1.41 oz
Scottish smoked salmon (or other high-quality smoked salmon), thinly sliced	2 kg	4 lb 6.4 oz
Pickled Ramps (page 338)	100	100

1. **FOR THE VIDALIA ONION MAYONNAISE:** Combine all of the ingredients in a Robot Coupe and process to obtain a homogeneous mix. Adjust the seasoning. Reserve in the refrigerator. The mayonnaise will hold for up to 2 days in the refrigerator.

2. **TO PICK UP:** Cut a ciabatta bun in half. Spread 30 g/1.05 oz of Vidalia onion mayonnaise on the bottom bun half.

3. Toss 50 g/1.76 oz of arugula in a bowl with 7 g/.24 oz of extra-virgin olive oil and 2 g/.07 oz of fleur de sel. Place the dressed arugula on top of the mayonnaise and fluff the arugula for height.

4. Layer 200 g/7.05 oz of smoked salmon on top of the arugula. Do not put it on flat; try to give it some height by folding it onto itself or slightly curling it.

5. Place 5 pickled ramps evenly spaced on top of the salmon. Serve.

PROSCIUTTO AND RONNYBROOK BUTTER ON BAGUETTE

yield: 20 portions

INGREDIENT	METRIC	U.S.
Baguettes (page 109)	10	10
Ronnybrook butter, soft	600 g	1 lb 5.12 oz
Prosciutto, thinly sliced	1 kg	2 lb 3.2 oz

1. Cut the ends off of a baguette and cut the baguette vertically in half. Each half will be used for 1 portion. Cut one of the halves horizontally in half.

2. Spread 30 g/1.05 oz of butter on the bottom half of the baguette.

3. Lay 50 g/1.76 oz of the prosciutto slices on top of the butter. Put the top half of baguette on the prosciutto. Cut in half and serve.

SMOKED TROUT WITH CUCUMBER AND YOGURT WITH DILL AND CHIVES ON COUNTRY BREAD

yield: 20 portions

INGREDIENT	METRIC	U.S.
Plain whole-milk yogurt	600 g	1 lb 5.12 oz
Dill, finely chopped	15 g	.53 oz
Chives, finely chopped	20 g	.71 oz
Salt	3 g	.11 oz
Country Bread Bâtard (page 114), cut to 1-cm-thick slices	40 slices	40 slices
English cucumber, peeled and thinly sliced	600 g	1 lb 5.12 oz
Smoked trout, broken by hand into small pieces	1 kg	2 lb 3.2 oz

1. Combine the yogurt with the dill, chives, and salt in a bowl. Stir to incorporate. Reserve in an airtight container in the refrigerator. The yogurt mixture will hold in the refrigerator for up to 2 days.

2. **TO PICK UP:** Spread about 30 g/1.05 oz of yogurt on a slice of bread.

3. Shingle 7 slices (about 30 g/1.05 oz) of cucumber on top of the yogurt. Place 100 g/3.53 oz of smoked trout on top of the cucumber.

4. Place another slice of bread on top of the trout, and serve.

COACH FARMS TRIPLE-CREAM GOAT CHEESE WITH FIGS, WALNUTS, AND SORREL ON SLICED BRETON

yield: 20 portions

INGREDIENT	METRIC	U.S.
Port	250 g	8.82 oz
Sugar	500 g	1 lb .16 oz
Black mission figs (about 40)	1 kg	2 lb 3.2 oz
Breton Miche (page 115), cut into 1-cm/.4-in slices (will need 2 miches for this)	40 slices	40 slices
Coach Farms triple-cream goat's milk cheese, tempered	3 kg	6 lb 9.76 oz
Sorrel	100 g	3.53 oz
Aged balsamic vinegar (5 years)	20 g	.7 oz
Extra-virgin olive oil	40 g	1.41 oz
Salt	10 g	.35 oz
Toasted walnuts, coarsely chopped	200 g	7.05 oz

1. In a small sauce pot, combine the port and the sugar. Cook over medium-high heat until the liquid becomes syrupy.

2. In the meantime, trim the stem and the base of the figs and cut an "X" at the top and at the bottom. Put the figs in a single layer in a half hotel pan.

3. Once the liquid is ready, pour it over the figs to coat them. Cover the hotel pan tightly with plastic wrap and let them cool to room temperature.

4. Once they have cooled, leave them at room temperature during service. The figs will keep for 12 hours at room temperature or up to 3 days in the refrigerator.

5. **TO PICK UP:** Cut 2 figs into quarters and lay them over a slice of bread.

6. With a sharp, warm knife, cut 150 g/5.29 oz of the cheese into thin slices and place them over the figs. This cheese has a soft, edible rind that should be kept on. It is meant to be eaten.

7. In a small bowl, toss 5 g/.17 oz of sorrel leaves with a quick drizzle of balsamic vinegar and olive oil and a pinch of salt. Place the sorrel on top of the cheese.

8. Sprinkle 10 g/.35 oz of toasted walnuts over the sorrel. Cover the sandwich with another slice of bread and serve.

note To temper the goat cheese, remove it from the refrigerator during service.

ROAST BEEF WITH CABRALES CHEESE, HORSERADISH CREAM, AND CARAMELIZED ONIONS ON FRANCESE

yield: 20 portions

INGREDIENT	METRIC	U.S.
ROAST BEEF		
Aged sirloin beef, bone-in	4 kg	8 lb 13.12 oz
Canola oil	100 g	3.53 oz
Salt	50 g	1.76 oz
Freshly ground black pepper	5 g	.18 oz
HORSERADISH SPREAD		
Grated horseradish	100 g	3.53 oz
Crème fraîche	500 g	1 lb 1.6 oz
Mayonnaise	500 g	1 lb 1.6 oz
Caramelized Onions (page 331)	2.5 kg	5 lb 8.2 oz
Francese (page 117), cut into 1.25-cm-/.5-in-thick slices	40 slices	40 slices
Cabrales	1.6 kg	3 lb 8.48 oz

1. **FOR THE ROAST BEEF:** Set a static oven to 90°C/200°F.

2. In a large sauté pan, heat the canola oil over high heat.

3. Rub the beef with the salt and pepper. When the oil starts to shimmer, place the meat in the pan and brown it on all sides. Once it is browned, transfer the pan to the oven. Cook the meat until it reaches an internal temperature of 60°C/140°F for medium doneness, 50°C/125°F for rare, and 70°C/160°F for well-done. This might take between 2 and 3 hours, depending on the oven.

4. Let the beef cool to room temperature, and then place it in the refrigerator, covered with plastic wrap. It will keep for up to 2 days in the refrigerator. Once chilled, slice as thinly as possible on a slicer. Cover with plastic wrap and refrigerate.

5. **FOR THE HORSERADISH SPREAD:** Combine all of the ingredients in a bowl. Add more horseradish as desired.

6. **TO PICK UP:** Spoon 125 g/4.41 oz of caramelized onions on a slice of the Francese. Spread it evenly over the bread.

7. Place 200 g/7.05 oz of the roast beef on top of the onions.

8. Spoon 55 g/1.94 oz of horseradish spread on top of the roast beef.

9. Cut about 80 g/2.82 oz of thin slices of Cabrales with a sharp knife and place them on top of the horseradish spread. Always cut this cheese to order.

10. Top with a slice of Francese on top of the cheese and serve.

BACON, LETTUCE, TOMATO, AND AVOCADO ON COUNTRY BREAD

yield: **20 portions**

INGREDIENT	METRIC	U.S.
Niman Ranch uncured applewood smoked bacon, sliced 3 mm/.12 in thick	4 kg	8 lb 13.52 oz
Country Bread (page 114), cut into 2.5-cm-/1-in-thick slices (4 to 5 bâtard loaves)	40 slices	40 slices
Mayonnaise	900 g	1 lb 15.68 oz
Iceberg lettuce, separated into whole leaves	600 g	1 lb 5.12 oz
Avocado, sliced to order	1.5 kg	3 lb 4.96 oz
Ripe tomatoes, thinly sliced	2 kg	4 lb 6.56 oz
Sea salt	20 g	.64 oz
Freshly ground black pepper	10 g	.32 oz

1. Preheat a convection oven to 160°C/320°F.

2. Lay the sliced bacon on a sheet pan lined with parchment paper. Bake in the oven until crisp, 12 to 15 minutes. It is crucial that the bacon be crisp.

3. Cool the bacon to room temperature. Discard after service.

4. **TO PICK UP:** Spread a slice of bread with 45 g/1.6 oz of mayonnaise.

5. Place 2 to 3 leaves of iceberg lettuce on top of the mayonnaise. It is important to use iceberg lettuce because, although it may not have any nutritional value, it is the crispest of all lettuces.

6. Lay 75 g/2.64 oz of sliced avocado onto the lettuce. Always cut or portion avocado to order.

7. Place 200 g/7.05 oz of bacon, or more if desired, on top of the avocado.

8. Place 5 slices of tomato on top of the bacon. Sprinkle a pinch of sea salt and some black pepper on top of the tomato. Put a slice of bread on top of the tomato, and serve.

note Uncured bacon is used in this sandwich because it gives all of the flavor needed from bacon minus the salt.

BRAISED PORK SHOULDER WITH PICKLED ONIONS AND JALAPEÑOS, BIBB LETTUCE, AND CHIPOTLE MAYONNAISE ON BRIOCHE BUN

yield: **20 portions**

INGREDIENT	METRIC	U.S.
Brioche Dough (page 10)	2.84 kg	6 lb 4.16 oz
BRAISED PORK SHOULDER		
Pork shoulder	4 kg	8 lb 13.12 oz
Chicken stock, or as needed	6 kg	13 lb 3.68 oz
Salt	100 g	3.53 oz
Chipotle peppers in adobo sauce	150 g	5.29 oz
PICKLED ONIONS		
Water	300 g	10.58 oz
Red wine vinegar	600 g	1 lb 5.12 oz
Salt	30 g	1.07 oz
Sugar	30 g	1.07 oz
Black peppercorns	6	6
Thyme sprigs	7	7
Jalapeños, stemmed, seeded, and thinly sliced	150 g	5.28 oz
Red onions, thinly sliced (about 1½)	600 g	1 lb 5.12 oz
CHIPOTLE MAYONNAISE		
Mayonnaise	750 g	1 lb 10.4 oz
Chipotle peppers in adobo sauce	150 g	5.28 oz
Bibb lettuce	600 g	1 lb 5.12 oz

1. **FOR THE BRIOCHE BUNS:** See the brioche recipe on page 10. Portion out 142-g/5-oz pieces and shape into rounds. Score the top with a sharp lamé. Follow the proofing and baking instructions for brioche on page 15.

2. **FOR THE PORK SHOULDER:** Combine the pork shoulder with the chicken stock, salt, and the chipotle peppers in a pot. The shoulder should be completely submerged in the stock.

3. Bring the stock to a boil, and then reduce the heat to a simmer. Cook until the pork is fork-tender, 3 to 4 hours.

4. Remove the pork from the chicken stock. Shred the pork with a fork into bite-size morsels and place into a hotel pan. Keep the pulled pork in an Alto-Shaam set to 60°C/140°F during service. Discard any left over after service.

5. **FOR THE PICKLED ONIONS:** Bring the water, vinegar, salt, sugar, peppercorns, thyme sprigs, and jalapeños to a boil in a pot.

6. Add the onions and reduce the heat to a simmer. Cook the onions and jalapeños until wilted, about 5 minutes.

7. Cool over an ice bath. Reserve in the refrigerator. The onions will hold for up to 5 days in the refrigerator.

8. **FOR THE CHIPOTLE MAYONNAISE:** Combine the mayonnaise and the chipotle peppers in a blender cup. Purée until thoroughly combined. Transfer to an airtight container and reserve in the refrigerator. The mayonnaise will hold for up to 1 week.

9. **TO PICK UP:** Cut the brioche bun open. Spread 45 g/1.6 oz of mayonnaise over the bottom piece of bread.

10. Place 2 to 3 leaves of Bibb lettuce on top of the mayonnaise.

11. Place 200 g/7.05 oz of pork shoulder on top of the lettuce and 60 g/2.11 oz of pickled onions and jalapeños on top of the pork. Cover with the top piece of brioche and serve.

SERRANO HAM WITH FRIED EGG AND BUTTER ON BAGUETTE

yield: 20 portions

INGREDIENT	METRIC	U.S.
Baguettes (page 109)	10	10
Butter, soft	1.8 kg	3 lb 15.52 oz
Serrano ham, thinly sliced	2 kg	4 lb 6.4 oz
Eggs	40	40

1. Cut the ends off of a baguette, and then cut it in half. Cut one half of the baguette horizontally. Spread 45 g/1.6 oz of butter on the bottom slice of baguette.

2. Place 100 g/3.53 oz of Serrano ham on top of the butter.

3. Heat 45 g/1.59 oz butter in a small sauté pan over high heat.

4. Crack 2 eggs into a ramekin and gently pour them into the pan when the butter starts to bubble. Turn the heat down to medium-low.

5. Cook for about 2 minutes or until the whites are completely cooked but the yolks are still runny. Use a nonstick pan if needed.

6. Put both eggs on top of the Serrano ham, place the top piece of baguette on the eggs, and serve.

note I had this particular sandwich once in Spain, but instead of Serrano ham it had jamón de Jabugo, which is the best cured ham, in my opinion. It is also prohibitively expensive.

DEEP-FRIED BATTERED SKATE WITH SAUCE RÉMOULADE ON BRIOCHE BUN

yield: **20 portions**

INGREDIENT	METRIC	U.S.
BRIOCHE HOT DOG BUNS		
Brioche Dough (page 10)	3 kg	6 lb 9.76 oz
Egg Wash for Brushing (page 13)	as needed	as needed
Sesame seeds	40 g	1.41 oz
Sauce Rémoulade (page 373)	900 g	1 lb 15.75 oz
Butter	600 g	1 lb 5.16 oz
Skate wing, cut into 2.5-cm-/-1-in-wide strips	4 kg	8 lb 13.12 oz
Beer Batter (page 335)	2 kg	4 lb 6.4 oz

1. The brioche hot dog buns are made with the brioche recipe on page 10. Divide the dough into 50-g/1.76-oz pieces. Roll each piece into 30-cm-/12-in-long strands. Make a braid with 3 strands, pinching the ends and tucking them in under the braid. Brush the top with egg wash. Follow the proofing and baking instructions for brioche on page 15. Sprinkle 2 g/.07 oz of sesame seeds on each braid just before baking.

2. To pick up: Heat a fryer to 190°C/375°F.

3. Portion 30 g/1.05 oz of sauce rémoulade into a ramekin or jar and set aside. The sauce can be pre-portioned before service; keep well covered with plastic to prevent a skin from forming on the top if it is in ramekins. Reserve refrigerated.

4. Cut a hot dog bun in half and spread about 15 g/.52 oz of butter on each half. Toast butter side up in a salamander until it turns a light brown.

5. Meanwhile, dip 200 g/7.05 oz skate wing pieces in the beer batter. Spoon them out with a slotted spoon and fry them until they are amber brown and crisp, about 2 minutes. Remove them from the fryer and place them on a clean, heavy-duty paper towel or kitchen towel to absorb excess oil.

6. Place the fried fish inside the toasted brioche bun. Serve with the sauce rémoulade on the side.

notes If desired, season the fish with additional salt and pepper, but the beer batter should provide sufficient flavor.

Always use a separate fryer for frying fish. The oil absorbs the flavor of fish and then permeates other foods fried in it. Thus French fries cooked in the fish fryer will taste like fish.

The sauce is served in a ramekin so that the customer can put it on the fish him/herself; if it is put on the hot fried fish, it will break the emulsion by the time it gets to the customer, and it will be very unsightly.

Malt vinegar is traditionally served with fried foods in Great Britain, especially fish and chips.

This sandwich would go well with a side salad of plain mixed greens and vinaigrette.

SAUCE RÉMOULADE

yield: 1.18 kg/2 lb 9.62 oz

INGREDIENT	METRIC	U.S.
Mayonnaise	750 g	1 lb 10.4 oz
Crème fraîche	250 g	8.82 oz
Capers, finely chopped	60 g	2.12 oz
Gherkins, finely chopped	60 g	2.12 oz
Chives, finely chopped	8 g	.28 oz
Chervil, finely chopped	8 g	.28 oz
Tarragon, finely chopped	4 g	.14 oz
Dijon mustard	15 g	.53 oz
Apple cider vinegar	18 g	.63 oz
Anchovy paste	5 g	.18 oz
Salt	3 g	.11 oz
Freshly ground black pepper	1 g	.04 oz

1. Combine all of the ingredients in a bowl.

2. Adjust seasoning with salt and pepper. Reserve refrigerated in an airtight container. The sauce will keep for up to 2 days in the refrigerator before the fresh herbs start to discolor.

GRILLED FLANK STEAK WITH TOMATO, ICEBERG LETTUCE, AND CHIMICHURRI ON GRILLED CIABATTA

yield: 20 portions

INGREDIENT	METRIC	U.S.
FLANK STEAK		
Flank steak	4 kg	8 lb 13.12 oz
Salt	12 g	.42 oz
Freshly ground black pepper	3 g	.11 oz
CHIMICHURRI SAUCE		
Parsley leaves, medium-finely chopped	75 g	2.65 oz
Cilantro leaves, medium-finely chopped	75 g	2.65 oz
Capers, finely chopped	30 g	1.07 oz
Garlic cloves, finely chopped	10 g	0.35 oz
Red wine vinegar	30 g	1.07 oz
Salt	15 g	.53 oz
Red pepper flakes	10 g	.35 oz
Freshly ground black pepper	2 g	.07 oz
Extra-virgin olive oil	130 g	4.59 oz
Ciabatta Buns (page 112)	20	20
Iceberg lettuce	400 g	14.11 oz
Beefsteak tomatoes, ripe, sliced 1.25 cm/.5 in thick	1.2 kg	2 lb 10.4 oz
Maldon sea salt	20 g	.7 oz
Freshly ground black pepper	2 g	.07 oz

1. **FOR THE FLANK STEAK:** Heat the grill to high.

2. Season the flank steak on both sides with salt and pepper. Grill for about 8 minutes per side for medium/medium-rare. Turn the meat only once.

3. Once the meat is grilled, let it rest for 10 minutes off the grill. Transfer it to a hotel pan and hold in an Alto-Shaam at 60°C/140°F during service. Discard after 12 hours.

4. **FOR THE CHIMICHURRI:** Place all of the ingredients in a bowl and stir to combine. Adjust the seasoning if needed. The sauce will keep for up to 3 days in the refrigerator.

5. **TO PICK UP:** Cut the ciabatta bun in half lengthwise. Place 2 to 3 iceberg lettuce leaves on the bottom piece of bread.

6. Remove the flank steak from the Alto-Shaam and cut off a 200-g/7.05-oz piece.

7. Slice the meat into 5 or 6 thin slices, cutting against the grain. Place the meat on top of the lettuce.

8. Spoon 30 g/1.05 oz of chimichurri on top of the meat. Put 3 slices of tomato on top of the meat.

9. Season with 1 g/.03 oz of Maldon sea salt and black pepper. Place the top slice of ciabatta on top of the tomatoes, and serve.

All of the sandwiches that follow are pressed in a sandwich press except for the Monte Cristo, which is fried.

SALTED CARAMEL WITH BANANAS AND CHOCOLATE ON BRIOCHE

yield: **20 portions**

INGREDIENT	METRIC	U.S.
Pullman Loaf (page 37)	3	3
Clarified butter, melted	600 g	1 lb 5.16 oz
Bananas, small	20	20
Salted Caramel (page 262)	1 kg	2 lb 3.2 oz
Chocolate batons	1 kg	2 lb 3.2 oz

1. Freeze the Pullman loaves for about 30 minutes or until they are semi-frozen. Cut the Pullman loaves in half widthwise, and trim the crusts off.

2. Cut each loaf into 1-cm-/.4-in-thick slices with a serrated knife. Each loaf should yield 16 slices per loaf, or 8 portions.

3. Brush 15 g/.52 oz of clarified butter on 2 slices of brioche. The side that has been brushed is the side that will be in direct contact with the press, so once the clarified butter has been brushed on, flip the slices over.

4. Trim the ends off of a small banana and cut it into 3 evenly thick slices lengthwise. Place the slices on the bread.

5. Spoon 50 g/1.76 oz of caramel on top of the bananas. Put about 50 g/1.76 oz of batons on top of the caramel per sandwich, making sure they are evenly lined up.

6. Close the sandwich with the second slice of brioche and put it on a hot sandwich press. Press it for a few minutes until there are visible press marks, then turn the sandwich 45 degrees and continue to press until another set of visible press marks is achieved. The pressing time depends on the model of press used. It does go quickly with brioche though, so be very attentive.

7. Once the sandwich is done, remove it from the press and cut it on the diagonal to obtain 2 triangles. Put one piece on a plate, and then the other piece on top. Serve.

notes This sandwich falls into many categories. It can really be eaten at any time (breakfast, lunch, or dinner), as a sandwich or even as dessert.

The chocolate batons are the same ones used for the pain au chocolat on page 47 (see note), because they have a higher resistance to heat.

MONTE CRISTO: CYPRESS GROVE TRUFFLE TREMOR CHEESE AND JAMBON DE BAYONNE

yield: 20 portions

INGREDIENT	METRIC	U.S.
Jambon de Bayonne	2 kg	4 lb 6.4 oz
Cypress Grove Truffle Tremor cheese	2 kg	4 lb 6.4 oz
White sandwich bread, unsliced	4 loaves	4 loaves
Eggs	1.5 kg	3 lb 4.96 oz
Milk	1.25 kg	2 lb 12.16 oz
Salt	10 g	.35 oz

1. Line the inside of a sheet pan with plastic wrap.

2. Slice the jambon de Bayonne as thinly as possible, and then lay half of the slices (1 kg/ 2 lb 3.2 oz) shingled in a single layer on top of the plastic wrap.

3. Cut the cheese into very thin slices. It is important that the cheese be chilled so that it can be easily cut. Place the cheese slices on top of the sliced ham in a single layer (do not shingle).

4. Cover the cheese with the remaining sliced ham. Place a sheet of plastic wrap on top of the ham and a flat sheet pan on top of the plastic. Weigh it down with a heavy cutting board. Refrigerate the setup overnight.

5. The next day, cut 6.25-cm/2.5-in squares out of the layered cheese and ham, using a very sharp knife.

6. Cut the bread into twenty 5.5-cm-/2.2-in-thick slices, using a boning knife cut a slit down the middle of the side of each slice. The pocket should be 7 cm/2.8 in wide. Insert a cheese-and-ham square into this slit. The assembled sandwiches can be held in the refrigerator for up to 2 days.

7. Combine the eggs, milk, and salt in a bowl. Stir with a whisk until evenly mixed, and then pass through a fine-mesh sieve. Reserve in a hotel pan in the refrigerator during service. Otherwise, reserve in an airtight container in the refrigerator. Discard after 3 days.

8. **TO PICK UP:** Heat a fryer to 190°C/375°F.

9. If necessary, place the custard in a hotel pan or other container in which the assembled sandwich can be completely submerged.

10. Dip a sandwich in the custard for 4 seconds. Let the excess drip off the sandwich, and place it in a hotel pan. Repeat with the other sandwiches. Place this hotel pan in an Alto-Shaam set to 60°C/140°F for at least 1 hour before service. This ensures that the sandwich will be warm throughout. A sandwich this thick takes a long time to get fully hot in the fryer.

11. **TO FINISH PICK-UP:** Carefully drop a sandwich into the hot oil. Fry until golden brown, flipping the sandwich over to obtain even browning. Remove the sandwich from the fryer and place it on a clean, heavy-duty paper towel or kitchen towel to absorb excess oil. Serve immediately.

notes Cypress Grove Truffle Tremor cheese is a bloomy cheese with an edible rind, truffle pieces, and a soft interior made from goat's milk. It is made in Humboldt County, California (see Resources, page 540).

Jambon de Bayonne is the French equivalent of prosciutto; it is subtler, less salty, and easier to bite into.

SAINT MARCELLIN WITH TOASTED SICILIAN PISTACHIOS AND BING CHERRY COMPOTE ON BAGUETTE

yield: **20 portions**

INGREDIENT	METRIC	U.S.
BING CHERRY COMPOTE		
Bing cherries, pitted	1.5 kg	3 lb 4.96 oz
Sugar	750 g	1 lb 10.4 oz
Water	750 g	1 lb 10.4 oz
Cinnamon sticks	7	7
Vanilla pods, split and scraped	3	3
Baguettes (page 109)	10	10
Clarified butter, melted	600 g	1 lb 5.12 oz
Sicilian pistachios, toasted (see page 19)	1 kg	2 lb 3.2 oz
Saint Marcellin cheese	20 wheels	20 wheels

1. **FOR THE CHERRY COMPOTE:** Combine the cherries, sugar, water, cinnamon, and vanilla pods and beans in a sauce pot. Bring to a quick boil over high heat, and then turn the heat down to simmer the cherries. Cook until the cherries are tender, about 20 minutes.

2. Remove the pot from the heat and transfer the cherries and liquid to a hotel pan to cool to room temperature. Remove the vanilla pods.

3. Once they have cooled, strain the cherries from the cooking liquid, transfer them to an airtight container, and refrigerate. They will keep for up to 5 days in the refrigerator. Reserve the liquid to cook the next batch of cherries. The flavor will intensify each time.

4. **TO PICK UP:** Preheat a convection oven to 160°C/320°F. Cut the ends off of a baguette, and then cut the baguette in half. Cut one half in half lengthwise. Trim the top crust off.

5. Spread 15 g/.52 oz of clarified butter on each half. Flip the bread over, and spoon 75 g/2.64 oz of cherries on the bottom half of the baguette.

6. Close the sandwich with the top piece of baguette, crumb side out. Place the sandwich on a hot sandwich press.

7. Meanwhile, place 50 g/1.76 oz of toasted Sicilian pistachios over the surface of a Saint Marcellin wheel and warm up in a 160°C/320°F oven while the sandwich gets pressed. Do not melt the cheese all the way; merely soften it.

8. Once the sandwich is toasted, put it on a plate with the warmed Saint Marcellin. Place the Saint Marcellin on a paper doily or serviette to keep it in place, and serve.

notes Saint Marcellin is a bloomy cow's milk cheese from the French Alps with a soft ring outside and a creamy soft interior, and it is just stinky enough. It comes in a small clay ramekin, which makes it ideal for warming it in an oven. It is also small enough that it can be for one person alone.

For extreme funk, try this sandwich with a real Alsatian Muenster cheese. This cheese, however, is not for the meek. It really, really stinks.

To eat this sandwich, either dip the sandwich in the warmed cheese or spoon the warmed cheese onto the sandwich before each bite.

MAHON GRILLED CHEESE WITH PADRÓN PEPPERS AND AÏOLI ON SOURDOUGH BREAD

yield: 20 portions

INGREDIENT	METRIC	U.S.
AÏOLI		
Garlic	10 g	.35 oz
Salt	4 g	.14 oz
Pasteurized egg yolks	170 g	6 oz
Red wine vinegar	7 g	.25 oz
Lemon juice	10 g	.35 oz
Lemon zest	2 g	.07 oz
Canola oil	720 g	1 lb 9.44 oz
Extra-virgin olive oil	240 g	8.47 oz
PADRÓN PEPPERS		
Extra-virgin olive oil	150 g	5.29 oz
Padrón peppers, stemmed	1.5 kg	3 lb 4.96 oz
Sea salt	12 g	.42 oz
Sourdough Bâtards (page 121), cut into 1-cm/.4-in slices (4 to 5 bâtards)	40 pc	40 pc
Mahon, rind cut off, thinly sliced	2 kg	4 lb 6.4 oz

1. **FOR THE AÏOLI:** Chop the garlic very finely on a cutting board with a pinch of salt. Make a paste with your knife, using the side of the blade against the cutting board. Alternatively, use a garlic press.

2. Anchor down a bowl with a damp cloth towel. Place the egg yolks, garlic, vinegar, lemon juice, lemon zest, and salt in it. Whisk until evenly mixed.

3. Combine both oils, and slowly pour them into the bowl while whisking vigorously to create an emulsion.

4. Reserve in an airtight container with plastic placed directly on the surface of the aïoli. The aïoli will hold for up to 3 days in the refrigerator.

5. **FOR THE PADRÓN PEPPERS:** Pour the extra-virgin olive oil into a large sauté pan over high heat. When the oil starts to shimmer, add the peppers and quickly sauté until their skin is blistered, 30 to 45 seconds.

6. Remove the sauté pan from the heat and spoon the peppers out of the pan with a slotted spoon onto a clean, heavy-duty paper towel or kitchen towel. Sprinkle with sea salt. Reserve the peppers at room temperature during service. Discard any leftover cooked peppers after service.

7. **TO PICK UP:** Brush 2 slices of sourdough with 50 g/1.76 oz aïoli on one side only. These will be the sides that come in direct contact with the sandwich press, so flip them over after spreading them with aïoli.

8. Place 75 g/2.64 oz of Padrón peppers on the bottom slice of bread. Place 100 g/3.53 oz of Mahon on top of the peppers. Cover with the remaining slice of bread.

9. Press on a hot sandwich press until the bread is toasted and the cheese is melted, about 5 minutes. Cut the sandwich in half on the diagonal and serve.

notes Mahon cheese is a Spanish cheese made from raw cow's milk; it melts very well, almost like mozzarella (see Resources, page 540).

Padrón peppers are small green peppers that are mostly harmless. They are mostly harmless because, on average, one in ten or twelve peppers is hot. It's like chile pepper roulette. You never know when you'll get one.

This sandwich uses aïoli brushed on the bread as the fat that will crisp the bread in the press. It will also add a good amount of flavor. The only downside to using aïoli is that it will really make a mess on the press, so it will need to be cleaned frequently.

TILLAMOOK GRILLED CHEESE WITH MAPLE BACON, TRUFFLE BÉCHAMEL, AND AÏOLI ON COUNTRY BREAD

yield: 20 portions

INGREDIENT	METRIC	U.S.
Aïoli (page 380)	800 g	1 lb 12.16 oz
Country Bread (page 114), cut into 1-cm/.4-in slices (about 2 miches)	40	40
Truffle Béchamel (page 302)	1.2 kg	2 lb 10.4 oz
Maple Bacon (page 335)	1.65 kg	3 lb 10.2 oz
Tillamook Cheddar, thinly sliced	3 kg	6 lb 9.46 oz

1. Spread 20 g/.7 oz of aïoli on each slice of bread. These will be the sides that are in direct contact with the press, so flip the slices of bread over after spreading them with aïoli.

2. Spread 60 g/2.11 oz of truffle béchamel over the bottom slice of bread. Place 75 g/2.64 oz of maple bacon on top of the béchamel.

3. Place 150 g/5.29 oz of sliced cheddar on top of the bacon. Put the top slice of bread on top of the cheese, with the aïoli side facing out.

4. Press the sandwich on a hot sandwich press until the bread is toasted and crisp and the cheese is melted. Cut the sandwich in half on the diagonal and serve.

note Tillamook Cheddar is a cheese made in Oregon. You can substitute any other kind of quality Cheddar. This is a grilled cheese all grown up.

entrées

Entrées are items that come very close to blurring the line between a restaurant and a café. It is important to offer entrée portions in a café because your customers will expect it. You can't eat salads or sandwiches every day, and you can't really serve them for dinner. Entrées will be more popular toward the evening hours because people don't usually have sandwiches for dinner.

There aren't rules written in stone about what constitutes an entrée. It should theoretically be a larger portion size than what you would typically serve as an appetizer, as a whole, not necessarily a single component. For example, the pork component in the crisp pork belly and wilted vegetable salad on page 320 will weigh the same as the pork belly entrée in this section (350 g/12.35 oz), because any more than that is just too much. Some might say that there is no such thing as too much pork, but with something so rich, you really shouldn't overdo it when it comes to the size of the portion. That said, when it comes to entrées, the secondary components can increase in size. However, you shouldn't serve entrées that weigh more than 600 g/1 lb 5.12 oz, because such a large portion of food can be overwhelming to the average person.

As far as actual components of an entrée, a classical view of entrées is to always include a protein, a starch, a sauce, and two vegetables. However, that doesn't mean you can't or shouldn't be able to change that. These recipes will usually do without a sauce in the strict sense of the word. For example, the dressing for the frisée in the pork belly acts as a sauce, the poblano butter for the hanger steak fulfills the functions of a sauce, and the same goes for the runny egg yolk from the fried egg. A sauce can be many things.

When deciding upon a menu, you will probably be cooking what you know how to cook and what you like to cook. But within those items, offer a variety of products. Think of the different proteins that are available. Beef, chicken, and fish are the obvious choices, but don't forget about vegetarian or meatless options. The most important factor to consider is how fast you will be able to plate this food. Café cuisine is mostly about how far ahead you can take your mise en place to have a quick, efficient pickup.

the immersion thermocirculator

ONE OF THE DOWNSIDES OF MOST COOKING METHODS is that whatever is being cooked suffers a certain amount of moisture loss during the cooking process. This occurs because water evaporates at 100°C/212°F, and, since most cooking occurs well above these temperatures, there will be a corresponding percentage of moisture loss. Moisture retention is the first and foremost benefit gained from cooking food inside a Cryovac with a thermocirculator; a close second benefit is that the temperature is constant. I would recommend reading *Sous-Vide Cuisine* by Joan Roca and Salvador Brugués for in-depth information, but this is a brief description of how the machine works.

An immersion thermocirculator is a piece of equipment that has an electronic adjustable temperature setting, a water circulator and a heating element that are both submerged in water. There are models that are comprised of just the heating element and the circulator, with the electronic component perched on a plastic or metal bath. The size of the bath depends on the capacity of the thermocirculator; there are other models that come attached to a bath. In any of the machines, the key is that the heating element, along with the water circulator, will keep the water at a constant temperature throughout the entire bath.

Cryovac foods are not the only way to cook in the thermocirculator. You could introduce food directly into the water, or use stock or even extra-virgin olive oil in the bath. However, tightly sealing the food in an anaerobic environment such as the Cryovac is truly the best way to lock in the moisture and flavor. Additionally, cleaning the circulator after it has been circulating oil is no easy task.

While the temperature is effectively controlled, the time the product spends in the water depends on the person doing the cooking. It is also important to shock the cooked item in an ice bath as soon as it is finished cooking to stop the cooking process completely. In order to determine cooking time and temperature, you will need to perform a few trials and risk wasting food, which is necessary in order to obtain a product with which you are satisfied. One effective method is to take the actual internal temperature of the item that is being cooked. This applies to animal proteins mostly, not necessarily to vegetables or fruit. In order to do this, you need a thermocoupler thermometer (see Resources, page 540), which has a needle-thin probe that can easily puncture the bag. Apply a small piece of special Cryovac tape to the surface of the bag before doing so (see Resources, page 540) to ensure that the seal will not be compromised. Once you have determined the time it takes to cook the protein to your liking, it should always be the same as long as your thermocirculator is working properly, and you won't have to take the internal temperature each time.

Given a choice, it is preferable to cook with a thermocirculator rather than with an Alto-Shaam or combi oven, since the food is truly better protected and encased, and it is a surefire way to infuse flavors and get the best textures from the food. Some items that are cooked in this way will need to be cooked a second time. For example, the hanger steak on page 392 is cooked in a Cryovac first to an internal temperature of 60°C/140°F, then shocked in an ice bath and refrigerated. The steaks are tempered for at least 30 minutes before being finished on the grill for a few minutes to char the outside. Cooking it this way will result in a much faster pickup than if the meat is cooked solely on the grill. It also protects against the loss of volume from evaporation in the meat during the cooking process.

BERKSHIRE PORK BELLY WITH POTATO TERRINE, FRISÉE, AND BALSAMIC CARAMEL

yield: 20 portions

INGREDIENT	METRIC	U.S.
Berkshire pork belly	6 kg	13 lb 3.68 oz
Garlic	300 g	10.58 oz
Shallots	200 g	7.05 oz
Salt	20 g	.71 oz
Thyme sprigs	60	60
Brown sugar	200 g	7.05 oz
Freshly ground black pepper	10 g	.35 oz
Chicken stock	3 kg	6 lb 9.76 oz
POTATO TERRINE		
Capers	800 g	1 lb 12.16 oz
Parsley leaves	75 g	2.64 oz
Yukon gold potatoes	3.6 kg	7 lb 15.04 oz
Freshly ground black pepper	4 g	.14 oz
BALSAMIC CARAMEL		
Balsamic vinegar	400 g	14.11 oz
Sugar	100 g	3.53 oz
Frisée lettuce	300 g	10.58 oz
Extra-virgin olive oil	300 g	10.58 oz
Salt	5 g	.18 oz
Freshly ground black pepper	1 g	.04 oz

1. **FOR THE PORK BELLY:** Trim the skin from the belly. Remove all but a .5-cm/.2-in layer of fat from the belly. Score the fat in a diamond grid, cutting all the way through just to the flesh but without cutting into the flesh. The diamonds should measure 1 cm/.4 in.

2. Smash the garlic coarsely and chop the shallots coarsely. In a roasting pan that will fit the belly completely, sprinkle the area where the belly will be placed with half of the salt. Spread one-third of the garlic, shallots, and thyme over the salt.

3. Place the belly in the pan, fat side up. Sprinkle the remaining salt, the brown sugar, and the black pepper evenly over the entire surface and rub it into the scoring in the fat. Cover the belly with the rest of the garlic, shallots, and thyme, making sure to press them into the fat.

4. Preheat a conventional static oven to 150°C/302°F.

5. Pour the chicken stock into the roasting pan. It should come three-quarters of the way up the belly; all of the stock may not be needed. Wrap the pan in aluminum foil to keep in the steam.

6. Braise the pork belly for 3 to 4 hours, or until the meat is meltingly tender and most of the fat has rendered away. Check the pan at the 2-hour mark to make sure there is enough stock in the pan. If not, pour in more stock.

7. Cool the belly in the pan. Place a pan filled with ice underneath the roasting pan, and place this setup in a reach-in or walk-in refrigerator. Do not discard the braising liquid; the pork will be stored in this liquid.

8. Put plastic wrap directly on top of the belly. Place another pan on top of the belly with a weight on top (three #10 cans will work well). This will weigh the belly down and form it into an even piece. Allow it to chill overnight in the refrigerator.

9. Once it is chilled, cut the belly into 200-g/7.05-oz portions that measure about 5 by 9 cm/ 2 by 3.6 in. Trim enough fat from the top so that there is only about 3 mm/.11 in left. The portions can be reserved in the refrigerator at this point for up to 48 hours, in an airtight container.

10. Thirty minutes before service, reheat the pork belly in a 160°C/320°F convection oven. Reserve the pork belly in an Alto-Shaam oven set to 60°C/140°F, covered with plastic. Discard any left over after 12 hours.

11. **FOR THE POTATO TERRINE:** Chop the capers and parsley together until the mixture almost forms a sort of paste.

12. Place the potatoes in enough cold, salted water to cover, and bring to a boil. Boil the potatoes until just cooked. Drain the water. Let the potatoes cool in a hotel pan.

13. Line a loaf pan or terrine mold with plastic wrap, using enough plastic so that there are large flaps of plastic wrap on either side of the mold. As soon as the potatoes cool down to a manageable temperature but are still warm, cut them into 1.75-cm-/.5-in-thick slices. Lay one layer of sliced potatoes at the bottom of the mold and push them down with your hands to fill in any gaps. Put a layer of caper and parsley paste (about 120 g/4.23 oz) down over the potatoes, then sprinkle with black pepper. Repeat this procedure 2 more times. The mold should be filled to over 1 cm/.4 in from the top, so if more layers are needed to achieve this height, add more layers. Cover the last layer of potatoes with the plastic wrap flaps. For 20 portions, a second terrine might need to be built the same way.

14. Place a heavy cutting board on top of the terrine(s) and refrigerate overnight. The next day, remove the potato terrine(s) from the mold(s) and put on a cutting board. Do not take the plastic off. Reserve in the refrigerator for up to 36 hours.

15. **FOR THE BALSAMIC CARAMEL:** Combine the balsamic vinegar with the sugar in a small sauce pot. Bring it to a boil, and then turn the heat down to medium-low. Cook until it has reduced to one-quarter of its original weight. Let it cool to room temperature. Reserve in an airtight container at room temperature. Discard after 2 months.

16. **TO PICK UP:** Place a portion of the pork belly on a sizzle platter with the fat side facing down and place in a 260°C/500°F static oven or impinger oven for 5 minutes to crisp up the outer layer. If necessary, flip it over, fat side up, and heat it for a few more minutes to help crisp up the fat.

17. Meanwhile, cut a 1.25-cm/.5-in slice of the potato terrine with a thin slicing knife. Put the slice on a plate, laying it on its side.

18. Toss 15 g/.52 oz of frisée with 15 g/.52 oz of extra-virgin olive oil, a pinch of salt, and some black pepper. Put the dressed lettuce over the terrine.

19. Once the pork belly is crisp and hot, put it on the plate next to the potato terrine. Drizzle about 5 g/.17 oz of balsamic caramel over the pork belly and around the plate, and serve immediately.

note Make sure to use high-quality canned fillets for the terrine.

table service at the café

THE MOST VALUED CHARACTERISTIC OF SERVICE IN A CAFÉ IS EFFICIENCY. A café is the place where people will go to get excellent food, quickly. It should be attentive and detail oriented, but not to the extent of being overwhelmingly stuffy. Having said that, all of the different areas of the café need to be in sync. If you consider that the majority of the menu (about two-thirds on average) is already made (bread, breakfast pastries, cakes, desserts, ice cream, chocolates, and so forth.), it should be as simple as taking an order, charging it, packaging it, and sending it out. For more involved items, even a cappuccino, the process slows down to some extent. This is why it is so important to understand the true meaning of café food. If you look through the recipes in this chapter, you will see that the mise en place for these items is very advanced, to the point where the pickup should take no more than 5 minutes, even for a grilled hanger steak.

It is very important to have the equipment and know how to be able to work quickly, and it is also important to train your staff to be in the same mindset. However, keep in mind that customers should not feel rushed. There is such a thing as being too efficient. Take the time to give each customer the attention he or she deserves, especially if the customer has chosen to take a seat in your dining room instead of taking food to go. This is an opportunity to engage with customers to an extent and ensure their return.

PASTA NECKERCHIEF "CARBONARA": FRESH PASTA AND FRIED EGG WITH BACON LARDONS

yield: 20 portions

INGREDIENT	METRIC	U.S.
Duck eggs	20	20
Slab bacon, outer rough skin trimmed off and cut into lardons	2 kg	4 lb 6.56 oz
CARBONARA SAUCE		
Parmesan, grated	400 g	14.08 oz
Pecorino Tartufo, grated	400 g	14.08 oz
Butter, soft	375 g	13.23 oz
Heavy cream	375 g	13.23 oz
Crème fraîche	550 g	1 lb 3.36 oz
Duck fat	1.5 kg	3 lb 4.96 oz
Fresh pasta, cut into rectangles 10 by 20 cm/4 by 8 in	7 kg	15 lb 6.91 oz
Parsley leaves, coarsely chopped	40 g	1.44 oz
Maldon sea salt	10 g	.35 oz

1. To cook the eggs, see the procedure for coddled eggs on page 335.

2. To cook the bacon lardons, cut the bacon into pieces 1.25 by 2.5 by 1.25 cm/.5 by 1 by .5 in. Place them in a sauté pan over low heat and render the fat out. Cook until the bacon is crisp.

3. Remove the crisp lardons from the fat with a slotted spoon and pat them dry on a clean, heavy-duty paper towel. Reserve uncovered at room temperature during service. Discard after 12 hours.

4. **FOR THE CARBONARA SAUCE:** Combine both cheeses with the butter, heavy cream, and crème fraîche in a pot. Bring the contents to a boil, and then reduce the heat to low. Keep it covered during service. Discard after 12 hours.

5. **TO PICK UP:** Keep a large pasta pot with salted water ready for service. Place it over high heat and keep it at a boil, replenishing the water as needed during service. This is the pot that will be used to cook the pasta. These pots can usually handle four different orders at a time since they are fitted with four "quarter-circle" baskets that fit together inside the pot.

6. Put the duck fat in a sauce pot over medium-low heat and keep it at 175°C/350°F.

7. Place a sheet of pasta in a basket and cook until al dente. Meanwhile, crack open one of the eggs and carefully fry it in the duck fat until golden brown, turning it occasionally to ensure even browning. Remove the egg from the fryer with a slotted spoon and put the spoon down onto a clean, heavy-duty paper towel to drain off any excess fat.

8. Remove the pasta from the boiling water and drain off the excess water. Put the cooked sheet of pasta into the sauce pot with the carbonara sauce. Toss the pasta with a large fork or prongs until it is evenly coated.

9. Roll the pappardelle up with the prongs and gently put it in a serving bowl. Sprinkle 2 g/.07 oz of parsley over it, then 5 g/.17 oz of crisp lardons, and then put the fried egg on top, with a pinch of Maldon salt over that. Serve immediately.

DUCK CONFIT WITH WARM LENTILS AND PEARL ONIONS

yield: **20 portions**

INGREDIENT	METRIC	U.S.
DUCK CONFIT		
Salt	1 kg	2 lb 3.2 oz
Duck legs, quartered	20	20
Duck fat	5 kg	11 lb .32 oz
Thyme sprigs	7	7
Pearl onions, root ends trimmed and outer layers of skin removed	100	100
LENTILS		
Green Puy lentils	3 kg	6 lb 9.76 oz
Chicken stock	3 kg	6 lb 9.76 oz
Onions, finely diced	600 g	1 lb 5.12 oz
Carrots, finely diced	300 g	10.56 oz
Celery, finely diced	300 g	10.56 oz
Garlic, crushed	20 g	.64 oz
Thyme sprigs	3	3
Slab bacon, diced	200 g	7.05 oz
Salt	35 g	1.23 oz
Chicken stock	2 kg	4 lb 6.4 oz

1. **FOR THE DUCK CONFIT:** Sprinkle 250 g/8.82 oz of salt in an even layer into each of 2 hotel pans.

2. Put 10 duck-leg quarters into each hotel pan and sprinkle 250 g/8.82 oz of salt on top of each hotel pan, covering the duck legs. Cover both hotel pans and refrigerate for 24 hours to cure the duck legs.

3. The next day, rinse the salt off the duck legs and pat them dry.

4. Heat an oven to 120°C/250°F.

5. Melt the duck fat in a rondeau large enough to fit all the duck legs and the duck fat.

6. Put the duck-leg quarters in the melted fat, along with the thyme and the pearl onions. The duck-leg quarters should be completely submerged in the fat.

7. Cover the rondeau with a lid or with foil. Put in the oven and cook the duck legs until the meat is tender and almost falling off the bone, about 3 hours. The fat should never get too hot, or else the duck meat will cook too quickly and become hard instead of tender. If the pearl onions are cooked before the duck legs are, spoon them out of the fat with a slotted spoon when they are just cooked and put them in a hotel pan to cool at room temperature. Reserve them covered at room temperature during service.

8. Once the duck legs are cooked, transfer them to a deep hotel pan, keeping them in the fat. Put the hotel pan in an Alto-Shaam set to 60°C/140°F. If there are any left over after service, they can be used the next day. If the duck is left to cool in the fat in the refrigerator and they are left in the solidified fat in the refrigerator, they can keep for up to 1 month. Duck confit was originally meant to preserve the duck before refrigeration was invented.

9. **FOR THE LENTILS:** Place the lentils in a sauce pot and cover them with water. Bring to a boil, and then strain them.

10. Put them back in the sauce pot with enough chicken stock to cover them. Add the onions, carrots, celery, garlic, thyme, and bacon. Simmer until the lentils are no longer covered with chicken stock, about 40 minutes. Add more chicken stock until they are once again covered.

11. Continue to cook until the lentils are tender. If necessary, continue to add more chicken stock, and season with salt, but be careful when seasoning since the bacon not only contributes flavor, it also adds salt.

12. Once the lentils are cooked, transfer them to a hotel pan and adjust seasoning if needed (stirring the salt in). Let them cool in the refrigerator. Remove the visible pieces of carrots, celery, onions, thyme sprigs, and garlic. Reserve in the refrigerator during service. Discard after 12 hours.

13. **TO PICK UP:** Place a duck-leg quarter on a sizzle platter, skin side up, and put it in a hot salamander, a static oven set to 260°C/500°F, or an impinger oven set to the same temperature. Cook the duck confit for 10 minutes to crisp the skin and heat the meat thoroughly. Some chefs like to crisp the skin up in a sauté pan over a high flame with the skin facing down, but an oven or impinger oven gives you better control over the outcome.

14. While the skin is getting crisp, heat 45 g/1.6 oz of duck fat in a sauté pan over high heat. Add 10 pearl onions and 250 to 300 g/8.82 to 10.58 oz of lentils, plus 30 g/1.05 oz of chicken stock. Cook until all of the components are very hot.

15. Place the lentils and the pearl onions on a plate or, preferably, in a bowl. Lean the crisp duck-leg quarter on the lentils, with the bone pointing up for height. Serve immediately.

GRILLED HANGER STEAK WITH POBLANO BUTTER AND FRENCH FRIES

yield: 20 portions

INGREDIENT	METRIC	U.S.
Hanger steak	7 kg	15 lb 6.88 oz
Salt	45 g	1.59 oz
Freshly ground black pepper	8 g	.28 oz
POBLANO BUTTER		
Salted butter	600 g	1 lb 5.12 oz
Garlic, minced	10 g	.53 oz
Poblano pepper, blistered, skinned, seeded, stemmed, and cut into brunoise	50 g	1.76 oz
French Fries (page 358), **par-cooked** (see Notes)	5 kg	11 lb .32 oz
Salt	as needed	as needed

1. Season the hanger steaks with salt and pepper. The weight given is an approximate amount for twenty 350-g/12.35-oz pieces. Cryovac each piece individually.

2. Set an immersion thermocirculator to 65°C/150°C. Cook the hanger steak for exactly 20 minutes, or until it reaches an internal temperature of 60°C/140°F. See the sidebar on page 383 to check internal temperatures of Cryovac foods. Shock the steaks in an ice bath to stop the cooking process. Reserve in the refrigerator for up to 2 days.

3. **FOR THE POBLANO COMPOUND BUTTER:** Mix all of the ingredients together in the bowl of an electric mixer using a paddle attachment.

4. Lay a piece of plastic wrap 25 x 45 cm/10 by 18 in on a flat surface. Remove the butter from the bowl and put it on the plastic wrap. Roll the plastic up to form a tube. Tighten the ends by rolling them up; this will also help to form a straight tube. Place the tube on a sheet pan and refrigerate.

5. Once it is firm, cut the butter into 30-g/1.05-oz pieces and reserve refrigerated, with the plastic still wrapped around it. It will keep for up to 3 days in the refrigerator.

6. **TO PICK UP:** Heat a grill to as hot as possible. Heat a fryer to a 190°C/375°F.

7. Remove a few orders of hanger steak from the refrigerator during service. Take out as many as you think you will sell in the course of 3 hours. Meat cooks much better and faster if it is tempered, but don't leave the meat out for more than 3 hours, since it can generate food-borne bacteria growth.

8. Remove a parcooked piece of hanger steak from its Cryovac bag and place it on the grill. The outer surface should just be crisped. If wanting to cook the meat to a higher internal temperature, then do so. For medium, which is what it was cooked to in the first place, cook the steak for 2 minutes on each side. For higher internal temperatures, use a thermometer. While the meat is cooking on the grill, drop 250 g/8.82 oz of par-cooked French fries into the fryer.

9. Once the meat is cooked, take it off the grill and let it relax for 3 minutes, and then slice it with a very sharp knife against the grain into 1.25-cm-/.5-in-thick slices. Place the sliced meat on a plate, and then put a disc of poblano butter on top of the center piece of meat, making sure to remove the plastic wrap around it first.

10. Take the fries out of the fryer and toss them with salt in a bowl. Put the seasoned fries next to the meat, and serve immediately.

notes This cut of meat tends to lose a lot of weight in the form of moisture when it is grilled, shrinking considerably in size; this is why we cook it to medium doneness in a thermocirculator. It will finish cooking on the grill on the pickup.

Use the French Fries recipe on page 358, but do not use truffle salt for this preparation, unless desired.

BEVERAGES

ONE OF THE EASIEST WAYS to make money in a café is to sell beverages. Their cost is minimal, in most cases the labor involved is also minimal, and they enjoy a longer shelf life than prepared foods. The trick lies in making them well and serving them at the proper temperature, especially those that are brewed or steeped, such as coffee and espresso drinks and teas and tisanes (infusions). These beverages will be covered in this chapter, as well as non-alcoholic drinks and some beer and wine drinks. Cocktails, in the strict sense of the word, are not covered in this book, but that doesn't mean that a café cannot offer them.

ANYONE CAN MAKE a cup of coffee, but you need to know how to make a better cup of coffee than anyone else—or at least, better than anyone close to your café. Coffee is the main example here because coffee is one of the main draws for a café. It is one of the first things that will bring someone into your establishment, and will ideally keep them coming back, and not just for coffee, but for everything else you have to offer. If the coffee is bad or just average, customers will probably not return unless they absolutely must. But if the coffee is good, they will go out of their way to get it. As with everything else in this book, the perfect (or close to perfect) product is the result of proper technique, execution, and use of equipment. You can spend thousands of dollars on the ultimate espresso machine, but if you have bad coffee beans, there goes your money.

COFFEE AND ESPRESSO

Good coffee is largely a matter of personal taste, but there are a few factors to consider when looking at the quality of the bean. The two most common species of coffee beans are *robusta* and *arabica*. *Arabica* is the species from which all great coffees are made. About three-quarters of all the coffee that is harvested in the world is from this species. Only 10 percent of that amount is considered "specialty" coffee, and within that 10 percent, only 1 to 2 percent is considered exceptional coffee, also called "grand crus." *Robusta* plants produce almost twice as many beans as *arabica*, and their beans contain twice the amount of caffeine, but they do not produce the same quality of flavor, aroma, or body as *arabica* beans.

Ideally, *arabica* plants are grown at high altitudes—between 4,000 and 6,000 feet—in specific mountainous tropical regions between the Tropic of Cancer and the Tropic of Capricorn. They are grown at temperatures that range between 16°C/60°F and 21°C/70°F. Besides all of these specific environmental conditions, the coffee beans require special handling and should be picked at their peak of ripeness. Not all the beans on a plant will ripen at the same time, which is where the harvesting can get challenging. Imagine having to sift through an entire plant with hundreds of beans just to get those that are at their peak. The period of time between harvest and roasting is anywhere from two to six months. Once the beans are roasted, they will be at their peak for five days and are usable for seven more days, unless they are specially packed (see the following text on one-way valve pack). If they are properly packaged, they will keep for up to two months before they become stale.

Coffee can be purchased with the following denominations.

blends

As the name states, blends are a mixture of one variety of coffee beans from different countries. Rarely will you drink a cup of coffee made from one particular type of bean. They should be mixed and combined until the ideal balance is achieved. This ideal balance is determined by the preference of the person who brews it and eventually drinks it, and it is hoped it will be that of the customer as well. Not all coffees are blends, though; the majority of coffee sold is known as "single-origin" coffee.

single-origin coffee

This refers to a combination of a variety of beans from one specific country or a region in a country.

roasting

Roasting is one of the last steps in the coffee-making process, and it is what makes coffee the product we know. It is by no means the most laborious, but it is what can make or break the final product. The whole process takes from ten to fifteen minutes and starts with the dried green coffee beans. They are placed in the roasters, which are essentially just cylinders or barrels, and are spun around a heating element until properly roasted. The size of the roasters can vary widely. Some roast hundreds of pounds at a time, while some personal roasters roast a pound at a time. Those people who are experienced coffee roasters know the approximate time and temperature it takes to roast certain beans, but they are also guided by smell and sight and make adjustments for each batch. Once the beans have cooled, they should not be brewed for forty-eight hours since they haven't reached the optimum state (the point at which they are ideally brewed). At this point they need to be packaged in one-way valve bags, or if they aren't, they need to be used in the next ten days maximum. A one-way valve bag will allow CO_2 to escape, but will not let oxygen in or out, thus significantly extending the shelf life of the coffee. Many off-the-shelf coffees are not treated this way, and it is quite likely that most of it is sold stale. Any other package but the one-way valve bag will quickly make the coffee stale, because if the CO_2 that the beans expel after roasting is not released, it will have a staling effect.

Coffees are generally sold with the degrees of roast listed below. Some coffee beans can be purchased with a mixture of various beans roasted to different degrees. The difference between coffee beans that are roasted for coffee and beans that are roasted for espresso is that the latter are generally

organic coffee and tea

COFFEE AND TEA PRODUCERS are not allowed to simply state that their product is "organic." There is a third party involved that designates what is organic and what is not organic. In the U.S. it is the United States Department of Agriculture, which not too long ago didn't have specific guidelines as to what constituted organic and what did not.

The USDA now has very strict regulations as to what is and what is not organic, and it provides a seal with a logo that can be printed on any type of packaging. For a coffee or tea to be designated as organic, it will need to have been propagated, grown, processed, transported, stored, and roasted (coffee) or fermented (some teas) without ever coming in contact with synthetic chemicals. The chemicals of greatest concern are pesticides and herbicides, which can have adverse effects on the human body. Organic is assumed to be better for your body than non-organic or inorganic foods. However, the actual coffee beans or tea leaves are put through a number of processes before they are brewed, and they are essentially used to flavor water and aren't meant to be eaten whole, like a cucumber or an apple. Is there a huge impact on the body if you drink coffee or tea that is not organic? It's something to think about.

Organic practices are good for the environment when they are properly followed. Synthetic pesticides and herbicides can cause a very negative impact on plants and animals, which will indirectly impact you at one point or another. There are such things as organic pesticides and herbicides.

roasted dark brown, but not black. That said, any type of roast or bean or mix of beans can be used to make espresso. The defining characteristic of espresso is the size of the grind; it should be the finest for espresso.

There are two ways to categorize coffee roasts. First is by the fancy name, which is used for marketing but doesn't really describe the degree of roast. These are two examples of the terms used to describe the two most popular types of roasts used today.

VIENNA OR "FULL CITY"

This roast is medium to dark brown and has a shiny bloom from the beans' oils. This type of roast is focused on bringing out the body of the coffee and, to a lesser degree, the acidity and aroma.

DARK ITALIAN OR DARK FRENCH

This is the darkest type of roast, which will result in a flavor determined mostly by the roast rather than by the actual nature of the bean. Regular Italian roast is typically used for espresso and is also known as espresso roast.

And then there is the accurate naming of roasts, established by the Specialty Coffee Association of America (SCAA). These are the categories:

Light brown: This denotes the lightest roast. Market names: light, cinnamon, New England. Mostly used for less expensive commercial blends.

Medium brown: This indicates the middle of the range. Market names: American, medium, city, regular. Classic American coffee with full flavor development.

Medium-dark brown: Market names: Viennese, full city, light French, espresso, continental, light espresso. The standard for Italian espresso. Acidity is decreased, and the body and sweetness increase.

Dark brown: Market names: espresso, French, dark, Italian, Turkish. Not very acidic. Bittersweet. Used for American-style espresso.

Very dark brown: This denotes the darkest roast. Market names: Italian, dark, French, heavy, Spanish, Neapolitan. Zero acidity. Bittersweet with some charred flavors that are not necessarily unpleasant.

Black-brown: Market names: Dark French, Spanish, Neapolitan. Dominated by a burned taste. Very thin body. The more the bean roasts, the less body it will have.

That's it. With these standard terms, it is easier for coffee buyers to understand what roast they are getting.

brewing coffee

Good brewed coffee is the result of following a recipe and a technique using the proper tools and equipment. It is no different from everything else that is made in the café. And any good recipe begins with good-quality ingredients, in this case the coffee beans and water. About 98 percent of a cup of coffee is water, and the rest is the soluble parts of the coffee bean. These soluble parts constitute about 30 percent of the total weight of the bean, but only 20 percent of the total weight of the bean is the actual desirable solubles. The other 10 percent is just bitter, unpleasant flavors. Using good water is crucial. If you are fortunate enough to live in an area where the tap water is not too heavy (high in minerals) and is clean, you are halfway there. Otherwise, use bottled water, which could be pricey in the long run, or a good filtering system.

The main objective of brewing coffee is to extract the largest amount of good flavors from the ground coffee beans. Following are the elements of a proper cup of coffee, in no particular order. They all are important to the end result.

ROASTING TIME
How long were the beans roasted? The roast is a matter of personal preference (see roast list above).

FRESHNESS
Don't forget, beans are at their peak for five days after they rest for forty-eight hours post-roasting. After that, they only have seven more days when they are usable. If they are packed in the airtight one-way valve bags, they will keep for up to two months. Beans that are no longer fresh will not brew to their full capacity and will result in a weak cup of coffee or espresso, often with a stale flavor. These beans can be used to make ice cream, though.

SIZE OF GRIND
Each type of brewed coffee requires a particular size grind. The grind will determine how much exposed surface area of the coffee bean will come in contact with water. The best result will come from grinding the bean just enough so that the right amount of the coffee bean's solids are extruded into the water used to brew them. In other words, the type of grind depends on the

brewing time. A fine grind will cause the water to take too long to pass through the beans, and result in an overly bitter-tasting coffee if the wrong brewing method is used. If the grind is too big, there will barely be any solids dissolved. The best way to grind coffee beans is to use a commercial burr grinder, since its disc blades will produce an evenly sized grind, cutting the beans rather than crushing them. Blade grinders are passable for home use, but not for commercial use; since they do not yield very consistent results and these grinders actually crush rather than cut the bean. Keep in mind that while whole coffee beans can go stale in a couple of weeks unless they are stored in airtight one-way valve bags, coffee will become stale within hours of being ground. Many commercial grinders can be programmed to grind a specific amount for a specific time. Grind the coffee just before brewing for optimum results.

WATER QUALITY AND TEMPERATURE
If your espresso machine or the water you use to brew coffee in any type of brewing method is not filtered, it can result in certain mineral off flavors in the coffee. Furthermore, hard waters will eventually damage the expensive machines, clogging the very delicate mechanisms that brew the beans. Also, off temperatures (if the water is too hot or too cold) will ruin the brewing. The temperature needs to be within range in order to obtain the most efficient brew.

RATIO OF COFFEE TO WATER
As ambiguous as it sounds, always use just the right amount of water or a little more (see proportions under Brewing Methods below). When you brew fewer coffee beans than required for a specific amount of water, the coffee will be watered down. You can always add a few extra coffee beans, and if the brew is too strong, dilute it with some equally hot plain water.

HOLDING TIME
Only coffee that has been brewed in automatic drip brewers in large amounts can be held, and the ideal temperature for this is between 85°C/185°F and 88°C/190°F. The longest possible time to hold coffee for is one hour (the first twenty minutes are when it is at its peak), since it oxidizes as time goes by. Try to keep a timer set to forty-five minutes (one hour is too late, since someone might get an hour-old cup and take fifteen or more minutes to drink it) next to each brewer, and, when it goes off, discard any coffee left in it.

brewing methods

A standard cup of coffee is about 160 mL/5.5 fl oz. It starts out as 180 mL/6 fl oz, but some of the water is absorbed by the ground coffee. A standard recipe for coffee is 55 g/1.96 oz ground coffee for every 1 kg/ 2 lb 3.2 oz of water. However, this ratio of beans to coffee could go lower or higher, from 50 g/1.76 oz up to 70 g/2.47 oz. This recipe holds true for any method or equipment used for brewing, but what will vary is the size of the grind (see the chart on page 402). As far as choosing a method, it largely depends on what works for the establishment. In any case, always keep the coffee cups and all other vessels meant for hot drinks warm. A good place to achieve this is on top of an espresso machine, or use coffee-cup warmers. The main reason to keep them warm is to extend the time that the coffee stays hot. If it is poured into a room-temperature cup, it will drop its temperature much faster.

decaffeinated coffee

HOW MANY TIMES HAVE YOU BEEN TO A COFFEE SHOP OR CAFÉ that makes great coffee but bad decaf versions of their coffee and espresso? Decaf coffee does contain a small percentage of caffeine, about one-fortieth of the original amounts. The decaffeination process consists of dissolving the caffeine in the coffee beans while they are still green (it will dissolve out of the beans at that point). Therein lies the problem. When the caffeine is dissolved, some of the other desirable solids found in coffee beans that are responsible for flavor and aroma are also dissolved. No matter how well the decaffeination process goes, the final result will never be the same as regular coffee. Keeping that in mind, it is still possible to obtain a high-quality decaffeinated coffee bean.

There are three different processes for decaffeinating coffee beans:

Solvents
The still-green beans are steamed to open their pores, and then they are soaked in a solvent that binds to caffeine. The beans are steamed again to remove the solvent along with the caffeine. This is the most widely used method. The solvents used in today's processes are either methylene chloride or, more recently, ethyl acetate. The use of methylene chloride is harmful to the environment but ethyl acetate is not.

Carbon Dioxide
When compressed, CO_2 binds to caffeine. The beans are steamed and then bathed in CO_2, and then the caffeine is removed through charcoal filtering. This method best preserves the flavors of the bean, but it is newer than the solvent method and it has been slow to catch on. It is not harmful to the environment.

Water Process
The beans are soaked in very hot water and the beans then release their caffeine, which is then filtered through charcoal. The beans are returned to the water they were soaked in to reabsorb the other solids responsible for flavor and aroma. This process is costly and time-consuming, and some coffee experts argue that the results are not worth it. This method is not harmful to the environment.

So, where does all that caffeine go? In the first two processes it can be recovered and sold. Some major national coffee chains add caffeine to their coffee to give you that extra jolt. In the water process, it is trapped in the charcoal and is impossible to remove.

The method that is best depends on your personal taste. While the CO_2 method seems to yield the best results, it is not widely available. If you can find it, buy it; or purchase decaffeinated coffee that uses the ethyl acetate solvent method.

AUTOMATIC DRIP BREWERS

For general purposes, the most efficient method for brewing quality coffee in large amounts is a drip brewer, and it uses the same principles as the cone filter drip. The essence of this method is to saturate the ground coffee with hot water in a paper filter, and the resulting brewed coffee is held hot for a period of time. This process is done automatically, which means that the brewer dispenses the preprogrammed amount of water at a preprogrammed temperature for a preprogrammed amount of time, and it holds the resulting coffee at a preprogrammed temperature. Try not to purchase brewers that have a capacity larger than 6 liters/1.5 gallons, since keeping such an amount of coffee hot is challenging, let alone larger amounts.

CONE FILTER DRIP (MANUAL DRIP)

Cone filter drips operate by the same principles as the automatic drips, but the brewing is done by hand. In this case, the water temperature is controlled by a human being. The ground coffee is placed inside a paper filter, which is then placed inside a cone filter. Ideally the filters are made of porcelain, but some are made of plastic. This cone is placed over a coffee cup or mug, and hot water is poured over the ground coffee slowly, so as to saturate it with water. This is also known as blooming the coffee. Be careful to not add so much water that the coffee floats. Once the initial amount of water has passed through the filter, the process is repeated until the cup or mug is full. The disadvantage of this method is that it is time-consuming, since the barista has to constantly tend to the brewing process. There are some clever solutions to this time delay, however, and one of them consists of an apparatus that holds four or five cone filters on a stand with the same amount of cups or mugs underneath them, so the barista can pour the first amount of water into the first cone and so on for the other cups, so as to not have to wait for the water to pass through the filter of just one cup. The problem with that is that this is contingent on getting four or five orders at the exact same time, which is rare.

There is another brewer known as the Chemex, which is made of two cones attached at the narrow end. The top cone is lined with a filter, and then the finely ground coffee beans are placed in the filter. In principle, it is similar to the cone filter, but the resulting coffee needs to be poured into a cup after it is brewed, while the cone filter drips directly into the cup.

The reason why the cone filter is worth the trouble is that it yields a terrific cup of coffee with no sediment. Sediment is in itself is not a bad thing, but some people just don't like to see it at the bottom of their cup. One downside to using paper filters is that some of the essence of the coffee is absorbed into the paper and therefore lost. The alternative is a gold-washed cone filter, which, if properly cared for, can keep for years.

FRENCH PRESS (Plunger Pot or Cafetière)

This is my preferred method of brewing coffee. A French press is an apparatus that brews small amounts of coffee at a time, anywhere from two to eight portions depending on the size and capacity of the press. Coarsely ground coffee is poured into the press, and then hot water is poured in almost to the top. The lid is placed over the top of the press, the coffee is left to brew for four to six minutes (ideally five), and then the fine-mesh strainer is pushed down on the press. This method extracts all of the positive soluble flavors from the coffee beans, and the resulting coffee is extraordinary. This method also carries a lot

A French press is the most efficient and economical method of brewing extraordinary coffee.

of weight with customers, since it is coffee that was brewed especially for them. The only downside is that the coffee grounds are still in contact with the water, so if it is not consumed within a reasonable amount of time, the bad soluble flavors will be combined with the coffee. Additionally, the more the grounds sit in the hot water, the more caffeinated it will become. In any case, the French press is the most economical and efficient way to make excellent coffee. Some companies make a plastic version, which is just as good as the glass press but will cost less and have a longer lifespan. In a busy café, replace the presses every six months or so. They are rather inexpensive, which is a good thing, since some customers can grow attached to them and decide to take them home. Sometimes it happens.

VACUUM POT BREWER

This pot looks like something you would find in a laboratory. It consists of two glass spheres, one on top of the other, attached by a seal. Between the two spheres is a very fine-mesh sieve inside a funnel into which the ground coffee beans will be placed. This funnel connects the bottom sphere to the top sphere. The way it works is as follows: Pour water into the bottom glass sphere and place the jug over a stovetop, with a diffuser between the sphere and the stove. The funnel and sieve are attached to the top sphere, and the sphere is then attached to the handle on the bottom sphere. At this point, the ground coffee is poured into the funnel. Turn the stove on high, and as the water boils it will pass through the funnel up into the top sphere. It passes through the ground coffee; some water will remain in the bottom sphere. This is not a bad thing and it won't water down the coffee; it needs to be there to keep the bottom sphere from cracking over the heat. Take the brewer off the heat; the coffee is now brewed and will pour down on its own into the bottom sphere because of gravity. If it does not pour down, it just needs to be put over the stove again, and then it will pour right down. The coffee is now ready to be poured and drunk.

This type of coffee brewing is visually impressive, and the vacuum pot brews an excellent pot of coffee. There are two downsides, though, as far as convenience goes. One is that it is an expensive piece; second, it requires a stove to be placed next to the barista work area, which makes for an awkward work space.

Using a Vacuum Pot Brewer

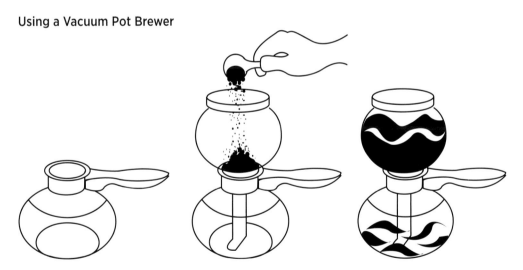

To use a vacuum pot brewer: Pour water into the bottom glass sphere and place over a stovetop. Attach the funnel and sieve to the top sphere and attach the top sphere to the handle on the bottom sphere. Pour the ground coffee into the funnel. Turn the stove on high, and as the water boils it will pass through the funnel up into the top sphere. When the coffee is brewed, it will pour down into the bottom sphere because of gravity.

general brewing guidelines

type of grind	type of brew	grind time*	brewing time	water temperature
Coarse	French press	10 seconds	4 to 6 minutes (ideally 5 minutes)	90°C/195°F to 96°C/205°F
Medium	Automatic drip brewer	15 seconds	4 to 6 minutes	90°C/195°F to 96°C/205°F
Fine	Cone filter drip (manual drip)	25 seconds	1 to 5 minutes, depending on the paper filter and the size of the cone	90°C/195°F to 96°C/205°F
Very fine	Espresso machine	30 seconds	20 to 30 seconds (ideally 22 seconds)	90°C/195°F to 96°C/205°F

*The grind time depends on the type of grinder, but this is a good range for most commercial burr grinders.

iced coffee

Any of the above methods will do when making iced coffee, but keep in mind that the addition of water in the form of ice will dilute the coffee. There are three options to resolve this:

- Brew a large amount of coffee and then quickly cool it down in an ice bath. Reserve the coffee cold.

- To brew to order, use twice the amount of ground coffee when brewing, and when the ice is added, it will melt. The resulting liquid will be just right.

- Make ice cubes with coffee, brew a regular cup of coffee to order, and use the coffee ice cubes to cool it down.

tasting coffee

There are four predominant categories that pertain to tasting coffee. The most important, as with anything we consume, is flavor, and it is the broadest of all the categories. It encompasses the next two categories, aroma and acidity, and is an indicator of intensity. The aroma is perceived well before the coffee is drunk and can be extremely complex. Acidity is not a bad thing; in fact, it is the benchmark for quality coffee. The fourth and final quality category is body, which can be light, medium, or full, and is directly proportionate to the brewing method and type of bean.

The ideal scenario as a café owner/operator is not to buy any brand of coffee from the supermarket shelf or online; establish and develop a relationship with a reputable coffee roaster and purveyor. Don't

frown upon larger companies just because they are big, and don't go with microroasters just because they are small. Go with the company that has your best interests at heart and will work closely with you to produce the results you are looking for. Most

For a unique touch, brew a cup of coffee to order and chill it with frozen coffee ice cubes.

importantly, they should roast coffee well. These types of companies will often roast the beans to your liking and create specific blends for your establishment (for Resources, see page 540). Also, you will always know when the beans were roasted, so that you can be guaranteed that they won't be stale. Some roasters might even provide the brewing equipment, which can be very costly, and training for your employees, as long as you buy their product.

Establishing this relationship can be one of the smartest decisions you make, since having a deep knowledge of coffee and how to make it is what truly will set you apart from any competition. Don't forget, one of the top reasons for opening a café is to sell coffee, and it should never be an afterthought. In many establishments, including restaurants, coffee, espresso, and the drinks that can be made with them are often rushed and aren't very good. Good coffee takes a lot of care and a well-trained hand. The person who makes the coffee, the barista, needs to make sure, among many things, that the right amount of coffee is being used, that the water is at the right temperature, and that it is coming out with the right pressure, often making adjustments from cup to cup.

Selling coffee by the pound is also a smart way to make money. If your customers like your coffee, they might buy a pound or two for themselves or as a gift. In this transaction, there is practically no labor involved on your part.

bad coffee troubleshooting

If it is weak:

- There is not enough coffee.

- The coffee is not ground to the correct size. Typically it is too big.

- The water was not hot enough.

- The coffee was not brewed long enough.

If it is too bitter:

- The coffee was ground too finely.

- There was insufficient coffee.

- The coffee is old and has been in the brewer or pot for too long.

- The brewing took too long.

brewing espresso

Espresso is defined by the Specialty Coffee Association of America as "a coffee beverage prepared using water under pressure and served in a preheated demitasse cup. When made correctly, espresso has a top layer of golden foam, known as crema." A more extensive definition by the World Barista Championship association is:

> An espresso is a one-ounce beverage (25 to 35 ml including crema) prepared with an appropriate and consistent amount of coffee (depending on the coffee and the grind) though which clean water of 195–205 degrees F (95–96 degrees C) has been forced at 8.5 to 9.5 atmospheres of pressure, and where the grind of the coffee is such that the brewing flow time is between 20 and 30 seconds. While brewing, the flow of espresso should appear to have the viscosity of warm honey, and the resulting beverage should exhibit a thick, dark, golden cream-foam (crema).

All of the precautions that need to be taken for brewing coffee must be followed even more strictly when it comes to brewing espresso properly. It requires extreme precision and speed. The whole process is very quick, so the barista needs to be aware during the entire process. Make sure to have a warm cup before brewing the espresso. It can be warmed over the espresso machine or rinsed with hot water. This process is generally as follows:

1. The coffee beans are always ground to order in a tamper. A good burr grinder with a tamper is extremely expensive but well worth it. The average weight of one tamper, or the amount for one shot of espresso, is 7 to 9 g/.25 to .32 oz. The grind is extremely fine. If you were to spread out 7 g/.25 oz of ground espresso in a single layer, it would occupy three square feet.

2. The portafilter is the part of the espresso machine that holds the espresso beans and is detachable. Rinse it under hot water from the espresso machine's spout and put it under the burr grinder. The portafilter should be compatible with the grinder, since it will need to attach tightly to the grinder in order for all the ground coffee to fall into place and to be tamped. It shouldn't be tamped too tight, just enough to let the water through efficiently. Grinders with proper tampers are very expensive because they have the technology that takes the guesswork out of how much coffee is needed and how tightly the ground coffee should be packed into the portafilter. If you cannot afford a proper tamper, you and your barista will need to practice with a separate manual tamper until you find the most

adequate pressure to apply on the portafilter. If there is any ground coffee around the portafilter, wipe it off.

3. Insert the portafilter into the espresso machine and start brewing immediately. The espresso is "pulled" through hot water at 90° to 96°C/195° to 205°F on the espresso machine for 20 to 30 seconds at about 130 psi. That is the pressure with which the water is forced through the ground coffee; psi stands for pounds per inch. This amount can also be expressed in atmospheres, and its equivalent is 9 atmospheres. It should result in exactly 1.25 fl oz for a perfectly pulled espresso, and it should be served in a 3-fl-oz demitasse. Anything less than this amount is known as a *corto* or a *ristretto,* which is just shy of an ounce, and anything more is known as a *lungo,* about 1.5 fl oz. An espresso with a lemon twist is known as an *espresso romano.*

4. The espresso should be served immediately or used to make an espresso drink.

5. Take the portafilter off the machine and knock the used grounds out using the "knockout" box. This box is a metal pan with a bar that goes across the top of the pan, onto which you will tap the portafilter. The bar is covered in foam or rubber to keep the portafilter from getting damaged as you tap it. Rinse the portafilter and reattach it to the espresso machine to keep it hot.

Brewing Espresso

FROM LEFT TO RIGHT:

1. Brewing espresso requires extremely fine grounds, best achieved with a burr-type grinder.
2. The liquid will look gradually thicker and lighter as it pours out of the portafilter.
3. A properly brewed cup of espresso will have a uniform layer of creamy, caramel-colored foam, called crema, on its surface.

espresso machines

THIS IS ONE MACHINE for which you will have to resign yourself to investing a large chunk of money. Try not to skimp on it or buy a secondhand machine. If you care for your machine and use it properly, you will have a line going out the door of people wanting a cup of your espresso.

When looking for an espresso machine, look for one with a dual boiler or two separate water heaters. Remember, espresso is brewed with water that is at a lower temperature than the water that is needed to steam milk. If you have a single boiler, you will have a good espresso with a poor steamer, or vice versa. The need for two boilers is partially what can make the machine so expensive. Keeping this is in mind, the machine should have two separate water sources. Besides the dual boiler, it should have an accurate thermostat. Perform weekly tests on the temperature of the water that the machine is putting out and make adjustments as needed. The brew heads, or where the brewing takes place in the machine, need to be made of a heavy-gauge stainless steel. This ensures that the water temperature can be held consistently with minor fluctuations, and it will also result in a longer life for the machine.

Make sure to assess the volume you will be making daily. If you have a tiny machine, you won't be able to keep up with orders; if you have a giant machine and not so many customers, you spent too much money unwisely. Finally, make sure the manufacturer offers training for your staff and a preventive maintenance program. Maintaining your machine is worth every penny.

KEY POINTS TO LOOK FOR WHILE BREWING A PROPER ESPRESSO

- The brewing time should be between 20 and 30 seconds, no more and no less.

- When the water pours out of the portafilter into the cup, it will start very fluid and then it will appear to be thicker or fuller and go from a dark brown to a lighter brown.

- The top of the espresso in the cup should be covered by what is known as the crema (see below).

- Taste: A properly brewed espresso should be lightly sweet, smoky, and robust.

Crema is a creamy, caramel-colored foam that forms on top of a properly brewed espresso. If it is properly made, it is sweet, uniform with no holes, and long lasting. It is made of vegetable oils, proteins, and sugars, with elements of foam colloid and emulsions. The portafilter contains a small amount of CO_2 at such a high pressure, so when the hot water passes through the coffee beans, there will be thousands of minuscule bubbles formed inside the resulting brew in the cup. These bubbles make up the foam, which is a dispersion of a gas in a liquid. Since these bubbles are lighter than the liquid part of the espresso, they will float to the top. CO_2 bubbles on their own have a very short lifespan, but coffee beans contain a compound called melanoidin, polymers that form when sugars and amino acids are combined through the Maillard reaction (see page 5). They are also found in breads. These polymers wrap themselves around the bubbles, since they are repelled by water, and they will in turn face any air around them, extending the life of the bubble for a short period of time. The foam is not permanent, since coffee does contain a proportion of fat, which makes foams unstable. The crema that forms on top of a properly pulled espresso will last longer and have a thicker body than that on top of espresso was made too quickly. The color of the crema in a properly brewed espresso will go from dark brown to light caramel as the brewing progresses.

The four points to making great espresso (also known as the four "M's") are:

- *Macchina* **or** *Macinazione:* The type of espresso machine used will determine the positive or negative outcome.

- *Miscela:* The coffee bean blend.

- *Molino:* The grinder, preferably a burr-type grinder.

- *Mano:* The hand that makes the espresso. You can have the latest and greatest machinery, but if you do not have an intelligent and efficient barista, there is no point to all the money spent. Always keep in mind that you will need to sell a lot of coffee, espresso, and drinks made from these to turn a profit.

Spend as much as you can on a high-quality espresso machine and a grinder/tamper, or better yet, have your coffee roaster sponsor one for you. The best home-use model will never produce the same results as a full-fledged professional one, and even among professional machines, there are but a few truly exceptional machines. The espresso machine has many different components and elements that need to work precisely and simultaneously, whereas an automatic drip brewer is much simpler.

It is often thought that espresso, because of its strong flavor, contains much higher amounts of caffeine than a cup of coffee. This is in fact not true. Espresso is usually consumed in very small amounts, and it typically contains 50 to 70 milligrams of caffeine, while a cup of coffee contains well over 100 milligrams. The ground espresso beans spend such a short time with the water during the brewing process that there is very little opportunity to extract as much caffeine as is extracted with an automatic drip brewer or other coffee brewing method.

COFFEE AND ESPRESSO DRINKS

Once you understand the basics of making coffee and espresso, it is important to learn all of the different drinks that can be made from them. They are essentially different combinations of coffee and dairy, and sometimes they are flavored. The first step

is to know how to steam and froth milk. Once you can do this properly, you will be able to make any kind of coffee and espresso drinks. Different types of milk or milk alternatives can be steamed and frothed, but the results will be different. Do not steam milk for iced drinks; instead use a mini frother with cold milk.

The biggest challenge with steaming and frothing milk is that it requires a higher water temperature than needed to brew espresso. Water steams at 100°C/212°F, and espresso brews at 90° to 96°C/195° to 205°F. These two functions are usually part of the same espresso machine. The better espresso machines will have two separate thermostats and the water for the espresso will be completely separate from the water for steaming; if you only had one water temperature, you would be sacrificing the quality of one of the components. Most espresso machines on the lower end of the price range will only have one temperature. Machines with dual temperatures are drastically more expensive.

STEPS TO STEAMING AND FROTHING MILK

1. Turn the steam wand on and off quickly to force any impurities out.

2. Pour the milk into a metal pitcher. On average, the amount needed is about 160 g/5.64 oz for one cappuccino, and it is always better to make a little (not too much) more than you need, since it will foam better when there is more milk in the pitcher than when there is too little. When there is too little milk in the metal pitcher, the milk tends to boil quickly and large bubbles tend to form instead of nice minuscule ones. The downside to using more milk is that milk cannot be reheated more than once with the same results, since milk is an emulsion and heat breaks that emulsion. Always keep in mind that you should use an appropriately sized pitcher to steam and froth the milk, since it will triple in volume.

3. Submerge the wand in the milk and turn the steam on to the highest setting. Pull the pitcher down so that the tip of the wand is barely submerged in the milk. The ideal serving temperature for steamed milk is between 65° and 71°C/150° and 160°F. Hotter temperatures will damage the milk and are difficult to drink. Use a thermocoupler thermometer to take the correct real-time temperature of your milk. It is a pricey thermometer, but it has the advantage

of speed and accuracy, unlike most economical thermometers. When the milk reaches the proper temperature range, it will make a deep whirring or a low rumbling sound, the sign of a proper foam. A high-pitched sound comes from loose milk that has not been frothed to its ideal state; continue to steam and froth until the high pitch is no longer heard.

4. Turn the steam off and pull the pitcher away from the milk. Never pull the pitcher away while the steam is on or else the milk might explode out of the pitcher and you might end up wearing it.

5. Turn the steam wand on and off quickly to force any impurities out after steaming the milk.

6. Once the milk is steamed, tap it on a cloth towel to pop any large bubbles and swirl the pitcher slightly to keep the foam even. This foam will be maintained for a few minutes, but be sure to brew your espresso or finish making your coffee drink quickly.

Steaming and Frothing Milk

FROM LEFT TO RIGHT:

1. Keep the tip of the wand submerged in the milk until it reaches the proper temperature and you no longer hear the high-pitched sound of loose milk.
2. Ideal foam consistency can be achieved by an attentive barista with proper frothing technique.
3. Immediately pour the steamed milk into the coffee drink and use a spoon to top with the foam.

coffee and espresso drinks

drink	ratio
Americano	Two shots of espresso plus one espresso cup's worth of hot water
Café Latte	One shot of espresso "pulled" for the equivalent amount of time of 1.5 espressos, steamed milk on top, plus 6 mm/.25 in milk foam
	Double latte: two shots of espresso "pulled" for the equivalent amount of time of 3 espressos, plus steamed milk and 6 mm/.25 in milk foam
Cappuccino	Two shots of espresso, steamed milk to fill ⅔ of the cup, plus milk foam in the remaining ⅓ of the cup. In other words: ⅓ espresso, ⅓ steamed milk, and ⅓ foam.
Café Mocha	Two shots of espresso, steamed milk with no foam, and 30 g/1 oz of high-quality chocolate syrup. Some customers may want it to be topped with whipped cream.
Macchiato	Two shots of espresso plus a spoonful of milk foam
Café au lait	180 mL/6 fl oz cup coffee plus 60 mL/2 fl oz cup steamed milk
Mochaccino	Same recipe as a cappuccino plus 30 g/1 oz high-quality chocolate syrup
Red eye	Cup of coffee plus two shots of espresso
Affogato	A shot of espresso served over vanilla gelato

Café au Lait

Affogato

There are other varieties of drinks made with coffee and espresso, but these are the most popular types. These drinks can also be made into iced beverages. Do not steam the milk for the latter, though; instead, use a mini frother. They can also be decaffeinated. You may have customers who request their drinks with whipped cream; use a cream whipper with fresh, lightly sweetened cream.

There are some high-quality syrup brands available (see Resources, page 540), and there are many flavors to choose from. The higher-quality syrups are somewhat more expensive, but they are recommended since they will not cover up the taste of the coffee or espresso. When used correctly, they will act as more of a background flavor.

When flavoring a hot drink, always pour the flavor in first and then add the brewed coffee or espresso. You needn't stir, since the syrup will dissolve as the liquid is poured into the cup. Drinks can also be flavored with spices, such as nutmeg, cinnamon, clove, allspice, and cardamom. It is not recommended to brew with them, however.

average cup capacities

type of cup	serving size	total capacity (filled to the top)
300 mL/10 fl oz to-go plastic cup for small to-go iced coffee and espresso drinks	245 g/8.64 oz	307 g/10.83 oz
480 mL/16 fl oz to-go plastic cup for large to-go iced coffee and espresso drinks	467 g/1 lb .32 oz	548 g/1 lb 3.2 oz
600 mL/20 fl oz drinking glass for most iced coffee and espresso drinks	508 g/1 lb 1.76 oz	573 g/1 lb 4.16 oz
Small coffee to-go cup	348 g/12.27 oz	413 g/14.57 oz
Large coffee to-go cup	413 g/14.57 oz	505 g/1 lb 1.76 oz
Coffee mug	246 g/8.68 oz	302 g/10.65 oz
Espresso cup	62 g/2.18 oz	90 g/3.17 oz
Espresso to-go cup	62 g/2.18 oz	112 g/3.95 oz
Cappuccino mug	180 g/6.35 oz	215 g/7.58 oz
Latte mug	241 g/8.5 oz	302 g/10.65 oz
Latte small to-go cup	346 g/12.2 oz	413 g/14.57 oz
Large (double) latte cup	433 g/15.27 oz	505 g/1 lb 1.76 oz
Cappuccino small to-go cup	350 g/12.35 oz	413 g/14.57 oz
Large (double) capuccino cup	376 g/13.26 oz	505 g/1 lb 1.76 oz

A coffee mug is typically used for coffee, latte, café mocha, chai latte, hot chocolate, and hot tea.

TEA

While coffee, espresso, and the drinks that are made with them will constitute the majority of the beverage sales, tea should be given the same amount of care; it is just as important as any other of the items you produce and sell.

All teas come from a single species of tree, *Camellia sinensis.* Any "teas" that do not come from this tree are called infusions or tisanes and are incorrectly referred to as teas (see infusions, page 414). This tree's lifespan ranges from 30 to 100 years, growing to between 45 and 60 feet tall with at least five hours of sun a day in warm and humid climates. The trees that can grow at the highest altitudes of 4,000 feet or more produce the best-quality teas. For the most part, the tree's leaves are harvested from spring to fall, with their flavor changing depending on the season in which they were picked, and the climate, soil, and conditions in which the leaves are kept.

Tea leaves contain caffeine, mineral ions, amino acids, polyphenolic flavanols, and carbohydrates, which give tea its color and flavor. They contain a large percentage of water (about 80 percent), which is further reduced to about 70 percent during the initial withering of the leaves. It is when the leaves are oxidized, or fermented, that the polyphenolic flavanols in the leaves come into contact with oxygen and the different flavors that are unique to each type of tea are created. The drying process breaks down the enzyme that is responsible for oxidation. When this process begins will decide the outcome of the tea. The sooner the leaves are dried, the sooner the fermentation will stop. Fermentation is not necessarily a sign of quality or lack thereof. It is just a matter of personal taste.

All teas contain a portion of caffeine, but the content will vary depending on the darkness of the leaf. Green tea has less caffeine than an Earl Grey (black tea), for example.

There are close to 3,000 varieties of tea produced in the world, which fall into four major categories: white, green, oolong, and black (with three subcategories that apply to each of the previous categories, such as scented, compressed, and organic).

white tea

White tea is made from unfermented tea tree buds or "tips." While the tea tree leaves produce high-quality teas, the buds are prized for their subtle, almost sweet flavor, and should be drunk without sugar, milk, or cream to optimize their flavor. The highest-quality white teas are composed exclusively of buds, while lower-quality white teas will have a few leaves. The liquid that results from the infusion with hot water is a very pale amber color. Pure white tea buds are simply withered and then sun-dried to prevent fermentation, while the buds found in black teas are fully fermented.

green tea

Green tea is comprised of unfermented leaves with no oxidation. Green teas will contain mostly leaves and a few buds or tips, which is the main difference between green tea and white tea. They are processed the same way (wilting and then sun-drying) to prevent fermentation.

oolong tea

Semi-fermented with mild oxidation and also known as *pouchong* in China, oolongs are considered the finest teas in the world. China and Taiwan produce the best oolong teas. The highest quality of oolong tea is fermented 50 percent (three to four hours), while those fermented 30 percent (one to two hours) are the most common. Purists prefer not to add anything to oolong teas that will interfere with their subtle flavor and aroma. These tea leaves are wilted, rolled (which gives green and black teas their characteristic shape), sifted, mildly fermented, and then sun-dried.

black tea

Black teas are fully fermented and have total oxidation. There is a variety of black tea called *pu-huer* tea, which is fermented twice. As seen in the list on page 411, whole-leaf black teas can contain buds, and the more they contain, the higher the quality. The darker the tea, the higher the amount of caffeine it will contain. Creating black tea leaves is accomplished through five steps: wilting, rolling, sifting, fermenting (up to seven hours), and drying. Black tea is the most popular variety of tea in the world. It is also the one that has the largest number of subcategories.

scented teas

These are teas that have an extra ingredient added to enhance the existing flavors or to add another flavor profile. For example, jasmine tea is essentially either black or green tea with dried jasmine blossoms. There are other flower-scented teas as well as fruit-scented teas, which are actually a combination of an infusion and tea. Classic varieties include jasmine, orchid, litchi (Litchi Hongcha), and rose.

compressed teas

These are packed teas or compressed tea cakes. The leaves are initially steamed to soften them and are then formed into a specific shape. The most common shapes are spheres, nests, and bricks. There are many very visually arresting compressed teas that combine a variety of teas with flowers and that make a very dramatic steeping.

organic teas

These are any variety of tea harvested and treated within organic standards. As with anything organic, they have become incredibly popular, and almost every single type of tea is available grown organically.

tea grading

The following shows how teas are commercially graded; bear in mind that this grading is based on leaf size. Leaf size has little to do with quality; it has to do with brewing time. The smaller the leaf, the quicker the brew. There will be varying qualities among same-size tea leaves.

DENOMINATIONS FOR ALL TEAS

whole-leaf tea: Whole-leaf tea can only be sold if it has undamaged whole leaves. The tea will contain some tips or buds. Following are the denominations for whole-leaf tea:

- **Souchong:** the lowest grade of black tea
- **Pekoe (P):** low-quality black tea
- **Orange Pekoe (OP):** medium to low quality
- **Flowery Orange Pekoe (FOP):** medium quality
- **Golden Flowery Orange Pekoe (GFOP):** contains a few golden tips or buds; medium quality
- **Tippy Golden Flowery Orange Pekoe (TGFOP):** contains many tips or buds; medium-high quality
- **Finest Tippy Golden Flowery Orange Pekoe (FTGFOP):** high-quality Flowery Orange Pekoe
- **Special Finest Tippy Golden Flowery Orange Pekoe (SFTGFOP):** highest-quality Flowery Orange Pekoe

Brewing Compressed Tea

FROM LEFT TO RIGHT:
1. Compressed teas are packed into a specific shape and steeped in the same way as any loose-leaf tea.
2. A variety of teas may be combined with flowers not only for flavor but also for a more dramatic steeping process.
3. After 10 minutes, the compressed sphere is fully opened and the cup of tea is finished steeping.

broken-leaf tea: In this tea, the leaves are cut accidentally or on purpose. It cannot be considered whole-leaf tea at this point. They have a stronger flavor and are usually mixed with milk. They are also classified according to the presence of tips or buds. The list below is not arranged by quality as is the list above; it is simply the different varieties of broken-leaf tea.

- Broken Orange Pekoe (BOP)
- Golden Broken Orange Pekoe (GBOP)
- Flowery Broken Orange Pekoe (FBOP)
- Golden Flowery Broken Orange Pekoe (GFBOP)
- Tippy Golden Flowery Broken Orange Pekoe (TGFBOP)
- Tippy Golden Broken Orange Pekoe (TGBOP)
- Broken Pekoe (BP)
- Broken Pekoe Souchong (BPS)

fanning-leaf tea: This is also known as "Dusts" or "Fines." The leaves are cut or broken into very small pieces and the tea is even stronger than broken-leaf teas. They are mostly used for tea bags, which are brewed quickly.

- Orange Fannings (OF)
- Broken Orange Pekoe Fannings (BOPF)
- Pekoe Fannings (PF)
- Broken Pekoe Fannings (BPF)
- Pekoe Dust (PD)
- Broken Mixed Fannings (BMF)
- Fine Dust (FD)
- Red Dust (RD)
- Super Red Dust (SRD)
- Golden Dust (GD)
- Super Fine Dust (SFD)

Once tea is processed, it is either packed or blended with other teas of the same variety that are grown in different regions or countries. Not all tea leaves are the same; like grapes for wine, they can be combined from different areas to produce a specific result. This blending method is very common, because some tea drinkers who buy a specific brand expect to have the same flavors every time they purchase a specific kind of tea. Other people might prefer what is

known as "single-source," "specialty," or "garden" teas, which are not blended teas. They enjoy tasting the subtle differences between each batch of tea from a specific area.

classic blended teas

- **Earl Grey:** Blended Chinese or Indian and Chinese teas with bergamot fruit oil; bergamot is a type of orange.
- **Irish breakfast:** Generally, it is comprised of blended Assams.
- **English breakfast:** This is typically a blend of Assam, African, and Ceylon teas.
- **Russian Caravan:** This is a blend of oolong or black teas.

what type of tea should you sell?

There is no one answer to this question. As far as quality goes, loose leaf is always the best quality, but it gets complicated when brewing individual loose-leaf teas to go. There are some high-quality tea bags available and some are even nice to look at, but they can't compare to brewed loose-leaf tea. They are more a matter of convenience rather than quality. Tea bags have a four- to six-month lifespan, while loose-leaf teas keep for over two years if they are kept in an airtight, opaque container in a cool, dry place. You can brew individual portions of loose-leaf teas, but you essentially have to make an actual tea bag. Portion the tea into a porous bag similar to a coffee filter, which can be made of paper, fine-mesh nylon, or other synthetic materials. Some of these bags can be sealed shut with an iron or with the sealer element from a Cryovac machine, which can seal many at one time. This system works well for both to-stay and to-go individual cups, but there is some labor involved. There are other paper tea bags that have two perforations on either side of the bag. You can slide a skewer through them and the tea bag will sit on the top of the cup, so that after the tea has brewed, it can be removed easily. The only problem with this system is that it makes it impossible to put a lid on the to-go cup, but it works very well for individual orders to stay. There are also longer paper bags that can hang over the side of the cup. They can easily be removed, but the paper will absorb the water continuously, soaking the flap that hangs over the side of the cup and making for a big wet mess. The ideal option for to-stay teas is a more traditional approach. Instead of using paper, there are metal alternatives, such as a spring-headed infuser (a fine-mesh wire sphere that opens and closes similarly to a pair of scissors; the tea is placed inside the sphere), a mesh tea ball (a fine-mesh wire sphere that latches shut; the tea is placed inside the sphere), and a tea ball infuser (similar to the mesh tea ball but not as fine), among others. They have the advantage of being able to be used more than once.

Regardless of the type of bag you use for loose-leaf teas, remind your customers that the brewing time is longer than that of a regular tea bag. See the brewing times for each type of tea in the table below. Not all teas are in this section, only those that are the most popular. Loose-leaf tea takes two to five minutes to fully brew on average.

BREWING TEA

There is always the possibility that you will have customers who will order a pot of tea, and in this case you should know how to brew a pot of tea properly. When hot water is poured onto tea, its solubles are released into the water. The correct water temperature will ensure a favorable flavor extraction and result in a good cup of tea. The steps are as follows:

1. As with coffee, the quality of the water is crucial. Make sure to use either spring water or adequately filtered water. The water should be at 95°C/203°F on average, but it can vary from tea to tea. Have a hot water dispenser preset to this temperature and keep your teapots warm. Use a teapot that has an infuser canister and a plunger; they work very similarly to a French press pot for coffee.

2. Fill the infuser canister with the desired amount of loose-leaf tea. Typically, the ratio is one teaspoon per cup of tea. There's a reason why a teaspoon is used for tea.

3. Pour the hot water into the teapot and insert the infuser canister. Let it steep for the required amount of time, and then push the plunger down. Take the infuser out of the tea pot and put the lid back on it. Serve immediately with warm tea cups.

The brewing points about water temperature, using warmed tea cups, and steeping time apply to to-go cups or single-to-stay cups. Remind your customer about steeping time for to-go cups. They can always leave the bag in the cup if they choose to do so, but the tea will eventually become oversteeped and bitter tasting.

general brewing times for popular types of tea

type of tea	brewing temperature	brewing time	ratio
Assam (all types except green)	95°C/203°F	3 to 4 minutes	1 teaspoon: 1 cup water
Assam green	95°C/203°F	2 to 2.5 minutes	2 teaspoons: 1 cup water
Darjeeling (all types)	95°C/203°F	2 to 3 minutes	1.5 teaspoons: 1 cup water
China white teas	85°C/185°F	7 minutes and up to 15 for some varieties	2 teaspoons: 1 cup water
China green teas	70°C/158°F	3 to 4 minutes	2 teaspoons: 1 cup water
China oolong teas (includes pouchong)	95°C/203°F	5 to 7 minutes	1 teaspoon: 1 cup water
China black teas	95°C/203°F	5 to 7 minutes	1 teaspoon: 1 cup water
Indonesian teas	95°C/203°F	3 to 4 minutes	1 teaspoon: 1 cup water

iced tea

To make iced tea, follow the basic principles for brewing tea, but use one of these three methods to obtain a better final result:

- Brew twice the amount of tea that you would for a regular hot cup of tea. Pour it into a glass with ice to cool down and to dilute it to the proper strength.

- Brew a regular batch of tea and cool it over an ice bath. Reserve chilled. Serve in a glass with ice.

- Brew a regular batch of tea and cool it over an ice bath. Freeze half of it in ice cube trays and reserve the rest chilled. Serve the tea with the tea ice cubes to get the best result.

Iced tea is typically not served sweetened; it is sweetened by the person who is drinking it. Serve iced tea with a small pitcher of simple syrup so that the sugar will dissolve in the tea. And if it is infused with a vanilla bean, all the better.

infusions (tisanes)

Everything that can be brewed and is not tea or a coffee bean is known as an infusion (although technically coffee is an infusion too). Remember, if it does not come from the tea tree, it cannot be called tea. There are also herbal teas, but that label is only correct if the mixture is a blend of herbs and tea. For example, it is a common misconception that chamomile is a type of tea, when it is really a flower. Most infusions (also known as tisanes) can be made with the ingredients listed below, either alone or in combination. The combination can contain a type of tea. Chai latte is a perfect example of a combination of tea, typically Assam, and a tisane, using ginger, cardamom, clove, cinnamon, and sometimes peppercorns. Chai latte is steeped into a combination of equal parts water and milk.

- **Spices:** Cinnamon, nutmeg, allspice, clove, ginger, and cardamom can all be used. Chai latte, which is spice based, is considered an infusion.

- Vanilla pods/beans

- **Dehydrated flowers:** Examples include jasmine, chrysanthemum, rose petals, chamomile, lavender, geranium, hibiscus, violet, and lilac.

- **Dehydrated citrus peel:** Examples include orange, grapefruit, lime, lemon, and kaffir lime.

- **Dehydrated fruit:** Examples include pineapple, apple, cranberry, berries, coconut, peach, apricot, cherry, mango, and pomegranate.

- **Herbs:** Examples include mint, basil, lemon verbena, rosemary, thyme, sage, yerba maté, lemon myrtle, peppermint, and spearmint.

- **Leaves:** Examples include eucalyptus, rooibos, bay leaf, and kaffir lime leaf.

- **Other:** cocoa nibs, toasted barley

A general ratio for brewing tisanes is one tablespoon of tisane ingredient per cup of water. The problem with this is that the size of the tisane components can vary wildly. If using cinnamon sticks, whole litchis, or rosemary stems, for example, they can't be measured in a spoon measure. Having said that, a better way to measure the amount needed to make a tisane is to weigh out 10 or 11 g/.35 to .39 oz of tisane ingredient per 250 g/8.82 oz of water, or roughly a cup.

BREWING INSTRUCTIONS

Make sure the cup used is warm.

1. Measure out the tisane. Tisane can be brewed in the same ways as tea (see page 413). Portion it into a paper tea bag or a metallic infuser. Use a French press pot if possible, since there will be no need for paper and it will keep all the infusion ingredients in one place. There are individually sized French press pots, but the downside is that these are impossible to use for to-go orders. Unless your customers feel like waiting a few minutes, use paper bags for to-go orders.

2. Bring the water up to just under a boil. Pour the water into the cup or French press pot. Let the tisane steep for 5 to 7 minutes. It differs from tea in that the infusion ingredient does not need to be removed from the water. Tea becomes bitter if it is oversteeped. Tisane does not, but it needs at least 5 to 7 minutes to fully infuse.

Teas and tisanes can be purchased in bulk for your establishment's needs, but you can also repackage them in an airtight tin or other airtight container with your establishment's logo and resell them. For legal reasons, you need to mention the name of the company that produced the tea or tisane somewhere on the package, unless you make your own teas and tisanes. Make sure that the container is airtight and opaque so that light will not pass through it. Light oxidizes tea and some tisanes.

EXAMPLES OF TISANES

You could make your own tisanes if you are so inclined, but there are some very high-quality products available that will make your life easier (see Resources, page 540). The most important thing is to provide your customers with a quality product.

- **Blood orange and pear:** Serve chilled or hot.
- **Chamomile and lavender:** Serve chilled or hot.
- **Chrysanthemum and vanilla pod:** Serve hot.
- **Kaffir lime leaf and vanilla pod:** Serve chilled.
- **Jasmine dragon phoenix pearls with rooibos:** Can be served hot or chilled.
- **Rosebud and ginger:** Serve chilled.
- **Lemon verbena and peach:** Serve chilled.
- **Rose of suzhou:** Serve hot.
- **Rosemary, mint, raspberry, and honeycomb:** Serve chilled.
- **Blueberry and lemon:** Serve chilled.

Chrysanthemum and Vanilla Infusion

NON-ALCOHOLIC DRINKS

This section discusses beverages that are not coffee, espresso, tea, or tisane in the strict sense of the words but that could include one or more of those items. They are combinations of different liquids, and often some solids added as garnishes, that are for the same purpose: drinking. They don't fall into one single general category, but they do have something in common, and that is that they do not contain alcohol.

When you are deciding on a menu mix, you have to consider not only your personal tastes, but your customer's tastes as well. Most importantly, though, try to use ingredients that are in season, because they will be more economical and because it is environmentally friendlier.

Try to keep tisane-type ingredients to a minimum and not use them as a main component, since there are other great options available. This is where fresh and seasonal ingredients can be used in a different way.

Non-alcoholic drinks can be grouped into two very general categories: cold and frozen drinks and hot drinks (see page 424).

cold and frozen drinks

Cold and frozen drinks can be made with but are not limited to fruit juices and purées, vegetable juices and purées, and sodas. This is when a good juicer comes in handy. The Champion juicer truly extracts more water out of a fruit or vegetable than any other juicer I have used, and it leaves the pulp and other solids behind.

Solid garnishes such as fruit cut into morsel-size pieces, tapioca (bubble, large, medium, small), seeds such as passion fruit, basil, and cucumber, and crushed herbs can be added to these drinks. Additionally, they can include a frozen component like sorbet, granité (or granita), ice cream, or even a flavored foam. It is really up to the chef how the drink is garnished, if at all.

SODAS

It is also possible to make your own sodas. Assemble at least one soda siphon, since most hold only one liter, and CO_2 chargers. There are more industrial-size machines to carbonate drinks, but you have to consider the cost benefit of purchasing such an apparatus and the space it's going to take. The siphon and chargers are essential to make your own carbonated water. This liquid can be naturally flavored, but it needs to be as fluid as water so that it can pass through the siphon. Thicker liquids cannot be extruded from the very fine spout on the siphon. See the Granny Smith Apple Soda on page 420 as an example.

Brand-name sodas are not included in this chapter, although technically they do fall into this category. The variety you can offer besides the usual brands is something your customers will appreciate. There are quite a few "artisan" soda makers, which make high-quality products with real flavorings and no high-fructose corn syrup.

FROZEN DRINKS

Frozen drinks are also called granitas or granités. They are commonly known as "slush" and they are in fact an icy slush. The principle behind these types of drinks is that they are essentially a frozen fruit juice or other flavored liquid with a precise concentration of sugar. Typically, this is around 16° Brix. Brix is the percentage of sugar found in a liquid, and it is measured with a refractometer; a liquid with 16° Brix will contain 16 percent sugar. The liquid can be dairy based as long as it is fat-free, such as milk and even yogurt. The machine that freezes and dispenses the slush is similar to an ice cream batch freezer (see Resources, page 540). It paddles the sweetened liquid around a barrel that contains tubes filled with Freon gas or nitrogen, in some cases, and freezes the liquid to a semisolid slush. Typically these machines will hold up to two different flavors.

There are many flavor possibilities for granitas, but the liquid has to be fat-free. Fat will congeal as the granita freezes, producing unpleasant, grainy lumps of milk fat. This machine does require a substantial investment, but the cost of the ingredients to make the granitas is minimal, and in the warm summer months you will possibly have a hard time keeping up with demand, especially if you use high-quality ingredients. Granitas can be served on their own, or with another liquid component and a solid garnish.

You cannot make granitas with a blender; they will not yield the smooth product that a granité machine does. If you do in fact use a blender, you will be making a product called a frappé, which is basically a flavored liquid (such as coffee, tea, or fruit juice) blended with ice; it typically has a very short lifespan.

ELDERFLOWER WITH BOSC PEAR–INFUSED WATER AND BOSC PEAR SORBET

yield: 10 drinks

INGREDIENT	METRIC	U.S.
BOSC PEAR WATER AND SORBE		
Bosc pears	3 kg	6 lb 9.76 oz
Water	3 kg	6 lb 9.76 oz
Superfine sugar	500 g	1 lb 1.64 oz
Tahitian vanilla pods, split and seeds scraped	3	3
Salt	2 g	.07 oz
Elderflower Syrup (see Resources, page 540)	500 g	1 lb .16 oz

1. Assemble ten 600-mL/20-fl-oz glasses.

2. **FOR THE PEAR WATER:** Peel and core the pears. There should be 2 kg/4 lb 3.6 oz of fruit with no seeds, stems, or skin.

3. Place the pears in a sauce pot with the water, sugar, vanilla pods and seeds, and salt and gently simmer over medium heat until the pears are tender and cooked through. Let the pears sit in the poaching water overnight, covered, in the refrigerator.

4. Remove the pears from the water. Pass the water through a fine-mesh sieve lined with cheesecloth and reserve.

5. Purée the pears in a commercial blender on high speed until smooth. You will not need to add water or more sugar since it has already been absorbed by the pears.

6. Churn in a batch freezer until frozen. Reserve the sorbet in the freezer for up to 48 hours.

7. **TO PICK UP:** Scoop 150 g/5.29 oz of pear sorbet into one of the glasses. Pour 300 g/10.58 oz of pear water and 50 g/1.76 oz of elderflower syrup into the glass. Serve with a straw.

note You can also add vanilla bean (or other spice) and a pinch of salt to the pear poaching liquid. A small amount of acid, such as fresh lemon juice (about 100 g/3.53 oz), added to the poaching liquid will help accentuate flavors and slow down the pear's oxidation.

SPARKLING LEMONADE WITH LEMON SORBET AND POMEGRANATE TAPIOCA

yield: 10 drinks

INGREDIENT	METRIC	U.S.
LEMONADE		
Fondant sugar or other fine crystal sugar	400 g	14.08 oz
Water	2.5 kg	5 lb 8.16 oz
Fresh lemon juice	300 g	10.58 oz
POMEGRANATE TAPIOCA		
Medium pearl tapioca	300 g	10.58 oz
Pomegranate juice	1 kg	2 lb 3.2 oz
Corn syrup	100 g	3.53 oz
Lemon sorbet	1 kg	2 lb 3.2 oz
Gold leaf sheets	10	10

1. Assemble ten 600-mL/20-fl-oz glasses.

2. **FOR THE LEMONADE:** Combine the fondant sugar with the water in a bowl and stir to dissolve the sugar. Add the lemon juice. Taste and adjust acidity and/or sweetness. This amount should be enough to fill a siphon 5 times (each siphon generally holds 1 liter). Fill the siphon according to the manufacturer's instructions.

3. Charge the siphon with CO_2. Some siphons require 1 charge, some need 2. Refrigerate until needed. Refrigerate the remaining liquid and fill the siphon as needed.

4. **FOR THE POMEGRANATE TAPIOCA:** Place the tapioca in a pot with enough cold water to cover it by 2.5 cm/1 in.

5. Bring it up to a boil, and then strain the tapioca through a sieve. Rinse the tapioca with hot water and put in the pot again with enough water to cover it by 2.5 cm/1 in. Bring it back up to a boil, and then strain it again. Repeat this process until the tapioca is translucent.

6. Place the tapioca back in the pot and add the pomegranate juice. Bring to a simmer, and simmer for about 5 minutes. Let the tapioca sit in the juice for 10 to 15 more minutes or until the tapioca has absorbed the juice.

7. Strain the tapioca and rinse in cold water. Once it has cooled, toss it in the corn syrup and reserve in the refrigerator to keep the tapioca pearls from sticking to each other. Discard after 1 day of service. The tapioca will absorb twice its weight in liquid.

8. **TO PICK UP:** Spoon 60 g/2.11 oz of tapioca into a glass.

9. Scoop 100 g/3.53 oz of lemon sorbet into the glass. Put a sheet of gold leaf on the sorbet.

10. Dispense the sparkling lemonade tableside to fill the glass. Serve with a straw.

STRAWBERRY JUICE WITH VANILLA SHERBET, CRUSHED BASIL, AND BASIL SEEDS

yield: 10 drinks

INGREDIENT	METRIC	U.S.
STRAWBERRY JUICE		
Strawberries, stemmed	12 kg	26 lb 7.36 oz
Fondant sugar or other fine crystal sugar	450 g	15.87 oz
Basil seeds	150 g	5.28 oz
Basil leaves	50	50
Vanilla Sherbet (recipe follows)	750 g	1 lb 10.4 oz

1. Assemble ten 600-mL/20-fl-oz glasses.

2. **FOR THE STRAWBERRY JUICE:** Place the strawberries in a large bowl over a simmering hot water bath. This will slowly release the liquid from the strawberries and leave the pulp behind, so the result will be a clear, pink liquid with an intense strawberry flavor.

3. Cool the liquid over an ice bath. Stir in the fondant sugar until dissolved. Add more sugar if needed. Discard after 48 hours

4. Place the basil seeds in a bain marie and cover them with cold water. Let them soak for at least 1 hour before using. The basil seeds will form a gelatinous shell around the seed. Discard after 24 hours.

5. **TO PICK UP:** Place 5 basil leaves in a cup and crush the leaves inside the glass with a mortar. Scoop 75 g/2.64 oz of vanilla sherbet on top of the basil.

6. Spoon 15 g/.52 oz of soaked basil seeds on top of the sherbet. Pour the strawberry water over the basil seeds to fill the glass (about 450 g/15.87 oz).

VANILLA SHERBET

yield: 750 g/1 lb 10.4 oz

INGREDIENT	METRIC	U.S.	%
2% milk	540 g	1 lb 3.04 oz	72%
Tahitian vanilla pod, split and scraped	2	2	
Simple syrup, at 50° Brix	210 g	7.41 oz	28%

1. Bring the milk to a boil with the vanilla pod and beans. Turn the heat off and let the vanilla steep for 30 minutes. Strain the mixture and cool the milk over an ice bath.

2. Add the simple syrup. Refrigerate or churn in an ice cream batch freezer. Reserve in the freezer in an airtight container for up to 48 hours.

GRANNY SMITH APPLE SODA

yield: 10 drinks

INGREDIENT	METRIC	U.S.	%
Granny Smith apples	15 kg	33 lb 1.12 oz	95.18%
Ascorbic acid	10 g	.35 oz	.06%
Fondant sugar or other fine crystal sugar	750 g	1 lb 10.4 oz	4.76%
Salt	as needed	as needed	

1. Assemble ten 600-mL/20-fl-oz glasses.

2. Cut the apples coarsely into eighths. As you are cutting, someone should be juicing the apples. Ideally this is done by two people. Speed is important to prevent the juice from oxidizing. As the juice is coming out of the juicer, it is a good idea to put a small amount of ascorbic acid in the juice. If you wait until all the apples have been juiced to add the ascorbic acid, the juice will have started oxidizing.

3. Stir the fondant sugar into the apple juice. Adjust sweetness if needed. Add a pinch of salt. Strain the liquid through a fine-mesh sieve.

4. Fill a siphon with the apple juice according to the manufacturer's instructions. Load the siphon with one or two CO_2 chargers and reserve in the refrigerator. Refill the siphon as needed. Reserve the remaining juice in the refrigerator.

5. **TO PICK UP:** Fill a glass halfway full with ice. Dispense the juice from the siphon into the glass and serve with a straw.

MEYER LEMON GRANITA WITH HUCKLEBERRY JUICE AND HUCKLEBERRIES

yield: 10 drinks

INGREDIENT	METRIC	U.S.
MEYER LEMON GRANITA		
Meyer lemon juice	3.9 kg	8 lb 9.6 oz
Simple syrup, at 50° Brix	1.1 kg	2 lb 6.88 oz
Salt	3 g	.10 oz
HUCKLEBERRY JUICE		
Huckleberries	500 g	1 lb 1.64 oz
Water	200 g	7.05 oz
Sugar	400 g	14.11 oz

1. Assemble ten 600-mL/20-fl-oz glasses.

2. **FOR THE GRANITA:** Combine the Meyer lemon juice, the simple syrup, and the salt.

3. Pour into the granita machine and freeze. If you do not have a granita machine, churn the liquid in an ice cream batch freezer and blend it to order with an additional small amount of sweetened Meyer lemon juice. The granita should be of a drinkable/pourable consistency.

4. **FOR THE HUCKLEBERRY JUICE:** Combine the huckleberries, water, and sugar in a sauce pot and bring to a boil. Reduce the heat to low and simmer for 5 minutes. Turn the heat off and strain the huckleberries out; reserve them in the refrigerator. Discard after 4 days.

5. Reduce the resulting liquid by half in a pot over high heat. Cool over an ice bath and reserve in the refrigerator.

6. **TO PICK UP:** Scoop 500 g/1 lb .16 oz of Meyer lemon granita into a glass. Spoon 50 g/1.76 oz of huckleberries into the glass. Pour 50 g/1.76 oz of huckleberry juice into the glass. Serve with a straw.

PASSION FRUIT GRANITA WITH COCONUT FOAM AND SHREDDED COCONUT

yield: 10 drinks

INGREDIENT	METRIC	U.S.
PASSION FRUIT GRANITA		
Passion fruit purée concentrate	1.8 kg	3 lb 15.52 oz
Orange juice	1.8 kg	3 lb 15.52 oz
Simple syrup, at 50° Brix	1.4 kg	3 lb 1.44 oz
COCONUT FOAM		
Sweetened coconut milk	1 kg	2 lb 4.2 oz
Gelatin sheets, bloomed	10 g	.35 oz
Unsweetened shredded coconut	300 g	10.58 oz

1. Assemble ten 600-mL/20-fl-oz glasses.

2. **FOR THE GRANITA:** Combine the passion fruit purée, orange juice, and simple syrup. Pour into the granita machine and freeze. If you do not have a granita machine, you can churn the liquid in an ice cream batch freezer and blend it to order with an additional small amount of sweetened passion fruit and orange juice The granita should be of a drinkable/pourable consistency.

3. **FOR THE COCONUT FOAM:** Combine the coconut milk and the gelatin sheets in a bowl and place over a simmering hot water bath. Stir until the gelatin has dissolved.

4. Cool over a cold water bath. Do not use an ice bath, since it will set the gelatin. Discard after 3 days.

5. Fill a heavy cream whipper with the coconut-gelatin mix. Close it tightly, and fill it with 2 chargers, shaking the whipper between charges. Reserve in the refrigerator.

6. **TO PICK UP:** Pour 500 g/1 lb .16 oz of granita into a glass. Dispense coconut foam over the top of the granita; some of it should dome above the rim of the glass. Coat the foam with shredded coconut. Serve with a straw.

CONCORD GRAPE SODA WITH BUTTERMILK SHERBET

yield: 10 drinks

INGREDIENT	METRIC	U.S.
CONCORD GRAPE JUICE		
Concord grapes, stemmed	2.1 kg	4 lb 10.08 oz
Water	700 g	1 lb 8.64 oz
Sugar	700 g	1 lb 8.64 oz
Buttermilk Sherbet (recipe follows)	1.5 kg	3 lb 4.96 oz

1. Assemble ten 600-mL/20-fl-oz glasses.

2. **FOR THE CONCORD GRAPE JUICE:** Combine the grapes, water, and sugar in a pot and bring to a boil. Turn off the heat. Strain the grapes through a coarse-mesh sieve, pushing down with a ladle to extrude as much juice from the grapes as possible.

3. Pass the remaining liquid through a fine-mesh sieve and then through cheesecloth, and then chill over an ice bath. Adjust the sweetness if necessary. There should be 3.5 kg/7 lb 11.36 oz of juice. Discard after 3 days.

4. Fill a soda siphon with the juice as per the manufacturer's instructions and charge with 1 or 2 CO_2 chargers. Reserve in the refrigerator. Reserve the remaining liquid chilled and refill the siphon as needed.

5. **TO PICK UP:** Remove 3 tubes of buttermilk sherbet from the freezer and unwrap them. Put them in the glass in a standing position.

6. Dispense the grape soda at the last minute or, better yet, tableside. Serve with a straw and a long spoon.

BUTTERMILK SHERBET

yield: 1.5 kg/3 lb 4.8 oz

INGREDIENT	METRIC	U.S.	%
Buttermilk	780 g	1 lb 11.52 oz	52%
2% milk	285 g	10.05 oz	19%
Simple syrup, at 50° Brix	435 g	15.34 oz	29%

1. Combine all of the ingredients in a bowl.

2. Line 30 stainless-steel or PVC tubes 2.5 by 10 cm/1 by 4 in with acetate and freeze them in a standing position on a sheet pan lined with a nonstick rubber mat.

3. Churn the buttermilk sherbet in an ice cream batch freezer. Extrude the sherbet into a piping bag, and pipe the sherbet into the prepared tubes. Even out the tops with a small offset spatula. Freeze to harden.

4. Once hardened, push the sherbet tubes out of their molds and reserve frozen with the acetate still on (this will prevent freezer burn). These will hold a semismooth consistency for 2 days in the freezer. After that, if there are any tubes left over, melt them down and churn them again.

hot drinks

Hot drinks are more popular in cooler climates and in the colder seasons like fall, winter, and early spring. The following examples of hot drinks can be made and held hot for long periods of time. This is a huge advantage over coffee and tea, as well as the drinks made with them, which can have a very short lifespan. For this to work, though, you will need to invest in the proper holding equipment.

The most common and easiest way to preserve hot liquids is to use thermally insulated containers, which come in a variety of sizes and insulating capacities. Typically, the longer it can preserve the heat, the better the insulation in the container, but it will also be more expensive since the capacity to insulate is what makes the difference between a good thermal container and a bad one. If possible, have three or four of these containers for the same liquid filled during service, so that as you dispense from one container, the others will remain hot for longer periods of time. Alternatively, you can make hot drinks at different times during the day.

HOT CHOCOLATE

Hot chocolate is one of those items that can easily be made well but is usually poorly made. Just get a few basic ingredients of the highest quality, and the rest takes care of itself. As long as you respect the quality of the ingredients and you make it fresh each day, there should be no reason not to obtain an excellent product.

One of the recurring defects that occurs with hot chocolate is that after it sits for extended periods of time (cold or hot), some of the fat tends to separate to the top and some of the chocolate solids sink to the bottom. To resolve this problem, try adding powdered soy lecithin, a natural ingredient, at less than 1 percent of the total weight of the entire recipe.

Hot chocolate is very versatile as far as its thickness, which can be changed simply by adjusting ingredient quantities and also the seemingly endless numbers of flavors that can be added simply by steeping them in the original amount of milk. At the end of this section there are some examples and amounts of the flavors that can be added to hot chocolate.

MULLED CIDER

Mulled cider's function is twofold: not only is it a hot drink, but the aroma of hot mulled cider brings back fond memories to many people. Cinnamon, cloves, and apples are all things that are associated with the holidays, and therefore have a nostalgic, feel-good aroma. Not that this will necessarily help you sell more mulled cider (it might), but it will certainly make for a warm and very welcoming dining room. It is a good idea to make the mulled cider in the dining room area so that all of those aromas are appreciated there. Keep a small pot with some mulled cider over very low heat in a hidden area by the dining room to keep that aroma going throughout the day. The rest should be kept in thermally insulated containers. When an order comes in, it is a good idea to get the cider a lot hotter than when it comes out of the container, because at that point it will only be somewhat hot. Pour the cider into a mug, and then get the cider very hot by using the steam spout from the espresso machine.

THIN HOT CHOCOLATE

yield: 2.4 L/10 cups (served in a 270-mL/9-fl-oz cup)

INGREDIENT	METRIC	U.S.	%
Whole milk	1.81 kg	4 lb	72.6%
Dark chocolate (64%) coins	681 g	1 lb 8 oz	27.22%
Fleur de sel	.91 g	.3 oz	.04%
Soy lecithin, powdered	4 g	.13 oz	.15%

1. Bring the milk to a boil and pour it over the chocolate. Ideally, place it in a bain marie or similar tall metallic cylinder.

2. Using an immersion blender, blend the milk with the chocolate. Meanwhile, add the salt and the soy lecithin. Blend until you obtain a uniform mixture.

3. Strain and hold at 80°C/176°F. Reheat each order by pouring the hot chocolate in a mug or cup and then using the steam spout from the espresso machine to heat it further. While the hot chocolate comes out hot from the thermal container, it is a much better product if it can be served piping hot. Discard after service.

THICK HOT CHOCOLATE

yield: 2.4 L/10 cups (served in a 270-mL/9-fl-oz cup)

INGREDIENT	METRIC	U.S.	%
Whole milk	1.24 kg	2 lb 12 oz	49.91%
Heavy cream	416 g	14.67 oz	16.64%
Dark chocolate (64%) coins	833 g	1 lb 13.28 oz	33.27%
Fleur de sel	1 g	.04 oz	.05%
Soy lecithin, powder	3 g	.12 oz	.13%

1. Combine the milk and the cream in a sauce pot and bring to a boil.

2. Pour over the chocolate. Ideally place it in a bain marie or similar tall metallic cylinder.

3. Using an immersion blender, blend the milk and cream with the chocolate. Meanwhile, add the salt and the soy lecithin. Blend until you obtain a smooth, uniform mixture.

4. Strain and hold at 80°C/176°F. Reheat each order by pouring the hot chocolate in a mug or cup and then using the steam spout from the espresso machine to heat it further. While the hot chocolate comes out hot from the thermal container, it is a much better product if it can be served piping hot. Discard after service.

recommended flavorings

To steep the following flavors, put them in the milk or the milk and cream before it boils. Bring them to a boil together and then turn off the heat. Cover the pot with plastic wrap and steep the flavors for a few minutes. As a rule, steep the mixture for 5 minutes maximum if steeping teas and 15 to 20 for other flavors. Strain them into another pot using a fine-mesh sieve and return the liquid to a second boil before pouring over the chocolate. The amounts are for the yields for the recipes above. Try using a combination of these flavors as well. You can also use Mexican chocolate as a substitute in the recipes above. It will result in an intense chocolate taste with a hint of cinnamon.

Earl Grey tea: 40 g/1.41 oz

Jasmine tea: 40 g/1.41 oz

Nutmeg: 7 whole nutmegs, crushed

Star anise, toasted: 20 g/.71 oz

Cinnamon sticks, toasted: 40 g/1.41 oz

Mexican cinnamon, toasted: 25 g/.88 oz

Vanilla pods, split and scraped: 2

Cloves, toasted: 12 g/.42 oz

Pink peppercorns, lightly toasted: 12 g/.42 oz

Cardamom pods, toasted: 10 g/.35 oz

Orange zest: 30 g/1.07 oz

Lemon zest: 24 g/.84 oz

Lime zest: 16 g/.56 oz

Crushed candy canes: 175 g/6.17 oz

Toasted nuts (almonds, hazelnuts, pecans, macadamia nuts, cashews, pistachios): 375 g/13.23 oz. In this case you will need to steep the nuts with 25 percent more liquid than the recipe calls for, since the nuts will absorb some of the liquid.

Toasted unsweetened coconut: Follow the same instructions as for the nuts.

MARSHMALLOW

yield: 976 g/2 lb 2.43 oz

INGREDIENT	METRIC	U.S.	%
Cornstarch	100 g	3.53 oz	
Confectioners' sugar	100 g	3.53 oz	
Sugar	450 g	15.87 oz	46.11%
Light corn syrup	75 g	2.65 oz	7.68%
Water	130 g	4.59 oz	13.32%
Egg whites	300 g	10.58 oz	30.74%
Gelatin sheets, silver, bloomed in cold water, drained, excess water squeezed off	21 g	.74 oz	2.15%

1. Combine the cornstarch and confectioners' sugar. Dust a half sheet pan lined with a non-stick rubber mat with half the mixture.

2. Combine the sugar and corn syrup in a sauce pot with the water and mix to obtain a "wet sand" texture. Place the pot over high heat and cook to 155°C/311°F. Meanwhile, in the bowl of an electric mixer fitted with the whip attachment, whip the egg whites on high speed to stiff peak. Keep the mixer running.

3. Turn the heat off and whisk the bloomed gelatin into the sugar syrup. Remove the pan from the heat and pour the mixture into the whipping egg whites.

4. Spread the mixture evenly over the prepared sheet pan. Once spread, dust the remaining cornstarch-sugar mixture over the marshmallow. Let the marshmallow slab set overnight.

5. Once set, flip the marshmallow onto a cutting board, and using a sharp knife cut the marshmallow into 2.5-cm/1-in cubes. Reserve in an airtight container. Discard after four days or freeze for up to 2 months.

MULLED CIDER

yield: 2.4 L/10 cups (served in a 270-mL/9-fl-oz cup)

INGREDIENT	METRIC	U.S.	%
Apple cider	2.19 kg	4 lb 13.28 oz	85.91%
Orange juice	137 g	4.83 oz	5.37%
Lemon juice	82 g	2.9 oz	3.22%
Sugar	131 g	4.64 oz	5.15%
Cloves, toasted	9 g	.31 oz	.34%
Cinnamon sticks, toasted	5	5	
Oranges, quartered	3	3	
Lemons, quartered	2	2	

1. Mix all of the ingredients together in a sauce pot and bring to a boil. Simmer for 10 minutes or until fully aromatic.

2. Strain and reserve at 80°C/176°F. Reheat each order by pouring the mulled cider in a mug or cup and then using the steam spout from the espresso machine to heat it further.

BEER AND WINE

While an entire book could be written on either subject, and a very large book it would be, this chapter will not dissect the intricacies of beer and wine. This section will encompass beverages that are made with them and offer a few suggestions on serving them alone.

Serving beer and wine alone can be profitable if you know how to sell them, since they require little labor and are shelf stable for long periods of time, plus the upsell can be significant. A 30 to 50 percent markup on wine is a generally accepted practice. Wine cannot be marked up as much in a café as in a restaurant, though. Beer is a much easier sell, since it is already an individual portion, it is easily served, and it is even prepackaged to go. You should expect to sell moderately priced wine by the glass, so make sure to offer several high-quality wines (expensive doesn't necessarily mean better) at an appropriate price. Rarely will you have a customer order an entire bottle of wine with his or her lunch, unless there is large crowd involved. That is expected in a restaurant environment more than in a café. Try to offer six to ten wines by the glass, half white and half red. You can include a sparkling wine or Champagne every now and then, but you should expect a short shelf life on the carbonation, no matter how technologically advanced a stopper system you have. Red and white wine can be preserved for a longer period of time. After the bottle is opened, use a vacuum stopper. This is essentially a rubber cork with a small hole, into which you insert a pump to extract any oxygen from the bottle, thus extending its shelf life. The bottle will need to be vacuumed out after each pour. Do not hold wine that has been opened for more than 36 hours. Another preserving system uses the same type of rubber cork, but instead injects argon gas into the bottle. This device holds the argon gas cartridge, and then it is fitted with a nozzle that fits inside the rubber cork's opening, into which the gas is dispensed. This system is more effective than vacuuming oxygen out of the bottle. It may extend the life of the wine by an extra day, and it takes less time than pumping the oxygen out by hand, but it can be more expensive because of the argon gas cartridges. There are also automatic vacuums that suck the oxygen out of the bottle so that you don't have to do it yourself, but these can get very pricey. Think of investing in wine preserving this way: If you sell enough wine, you won't need to invest any money trying to figure out how to preserve it. Any wine that is left over at the end of the day can be used to make wine-based drinks (see the following text).

A good wine refrigeration system is a practical and not-too-expensive investment. Some can hold both red and white wine at different temperatures, and this is crucial to serving wine properly.

wine- and beer-based drinks

Most but not all of these drinks follow the basic principles of a classic Spanish sangria: wine and fruit juice combined with fruit. This can produce a large amount of variations on the theme, but keep in mind that a typical wine used for sangria is not of the highest quality. The idea behind making these types of drinks is to use open wine that has peaked in order to keep it from going to waste and to use it in a way that still creates a high-quality product. Of course, if the wine is corked, stale, or turning to vinegar, never, ever use it. You can pop open a fresh bottle of wine for mixed wine drinks, but again, do not use expensive bottles for this purpose.

The combination used for alcohol-based drinks in this book is not limited to wine; you can use beer or a combination of wine and a liquor, or beer and a liquor. Drinks made with beer will have to be mixed to order to keep them from losing their carbonation. The garnish is not limited to fruit, either. As you will see in the recipes that follow, some do not contain any solid garnishes. These mixed drinks can be very popular during warm-weather months, or if you are located in an area that is warm year round, all the better.

These drinks can be sold by the glass or by the pitcher (four to six servings per pitcher).

The general ratio for the following drinks is one part fruit juice to one part wine. The fruit garnish used, if any, is particular to each recipe. These drinks should be served in a 480-mL/16-fl-oz glass (filled to 450 mL/15 fl oz). Ice is optional for beer and wine drinks, since the ingredients should be kept chilled to begin with. If you choose to use ice, the recipe will yield 50 percent more. If using ice, use finely shaved ice, since it keeps the drink colder than ice cubes do. There are machines that shave ice quickly and easily. Contrary to what one might think, shaved ice does not melt faster than ice cubes. When you pour the liquid over the shaved ice in the glass, the outer surface of the ice melts but it immediately freezes again, forming a sort of large, porous ice cube, which takes longer to melt than a regular ice cube because of its size. Serve the drinks with a long-handled, thin demitasse spoon, to make eating the garnish easier.

MERLOT WITH MEYER LEMON LEMONADE AND CANTALOUPE

yield: 10 drinks

INGREDIENT	METRIC	U.S.	%
MEYER LEMON LEMONADE			
Water	900 g	1 lb 15.75 oz	48%
Meyer lemon juice	600 g	1 lb 5.12 oz	32%
Fondant sugar or other fine crystal sugar	375 g	13.23 oz	20%
Cantaloupe, scooped with a small Parisienne scoop	900 g	1 lb 15.68 oz	20%
Merlot	1.8 kg	3 lb 15.52 oz	40%
Meyer Lemon Lemonade	1.8 kg	3 lb 15.52 oz	40%

1. **FOR THE MEYER LEMON LEMONADE:** Combine all of the ingredients in a bowl or pitcher. Stir to dissolve the sugar. Adjust sweetness if needed. Reserve in an airtight container in the refrigerator. Discard after 48 hours.

2. **TO PICK UP:** Scoop the cantaloupe to the desired scoop size, the smaller the better.

3. Combine the Merlot and Meyer lemon lemonade with the cantaloupe and reserve chilled. This particular sangria tastes better after 24 hours, once the cantaloupe has completely absorbed the flavors of the wine and the lemonade.

4. Stir before serving in a 480-mL/16-fl-oz glass filled to 450 mL/15 fl oz without ice. Discard after 72 hours.

PINOT GRIGIO WITH ORANGE JUICE AND CITRUS FRUITS

yield: 10 drinks

INGREDIENT	METRIC	U.S.	%
Pinot Grigio	1.8 kg	3 lb 15.52 oz	40%
Orange juice, fresh	1.8 kg	3 lb 15.52 oz	40%
Valencia orange suprêmes	300 g	10.58 oz	6.67%
Grapefruit suprêmes	300 g	10.58 oz	6.67%
Blood orange suprêmes	300 g	10.58 oz	6.67%

1. Combine the Pinot Grigio with the orange juice and the citrus suprêmes gently, to prevent them from breaking up.

2. Reserve in the refrigerator. Stir before serving in a 480-mL/16-fl-oz glass filled to 450 mL/ 15 fl oz without ice. Discard after 48 hours.

RIESLING WITH CRANBERRY JUICE AND POMEGRANATE SEEDS

yield: 10 drinks

INGREDIENT	METRIC	U.S.	%
Pomegranate seeds (about 4 whole pomegranates)	900 g	1 lb 15.68 oz	20%
Riesling	1.8 kg	3 lb 15.52 oz	40%
Cranberry juice	1.8 kg	3 lb 15.52 oz	40%

1. Extract the seeds from the pomegranate by cutting the fruit in half and tapping the seeds out with a wooden spoon. Remove any white membrane.

2. Combine the Riesling and cranberry juice with the pomegranate seeds. Reserve in the refrigerator. Stir before serving in a 480-mL/16-fl-oz glass filled to 450 mL/15 fl oz without ice. Discard after 48 hours.

CHARDONNAY WITH PEACH NECTAR AND BUBBLE TAPIOCA

yield: 10 drinks

INGREDIENT	METRIC	U.S.	%
Bubble tapioca	900 g	1 lb 15.68 oz	20%
Corn syrup	100 g	3.53 oz	
Chardonnay	1.8 kg	3 lb 15.52 oz	40%
Peach nectar	1.8 kg	3 lb 15.52 oz	40%

1. **FOR THE BUBBLE TAPIOCA:** Check the manufacturer's instructions for cooking. Generally speaking, all parcooked bubble tapioca is cooked the same way. Weigh the tapioca and place water in the amount of 3 times the weight of the tapioca in a pot. Bring the water up to a boil, and then pour in the tapioca, stirring gently so that the pearls do not scorch or stick to the bottom of the pot.

2. Wait until the tapioca pearls float to the top, and then cover the pot with a lid. Cook for 25 to 30 more minutes, or until halfway cooked. Break a pearl open and look to see if the center is still hard; the exterior should be soft and chewy.

3. Remove the pot from the heat and let it sit for 25 to 30 minutes with the lid still on.

4. Strain the pearls and rinse them in cold water to stop the cooking process.

5. Toss them in a bowl with just enough corn syrup to coat the pearls evenly. They must be used within 24 hours of being made; otherwise they will go from being pleasantly chewy to crumbly.

6. **TO PICK UP:** Combine all the ingredients. Reserve in the refrigerator. Stir just before serving in a 470-mL/16-fl-oz glass filled to 450 mL/15 fl oz without ice. Discard after 24 hours.

CAVA WITH PASSION FRUIT JUICE AND PASSION FRUIT SEEDS

yield: 10 drinks

INGREDIENT	METRIC	U.S.	%
Passion fruit seeds	300 g	10.58 oz	6.67%
Passion fruit juice	2.1 kg	4 lb 10.08 oz	46.67%
Cava (or Prosecco or other dry sparkling white wine)	2.1 kg	4 lb 10.08 oz	46.67%

1. **TO PICK UP:** This drink needs to be made to order. Place 30 g/1.06 oz of passion fruit seeds in a 480-mL/16-fl-oz glass.

2. Fill the glass halfway with passion fruit juice. Pour in the Cava tableside or at the last minute. The glass should be filled to 450 mL/15 fl oz without ice.

note Passion fruit juice (sometimes called nectar) is labeled as such. Do not get it confused with the purée, which is oftentimes concentrated and mostly used for pastry production. You can use the purée, but keep in mind that if it is concentrated you will have to cut it down with an equal part of orange juice or water, and then sweeten it.

ASTI SPUMANTI WITH APRICOT NECTAR AND RASPBERRIES

yield: 10 drinks

INGREDIENT	METRIC	U.S.	%
Fresh raspberries	500 g	1 lb 1.64 oz	11.11%
Apricot nectar	2 kg	4 lb 6.4 oz	44.44%
Asti Spumanti	2 kg	4 lb 6.4 oz	44.44%

1. This drink is assembled to order. Place 50 g/1.76 oz of fresh raspberries in a 480-mL/16-fl-oz glass.

2. Pour in the apricot nectar to fill the glass halfway.

3. Pour the Asti Spumanti into the glass tableside or at the last minute. The glass should be filled to 450 mL/15 fl oz without ice.

FRANZISKANER HEFE-WEISSE WHEAT BEER AND LEMONADE

yield: 10 drinks

INGREDIENT	METRIC	U.S.	%
LEMONADE			
Water	900 g	1 lb 15.68 oz	60%
Lemon juice	300 g	10.58 oz	20%
Fondant sugar or other fine crystal sugar	300 g	10.58 oz	20%
Lemon wedges	10	10	
Light Hefe-weisse beer	3 kg	6 lb 9.76 oz	66.67%

1. **FOR THE LEMONADE:** Combine the water, lemon juice, and sugar in a bowl or pitcher and stir until the sugar has dissolved. There should be 1.5 kg/3 lb 4.96 oz of lemonade. Reserve in an airtight container in the refrigerator. Discard after 2 days.

2. **TO PICK UP:** This drink needs to be made to order. Fill a 480-mL/16-fl-oz glass one-third of the way with lemonade. Put a wedge of lemon on the rim of the glass.

3. Serve with a full bottle of Hefe-weisse beer on the side.

notes This drink is European in origin, known in France as a panaché, in Britain as a shandy, and in Germany as a radler. It consists of mixing equal parts beer and lemon-lime soda. This recipe uses actual lemonade. In Britain, if you ask for lemonade, you will get a lemon-lime soda.

This drink works well with lager and pilsner beers as well. Dark beers don't work as well with the lemonade.

CHAMPAGNE WITH BLACKBERRIES, CRÈME DE VIOLETTE LIQUEUR, AND VIOLET SYRUP

yield: 20 drinks

INGREDIENT	METRIC	U.S.	%
Blackberries	30	30	
Violet syrup	100 g	3.53 oz	4%
Crème de violette	300 g	10.58 oz	12%
Champagne	2.1 kg	4 lb 10 oz	84%

1. This drink is assembled to order. Place 3 blackberries in a champagne flute.

2. Pour 10 g/1.35 oz of violet syrup and 30 g/1.06 oz of crème de violette on top of the blackberries.

3. Pour the Champagne tableside or at the last minute. The glass should be filled to 240 mL/8 fl oz without ice.

notes Violet syrup is purchased premade; see Resources, page 540.

ROGUE CHOCOLATE STOUT WITH VANILLA ICE CREAM

INGREDIENT	METRIC	U.S.	%
VANILLA ICE CREAM			
Heavy cream	1 kg	2 lb 3.2 oz	48.78%
Milk	500 g	1 lb 1.64 oz	24.39%
Tahitian vanilla pods, split and scraped	2	2	
Sugar	250 g	8.82 oz	12.2%
Egg yolks	300 g	10.58 oz	14.63%
Rogue chocolate stout	3.9 kg	8 lb 9.6 oz	86.67%

1. **FOR THE VANILLA ICE CREAM:** Prepare an ice bath to cool the base down once it is cooked. Place a bain marie or hotel pan directly into the ice bath so that it is ready. It is crucial to stop the cooking process as quickly as possible to prevent the eggs from cooking too far.

2. Combine the cream, milk, vanilla pods and seeds, and half the sugar in a pot over medium-high heat. Do not stir.

3. Combine the yolks and the other half of the sugar in a bowl, and mix to obtain a homogenous mass.

4. Once the liquid comes to a boil, temper it into the egg yolk mixture, whisking constantly. Return the mixture to the pot and place it over medium-low heat.

5. Whisk constantly until the mixture reaches 85°C/185°F. Immediately turn off the heat and take the pot off the heat.

6. Whisk for 1 more minute, and then strain through a fine-mesh sieve into the prepared bain marie or hotel pan over the ice bath. Cool down quickly by stirring the base constantly in the ice bath.

7. Churn in an ice cream batch freezer and reserve in the freezer. Only churn what is needed for that day. Any leftover vanilla ice cream can be thawed and churned one more time. After that, if there is any left over, it must be discarded.

8. **TO PICK UP:** This drink needs to be made to order. Scoop 60 g/2.11 oz of vanilla ice cream into a 480-mL/16-fl-oz glass. Serve with a bottle of chocolate stout on the side.

notes This recipe yields more ice cream than you need for this drink recipe. It is better to make more than to make such a minuscule amount; otherwise the ingredients won't be able to do all they have to do to become a proper ice cream base.

TXAKOLI ROSÉ WITH LITCHIS, RASPBERRIES, AND ELDERFLOWER

yield: 10 drinks

INGREDIENT	METRIC	U.S.	%
Litchis, skinned and pitted	20	20	
Raspberries, fresh	30	30	
Elderflower Syrup (see Resources, page 540)	300 g	10.58 oz	12%
Txakoli rosé	2.2 kg	4 lb 13.6 oz	88%

1. This drink needs to be made to order. It can be served in a champagne flute. Place 2 whole litchis and 3 raspberries in the flute. Pour in 30 g/1.06 oz of elderflower syrup.

2. Pour the Txakoli rosé tableside or at the last minute. The glass should be filled to 240 mL/8 fl oz without ice.

note Txakoli (pronounced chà-Ko-lee) is a Basque wine, slightly sparkling and usually dry. It is typically white, but is also available in rosé. See Resources, page 540.

GINGER BEER WITH BASIL SEEDS, BASIL, AND DOMAINE DE CANTON GINGER LIQUEUR

yield: 10 drinks

INGREDIENT	METRIC	U.S.	%
Basil seeds	200 g	7.05 oz	4.44%
Basil leaves	30	30	
Domaine de Canton ginger liqueur	300 g	10.58 oz	6.67%
Ginger beer	4 kg	8 lb 13.12 oz	88.89%

1. Soak the basil seeds overnight in enough cold water to cover by 5 cm/2 in. They will absorb twice their weight in water.

2. This drink needs to be made to order. Spoon 40 g/1.41 oz of soaked basil seeds into a 480-mL/16-fl-oz glass.

3. Pour 30 g/1.06 oz of ginger liqueur into the glass. Pour 400 g/14.11 oz of ginger beer into the glass. It should be filled to 450 mL/15 fl oz without ice. Garnish with basil leaves and serve immediately.

notes Technically ginger beer is not beer, but neither is root beer. Use ginger ale if you find that ginger beer is too abrasive. And technically this is more a cocktail than anything else.

Domaine de Canton ginger liqueur is a cognac infused with ginger (see Resources, page 540).

Ginger Beer with Basil Seeds, Basil, and
Domaine de Canton Ginger Liqueur

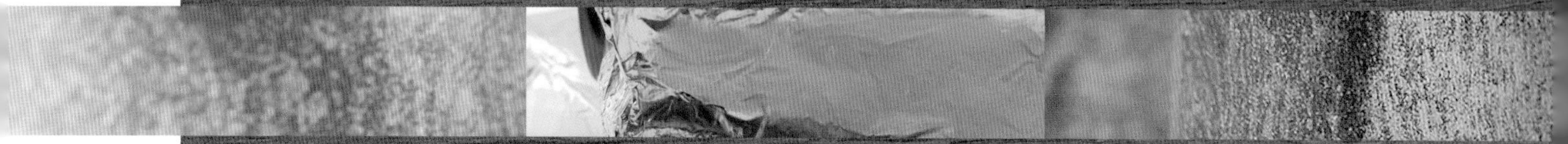

THE RETAIL SHELF

SO FAR, THE CHAPTERS IN THIS BOOK HAVE COVERED all of the
basic and indispensable products that make for a successful café:
breads, breakfast pastries, cakes, desserts, cookies, savory items,
and beverages. Another facet of the café is that the possibilities to
extend your products and services to your patrons can be virtually
endless through the retail shelf. If you detect a need from your
customers, you can easily incorporate it there. There may not even
be an expressed need; sometimes you can start offering an item that
your customers will want to buy. With this type of flexibility, it is also
just as easy to eliminate a product that is not selling without putting
a damper on your other offerings. Let's say that the café and its
retail shelf are much more versatile than a restaurant can ever hope
to be. Not better, just much more versatile.

THAT'S NOT TO SAY that new items will come out of thin air. There are labor, space, and equipment to consider. For this reason you have to make sure that you will make the right investment. For example, if your café is in a very humid climate, such as the Caribbean, don't spend time making hard candy or much cooked sugar work, since no matter how cool the shop is, the humidity will damage the product. If your café is in an area where it snows eight months out of the year, you probably wouldn't sell much ice cream. Always be aware of the environment.

This chapter will cover chocolates; confections; jams, marmalades and jellies; spices, salts and other condiments; frozen desserts (ice creams, sorbets, and other varieties); and special-occasion items. And these are just a few of the possibilities. All of these products require that special attention be paid to how they will be packaged. Each case is different, but they all have a unifying characteristic; they will in all likelihood be consumed in a place other than the café and are generally given away as gifts or are a part of a special celebration. It is because of this that you must always consider that the packaging is in reality gift wrapping.

CHOCOLATES

Is there any other type of gift that is so well received? Even bad chocolate is appreciated. This is an area of opportunity to stand out. There are a large number of quality chocolate shops in the world, and, for the most part, chocolate and chocolate products are exclusively what they sell. This is not your direct competition, however, because your café is not only a chocolate shop. That said, chocolates may very well become an extension of your brand.

The most important consideration for chocolate is that it requires a specific set of skills and solid techniques. If you do decide to go this route, make sure that you have the know-how or can teach your staff how to work with chocolate. You will also need to have an adequate space, and this space not only means an adequately sized chocolate manufacturing room, but also a temperature-controlled room. You must have air conditioning for most of the year. Air conditioning can be an expensive investment, but chocolate can't be tempered in a hot pastry shop. Ideally, the storage area for chocolate will be between 17° and 21°C/63° and 70°F. Humidity must be kept to a minimum, since water particles in the air will dull the shine of the chocolate.

This section will cover hand-dipped chocolates, molded chocolates, truffles, and chocolate bars.

basic tempering method

This section bypasses classic tempering methods, which can be achieved mechanically or manually by seeding or tabling, in favor of one that is simpler. The chocolate is tempered with the addition of a small amount of powdered cocoa butter. The classic tempering methods are tried and true, but the cocoa butter method is valued for its simplicity and because it will result in a very shiny chocolate. In classic tempering methods, the chocolate is brought to 40°C/104°F, either in a microwave or over a double boiler, and then it is cooled to 28°C/82.4°F by seeding or tabling. The chocolate is then reheated to 31° to 33°C/87.8° to 91.4°F for dark chocolate or 29° to 30°C/84.2° to 86°F for milk, white, or colored chocolate. The cocoa butter method is as follows:

1. Weigh the desired amount of chocolate.

2. Weigh the powdered cocoa butter. Its commercial name is Mycryo (see Resources, page 540). The amount needs to be 1 percent of the total weight of the chocolate.

3. Melt the chocolate in a microwave or over a double boiler to 37° to 38°C/98.6° to 100.4°F. Place the bowl over a stand such as a cake ring or whatever will keep it from being in direct contact with a work surface. Let it to cool to 34° to 35°C/93.2° to 95°F with a probe thermometer in the chocolate. Once it reaches this temperature, slowly add the cocoa butter using a beurre mixer. Make sure the blade is submerged in the chocolate to prevent bubbles from forming in the chocolate. It is impossible to get rid of all of them if they form, and they might show up in the product, but try to avoid them. Sprinkle in the cocoa butter. Blend until the cocoa butter has been homogeneously mixed with the chocolate.

4. Let the chocolate cool to 31° to 33°C/87.8° to 91.4°F for dark chocolate or 29° to 30°C/84.2° to 86°F for milk, white, or colored chocolate.

5. At this point, the chocolate is ready to work with. It is crucial to have all the mise en place ready before the chocolate is at proper temper, since the chocolate will cool further while you are searching for tools, molds, etc. This is another advantage to this method; you can gather your mise en place while the chocolate is cooling. When seeding and tabling, get all of the mise en place together before you start tempering the chocolate. The cocoa butter method is more efficient. Some argue that the addition of cocoa butter corrupts the integrity of the chocolate and might affect

or dull its flavor. It is seen as the magic powder that does the work for you. However, 1 percent of the total weight of the chocolate will have zero noticeable impact on flavor. Ultimately it is up to you which method you want to use.

If you have a chocolate tempering machine you won't have to worry about any of this. But if you do, you must know your machine inside and out. A chocolate tempering machine can be finicky, but when used properly you can have large amounts of chocolate tempered and ready to go.

molded chocolates

High-quality chocolate molds are made out of polycarbonate, and they are available in thousands of shapes and sizes. Molds that have smooth surfaces feature the chocolate's shine, and thus it can be better seen and appreciated (see Resources, page 540). Making a large amount of molded chocolates requires a lot of planning, space, and organization.

QUALITY ASPECTS OF MOLDED CHOCOLATES

The shell and the base or cap should be thin and even. A common mistake is that the base or cap is often thicker than the shell, because one of the trickiest things about molded chocolates is putting in just the right amount of filling. If there is too little, the cap will be thick. If there is too much, the filling might overflow from the mold, making capping impossible or at the very least sloppy. Thick shells are not very pleasant to eat and are a sure sign that the person making the chocolate needs further practice and instruction in the craft.

The cap should have no overhangs, also known as "feet." This occurs when the chocolate is applied to the mold once the filling has been piped in, and the chocolate is not properly scraped off. The cap and the shell should be one solid piece as well. It sometimes occurs that the place where the cap and shell meet are cracked. This happens when the shell has already set, by the time the cap is applied, so when the cap is setting it pulls in and cracks. This mostly occurs in larger pieces of molded chocolate such as candy bars. To prevent this from happening, apply an industrial confectioners' blow dryer set on cool to the border of the shell just before applying the cap portion of chocolate. This will soften it without melting the shell or the filling. It will also cause both chocolates to set at more or less the same rate and prevent any cracking.

FILLINGS FOR MOLDED CHOCOLATES

Determine what you want for the filling consistency. Do you want it to be semifirm so that when you bite into it, it stays in place? Or do you want it to be chewy, like a caramel? In either case, the filling should not make a mess when the chocolate is being eaten. Otherwise think about making smaller chocolates that are meant to be eaten in a single bite, not bar-size pieces or even two-bite pieces. It is fine to have fluid fillings in this case.

Is the filling smooth? If it is grainy or chalky, something went very wrong during the making of the filling. If a ganache is grainy or chalky, it may have separated, and when it sets it also sets separately. In this case, the fats in the ganache didn't emulsify and didn't have a chance to combine. Ganache is not the only filling used for molded chocolates. As seen further on, there are many varieties of fillings, and within those fillings you can incorporate other textures to enhance or contrast the principal filling. Examples of non-ganache fillings are caramel, fruit jellies (pâte de fruit), fluid pralines, liquors and liqueurs, fondant, marzipan, nougat, gianduja, and even aerated chocolate. Examples of textures that can be added are croquants, caramelized puffed rice, feuilletine, popping candy, brittles, and candied nuts.

Is the chocolate shiny? If not, there is a chance that in the tempering process the chocolate bloomed. It could be that the fat component bloomed, meaning that the fat components in the chocolate did not emulsify and the cocoa butter rose to the surface of the chocolate and set there. Or it could be that the sugar component bloomed, which is caused by condensation on the surface of the chocolate, which occurs if the chocolate is refrigerated and then taken out of the refrigerator. The moisture then evaporates and the sugar crystallizes on the chocolate's surface. Keep in mind that chocolate reflects the surface on which it is molded, so if the mold was not properly cleaned, polished, and buffed before using, the chocolate, even though it might be perfectly tempered, might be dull or spotty as a result of a dull or spotty mold. Pour tempered chocolate on parchment paper and it will have a dull appearance. Pour tempered chocolate over a clean glass surface and it will shine.

Does the chocolate "snap" when you bite into it? A good snap is the sign of a properly tempered chocolate. Is the surface smooth? Air pockets can easily get trapped inside a chocolate mold if you are not careful. They usually like to find corners or borders, where they can easily stay put.

basic principles for making ganache

Ganache is an emulsion and a suspension. It is first and foremost an emulsion because it is a stable mixture of fat and water, but it is also, to a lesser degree, a suspension because there are non-soluble elements evenly suspended in liquid elements. If the ganache is not emulsified properly, it will break and result in an unpleasant, grainy texture. Smoothness is the goal. That smoothness is intended to be a contrast in texture to the snap of the chocolate that envelops the ganache. The texture of the ganache is determined by the proportion of ingredients used; the higher the amount of the chocolate, the denser it will be, and the higher the amount of liquid, the smoother it will be. It is this amount of water in a recipe that will also determine the shelf life of a ganache: The higher the water activity (Aw), the shorter the shelf life. The challenge lies in striking the correct balance of ingredients to obtain an optimum result of a smooth, flavorful ganache with a shelf life of at least two weeks. This ratio of ingredients will also determine how the ganache will be used. The ganache for molded chocolates should be pourable into a mold lined with chocolate. Truffles are made with pipeable ganache that sets at room temperature and can be coated in tempered chocolate or piped into a truffle shell. The ganache for hand-dipped chocolates should be pourable to fill a plastic or metal frame and, once it sets, firm enough to be cut and hold its shape while it is dipped. Ganache that is piped into molded starch or silicone molds should set and then be able to be coated in tempered chocolate.

Ganache is essentially a chocolate and cream mixture with a high percentage of fat. The typical components of a ganache are chocolate and cream, to which butter, other liquids, and soluble or non-soluble flavoring can be added. Adding butter to dark and milk chocolate ganache not only adds richness, it also makes for a final product that is smooth yet firm at the same time. Do not add butter to a white chocolate ganache, since it has a higher fat content to begin with. Think of what butter looks like when it is cold and when it is at room temperature. It looks the same and, because of its high fat-solid content, it is easily spread, but it also holds its shape. The flavoring added to the ganache should not overwhelm the other ingredients; it should enhance them.

method #1 for making ganache

1. Weigh the chocolate into a stainless-steel bowl, making sure its size is appropriate.

2. Weigh the butter, making sure it is soft. Never use refrigerated butter.

3. Bring the heavy cream to a rolling boil. Some flavors can be added to heavy cream. If a recipe calls for glucose, corn syrup, or sorbitol, those need to be added at this point as well.

4. Pour the cream over the chocolate and let it sit for 1 minute to begin the melting process. Stir the ingredients gently and carefully with a rubber spatula until a homogeneous mix is obtained. Using a whisk to stir the ganache may add unwanted bubbles.

5. Allow the mixture sit at room temperature until it reaches 35°C/95°F, and then stir in the soft butter with a rubber spatula until a homogeneous mix is obtained. At this point the ganache should be a smooth and shiny and ready to be portioned.

6. Once portioned, the ganache needs to set at room temperature and be served between 18° and 21°C/64° and 70°F.

Sorbitol is a type of alcohol that is derived from fruits such as apples and pears. When it is added to a ganache recipe, it reduces the water activity and thus extends its shelf life. It also has half of the sweetening power of regular crystalline sugar. It is available in liquid and in powder form. The recipes in this book that contain sorbitol use the liquid form.

method #2 for making ganache

This method is used for ganache that is more fluid. The ratio of heavy cream to chocolate is almost the same, but when it sets, it sets firm yet soft. This is a good ganache for molded chocolates, not for cutting on a guitar.

1. Bring the heavy cream to a boil and pour it over the chocolate in a bowl. Stir to dissolve the chocolate completely. Once the chocolate is dissolved, stir in the soft butter.

2. Allow the mixture to sit for 20 to 30 minutes to cool down before piping. If warm ganache is poured into a chocolate shell, the shell might melt or at least soften and lose its temper and bloom.

Always use chopped chocolate or chocolate coins to make ganache; it will melt better and faster than larger pieces of chocolate.

BASIC PRINCIPLES FOR MOLDED CHOCOLATE MANUFACTURE

1. Make sure the molds are washed and dried.

2. Polish them thoroughly with a lint-free cloth until the plastic squeaks. Use cheesecloth to get into difficult corners.

3. In order to obtain a very shiny shell, coat the inside of the molds with a mixture of equal parts chocolate and cocoa butter. Melt them together and then cool them over an ice bath until the mixture reaches 32°C/90°F. Use a compressor and paint gun or an airbrush to spray the mixture directly into the molds. Allow the spray to set. You can spray with any type of chocolate and create interesting contrasts. You can also spray with colored cocoa butter to give the shell a particular hue. In order to do this, you must use cocoa butter colored with a fat-based food coloring in liquid or powder form. The liquid form mixes in much more easily than the powdered form. Pre-colored cocoa butter can also be purchased. Cool this mixture down to 26°C/79°F before spraying the molds. You can also brush the cocoa butter–chocolate mixture or the colored cocoa butter into the molds using a clean, smooth brush if you do not have a compressor with a paint gun or an airbrush. However, it won't be as even.

4. Garnish the molds. At this point, temper small amounts of any particular chocolate or colored cocoa butter and drizzle or brush it into the molds. You can also brush powdered colors onto the molds or apply gold leaf, for example. Remember, this is all preparatory work for later.

5. Gather the necessary tools and equipment. Assemble the following equipment:
   - 17.5-cm/7-in chocolate spatula
   - 30-cm/12-in chocolate spatula
   - 227- or 340-g/8- or 12-oz ladle. The choice in ladle should be determined by whichever you can handle comfortably.
   - Sheet pans lined with parchment paper and wire racks large enough to hold all of the molds
   - Two cloth towels, folded in half and stacked on top of each other next to the bowl with tempered chocolate
   - Empty bowl for chocolate scrapings
   - Piping bags
   - Enough clean sheet pans lined with parchment paper to hold all of the molded chocolates
   - Blow dryer
   - Cotton gloves to handle the molded chocolate

6. Temper the chocolate. Hold the mold horizontally over the tempered chocolate.

7. Using the ladle, carefully pour the chocolate into the mold until the cavities are full. If there is too much chocolate, you will have a mess on your hands. If there is too little, you will have to refill the ladle. The less you refill the ladle, the better.

8. Once the mold is filled to the top, turn it over 180 degrees on top of the chocolate bowl to pour the excess out. Tap the mold gently on the sides with the long chocolate spatula. Once the chocolate isn't pouring out of the mold any longer, keep the mold in the same position facing the chocolate and, using the spatula, scrape the excess chocolate off. You need such a wide spatula so that you can scrape the chocolate off the entire mold in one shot. Narrower spatulas will require you to scrape two or three more times, and it can end up being uneven. If the mold has some detailing or intricate design or deep crevice, turn the mold over and tap it on the two cloth towels you have set aside next to the chocolate bowl. This will help pop any bubbles or air pockets. Turn the mold back over to face down and tap it again so that the chocolate coats the shell evenly.

9. Do not turn the mold back over. This can cause the chocolate to settle at the bottom of the mold, and thus the shell will not be an even thickness throughout. Put the mold on top of the wire rack, facing down so that any excess chocolate can drip out. Keep filling the remaining molds.

10. After a few minutes, the first mold that was coated will start to set. Turn it over. There may be some "feet" or overflow of chocolate around the chocolate shell. At this point the chocolate is semifirm and not completely hard, so you can scrape the feet off with the wide chocolate spatula. Let the chocolate set facing up now. This will help the chocolate set faster than if it were facing down, since air will circulate faster through it facing up. The faster the chocolate sets, the shinier it will be and the less chance of the chocolate blooming. The spatula will need to be cleaned after every few molds since the chocolate will be setting on it and it might make evenly scraping the chocolate off the mold difficult.

Using the smaller spatula, scrape the larger spatula clean by scraping it into a bowl or over a sheet of parchment paper.

11. Check the temper of the chocolate. If the chocolate is getting cold, warm it up over a hot water bath. Place the bowl over the simmering, not boiling, water for a few seconds, stirring constantly, and then take it off. Repeat until the chocolate is back in temper.

12. Once all of the molds have shells, proceed with making the fillings. Ideally, ganaches are made just before they are needed so that they are liquid enough to pour into the shells and settle inside them gently. Other fillings, such as caramel, can be made well ahead of time. Reheat the chocolate used to coat the molds. It will be tempered later to cap the shells.

13. Fill the shells just enough so that the fillings are just under the tops of the shells. Remember that this will determine the thickness of the cap. Once the molds are filled, tap them gently on the cloth towels. This will help the filling smooth itself out. Inspect the mold closely at eye level. If any filling is protruding, use a toothpick or skewer to even it out. Check to see if the molds could use a little more filling. Remember that the filling is still fluid, so this is a good time to make these adjustments. Once the filling sets, it is impossible to smooth it out.

14. Once the molds are filled, allow the fillings to set. Each ganache might be different. Do not refrigerate the molds to speed up the process.

15. Temper the chocolate again. Use what was reserved earlier from coating the shells. Reheat it and temper it.

16. Place the mold facing up horizontally over the bowl with the tempered chocolate. Using a clean ladle, pour the chocolate over the mold. Try to use just the right amount so as not to make a mess. Scrape off the excess chocolate with the wider chocolate spatula. Repeat with all of the molds, keeping the chocolate in temper throughout the process. Let the chocolates set at room temperature. You will know when the chocolates are set because you will be able to see through the mold that they have pulled away from it. In some cases it is acceptable to put the molds in the refrigerator for a few seconds to set the chocolate all the way if it looks like it is partially stuck on the mold. Don't keep them refrigerated for long, since some sugar bloom may occur.

To unmold the chocolates:

1. Set up a clean area and line it with parchment paper. Have a few sheet pans lined with parchment paper ready.

2. Put on cotton gloves. These gloves are ideal for handling chocolate since they won't scuff the surface. Other types of gloves, such as vinyl or latex, can leave marks, and bare hands are not recommended.

3. Carefully turn the mold onto the parchment paper. The closer to the parchment you work the better, since the chocolate won't have to fall too far and risk breaking. If they seem stuck even though they look like they have pulled away from the mold, gently tap them with a spatula to help them to come out.

4. Once they fall onto the parchment, transfer the chocolates to the sheet pans that are lined with parchment paper.

5. Switch out the parchment paper on the work surface or clean it up before unmolding another mold. Flecks of chocolate can cling to the chocolates and make them look bad.

6. Store the chocolates in a cool, dry place. Do not wrap them with plastic or refrigerate them. Pack them, box them, or wrap them. Make sure to write an expiration date on them. The chocolates in this book have a shelf life of a least a month.

This method applies to individual molds, magnetic molds, and candy bar molds.

MAGNETIC MOLDS

Magnetic molds offer another option for molded chocolates. They have two components, one of them being the lid. The lid and the main frame have strong magnets that keep them tightly joined together. It is between this lid and the frame that you can place a sheet of acetate or a transfer sheet with an image on it. Be sure that the transferable image faces the inside of the frame.

Packing a Box of Chocolates

FROM LEFT TO RIGHT:

1. Choose an appropriately sized box, and take great care in placing each chocolate inside.
2. Secure the box with a ribbon, making sure that the bow is tight and even.
3. Impeccable packaging is fundamental to increasing your café's retail sales.

holiday molded chocolates

A CHOCOLATE SHOWPIECE is typically associated with large sculptures that are made for show only and are not really meant to be eaten. In this case they are small enough to be portable and are meant to be eaten.

Chocolate is often used to represent items associated with a particular holiday because people like to eat chocolate regardless of the date. One favorite is Easter eggs in all sizes. They can be filled with truffles or candied nuts.

Method for Holiday Molded Chocolates

The method is based on the molded chocolate method on page 441. The only difference is that the molds for the holiday pieces are comprised of two polycarbonate mold halves that are "glued" together with chocolate to form the mold.

When both molds are cast and semi-set, they are put together. The chocolate at this point should not be completely set, which will help bind both pieces together. However, if the chocolate seems to have set too much, pipe a thin line of tempered chocolate along the border of each piece and join them together. Some of these molds have magnets or are made so that they are attached by pressure. If these molds are not what you are using, use heavy-duty clamps to keep both pieces together. It is crucial to have an even coat of chocolate in these molds, because if it is thicker in some areas and thinner it others it can throw the balance of weight off. The chocolate will either crack or, in the case of an egg-shaped chocolate, have a hard time finding its balance. Since the molds are typically larger, they should have a thicker layer of chocolate. Also, it is important that the seam be as invisible as possible. Some examples of holiday chocolate pieces are:

- **Easter:** Easter bunnies, eggs, chickens, baskets, lambs, squirrels
- **Halloween:** pumpkins, bats, ghosts, witches, cats
- **Winter holidays:** Santa Claus, snowmen, candy canes, snowflakes, dreidels, Christmas trees, gingerbread houses
- **Thanksgiving:** turkeys, ears of corn, acorns
- **Valentine's Day:** hearts, cupids, lips
- **Fourth of July:** Liberty Bell, American flag, stars

For the Easter eggs in the photo on page 445, the egg molds used measured (from front to back): 8.75 by 12.5 cm/3.5 by 5 in (three chocolate "wood grain"), 11.25 by 16.25 cm/4.5 by 6.5 cm (Dark Chocolate "Aztec Gold"), 20 by 28.75 cm/8 by 11.5 in (white egg with red stripe), 25 by 31.25 cm/10 by 12.5 in (Dark chocolate, white cocoa butter spray, dark drizzle), and 30 by 40 cm/12 by 16.5 in (large dark egg, white and colored cocoa butter).

chocolate thimbles

Chocolate thimbles are essentially uncapped molded chocolates. They are a chocolate cup with one or more fillings, which can have the addition of a solid garnish as texture and can be decorated on top, almost like a cupcake. There are a variety of cup-shaped molds available. The ones used in this section have a 30-g/1.06-oz capacity, which means they are meant to be eaten in a couple of bites. All shells are made with dark chocolate.

Review the method for molded chocolate on page 441. Do not complete the capping step.

CARAMEL THIMBLES

yield: 48 cups

components

48 Dark Chocolate Cups (see method on page 441)

720 g/1 lb 9.28 oz Caramel

1 kg/2 lb 3.2 oz Chocolate Piping Cream

48 large Maldon sea salt flakes

1. Fill each cup halfway with caramel.

2. Pipe a rosette of chocolate piping cream to 2.5 cm/1 in above the top of the cup.

3. Garnish each cup with 1 large flake of Maldon sea salt. Discard after 1 month.

CARAMEL

yield: 720 g/1 lb 9.28 oz

INGREDIENT	METRIC	U.S.	%
Glucose syrup	146 g	5.13 oz	20.23%
Sugar	291 g	10.25 oz	40.46%
Heavy cream	182 g	6.41 oz	25.28%
Butter	91 g	3.2 oz	12.64%
Salt	10 g	.35 oz	1.39%

1. See the procedure for caramel on page 33.

2. Cool completely before using.

3. Reserve at room temperature. Discard after 1 month.

CHOCOLATE PIPING CREAM

yield: 1 kg/2 lb 3.2 oz

INGREDIENT	METRIC	U.S.	%
Butter, soft	250 g	8.82 oz	25%
Pretacao cocoa paste	250 g	8.82 oz	25%
Dark chocolate (64%), tempered	500 g	1 lb 1.64 oz	50%

1. Combine the butter with the cocoa paste in a bowl using a rubber spatula.

2. Stir in the tempered chocolate. Mix until homogeneous.

3. Pour into a piping bag fitted with a fluted piping tip. Pipe immediately; this will set firm when it is completely cooled.

SACHER THIMBLES

yield: 48 cups

components

150 g/5.29 oz slivered almonds

6 dried apricots

500 g/1 lb 1.64 oz **Apricot Pâte de Fruit** (page 480)

75g/2.64 oz superfine sugar

48 **Dark Chocolate Cups** (see method on page 441)

600 g/1 lb 5.12 oz **Chocolate Piping Cream** (recipe above)

1. Preheat a convection oven to 160°C/320°F.

2. Toast the almonds until golden brown and aromatic. Cool them to room temperature. Reserve 48 pieces and chop the remaining almonds to put on top of the pâte de fruit inside the chocolate cup.

3. Cut the apricots in half lengthwise, then in half lengthwise again, to obtain 4 quarters. Cut each quarter in half widthwise to obtain 48 slivers.

4. Cut 1.25-cm/.5-in discs out of the pâte de fruit using a ring cutter. Coat the discs in the superfine sugar.

5. Place a disc of pâte de fruit inside each chocolate cup. Reserve uncovered at room temperature. Sprinkle 2 g/.07 oz of chopped toasted almonds into each cup.

6. Pour the chocolate cream into a piping bag fitted with a plain #4 piping tip. Pipe the cream on top of the toasted almonds.

7. Place 2 apricot slivers on top of the ganache in the cup. Lean a whole almond sliver on the apricot. Discard after 2 weeks.

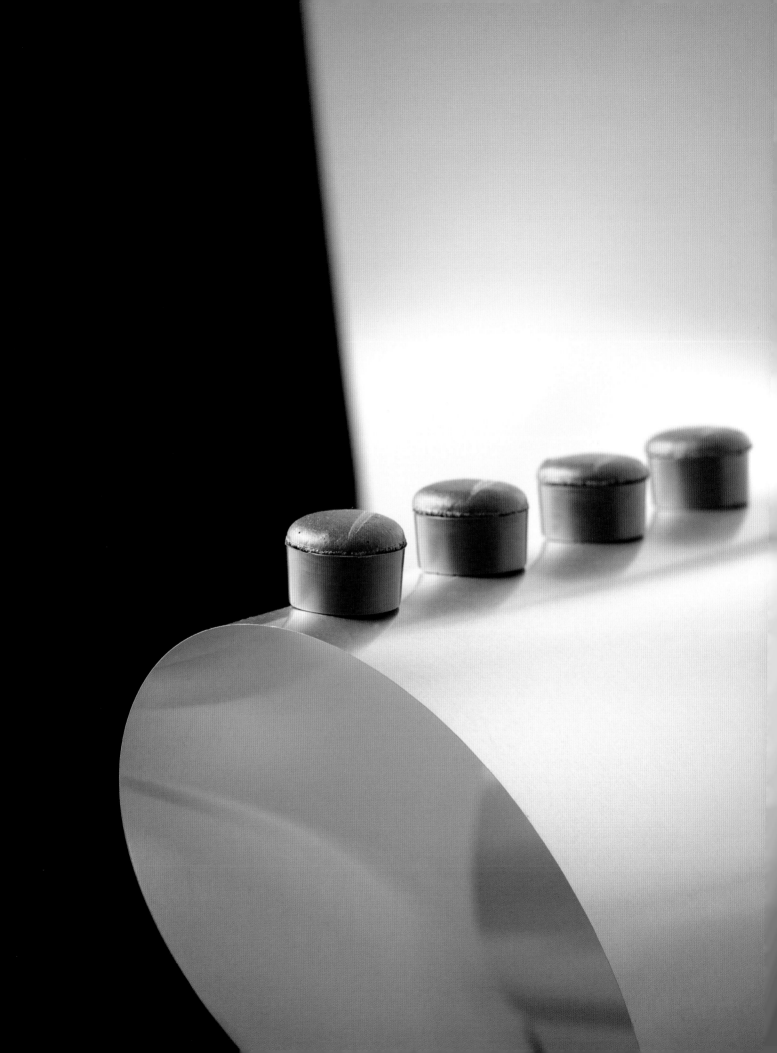

TIRAMISU THIMBLES

yield: 48 cups

components

48 Dark Chocolate Cups (see method on page 441)

703 g/1 lb 8.64 oz Espresso Cream

100 g/3.53 oz dark chocolate–covered puffed rice (see Resources, page 540)

800 g/1 lb 12.16 oz Chocolate Marsala Ganache

48 Brown Macarons brushed with gold dust (page 275)

1. Fill each cup halfway with espresso cream.

2. Pour 2 g/.07 oz of chocolate-covered puffed rice over the espresso cream. Reserve at room temperature.

3. Pipe the ganache into the chocolate cup and fill to the top.

4. Garnish with a macaron. Let set at room temperature. Discard after 1 month.

ESPRESSO CREAM

yield: 703 g/1 lb 8.64 oz

INGREDIENT	METRIC	U.S.	%
Heavy cream	175 g	6.17 oz	24.89%
White chocolate coins	525 g	1 lb 2.56 oz	74.68%
Espresso concentrate	3 g	.11 oz	.43%

1. Bring the cream to a boil, and pour it over the white chocolate in a bowl. Pour in the espresso concentrate. Stir to dissolve the chocolate.

2. Since there is a large amount of chocolate compared to the amount of cream, it might not melt the chocolate all the way. To melt the chocolate if necessary, place the bowl over a hot water bath.

3. Cool and reserve at room temperature. Discard after 1 month.

CHOCOLATE MARSALA GANACHE

yield: 800 g/1 lb 12.16 oz

INGREDIENT	METRIC	U.S.	%
Heavy cream	250 g	8.82 oz	24.39%
Glucose	100 g	3.53 oz	9.76%
Dark chocolate (64%) coins	150 g	5.29 oz	14.63%
Milk chocolate coins	150 g	5.29 oz	14.63%
White chocolate coins	150 g	5.29 oz	14.63%
Pretacao cocoa paste	150 g	5.29 oz	14.63%
Marsala	75 g	2.65 oz	7.32%

1. Bring the cream and glucose to a boil. Pour over all of the chocolates and cocoa paste in a bowl and stir until a homogeneous mass is obtained.

2. Stir in the Marsala.

3. Pour into a piping bag if using soon; otherwise reserve in an airtight container at room temperature. Discard after 1 month.

PUMPKIN THIMBLES

yield: 48 cups

components

48 Dark Chocolate Cups (see method on page 441)

600 g/1 lb 5.12 oz Pumpkin Butter

150 g/5.29 oz praline croquant

1 kg/2 lb 3.2 oz Praline Cream

1. Fill each cup halfway with pumpkin butter.

2. Pour 2 g/.07 oz of praline croquant into each cup. Reserve uncovered at room temperature.

3. Pour the praline cream into a piping bag fitted with a plain #6 piping tip.

4. Pipe a "kiss" to 2.5 cm/1 in above the top of the cup.

5. Sprinkle about 1 g of praline croquant on top of the cream before it sets.

6. Discard after 10 days. The pumpkin butter has a shorter shelf life than other fillings since it contains a higher water activity level (Aw).

PUMPKIN BUTTER

yield: 600 g/1 lb 5.12 oz

INGREDIENT	METRIC	U.S.	%
Sugar pumpkin, peeled, seeded, and cut into medium dice	978 g	2 lb 2.56 oz	65.18%
Butter	163 g	5.75 oz	10.86%
Sugar	359 g	12.67 oz	23.95%
Tahitian vanilla pods, split and scraped	2	2	
Cinnamon sticks	4	4	

1. Place all of the ingredients in a pot and bring to a boil, and then reduce the heat to a simmer.

2. Cook until the mixture is reduced by half, about 2 hours, stirring every 5 to 10 minutes.

3. Remove the vanilla pods and cinnamon sticks. Pass the mixture through a food mill and cool to room temperature. Reserve the pumpkin butter in the refrigerator if not using soon. The pumpkin butter will keep for 3 weeks if stored in the refrigerator or 10 days if kept at room temperature.

note The recipe total for the pumpkin is higher, but there will be a loss of weight during the cooking process due to evaporation.

PRALINE CREAM

yield: 1 kg/2 lb 3.2 oz

INGREDIENT	METRIC	U.S.	%
Butter, soft	250 g	8.82 oz	25%
Praline paste	250 g	8.82 oz	25%
Milk chocolate, tempered	500 g	1 lb 1.64 oz	50%

1. Combine the butter with the praline paste in a bowl using a rubber spatula.

2. Stir in the tempered milk chocolate. Mix until homogeneous. Use this cream as soon as it is made; once it sets, it gets hard and it cannot be softened again. Discard after 1 month.

assorted individual molded chocolates

This section is about molded chocolates that are individually portioned. There is no recipe for the actual shell; follow the procedure on page 441 to prepare the molds. However, the recommended elements used for each chocolate mold appear at the beginning of each filling's recipe. The capacity of each mold varies. The amounts below will be enough for about 48 pieces (2 molds with 24 cavities, which is an average amount for large range of molds). There is no standard amount for polycarbonate chocolate molds, though; they range from 1 piece for candy bars to as many as 48 pieces for coffee bean molds, for example.

MEXICAN CHOCOLATE GANACHE

yield: 48 pieces

INGREDIENT	METRIC	U.S.	%
Dark Chocolate Spray (page 264)	as needed	as needed	
Edible gold dust	as needed	as needed	
Dark chocolate (64%), tempered	as needed	as needed	
GANACHE			
Heavy cream	244 g	8.61 oz	33.9%
Glucose	43 g	1.51 oz	5.93%
Sorbitol	31 g	1.08 oz	4.24%
Mexican chocolate, chopped	366 g	12.91 oz	50.85%
Butter, soft	37 g	1.29 oz	5.08%

1. To prepare the molds, spray or brush the insides of the molds with dark chocolate spray. This spray should be made of equal parts cocoa butter and dark chocolate that is melted and then cooled to 32°C/89°F.

2. Brush edible gold dust into the molds. Line the molds with tempered dark chocolate following the procedure for molded chocolates on page 441.

3. **FOR THE GANACHE:** Combine the cream, glucose, and sorbitol in a small sauce pot and bring to a boil.

4. Pour the mixture over the chocolate in a bowl and stir until the chocolate has dissolved.

5. Allow the mixture to cool to 30°C/86°F, and then stir in the butter.

6. Pipe the ganache into the molds and tap the molds to even out the ganache. Cap the shells and unmold following the procedures for molded chocolates on page 444. Discard after 1 month.

note These were made in a dome-shaped mold with a 15-g/.53-oz capacity for each piece.

Assorted Molded
Chocolates

CINNAMON GANACHE

yield: 48 pieces

INGREDIENT	METRIC	U.S.	%
Red cocoa butter, tempered	as needed	as needed	
Dark chocolate (64%), tempered	as needed	as needed	
GANACHE			
Heavy cream	244 g	8.61 oz	33.9%
Cinnamon sticks, toasted and crushed	2	2	
Glucose	43 g	1.51 oz	5.93%
Sorbitol	31 g	1.08 oz	4.24%
Dark chocolate (72%) coins	366 g	12.91 oz	50.85%
Butter, soft	37 g	1.29 oz	5.08%

1. Spray or brush the tempered red cocoa butter inside the molds. Line the molds with tempered dark chocolate following the procedure for molded chocolates on page 441.

2. **FOR THE GANACHE:** Combine the cream and cinnamon sticks in a sauce pot and bring to a boil. Remove the pan from the heat and let the mixture steep for 15 minutes. Add the glucose and sorbitol to the infused cream and bring to a boil.

3. Strain over the chocolate in a bowl and stir until the chocolate has dissolved.

4. Allow the mixture to cool to 30°C/86°F, and then stir in the butter.

5. Pipe the ganache into the molds and tap the molds to even out the ganache. Cap the shells and unmold following the procedures for molded chocolates on page 444. Discard after 1 month.

note These chocolates were made in square molds with an Aztec design with a 15-g/.53-oz capacity per piece.

GIANDUJA GANACHE

yield: 48 pieces

INGREDIENT	METRIC	U.S.	%
Milk chocolate spray (page 264)	as needed	as needed	
Dark chocolate (64%), tempered	as needed	as needed	
Milk chocolate, tempered	as needed	as needed	
GANACHE			
Heavy cream	250 g	8.82 oz	35.21%
Glucose	100 g	3.53 oz	14.08%
Praline paste	100 g	3.53 oz	14.08%
Milk chocolate coins	250 g	8.82 oz	35.21%
Cognac	10 g	.35 oz	1.41%

1. To prepare the molds, spray or brush the insides of the molds with milk chocolate spray. This spray should be made of equal parts cocoa butter and milk chocolate that is melted and then cooled to 32°C/89°F.

2. Brush 1 brushstroke of tempered dark chocolate inside each mold. Line the molds with tempered milk chocolate following the procedure for molded chocolates on page 441.

3. **FOR THE GANACHE:** Bring the cream and glucose to a boil in a sauce pot, and then pour it over the praline paste and milk chocolate in a bowl.

4. Stir until the chocolate is dissolved, and then add the cognac.

5. Allow the mixture to cool to between 21° and 28°C/70° and 82°F before piping.

6. Pipe the ganache into the molds and tap the molds to even out the ganache. Cap the shells and unmold following the procedures for molded chocolates on page 444. Discard after 1 month.

notes This recipe does not contain sorbitol, but it does contain most ingredients that have a low water activity level (Aw).

These were made with an offset-dome mold with a 15-g/.53-oz capacity per piece.

LEMON GANACHE AND POPPING CANDY

yield: **48 pieces**

INGREDIENT	METRIC	U.S.	%
Dark chocolate (64%), tempered	as needed	as needed	
White chocolate, tempered	as needed	as needed	
GANACHE			
Heavy cream	267 g	9.41 oz	32.68%
Lemon zest	3 g	.09 oz	.33%
Glucose	47 g	1.65 oz	5.72%
Sorbitol	33 g	1.18 oz	4.08%
Dark chocolate (64%) coins	400 g	14.11 oz	49.02%
Butter, soft	40 g	1.41 oz	4.9%
Popping candy, unflavored	27 g	.94 oz	3.27%

1. Drizzle thin lines of tempered dark chocolate inside the molds in a crisscross pattern.

2. Line the molds with tempered white chocolate following the procedure for molded chocolates on page 441.

3. **FOR THE GANACHE:** Combine the cream and lemon zest in a sauce pot and bring to a boil. Remove the pot from the heat and let the zest steep for 10 minutes. Add the glucose and sorbitol and return to a boil. Strain it over the chocolate in a bowl. Stir until the chocolate is dissolved.

4. Allow the ganache to cool to 30°C/86°F, and then stir in the butter. Stir in the popping candy.

5. Pipe the ganache into the molds and tap the molds to even out the ganache. Cap the shells and unmold following the procedures for molded chocolates on page 444. Discard after 2 weeks.

note These chocolates were made in plain square molds with a 15-g/.53-oz capacity per piece.

JASMINE TEA GANACHE AND CARAMELIZED PUFFED RICE

yield: 48 pieces

INGREDIENT	METRIC	U.S.	%
Dark Chocolate Spray (page 264)	as needed	as needed	
Dark chocolate (64%), tempered	as needed	as needed	
GANACHE			
Heavy cream	267 g	9.41 oz	32.68%
Jasmine tea	3 g	.09 oz	.33%
Glucose	47 g	1.65 oz	5.72%
Sorbitol	33 g	1.18 oz	4.08%
Dark chocolate (64%) coins	400 g	14.11 oz	49.02%
Butter, soft	40 g	1.41 oz	4.9%
Caramelized puffed rice (see Resources, page 540)	27 g	.94 oz	3.27%

1. Spray or brush the insides of the molds with dark chocolate spray. This spray should be made of equal parts cocoa butter and dark chocolate that is melted and then cooled to 32°C/89°F.

2. Line the molds with tempered dark chocolate following the procedure for molded chocolates on page 441.

3. **FOR THE GANACHE:** Bring the cream and tea to a boil in a sauce pot. Remove the pot from the heat and let the tea steep for 5 minutes. Strain the tea leaves out. Add the glucose and sorbitol and bring back to a boil. Strain the mixture over the chocolate in a bowl and stir until the chocolate is dissolved.

4. Allow the mixture to cool to 30°C/86°F, and then stir in the butter. Stir in the caramelized puffed rice.

5. Pipe the ganache into the molds and tap the molds to even out the ganache. Cap the shells and unmold following the procedures for molded chocolates on page 444. Discard after 2 weeks.

note These chocolates were made in square molds with a cocoa pod design with a 15-g/.53-oz capacity per piece.

COCONUT GANACHE

yield: 48 pieces

INGREDIENT	METRIC	U.S.	%
White chocolate, tempered	as needed	as needed	
Dark chocolate (64%), tempered	as needed	as needed	
COCONUT GANACHE			
Unsweetened coconut milk	150 g	5.29 oz	21.43%
White chocolate coins	450 g	15.87 oz	64.29%
Desiccated coconut	100 g	3.53 oz	14.29%

1. To prepare the molds, brush the insides of the molds with tempered white chocolate.

2. Line the molds with tempered dark chocolate following the procedure for molded chocolates on page 441.

3. **FOR THE GANACHE:** Bring the coconut milk to a boil and pour over the white chocolate. Stir until the chocolate is dissolved. It might not dissolve completely because there is a high ratio of chocolate to coconut milk (3:1). If necessary, finish melting the chocolate over a hot water bath.

4. Stir in the coconut. Allow the mixture to cool to between 21° and 28°C/70° and 82°F/ before piping.

5. Pipe the ganache into the molds and tap the molds to even out the ganache. Cap the shells and unmold following the procedures for molded chocolates on page 444. Discard after 2 weeks.

note These chocolates were made in oval molds with Mayan graphics, with a 15-g/.53-oz capacity per piece.

chocolate bars

Candy bars are made using the exact same method as individual molded chocolates; the main difference, other than size, is that they are usually packaged and sold individually. This is an opportunity to use high-end packaging. Use foil alone or foil and decorated paper or gift wrap. You could even use a box lined with decorated paper that can fit the chocolate bar comfortably. Don't bother too much with any particular design for the bar's surface, since it is going to be wrapped anyway. If desired, drizzle white chocolate on the mold and then use dark chocolate as the shell, but it is a waste of time to spray or brush a coat of tempered chocolate and cocoa butter on it.

Chocolate bars don't always need to be filled with a ganache. Some molds are too thin for any filling. They can be filled with plain chocolate, flavored chocolate, or chocolate with a garnish like praline croquant or chopped toasted almonds added to it.

This is a particularly nice item, since, when proper technique is applied, it makes a very sophisticated version of what has become a very common item, the mass-produced candy bar.

PASSION FRUIT CREAM CHOCOLATE BARS

yield: 18 bars (35 g/1.23 oz each)

INGREDIENT	METRIC	U.S.	%
Dark chocolate (60% if possible), tempered	as needed	as needed	
PASSION FRUIT CREAM			
Passion fruit purée concentrate	81 g	2.87 oz	12.5%
Orange juice	81 g	2.87 oz	12.5%
White chocolate coins	488 g	1 lb 1.12 oz	75%

1. Line the molds with tempered dark chocolate following the procedure for molded chocolates on page 441.

2. **FOR THE CREAM:** Bring the passion fruit purée and orange juice to a boil in a sauce pot. Pour over the chocolate in a bowl and stir until the chocolate has dissolved. It might not dissolve completely because there is a large ratio of chocolate to passion fruit (3:1). If necessary, finish melting the chocolate over a hot water bath.

3. Allow the mixture to cool to between 21° and 28°C/70 and 82°F/before piping.

4. Pipe the ganache into the molds and tap the molds to even out the ganache. Cap the molds and unmold following the procedures for molded chocolates on page 444. Wrap or package the candy bars, date the package, and store for up to 1 month.

PRALINE CREAM AND MEYER LEMON PÂTE DE FRUIT CHOCOLATE BARS

yield: 6 bars (500 g/1 lb 1.64 oz each)

INGREDIENT	METRIC	U.S.	%
Dark chocolate (72% if possible), tempered	as needed	as needed	
MEYER LEMON PÂTE DE FRUIT			
Water	166 g	5.86 oz	11.08%
Glucose	446 g	15.73 oz	29.75%
Sugar, or as needed	703 g	1 lb 8.8 oz	46.83%
Pectin	19 g	.67 oz	1.27%
Meyer lemon juice	166 g	5.86 oz	11.08%
Praline Cream (page 451)	1.2 kg	2 lb 10.33 oz	

1. Line the molds with tempered dark chocolate following the procedure for molded chocolates on page 441.

2. **FOR THE PÂTE DE FRUIT:** Prepare a frame that measures 33 by 40 by 1.75 cm/13.2 by 16 by .5 in on a marble surface lined with a nonstick rubber mat. This frame will be used to obtain 6 pieces that measure 11 by 16 cm by 1.25 cm/4.4 by 6.4 by .5 in. Sprinkle superfine sugar over the surface of the mat.

3. Combine the water and 152 g/5.36 oz glucose in a sauce pot. Mix until the glucose has dissolved.

4. Combine 76 g/2.68 oz sugar and the pectin and slowly pour into the glucose mixture while whisking constantly.

5. Bring the mixture to a boil, and then add the remaining glucose. Add the remaining sugar.

6. Cook the mixture to 107°C/225°F. Remove the pot from the heat and stir in the Meyer lemon juice until a homogeneous mass is achieved.

7. Pour the pâte de fruit into the prepared frame. Let it set for a few minutes, and then sprinkle the entire surface with superfine sugar.

8. Once the pâte de fruit has set, cut it into pieces 11 by 16 cm/4.4 by 6.4 in. Keep the pâte de fruit covered. Discard after 1 month or after the outer layers start to get dried out.

9. Pour the praline cream into a piping bag fitted with a #2 plain tip. Pipe 200 g/7.05 oz into each mold. Place the mold on a scale to obtain a consistent amount in each bar.

10. Once the molds are halfway filled with praline cream, place the Meyer lemon pâte de fruit rectangles on top of the praline cream.

11. Cap the molds and unmold following the procedures for molded chocolates on page 444. Wrap or package the candy bars, date the package, and store for up to 1 month.

PEANUT BUTTER AND MILK CHOCOLATE CHOCOLATE BARS

yield: 18 bars (50 g/1.76 oz each)

INGREDIENT	METRIC	U.S.	%
Milk chocolate, tempered	as needed	as needed	
PEANUT BUTTER FILLING			
Peanut butter, smooth	450 g	15.87 oz	50%
Milk chocolate, tempered	450 g	15.87 oz	50%

1. Line the molds with tempered milk chocolate following the procedure for molded chocolates on page 441.

2. **FOR THE FILLING:** Warm the peanut butter over a hot water bath until it reaches 31°C/88°F. Mix the peanut butter with the tempered milk chocolate in a bowl until a homogeneous mass is achieved. Pour the mixture into a piping bag.

3. Pipe the filling into the molds and tap the molds to even out the filling. Cap the molds and unmold following the procedures for molded chocolates on page 444. Wrap or package the candy bars. This item has a very long shelf life, of about 1 year, which is the average shelf life of both peanut butter and chocolate. You will be able to tell if it is still good only by tasting it, since mold does not grow on peanut butter or chocolate; what will happen is that it will go stale. Ideally the candy bars won't sit on the shelf for a year.

truffles

The truffles in this book are made using hollow truffle shells. Other methods, such as piping the ganache, shaping it by hand, and then coating the truffle, can be too laborious to be cost-effective. Using a high-quality truffle shell resolves many issues:

- They produce consistent results.

- They reduce labor costs.

- They are easy to store and take up less space since they can be stored in close proximity to each other without scuffing each other (this would be impossible with molded chocolates).

- Fluid types of fillings, such as caramel and fondant, can be used in truffle shells but not in hand-shaped truffles.

In principle, truffles were given that name because they were meant to resemble the fungus that grows underground; this means that they should really be irregularly shaped. I personally find that it is more visually desirable to have sameness or consistency in size. Truffle shells are available in dark, milk, and white chocolate; they are also available in different sizes.

METHOD FOR FILLING AND COATING TRUFFLES

1. Make the filling. Ganache is the most widely used type of filling for truffles, although other types of fillings, such as caramel and fondant, can be used.

2. Once the ganache reaches a temperature below 30°/86°F, pipe it into the truffle shells just until it reaches the opening of the truffle shell.

3. Let the ganache set for at least 2 hours. In the meantime, temper the chocolate to coat the truffles. It should be the same type of chocolate as the shells. Assemble the coating(s) you will use to cover the truffles after they have been coated in chocolate. Some examples include cocoa powder, dextrose, chopped toasted nuts, coconut, sesame seeds, feuilletine, cocoa nibs, or puffed rice. This ingredient should be put in a flat container, such as a hotel pan or a sheet pan.

4. Put on a pair of gloves and dip your palms in the tempered chocolate. Place 2 or 3 truffles in your hands to coat them evenly with chocolate. Immediately after they are coated, toss them in the desired coating so that it will adhere to the surface of the truffle. If you wait too long to do this, the chocolate will set and the coating will not adhere to it. To prevent a mess, do not dip your chocolate-covered hands in the coating. Simply slide the pan back and forth to toss the truffles around in the coating.

5. Store the truffles in the coating or package them. Depending on the filling, if it has a low water activity (Aw) level, the truffles can have a long shelf life, about 2 months.

OATMEAL STOUT TRUFFLES

yield: about 100 pc (9 g/.32 oz each)

INGREDIENT	METRIC	U.S.	%
GANACHE			
Oatmeal stout	239 g	8.43 oz	26.55%
Sorbitol	64 g	2.25 oz	7.08%
Milk chocolate coins	518 g	1 lb 2.24 oz	57.52%
Butter, soft	80 g	2.81 oz	8.85%
Dark chocolate shells	100	100	
Dark chocolate (64%), tempered	as needed	as needed	
Salted roasted peanuts, chopped	as needed	as needed	

1. **FOR THE GANACHE:** Bring the oatmeal stout to a boil in a sauce pot, and then add the sorbitol. Pour over the chocolate in a bowl and stir until the chocolate has dissolved.

2. Allow the mixture to cool to 27°C/81°F, and then stir in the butter.

3. Pipe the ganache into the truffle shells. Coat in tempered dark chocolate and then in peanuts according to the procedure on page 462. Discard after 2 weeks.

COCONUT TRUFFLES

yield: about 100 pc (9 g/.32 oz each)

INGREDIENT	METRIC	U.S.	%
COCONUT FILLING			
Heavy cream	165 g	5.82 oz	18.12%
Unsweetened coconut milk	99 g	3.49 oz	10.87%
Glucose	26 g	.93 oz	2.9%
Dark chocolate (60%) coins	561 g	19.79 oz	61.59%
Butter, soft	33 g	1.16 oz	3.62%
Malibu coconut rum	26 g	.93 oz	2.9%
White chocolate shells	100	100	
White chocolate, tempered	as needed	as needed	
Desiccated coconut	as needed	as needed	

1. **FOR THE FILLING:** Bring the cream, coconut milk, and glucose to a boil in a sauce pot. Pour over the chocolate in a bowl and stir to dissolve the chocolate.

2. Allow the mixture to cool to 27°C/81°F, and then stir in the butter. Stir in the rum.

3. Pipe the filling into the truffle shells. Coat in tempered white chocolate and then in desiccated coconut according to the procedure on page 462. Discard after 2 weeks.

NUTMEG TRUFFLES

yield: about 100 pc (9 g/.32 oz each)

INGREDIENT	METRIC	U.S.	%
NUTMEG FILLING			
Heavy cream	277 g	9.77 oz	30.77%
Nutmeg seeds, crushed	2	2	
Glucose	69 g	2.44 oz	7.69%
Milk chocolate coins	277 g	9.77 oz	30.77%
Dark chocolate (64%) coins	277 g	9.77 oz	30.77%
Milk chocolate shells	100	100	
Milk chocolate, tempered	as needed	as needed	
Dark, milk, and white chocolate–covered puffed rice (see Resources, page 540)	1.5 kg	3 lb 4.91 oz	

1. **FOR THE FILLING:** Bring the cream and nutmeg to a boil in a saucepot. Remove the pot from the heat, cover it with plastic wrap, and let the nutmeg steep for 20 minutes.

2. Strain the nutmeg out, stir in the glucose, and bring the mixture to a boil again. Pour over the chocolates in a bowl and stir to dissolve the chocolates.

3. Allow the filling to cool to 30°C/86°F before filling the truffle shells. Pipe the filling into the truffle shells.

4. Let the filling set for at least 2 hours. Coat the truffles in tempered milk chocolate and immediately roll them in the chocolate-covered puffed rice. This recipe will need about 500 g/1 lb 1.6 oz of each kind of puffed rice. Simply combine them in a hotel pan, put the just-coated truffles into the pan, and stir them around in the pan to completely coat them.

5. Reserve the truffles in an airtight container in a cool, dry place or package them. Discard after 2 weeks.

dipped chocolates

For dipped chocolates, the shape of the chocolate is determined by the filling rather than by a mold. Hand-dipped chocolates consist of one or two layers and sometimes three components that are stacked and cut to a specific shape. They then are dipped either manually or mechanically in chocolate and often garnished. The components, also known as centers or fillings, can be ganache, pâte de fruit, praline, nougat, marzipan, or caramel (firm or semifirm). These fillings can be cut and dipped on their own, or they can be stacked with one or more of the other types of centers.

Once the filling is made, it is poured into a frame. These frames are generally made of steel bars and are meant to be heavy and heat resistant in order to contain a warm or sometimes very hot liquid without losing their shape. The frame is made of four separate bars that can be assembled in a variety of square or rectangle sizes. Some bars are available as a one-piece frame that cannot be altered. The recipes for the fillings in this book are made to fit inside a rectangular frame made with bars 30 by 45 by 1.25 cm/12 by 18 by .5 in thick. If you only have bars or frames that are 30 by 30 by 1.25 cm/12 by 12 by .5 in thick, cut the recipe by 25 percent. The yield will depend on how the confections are cut. The items in this book are hand dipped, not machine dipped.

HAND-DIPPED CHOCOLATE METHOD

1. Prepare a frame. Place 4 steel bars on a marble surface lined with a nonstick rubber mat.

2. Line a very flat sheet pan with an acetate sheet. This will be where the chocolates will be placed as soon as they are dipped.

3. Have the garnishes ready if using. Examples of garnishes include solid garnishes such as candied citrus zest, salt, candied flowers, chocolate drizzle, transfer sheets, or nuts. Not all dipped chocolates require a solid garnish. Some pastry chefs prefer to use the actual dipping tool to leave a pattern over the top of the chocolate. Textured acetate sheets can also be used to create an imprint on top of the dipped chocolate (see Resources, page 540).

4. Make the filling and pour it into the frame. Even out the top of the filling, if necessary, with a plastic, steel, or Plexiglas bar. Let the filling set at room temperature. The time it takes to set depends on each particular filling.

5. Spread a thin layer of tempered chocolate over the surface of the filling, let it set, and then flip it over. This thin layer of chocolate, also known as the foot, will help keep the filling's shape and make it easier to handle and dip. Stack another filling or fillings on top, if desired.

6. Cut the filling by hand using a thin, sharp knife, or preferably a guitar for precise, quick cutting. A guitar is an instrument that has two main parts to it. There is a base and a cutter frame with evenly spaced wire strings attached to one end of the base (the actual guitar). The base is meant to hold the ganache, but it can also hold pâte de fruit, marzipan, caramels, and other confections. This base has many small grooves, so when the cutter comes down on the base, the thin wires on the frame can go through the base and cut all the way through the ganache or other confection. Rotate the ganache 90 degrees so that you can cut the ganache again to obtain even squares or rectangles. The guitar usually comes with a flat, thin sheet of stainless steel with the same dimensions as the base, which you can slide under the ganache to move it anywhere you need to.

7. Once all of the pieces are cut, temper the chocolate needed to dip the chocolates.

8. Using the appropriate dipping tool (similar to a fork), carefully dip each piece into the tempered chocolate. Scrape the bottom of the dipping tool against the side of the bowl to get rid of excess chocolate. Gently transfer each dipped piece onto the prepared sheet pan.

9. Garnish the chocolate before it sets. Once the chocolate sets, store it in a cool dry place or package it.

MALDON SEA SALT CHOCOLATES

yield: 2 kg/4 lb 6.4 oz (about 98 pc) at 20 g/.7 oz each before dipping

INGREDIENT	METRIC	U.S.	%
MALDON SEA SALT GANACHE			
Maldon sea salt	7 g	.25 oz	.36%
Heavy cream	783 g	1 lb 11.68 oz	39.15%
Glucose	107 g	3.77 oz	5.34%
Dark chocolate (64%) coins	996 g	2 lb 3.2 oz	49.82%
Butter, soft	107 g	3.77 oz	5.34%
Dark chocolate (64%), tempered	as needed	as needed	
Large Maldon sea salt crystals	98	98	

1. **FOR THE GANACHE:** Combine the sea salt, heavy cream, and glucose in a pot and bring it to a boil. Pour over the chocolate in a bowl and stir to dissolve the chocolate. Allow the mixture to cool to 27°C/81°F, and then stir in the butter.

2. Pour the ganache into a frame 30 by 45 by 1.25 cm/12 by 18 in by .5 in. If the filling seems too firm, place a sheet of acetate over the ganache and roll it out to the size of the frame using a rolling pin. Otherwise spread it with an offset spatula and even it out with a firm plastic or Plexiglas bar. Let the filling set at room temperature.

3. Once it has set, spread a thin layer of tempered dark chocolate over the surface. Let it set, and then flip the filling over.

4. Using a guitar, cut the ganache into rectangles 2 by 4 cm/.8 by 1.6 in.

5. Dip the ganache in the dark chocolate according to the procedure for hand-dipping chocolates on page 466. Before the chocolate sets, place a single Maldon salt crystal on each piece of dipped ganache on the top right corner. Drizzle 3 thin lines of tempered dark chocolate across the middle of the chocolate.

6. Package the chocolates. Discard after 2 weeks.

OLIVE OIL LOGS WITH BLACK OLIVE PRALINE

yield: 2 kg/4 lb 6.4 oz (about 70 pc) at 28 g/1 oz each before dipping

INGREDIENT	METRIC	U.S.	%
BLACK OLIVE PRALINE			
Black olives, pitted	1 kg	2 lb 3.2 oz	71.43%
Sugar	400 g	14.11 oz	28.57%
OLIVE OIL GANACHE FILLING			
Butter, soft	478 g	1 lb .8 oz	23.89%
Dark chocolate (72%), tempered	1.14 kg	2 lb 8.48 oz	57.32%
Extra-virgin olive oil	121 g	4.27 oz	6.05%
Black olive praline	255 g	8.99 oz	12.74%
Dark chocolate (72%), tempered	as needed	as needed	
White chocolate, tempered	as needed	as needed	
Vodka or rum	as needed	as needed	
Edible gold powder	as needed	as needed	

1. **FOR THE BLACK OLIVE PRALINE:** Chop the olives coarsely and toss in the sugar.

2. Place the olives in a dehydrator set to 60°C/140°F for 3 days (or in an oven with only the pilot heat on for 24 hours). They will look like dried-out raisins when they are done, and they will feel dry and brittle.

3. Once they are dehydrated, chop them by hand as finely as possible. Reserve in a cool, dry place at room temperature in an airtight container. They will keep for many years if kept in a dry environment.

4. **FOR THE OLIVE OIL GANACHE:** Stir the butter into the tempered chocolate, and then add the olive oil and the black olive praline.

5. Spread the ganache into a frame 30 by 45 by 1.25 cm/12 by 18 by .5 in. If the filling seems too firm, place a sheet of acetate over the ganache and roll it out to the size of the frame using a rolling pin. Otherwise spread it out in the frame with an offset spatula and even it out with a firm plastic or Plexiglas bar. Allow the filling to set at room temperature.

6. Once it has set, spread a thin layer of tempered dark chocolate over the surface. Let it set, and then flip the filling over.

7. Cut the filling into three 6-cm-/2.4-in-wide rows using a long, thin slicing knife.

8. Transfer the ganache to a guitar and cut with the 1.75-cm-/.5-in-wide slicer.

9. Dip the ganache rectangles in tempered dark chocolate according to the procedure on page 466.

10. Once the chocolate has set, drizzle a single line of tempered white chocolate horizontally across the left third of each rectangle.

11. Combine the vodka or rum with the gold powder. It should have the consistency of a thin paste. Brush the left end of the bar next to the white stripe with it to coat it completely.

12. Package the logs. Discard after 1 month.

note The recipe for the praline will yield less than 40 percent of the total original weight, since there will be large amount of moisture evaporation during the dehydration process.

BLACK CURRANT AND HIBISCUS CHOCOLATES

yield: 2 kg/4 lb 6.4 oz (about 81 pc) at 24 g/.84 oz each before dipping

INGREDIENT	METRIC	U.S.
CRYSTALLIZED HIBISCUS FLOWERS		
Hibiscus flowers, dried	10	10
Water	1 kg	2 lb 3.2 oz
Sugar	500 g	1 lb 1.64 oz
BLACK CURRANT GANACHE		
Black currant purée	412 g	14.55 oz
Sorbitol	41 g	1.45 oz
Dark chocolate (64%) coins	893 g	1 lb 15.52 oz
Invert sugar	69 g	2.42 oz
Violet liqueur	137 g	4.85 oz
Butter, soft	447 g	15.76 oz
Dark chocolate (65 %), tempered	as needed	as needed

1. **FOR THE CRYSTALLIZED FLOWERS:** Combine the hibiscus with the water in a medium sauce pot and bring to a boil. Remove the pan from the heat. Let the flowers steep for 30 minutes.

2. Strain the flowers out and pat them dry with a paper towel. Reserve the liquid and use it make granitas or other cold beverages.

3. Combine the flowers with the sugar, making sure the flowers are covered with the sugar. Reserve overnight, uncovered.

4. Dry the flowers in a dehydrator set to 60°C/140°F or a very low-temperature oven until the flowers are brittle.

5. Once the flowers are crystallized, break them up into small pieces about .5 cm/.2 in long; these pieces will be used as garnish. Reserve until needed. If kept in a cool, dry environment, they will keep for many years.

6. **FOR THE BLACK CURRANT GANACHE:** Bring the purée and the sorbitol to a boil in a sauce pot. Pour over the chocolate in a bowl and stir to dissolve the chocolate. Stir in the invert sugar to obtain a homogeneous mix. Stir in the violet liqueur and let the ganache cool to 27°C/81°F. Stir in the butter.

7. Pour the ganache into a frame 30 by 45 by 1.25 cm/12 by 18 in by .5 in. If the filling seems too firm, place a sheet of acetate over the ganache and roll it out to the size of the frame using a rolling pin. Otherwise spread it with an offset spatula and even it out with a firm plastic or Plexiglas bar. Let the filling set at room temperature.

8. Once it has set, spread a thin layer of tempered dark chocolate over the surface. Let it set, and then flip the filling over.

9. Using a guitar, cut the ganache into 3-cm/1.2-in squares.

10. Dip the ganache according to the procedure for hand-dipping chocolates on page 466. Before the chocolate sets, put on a single piece of crystallized hibiscus on each piece of dipped ganache.

11. Package the chocolates. Discard after 1 month.

Maldon Sea Salt Chocolates (rectangle) (page 467), Black Currant and Hibiscus Chocolates (square) (page 470), Espresso Palet D'or (round) (page 474)

ELDERFLOWER GANACHE POPS

yield: 2.16 kg/4 lb 12.19 oz (about 36 pc)

INGREDIENT	METRIC	U.S.	%
ELDERFLOWER GANACHE			
Sugar	300 g	10.58 oz	13.64%
Heavy cream	480 g	1 lb 9.6 oz	21.82%
Dark chocolate (60%) coins	1 kg	2 lb 3.2 oz	45.45%
Elderflower liqueur (St-Germain)	120 g	4.23 oz	5.45%
Butter, soft	300 g	10.58 oz	13.64%
Dark chocolate (64%), tempered	as needed	as needed	
White chocolate, tempered	as needed	as needed	
Crystallized lilac petals (see Resources, page 540)	36	36	

1. Line 36 PVC tubes 7.5 cm long by 2.5 cm diameter/3 by 1 in with acetate. Place them in a standing position on a flat sheet pan lined with a nonstick rubber mat.

2. Make a caramel with the sugar and the cream (see page 33), and then bring it to a boil. Pour the liquid over the chocolate in a bowl and stir to dissolve the chocolate. Allow the mixture to cool to 27°C/81°F. Stir in the elderflower liqueur and the butter.

3. Pour the ganache into a piping bag. Pipe the ganache into the prepared tubes and even out the top with an offset spatula.

4. Let the ganache set at room temperature. Once it is set, push a lollipop stick halfway into each tube.

5. Refrigerate the ganache for 2 hours.

6. Remove the ganache from the PVC tubes and take off the acetate.

7. Dip the ganache into tempered dark chocolate using the lollipop stick, letting the excess drip off the top.

8. Once the chocolate sets, garnish with a drizzle of white chocolate and a crystallized lilac petal. Reserve in a cool dry place in an airtight container. Discard after three weeks.

ESPRESSO PALET D'OR

yield: 2 kg/4 lb 6.4 oz (about 121 pc) at 16 g/.56 oz each before dipping

INGREDIENT	METRIC	U.S.	%
ESPRESSO CARDAMOM GANACHE			
Heavy cream	524 g	1 lb 2.56 oz	26.21%
Soluble coffee crystals	8 g	.28 oz	.39%
Pretacao cocoa paste	79 g	2.77 oz	3.93%
Dark chocolate (72%) coins	524 g	1 lb 2.56 oz	26.21%
Milk chocolate coins	786 g	1 lb 11.68 oz	39.32%
Butter, soft	79 g	2.77 oz	3.93%
Dark chocolate (64%), tempered	as needed	as needed	
Gold transfer sheets	as needed	as needed	

1. **FOR THE GANACHE:** Combine the cream, coffee crystals, and the cocoa paste in a sauce pot and bring to a boil. Pour over the chocolates in a bowl and stir to dissolve the chocolates. Allow the mixture to cool to 27°C/81°F, and then stir in the butter.

2. Pour the ganache into a frame 30 by 45 by 1.25 cm/12 by 18 by .5 in. If the filling seems too firm, place a sheet of acetate over the ganache and roll it out to the size of the frame using a rolling pin. Otherwise spread it with an offset spatula and even it out with a firm plastic or Plexiglas bar. Let the filling set at room temperature.

3. Once it has set, spread a thin layer of tempered dark chocolate over the surface. Let it set, and then flip the filling over.

4. Cut the ganache into 2.5-cm-/1-in-diameter rings using a warm ring cutter. Dip the ring in hot water and pat it dry; repeat between each cut.

5. Dip the ganache in the dark chocolate according to the procedure for hand-dipping chocolates on page 466. Before the chocolate sets, place a single piece of transfer sheet on top of each chocolate. It should cover the entire surface. Once the chocolate sets, remove the transfer sheet. Some transfer sheets are available precut to 2.5-cm/1-in squares; if these are not available, cut 2.5-cm/1-in squares out of the sheet of acetate using a ruler and an X-Acto knife.

6. Package the chocolates. Discard after 2 weeks.

confections

These particular items have the added benefit of a long shelf life since they have a very low to nonexistent water activity level (Aw). Chocolates, no matter how low their water activity level, do not have as long a shelf life as do most confections. However, confections will be more sensitive to a humid environment than chocolates. There are many varieties of confections, but this section will focus on three varieties: caramels, pâte de fruit, and lollipops. Each one of them is considered a confection, but they are very different in nature and final texture as well as in method of preparation. That said, they are all based on cooking sugar to a particular temperature that will determine their final texture, from soft like a caramel to hard like a lollipop.

CARAMELS

The following recipes fit inside a square frame made with steel bars that measure 30 cm square by 1.25 cm thick/12 by .5 in, with a yield of 2 kg/4 lb 6.4 oz. The frame is placed over a nonstick rubber mat on a marble surface. All caramels are meant to be cut into 3-cm/ 1.2-in squares, preferably using a guitar. The idea is that if they all have the same measurement, you can pack boxes with assorted caramels and they will all fit nicely.

The general method for making caramels is to cook sugar (either granulated by itself or combined with another variety, such as glucose, corn syrup, invert, or isomalt) to a certain temperature and then combine it with another ingredient (almost always a dairy product or a dairy product combined with another ingredient) to obtain a caramel that can hold its shape but still be soft and palatable. The temperature to which the sugar is cooked will determine how soft or firm the resulting caramel will be, as will the proportion of sugar to secondary ingredients, such as chocolate, cream, butter, or fruit juices or purées. In this section there are three varieties of caramel, one with a fruit juice (passion fruit) and chocolate, one with dairy (heavy cream and butter), and one with chocolate and heavy cream.

Remember to always use a clean pot when cooking sugar to prevent any contaminants from crystallizing the sugar, and to clean the sides of the pot with a wet, clean brush as the sugar is cooking to remove any sugar crystals that could crystallize the sugar in the pot. It is a good idea to have a brush (or two) in the shop that is exclusively for this purpose, because if you use a general purpose brush that has traces of glaze, syrup or egg wash, they will contaminate the sugar and thus defeat the purpose of keeping the sides of the pot clean from sugar crystals.

Always cool the caramels at room temperature (this will also prevent crystallization), preferably over a marble surface lined with a nonstick rubber mat. Use a nonstick rubber mat at least while the caramel is cooling down, and then transfer the nonstick rubber mat with the caramel to a flat sheet pan.

If possible, always pour the caramel into caramel bars. These bars are made of steel and are sturdy enough to stay in place and contain the hot caramel. Caramel bars come in different lengths and thicknesses, with which you can create a countless amount of different size squares and rectangles to suit your needs and the recipe yields.

FLEUR DE SEL CARAMELS

yield: 2 kg/4 lb 6.4 oz

INGREDIENT	METRIC	U.S.	%
Glucose	123 g	4.35 oz	6.16%
Sugar	821 g	1 lb 12.96 oz	41.07%
Fleur de sel	10 g	.36 oz	.51%
Butter	657 g	1 lb 7.2 oz	32.85%
Heavy cream	388 g	13.69 oz	19.4%

1. Combine the glucose, sugar, and fleur de sel in a pot and cook until it reaches 145°C/293°F. This is done as a dry caramel with no water, so it will need to be stirred frequently.

2. Meanwhile, combine the butter and cream in a sauce pot and bring it up to a boil.

3. Once the sugar mixture reaches 145°C/293°F, slowly and carefully pour the cream and butter into the pot with the sugar, whisking constantly.

4. Bring the mixture up to 122°C/252°F, stirring constantly. Pour into the prepared steel frame measuring 30 cm square by 1.25 cm thick/12 by .5 in.

5. Let the caramel cool to room temperature.

6. Once cooled, cut into 3-cm/1.2-in squares using the guitar or by hand with a thin, sharp knife. Wrap each piece with 6-cm/2.4-in cellophane squares.

7. Reserve in a dry, cool place, in an airtight container or package. Discard after 6 months.

PASSION FRUIT CARAMELS

yield: 2 kg/4 lb 6.4 oz

INGREDIENT	METRIC	U.S.	%
Sugar	800 g	1 lb 12.16 oz	40%
Passion fruit purée (concentrate)	240 g	8.47 oz	12%
Butter	200 g	7.05 oz	10%
White chocolate coins	760 g	1 lb 10.88 oz	38%

1. Cook the sugar, purée, and butter in a 4-quart sauce pot over high heat, stirring regularly, until the mixture reaches 120°C/248°F. Remove the pot from the heat.

2. When the mixture stops bubbling, stir in the chocolate. Pour the mixture into the prepared steel frame measuring 30 cm square by 1.25 cm thick/12 by .5 in.

3. Allow it to cool to room temperature. Once cooled, cut the caramels into 3-cm/1.2-in squares using the guitar or by hand with a thin, sharp knife. Wrap each piece with 6-cm/2.4-in cellophane squares.

4. Reserve in a dry, cool place, in an airtight container or package. Discard after 6 months.

CHOCOLATE CARAMELS

yield: 2 kg/4 lb 6.4 oz

INGREDIENT	METRIC	U.S.	%
Sugar	725 g	1 lb 9.6 oz	36.27%
Glucose	73 g	2.56 oz	3.63%
Water	167 g	5.91 oz	8.37%
Heavy cream	419 g	14.76 oz	20.93%
Butter	307 g	10.83 oz	15.35%
Baking soda	1 g	.04 oz	.06%
Salt	1 g	.04 oz	.06%
Dark chocolate couverture, chopped	307 g	10.83 oz	15.35%

1. Combine the sugar, glucose, and water in a pot. Cook the mixture to 145°C/293°F.

2. Meanwhile, combine the cream, butter, baking soda, and salt in a pot and bring to a boil.

3. Once the sugar mixture reaches 145°C/293°F, pour the hot cream mixture into the sugar slowly, while whisking constantly.

4. Stir in the chocolate couverture and bring the mixture back up to 118°C/244°F, stirring constantly.

5. Pour into the prepared steel frame measuring 30 cm square by 1.25 cm thick/12 by .5 in.

6. Let the caramel cool to room temperature.

7. Once cooled, cut into 3-cm/1.2-in squares using the guitar or by hand with a thin, sharp knife. Wrap each piece with 6-cm/2.4-in cellophane squares.

8. Reserve in a dry, cool place, in an airtight container or package. Discard after 6 months.

pâte de fruit

This confection is a combination of pectin-gelled fruit and cooked sugar. The following recipes were made using fruit purées to ensure consistency, since fruit purées contain the same amount of water, solids, and sugar from container to container. Using fresh fruit, while it may sound appealing, will not always yield a consistent result. The recipes below all fit inside steel frame measuring a 30 cm square by 1.25 cm thick/ 12 by .5 in.

PÂTE DE FRUIT METHOD

1. Prepare a steel frame measuring 30 cm square by 1.25 cm thick/12 by .5 in. Place the frame on a nonstick rubber mat on a marble surface. Sprinkle enough superfine or bakers' sugar on the mat to coat the entire surface with an even layer. All of the pâte de fruit are meant to be cut into 3-cm/1.2-in squares, preferably using a guitar. The idea is that if they all have the same measurement, you can pack boxes with assorted pâte de fruit and they will all fit nicely.

2. Whisk together the pectin and one-third of the sugar in a bowl to ensure a homogeneous mix. Place the mixture in a pot and whisk in the fruit purée.

3. Bring the mixture to a boil. Combine the remaining sugar with the glucose powder and slowly pour it into the pot while whisking constantly to avoid sugar clumps. Insert a probe thermometer or thermocoupler into the pot to monitor the temperature constantly.

4. Bring the mixture to 107°C/225°F. Remove the pot from the heat and add the citric acid, stirring constantly.

5. Pour into the prepared frame and let it set at room temperature. When it is halfway set, sprinkle superfine or bakers' sugar over the entire surface. Once it has fully set, remove the bars and flip the pâte de fruit over onto another nonstick rubber mat. Sprinkle the surface of the pâte de fruit with sugar.

6. Let the pâte de fruit set overnight without wrapping.

7. Once it is set, cut on a guitar or by hand into 3-cm/1.2-in squares. Once they are cut, toss them in more sugar. Shake the excess sugar off and wrap or package the pâte de fruit. If properly wrapped or packaged, pâte de fruit can keep for up to 2 months before it starts drying out.

Citric acid can be purchased in powder or liquid form. This recipe requires that the citric acid be added in liquid form. If you only have powdered citric acid, combine it with an equal amount of hot water and stir to dissolve the crystals. This mixture has an indefinite shelf life if kept in an airtight container.

recipes

The following recipes will yield about 100 pieces with little to no waste. Follow the method given above for all of the following recipes.

INGREDIENT	METRIC	U.S.	%
Pectin	20 g	.71 oz	1.1%
Sugar	798 g	1 lb 12.16 oz	43.38%
Cherry purée	840 g	1 lb 13.6 oz	45.66%
Glucose powder	168 g	5.93 oz	9.13%
Liquid citric acid	13 g	.46 oz	.73%

INGREDIENT	METRIC	U.S.	%
Pectin	17 g	.59 oz	.84%
Sugar	957 g	2 lb 1.76 oz	47.97%
Raspberry purée	840 g	1 lb 13.6 oz	42.13%
Glucose powder	168 g	5.93 oz	8.43%
Liquid citric acid	13 g	.46 oz	.63%

INGREDIENT	METRIC	U.S.	%
Pectin	20 g	.71 oz	1.07%
Sugar	924 g	2 lb .64 oz	49.13%
Strawberry purée	840 g	1 lb 13.6 oz	44.66%
Glucose powder	84 g	2.96 oz	4.47%
Liquid citric acid	13 g	.46 oz	.67%

INGREDIENT	METRIC	U.S.	%
Pectin	22 g	.78 oz	1.11%
Sugar	971 g	2 lb 2.24 oz	48.65%
Williams Pear purée	882 g	1 lb 15.1 oz	44.23%
Glucose powder	106 g	3.73 oz	5.31%
Liquid citric acid	14 g	.5 oz	.71%

INGREDIENT	METRIC	U.S.	%
Pectin	21 g	.74 oz	1.05%
Sugar	966 g	2 lb 2.08 oz	48.1%
Mango purée	840 g	1 lb 13.6 oz	41.82%
Glucose powder	168 g	5.93 oz	8.36%
Liquid citric acid	13 g	.46 oz	.67%

INGREDIENT	METRIC	U.S.	%
Pectin	20 g	.71 oz	.95%
Sugar	958 g	1 lb 1.76 oz	45.09%
Apricot purée	840 g	1 lb 13.6 oz	39.56%
Glucose powder	294 g	10.37 oz	13.84%
Liquid citric acid	12 g	.41 oz	.55%

BLACK CURRANT

INGREDIENT	METRIC	U.S.	%
Pectin	21 g	.74 oz	1.04%
Sugar	983 g	2 lb 2.72 oz	48.55%
Black currant purée	840 g	1 lb 13.6 oz	41.49%
Glucose powder	168 g	5.93 oz	8.30%
Liquid citric acid	13 g	.46 oz	.62%

MANDARIN ORANGE

INGREDIENT	METRIC	U.S.	%
Pectin	22 g	.77 oz	1.15%
Sugar	966 g	2 lb 2.08 oz	50.88%
Mandarin orange purée	840 g	1 lb 13.6 oz	44.25%
Glucose powder	59 g	2.07 oz	3.1%
Liquid citric acid	12 g	.41 oz	.62%

BLUEBERRY

INGREDIENT	METRIC	U.S.	%
Pectin	18 g	.65 oz	1.02%
Sugar	882 g	1 lb 15.1 oz	48.7%
Blueberry purée	840 g	1 lb 13.6 oz	46.38%
Glucose powder	59 g	2.07 oz	3.25%
Liquid citric acid	12 g	.41 oz	.65%

GRANNY SMITH APPLE

INGREDIENT	METRIC	U.S.	%
Pectin	15 g	.54 oz	.88%
Sugar	798 g	1 lb 12.16 oz	46.07%
Granny Smith apple purée	840 g	1 lb 13.6 oz	48.49%
Glucose powder	67 g	2.37 oz	3.88%
Liquid citric acid	12 g	.41 oz	.68%

Lollipops are a variety of hard candy, which is the direct result of cooking sugar to a high temperature. In this chapter, two shapes of lollipops will be made, flat rectangles and spheres. The base recipe that follows can be flavored and colored. Always use water-soluble liquid food coloring and oil-based flavors rather than alcohol-based flavors, which tend to be more pronounced.

LOLLIPOP

yield: about 30 lollipops

INGREDIENT	METRIC	U.S.	%
Sugar	1.15 kg	2 lb 8.64 oz	65.49%
Glucose	360 g	12.7 oz	20.50%
Water	240 g	8.47 oz	13.67%
Cream of tartar	6 g	.21 oz	.34%
Flavoring (oil based), or as needed	2 to 3 drops	2 to 3 drops	
Food coloring (alcohol or water based), or as needed	2 to 3 drops	2 to 3 drops	

1. Assemble the lollipop molds. For the sphere lollipops, use 3.75-cm/1.5-in silicone spheres (see Resources, page 540), and for the flat, rectangular lollipops, use a 1-cm-/.4-in-thick neoprene mat with rectangles measuring 2.5 by 7.5 cm/1 by 3 in cut out along the border using an X-Acto knife and a ruler. There are molds that are specific for making lollipops, which you can use as well. However, the neoprene mat allows you to cut out any shape or size you want.

2. If using a flat mat, place the lollipop sticks down the center of the cutout. Use tape to anchor down the stick, since it might move when the cooked sugar is poured into the mold. If using sphere molds, wait for the sugar to set halfway before inserting the stick, otherwise it will sink to the bottom and won't stand straight. You can speed up the process by spraying the top of the mold with nitrogen, also known as cold spray (see Resources, page 540).

3. Combine the sugar, glucose, water, and cream of tartar thoroughly in a sauce pot. Clean the inside of the pot with a brush and water.

4. Cook over high heat, preferably over an induction burner, stirring until the mixture starts to boil. Stop stirring and continue to cook until the sugar reaches 156°C/313°F.

5. Remove the pot from the heat and add the flavoring and the coloring as needed, swirling the pot to mix the ingredients evenly.

6. When the mixture stops bubbling, transfer it to a funnel gun. Keep the funnel warm by keeping it filled with very hot water before pouring in the sugar. This will prevent the sugar from setting inside the funnel, especially at the tip. Empty the funnel and dry it out thoroughly before pouring the cooked sugar into it.

7. Dispense the cooked sugar into the prepared molds.

8. Let the lollipops set at room temperature. Reserve in an airtight container with silica gel packs at room temperature, or package them. They will keep indefinitely if they are kept in a cool, dry environment.

notes If using the sphere molds, you can put a garnish such as dragées or candied flowers inside the molds before dispensing the sugar.

If the sphere lollipops or rectangular lollipops happen to have bubbles on their surface or a slightly uneven edge (for the rectangles), briefly touch them with the torch. This will smooth out the surface and also make it shinier.

To achieve a shimmered copper look, swirl edible copper powder into the cooked sugar (about 15 mL/.5 fl oz per recipe) using a small offset spatula before pouring it into the funnel. You may also use gold or silver shimmer dust.

flavors used for this book

Blue and Clear Sphere

Acai berry flavor. For 30 lollipops, garnish 30 silicone sphere molds with a small piece of silver leaf. Two sheets will be plenty for 30 lollipops. Cook the sugar as per the instructions on page 482; add a few drops of acai flavoring. Place half of the sugar in another pot and swirl in blue food coloring. Portion the blue sugar in first, and then portion the clear sugar.

Black and Gold Rectangle

Blackberry flavor. Make a paste with 5 g/.18 oz vodka or rum and .5 g/.02 oz gold powder. Set aside, covered. Cook the sugar as per the instructions on page 482. Flavor it with 2 or 3 drops of blackberry flavor. Color half of the sugar black; keep the remaining sugar warm over low heat in a pot. Pour the black sugar into the prepared mat. Let it cool, and then brush 1 brushstroke of gold vertically across the lollipop. Portion the clear sugar on top of the black sugar. Let it set completely before removing it from the mat.

Orange Rectangle

Orange flavor. Color 100 g/3.53 oz of rolling fondant black. Put it inside a clay forming tool with the attachment for thin string (see Note). Leave it there while cooking the sugar for the lollipops. Cook the sugar as per the instructions on page 482. Color it orange and flavor it with a few drops of orange flavoring. Portion the sugar to fill the rectangular mat halfway up. Extrude about 10 cm/4 in of fondant string over each piece of sugar, looping it around the surface to create a random loop pattern. Portion the remaining sugar to the top of the mold. Let it set completely before unmolding.

Brown and Gold Rectangle

Root Beer Float: root beer (brown with copper shimmer) flavor and vanilla (clear) flavor. Cook the sugar intended for the root beer first; add a few drops of dark brown food coloring and root beer extract to the cooked sugar. Add gold shimmer to the sugar. See the instructions for the shimmer amount and how to add it at top of page. Portion onto the rubber mat to fill it halfway. Place an oval silver dragée over the still-warm sugar so that it will adhere. Cook the second sugar and add a few drops of vanilla extract. Portion to fill the mat to the top. Let it set completely before unmolding.

Light Brown and Copper Rectangle

Coffee and caramel flavor. Cook the sugar intended for the coffee flavor first. Add a few drops of coffee extract and light brown food coloring to the sugar. Add copper shimmer to the sugar. See instructions for the shimmer amount and how to add it at top of page. Fill the rubber mat halfway. Cook the sugar intended for the caramel next; add a few drops of caramel extract to the sugar and portion it to fill the mold. Place a single blue dragée over the lollipop before the sugar sets completely so that it will adhere. Let it set completely before unmolding.

Red Rectangle

Strawberry and black pepper flavor. Roll out 100 g/3.53 oz of light blue rolling fondant to 1 mm/.04 in thick. Cut out 150 circles measuring 3 mm/.12 in diameter; let them dry out at room temperature, uncovered, for about 1 hour before needed. Cook the sugar as per the instructions on page 482; add red food coloring and strawberry flavoring. Portion into the molds to fill them halfway. Place 5 fondant circles over the sugar before it sets so that they will adhere. Finish filling the mold with the rest of the cooked sugar. If it is too hard to portion, warm it up in a pot over low heat to loosen it. Before the sugar sets, crack fresh black pepper over the surface of all the lollipops; use about 10 g/.35 oz for all 30 lollipops.

Yellow Sphere

Lemon flavor. Color 100 g/3.53 oz of rolling fondant black. Put it inside a clay forming tool with the attachment for thin string (see Note), and leave it there while you cook the sugar for the lollipops. Cook the sugar as per the instructions on page 482; color it light yellow and add a few drops of lemon extract. Fill the sphere molds halfway with the hot sugar. Extrude a thin string of black fondant into each mold to form a flower. Fill the molds with the remaining hot sugar.

note Clay forming tools are available at most craft supply stores. They are used to extrude clay in many shapes and forms, but they work very well for rolling fondant and marzipan.

JAMS, MARMALADES, AND JELLIES

These items, if you are not careful when making and packaging them, can breed bacteria and cause food-borne illnesses. The most important concerns when making them are to work as cleanly as possible and to always follow the basic canning principles in order to avoid the formation of mold or botulism, which is lethal.

Take the time to think about the packaging of these items. Sometimes they can easily look very "rustic." Some shops add twine and a piece of cloth to the jar to make it look homier. And that's fine, if that's what you are after, but there are other packaging options to consider.

Check your local legislation and health department for regulations on canning. Some states don't allow the production and/or sale of canned items without a license or permit. You can make it at home and eat it at home, but when you make larger amounts to sell, it can become a health hazard.

BASIC CANNING PRINCIPLES

1. Only use jars that are specific for canning. Sanitize the jars by submerging them in boiling water for at least 10 minutes. Once they are sanitized, prepare a clean plastic sheet pan by lining it with a sheet of acetate, then a sheet of silicone paper, and finally a layer of heavy-duty paper towels. Place the jars over the paper towels with the opening facing down. This achieves two things: The excess water can drip out, and it prevents anything from getting inside the jar. The lids should be sanitized just before the jars are closed up. These lids are specially designed so that they expand when they are hot and contract when they cool down, thus creating a tight seal between the jar and the lid. The lid, depending on the manufacturer, will dip or shrink as the jars cool down, because a vacuum is created that squeezes all the air out of the jar. This vacuum will preserve the contents of the jar. The lids can also be coated in a thin rubber or plastic layer. This helps the seal on the jar become tighter and also prevents the metal on the lid from rusting.

2. Once the jars have been sanitized, make the jam, marmalade, jelly, or fruit butter. Once it is made, portion it into the jars while they are still hot. Use a funnel to prevent any product from splattering on the rim of the jars. This could compromise the seal and promote bacteria growth.

3. While portioning the product into the jars, sanitize the lids by boiling them in water for 10 minutes. Take them out of the water as needed.

4. When all of the jars have been filled, put the hot lids on the jars and close them tightly. Place all of the jars in a pot with boiling water. Make sure the jars are covered by at least 1 inch of water. Boil for at least 10 and up to 20 minutes. Alternatively, if you have a steamer, you can steam the jars for 10 minutes.

5. Let the jars cool overnight at room temperature.

6. Label the jars. The label should include the name of the café, name of the product, amount contained in the jar (weight), manufacture date, ingredients, expiration date (2 years after manufacture), and the following note: *Refrigerate after opening*. This is the minimum amount of information. Check with your local health department about labeling requirements.

jams

A jam is a mixture of fruit and sugar, cooked to break down the fruit and obtain a spreadable mixture. Jams can be thickened just by cooking or by the addition of pectin. Adding pectin shortens the cooking time and therefore preserves the flavor of the fruit better. Some fruit contains natural pectin (apples, grapes, and berries, for example) and does not require the addition of pectin to set properly. The jams in this book are made without pectin.

PROCEDURE FOR MAKING JAMS

1. Sanitize the jars and lids.

2. Combine the fruit with the sugar and lemon juice in an appropriate-size pot and place it over high heat. Stir constantly to dissolve the sugar. Bring to a boil and continue to stir until the mixture thickens.

3. Test the gel. There are 3 ways to do this: (1) Take the temperature, which should read 104°C/220°F. (2) Take a refractometer reading: Cool a small amount of jam to 20°C/68°F. This is very important. If the liquid is hot, the refractometer will not give an accurate reading. Take a reading. It should read 65° Brix. This is the preferred method. (3) The least accurate test is the refrigerator test. This consists of putting a small amount of jam on a plate and putting it in a refrigerator, waiting a few minutes for it to cool, and then passing your finger through it. A mixture that has set will not spread after you run your finger through it and the surface will wrinkle when the edge of the jam is pushed.

Blueberry and Raspberry Jam

BERRY JAM

yield: 5.5 kg/12 lb 2.08 oz

INGREDIENT	METRIC	U.S.	%
Berries	2.8 kg	6 lb .88 oz	50.94%
Sugar	2.48 kg	5 lb 15.52 oz	45.21%
Lemon juice	206 g	7.27 oz	3.75%
Salt	6 g	.22 oz	.11%

Follow the basic canning principles on page 485. This recipe yields enough jam to fill twenty 227-g/8-oz jars. There will be some evaporation during the cooking process.

note This recipe can be used for blueberries, blackberries, and raspberries as well as for less common berries such as loganberries, boysenberries, and gooseberries.

STRAWBERRY AND TAHITIAN VANILLA BEAN JAM

yield: 5.5 kg/12 lb 2.08 oz

INGREDIENT	METRIC	U.S.	%
Strawberries, stemmed and sliced	2.89 kg	6 lb 5.92 oz	52.57%
Sugar	2.4 kg	5 lb 4.8 oz	43.74%
Lemon juice	199 g	7.03 oz	3.62%
Salt	4 g	.14 oz	.07%
Tahitian vanilla pods, split and scraped	3	3	

Follow the basic canning principles on page 485. Remove the vanilla pods before portioning the jam into the jars. This recipe yields enough jam to fill twenty 227-g/8-oz jars. There will be some evaporation during the cooking process.

PLUM AND CINNAMON JAM

yield: 5.5 kg/12 lb 2.08 oz

INGREDIENT	METRIC	U.S.	%
Red plums, pitted and chopped	2.86 kg	6 lb 5.12 oz	52.14%
Water	558 g	1 lb 3.68	10.14%
Sugar	1.91 kg	4 lb 3.52 oz	34.76%
Lemon juice	159 g	5.62 oz	2.9%
Salt	3 g	.11 oz	.06%
Vietnamese cinnamon sticks	5	5	

Follow the basic canning principles on page 485. Remove the cinnamon sticks before portioning the jam into the jars. This recipe yields enough jam to fill twenty 227-g/8-oz jars. There will be some evaporation during the cooking process.

A marmalade is essentially a suspension of fruit or vegetables and pulp in a jelly. Marmalades can be made by simply cooking the fruit with the sugar until it reaches the desired consistency. The most popular marmalades are those made with citrus fruits, but they are not the only type of ingredient that can be used for marmalade. There is no one method for making marmalade.

RED ONION MARMALADE

yield: 5.5 kg/12 lb 2.08 oz

INGREDIENT	METRIC	U.S.	%
Red onions, peeled and thinly sliced	1.35 kg	2 lb 15.84 oz	24.69%
Brown sugar	136 g	4.79 oz	2.47%
Dried cranberries, finely chopped	272 g	9.58 oz	4.94%
White wine vinegar	113 g	3.99 oz	2.06%
Powdered pectin	113 g	3.99 oz	
Sugar	1.81 kg	3 lb 15.84 oz	32.92%
Apple juice, unsweetened	1.69 kg	3 lb 11.84 oz	30.86%

1. Follow the canning principles on page 485 when making marmalade.

2. Sanitize the jars. This recipe yields enough marmalade to fill twenty 227-g/8-oz jars. There will be some evaporation during the cooking process.

3. Combine the onions, brown sugar, cranberries, and vinegar and cook over medium heat until the onions are translucent.

4. Whisk the pectin together with 200 g/7.05 oz of sugar in a bowl.

5. In a large sauce pot, combine the onion mixture and the apple juice. Whisk in the pectin mixture, pouring it in slowly and whisking constantly.

6. Bring to a boil while whisking constantly. Add the remaining sugar and bring the mixture back to a boil. Boil for about 1 minute. Perform a gel test using the refractometer. If it is ready, remove the pot from the heat and skim the surface; if not, continue to cook until it is ready.

7. Finish canning as per the basic canning principles on page 485.

note This item is recommended for savory applications.

CHERRY AND VANILLA MARMALADE

yield: 5.96 kg/13 lb 2.24 oz

INGREDIENT	METRIC	U.S.	%
Oranges, chopped and seeded	440 g	15.52 oz	7.38%
Rainier cherries or other cherry variety, pitted	2.4 kg	5 lb 4.64 oz	40.27%
Lemon juice	320 g	11.29 oz	5.37%
Tahitian vanilla pods, split and scraped	3	3	
Sugar	2.8 kg	6 lb 2.72 oz	46.98%

1. Follow the canning principles on page 485 when making marmalade.

2. Sanitize the jars. This recipe yields enough marmalade to fill twenty 227-g/8-oz jars. There will be some evaporation during the cooking process.

3. In a large rondeau, combine the oranges, cherries, lemon juice, and vanilla pods and seeds. Bring to a boil over medium high-heat. Reduce the heat to medium-low until the mixture is barely bubbling. Continue to cook until the orange peel is tender, about 35 minutes. As the mixture simmers, slowly stir in the sugar.

4. Bring the mixture back to a rolling boil, stirring constantly, until the mixture gels. This can take from 30 minutes to 1 hour.

5. Perform a gel test using the refractometer. If it is ready, remove the pot from the heat and skim the surface; if not, continue to cook until it is ready. Remove the vanilla pods.

6. Finish canning as per the basic canning principles on page 485.

GINGER AND PEAR MARMALADE

yield: 5.5 kg/12 lb 2.08 oz

INGREDIENT	METRIC	U.S.	%
Limes	7	7	
Ripe but semifirm Bosc pears, stemmed, peeled, cored, and coarsely chopped	2.92 kg	6 lb 7 oz	53.17%
Sugar	1.79 kg	3 lb 15.14 oz	32.72%
Crystallized ginger, finely chopped	101 g	3.56 oz	1.84%
Water	675 g	1 lb 7.8 oz	12.27%

1. Follow the canning principles on page 485 when making marmalade.

2. Sanitize the jars. This recipe yields enough marmalade to fill twenty 227-g/8-oz jars. There will be some evaporation during the cooking process.

3. Peel the limes and then cut the peel into julienne. Reserve until needed.

4. Cut the peeled limes in half and squeeze the juice into a large rondeau. Add the pears and toss them in the juice to coat. Add the sugar and the ginger. Mix until a homogeneous mass is obtained. Keep the mixture covered with plastic wrap for 1 hour.

5. In a small sauce pot, combine the lime julienne and the water and bring to a boil. Continue to cook until the water has almost evaporated. Strain the liquid onto the pears and reserve the lime julienne.

6. Bring the pear mixture to a rolling boil over high heat, stirring constantly, for about 20 minutes. Add the lime julienne and boil for 5 to 10 more minutes. Perform a gel test using the refractometer. If it is ready, remove the pot from the heat and skim the surface; if not, continue to cook until it is ready.

7. Finish canning as per the basic canning principles on page 485.

jellies

A jelly is a clear juice that is combined with sugar, pectin, and an acid and cooked until it gels. Most jellies are made with pectin because there are very few fruits that contain natural pectin. Additionally, gelling with pectin reduces the jellies' cooking time, which will result in a better and more pronounced fruit flavor.

The most challenging part of making jellies is extracting the water or juice from the fruit so that it is free of any pulp. Below are the different methods used to extract the juice from different types of fruit.

CONCORD GRAPE JELLY

yield: 5 kg/11 lb .32 oz

INGREDIENT	METRIC	U.S.	%
CONCORD GRAPE JUICE			
Concord grapes	10.14 kg	22 lb 5.76 oz	84.52%
Water	1.85 kg	4 lb 1.6 oz	15.48%
CONCORD GRAPE JELLY			
Sugar	2.4 kg	5 lb 4.65 oz	48%
Powdered pectin	100 g	3.53 oz	2%
Concord grape juice	2.5 kg	5 lb 8.16 oz	50%

1. **FOR THE CONCORD GRAPE JUICE:** Combine the grapes and water in a large rondeau and bring to a boil over high heat. Boil for about 1 minute, and then remove the pot from the heat and cover it with plastic wrap. Allow the mixture to sit for about 45 minutes.

2. Pass the liquid through a large-mesh sieve to remove the seeds.

3. Line a large-mesh sieve with 3 layers of cheesecloth and put it over a large bain marie. Pour the strained Concord grape juice into the sieve and let the juice strain for about 2 hours. Do not try to push or force it out.

4. Reserve the remaining liquid.

5. Follow the canning principles on page 485 when making jelly.

6. Sanitize the jars. This recipe yields enough jelly to fill twenty 227-g/8-oz jars. There will be some evaporation during the cooking process.

7. **FOR THE JELLY:** Whisk together 400 g/14.11 oz of sugar with the pectin in a bowl.

8. Pour the juice into an appropriate-size sauce pot. Pour in the pectin mixture slowly, whisking constantly. Whisk until it dissolves. Bring to a boil over high heat, stirring frequently.

9. Add the remaining sugar and return to a rolling boil, stirring constantly. Boil for 1 more minute. Take the pot off the heat and skim the surface; perform a gel test or check the Brix degrees on a refractometer.

10. Finish canning as per the basic canning principles on page 485.

RED CURRANT JELLY

yield: 5 kg/11 lb .32 oz

INGREDIENT	METRIC	U.S.	%
RED CURRANT JUICE			
Red currants	12 kg	26 lb 7.36 oz	96%
Water	500 g	1 lb 1.64 oz	4%
RED CURRANT JELLY			
Sugar	2.14 kg	4 lb 11.68 oz	42.93%
Powdered pectin	85 g	3 oz	1.7%
Red currant juice	2.76 kg	6 lb 1.6 oz	55.37%

1. **FOR THE RED CURRANT JUICE:** Combine the currants and water in a large rondeau and bring to a boil over high heat. Boil for about 1 minute, and then remove the pot from the heat and cover it with plastic wrap. Allow the mixture to sit for about 45 minutes.

2. Pass the liquid through a large-mesh sieve to remove the seeds and stems.

3. Line a large-mesh sieve with 3 layers of cheesecloth and put it over a large bain marie. Pour the strained red currant juice into the sieve and let the juice strain out for about 2 hours. Do not try to push or force it out.

4. Reserve the remaining liquid.

5. Follow the canning principles on page 485 when making jelly.

6. Sanitize the jars. This recipe yields enough jelly to fill twenty 227-g/8-oz jars. There will be some evaporation during the cooking process.

7. **FOR THE JELLY:** Whisk together 400 g/14.11 oz of sugar with the pectin in a bowl.

8. Pour the juice into an appropriate-size sauce pot. Pour in the pectin mixture slowly, whisking constantly. Whisk until it dissolves. Bring to a boil over high heat, stirring frequently.

9. Add the remaining sugar and return to a rolling boil, stirring constantly. Boil for 1 more minute. Take the pot off the heat and skim the surface. Perform a gel test or check the Brix degrees on a refractometer.

10. Finish canning as per the basic canning principles on page 485.

GRANNY SMITH APPLE JELLY

yield: 5 kg/11 lb .32 oz

INGREDIENT	METRIC	U.S.	%
APPLE WATER			
Granny Smith or other tart apples, quartered and cored	7 kg	15 lb 8.48 oz	65.12%
Water	3.75 kg	8 lb 4.32 oz	34.88%
GRANNY SMITH APPLE JELLY			
Sugar	2.59 kg	5 lb 11.52 oz	51.85%
Powdered pectin	93 g	3.27 oz	1.85%
Granny Smith apple juice	2.31 kg	5 lb 1.6 oz	46.3%

1. **FOR THE APPLE WATER:** Combine the apples and water in a large rondeau. The water should cover the apples completely. Bring to a boil over high heat, stirring frequently.

2. Turn the heat down and cover with plastic wrap. Simmer gently, stirring and crushing the apples occasionally, for 30 to 45 minutes.

3. Line a large-mesh sieve with layers of cheesecloth and place it over a bain marie. Pour the liquid and the apples into the sieve and let the liquid drip through for 2 to 3 hours. Do not try to force the liquid through.

4. Reserve the remaining liquid.

5. Follow the canning principles on page 485 when making jelly.

6. Sanitize the jars. This recipe yields enough jelly to fill twenty 227-g/8-oz jars. There will be some evaporation during the cooking process.

7. **FOR THE JELLY:** Whisk together 400 g/14.11 oz of sugar with the pectin in a bowl.

8. Pour the juice into an appropriate-size sauce pot. Pour in the pectin mixture slowly, whisking constantly. Whisk until it dissolves. Bring to a boil over high heat, stirring frequently.

9. Add the remaining sugar and return to a rolling boil, stirring constantly. Boil for 1 more minute. Take the pot off the heat and skim the surface. Perform a gel test or check the Brix degrees on a refractometer.

10. Finish canning as per the basic canning principles on page 485.

variation For McIntosh Apple Jelly, substitute an equal amount of McIntosh apples for the Granny Smith apples.

ICE CREAM AND OTHER FROZEN ITEMS

Of course, ice cream is an item that is more popular in warm climates or during warm seasons. If you live in a region where it is not warm year-round, you could experience a nosedive in frozen dessert sales during the winter. Frozen desserts that are to be scooped should be churned every day. Any frozen dessert that contains dairy such as ice cream, gelato, or sherbet can be churned only twice. When ice creams are churned once, they have already gone through a foaming process as they are churned. When they are melted down, most of the foam or air bubbles still remain in the melted base. When they are churned again, they will get even more air incorporated than in the original base, so if you initially had an overrun of 40 to 50 percent, on a second churn it will be 55 to 60 percent, which has a direct effect on the texture and structure of the ice cream. Sorbets can be churned over and over again. This can be a problem in the winter when you have to pay someone to churn the items fresh daily when you won't be selling enough frozen desserts to justify the labor incurred in their production. There are two possible solutions to this

problem. The first solution is to sell frozen desserts that are packaged or preportioned into containers that will keep the frozen items protected from freezer burn. This is a way to offer items that are a single portion or large enough for four people. The second part of the solution is to adjust the temperature of the display freezer. The ideal temperature for holding frozen desserts in a display case is –10°C/14°F, if they are to be scooped. Some pastry chefs prefer –18°C/0°F, but this could make the frozen item too hard and unpalatable. By turning the temperature up to –7°C/19°F, the product that has been pre-portioned will become very smooth and will not crystallize in the freezer; this however would be almost too soft for scooping so setting the freezer to –7°C/19°F is best for preportioned frozen desserts. Again, this only works for preportioned and packaged frozen desserts in the display case. Additionally, having the product already packaged expedites service; there is no scooping involved, which makes for one less step. This is another opportunity to invest in proper packaging, and there are many possibilities for this.

The frozen desserts in this book are all pre-packaged and meant to be displayed as is, but the actual recipes can be churned and served as scoops.

There are many varieties of frozen desserts, and they can be categorized into three large groups: dairy-based, machine-churned products; non-dairy-based, machine-churned, scraped or shaved, and non-aerated stillfrozen products; and aerated stillfrozen desserts. Aerated stillfrozen desserts such as parfaits, bombes, semifreddos, soufflés, and frozen mousses will not be part of this chapter.

dairy-based, machine-churned products

ICE CREAM
Ice cream is a combination of dairy (milk or milk and heavy cream), sugar, and a flavor. Simply put, an ice cream is an emulsion and then, after churning, is a foam in which the air bubbles are stabilized by freezing a large amount of the liquid around them. How much of the liquid is frozen depends on the sugar content of the base. Ice cream is churned until it has an overrun of between 40 and 60 percent (see the sidebar on page 495).

CUSTARD-BASE ICE CREAM
This is the same as ice cream but includes egg yolks, which act as an emulsifier.

GELATO
There are many confusing opinions as to what defines a gelato. Some examples of these conflicting definitions are: Gelato has little or no fat; gelato is made with milk only; gelato contains no eggs; a special machine is needed to churn gelato; gelato should be kept in a freezer at slightly higher temperatures than ice cream and sorbet since it is denser and can't be frozen as cold or it would be unpalatable; and gelato is made with cornstarch as a thickener. These are all misconceptions. If you ask an Italian pastry chef what gelato means, he will say, "ice cream." Gelato can be made as ice cream or as custard-base ice cream, with milk, milk and heavy cream, or milk and heavy cream and eggs. What really distinguishes gelato is its overrun percentage, which is typically around 20 percent. That does in fact make it denser than regular ice cream, since it has less air forced into it.

SHERBET
Sherbet is an ice containing less than 50 percent dairy in the total liquid, which can be water, fruit purée, or fruit juice, or a combination of these three items. Sherbet should contain 1 to 2 percent milk fat and 2 to 5 percent milk solids. The dairy content is very small compared to the remainder of the liquid. It also has about twice the amount of sugar of whole-fat ice cream so that it can form small ice crystals.

FROZEN YOGURT
The main dairy ingredient is yogurt. The yogurt can be whole fat, which produces the best results, or low- to nonfat yogurt, in which case the sugar is increased to produce a smooth, ice-crystal-free frozen yogurt.

MANUFACTURING PROCESS FOR DAIRY-BASED FROZEN DESSERTS

There are six major steps involved in the manufacture of ice cream, gelato, and sherbet. These steps hold true no matter the size of production. All of the items in this section will have to go through all of these steps in order to produce a quality product.

1. Making the Base: The desired ingredients are scaled out based on the formula, and the base is made according to the appropriate method (see production methods below).

2. Pasteurization: In this step, the liquid is heated to 85°C/185°F for a certain amount of time in order to destroy all pathogenic bacteria. The preferred method for small-batch production is known as HTST (high temperature, short time). The base is heated up to 85°C/185°F, removed from the heat, and then stirred for 2 minutes. This stirring accomplishes three things. It ensures that the base is evenly pasteurized, that the ingredients are "homogenized" (see below), and that certain ingredients, such as stabilizers and proteins, are hydrated. Another form of pasteurizing is LTST (low temperature, short time). This is performed in batch pasteurizers, which have the same purpose of killing bacteria, but the process is slower since the liquid doesn't get as hot as with the HTST method. In LTST, the mixture maintains a 65°C/149°F temperature for 30 minutes. This process is more convenient for industrial production, where larger amounts of liquid will take longer to come down to safe temperatures and therefore the base spends less time in the danger zone. If the large amount of liquid is not as hot as with the HTST method, it won't take it as long to cool down: if you have 100 liters/104 quarts at 65°C/149°F and 100 liters/104 quarts at 85°C/185°F, it will take the second amount longer to cool down than the first 100 liters at a lower temperature. It is also used for bases with ingredients that are sensitive to higher temperatures.

3. Homogenization: A fat emulsion is formed through constant agitation or stirring of the mix at pasteurization temperatures. The fat globules break up more readily and they do not tend to clump at that point. Clumps of fat will cause a thick base, and thinner bases incorporate air better and form smaller, more uniform air bubbles. This in turn will make for a smoother, more stable, and more "heat-shock" resistant product.

4. Aging: After the product has been homogenized, strained, and cooled over an ice bath to 4°C/39°F, it needs time to "age." During this time, the proteins and stabilizers become fully hydrated and the fat cools down and crystallizes. Protein and emulsifier networks are developed during this time. Aging or "maturing" will improve the whipping properties of the base, which in turn will make for a smoother frozen product with a high tolerance to heat shock. Aging time ranges from a minimum of 4 hours to a maximum of 24 hours. If there is a flavor being steeped, this time will also allow it to infuse a stronger flavor into the base.

5. Churning or Freezing: This is the process in which the base's water is partially frozen and air is whipped into the mix. This particular process takes place in a batch freezer.

6. Hardening: When an ice cream is extracted from a batch freezer, it is frozen, but not frozen enough to serve. The consistency is similar to soft-serve ice cream, since it is between −4°C/25°F and −6°C/21°F. At this point it is not scoopable. It needs to reach a minimum of −8°C/18°F or a maximum of −10°C/14°F to make it hard enough to scoop easily but still have it retain a smooth texture. The time it takes for a frozen product to reach this ideal temperature depends on the freezer. A good compressor equals quick hardening. A blast freezer set to −30°C/−22°F will harden 2 L/2 qt in 30 minutes. A conventional freezer can take up to 4 hours. Do not set the blast freezer any lower than −30°C/−22°F, because no matter how well you have made your base and no matter what sort of stabilizers and emulsifiers you have added to it, it will become too hard to scoop.

DAIRY-BASED FROZEN DESSERT PRODUCTION METHOD

There are a few different methods for making these varieties of frozen desserts. The desserts in this book are made with the following method.

1. Scale all of the ingredients accurately.

2. Mix 10 percent of the sugar with the stabilizer (which can be combined with the emulsifier or emulsifiers). The emulsifiers and stabilizers should not be added to the liquid without mixing them with the sugar, since adding them alone will cause them to clump. These clumps are impossible to break down, and they will render the stabilizer/emulsifier properties at least weaker than they would be in a soluble powder form, if not useless.

3. Place the milk in a pot over high heat.

4. Once it reaches 25°C/77°F, add the milk powder, if using, and liquid flavoring. Solid flavorings such as chocolate should be added once the base is made. From this point on, whisking should be constant to prevent any of the ingredients from settling to the bottom of the pot.

5. At 35°C/95°F, pour in and mix all of the sugars until dissolved. This refers to any type of sugar, either in solid, granulated form or in liquid form, like trimoline. Some recipes might contain egg yolks. If so, they should be whisked in at this point.

6. At 45°C/113°F, add the heavy cream, if using.

7. Before the mixture reaches 50°C/122°F, add the stabilizer-sugar mix in a slow pouring motion while whisking constantly.

8. Bring the mixture up to 85°C/185°F, take off the heat, and cook for 2 more minutes while whisking constantly to pasteurize and homogenize the mixture.

9. Pass the mixture through a fine-mesh sieve and chill down to 4°C/39°F as quickly as possible using an ice bath. If steeping flavors, chill over an ice bath but do not pass through a fine-mesh sieve until just before churning.

10. Let the mixture age for at least 4 hours or ideally for 12 hours.

11. Before churning, give the base a good stir. Churn to −8°C/18°F.

12. Place the churned product in a −10°C/14°F freezer.

overrun

OVERRUN IS THE PERCENTAGE INCREASE IN VOLUME from the liquid base of an ice cream, custard-base ice cream, gelato, sherbet, or sorbet that is a direct result of churning. For example, if you started with 2 liters of raspberry sorbet base and obtained 3 liters after churning, the volume has increased by 50 percent. This number represents the overrun.

Overrun can also be calculated with garnished bases, such as chocolate chips. The following formula can be used to determine overrun in a variety of situations, assuming that the equipment used to freeze the product performs consistently.

Determining overrun in a frozen ice cream, custard-base ice cream, gelato, sherbet, or sorbet with no garnish:

(volume of frozen product – volume of base)/volume of base x 100% = % overrun

Example: 1 liter of plain ice cream base gives 1.75 liters frozen ice cream

(1.75 liter – 1 liter)/1 liter x 100% = 75% overrun

It is very important to calculate the overrun on your products in order to establish consistency in the finished product and in the yield. The longer the base churns in the batch freezer, the more air will be incorporated. When testing a recipe, it might take a few tries before obtaining the desired overrun, which will depend on the desired consistency. Once the desired overrun is established, however, it will be sufficient to record the time it took from its liquid stage to its frozen stage at the desired overrun rather than to calculate the overrun each time you churn a batch of ice cream. When the product is churned subsequently, all you need to do is set the timer on the machine so that it stops freezing at the precise moment you desire. Remember, though, that this only applies to items churned in the batch freezer, and that you will need to churn the same amount each time.

non-dairy-based, machine-churned, and scraped or shaved products

SORBET

A sorbet is an aerated non-dairy frozen product that is churned in a batch freezer. They are made mainly of a fruit or vegetable juice, a fruit or vegetable purée, an infused or flavored liquid, a wine, or a liqueur. They contain a percentage of sugar that is dependent on the desired sweetness and the sweetness of the main component. Typically it is 25 to 32 percent for dessert preparations. This sugar is the total sugar that may be found in any of the ingredients, such as a fruit purée, plus the added sweetener. A sorbet is not necessarily a dessert. An acid, generally in the form of lemon juice, is sometimes added to intensify the flavor and control sweetness.

FRAPPÉ

A frappé is a combination of a fruit sorbet and another liquid or dairy product that is mixed in a blender until it obtains a slush-like consistency. The liquid can be flavored or infused water, a fruit or vegetable juice, soy milk, wine, or liqueur. If dairy is being used, it should be low-fat or fat-free milk or fat-free yogurt, because if there is a significant amount of fat present, it will seize as it is processed in the blender due to the friction of the blade. The proportion of sorbet to the added liquid or dairy product is not written in stone, but there should be a majority of sorbet in the finished product.

GRANITÉ (OR GRANITA)

Granité is French for "granite," and the dessert is named for the stone because of their similarity in appearance. It is also known as *granita* in Italian. A granité is a semisolid mass of small but visible ice crystals that are formed by occasionally scraping or stirring a liquid that has been placed in the freezer. Granités are mainly composed of a fruit or vegetable juice, an infused or flavored liquid, or a wine. This liquid is scraped or stirred at various times during the freezing process to prevent the liquid from freezing into a solid block of ice, and so it forms small ice crystals instead. Ideally the liquid is scraped or stirred with a fork every 15 to 30 minutes in a freezer that is at −18°C/0°F. It is important not to let the semi-frozen liquid sit for too long in the freezer, especially toward the beginning of the freezing process. The flavors and sugar can separate from the remaining ingredients, and the flavor and the sweetness will not be evenly distributed throughout the finished product. Although the granité's ice crystals should be very small, they are still visible. This is one of the big differences between granités and sorbets, in which ice crystals are minuscule and should not be visible to the human eye.

It is important to mention that there is a difference between the granités or granitas that are meant to be drunk and those that are scraped. Those that are meant to be drunk are kept in a looser state in a machine specially designed for that purpose than those that are scraped, because otherwise they will not go through a straw as easily. Scraped granités are meant to be eaten with a spoon.

SHAVED ICES

A variation on a granité is the shaved ice, which is made by simply freezing water or a flavored liquid and then shaving the resulting ice block with a fork, ice pick, or ice shaver to obtain small, pure ice crystals. The shaved ice is placed in an appropriate vessel such as a bowl or glass, and, once it is placed in front of the customer, a flavored liquid can be poured in.

ICES OR ICE POPS

An ice can have the same ratio of ingredients and physical attributes as a granité as far as being water-like. The sugar content of 16° to 19° Brix stays the same, yet it is left to freeze as a solid piece in order to make the finished product. The liquid base for an ice can also have the same base as a granité, such as fruit or vegetable juice, an infused or flavored liquid, or a wine, but ices can also be made with a fruit purée because purées freeze much better when they are left as a solid piece.

The shape of the ice is only limited by the pastry chef's imagination, but it must be something that will be easy to eat. It should be easy to bite, chew, and hold and should not make a huge mess or be awkward to eat, especially in a fine dining establishment.

NON-DAIRY-BASED, MACHINE-CHURNED, AND SCRAPED OR SHAVED METHOD FOR MAKING BASES

using a refractometer

The basic concept behind this method is to combine the main liquid, be it a fruit or vegetable purée, a fruit or vegetable juice, any flavored or infused liquid, or a wine, with a simple syrup at 50° Brix. There are two key points to consider:

1. The ratio of sugar to water in the simple syrup. Simple syrup is just a mixture of water and sugar that has been boiled to create a uniform liquid in which the sugar crystals have dissolved. The classic ratio of sugar to water in simple syrup for sorbet production is 65 percent sugar and 35 percent water. This will give us a simple syrup at 65° Brix. This ratio is not written in stone. A 50° Brix simple syrup can yield excellent results as well. The sorbet recipes in this book use a specially formulated syrup that contains different sugars and sorbet stabilizers (see recipe on the following page), which will ensure a smooth final product. For granités, ice pops, and popsicles, use a 50° Brix simple syrup. Keep in mind that whichever ingredient is the majority of the base will have a direct effect on the base. For example, if there is too much water, the main flavor will be watered down, but if there is too much sugar, it will be too thick. Also, always add the simple syrup to the base after it has cooled to room temperature.

2. The final reading of the base in a refractometer should be between 25° and 32° Brix, with 30° to 32° Brix being ideal for dessert sorbets and 16° to 19° Brix for granités, ice pops, and popsicles. The ideal environment in which to take a Brix reading is one where the temperature is 20°C/68°F and the liquids are at the same temperature. If the mixture is too cold or too hot, the refraction will be inaccurate.

PROCEDURE FOR MAKING SORBET BASES, GRANITÉS, AND ICE POPS USING THE REFRACTOMETER

1. Place the main liquid in a stainless-steel bowl. This main liquid should be free of solid particles and previously strained through a fine-mesh sieve. It can be a fruit or vegetable juice or purée, infusion, tea, coffee, liquor, or wine.

2. If the main liquid was refrigerated, remember to temper it to 20°C/68°F. To temper the main liquid, place the bowl in a larger bowl that is filled halfway with warm water at 40°C/104°F. Stir until the main liquid reaches 20°C/68°F.

3. Pour in some sorbet syrup to make sorbet bases or simple syrup for granités and ice pops and mix with a whisk. The syrup amount should be the equivalent of 20 percent of the weight of the main liquid.

4. Take a reading with the refractometer. If the refractometer reads below the desired Brix degrees, add more syrup. If the base has a Brix that is too high, simply add more of the main liquid. Acidic or bitter liquids will require more simple syrup than sweeter ones, unless a more savory result is desired.

5. Once the desired Brix has been reached, the base can be refrigerated for up to 3 days in most cases, or it can be processed immediately.

6. Churn the sorbet base, freeze and scrape the granité, or freeze the ice pops, and transfer to a –10°C/14°F freezer.

7. Let the sorbet harden in the freezer for 2 to 4 hours before serving. Freeze the granité, popsicles, or ice pops completely before serving.

SORBET SYRUP

yield: 10 kg/22 lb .73 oz

INGREDIENT	METRIC	U.S.	%
Sugar	4.2 kg	9 lb 4.32 oz	42.03%
Sorbet stabilizer	69 g	2.43 oz	.69%
Glucose powder	1.81 kg	4 lb .16 oz	18.18%
Water	3.91 kg	8 lb 9.92 oz	39.1%

1. Combine 10 percent of the sugar with the sorbet stabilizer and mix thoroughly.

2. Place the remaining sugar, glucose powder, and water in a pot over high heat. Stir constantly using a whisk.

3. When the mix reaches 40°C/104°F, slowly pour in the sorbet stabilizer-sugar mix while stirring. If the mix is poured in too quickly, the stabilizer will clump up and not work.

4. Continue stirring until the mixture reaches 85°C/185°F. At this temperature the stabilizers will fully hydrate and the sugars will dissolve completely.

5. Take the pot off the heat and transfer the liquid mix to an ice bath. Let the syrup cool completely before adding it to the main ingredient.

6. After combining the sorbet syrup with the main ingredient and water, let the mix "mature" or age for 2 hours minimum or ideally 6 hours. This will give the stabilizers and sugars time to bind with the main ingredient to produce a high-quality sorbet.

7. Reserve the syrup in an airtight container at room temperature for up to 2 weeks, or refrigerate for up to 2 months. Ideally it is left at room temperature in order to take an accurate reading on the refractometer.

YUZU SORBET MOCHI

yield: 50 portions (1 sphere per portion)

components

50 Yuzu Sorbet Spheres

3 kg/6 lb 9.76 oz Mochi Dough

100 g/3.53 oz rice flour (to coat the mochi dough)

1. **TO ASSEMBLE:** Pull out only 1 sphere at a time from the freezer.

2. Cut out a 5-cm/2-in square piece of mochi dough using a knife or scissors. Coat your gloved hands with rice flour.

3. Place the piece of mochi over the sphere and push the sphere into it while holding the dough in place with your other hand. It should stretch the mochi dough to a very thin layer. Once you have enveloped the entire sphere, cut the end of the dough off by squeezing it with your thumb and index finger. This will seal the sphere inside the dough.

4. Coat the sphere in rice flour, dust the excess dough, and return to the freezer. Getting this right will take a few tries and practice.

5. Display inside mini dim-sum steamers lined with decorative foil. Allow the sorbet to temper for 5 minutes before eating for the ideal texture. Discard after 4 days.

YUZU SORBET SPHERES

yield: 2 kg/4 lb 6.4 oz (about 50 spheres)

INGREDIENT	METRIC	U.S.	%
Yuzu juice	780 g	1 lb 11.52 oz	38.98%
Sorbet syrup	1.21 kg	2 lb 11.04 oz	60.98%
Salt	.8 g	.03 oz	.04%

1. Combine all of the ingredients in a bowl. Perform a refractometer test; it should be at 30° Brix, so make adjustments if necessary.

2. Churn the sorbet. Pipe it into 3.13-cm/1.25-in diameter silicone spheres (see Resources, page 540). If these sphere molds are not available, pipe into fleximold demi-spheres of the same diameter and freeze them. Once they have hardened, unmold them and fuse 2 halves together to form a sphere.

3. Even out the tops of the sphere molds and freeze until hardened in a blast freezer. Once they are firm, push them out of the mold and reserve frozen. Discard after 4 days.

MOCHI DOUGH

INGREDIENT	METRIC	U.S.	%
Sweet rice flour (glutinous), or as needed	876 g	1 lb 14.88 oz	30.31%
Superfine or other fine crystal sugar	964 g	2 lb 1.92 oz	33.36%
Hot water, at 82°C/180°F	1.05 kg	2 lb 5.12 oz	36.33%

1. Combine the rice flour and the sugar in a bowl. Pour in the hot water and stir until there are no lumps, using a gloved hand or wooden spoon.

2. Microwave for 40 to 60 seconds on high power in a commercial microwave; stir, then microwave again. This process may need to be done 3 to 5 times depending on the microwave. The dough is done cooking when it is elastic and almost translucent, with a white opaque hue. Sprinkle some rice flour on a sheet pan lined with a nonstick rubber mat, and place the mochi on the flour. Cover it with plastic wrap and let it cool in the refrigerator or at room temperature.

3. Once it is cool, stretch the dough to .5 cm/.2 in thick by hand or using a rolling pin. Keep it covered with plastic wrap. Discard after 2 days.

note Mochi is a Japanese dough made with glutinous rice flour. It is very chewy and soft. Some use it with a filling of red bean paste, but we will use it to wrap around a yuzu sorbet. It stays soft even when it is frozen. Make sure to use glutinous rice flour, or else it won't work.

ROOT BEER SORBET AND VANILLA ICE CREAM "FLOAT"

components

7.5 kg/16 lb 8.48 oz Root Beer Sorbet Base

50 Vanilla Ice Cream Spheres

1.23 kg/2 lb 11.36 oz Root Beer Foam

1. To assemble: Place fifty 227-g/8-oz jars in a freezer.

2. Churn the root beer sorbet and fill the jars halfway by piping it in.

3. Place 1 sphere of vanilla ice cream into each jar and push down so that it is completely covered by the sorbet.

4. Pipe more sorbet into the jars until they are filled to the top. Even out the top with an offset spatula.

5. Blend the root beer foam. Once there is a nice head of foam, start spooning it on top of the jars into a mound. Freeze immediately so the bubbles set and don't pop.

6. Freeze and then serve. The foam will need to be refreshed daily. Allow the dessert to temper for 5 minutes before eating for the ideal texture. Discard after 5 days.

note This is a take on the classic root beer float, but in this case all the components are frozen, even the foam on top.

Root Beer Sorbet
and Vanilla Ice Cream
"Float"

VANILLA ICE CREAM SPHERES

yield: 2 kg/4 lb 6.4 oz (about 50 spheres)

INGREDIENT	METRIC	U.S.	%
Milk	1.47 kg	3 lb .3.92 oz	73.59%
Milk powder	61 g	2.16 oz	3.06%
Granulated sugar	213 g	7.52 oz	10.66%
Tahitian vanilla pod, split and scraped	4	4	
Glucose powder	80 g	2.82 oz	4%
Invert sugar	27 g	.94 oz	1.34%
Ice cream stabilizer	7 g	.25 oz	.35%
Yolks	140 g	4.94 oz	7%

1. To make the ice cream base, see the method for making dairy-based frozen desserts on page 493.

2. Churn the ice cream. Pipe the ice cream into 3.13-cm/1.25-in diameter silicone spheres (see Resources, page 540). Freeze until hardened in a blast freezer. Once they are firm, push them out of the mold and reserve frozen in an airtight container in a single layer.

ROOT BEER FOAM

yield: 1.23 kg/2 lb 11.38 oz

INGREDIENT	METRIC	U.S.	%
Gelatin sheets, bloomed	27 g	.94 oz	2.16%
Root beer, at room temperature	1.2 kg	2 lb 10.4 oz	97.35%
Soy lecithin, powdered	6 g	.21 oz	.49%

1. Melt the gelatin over a warm water bath with 200 g/7.05 oz of root beer, and then stir it into the remaining root beer.

2. Add the soy lecithin to the root beer mixture and foam it using a handheld blender, tilting the bowl and exposing the blade halfway to incorporate air better.

3. Use the foam immediately. Any leftovers that are not used cannot be saved. This needs to be made fresh each time you need it, since the gelatin will set and make any foaming impossible, even after you remelt it.

ROOT BEER SORBET BASE

yield: 7.5 kg/16 lb 8.48 oz

INGREDIENT	METRIC	U.S.	%
Root beer	6.76 kg	14 lb 14.72 oz	90.25%
Root beer extract	51 g	1.79 oz	0.68%
Sorbet syrup	677 g	1 lb 7.84 oz	9.03%
Salt	3 g	.12 oz	0.05%

Combine all of the ingredients in a bowl. Adjust the Brix if necessary to achieve 30° Brix. Reserve refrigerated.

CASSIS SORBET, MARZIPAN ICE CREAM, AND CHOCOLATE ICE CREAM BOX

yield: 50 boxes

components

7.5 kg/16 lb 8.48 oz Cassis Sorbet Base

7.5 kg/16 lb 8.48 oz Marzipan Ice Cream Base

7.5 kg/16 lb 8.48 oz Chocolate Ice Cream Base

1. **TO ASSEMBLE:** Churn all 3 frozen bases and extrude them into piping bags. Each flavor will require 5 or 6 piping bags.

2. Let them harden slightly in a freezer; meanwhile, freeze the cubes.

3. Pipe a small amount of each frozen item into the cubes, alternating flavors, until each cube is filled.

4. Place the lid on each cube and let the items harden in a freezer before displaying. Allow the box to temper for 5 to 7 minutes before eating for the ideal texture. Discard after 5 days.

note This is displayed in cubes that measure 10 cm/4 in on each side. Inside the cube are all the frozen items, randomly piped but in equal amounts in each cube. The cube has a plastic lid (see Resources, page 540).

CASSIS SORBET BASE

yield: 7.5 kg/16 lb 8.48 oz

INGREDIENT	METRIC	U.S.	%
Cassis (black currant) purée	3.43 kg	7 lb 8.96 oz	45.75%
Water	858 g	1 lb 14.24 oz	11.44%
Sorbet syrup	3.2 kg	7 lb 1.12 oz	42.77%
Salt	3 g	.11 oz	.04%

1. Combine all the ingredients in a bowl. Adjust the Brix if necessary to achieve 30° Brix.

2. Follow the sorbet procedure on page 497.

MARZIPAN ICE CREAM BASE

yield: 7.5 kg/16 lb 8.48 oz

INGREDIENT	METRIC	U.S.	%
Milk	4.76 kg	10 lb 8.16 oz	63.59%
Milk powder	229 g	8.16 oz	3.06%
Sugar	800 g	1 lb 12.16 oz	10.67%
Glucose powder	300 g	10.58 oz	4%
Invert sugar	100 g	3.53 oz	1.33%
Ice cream stabilizer	26 g	.96 oz	.35%
Egg yolks	525 g	1 lb 2.56 oz	7%
Marzipan	750 g	1 lb 10.4 oz	10%

Follow the procedure for ice cream production on page 493. Add the marzipan after the base reaches 85°C/185°F. Incorporate it into the mixture using a beurre mixer, and then strain through a fine-mesh sieve and cool down in an ice bath. Age overnight.

CHOCOLATE ICE CREAM BASE

yield: 7.5 kg/16 lb 8.48 oz

INGREDIENT	METRIC	U.S.	%
Milk	4.93 kg	10 lb 14.24 oz	65.84%
Milk powder	206 g	7.28 oz	2.75%
Sugar	694 g	1 lb 8.48 oz	9.26%
Glucose powder	270 g	9.52 oz	3.6%
Trimoline	90 g	3.18 oz	1.2%
Ice cream stabilizer	26 g	.93 oz	.35%
Egg yolks	525 g	1 lb 2.56 oz	7%
Dark chocolate (64%) coins	750 g	1 lb 10.4 oz	10%

Follow the procedure for ice cream production on page 493. Add the chocolate after the base reaches 85°C/185°F. Incorporate it into the mixture by whisking until the chocolate has dissolved, strain through a fine-mesh sieve, and cool down in an ice bath. Age overnight.

PASSION FRUIT SORBET AND COCONUT MACARON SANDWICH

yield: 50 portions

components

3 kg/6 lb 9.76 oz Passion Fruit Sorbet Base

100 Coconut Macarons

1. **TO ASSEMBLE:** Churn the sorbet base and extrude it into a piping bag.

2. Remove the macarons from the freezer. Pipe about 60 g/2.11 oz onto the flipped-over macarons.

3. Place the other macaron on top at a slant. Freeze to harden.

4. Ideally this sorbet sandwich is wrapped with foil or placed inside a plastic cube. Allow the sandwich to temper for 5 minutes before eating for the ideal texture. Discard after 5 days.

note This is a variation on an ice cream sandwich, using a sorbet and a macaron cookie to sandwich it.

PASSION FRUIT SORBET BASE

yield: 3 kg/6 lb 9.76 oz

INGREDIENT	METRIC	U.S.	%
Passion fruit purée (see Note)	1.07 kg	2 lb 5.76 oz	35.72%
Water	964 g	2 lb 2.08 oz	32.14%
Sorbet syrup	964 g	2 lb 2.08 oz	32.14%

Combine all of the ingredients in a bowl. Adjust the Brix if needed to achieve 30° Brix.

note If using concentrated purée, use half purée and half orange juice for the total amount of the purée.

COCONUT MACARONS

yield: about 100 cookies

INGREDIENT	METRIC	U.S.	%
Egg whites, at 21°C/70°F	210 g	7.41 oz	21.01%
Superfine sugar, ground in a coffee grinder	53 g	1.85 oz	5.25%
Cream of tartar	1 g	.04 oz	.11%
Fondant sugar	473 g	1 lb 0.64 oz	47.27%
Blanched almond flour	263 g	9.26 oz	26.26%
Salt	1 g	.04 oz	.11%
Desiccated coconut, very finely chopped	200 g	7.11 oz	

1. Follow the procedure for macarons on page 271.

2. Pipe macarons to 6.25-cm/2.5-in diameter circles. Sprinkle the coconut to cover each macaron completely.

3. Once they are baked (see baking instructions on page 275; they will take between 4 and 6 more minutes to bake than smaller macarons), flip half of the cookies over and freeze them all.

LEMON MYRTLE ICE CREAM WITH STRAWBERRY JAM IN A SHORTBREAD COOKIE BOX

yield: 50 portions

components

5 kg/11 lb .32 oz Strawberry Jam

8 kg/17 lb 10.19 oz Lemon Myrtle Ice Cream Base

1 sheet pan Shortbread Cookie Morsels

1. **TO ASSEMBLE:** Freeze fifty 280-g/10-oz cubes. The cubes should measure 5 by 10 by 5 cm/2 by 4 by 2 in. These cubes must have lids (see Resources, page 540).

2. Place the jam into piping bags.

3. Churn the ice cream and extrude into piping bags. Freeze for about 30 minutes to harden.

4. Work on 6 to 8 cubes at a time. Fill the cubes one-third of the way with ice cream, and place about 20 g/.7 oz of cookie morsels over the ice cream. Pipe 30 g/1.06 oz of jam on top of the cookies. Repeat the process 2 more times. The final layer should be jam.

5. Freeze all the cubes to harden the ice cream. Allow this dessert to temper for 5 minutes before eating for the ideal texture. Discard after 5 days.

STRAWBERRY JAM

yield: 5 kg/11 lb .32 oz

INGREDIENT	METRIC	U.S.	%
Fresh strawberries, hulled, stemmed, and quartered	3.75 kg	8 lb 4.32 oz	50%
Sugar	3.75 kg	8 lb 4.32 oz	50%
Madagascar vanilla pods, split and scraped	5	5	

1. Combine the ingredients in a sauce pot. Bring to a boil, and then simmer until the liquid reaches 65° Brix (cool a small amount down on a cold plate to 20°C/68°F and use a refractometer to accurately measure Brix). Remove the vanilla pods.

2. Cool the jam in an ice bath. Once the jam has cooled, refrigerate it in an airtight container. It will keep for up to 1 month.

note The weight of the recipe totals 7.5 kg/16 lb 8.48 oz, but there will be a significant loss of volume due to evaporation during the cooking process.

LEMON MYRTLE ICE CREAM BASE

yield: 8 kg/17 lb 10.19 oz

INGREDIENT	METRIC	U.S.	%
Milk	5.74 kg	12 lb 10.56 oz	71.8%
Milk powder	239 g	8.41 oz	2.98%
Lemon myrtle	195 g	6.88 oz	2.44%
Sugar	832 g	1 lb 13.44 oz	10.4%
Glucose powder	312 g	11.01 oz	3.9%
Trimoline	104 g	3.68 oz	1.3%
Ice cream stabilizer	27 g	.96 oz	.34%
Egg yolks	546 g	1 lb 3.2 oz	6.83%

Follow the procedure for ice cream production on page 493. Add the lemon myrtle in with the milk.

SHORTBREAD COOKIE MORSELS

yield: 1 full sheet pan

INGREDIENT	METRIC	U.S.	%
All-purpose flour	1.05 kg	2 lb 4.96 oz	40.89%
Rice flour	150 g	5.29 oz	5.84%
Salt	18 g	.63 oz	.7%
Butter, soft	900 g	1 lb 15.75 oz	35.05%
Sugar	450 g	15.87 oz	17.52%

1. Line a sheet pan with silicone paper.

2. Follow the shortbread cookie method on page 282. Place the dough on a full-size sheet pan lined with a nonstick rubber mat and roll it out to the size of the sheet pan; try to keep it as evenly thick as possible. Freeze the dough until firm and then dock it throughout with a fork. The dough is to be baked in one piece.

3. Once the baked shortbread is cool, chop the sheet of cookie into bite-size pieces. Reserve frozen in an airtight container. Discard after 1 month.

PETITE BEURRE COOKIE AND SALTED CARAMEL ICE CREAM SANDWICH

yield: 50 portions

components

100 Petite Beurre Cookies

5 kg/11 lb .32 oz Caramel Ice Cream Base

1. **TO ASSEMBLE:** Place all of the cookies in the freezer, flat side down.

2. Churn the ice cream and extrude it into piping bags. Let the bags freeze to harden a little, for about 30 minutes.

3. Remove the cookies from the freezer. Pipe the ice cream onto half of the cookies, working with 5 to 7 cookies at a time. Top with the remaining cookies to make sandwiches. The baked side of the cookie should be facing out for both pieces in order to obtain an even square.

4. Place the assembled sandwiches in the freezer to harden.

5. Wrap with foil and decorative paper. Allow the ice cream to temper for 5 minutes before eating for the ideal texture. Discard after 5 days.

PETITE BEURRE COOKIES

yield: 100 cookies

INGREDIENT	METRIC	U.S.	%
Salted butter, soft	1 kg	2 lb 3.36 oz	33.38%
Sugar	500 g	1 lb 1.64 oz	16.67%
All-purpose flour	1.16 kg	2 lb 9.28 oz	38.95%
Rice flour	167 g	5.9 oz	5.57%
Salt	20 g	.71 oz	.67%
Sugar for sprinkling, or as needed	143 g	5.04 oz	4.76%

1. Cream the butter and sugar together on medium speed in an electric mixer fitted with a paddle attachment until smooth, about 5 minutes.

2. Sift together the flours and salt. Add to the butter mixture and mix on low speed until incorporated.

3. Roll the dough to 5 mm/.25 in, wrap in plastic wrap, and refrigerate until hardened, about 1 hour.

4. Preheat a convection oven to 160°C/320°F.

5. Cut the shortbread into 10-cm/4-in squares with a square cutter, or use a ruler and a sharp knife.

6. Sprinkle sugar on top and dock with a fork in a 4x4 grid. Freeze for 20 minutes.

7. Bake until golden brown on the borders, about 5 minutes. Cut the edges of the cookies again while they are still warm in order to get a clean cut and uniform square shape.

8. Cool to room temperature. Reserve in an airtight container in the freezer. Discard after 1 month.

CARAMEL ICE CREAM BASE

yield: 5 kg/11 lb .32 oz

INGREDIENT	METRIC	U.S.	%
Milk	3.68 kg	8 lb 1.76 oz	73.6%
Milk powder	153 g	5.4 oz	3.06%
Tahitian vanilla pods, split and scraped	4	4	
Sugar	800 g	1 lb 12.16 oz	16%
Ice cream stabilizer	17 g	.6 oz	.34%
Yolks	350 g	12.35 oz	7%

1. Combine the milk, the milk powder, and the vanilla bean in a pot and bring to a simmer.

2. Meanwhile, make a dry caramel with the sugar. Place the sugar in a clean sauce pot over high heat without any water and stir it frequently with a wooden spoon until all of the sugar is caramelized to a dark amber brown (165°C/330°F). Once the sugar is at the correct temperature, whisk in the hot milk mixture slowly.

3. Allow the mixture to cool to 35°C/95°C. Proceed with the ice cream method on page 494.

note The final churned ice cream will have a very light caramel color.

These are hands down the easiest frozen desserts to make. They are also the most profitable, since the ingredients are very low in cost and the labor involved is minimal.

ICE POP PROCEDURE

1. The base is made in the same manner as a granité. It is a flavored liquid with the addition of simple syrup, or it can be just sugar dissolved into a flavored liquid. There should be enough sugar to result in a range of Brix between 16° and 19°, so it will freeze hard, but not as hard as water alone.

2. The ice pops in this book were made using Cryovac bags. These bags measure 30 by 45 cm/18 by 12 in. The bags were sealed every 4 cm/1.6 in widthwise using the sealer of the Cryovac machine, and then they were cut open using a ruler and an X-Acto knife on one end of the sealed lengths. This opens them up so that liquid can be poured into them. The bag is then rolled up loosely and placed in a bain marie in a standing position, with the open ends facing up.

3. Once the base is made, it is funneled into each opening. You can get up to 12 to 14 ice pops per each bag of this size. Before you portion the liquid into them, you can put a solid garnish in the bags and then funnel in the liquid.

4. Once the bags are filled, they are carefully sealed at the top with the Cryovac machine sealer and frozen until hardened.

5. When they have hardened, the bags can be separated from each other using a very sharp X-Acto knife; be careful to only cut through the sealed plastic and not the actual ice pop. It is a good idea to cut a slit on one of the short ends with the same X-Acto knife in order to make it easy for your customers to open each bag with their hands.

6. Reserve frozen. These items have a very long shelf life, of at least 6 months.

ESPRESSO AND AMARETTO ICE POP

yield: 7.5 kg/16 lb 8.48 oz (50 ice pops)

INGREDIENT	METRIC	U.S.	%
Freshly brewed espresso	1.4 kg	3 lb 1.44 oz	18.67%
Freshly brewed coffee	5 kg	11 lb .32 oz	66.67%
Amaretto	300 g	10.58 oz	4%
Superfine, fondant, or other fine-crystal sugar	800 g	1 lb 12.16 oz	10.67%

1. Combine all of the ingredients in a bowl.

2. Cool to 20°C/68°F and take a refractometer reading. Adjust the Brix if necessary to achieve 17° Brix. Taste the mixture as well; it has a strong espresso and coffee flavor that might not be suited to all people.

3. Follow the procedure for ice pops on page 497.

CHERRY AND VANILLA ICE POP

yield: 10.95 kg/24 lb 2.24 oz (50 pops)

INGREDIENT	METRIC	U.S.	%
Cherries, stemmed and pitted	2 kg	4 lb 6.55 oz	18.26%
Water	6.45 kg	14 lb 3.51 oz	58.9%
Tahitian vanilla pods, split and scraped	5	5	
Superfine, fondant, or other fine-crystal sugar	2.5 kg	5 8.18 oz	22.83%

1. Combine all of the ingredients in a pot. Cook over high heat until the cherries are tender.

2. Strain the cherries out, and then pass the liquid through a fine-mesh sieve. Remove the vanilla pods and cool the cherries in the refrigerator on a sheet pan lined with plastic wrap.

3. Cool the liquid to 20°C/68°F and take a refractometer reading. Adjust the Brix if necessary to achieve 17° Brix. Taste the base.

4. Once the cherries are cool, place 6 to 8 cherries into each bag.

5. Follow the procedure for ice pops on page 497.

note Liquid makes up 7.5 kg/16 lb 8.48 oz of the yield; the remainder is the cherries that will be put inside the ice pop bags.

PARAMOUR TISANE AND BLUEBERRIES ICE POP

yield: 9.75 kg/21 lb 8 oz (50 pops)

INGREDIENT	METRIC	U.S.	%
Paramour tisane	250 g	8.82 oz	2.56%
Water	6.4 kg	14 lb 1.76 oz	65.64%
Superfine, fondant, or other fine-crystal sugar	1.1 kg	2 lb 6.88 oz	11.28%
Blueberries or huckleberries	2 kg	4 lb 6.4 oz	20.51%

1. Combine the tisane, water, and sugar in a pot. Bring the mixture to a boil while stirring, and then turn off the heat. Let the tisane infuse for 5 minutes, and then strain it through a fine-mesh sieve.

2. Cool the liquid to 20°C/68°F and take a refractometer reading. Adjust the Brix if necessary to 17 ° Brix. Taste the base.

3. Fill each bag with 40 g/1.41 oz of blueberries, and then fill it with the tisane.

4. Follow the procedure for ice pops on page 497.

note Liquid makes up 7.5 kg/16 lb 8.48 oz of the yield; the tisane does not count toward the final yield.

CHAMPAGNE, ELDERFLOWER, AND RASPBERRIES ICE POP

yield: 9.5 kg/20 lb 15.04 oz (50 pops)

INGREDIENT	METRIC	U.S.	%
Champagne or Prosecco	5.75 kg	12 lb 10.88 oz	60.53%
Elderflower syrup	1.75 kg	3 lb 13.76 oz	18.42%
Raspberries	2 kg	4 lb 6.4 oz	21.05%

1. Combine the Champagne and elderflower syrup in a bowl. Bring the mixture to 20°C/68°F and take a refractometer reading. Adjust the Brix if necessary to 17° Brix. Taste the base.

2. Fill each bag with 40 g/1.41 oz of raspberries, and then fill it with the Champagne and elderflower mix.

3. Follow the procedure for ice pops on page 497.

note Liquid makes up 7.5 kg/16 lb 8.48 oz of the yield; the rest is raspberries.

special-occasion items

Not everybody is so well organized that they can order a cake weeks in advance for a special occasion such as a birthday, wedding, or other social gathering. I would include myself in that group. That is why it is always good to offer items, particularly cakes, to help your customers in this situation. Some are seasonal, such as the bûche de Noël cake that is for Christmas, but throughout the year, people have birthdays, weddings, and other celebratory occasions. Cake is one of the most popular ways to celebrate an event in a group gathering. Pie, especially apple, is a quick, easy dessert to take to a casual dinner party.

Oftentimes people ask for a cake at the last minute, and the standard response is typically that at least 48 hours advance notice is needed. While some cakes do take that long to prepare from beginning to end, there is an opportunity to be the place that can quickly bail out customers in dire need of cake. The mise en place needed to be able to produce a special-occasion cake or two and a birthday cake or two can be kept on hand on a daily basis. After a few weeks, the cakes might sell every day, when regular customers know they can come to the café for their last-minute cakes.

Now, it is important not to take advantage of the situation maliciously just because people are willing to pay more for these items. Instead, be nice and charge what you normally would. Everyone will appreciate that, and your customers' loyalty will be solid.

With other season-specific items, do take advance orders, but always have enough to offer for those people who did not place their orders on time. No matter how many you make, you will typically sell them all, especially around closing time.

FROM LEFT TO RIGHT: Birthday Cake (page 520), Mac-en-Bouche (page 517), Pumpkin Cake (page 522)

MAC-EN-BOUCHE

yield: 1 cake

components

150 assembled Macarons, piped to a 2-cm/.8-in diameter (page 275)

1 kg/2 lb 3.2 oz lime green rolled fondant

8 Crème Fraîche Sponge Cake Discs

3.02 kg/6 lb 10.72 oz Vanilla Diplomat Cream

750 g/1 lb 10.4 oz Buttercream (page 266)

1.5 kg/3 lb 4.8 oz light yellow–colored rolled fondant

200 g/7.05 oz melted chocolate

1. Assemble a wood base with a dowel going through the center of the base in order to support the cake. The base should be slightly larger than the cake and the dowel should be as tall as the cake. The dowel should be about 2 cm/.8 in thick. The size of the cake is completely adjustable. This cake is 45 cm/18 in tall and has a 20 cm/8 in diameter.

2. Reserve the macarons frozen.

3. Line the cake stand base with a thin layer of lime green fondant. Whenever coating a non-edible surface such as wood or Styrofoam, always coat it with a thin layer of shortening; this will help the fondant adhere to the wood. Wrap the bottom of the base with ribbon to give it a clean look.

4. Cut a 2-cm/.8-in ring out of the center of each crème fraîche sponge cake disc. Slide the 20-cm/8-in disc over the dowel.

5. Put the prepared base on a cake stand. This will help spin the cake as you pipe the diplomat cream.

6. Pipe a 2.5-cm-/1-in-thick spiral of diplomat cream on top of the bottommost layer of crème fraîche cake. Start at the center by the dowel and start spinning the cake stand; pipe until you have reached the edge of the sponge cake. It should protrude from the cake by 2 mm/.08 in.

7. Place the 17.5-cm/7-in disc over the dowel and on top of the diplomat cream. Repeat this process with the remaining cake discs and diplomat cream, going from largest to smallest when placing the cake rings over the dowel. Do not pipe any diplomat on top of the topmost cake disc.

8. Using an offset spatula, spread the protruding vanilla diplomat cream evenly to create a smooth exterior on the cone.

9. Freeze the cone for about 30 minutes.

10. Meanwhile, smooth out the buttercream and prepare the yellow fondant. Roll or sheet the fondant down to 3 mm/.12 in. It should be large enough to cover the cone completely; sheet it out to about the size of a sheet of parchment paper. Keep the fondant well covered with plastic wrap to keep it from drying out and cracking.

11. Remove the cake from the freezer and coat it in the buttercream. Try to get it as smooth as possible; any bumps and rough edges will show up on the fondant.

12. Wrap the cake in the yellow fondant, smoothing it out with your hand. Trim any excess off.

13. Using a cornet filled with melted chocolate, "glue" the macarons onto the cake, starting from the bottom and continuing to the top in an even pattern.

14. Reserve in the refrigerator. Discard after 3 days; the fondant helps protect the interior of the cake.

notes This is a play on the traditional French wedding cake that consists of mini pâte à choux puffs filled with pastry cream and covered with caramelized sugar, built to resemble a tall cone. This cake alternates layers of crème fraîche cake and vanilla diplomat cream, covered in rolled fondant, studded with French macarons. The recipe is for one cake only because it is quite tall and large.

You can choose one color and one flavor of macaron, as was done for this cake, or you can use a combination of colors and flavors. These macarons are green, filled with strawberry jam and buttercream.

To color fondant, knead the fondant on a smooth surface to soften it. Add a few drops of coloring (a few drops go a long way, so be careful to not add too much) and continue to knead until the fondant is evenly colored, with no swirls of white. Always keep it well wrapped in plastic when you are not using it.

CRÈME FRAÎCHE SPONGE CAKE DISCS

yield: 2.2 kg/4 lb 13.6 oz

INGREDIENT	METRIC	U.S.	%
All-purpose flour	387 g	13.66 oz	17.6%
Baking powder	32 g	1.14 oz	1.47%
Vanilla powder	3 g	.1 oz	.12%
Salt	5 g	.19 oz	.25%
Butter, at 21°C/70°F	408 g	14.38 oz	18.53%
Sugar	367 g	12.94 oz	16.67%
Eggs, at 21°C/70°F	270 g	9.51 oz	12.26%
Crème fraîche, at 21°C/70°F	728 g	1 lb. 9.6 oz	33.11%

1. Spray the inside border of a sheet pan with nonstick oil spray, then place a nonstick rubber mat on the sheet pan.

2. Preheat a convection oven to 160°/320°F.

3. Sift the flour, baking powder, vanilla powder, and the salt.

4. Cream the butter with the sugar on high speed in the bowl of an electric mixer fitted with the paddle attachment for 4 to 5 minutes or until the mixture is light and fluffy. Add the eggs in 4 additions, scraping the bowl and the paddle in between each addition.

5. Add the dry ingredients and pulse the mixer until a homogeneous mass is obtained. Be careful not to overmix.

6. Add the crème fraîche and pulse the mixer until a homogeneous mass is obtained.

7. Pour the batter onto the prepared sheet pan and spread it out evenly using an offset spatula. It will be about 2 cm/.8 in thick.

8. Bake until golden brown, 13 to 15 minutes.

9. Cool to room temperature, and then place in the refrigerator. Once the cake is cold, flip it over onto a cutting board and cut out circles with the following dimensions (one of each size): 20 cm/8 in, 17.5 cm/7 in, 15 cm/6 in, 12.5 cm/5 in, 10 cm/4 in, 7.5 cm/3 in, 5 cm/2 in, and 2.5 cm/1 in.

10. Reserve the cake circles, covered in plastic wrap, in a freezer or refrigerator. They will keep for up to 3 months frozen and 1 week in the refrigerator.

VANILLA DIPLOMAT CREAM

yield: 3.02 kg/6 lb 10.72 oz

INGREDIENT	METRIC	U.S.	%
PASTRY CREAM			
Milk	841 g	1 lb 13.6 oz	56.09%
Sugar	209 g	7.36 oz	13.92%
Salt	5 g	.16 oz	.31%
Tahitian vanilla pods, split and scraped	1.5	1.5	
Eggs	278 g	9.82 oz	18.55%
Cornstarch	83 g	2.95 oz	5.57%
Butter	83 g	2.95 oz	5.57%
VANILLA DIPLOMAT CREAM			
Gelatin sheets, bloomed	25 g	.87 oz	.82%
Heavy cream	1.5 kg	3 lb 4.96 oz	49.59%
Pastry cream	1.5 kg	3 lb 4.96 oz	49.59%

1. **FOR THE PASTRY CREAM:** Combine the milk with half of the sugar, the salt, and the vanilla pods and seeds in a sauce pot. Bring to a boil. Meanwhile, whisk together the eggs with the cornstarch to obtain a smooth paste. Stir in the other half of the sugar.

2. Once the liquid comes to a boil, temper in the egg yolk slurry.

3. Return the pot to the heat and turn the heat to medium-low. Stir constantly and vigorously until the pastry cream thickens and comes to a boil. Remove the pot from the heat and stir for 30 seconds. Stir in the butter, and then pour the pastry cream into a hotel pan. Remove the vanilla pods.

4. Cover the pastry cream with plastic wrap directly over its surface and place in the refrigerator (see Notes). Once cold, transfer it to an airtight container and refrigerate it with plastic directly on its surface. It will keep for 4 days in the refrigerator.

5. Have a piping bag fitted with a #6 plain tip ready.

6. Squeeze the excess water from the bloomed gelatin sheets and place them in a bowl. Melt over a warm water bath.

7. Meanwhile, whip the heavy cream until medium peaks form.

8. Soften the pastry cream and bring it up to room temperature, stirring it gently with a whisk in a bowl. Stir in the melted gelatin quickly to keep it from setting when it comes into contact with the cold pastry cream.

9. Fold in the heavy cream in 2 additions. Pour some of the mixture into a piping bag. Use immediately to assemble the cake; discard any leftover diplomat cream.

notes If making larger batches, cool down the pastry cream over an ice bath.

Add fresh berries to the diplomat cream once you have piped it on, but make sure they are in season.

BIRTHDAY CAKE

yield: 6 cakes

components

24 Devil's Food Cake Discs

400 g/14.11 oz melted dark chocolate

8.4 kg/18 lb 8.32 oz Chocolate Ganache

3 kg/6 lb 9.82 oz Buttercream (page 266)

3 kg/6 lb 9.82 oz fondant

1. **TO ASSEMBLE:** Place 6 cake rings 15 cm/6 in in diameter by 10 cm/4 in high over a sheet pan lined with a nonstick rubber mat. Line the inside of each mold with a piece of silicone paper of the same dimensions, slightly overlapping on the ends; it is only meant to fit the circumference of the mold.

2. Remove 6 cake discs from the refrigerator and coat the base of each with a thin layer of melted chocolate. Let the chocolate set, and then put 1 piece inside each ring with the chocolate side facing down.

3. Each cake will require between 1.3 and 1.4 kg/2 lb 13.76 oz and 3 lb 1.28 oz of ganache total. Pour in about 430 g/15.17 oz of ganache (about 1.5 cm/.6 in thick) and place another disc of cake on top. Repeat this procedure 2 more times so that there are 4 cake layers and 3 ganache layers in each cake. The last cake piece should protrude about .5 cm/.2 in from the ring; if not, the discs are too thin or there is not enough ganache.

4. Place a sheet of parchment paper on top of the cakes, then place another sheet pan on top of the parchment paper. Weigh it down with a heavy cutting board and place the setup in the freezer to harden.

5. Once the cakes have hardened, they can be wrapped individually while still in the mold and kept frozen for up to 6 months.

6. **TO FINISH THE CAKES:** Remove the cakes from the freezer. Push the cakes out of their molds and discard the silicone paper. Return to the freezer, leaving 1 cake out. Spread a thin, even coat of buttercream over the surface of the cake. This is known as masking the cake. Return to the freezer to harden. Repeat with the other cakes. Meanwhile, prepare the fondant.

7. Color the fondant with light blue coloring (water or alcohol based) and roll or sheet it down to 3 mm/.12 in on the sheeter or by hand.

8. Remove the cake from the freezer and place it on a cake base. Gently and carefully place the fondant over the cake. Smooth it out with your hands until it has no bumps or uneven areas. Trim the excess fondant at the base.

9. Cut out ribbon and attach it to the cake to resemble a gift box. I recommend using a glue gun (to glue ribbon on ribbon, not ribbon on the cake).

10. Display for up to 5 days at room temperature, covered, using a cake stand and dome.

note It is a pretty safe bet that most people will not argue with the combination of chocolate and chocolate. This cake alternates layers of devil's food cake and ganache and is coated with fondant. Since this cake contains ganache, it is perfectly safe to display it out of the refrigerator, and it will keep for up to 5 days. It is actually better to leave it at room temperature so that it is smoother and more palatable.

DEVIL'S FOOD CAKE DISCS

yield: (3 full sheets; eight 15-cm/6-in discs per sheet)

INGREDIENT	METRIC	U.S.
Devil's Food Cake batter (page 145)	6 kg	13 lb 3.64 oz

1. Divide the batter into 3 equal amounts and spread them in an even layer on the prepared sheet pans. Bake until when you press the center of the cake with your finger tips the cake will spring back, about 8 to 12 minutes.

2. Once the cake has cooled, cut out eight 15-cm/6-in discs per sheet for a total of 24 discs. Each cake will use 4 discs. Keep the discs in the refrigerator, because they are easier to handle when they are cold. They will keep for 3 to 4 days in the refrigerator. If they are well wrapped with plastic, they will keep for up to 1 month in the freezer.

CHOCOLATE GANACHE

yield: 8.4 kg/18 lb 8.32 oz

INGREDIENT	METRIC	U.S.	%
Heavy cream	4 kg	8 lb 13.12 oz	47.62%
Dark chocolate (64%) coins	3.6 kg	7 lb 15.04 oz	42.86%
Butter, soft	800 g	1 lb 12.16 oz	9.52%

1. Bring the cream to a boil and pour it over the chocolate in a bowl. Stir to dissolve the chocolate.

2. Once the chocolate has dissolved, stir in the butter. Stir until the butter has dissolved. This ganache will keep for 7 days at room temperature and for up to 1 month in the refrigerator.

PUMPKIN CAKE

yield: 6 cakes

components

Twelve 12.5-cm/5-in Pumpkin Pound Cake Discs

100 g/3.53 oz white chocolate, melted

5 kg/11 lb Thick Caramel

Twelve 15-cm/6-in Pumpkin Pound Cake Discs

Twelve 17.5-cm/7-in Pumpkin Pound Cake Discs

3.06 kg/6 lb 11.8 oz Pumpkin Spice Buttercream

3.4 kg/7 lb 7.93 oz rolled fondant

Green food coloring, as needed

Orange food coloring, as needed

Brown food coloring, as needed

1. Place six 12.5-cm/5-in pound cake discs, with the side that was in contact with the sheet pan up, on a sheet of parchment paper. Coat the base with a thin layer of white chocolate. Turn the discs over once the chocolate has set and place them on six 12.5-cm/5-in cake boards.

2. Place the caramel in a piping bag. Pipe a .5-cm-/.2-in-thick spiral of caramel around the surface of the pumpkin cake disc. Place a 15-cm/6-in disc of pumpkin pound cake on top of the caramel. Pipe a .5-cm-/.2-in-thick spiral of caramel around the surface of the pumpkin cake disc. Place a 17.5-cm/7-in disc of pumpkin pound cake on top of the caramel. Pipe a .5-cm-/.2-in-thick spiral of caramel around the surface of the pumpkin cake disc. Repeat this process with the remaining cake layers and caramel. The cakes should be placed in ascending order: 17.5-cm/7-in cake, 15-cm/6-in cake, 12.5-cm/5-in cake. Do not pipe caramel on top of the last layer of cake. Place the cakes in the freezer to harden.

3. Take the cake out of the freezer. Put on a pair of rubber gloves.

4. Using your hands, coat each cake with an even layer of buttercream (about 500 g/1 lb 1.6 oz); not too thick, just enough so that you cannot see the cake.

5. Using your index finger, indent the buttercream with "wedges" to simulate the look of a pumpkin. Smooth it out with your hands so that the wedge looks natural.

6. Place the cakes in the freezer.

7. Prepare the fondant. Color about 400 g/14.11 oz of fondant with water- or alcohol-based green food coloring. Keep it covered with plastic wrap until needed.

8. Color the remaining 3 kg/6 lb 9.76 oz of fondant with water- or alcohol-based orange food coloring. Divide it into 6 equal pieces and shape each piece into a round, flat disc. Remember to keep the fondant covered with plastic wrap when not using it, to prevent it from drying out.

9. Sheet each disc between 2 pieces of silicone paper to 3 mm/.12 in thick. Rotate the fondant 90 degrees as you sheet it to obtain a circle.

10. Remove the cakes from the freezer. Carefully place the fondant over each cake. Smooth it out with your hands until you obtain a smooth surface.

11. Put some orange food coloring inside the canister of an airbrush and spray it between the wedges of the pumpkin to give it a more natural look.

12. Place the cakes on a cake display board.

13. Form a stem, 3 large leaves, and 7 small leaves for each cake using the green fondant; use different shapes of leaf cutters for the leaves. Put the stem on top of the cake, anchoring it down with a toothpick, and then the leaves around the stem. Put some brown food coloring inside the canister of an airbrush and spray a light coat on all of the green elements of the cake. Spraying the brown on the green will give it a very natural look. If you want to cover up the base of the pumpkin, color about 100 g/3.53 oz of buttercream (per cake) with green food coloring and, using a leaf piping tip, pipe leaves around the base.

14. Display the cake at room temperature, covered, for 5 days maximum.

note This cake is ideal for the entire fall season and the first part of the winter. It is shaped like a pumpkin and finished to look like a pumpkin, but it is not intended only for Halloween and Thanksgiving. As with the birthday cake, it can be held and displayed at room temperature for 5 days or more, so long as it is kept covered.

PUMPKIN POUND CAKE

yield: 8 kg/17 lb 10.24 oz

INGREDIENT	METRIC	U.S.	%
Pastry flour	2.24 kg	4 lb 15.04 oz	28.01%
Baking powder	47 g	1.67 oz	.59%
Ground cinnamon	24 g	.84 oz	.30%
Ground ginger	11 g	.39 oz	.14%
Ground allspice	5 g	.17 oz	.06%
Grated nutmeg	5 g	.17 oz	.06%
Salt	17 g	.61 oz	.22%
Water	805 g	1 lb 12.32 oz	10.06%
Pumpkin purée	1.13 kg	2 lb 8.16 oz	14.2%
Butter, at 21°C/70°F	947 g	2 lb 1.44 oz	11.84%
Superfine or bakers' sugar	2.05 kg	4 lb 8.32 oz	25.65%
Eggs, at 21°C/70°F	710 g	1 lb 9.12 oz	8.88%

1. Preheat a convection oven to 160°C/320°F.

2. Spray a light coat of nonstick oil spray around the interior border of 4 sheet pans. Line them with a nonstick rubber mat.

3. Sift the flour, baking powder, spices, and salt together. Combine the water and the pumpkin purée in a bowl.

4. Cream the butter and the sugar on medium speed in the bowl of an electric mixer fitted with the paddle attachment until light and fluffy, 5 to 7 minutes. Slowly add the eggs in 4 additions. Stop the mixer, drop the bowl, and scrape it between each addition to ensure a homogeneous mix is obtained.

5. Turn the mixer off and add the dry ingredients. Pulse the mixer on low speed a few times to incorporate some of the dry ingredients. Mix on low speed just enough to obtain a homogeneous mass. Finally, add the pumpkin purée and mix just until it is fully incorporated.

6. Divide the batter into 4 equal parts that weigh 2 kg/4 lb 6.4 oz. Spread each portion evenly in each prepared sheet pan using an offset spatula.

7. Bake until golden brown, about 10 minutes. Check for doneness by pressing the center of the pound cake with your fingertips; when it is done, it will spring back.

8. Cool the cakes to room temperature, and then freeze them.

9. Once they are frozen, remove them from the sheet pan by passing a knife carefully around the border. Try not to cut through the rubber mat. Flip the sheet pan over and peel off the rubber mat.

10. Cut out the cake layers. Cut 12 layers each of the following dimensions: 12.5 cm/5 in, 15 cm/6 in, and 17.5 cm/7 in.

12. Freeze the discs until firm before assembling the cakes. Discard after 2 months.

THICK CARAMEL

yield: 5 kg/11 lb

INGREDIENT	METRIC	U.S.	%
Glucose syrup	1.01 kg	2 lb 3.68 oz	20.23%
Sugar	2.02 kg	4 lb 7.2 oz	40.46%
Heavy cream	1.26 kg	2 lb 12.48 oz	25.28%
Butter	632 g	1 lb 6.24 oz	12.64%
Salt	70 g	2.45 oz	1.39%

1. See the procedure for caramel on page 33.

2. Cool the caramel completely before using. Do not refrigerate; it will keep for up to 6 months in an airtight container at room temperature.

PUMPKIN SPICE BUTTERCREAM

yield: 3.06 kg/6 lb 11.8 oz

INGREDIENT	METRIC	U.S.	%
Ground cinnamon	30 g	1.07 oz	53.57%
Ground ginger	14 g	.49 oz	25%
Ground allspice	6 g	.21 oz	10.71%
Grated nutmeg	6 g	.21 oz	10.71%
Buttercream (page 266), cooled	3 kg	6 lb 9.76 oz	

Combine the cinnamon, ginger, allspice, and nutmeg in a bowl. Stir into the buttercream.

BÛCHE DE NOËL

yield: 6 cakes

components

6 Caramel Cremeur tubes

6 Gingerbread Sponge Cake rectangles

4.5 kg/9 lb 14.72 oz Dark Chocolate Mousse

3 kg/6 lb 9.7 oz Shiny Chocolate Glaze

12 Chocolate Square Plaques

4 g/.14 oz gold dust

4 g/.14 oz silver dust

6 Chocolate Spiral Décors

1. Spray 6 semicircle terrine molds measuring 7.5 by 20 by 7.5 cm/3 by 8 by 3 in with a light coat of nonstick oil spray.

2. Line each mold with a sheet of acetate that is as long as the mold, but 7.5 cm/3 in wider than the total interior width of the mold. The acetate should come up over the sides of the mold by 3.75 cm/1.5 in on each side. This overhang should be taped to the outside of the mold to keep it in place. Crease the protruding acetate with your fingers along the border of the mold so that the acetate is completely flush with it and not bowing out.

3. Take the acetate off of the frozen caramel cremeur inserts and reserve frozen. Have the gingerbread cake rectangles at hand in the freezer.

4. Pipe a 3.75-cm-/1.5-in-thick layer of chocolate mousse around the base of each mold.

5. Place a caramel mousse tube over the mousse in each mold, making sure they are centered. Push down gently until enough mousse comes up the sides of the caramel cremeur insert to completely envelop its sides only, but not the top.

6. Pipe enough chocolate mousse on top of the caramel insert to come within 2.5 cm/1 in of the top of the mold.

7. Remove the gingerbread cakes from the freezer. Place them on top of the mousse in the molds, chocolate side facing up. Push them down until the mousse comes up to the border of the mold. The cake and the mousse should be at the same level as the edge of the mold.

8. Place all of the assembled cakes on a sheet pan, and then place a sheet of acetate over the cakes. Put a flat sheet pan on top of the cakes and a heavy cutting board over the sheet pan to weigh the cakes down. Freeze the cakes to harden them.

9. Once they are frozen, they can be wrapped individually while still in the molds. Discard after 3 months.

10. **TO FINISH THE CAKES:** Melt the shiny glaze over a hot water bath. Once it is melted, let it cool to 38°C/100°F.

11. Assemble 6 cake boards that measure 7 by 18 cm/2.8 by 7.2 in.

12. Line a sheet pan with a sheet of parchment paper, and then place a wire rack over it.

13. While the glaze is cooling, remove the frozen cakes from the terrine molds. Dip a paring knife in very hot water and pass it between the interior of the short ends of the molds and the mousse. Release the cake by gently pulling it out using the acetate. Place the cakes over the cake boards as they come out of the molds. Put them on the wire rack.

14. Once all of the cakes are unmolded, glaze them if the glaze has cooled sufficiently, or keep them in the freezer until it does.

15. Glaze the cakes to coat them completely. Let the cakes set in the refrigerator.

16. Transfer the cakes to a cake display board or base.

17. Place 1 square plaque on each end of the cake, shiny side out. Sprinkle gold and silver dust evenly over the cake. Place the chocolate spirals on the cake. Display for up to 2 days.

note This is a traditional French cake made for the Christmas season. The classic version features a sheet of sponge cake covered with a layer of flavored buttercream, Bavarian, or mousse. It is then rolled up, coated in more buttercream or sometimes ganache, and decorated with meringues shaped as mushrooms and Christmas symbols. This version is a more contemporary cake while still preserving its classic log shape; after all, *bûche* means "log" in French. The flavors in this recipe—chocolate, gingerbread spice, and caramel—are closely related to the Christmas holiday.

CARAMEL CREMEUR

yield: 2.5 kg/5 lb 8.16 oz

INGREDIENT	METRIC	U.S.	%
CARAMEL BASE			
Sugar	390 g	13.76 oz	15.61%
Butter	130 g	4.59 oz	5.2%
Heavy cream	304 g	10.71 oz	12.14%
Eggs	260 g	9.18 oz	10.41%
Gelatin sheets, bloomed	18 g	.64 oz	.73%
Heavy cream	997 g	2 lb 3.2 oz	39.89%
Heavy cream stabilizer (liquid)	10 g	.37 oz	.42%
Dark chocolate–coated puffed rice (see Resources, page 540)	390 g	13.76 oz	15.61%

1. Line 6 PVC tubes 17.5 cm/7 in long by 5 cm/2 in diameter with acetate. Place them standing upright on a half sheet pan lined with parchment paper.

2. For the caramel base: In a small sauce pot, cook the sugar according to the procedure for dry caramel on page 33, stirring constantly with a wooden spoon until it turns a medium amber. Stir in the butter, then the cream. Remove from the heat.

3. Place the eggs over a hot water bath and heat them to 60°C/140°F while stirring constantly. Transfer them to the bowl of an electric mixer fitted with the whip attachment and whip until they have cooled to room temperature. While the eggs are whipping, stream in the caramel. Add the bloomed gelatin and whip until the gelatin dissolves and the mixture has cooled to 21°C/70°F.

4. Whip the cream and the stabilizer until medium peaks form. Fold into the caramel in 2 additions. Stir in the chocolate-covered puffed rice.

5. Pour the cremeur into a piping bag and pipe it into the prepared PVC tubes. Even out the top with an offset spatula. Place in the freezer to harden.

6. Once the caramel cremeur has hardened, take them out of the freezer and push them out of the molds. Keep them wrapped in the acetate in the freezer until needed. Discard after 2 months.

GINGERBREAD SPONGE CAKE

yield: 1.5 kg/3 lb 4.96 oz

INGREDIENT	METRIC	U.S.	%
Bread flour	185 g	6.51 oz	12.31%
Pastry flour	185 g	6.51 oz	12.31%
Salt	5 g	.16 oz	.3%
Ground ginger	9 g	.31 oz	.58%
Ground cinnamon	4 g	.15 oz	.29%
Ground allspice	3 g	.09 oz	.17%
Grated nutmeg	2 g	.06 oz	.11%
Egg yolks	660 g	1 lb 7.2 oz	43.98%
Dark brown sugar	369 g	13.03 oz	24.63%
Butter, melted but cool	62 g	2.2 oz	4.15%
Crystallized ginger, finely chopped	18 g	.62 oz	1.17%
Dark chocolate (64%), melted	100 g	3.53 oz	

1. Grease the border of a half sheet pan with nonstick oil spray and line it with a nonstick rubber mat.

2. Preheat a convection oven to 160°C/320°F.

3. Sift the flours, salt, and ground ginger, cinnamon, allspice, and nutmeg together.

4. Whip the egg yolks with the brown sugar on high speed in the bowl of an electric mixer fitted with the whip attachment until they reach the ribbon stage.

5. Fold in the dry ingredients by hand, then stir in the butter, and finally the crystallized ginger.

6. Pour the génoise into the prepared frame and spread it evenly with an offset spatula.

7. Bake until golden brown, about 15 minutes.

8. Cool to room temperature.

9. Once it has cooled, flip the cake onto a cutting board lined with silicone paper, and then flip it back onto a clean sheet pan lined with silicone paper. Remove the top sheet of silicone paper and reserve for another use.

10. Place a 2-cm-/.75-in-thick frame on top of the cake, and then trim the borders so that the cake fits inside the frame. Use a long serrated knife to cut the cake to the same thickness as the frame. The knife should be longer than the frame is wide so that the blade can use the frame as a guide to lean on while you cut it. If the cake is not staying flat as you cut it, press down with your hand close to the blade as you cut.

11. Freeze the cake to harden it.

12. Flip the cake over so that the base is facing up. Spread a thin layer of melted dark chocolate over it with an offset spatula and let it set.

13. Cut out 6 rectangles measuring 6.25 by 17.5 cm /2.5 by 7 in. Reserve them frozen.

DARK CHOCOLATE MOUSSE

yield: 4.5 kg/9 lb 14.72 oz

INGREDIENT	METRIC	U.S.	%
Eggs	911 g	2 lb .16 oz	20.24%
Sugar	375 g	13.23 oz	8.33%
Dark chocolate (64%) coins	1.2 kg	2 lb 10.56 oz	26.79%
Heavy cream	2 kg	4 lb 6.88 oz	44.64%

1. Combine the eggs with the sugar in a bowl and bring up to 60°C/140°F over a hot water bath while stirring constantly.

2. Remove from the heat and pour it into the bowl of an electric mixer fitted with the whip attachment. Whip on high speed until it cools to 35°C/95°F and reaches the ribbon stage, about 10 minutes. Meanwhile, melt the chocolate over a hot water bath or in a microwave. Allow it cool to 35°C/95°F.

3. Once both the eggs and the chocolate are at the right temperature, strain the egg mix through a sieve over the chocolate and mix with a whisk until a homogeneous mass is obtained.

4. Whip the cream to medium peaks.

5. Fold half of the whipped cream into the chocolate mixture. Fold in the remaining whipped cream. Fill a piping bag with the mousse. Follow the instructions for assembling the cakes.

SHINY CHOCOLATE GLAZE

yield: 3 kg/6 lb 9.7 oz

INGREDIENT	METRIC	U.S.	%
Sugar	1.24 kg	2 lb 11.84 oz	41.49%
Water	657 g	1 lb 7.2 oz	21.9%
Cocoa powder	380 g	13.42 oz	12.68%
Crème fraîche	380 g	13.42 oz	12.68%
Dark chocolate (55%) coins	277 g	9.75 oz	9.22%
Gelatin sheets, bloomed (17.4 sheets)	61 g	2.15 oz	2.03%

1. Bring the sugar, water, cocoa powder, and crème fraîche up to a boil while stirring constantly.

2. Once it comes to a boil, stir in the chocolate and whisk until dissolved.

3. Squeeze the excess water from the gelatin sheets. Add the bloomed gelatin to the chocolate and stir until dissolved.

4. Pass the mixture through a fine-mesh sieve.

5. Cool over an ice bath. Once cooled, transfer to an airtight container and store in the refrigerator. Discard after 2 weeks.

CHOCOLATE DECORATIONS

yield: about 20 square plaques and over 20 spiral décors

INGREDIENT	METRIC	U.S.	%
Dark chocolate (72%), tempered	1 kg	2 lb 4.2 oz	100%

1. **FOR THE PLAQUES:** Grease a marble surface with a light coat of nonstick oil spray. Smooth it out with a paper towel.

2. Place a sheet of acetate over the greased area.

3. Spread half of the tempered chocolate over the acetate in a thin layer using an offset spatula.

4. When it is semi-set, transfer the sheet to another section of the marble to avoid having the sheet stick to the marble (in case there was any chocolate overhanging the acetate).

5. Using a ruler and a paring knife, cut out as many 10-cm/4-in squares as possible. Extra squares can be used for future cakes.

6. Place the acetate over a clean sheet pan lined with parchment paper with the chocolate facing down. Put a heavy cutting board over the chocolate so that it doesn't bow or warp as it sets.

7. Once the chocolate has set, leave it on the acetate at room temperature in a cool, dry place.

8. **FOR THE SPIRALS:** Cut out 6 pieces of acetate 10 by 30 cm/4 by 12 in.

9. Grease a marble surface with a light coat of nonstick oil spray. Smooth it out with a paper towel.

10. Place the sheets of acetate over the greased area, making sure they are evenly spaced.

11. Pour about 75 g/2.64 oz of tempered chocolate onto each piece of acetate, and then spread it out evenly with an offset spatula. Using a chocolate comb, comb through the chocolate. The chocolate should take on a striped pattern that is about 4 mm/.16 in wide.

12. When it is semi-set, transfer the sheet to another section of the marble to avoid having the sheet stick to the marble (in case there was any chocolate overhanging the acetate).

13. Twist the acetate into a half-pipe, and let it set that way on the marble. Once it is set, carefully transfer the twists to a sheet pan lined with parchment paper and place in a cool, dry place.

note It is difficult to make only 6 spirals with tempered chocolate; use the leftover pieces for future cakes.

wedding cake

A good-tasting wedding cake is almost a contradiction in terms, so this is an area of great opportunity to make a beautiful cake that tastes good. Keep in mind that the café is not a wedding cake shop. The café doesn't have the same setup as a wedding cake maker, where that's all they make. A café environment really has to go out of its way and dedicate many resources to the project. You can certainly choose how far you are willing to go in order to accommodate the customer. One suggestion is to have one standard wedding cake, which allows for some flexibility without going too crazy. If your cake is blue, it can just as easily be red or yellow or white, but when the customer wants dozens of individual gum paste orchids, you just might not be able to pull it off. This cake should not be available on a daily basis. Establish a minimum 72- or 48-hour advance notice.

The cake here is a classic combination of layers of carrot cake and sweet cream cheese between the layers. Since the filling is cream cheese based, it is somewhat stable at room temperature. It can't be left out for 5 days, unlike the birthday cake, but it can be left out for the duration of a wedding party without it melting or spoiling. This recipe is for a single cake to serve between 40 and 50 people. If the wedding has more guests than that, you can make sheet-size cakes that are not displayed during the wedding but are kept in a serving area and cut when the wedding cake is cut. A full sheet cake feeds about 60 people. A half sheet cake feeds about 30, and so on. If the cake will be serving fewer than 40 to 50 people, make it shorter or smaller.

WEDDING CAKE

yield: 1 cake (serves between 40 and 50)

components

200 g/7.05 oz tempered dark chocolate

Five 30-cm/12-in Carrot Cake Squares

100 g/3.53 oz white chocolate

8.52 kg/18 lb 11.84 oz Cream Cheese Filling, soft

1.65 kg/3 lb 10.2 oz Buttercream (page 266)

2.5 kg/5 lb 8.2 oz rolled fondant

200 g/7.05 oz glycerin

200 g/7.05 oz water

100 g/3.53 oz rolled fondant, colored black

10 g/.35 oz rolled fondant, colored yellow

10 g/.35 oz rolled fondant, colored blue

10 g/.35 oz rolled fondant, colored green

10 g/.35 oz rolled fondant, colored red

Striped pattern printed on sugar paper

Man and woman images printed on sugar paper

1. Pour the tempered dark chocolate in the alphabet silicone mold letters "l", "o", "v" and "e". Let it set in the mold, and then remove them from the mold. Reserve until needed.

2. Coat the inside of a cake mold measuring 30 cm square by 20 cm tall/12 in square by 8 in tall with a thin layer of nonstick oil spray. Line the inside of the mold with silicone paper; it should be the exact dimensions of all 4 sides. Place the mold on a sheet pan lined with a nonstick rubber mat.

3. Coat a cake square with a very thin layer of white chocolate. Let the chocolate set. Place that layer inside the cake mold, chocolate side down.

4. Pipe 2.13 kg/4 lb 10.88 oz of cream cheese filling in a square spiral on top of the cake. Repeat with the remaining layers of cake and cream cheese frosting. The first and last layer should be cake. There should be 5 layers of cake and 4 layers of cream cheese filling. Place the cake in the freezer.

5. Once the cake is frozen, gently slide the cake mold off and discard the silicone paper. Place the cake over a cake board with the same dimensions those of the cake.

6. Coat the cakes with an even layer of buttercream. It is easier to do this if the cakes are put on a spinning cake stand, so that the stand can be moved as needed. Use an offset spatula to distribute the buttercream evenly. Return the cake to the freezer.

7. Prepare the cake presentation base. Grease the surface of a piece of plywood 1.75 cm thick by 37.5 cm diameter/.5 by 15 in diameter with shortening. This will help the fondant to adhere to it.

8. Sheet 500 g/1 lb 1.6 oz of the rolled fondant to 3 mm/.12 in thick. It should be about the size of a sheet of parchment paper.

9. Roll the fondant onto the presentation base and smooth it out with your hands. Trim off the excess. Attach a thin ribbon around the border to make the base look cleaner, if desired.

10. Remove the buttercream-covered cake from the freezer and place it on a cake stand.

11. Sheet out the remaining 2 kg/4 lb 6.4 oz of the rolling fondant to 3 mm/.12 in to cover the cake. There are 3 pieces of fondant needed to cover the cake. One needs to be the entire length of the cake, and it should measure 30 by 70 cm/12 by 28 in. The other 2 pieces should be rectangles that measure 20 by 30 cm/8 by 12 in. Place the 2 small rectangles on the cake, 1 on each side. Place the longer piece across the entire surface of the cake.

12. Once the entire cake has been covered with fondant, transfer it to the presentation base, using a large, wide, heavy-duty offset spatula. Make sure it is centered on the base. This cake is heavy, so you might need 2 people to lift it from the cake stand, using a large, wide heavy-duty spatula on either side of the cake.

13. Combine the glycerin and water. Brush the cake with a light coat of this mixture, and pat any excess off with a heavy-duty paper towel; this helps protect the cake and gives it shine, and fondant cutouts and sugar paper prints will adhere to it.

14. Place the black fondant in a clay forming tool with a large string attachment in place (see page 484). Extrude the black fondant onto the cake, looping it every few inches to create a random loop pattern. Place the yellow, blue, green, and red fondant inside each loop, alternating the colors. Place the striped pattern sugar paper on top of the cake and the man and woman images on top.

15. Reserve in the refrigerator for up to 2 days. When fondant is refrigerated for long periods of time, condensation hygroscopes the fondant and the sugar paper, and they start to look like they are melting away.

note Make sure to have sturdy boxes big enough to pack this cake before you take any orders.

CREAM CHEESE FILLING

yield: 8.5 kg/18 lb 11.84 oz

INGREDIENT	METRIC	U.S.	%
Cream cheese, soft	6.01 kg	13 lb 4.32 oz	70.82%
Superfine or bakers' sugar	2.4 kg	5 lb 4.96	28.33%
Tahitian vanilla paste	72 g	2.56 oz	.85%

1. Combine all of the ingredients in the bowl of an electric mixer fitted with the paddle attachment. Mix on low speed until a homogeneous mass is obtained. Adjust the sweetness if necessary.

2. Since it is now soft, it is the ideal consistency for spreading. If storing it in the refrigerator, soften it by paddling it with a mixer before using. It will keep for up to 1 month in the refrigerator.

CARROT CAKE LAYERS

yield: 14 kg/30 lb 13.76 oz (7 full sheets)

INGREDIENT	METRIC	U.S.	%
Bread flour	1.31 kg	2 lb 14.56 oz	9.43%
Pastry flour	953 g	2 lb 1.6 oz	6.81%
Baking soda	117 g	4.14 oz	.84%
Ground cinnamon	50 g	1.76 oz	.36%
Salt	50 g	1.76 oz	.36%
Butter, at 21°C/70°F	3.38 kg	7 lb 7.52 oz	24.19%
Superfine or bakers' sugar	3.73 kg	8 lb 3.84 oz	26.71%
Vanilla paste	44 g	1.55 oz	.31%
Eggs, at 21°C/70°F	1.75 kg	3 lb 14.08 oz	12.57%
Carrots, grated	1.58 kg	3 lb 7.84 oz	11.31%
Walnuts, toasted and chopped	997 g	2 lb 3.2 oz	7.12%

1. Spray the inside border of 5 sheet pans with a light coat of nonstick oil spray and line them with a nonstick rubber mat.

2. Preheat a convection oven to 160°C/320°F.

3. Sift the flours, baking soda, cinnamon, and salt together.

4. Cream the butter and the sugar together in an electric mixer fitted with the paddle attachment on medium speed until light and fluffy, about 4 minutes.

5. Add the vanilla paste to the eggs. Add this mixture to the creamed mixture in 4 additions. Stop the mixer, drop the bowl, and scrape the bottom and the paddle with a rubber spatula between each addition.

6. Add the sifted dry ingredients. Pulse the mixer a few times, add the carrots and walnuts, and then mix on low speed just to incorporate the dry ingredients and obtain a homogeneous mass.

7. Divide the batter into 5 equal parts that weight 2.8 kg/6 lb 2.72 oz each. Spread each portion of the batter evenly into a sheet pan with an offset spatula.

8. Bake the carrot cake sheets until golden brown, 10 to 12 minutes. Test the center of each cake for doneness by pushing the center of the cake with your fingers; if it springs back, it is done.

9. Let the cake cool to room temperature, and then freeze the cakes.

10. Once they are frozen, cut out five 30-cm/12-in squares. Using a 2.5-cm-/1-in-thick guide, cut out all of the discs using a serrated knife so that they are all evenly thick. Reserve the leftover cake to assemble other smaller cakes.

11. Reserve the cake squares in the freezer until needed. Discard after 2 months.

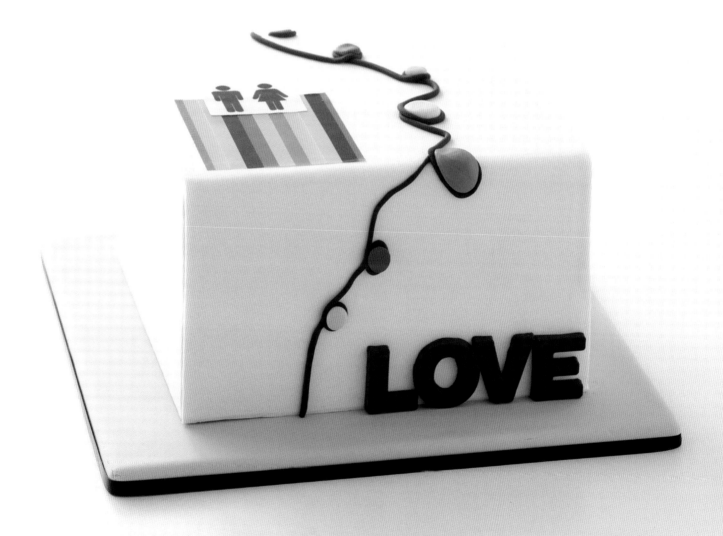

THE RETAIL SHELF

Your customers are the type of people who care about food and the quality of what they are consuming. Remember, the average consumers are more food savvy and sophisticated now than they were ten years ago. In the future, those numbers will surely grow, and one hopes, so will your business. These customers are probably friendly with or related to people who share the same or similar interests with them, and that little tin of special salt is probably just the right gift to give for any occasion. It is because of this that you can offer a variety of high-quality, shelf-stable products on the retail shelf. Don't forget that the packaging for them has to be not only beautiful but functional as well. People will actually be using these items in their homes, so the packaging should revolve around that idea. Don't get too complicated or too big. As with anything you package, bear in mind that the packaging will be a reflection of your business.

Chances are that you won't be harvesting your own cinnamon from Vietnam or sea salt from the marshes of the Blackwater River in England (where Maldon salt is from). Source these products from a high-quality spicemonger. There are vast differences in aroma and flavor between those large plastic jars you get at the supermarket and those that were specially harvested and cared for. There is also a price difference. High-quality spices are not cheap, but the quality is well worth the cost. And there is very little labor involved in selling spices and salts. All that has to be done is to put the spice, salt, or condiment in a package and label it. Most of these items are purchased in bulk, which can bring the price down. As long as you store your spices, salts, and other condiments properly, in cool, dry places in airtight containers, they will have a long shelf life. In some states, for legal purposes, you have to mention somewhere on the label the source where the spices, salts, or condiments came from.

One idea for the retail shelf is to sell themed, assorted boxes. For example, put together a box with four different varieties of pepper, or six different kinds of salt. You can charge a little bit less than it would cost to purchase all of the items individually in order to encourage your customers to purchase the product. Place these items close to a cash register to increase the odds of an impulse purchase. While your customers wait in line to place their order, they will have ample time to see what you have on the retail shelf and to grab a tin or two. You can also add a small printed document to your retail shelf, such as a flyer or pamphlet, that offers information, ideas, and recipes for how to use these ingredients.

The following table shows a few examples of items that might appear on the retail shelf. They are high-quality products. For example, not all nutmeg is equal. Grenadian nutmeg is the best quality nutmeg, bar none. These are only examples of the many varieties of spices, salts, and mixes that can be sold in the café.

salt	spices	others (mixes)
Maldon sea salt	Cinnamon (whole or ground):	Hot chocolate mix
Sel gris de Guerande	—Vietnamese	Mexican hot chocolate mix
Fleur de sel	—Indonesian	Mulling spices
Cyprus flake salt	—Mexican	Pumpkin spice
Hawaiian black sea salt	Grenadian nutmeg	
Truffle salt	Madagascar cloves	
Himalayan salt	Vanilla pods:	
Alderwood smoked salt	—Tahitian	
Murray River pink flake salt	—Madagascar	
Peruvian pink salt	—Bourbon	
Indian black salt	Pepper:	
	—Tellicherry peppercorns	
	—Malaysian white peppercorns	
	—Aleppo	
	—Cubeb	
	Hungarian paprika or pimentón dulce	
	Saffron	
	Piment d'espelette	
	Grains of paradise	

Dried herbs will not be as good as fresh herbs, but you can consider selling dried mushrooms, which retain most of their quality once they have been rehydrated. Other items that could be sold on the retail shelf are lollipops and other hard candy; chocolates (truffles, hand dipped, molded); caramels; jams, jellies, and marmalades; and tisanes, teas, and coffee beans.

packaging retail items

ONE OF THE HARDEST THINGS TO EXPLAIN is that the tiniest little detail will have an impact on your business, for better or for worse. Businesses that are not doing so well are often caught in a downward spiral of several small bad things that add up to impact the business. Business is rarely about one big event that will determine its success or failure; it is the smaller day-to-day successes that will determine it.

Packaging is one of those seemingly minor components of your café or restaurant. Think of it as advertising. And it is advertising that your customers take home, to friends, or to the office for others to see. The actual package can convey a lot of information about your establishment.

You have to make sure you do your homework when you choose your packaging. Make sure that it is not only attractive but also functional. These are a few questions you should ask yourself:

- Will it hold the product in place?

- Will it protect the product during transportation?

- Is it greaseproof?

- Does it stain easily?

- Is it recyclable?

- Is it the right size for the product?

- Is it easy to reorder?

- What is the cost?

- Does it fit the image of the café?

GLOSSARY

acid A substance having a sour or sharp flavor. Foods generally referred to as acids include citrus juice, vinegar, and wine. A substance's degree of acidity is measured on the pH scale; acids have a pH of less than 7.

aeration To incorporate air by beating or whipping ingredients.

Alto-Shaam An oven that cooks product and holds it at a preset temperature.

arabica The species from which about three-quarters of the world's coffee derives. It is known to have superior body, flavor, and aroma as compared to its counterpart, *robusta* coffee beans.

automatic drip brewer An automated system of brewing coffee where a preprogrammed amount of water at a desired temperature dispenses for a set amount of time and holds the resulting coffee at a pre-set temperature.

bakers' percentage The percentage of ingredients in a yeast-raised product as calculated from the percentage of the flour, which always equals 100 percent. It can be one type of flour or a combination of flours.

barista An individual responsible for preparing hot beverages including coffee, tea, and espresso drinks.

biga Italian for "an aged dough." A type of pre-ferment containing 50 to 60 percent water and ⅓ to ½ percent instant yeast.

bismarck Also known as a filling tip, it has a thin, long tube attached to a regular-shaped piping tip.

blast freezer A freezer that can drop down to –38°C/–36°F in a short period of time.

blending method A mixing method in which two or more ingredients (wet and dry) are combined just until they are evenly mixed.

braise: A cooking method in which the main item, usually meat, is seared in fat, and then simmered in stock or another cooking liquid in a covered vessel.

Brix scale A scale of measurement (decimal system), expressed in degrees, used to determine the density and concentration of sugar in a solution.

caramelization The process of cooking sugar in the presence of heat. The temperature range in which sugar caramelizes is 160° to 182°C/320° to 360°F. The browning of sugar enhances the flavor and appearance of food.

cocoa butter The fat extracted from the cacao bean.

combi oven A type of convection oven that can combine three modes of cooking in one oven at one time; it can poach, steam, roast, broil, and bake, and can reheat cooked food to the desired temperature. It can cook through hot air or steam, or a combination of both.

cone filter drip Similar to an automatic drip brewer, except that the water temperature for the brewing is controlled by a person instead of an automated machine.

confit An item cooked or preserved in its own fat or juices.

convection oven An oven that circulates hot air to heat the oven more uniformly.

creaming method To blend fats and sugar together to incorporate air.

crema A creamy, caramel-colored foam that forms on top of a properly brewed espresso. It is made of vegetable oils, proteins, and sugars, with elements of foam colloid and emulsions.

custard Any liquid thickened by the coagulation of egg proteins.

cut-in method This method consists of cutting or rubbing butter or another solid fat into flour. The fat is left in pea-size pieces, which results in a flaky pastry when baked.

CVap oven An oven that cooks products with steam and a quick temperature raise, which cooks the product evenly and with no loss of moisture.

dark Italian/dark French roast The darkest type of roast, which will result in a flavor determined mostly by the roast rather than by the bean itself.

dehydrator An appliance that removes moisture from items, generally fruit or vegetables.

Desired Dough Temperature (DDT) A method for determining the necessary temperature for water to be added to a dough by using the temperatures of other ingredients as well as the temperature of the environment.

fondant Sugar cooked with corn syrup, which is induced to crystallize by constant agitation in order to produce the finest possible crystalline structure. Fondant is used as centers in chocolate production, or as a glaze in pastries.

French press A pot that brews small amounts of coffee at a time (two to eight portions depending on the size of the press). Also called a plunger pot or cafetière.

frozen yogurt A smooth frozen dessert in which the main dairy component is whole-fat, low-fat, or fat-free yogurt.

ganache An emulsion of chocolate and cream. Ganache may also be made with butter or other liquids in place of the cream.

gelatin A protein derived from the skins and tendons of animals (generally pigs). Gelatin is used as a binder and stabilizer. It is available in granulated and sheet/leaf forms.

gelato An Italian-style ice cream that is denser than American-style ice cream. It has an overrun of 20 percent.

gellan gum A stabilizer that is obtained from fermented bacteria. Gellan gum is characterized by high gel strength, ease of use, clarity, flexibility, reliable supply, and the ability to be used in a variety of combinations.

gliadin A protein found in wheat flour. The part of gluten that gives it extensibility and viscosity.

glucose (1) A monosaccharide that occurs naturally in fruits, some vegetables, and honey. Also known as dextrose. (2) A food additive used in confections.

glutenin A protein found in wheat flour. The part of gluten that gives it strength and elasticity.

granité (or granita) A frozen mixture made with water, sugar, and flavoring such as fruit juice or wine; stirred frequently while freezing, it has an icy texture.

homogenize To mix ingredients together so that they become the same in structure.

hygroscopic Absorbing moisture from the air. Sugar and salt are both hygroscopic ingredients.

ice cream An ice cream is an emulsion and then, after churning, is a foam in which the air bubbles are stabilized by freezing a large amount of the liquid around them. Ice cream can be made with or without eggs.

immersion thermocirculator A piece of equipment with an electronic adjustable temperature setting, as well as a water circulator and a heating element that are both submerged in water. Because of the constantly circulating water, temperature will remain constant and little to no moisture will be lost from the item being cooked.

impinger An oven that heats by blowing hot air from the top and the bottom of the oven while a conveyor belt moves food along at a constant speed that can be adjusted based on your needs.

invert sugar (or Trimoline) Sucrose that has been broken down (inverted) into dextrose (glucose) and levulose (fructose). It is sweeter and more soluble than sucrose and does not crystallize as easily.

Italian meringue A meringue made from whipped egg whites and sugar syrup that has been cooked to 121°C/250°F. The syrup is poured slowly into the whipping egg whites when they have achieved stiff peak, and then the meringue is whipped to the desired peak.

lamination The technique of layering fat and dough through a process of rolling and folding to create alternating layers.

leavening Raising or lightening by air, steam, or gas (carbon dioxide). In baking, leavening occurs with yeast (biological), baking powder or baking soda (chemical), and steam (physical/mechanical).

Maillard reaction A complex browning reaction that results in the particular flavor and color of foods that do not contain much sugar, such as bread. The reaction, which involves carbohydrates and amino acids, is named after the French scientist who first discovered it.

mochi A soft, chewy Japanese dough made with glutinous rice flour.

mousse A French term that means "foam" or "froth"; also a soft, creamy food, either sweet or savory, lightened by adding whipped cream, beaten egg whites, or both; or a pâte à bombe.

nappé The consistency of a liquid that will coat or cover the back of a spoon. In English it means "to coat."

overrun The increase in volume of ice cream, sorbet, sherbet, or gelato caused by the incorporation of air during the freezing process.

parisienne scoop A small tool used for scooping balls out of fruits or vegetables. Also called a melon-baller.

pâte de fruit A confection that is a combination of pectin-gelled fruit and cooked sugar.

pâte fermentée A type of pre-ferment that contains many ingredients and is mixed to full gluten development, nearly resembling a dough itself. Literally a fermented dough.

pectin A gelling agent or thickener found in fruits, particularly in apples, quinces, and the skins of citrus fruits.

petit plaisir Literally translates into "small pleasure." Petits plaisirs are small, individually portioned desserts.

poach To cook gently in simmering liquid that is 70° to 82°C/160° to 185°F.

portafilter A detachable part of an espresso machine that holds the espresso beans.

pre-ferment A biga, poolish, pâte ferment, or white sour starter.

proof To allow yeast dough to rise.

Refractometric Index (RI) A measure of a fruit's sugar content. A refractometer, also called a Brix hydrometer, is used to determine the precise sugar content in bases of frozen desserts.

robusta These coffee plants produce about twice as many beans that have twice as much caffeine as those from the *arabica* species, but they are widely regarded as being lower in overall quality.

rondeau A shallow, wide, straight-sided pot with two loop handles.

sangria A Spanish beverage made by mixing wine, fruit, and fruit juice.

single-origin coffee Refers to a combination of a variety of beans from one specific country or a region in a country.

soda siphon A small appliance that, when used with CO_2 chargers, carbonates beverages.

sorbet An aerated non-dairy frozen product that is churned in a batch freezer or Pacojet. Sorbets are made mainly of fruit or vegetable juice, fruit or vegetable purée, and/or infused or flavored liquid, wine, or liqueur.

sorbitol A type of alcohol that is derived from fruits such as apples and pears; it has half the sweetening power of regular crystalline sugar. When it is added to

a ganache recipe, it reduces the water activity (Aw) and thus extends the shelf life of the product.

sponge A pre-ferment with one part water to two parts flour. This pre-ferment has more yeast added than a poolish, which makes it ferment more quickly.

stabilizer An ingredient that helps to develop the solid structure or "framework" of a finished product. Gelatin and pectin can act as stabilizers in ice cream bases.

straight method Mixing method used for breads in which all ingredients are placed in the bowl and the dough is mixed to full gluten development.

tapioca maltodextrin A flavorless modified tapioca starch that thickens and stabilizes fatty compounds.

temper (1) To melt, agitate, and cool chocolate to ensure that it retains its smooth gloss, crisp "snap" feel, and creamy texture. (2) To heat gently and gradually, as in the process of incorporating hot liquid into a liaison to gradually raise its temperature.

Thermomix blender A blender that is more powerful than most commercial blenders and that also allows the application of heat from 37° to 100°C/99° to 212°F.

tisane An infusion that is generally considered to be a type of tea, though it contains no tea leaves, such as herbal teas.

vacuum pot brewer A method to brew coffee that consists of two glass spheres, one on top of the other, attached by a seal. Between the two spheres there is a very fine–mesh sieve inside a funnel into which the ground coffee beans are placed. This funnel connects the bottom sphere to the top sphere, and water passes through it as it boils, the water passing though the ground coffee and eventually settling into the top sphere, and finally settling back into the bottom sphere.

Vienna (or "full city") Medium to dark brown roast that has a shiny bloom from the beans' oils.

water activity A measure of the amount of water available for chemical or enzymatic reactions, or for biological use. The water-activity level of a substance is always compared with that of pure water, which has a water-activity level of 1.00.

xanthan gum: A stabilizer that has great thickening power (it can thicken alcohol). It is soluble almost immediately as it comes into contact with a hot or cold liquid.

BIBLIOGRAPHY

Aduriz, Luis Andoni, and Jose Belmonte Rocandio. *Bestiarium Gastronomicae*. San Sebastian, Spain: Gourmandia. 2006.

Bertinet, Richard. *Crust*. London, England: Kyle Books. 2007.

Bilheux, R., A. Escoffier, D. Hervé, and J. M. Pouradier. *Special and Decorative Breads*. New York: Van Nostrand Reinhold. 1989.

Botella, Toni. *Cocktail Cuisine*. Barcelona, Spain: Montagud Editiores. 2002.

Calvel, Raymond, Ronald L. Wirtz, and James J. MacGuire. *The Taste of Bread*. Gaithersburg, MD: Aspen Publishers, Inc. 2001.

Chuen Kam, Lam, Lam Kai Sin, and Lam Tin Yu. *Way of Tea: The Sublime Art of Oriental Tea Drinking*. Hauppage, NY: Barron's Educational Series. 2002.

Colicchio, Tom. *Craft of Cooking*. New York: Clarkson Potter Publishers. 2003.

Cruz, Jordi. *Logical Cuisine*. Barcelona, Spain: Buffet & Ambigu, S.L. 2007.

Davids, Kenneth. *Coffee: A Guide to Buying, Brewing and Enjoying (Fifth Edition)*. New York: St. Martin's Griffin. 2001.

Davidson, Alan, Jane Davidson, Tom Jaine, and Helen Saberi. *The Oxford Companion to Food (Second Edition)*. New York: Oxford University Press. 2006.

Edwards, W. P. *The Science of Sugar and Confectionery*. Cambridge, UK: The Royal Society of Chemistry. 2000.

Figoni, Paula. *How Baking Works*. Hoboken, NJ: John Wiley & Sons, Inc. 2008.

Gautier, Lydia. *Tea: Aromas and Flavors around the World*. San Francisco, CA: Chronicle Books, LLC. 2006.

Hamelman, Jeffrey. *Bread: A Baker's Book of Techniques and Recipes*. Hoboken, NJ: John Wiley & Sons, Inc. 2004.

Henderson, Fergus. *The Whole Beast: Nose to Tail Eating*. New York: HarperCollins Publishers, Inc. 2004.

———, and Justin Piers Gellatly. *Beyond Nose to Tail*. New York: Bloomsbury USA. 2007.

Jenkins, Steven. *The Cheese Primer*. New York: Workman Publishing Company, Inc. 1996.

Kayser, Eric, Jean-Claude Ribaut, and Fabienne Gambrelle. *100% Pain*. Paris, France: Éditions SOLAR. 2003.

Knox, Kevin, and Julie Sheldon Huffaker. *Coffee Basics*. Hoboken, NJ: John Wiley & Sons, Inc. 1997.

Kutas, Rytek. *Great Sausage Recipes and Meat Curing (Third Edition)*. Buffalo, NY: The Sausage Maker, Inc. 2007.

L'Ecole Lenôtre. *Les Pains et Viennoiseries de l'Ecole Lenôtre*. Les Lilas, France: Éditions Jérôme Villette. 1995.

Loiseau, Bernard, and Gérard Gilbert. *Trucs de Pâtissier*. France: Marabout. 2000.

McGee, Harold. *On Food and Cooking: The Science and Lore of the Kitchen (Second Edition)*. New York: Scribner. 2004.

McNally, Keith, Riad Nasr, and Lee Hanson. *The Balthazar Cookbook*. New York: Clarkson Potter Publishers. 2003.

Migoya, Francisco. *Frozen Desserts*. Hoboken, NJ: John Wiley & Sons, Inc. 2008.

Morato, Ramón. *Chocolate*. Barcelona, Spain: Grupo Editorial Vilbo. 2007.

Pettigrew, Jane. *The Tea Companion: A Conoisseur's Guide*. Philadelphia: Quintet Publishing Limited. 2004.

Poilâne, Lionel, and Apollonia Poilâne. *Le Pain par Poilâne*. Paris, France: Le Cherche Midi Éditeur. 2005.

Reyanud, Stéphane. *Pork and Sons*. New York: Phaidon Press, Inc. 2007.

Rosich, Enric. *Renovación*. Barcelona, Spain: Montagud Editiores. 2007.

Ruhlman, Michael, and Brian Polcyn. *Charcuterie*. New York: W. W. Norton & Company, Inc. 2005.

The Culinary Institute of America. *Baking and Pastry: Mastering the Art and Craft*. Hoboken, NJ: John Wiley & Sons, Inc. 2004.

Wybauw, Jean-Pierre. *Chocolate without Borders*. Tielt, Belgium: Lannoo Uitgeverij. 2007.

Wybauw, Jean-Pierre. *Fine Chocolates—Great Experience*. Tielt, Belgium: Lanoo Uitgeverij. 2004.

INTERNET REFERENCES
coffee
www.countreculturecoffee.com
www.worldbaristachampionship.com

online conversion tools
www.onlineconversion.com

RESOURCES

EDIBLES

basil seeds
www.kalustyans.com

bubble tapioca and straws
www.bubbletea.com

butters (recommended for lamination)
Kerry Gold: www.kerrygold.com
Plugrá: www.kellerscreamery.com

candied chestnuts and chestnut purée
www.mastercaviar.com

candied lilacs and mimosas
www.markethallfoods.com

chestnut jam
www.petrossian.com

coquitos (baby coconuts)
www.melissas.com

elderflower syrup
www.lepicerie.com

gums
Gellan gum: www.mpbio.com
Carrageen gum, locust bean gum: www.ticgums.com

honey powder (Crumiel)
www.le-sanctuaire.com
www.tienda.com

flours
White Lily Flour: www.whitelily.com

fondant sugar, icing sugar
www.indiatree.com

freeze-dried fruit
www.harmonyhousefoods.com

fruit purées
Ravifruit: http://kerry.provnet.fr

luxardo cherries
www.wallywine.com

tisanes
www.serendipitea.com

universal pectin (or NH95 pectin)
www.pomonapectin.com

violet liqueur
www.absintheonline.com

violet syrup
www.greenbean-store.com

yeast
Lesaffre Yeast Corporation: www.bakipan.com

"Zirbenz" Stone Pine liqueur
www.winecommune.com/stores/item.cfm/storeID/68/lotID/2474773.html

strawberry powder and vanilla powder, chocolate décor chips, candied violets, macadamia nut paste, cold spray, mini apples, chocolate-covered puffed rice
Albert Uster Imports: www.auiswisscatalogue.com

silica gel packs, chocolate batons, neutral mirror glaze, cocoa butter spray, caramelized puffed rice
www.pastrychef.com

MOLDS AND PANS

CopyFlex silicone for mold-making
www.culinart.net/silicone

custom-made cake frames and molds (heavy-gauge aluminum)
www.frankencutters.com
E-mail: Info6@frankencutters.com or Frank Longmore at frank@frankencutters.com

flexible ice tray (oblong oval)
www.amazon.com

mini panettone molds
www.qualitapaper.com

rib-bake pans, loaf pan molds
Chicago Metallic: www.cmbakeware.com

silicone sphere molds
www.chefrubber.com

tubes for the apple jelly spaghetto kit
www.bienmanger.com

OTHER BAKING EQUIPMENT

croissant cutters, stainless-steel rings, financier molds, heavy cream whippers, soda siphons, bamboo cornets
www.jbprince.com

custom-made silk screens
http://friendsfabricart.com

edible printing paper, ink, and printer
www.icingimages.com

paper brioche cups, cupcake paper wrappers, edible printed wafer paper, dragées
www.fancyflours.com

pipettes
www.labdepotinc.com

silicone letter molds
www.chefrubber.com

textured acetate sheets/printed acetate sheets for hand-dippped chocolates
www.pcb-creation.fr

SERVING VESSELS

clear plastic boxes
www.amacbox.com

small glasses (votives) for desserts, assorted shapes
www.cudge.net

special dessert glasses (individual portions)
www.jbprince.com

INDEX

Page numbers in *italics* indicate illustrations